Communications
in Computer and Information Science 11

Max Mühlhäuser   Alois Ferscha
Erwin Aitenbichler (Eds.)

Constructing Ambient Intelligence

AmI 2007 Workshops
Darmstadt, Germany, November 7-10, 2007
Revised Papers

 Springer

Volume Editors

Max Mühlhäuser
Erwin Aitenbichler
Technische Universität Darmstadt
Hochschulstr. 10, 64289 Darmstadt, Germany
E-mail: {max, erwin}@informatik.tu-darmstadt.de

Alois Ferscha
Johannes Kepler Universität Linz
Altenbergerstr. 69, 4040 Linz, Austria
E-mail: ferscha@jku.ac.at

Library of Congress Control Number: 2008932557

CR Subject Classification (1998): H.4, C.2, D.4.6, H.5, I.2, K.4

ISSN   1865-0929
ISBN-10   3-540-85378-2 Springer Berlin Heidelberg New York
ISBN-13   978-3-540-85378-7 Springer Berlin Heidelberg New York

Springer is a part of Springer Science+Business Media

springer.com

© Springer-Verlag Berlin Heidelberg 2008
Printed in Germany

Typesetting: Camera-ready by author, data conversion by Scientific Publishing Services, Chennai, India
Printed on acid-free paper   SPIN: 12511433   06/3180   5 4 3 2 1 0

Preface

A foreword for the present workshop proceedings cannot be provided without first looking at the larger context of the AMI conference in which the workshops were organized. The AMI 2007 conference has roots in preceding events, but in many respects, AMI can be called a novel conference format and hence a premiere. Among the several aims that inspired and shaped this new conference format, the following two are particularly worth considering: (1) to provide a forum for the *ambient intelligence* flavor of research on the Post-PC era of computer science, complementing the *ubiquitous computing* and *pervasive computing* flavors emphasized by already-existing conferences; (2) to offer an event that attracts contributions from all over the globe yet emphasizes European strengths – with particular reference to the Information Society Technologies (IST) branch of the EU research framework programs (FPs), which carry the same label as the conference.

The workshop organization chairs reflected these unique characteristics of the new AMI conference series in the *call for workshop proposals* using two corresponding measures: (1) by particularly soliciting workshops on in-depth topics corresponding to the above-mentioned ambient intelligence flavor of Post-PC research; (2) by offering two different workshop threads: one 'usual' thread for advanced topics (called "SW workshops") and one thread for workshops related to concrete EU FP6 and FP7 projects (called "EU workshops").

Considering the new-born status of the conference format, we were more than satisfied with the response to our call. For both threads, we received substantially more submissions than we could accommodate. We established a careful review process, in which we involved other members of the AMI Organizing Committee, and tried to resolve conflicts and overlaps partially as submissions were announced or came in. In this respect, the final acceptance rate is hard to quantify exactly, but the ten workshops finally accepted and held represent a little more than 50% of the original submissions. We did not collect formal reviews after the workshops, but received a large number of very positive comments. In particular, the attendance finally rose to more than half of the total number of conference attendants, a fact that we consider a spectacular success.

The ten accepted workshops turned out to be well distributed over the two threads: six SW and four EU workshops were held. Among the SW workshops, SW1 followed the above-mentioned spirit of AMI in that it emphasized artificial intelligence methods for AMI. The papers addressed pertinent topics like reasoning, ontologies, pattern search, and intelligent information networks. SW4 looked at building blocks for AMI systems under the label "smart products." Business aspects related to consumer products and novel IT security aspects came into focus in this workshop due to the particular accepted papers. Two workshops were "putting the human in the center" of interest: SW3 looked at model-driven approaches to multimodal interaction for AMI, and SW6 at human factors of AMI in general. SW5 concentrated on a particular application domain, namely, ambient-assisted living (AAL); the nice collection of papers covered diverse aspects, ranging from requirements over development support to pilots and experiences, plus the pertinent topic of activity detection. The remaining workshop of this thread, SW2, was particular with respect to its emphasis on a "meta" problem, namely, user studies and user-centric evaluation of AMI systems in general.

The standard format proposed for EU workshops was a gathering for mutual updates on the status and achievements of the research work carried out in a particular large EU project; closed and open workshops were permitted. For such events, representation in the proceedings was restricted to summary and conclusion papers, typically one per workshop, in order to assure the scientific quality of the overall publication. The workshops on wirelessly accessible sensor platforms (WASP, EU2), on ambient knowledge discovery (KDubiq, EU5), and AAL (EU3, representing the two European projects SOPRANO and PERSONA, not to be confused with SW5) followed this format. The open, thoroughly reviewed workshop on the Amigo project (a large-scale EU activity on AMI in the home) deviated from the standard format for EU project workshops in that participants were allowed to contribute individual, quality-assured papers to the workshop proceedings. This exemption was given due to the high scientific standards observed by the organizers.

In conclusion, the valuable contributions compiled in this volume manifest the success and high scientific quality of the first set of workshops collocated with the AMI conference series. The workshop organizers would like to express their particular gratitude to Dr. Aitenbichler and Andreas Petter from Telecooperation, Technische Universität Darmstadt, and would like to thank the organizers of the individual workshops and all authors. These individuals – and more "helpers in the background" who must be left unmentioned for the sake of brevity – were truly instrumental for the realization and success of the AMI workshops. With the present proceedings, we are all privileged to harvest the fruits of hard work in the preparation, realization, and compilation of the AMI workshops. We hope that they are considered by the readers as worthwhile, valuable manifestations of creative scientific work.

January 2008

Max Mühlhäuser
Alois Ferscha

Table of Contents

Artificial Intelligence Methods for Ambient Intelligence

Evaluating Ubiquitous Systems with Users

Model Driven Software Engineering for Ambient Intelligence Applications

Smart Products: Building Blocks of Ambient Intelligence

Ambient Assisted Living

Human Aspects in Ambient Intelligence

Amigo

WASP - Wirelessly Accessible Sensor Populations

Conjoint PERSONA - SOPRANO Workshop

KDubiq Workshop

Workshop Summary: Artificial Intelligence Methods for Ambient Intelligence

Ralph Bergmann[1], Klaus-Dieter Althoff[2], Ulrich Furbach[3], and Klaus Schmid[2]

[1] University of Trier
Business Information Systems II
54286 Trier, Germany
bergmann@uni-trier.de
www.wi2.uni-trier.de
[2] University of Hildesheim
Department for Computer Science
Marienburger Platz 22
31141 Hildesheim, Germany
schmid@sse.uni-hildesheim.de
www.sse.uni-hildesheim.de
[3] University of Koblenz-Landau
Department of Computer Science
Universitätsstraße 1
56070 Koblenz, Germany
uli@furbach.de
www.uni-koblenz.de/FB4/Institutes/IFI/AGKI

1 Preface

We are pleased to present the workshop proceedings of the workshop Artificial Intelligence Methods for Ambient Intelligence, which took place as part of the European Conference on Ambient Intelligence on November 7, 2008 in Darmstadt, Germany. Ambient Intelligence (AmI) is the vision of our future environment. In this future environment we will be surrounded by various kinds of interfaces supported by computing and networking technology which will provide an intelligent, seamless and non-obtrusive assistance to humans. The ambient environment will be aware of the presence and identity of the humans, it will be able to communicate in multi-modal form and to anticipate the humans' goals and needs in order to provide best possible assistance to them. This broad vision addresses all areas of human life, such as home, work, health care, travel and leisure activities. A large amount of interdisciplinary research will be required in order to achieve this vision. Here, Artificial Intelligence (AI) provides a rich set of methods for implementing the "intelligence bit" of the AmI vision. Speech recognition, image interpretation, learning (from user interaction), reasoning (about users' goals and intensions) and planning (appropriate user interaction) are core features of AmI to which AI can contribute significantly. The goal of this workshop is to make a step forward towards a common understanding of how AI can contribute to the AmI vision and how to align AI research with it.

M. Mühlhäuser et al. (Eds.): AmI 2007 Workshops, CCIS 11, pp. 1–3, 2008.

The papers presented in this proceedings volume have been selected in peer-review process in which each paper was reviewed by at least two members of the Program Committee of the workshop. Five papers have been accepted for presentation and publication in this proceedings volume. In addition the first paper *AI Methods for Smart Environments: A Case Study on Team Assistance in Smart Meeting Rooms* by Martin Giersich, Thomas Heider, and Thomas Kirste was an invited paper summarizing the main achievements from recent projects within the Mobile Multimedia Information System research group of Thomas Kirste at the University of Rostock (Germany). In his invited talk Thomas Kirste focused on how AI technology can help to control ensembles of devices in smart environments, particularly meeting rooms. The focus of this work was on inferring the needs of groups of users and on applying AI methods such as planning for combining the available devices to best suite the users' needs.

In the paper *A Survey of Semantics-based Approaches for Context Reasoning in Ambient Intelligence* Antonis Bikakis et al. analyse how different systems and frameworks described in the AmI literature apply semantic web standards (e.g. XML, RDF, OWL) and reasoning approaches (e.g. description logic, rule-based reasoning, probabilistic reasoning, or case-based reasoning) for processing context information.

In the second paper *Distributed Reasoning with Conflicts in an Ambient Peer-to-Peer Setting* Antonis Bikakis et al. then present a new algorithm for reasoning with distributed rule theories in an ambient setting.

Fiemke Both et al. present the paper *Model-Based Default Refinement of Partial Information within an Ambient Agent* in which they address the problem that agents need a reasoning method to interpret the partial information available by sensing to generate one or more possible interpretations. They apply model-based default reasoning to address this problem and demonstrate their approach in two different case studies.

The paper *CAMPUS NEWS - Artifical Intelligence Methods Combined for an Intelligent Information Network* by Markus Maron et al. describes the use of ontologies and description logics for selecting relevant information based on a user profile and location information. The developed methods are demonstrated as part of an existing mobile information system in use at the University Campus in Koblenz, Germany.

The last paper *Searching for Temporal Patterns in AmI Sensor Data* by Romain Tavenard et al. addresses the problem of predicting user behavior based on temporal data coming from sensor networks. Different methods are discussed and evaluated that enable the extraction of temporal pattern in the data.

2 Workshop Organizers

- Ralph Bergmann, University of Trier, Germany
- Klaus-Dieter Althoff, University of Hildesheim, Germany
- Ulrich Furbach, University of Koblenz-Landau, Germany
- Klaus Schmid, University of Hildesheim, Germany

3   Program Committee

The international program committee was involved in the reviewing of the papers submitted to the workshop. The organizers thank all members of the program committee for their work and valuable feedback to the authors.

- Juan Carlos Augusto, University of Ulster, U.K.
- Michael Berger, Siemens, Germany
- Iryna Gurevych, TU Darmstadt, Germany
- Otthein Herzog, Uni Bremen, Germany
- Thomas Kirste, Uni Rostock, Germany
- Gerd Kortuem, Uni Lancaster, U.K.
- Ramon Lopez de Mantaras, IIIA, Barcelona
- Max Mühlhäuser, TU Darmstadt, Germany
- Jörg Müller, TU Clausthal, Germany
- Markus Nick, Fraunhofer IESE, Germany
- Mihaela Ulieru, The University of New Brunswick, Canada
- Reiner Wichert, Fraunhofer IGD, Germany
- Volker Wulf, Uni Siegen, Germany

AI Methods for Smart Environments
A Case Study on
Team Assistance in Smart Meeting Rooms

Martin Giersich, Thomas Heider, and Thomas Kirste

Department of Computer Science, Rostock University
Albert-Einstein-Straße 21
18059 Rostock, Germany
`first.last@uni-rostock.de`

Abstract. Ubiquitous computing aims for the realisation of environments that assist users autonomously and proactively in a non-distractive manner. Therefore smart environment infrastructures need to be able to identify users needs (*intention recognition*) and to plan an appropriate assisting strategy (*strategy generation*) without explicit user interaction. In our two-stage approach we address inferring the intention of a team of users during a meeting within a smart multiple display environment and the system decision process – what information to present on which display – on the strategy generation level.

1 Introduction

A central requirement for an assistance architecture for a smart meeting room is that it should support technical infrastructures that are built from individual components in an ad hoc fashion. Our solution approach is a two-stage design, where at the first stage the system components recognize the intention of a team of users, and at the second stage, the system components jointly generate a strategy that fulfills the needs of the team. In this paper we report the results of our current research and the ongoing evaluation. Part one of the paper presents results in intention analysis and part two represents strategy generation and evaluation. At this time we evaluated the parts separately. An evaluation of the complete integrated system will be matter of future work.

Intention recognition becomes a challenge, especially if multiple users are observed by noisy heterogenous sensors. We propose a *team behavior model* based on hierarchical dynamic Bayesian network (DBN) for inferring the current task and activity of a *team* of users. Given (noisy and intermittent) sensor readings of the team members' positions in a meeting room, we are interested in inferring the team's current objective.

A simulation data evaluation of our particle filter based team behavior model shows reasonable inference accuracy and speed for our implementation and demonstrates how additional unreliable knowledge about the meeting agenda improves

M. Mühlhäuser et al. (Eds.): AmI 2007 Workshops, CCIS 11, pp. 4–13, 2008.

prediction accuracy and speed. Here, we claim that even unreliable agendas improve intention recognition in smart environments for a compliant team behavior without sacrificing recognition accuracy for the non-compliant case.

We propose to cast the **Strategy generation** problem as an optimization task. As example problem we use the document-display mapping question, which is what to present on what display in a multi-user, multi-display environment. We suggest the definition of an *explicit global quality measure* to achieve coherent ensemble behavior for a team of multiple users with (maybe) diverging interests.

The evaluation of this part shows, that an automated document display mapping based on an explicit global quality measure leads to coherent ensemble behavior and is at least as effective as conventional manual assignment, while at the same time significantly reducing the number of required interactions. This claims are based on user performance data collected in the scope of a comparsion study.

2   Intention Recognition

Especially for the intention recognition used in our prototype smart meeting room we studied whether incomplete and unreliable (i.e., sometimes misleading) knowledge about the needs of a team of users (agenda) can be used to improve the quality of intention recognition. Specifically, we were interested in the usefulness of an unreliable agenda for improving the recognition of team activities during a meeting. Based on Bayesian filtering and an explicit probabilistic team behavior model we have carried on a simulation study that allowed us to answer the following questions:

- How accurate and how fast can we predict team behavior with an agenda assumption and history knowledge?
- What influence do deviations of the team from the planned agenda assumption have on prediction quality (i.e., does a wrong agenda degrade the quality of intention recognition)?
- How flexible does an agenda assumption need to be in order to optimally predict team behavior?

We chose simulation of data rather than real world data as this enabled us to configure the probability distribution of the sensor readings. We used Gaussian and Cauchy distributed sensor readings with a variety of different parameter settings to examine the influence of the sensor model on the prediction quality.

Team Behavior Model – Bayesian Filtering for identifying a user's current task has been successfully used in several projects that aimed at supporting user activities in classrooms, meeting rooms, and office environments [1,2,3]. Here, *dynamic Bayesian networks* (DBNs) were investigated increasingly for modeling a user's activities [4,5]. In our own work, we looked at using DBNs for inferring the current task and actions of a *team* of users. Given (noisy and intermittent) sensor readings of the team members' positions in a meeting room,

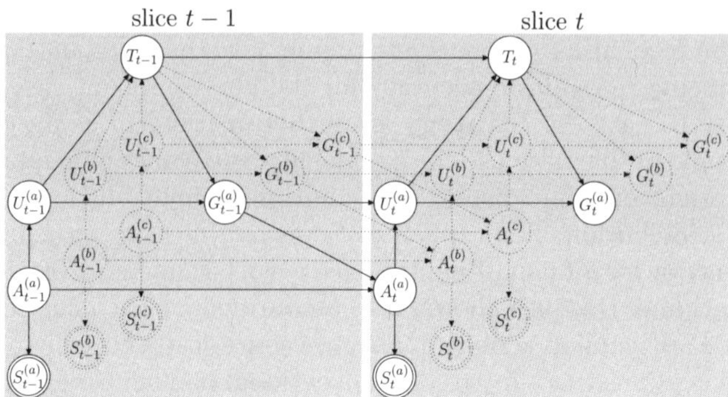

Fig. 1. Two-sliced dynamic Bayesian network (DBN) modeling team intention inference. It shows the intra-slice dependencies between observable (double-contoured) and hidden variables, as well as the inter-slice dependencies between consecutive states.

we were interested in inferring the team's current objective – such as having a presentation delivered by a specific team member, a moderated brainstorming, a round table discussion, a break, or the end of the meeting.

The basic structure of the DBN we propose for modeling the activities of such a team is given in Figure 1. With this DBN we try to model the behavior of a team of three users during a meeting. In order to exploit agenda information, we need a DBN structure that is able to incorporate an explicit agenda, and that represents the negotiation process between the team and its members during activity selection. At the top level, the team node T_t represents the current team intention. The team's intention at time t depends on what the team has already achieved (T at time $t-1$, T_{t-1}), and what the users i are currently trying to achieve (the $U_t^{(i)}$-nodes, $i \in \{a, b, c\}$). The $G_t^{(i)}$ nodes represent the new individual assignments if the team T will adopt a new intention. So at each time slice, the team looks at what the users have achieved so far and then decides what the users should do next. What the user is doing at time t depends on his previous action (e.g., the user's current position and velocity) and assignment – $A_{t-1}^{(i)}$ and $G_{t-1}^{(i)}$. Finally, the sensor observations of user i at time t – the nodes $S_t^{(i)}$ – depend on the user's activities at that time.

Note that these sensor nodes are the *only* observable nodes in our model: we estimate the team's negotiations from the observable behavior of the team members. Once a probabilistic model is available, it allows us to infer user and team intentions.

Experimental Design and Results – Clearly, agenda information should improve the quality of team intention recognition. However, as soon as a team deviates from the a-priori agenda, recognition quality may drop: The recognizer may be led to wrong conclusions by misleading a-priori information that potentially defeat any benefit. Objective of our evaluation has been to investigate, whether a-priori agenda information can be used to improve recognition quality

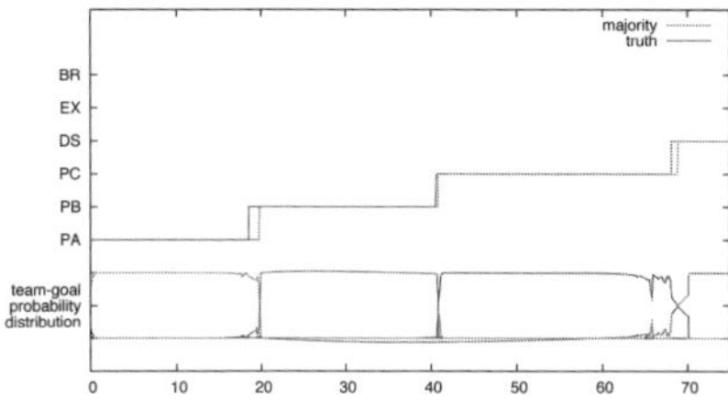
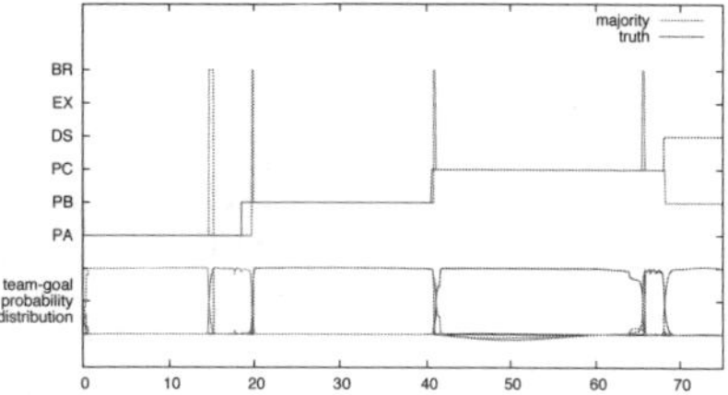

Fig. 2. Inference of a $\langle A, B, C, D \rangle$ truth from Cauchy distributed sensor data (delay 0.25, error 10.0) with the trackers $T_{.8}$ (left) and $T_{uniform}$ (right)

in case the team complies to the agenda, *without* sacrificing recognition quality in case of non-compliance with the agenda. We were interested in two main questions:

(a) How reliable is agenda based recognition in case of compliance and non-compliance, compared to an agenda-less tracking?

(b) How fast will an agenda based recognizer identify a change in the team objective for these cases?

To analyze the effect of an agenda on reliability and speed of intention recognition in case of compliance and non-compliance we chose three different conference sequences (one compliant, two non-compliant). Further we used four different parameter settings for the sensors. In two settings we used sensor data that is Gaussian distributed. The two other settings sensor data followed a Cauchy distribution. The settings for each distribution differed in delay between consecutive sensor readings and sensor error.

For the evaluation of recognition accuracy, we used four different models for a-priori agenda information – a random model where every activity has the same probability and history is not tracked ($T_{uniform}$) and three models with different start probabilities for user A {.6, .8, .95} and the other users respectively ($T_{.6}, T_{.8}, T_{.95}$). For every tracker model six runs were logged. The illustration of two typical representative of model $T_{.8}$ and model $T_{uniform}$ simulation runs in Figure 2 shows that the main uncertainty about the teams objective pervails during the phase of an objective shift. The left picture shows the advantage of agenda knowledge. For instance the objective shift from *B Presents* (PB) to *C Presents* (PC) around time slice 40 is recognized faster and more reliable. Further it shows that agenda knowledge leads to less misinterpretation of sensor readings. So the overall error rate shrinks. Figure 3 shows solid recognition also for non-compliant cases. Here, tracked with model $T_{.8}$.

The averages over 6 simulation runs for 48 different parameter settings give an delay between true objective shift of the team and the recognition of this shift of $7.36sec$ for $T_{.8}$ versus $10.95sec$ for $T_{uniform}$. The average intention recognition reliability for the best model $T_{.8}$ was measured with 91.16% correct versus 83.1% for the uniform model. Comparison of the reliability values for $T_{.8}$ and $T_{uniform}$ gives the most important result of this study:

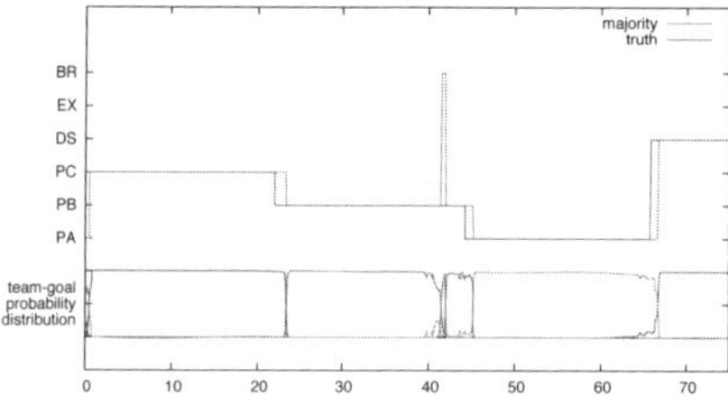

Fig. 3. Inference of the non-compliant truth $\langle C, B, A, D \rangle$ from Cauchy distributed sensor data (delay 0.25, error 10.0) with the trackers $T_{.8}$

It is possible to improve the recognition accuracy for the compliant case by using an agenda, *without* sacrificing recognition accuracy for the non-compliant case.

Therefore, it always pays to include available a-priori agenda information in the recognition system, even if the correlation between the agenda sequence and the true activity sequence is not very strong.

However, it is important to assign a suitable probability to the agenda's preferred sequence. If this value is too high (e.g., .95), the agenda becomes too rigid: it will tend to assume that the team follows the agenda, even if the sensor data does tell a different story. On the other hand, further increasing the looseness of the agenda (e.g., to .6) does not improve the recognition of the non-compliant action sequences. We suspect that unnecessary looseness will eventually degrade recognition capability, but we have not observed this in our data.

Finally, simulation results show that an agenda reduces the delay, specifically for the later team actions. (Clearly, the agenda will not reconsider items already worked off, an aspect favorably reducing the degrees of freedom in comparison to $T_{uniform}$.)

3   Strategy Generation

Multi-display environments support collaborative problem solving and teamwork by providing multiple display surfaces for presenting information [6,7]. One difficulty here is the *display mapping problem* – that is, deciding which information to present on what display in order to optimally satisfy the users' needs for information. Current approaches for controlling multi-display environments rely on manual assignment [8,9], using a suitable interactive interface and resolving conflicts by social protocols (negotiations). However, manual display assignment has to cope with the following problems:

- **Interest conflicts** between users might be solved faster by computer supported negotiation mechanism: It was observed that social protocols do not always suffice for coordinating the use of shared resources [10].

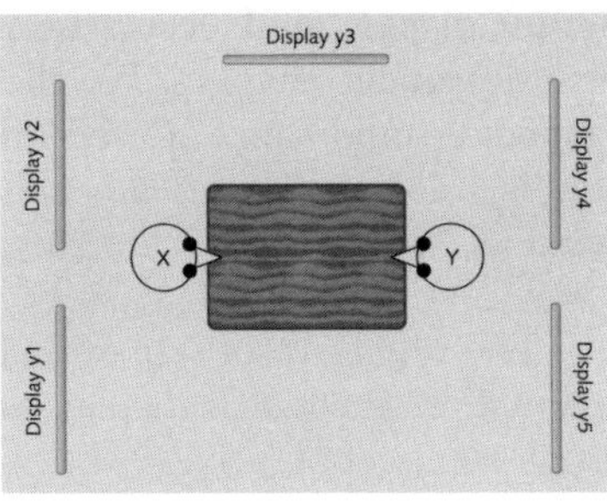

Fig. 4. Experimental setup for strategy generation comparsion study

- The need for **dynamic realignment** of display mapping is caused by topic changes in the user population: In this situation, the user's focus of attention will be on the changing topic rather than on convincing the display infrastructure to change the topic.

So, an automatic display assignment might be helpful in multiple display environments, specifically in multi-user settings. However, to our knowledge, it is not known if suitable automatic assignment heuristics can be found. This is the question we want to answer.

Display Mapping Quality Measure – A *display mapping* is a function m, which assigns documents to sets of displays. For a given document d, $m(d)$ gives the set of displays document d is assigned to. In order for automatic display mapping to be successful it is necessary to identify a well-defined quality measure that sufficiently captures the users needs. Clearly, at least the following aspects are reasonable:

Spatial Layout: For documents of high importance to a user, displays should be preferred that provide a good visibility for the user. Formally, this critierion for m can be defined as

$$q_s(m) = \sum_{\substack{u \in U \\ d \in D}} impt(d, u) * \max_{y \in m(d)} vis(y, u) \tag{1}$$

where $impt(d, u) \in [0 .. 1]$ denotes the importance of the document d to a user u, and $vis(y, u) \in [0 .. 1]$ the *visibility* of display y by user u. If a document is assigned to multiple displays, only the best one ("primary display") for a given user is considered when computing the quality for this user (this is the "max *vis*" term). Note, that deriving a reliable estimation of *impt* in general may be a substantial challenge. We think that additional informations available from intention recognition can be used as a surrogate (such as agenda listings, team members roles and associated documents, etc.).

Temporal Continuity: When considering a display for a document, the system should prefer already existing assignments: Documents should not unnecessarily change their place. A relevant display shift occurs between two mappings, if a user's primary display for a document changes. We then try to minimize these shifts relative to the document's importance. Based on these criteria, we have developed an algorithm that is able to automatically compute a display mapping for a set of users and documents (see [11]).

Experimental Design – The objective of our evaluation experiment was to measured the impact of manual vs. automatic display assignment on the performance of a team in solving a semi-cooperative task. In such tasks, the need of cooperation and joint use of information is not evident from the start, but rather arises while working on the task. We think that this kind of aspect pertains to many team processes.

Two-person teams had to solve a semi-cooperative set of comparison tasks as fast as possible. The two team members, X and Y, were given different agendas, each containing the description of an individual comparison. For X the task was to do a simple letter comparison of two documents A and B, for Y the task was to compare A and C. In addition, X and Y had to report time information and a random key from another document Time. The seemingly unrelated tasks for X and Y were linked into a cooperative task through the shared documents A and Time.

Every participant was given a simple user interface for document assignment. Manually assignment of a document to a display-surface is done through simple "drag & drop". For automatic assignment, the user just associates an importance value with the documents. As the agendas and task descriptions were mutually unknown, the sharing had to be discovered through a conflict in the manual assignment group.

For each experiment, we recorded the time required for completing the task, the number of interactions and the solution correctness (percentage of letter differences found). After each task set, the subjects were asked to answer a questionnaire regarding user satisfaction. After both task sets, the subjects were asked to complete a final questionnaire regarding the comparison of automatic versus manual assignment.

24 voluntary subjects were recruited from staff members and students of the local university. The teams had to solve two sets comparison tasks in sequence. Group A had to solve the first set using automatic assignment and the second set with manual assignment. The Group M was given the tasks in reverse order. In the evaluation of the results, we will call the first set "Initial Test" and the second "After Training", respectively. (See [12] for a more detailed discussion of both experimental setup and findings.)

Findings – When the teams were using automatic assignment, the average time to complete one set of a comparison task was $4{:}08min$, while they required an average time of $4{:}49min$ using manual assignment. The subjects needed 8.5 interactions on average with automatic and 15 interactions on average with manual assignment. This indicates that the automatic assignment is superior to manual assignment, regarding time and interactions.

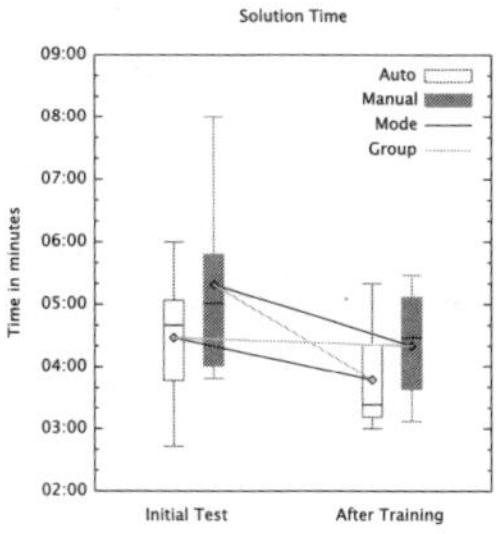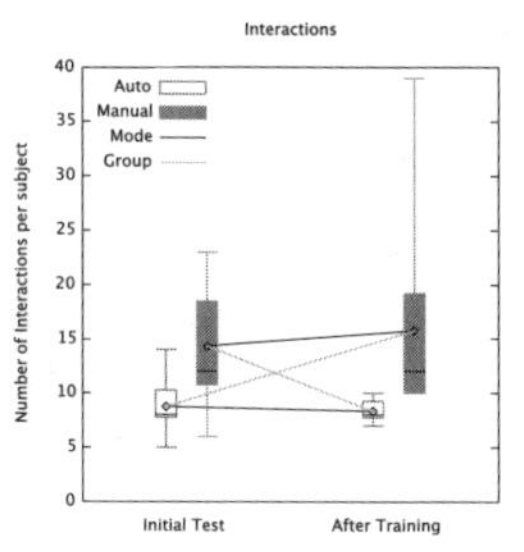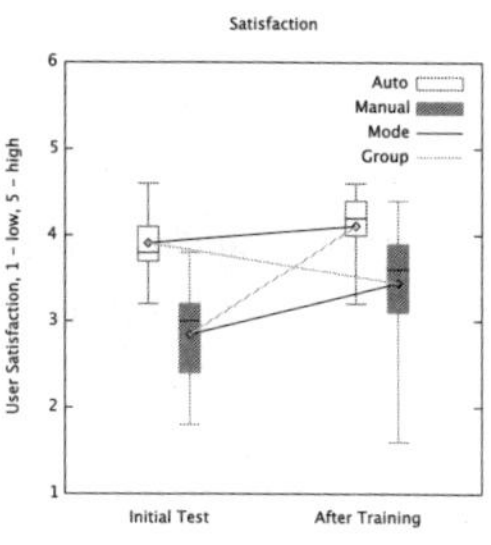

Fig. 5. Boxplots of solution time vs. mode, overall (left); interaction count vs. mode (middle); user satisfaction vs. mode (right)

An overview of the collected data is shown in the boxplots[1] in Figure 5. In these plots, "Mode" refers to the display assignment mode (manual vs. automatic). In the per-task-set plots, grey lines connect the mean values of the two consecutive task sets of a group (Group **A** or Group **M**), black lines connect consecutive task sets using the same assignment mode.

As can be seen in Figure 5, left, for both task sets the solution time is shorter when using automatic assignment. In addition, Group **M** was able to solve the task substantially faster in the second set (i.e., when switching from manual to automatic assignment), whereby Group **A** was not able to improve performance in the second set (i.e., switching from automatic to manual assignment). The number of interactions (Figure 5, middle) is smaller for the automatic method in both sets.

In the manual assignment mode, both groups initially had no idea that they needed to share documents. So they unwittingly "stole" the shared documents from each others "private" displays. It took a couple of interactions until the participants realized that they needed to cooperate and to assign some of the documents to a display visible to both users. This process of realization and negotiation was the reason for confusion and delay.

In the automatic assignment mode no such conflicts did arise as the system automatically displayed shared documents on a shared screen. If we use the number of interactions as indicator of occurred conflicts, the data shows that with the automatic mode the number of conflicts is considerably smaller than in the manual mode. A detailed survey of the log files showed that documents which had to be shared, very frequently were reassigned in the manual mode. This proves the presumption that resolving conflicts by social negotiation is – in some situations – inferior to a computer supported negotiation, which can be solved by an automatic assignment using a global quality function such as q.

For assessing user satisfaction, we used parts of the technology acceptance model (TAM)[13]. We included the following items, each to be answered on a scale from 1 (strongly disagree) to 5 (strongly agree):

---

[1] These boxplots show the minimum and maximum values, the 25% and 75% percentiles, the median (horizontal bar inside the box), and the mean (small circle inside the box).

> *The system is easy to use. – The system helps in solving the task effi-
> ciently. – It is easy to cooperate with the team partner. – The system
> helps in solving team conflicts. – I felt comfortable in using the system.*

The final questionnaire used the same items with the request to compare both approaches, automatic and manual assignment, on a scale from 1 (manual assignment strongly preferred) to 5 (automatic assignment strongly preferred).

The distribution of the user satisfaction data using per-questionaire averages is shown in Figure 5 (right). The overall user satisfaction is higher in the auto mode, for both task sets. In addition, user satisfaction *decreases* within a *group* when switching from auto to manual, while it *increases* when switching from manual to auto.

The correlation of the subjective user satisfaction with the objective data from the log files confirm our hypothesis that the automatic display assignment is superior to the manual assignment in multi-user, multi-display situations with conflicting and dynamic document sets.

4   Summary

We have discussed the problem of assisting teams in effectively using multi-display environments for working together and we have addressed the question whether it is possible to infer the intention of the team and to find well-defined quality criteria for automatic display assignment.

Our results regarding team intention recognition, inference accuracy and speed showed that despite noisy observable sensor data and a rather ad hoc prior probability distribution for the occurrence of agenda items a precise and robust inference is possible. Further adding agenda knowledge to a team behavior model was identified as improvement for the compliant case and as non-disturbing for the non-compliant case. So, we can claim that unreliable agendas are useful for inferring team intentions. We will now focus on in-depth development of an appropriate team behavior model and incorporate learning of probabiltiy distributions using *EM-algorithm*.

In the strategy generation part, we have been able to show that automatic assignment enables teams to solve their tasks in a shorter time, with less conflicts between team members, with greater satisfaction and with reduced cognitive load. Future investigations will have to show whether this benefit offers the universality and significance required to incorporate it generally into smart multiple display environments.

Finally the seamless integration of our two-stage design is an issue that we will address in the future work.

References

1. Franklin, D., Budzik, J., Hammond, K.: Plan-based interfaces: keeping track of user tasks and acting to cooperate. In: Proceedings of the 7th international conference on Intelligent user interfaces, pp. 79–86. ACM Press, New York (2002)

2. Bui, H.: A general model for online probabilistic plan recognition. In: IJCAI 2003: Proceedings of the 18th International Joint Conference on Artificial Intelligence, pp. 1309–1315 (2003)
3. Duong, T.V., Bui, H.H., Phung, D.Q., Venkatesh, S.: Activity recognition and abnormality detection with the switching hidden semi-markov model. In: CVPR 2005: Proceedings of the 2005 IEEE Computer Society Conference on Computer Vision and Pattern Recognition (CVPR 2005), Washington, DC, USA, vol. 1, pp. 838–845. IEEE Computer Society Press, Los Alamitos (2005)
4. Patterson, D.J., Liao, L., Fox, D., Kautz, H.A.: Inferring high-level behavior from low-level sensors. In: Proceedings of UBICOMP 2003: he Fifth International Conference on Ubiquitous Computing, October 12-15 (2003)
5. Patterson, D.J., Liao, L., Gajos, K., Collier, M., Livic, N., Olson, K., Wang, S., Fox, D., Kautz, H.A.: Opportunity knocks: A system to provide cognitive assistance with transportation services. In: Ubicomp, pp. 433–450. Springer, Heidelberg (2004)
6. Ferscha, A., Kortuem, G., Krüger, A.: Workshop on ubiquitous display environments. In: Proc. Ubicomp 2004, Nottingham, England, (September 7, 2004)
7. Back, M., et al.: Usable ubiquitous computing in next generation conference rooms: design, architecture and evaluation. In: Ubicomp Workshop 2006, Newport Beach, CA, USA, September 17 (2006)
8. Chiu, P., Liu, Q., Boreczky, J.S., Foote, J., Kimber, D., Lertsithichai, S., Liao, C.: Manipulating and annotating slides in a multi-display environment. In: Human-Computer Interaction INTERACT 2003: IFIP TC13 International Conference on Human-Computer Interaction (2003)
9. Johanson, B., Hutchins, G., Winograd, T., Stone, M.: Pointright: Experience with flexible input redirection in interactive workspaces. In: Proc. ACM Conference on User Interface and Software Technology (UIST2002), Paris, France, pp. 227–234 (2002)
10. Morris, M.R., Ryall, K., Shen, C., Forlines, C., Vernier, F.: Beyond social protocols: multi-user coordination policies for co-located groupware. In: CSCW 2004: Proceedings of the 2004 ACM conference on Computer supported cooperative work, pp. 262–265. ACM Press, New York (2004)
11. Heider, T., Giersich, M., Kirste, T.: Resource optimization in multi-display environments with distributed grasp. In: Proceedings of the First International Conference on Ambient Intelligence Developments (AmI.d 2006), Sophia Antipolis, France, September 19 - 22, 2006, pp. 60–76. Springer, Heidelberg (2006)
12. Heider, T., Kirste, T.: Automatic vs. manual multi-display configuration: A study of user performance in a semi-cooperative task setting. In: HCI 2007: HCI.but not as we know it, Lancaster, UK, September 3–7 (2007)
13. Davis, F.D.: Perceived usefulness, perceived ease of use, and user acceptance of information technology. MIS Quarterly, September 1989, vol. 13(3), pp. 319–340 (1989)

A Survey of Semantics-Based Approaches for Context Reasoning in Ambient Intelligence

Antonis Bikakis, Theodore Patkos, Grigoris Antoniou, and Dimitris Plexousakis

Institute of Computer Science, FO.R.T.H., Vassilika Voutwn
P.O. Box 1385, GR 71110, Heraklion, Greece
{bikakis,patkos,antoniou,dp}@ics.forth.gr

Abstract. A key issue in the study of Ambient Intelligence is reasoning about context. The aim of context reasoning is to deduce new knowledge, based on the available context data. The endmost goal is to make the ambient services more *"intelligent"*; closer to the specific needs of their users. The main challenges of this effort derive from the imperfect context information, and the dynamic and heterogeneous nature of the ambient environments. In this paper, we focus on semantics-based approaches for reasoning about context. We describe how each approach addresses the requirements of ambient environments, identify their limitations, and propose possible future research directions.

1 Introduction

Pervasive applications aim at providing the right information to the right users, at the right time, in the right place, and on the right device. In order to achieve this, a system must have a thorough knowledge and, as one may say, *"understanding"* of its environment, the people and devices that exist in it, their interests and capabilities, and the tasks and activities that are being undertaken. All this information falls under the notions of *context*.

The need for *reasoning* in context aware systems derives from the basic characteristics of context data. Two of these are *imperfection* and *uncertainty*. Henricksen and Indulska [1] characterize four types of imperfect context information: *unknown*, *ambiguous*, *imprecise*, and *erroneous*. Sensor or connectivity failures result in situations, that not all context data is available at any time. When the data about a context property comes from multiple sources, the context information may become ambiguous. Imprecision is common in sensor-derived information, while erroneous context information arises as a result of human or hardware errors. The role of reasoning in these cases is to detect possible errors, make predictions about missing values, and decide about the quality and the validity of the sensed data. The raw context data needs, then, to be transformed into meaningful information so that it can later be used in the application layer. In this direction, some suitable sets of rules can exploit the real meaning of some raw values of context properties. Finally, context reasoning may play the role of a decision making mechanism. Based on the collected context information, and

M. Mühlhäuser et al. (Eds.): AmI 2007 Workshops, CCIS 11, pp. 14–23, 2008.

on a set of decision rules provided by the user, the system can be configured to change its behavior, whenever certain changes are detected in its context.

If we also consider the high rates in which context changes and the potentially vast amount of available context information, the reasoning tasks become even more challenging. Overall, Knowledge Management in Ambient Intelligence should enable: *(a)* Reasoning with the highly dynamic and ambiguous context data; *(b)* Managing the potentially huge piece of context data, in a real-time fashion, considering the restricted computational capabilities of some mobile devices; and *(c)* Collective intelligence, by supporting information sharing, and distributed reasoning between the entities of the ambient environment.

In this paper, we present the various solutions that have been proposed to date, giving more attention to those that employ Semantic Web-based representations to describe context. The use of ontology languages is becoming common in such applications mainly because they offer enough representational capabilities to develop a formal context model that can be shared, reused, extended for the needs of specific domains, but also combined with data originating from other sources. Moreover, the development of the Semantic Web logic layer is resulting in rule languages that will enable reasoning with the user's needs and preferences and with the available ontology knowledge. According to the discussion on *Interactive Context-Aware Systems Interacting with Ambient Intelligence* in [2], ontology-based models manage to satisfy all demands placed concerning context modeling, such as distributed composition, partial validation, richness and quality of information, incompleteness and ambiguity, level of formality and, also, applicability to existing environments.

The rest of the paper is structured as follows: Section 2 focuses on ontological reasoning solutions, and Section 3 on rule-based approaches. Section 4 describes methods and techniques for distributed reasoning, while Section 5 discusses additional reasoning techniques concerning *learning, offline reasoning* and *probabilistic reasoning*. The last section proposes future research directions that may lead to more efficient reasoning solutions.

2   Ontological Reasoning

The SW Languages of RDF(S) and OWL are common formalisms for context representation. Along with their evolution, a number of SW Query languages (e.g. RDQL [3], RQL [4], TRIPLE [5]) and reasoning tools (e.g. FaCT [6], RACER [7], Pellet [8]) have been developed. Their aim is to retrieve relevant information, check the consistency of the available data, and derive implicit ontological knowledge. The studies of [9] and [10] describe the use of RDQL for accessing RDF context data, while the Context-Aware Guide described in [11] demonstrates the use of RQL in location-based mobile services. An interesting study that describes and evaluates the use of description logic for both representation and reasoning over context is presented in [12]. Below, we present representative examples of systems that reason with context data using Description Logics.

The P2P-based mobile environment in [13] consists of stations that provide semantic services and users with mobile devices, which manage their owner's semantic profile. Both the semantic services and the users' profiles are modeled as description logic predicates. The semantic matching between the services and the profiles, which determines whether a given profile is semantically compatible to a particular service and, if so, how well both do match, is accomplished by applying a set of DL rules, which are processed by a RACER reasoning engine.

In [14], they use a case study from the smart home domain (specifically a context-aware door-lock) to present their approach for modeling and reasoning about context using Description Logics. They have built an OWL schema to model the required context entities, and test three DL reasoners (RACER, its commercial successor RacerPro [15], and Pellet) using a real-case application scenario. However, their scenario is rather too simple to evaluate the performance of these reasoners in much broader context-aware applications.

The ontological reasoning approaches have two significant advantages. They integrate well with the ontology model, which is widely used for the representation of context; and most of them have relatively low computational complexity, allowing them to deal well with situations of rapidly changing context. However, their limited reasoning capabilities are a trade-off that we cannot neglect. They cannot deal with missing or ambiguous information, which is a common case in ambient environments, and are not able to provide support for decision making. Thus, we argue, that although we can use them in cases where we just want to retrieve information from the context knowledge base, check if the available context data is consistent or derive implicit ontological knowledge, they cannot serve as a standalone solution for the needs of ambient context-aware applications.

3   Rule-Based Reasoning

In the Ambient Intelligence domain, rules are primarily used to express policies, constraints and preferences. Below, we present some representative examples.

In the SOCAM architecture, they use FOL rules to reason about context ([16]). To resolve possible conflicts, they have defined sets of rules on the classification and quality information of the context data. They suggest that different types of context have different levels of confidence and reliability. For example, defined context is more reliable compared to sensed and deduced context. They also have different levels of quality; for example, an RFID-based location sensor may have a 80% accuracy rate whereas a Bluetooth-based sensor may only have a 60% accuracy rate. The reasoning engine is implemented in Jena2.

In the *Semantic Space* Architecture, there are two modules for retrieving and deriving new information from the OWL Knowledge Base ([17]). The Context Query Engine provides an interface for applications to extract desired context information from the knowledge base. The Context Reasoner enables the users to deduce higher level knowledge, based on the context data of the KB, using FOL rules. The system uses Jena2 to perform forward-chaining reasoning over the KB, based on the rules provided by the user. The same approach is also followed in the prototype context-aware implementation descibed in [18].

As part of *Gaia*, Ranganathan and Campbell propose a FOL-based context infrastructure ([19]). The context information is represented as first-order predicates, with the name of a predicate being the type of context described. The model allows both universal and existential quantification over variables. This allows parameterizing context and representing a much richer set of contexts. A predefined set of rules is used to deduce higher-level knowledge based on the raw context data. Whenever a change occurs in the system's context, the rules are re-evaluated and the new inferred context replaces the old one. To resolve conflicts that occur when multiple rules are activated in the same time, they have developed a priority base mechanism, allowing only one rule to fire at each time. For the evaluation of the rules, they use the XSB reasoning engine.

In [20], the use of OWL is proposed both for context representation data, and for the rules expressing the user preferences and security constraints. Once all the context knowledge has been loaded in system (implemented on Jess), some predefined forward-chaining rules are used to complete the core knowledge base. The service invocation rules, and the privacy enforcing rules, both represented as backward-chaining rules are then applied to the knowledge base.

The Semantic Context-Aware Access Control Framework in [21] uses a combination of Description Logics and Logic Programming reasoning. Specifically, they define two types of rules: (a)*context aggregation rules* to support reasoning using property path relationships; (b) *context instantiation rules* to provide OWL assertions for attribute values. Both types of rules are expressed according to the following pattern: *if context attributes $C_1...C_n$ then context attribute C_m*, which corresponds to a Horn clause, where predicates in the head and in the body are represented by classes and properties defined in the context and application-specific ontologies. A similar hybrid reasoning approach is also implemented in the context-aware service adaptation middleware described in [22]).

Rule languages provide a formal model for context reasoning. Furthermore, they are easy to understand and widespread used, and there are many systems that integrate them with the ontology model. However, all these approaches share a common deficiency; they cannot handle the highly changeable, ambiguous and imperfect context information. In many of the cases that we described, they had to build additional reasoning mechanisms to deal with conflicts, uncertainty and ambiguities. The proposed logic models suit better in cases, where we are certain about the quality of the collected data. Consequently, neither of these models can serve as the solution to the required reasoning tasks.

4   Distributed Reasoning Techniques

In an Ambient Intelligence environment, there coexist many different entities that collect, process, and change the context information. Although they all share the same context, they face it from different viewpoints based on their perceptive capabilities, their experiences and their goals. Moreover, they may have different reasoning, storage and computing capabilities; they may "speak" different languages; they may even have different levels of sociality. This diversity raises additional research challenges in the study of smart spaces, which only few recent studies have addressed. In the following paragraphs, we present these approaches, which have the common feature of employing methods and techniques from the field of Distributed Artificial Intelligence.

One such approach is *sTuples* ([23]). This framework extends Tuple Spaces using SW technologies to represent and retrieve tuples from a Tuple Space. The Tuple Space model uses a logically shared memory, where producers add tuples to a common space, while consumers read or extract tuples from the space using a search template. The sTuples model advances the space lookup operations using DAML+OIL for the representation of context entities and RACER as the reasoning engine. It provides a generic framework to implement clients and services in a pervasive environment by using service and data tuples. Data tuples are semantic descriptions of the context data that an entity is willing to share with other entities in the environment, while service tuples are advertisements of the services offered in the same environment. Each entity uses various types of agents to gain access to the Tuple Space, each of which has a distinct role. Examples of such roles are, managing the addition, removal and state changes of tuples, searching in the Tuple Space, recommending services to the user, and notifying the user about tuple changes.

Similar approaches, which combine SW technologies and shared memory models to support asynchronous communications in ambient environments, are the *Semantic Spaces* ([24]), and the context management framework presented in [25]. The latter follows a *blackboard*-based approach. A mobile terminal system uses a central context manager, which stores context information from any available source. Clients can directly query the manager to gain context information, subscribe to various context change notification services, or use higher level contexts transparently. In the latter case, the context manager assigns the reasoning tasks to dedicated recognition services.

The OWL-SF framework ([26]) combines the OMG's *Super Distributed Objects* (SDO) technology and the OWL language to allow the distribution of semantically annotated services for the needs of ambient context-aware systems. SDOs are logical representations of hardware and software entities that are used to enable distributed interoperability. The proposed framework integrates two basic building blocks, OWL-SDOs and Deduction Servers. The OWL-SDOs are semantic extensions of SDOs; they use the OWL language to describe their status, services and communication interface. Deduction servers are specific OWL-SDOs that provide reasoning services. They contain a deduction engine coordinating reasoning tasks, an RDF inference layer providing rule reasoning support and an OWL-DL reasoner. Besides providing reasoning support, they are responsible for collecting the status of SDOs published using the OWL format, and for building an integrated OWL description accessible to reasoning.

The main feature that distinguishes the latter study is the lack of a central reasoning or control entity; it is fully decentralized. Collecting the reasoning tasks in a central entity certainly has many advantages; we can achieve better control, and better coordination between the various entities that have access to the central entity. Blackboard-based and shared-memory models have been thoroughly studied and used in many different types of distributed systems and have proved to work well in practice. The requirements are, though, much different in this setting. Context may not be restricted to a small room, office or apartment; we must also study cases of broader areas. The communication with a central entity is not guaranteed; we must assume unreliable and restricted wireless communications. Thus, a fully distributed scheme is a necessity. The OWL-SF framework is a step towards the right direction, but certainly not the last one. In order to deal with more realistic ambient environments, we need to eliminate some of the assumptions that they make. For example, different entities are not required to use the same representation and reasoning models, and we cannot always assume the existence of dedicated reasoning machines.

5   Other Reasoning Techniques

This section presents additional techniques that have been used to enhance the reasoning capabilities of AmI applications to deal with certain challenges, such as the ambiguity of context information, and the vast amount of context data.

In AmbieSense ([27]), they deal with the potentially vast amount of context data, using *Case Based Reasoning*. The reasoning mechanism is split into two different parts; the on-line part that resides on the user's mobile device, and the off-line part that resides on the user's backbone system. When new information arrives from the context retrieval module, it is translated to fit a preexistent ontology and sent to a CBR agent. The agent tries to retrieve a known context or case, and classifies the current situation based on the retrieved one. The associated goal is then presented to the task decomposition agent, and the case is stored in the case base. Since the user is expected to experience a few different situations daily, the storage of the cases will quickly fill up the mobile device and the CBR searching process will be hampered. To remedy this, some of the reasoning process is moved into the user's backbone servers.

The ec(h)o audio museum guide, described in [28], uses DAML+OIL ontologies for the representation of context data and user profiles. Its reasoning engine uses a forward-chaining reasoning mechanism to select the sound objects to be presented. The rules use several criteria that correspond to the semantic descriptions of the museum artifacts, the visitor's profile, and the way the visitor moves and interacts with the artifacts. To perform reasoning more efficiently, they build a virtual network that keeps track of possible combinations of facts, and support rule activation using the RETE algorithm (implemented in Jess).

The use of a Bayesian network to deal with the ambiguity of context data has been proposed in some recent studies. In MIRA, a context-based retrieval system capable of recording and indexing MBone videoconferences, they use a Bayesian network, coupled to a cost model, to describe a context-retrieval service that provides performance measures based on reliability and resource usage cost ([29]). In [30], a probabilistic model is used to define uncertain contexts. This model extends the OWL ontology model of SOCAM, by attaching probability values to the context predicates. They also adopt a Bayesian network as an underlying reasoning mechanism, as it has efficient probabilistic reasoning capabilities and allows representing causal relationships between various contexts. Bayesian networks to recognize high-level contexts have also been used in [25].[1]

6   Discussion

The special requirements of ambient environments impose the need of logic models that inherently deal with the imperfect nature of context data. Models that embody the notions of uncertainty, temporal and spatial change, and incompleteness would provide more robust and efficient solutions. A possible solution is the use of *nonmonotonic* reasoning, which has already been studied and used in other settings with similar requirements, such as the Web, e-learning environments, business rules, security specifications, negotiation protocols, and others. Recently, a number of nonmonotonic rule languages have been studied and reasoners that integrate them well with ontologies have been developed.

The main drawback of this approach is its relatively higher computational complexity, which becomes even worse, if we consider the potentially vast amount of available context data. A possible solution is to partition the large knowledge bases into smaller pieces, share these pieces with other computing devices, and deploy some form of partition-based reasoning. This is of course not an easy task, and only few recent studies have focused on this problem. An interesting approach is proposed in [31], which studies the partitioning of a large OWL ABox with respect to a TBox so that specific kinds of reasoning can be performed separately on each partition and the results trivially combined in order to achieve complete answers. In [32], they propose algorithms for reasoning with partitions of related logical axioms in propositional and first-order logic, and a greedy algorithm that automatically decomposes a set of logical axioms into partitions. Applying these ideas in AmI seems to be a very promising research direction.

Finally, to achieve collective intelligence, we must study methods for integrating and reasoning with data coming from heterogeneous sources and possibly described in different vocabularies. Translating all the data in a common format (schema) and performing centralized reasoning (followed by most of the studies that we presented) is one of some possible solutions. This approach is described as the Local-As-View approach in the Data Integration research area ([33]). Other approaches, concerning mainly the integration of heterogeneous data, are the Global-As-View approach and the Both-As-View approach ([33]), which have been recently studied and implemented in semantic P2P management systems. GAV assumes a global virtual schema, which is defined as a set of views over the data source schemas. This enables writing queries and rules using the local language of each data source. In BAV, local schemas are mapped to

---

[1] The modeling and reasoning approaches, along with the architecture and the aim of the systems referenced in Sections 2-6 are summarized in Table 1.

Table 1. Main Features of Context-Aware Frameworks

System	Modeling	Reasoning	Architecture	Aim
CoBrA [9]	OWL	RDQL	centralized (agent-based)	context-aware services
Context Awareness Framework [10]	RDF	RDQL	centralized	service prioritization
CG Platform [11]	RDF	RQL	centralized	location-based services
Semantic Mobile Environment [13]	DL	DL	distributed (P2P)	profile-service matchmaking
Context-Aware Door Lock [14]	OWL	DL	centralized	automatic door lock
SOCAM [16],[30]	OWL	FOL + Bayesian	centralized (middleware)	middleware for mobile services
Semantic Space [17]	OWL	RDQL+FOL	centralized	smart space mobile services
Gaia Context Infrastructure [19]	FOL	FOL	centralized	context-aware services
CONON Prototype [18]	OWL	DL+FOL	centralized	context-aware services
eWallet [20]	OWL	Jess	centralized (agent-based)	context-aware services
Context-Aware Access Control Framework [21]	OWL	DL+LP	centralized	policy evaluation
CARE [22]	OWL	DL+LP	centralized (middleware)	service adaptation
sTuples [23]	DAML+OIL	DL	decentralized shared memory	mobile services
Semantic Spaces [24]	RDF		decentralized shared memory	information sharing
Context Management Framework [25]	RDF	Bayesian	decentralized (blackboard-based)	information sharing notification services
OWL-SF [26]	OWL	DL	distributed (SDOs)	distributed services
AmbieSense [27]	taxonomies	CBR	centralized	context management
ec(h)o system [28]	DAML+OIL	Jess	centralized	audio museum guide
MIRA [29]	XML	Bayesian	centralized	videoconferences management

each other using a sequence of schema transformations (*mappings*). Reasoning with multiple ontologies interrelated with semantic mappings is studied in [34]. Examples of totally distributed reasoning algorithms, where the whole reasoning procedure can be viewed as a chain of reasoning tasks performed by different entities, can be found in [35]. These approaches can also lead to new ideas on how to exploit the different reasoning capabilities of each entity in an ambient environment, in order to make the whole system of entities more intelligent.

References

1. Henricksen, K., Indulska, J.: Modelling and Using Imperfect Context Information. In: Proceedings of PERCOMW 2004, Washington, DC, USA, pp. 33–37. IEEE Computer Society Press, Los Alamitos (2004)
2. Schmidt, A.: Interactive Context-Aware Systems Interacting with Ambient Intelligence. In: Riva, G., Vatalaro, F., Davide, F., Alcaniz, M. (eds.) Ambient Intelligence, IOS Press, Amsterdam (2005)
3. Seaborne, A.: RDQL - A Query Language for RDF. W3C member submission, Hewlett Packard (2004)
4. Karvounarakis, G., Alexaki, S., Christophides, V., Plexousakis, D., Scholl, M.: RQL: a declarative query language for RDF. In: Proceedings of the 11th International World Wide Web Conference (WWW), pp. 592–603 (2002)
5. Sintek, M., Decker, S.: TRIPLE - A Query, Inference, and Transformation Language for the Semantic Web. In: Proceedings of the First International Semantic Web Conference, pp. 364–378. Springer, Heidelberg (2002)
6. FaCT: FaCT system website (2003), http://www.cs.man.ac.uk/~horrocks/FaCT/
7. Haarslev, V., Möller, R.: RACER System Description. In: IJCAR, pp. 701–706 (2001)
8. Parsia, B., Sirin, E.: Pellet: An OWL DL Reasoner. In: 3rd International Semantic Web Conference (ISWC 2004) (2004)
9. Chen, H., Finin, T., Joshi, A.: Semantic Web in a Pervasive Context-Aware Architecture. Artificial Intelligence in Mobile System, 33–40 (2003)
10. Forstadius, J., Lassila, O., Seppanen, T.: RDF-based model for context-aware reasoning in rich service environment. In: PerCom 2005 Workshops, pp. 15–19 (2005)
11. Patkos, T., Bikakis, A., Antoniou, G., Plexousakis, D., Papadopouli, M.: A Semantics-based Framework for Context-Aware Services: Lessons Learned and Challenges. In: Indulska, J., Ma, J., Yang, L.T., Ungerer, T., Cao, J. (eds.) UIC 2007. LNCS, vol. 4611, pp. 839–848. Springer, Heidelberg (2007)
12. van Bunningen, A.: Context aware querying - Challenges for data management in ambient intelligence. Technical Report TR-CTIT-04-51, Univ. of Twente (2004)
13. von Hessling, A., Kleemann, T., Sinner, A.: Semantic User Profiles and their Applications in a Mobile Environment. In: Fachberichte Informatik 2–2005, Universität Koblenz-Landau (2005)
14. Turhan, A.-Y., Springer, T., Berger, M.: Pushing Doors for Modeling Contexts with OWL DL a Case Study. In: PERCOMW 2006, Washington, DC, USA, IEEE Computer Society Press, Los Alamitos (2006)
15. Haarslev, V., Möller, R., Wessel, M.: RacerPro User Guide (2005), http://www.racer-systems.com/products/racerpro/users-guide-1-9.pdf
16. Gu, T., Pung, H.K., Zhang, D.Q.: A Middleware for Building Context-Aware Mobile Services. In: Proceedings of the IEEE Vehicular Technology Conference (VTC 2004), Milan, Italy (2004)
17. Wang, X.H., Dong, J.S., Chin, C.Y., Hettiarachchi, S.R., Zhang, D.: Semantic Space: an infrastructure for smart spaces. IEEE Pervasive Computing 3(3), 32–39 (2004)

18. Wang, X.H., Zhang, D.Q., Gu, T., Pung, H.K.: Ontology Based Context Modeling and Reasoning using OWL. In: PERCOMW 2004, Washington, DC, USA, p. 18. IEEE Computer Society Press, Los Alamitos (2004)
19. Ranganathan, A., Campbell, R.H.: An infrastructure for context-awareness based on first order logic. Personal Ubiquitous Comput. 7(6), 353–364 (2003)
20. Gandon, F.L., Sadeh, N.M.: Semantic web technologies to reconcile privacy and context awareness. Journal of Web Semantics 1, 241–260 (2004)
21. Toninelli, A., Montanari, R., Kagal, L., Lassila, O.: A Semantic Context-Aware Access Control Framework for Secure Collaborations in Pervasive Computing Environments. In: Proc. of 5th International Semantic Web Conference, November 2006, pp. 5–9 (2006)
22. Agostini, A., Bettini, C., Riboni, D.: Experience Report: Ontological Reasoning for Context-aware Internet Services. In: PERCOMW 2006, Washington, DC, USA, IEEE Computer Society Press, Los Alamitos (2006)
23. Khushraj, D., Lassila, O., Finin, T.: sTuples: Semantic Tuple Spaces. In: First Annual International Conference on Mobile and Ubiquitous Systems: Networking and Services (MobiQuitous 2004), pp. 267–277 (2004)
24. Krummenacher, R., Kopecký, J., Strang, T.: Sharing Context Information in Semantic Spaces.. In: OTM Workshops, pp. 229–232 (2005)
25. Korpipaa, P., Mantyjarvi, J., Kela, J., Keranen, H., Malm, E.-J.: Managing Context Information in Mobile Devices. IEEE Pervasive Computing 2(3), 42–51 (2003)
26. Mrohs, B., Luther, M., Vaidya, R., Wagner, M., Steglich, S., Kellerer, W., Arbanowski, S.: OWL-SF - A Distributed Semantic Service Framework. In: Workshop on Context Awareness for Proactive Systems (CAPS 2005) (2005)
27. Kofod-Petersen, A., Mikalsen, M.: Representing and Reasoning about Context in a Mobile Environment. Revue d'Intelligence Artificielle 19(3), 479–498 (2005)
28. Hatala, M., Wakkary, R., Kalantari, L.: Ontologies and rules in support of real-time ubiquitous application. Journal of Web Semantics, Special Issue on Rules and ontologies for Semantic Web 3(1), 5–22 (2005)
29. Castro, P., Mani, M., Mathur, S., Muntz, R.R.: Managing Context for Internet Videoconferences: The Multimedia Internet Recorder and Archive. In: Proc. of Multimedia and Computer Networks, San Jose, California (2000)
30. Gu, T., Pung, H.K., Zhang, D.Q.: A Bayesian Approach for Dealing with Uncertain Contexts. In: Proceedings of the Second International Conference on Pervasive Computing, Vienna, Austria, May 2004, Austrian Computing Society (2004)
31. Guo, Y., Heflin, J.: A Scalable Approach for Partitioning OWL Knowledge Bases. In: Second International Workshop on Scalable Semantic Web Knowledge Base Systems (SSWS 2006) (2006)
32. Amir, E., McIlraith, S.: Partition-based logical reasoning for first-order and propositional theories. Artif. Intelligence 162(1-2), 49–88 (2005)
33. Halevy, A.Y., Rajaraman, A., Ordille, J.J.: Data Integration: The Teenage Years. In: VLDB, pp. 9–16 (2006)
34. Serafini, L., Tamilin, A.: DRAGO: Distributed Reasoning Architecture for the Semantic Web. In: ESWC, pp. 361–376 (2005)
35. Adjiman, P., Chatalic, P., Goasdoue, F., Rousset, M.-C., Simon, L.: Distributed Reasoning in a Peer-to-Peer Setting: Application to the Semantic Web. Journal of Artificial Intelligence Research 25, 269–314 (2006)

Distributed Reasoning with Conflicts in an Ambient Peer-to-Peer Setting

Antonis Bikakis and Grigoris Antoniou

Institute of Computer Science, FO.R.T.H., Vassilika Voutwn
P.O. Box 1385, GR 71110, Heraklion, Greece
{bikakis,antoniou}@ics.forth.gr

Abstract. In ambient environments, there coexist many different entities that collect, process, and change the available context information. Although they all share the same context, they face it from different viewpoints based on their perceptive capabilities, experiences and goals. Moreover, they are expected to use distinct vocabularies; they may even have different levels of sociality. This diversity raises additional research challenges in the study of Distributed Artificial Intelligence. In this paper, we present an algorithm for reasoning with distributed rule theories in an ambient setting. The algorithm models the participating agents as nodes in a peer-to-peer system, and considers the potential conflicts that may arise during the integration of the distributed theories taking into account some special characteristics of context knowledge and ambient agents.

1 Introduction

The study of ambient environments and pervasive computing systems has introduced new research challenges in the field of Distributed Artificial Intelligence. These are mainly caused by the imperfect nature of the available context information and the special characteristics of the agents that provide and process this knowledge. Henricksen and Indulska in [1] characterize four types of imperfect context information: *unknown*, *ambiguous*, *imprecise*, and *erroneous*. Sensor or connectivity failures (which are inevitable in wireless connections) result in situations, that not all context data is available at any time. When the data about a context property comes from multiple sources, the context information may become ambiguous. Imprecision is common in sensor-derived information, while erroneous context information arises as a result of human or hardware errors.

The agents that operate in an ambient environment are expected to have different goals, experiences and perceptive capabilities. They may use distinct vocabularies; they may even have different levels of sociality. Due to the highly dynamic and open nature of the environment (various entities join and leave the environment at random times), they are not able to know a priori all other entities that are present at a specific time instance nor can they communicate directly with all of them.

Considering these requirements, three main challenges of knowledge management in Ambient Intelligence are to enable:

M. Mühlhäuser et al. (Eds.): AmI 2007 Workshops, CCIS 11, pp. 24–33, 2008.

1. Reasoning with the highly dynamic and ambiguous context data.
2. Managing the potentially huge piece of context data, in a real-time fashion, considering the restricted computational capabilities of some mobile devices.
3. Collective intelligence, by supporting information sharing, and distributed reasoning between the entities of the ambient environment.

So far, most pervasive computing frameworks have followed fully centralized approaches (e.g. [2,3,4,5,6,7,8,9,10,11]), while some others have employed models based on the *blackboard* and *shared memory* paradigms (e.g. [12,13,14]). Collecting the reasoning tasks in a central entity certainly has many advantages. It achieves better control, and better coordination between the participating entities. However, such solutions cannot meet the demanding requirements of ambient environments. The dynamics of the network and the unreliable and restricted (by the range of the transmitters) wireless communications inevitably lead to fully distributed solutions.

The goal of this study is to propose a distributed solution tailored to the special characteristics of ambient environments. The approach we propose to take models the agents of an ambient environment as nodes in a peer-to-peer system. Specifically, it considers nodes that have independent knowledge, and that interact with existing, *neighboring* nodes to exchange information. The internal knowledge is expressed in terms of rules, and knowledge is imported from other nodes through *bridging rules*.

Even if it is assumed that the theory of each node is locally consistent, the same assumption will not necessarily hold for the global knowledge base. The unification of the local theories, which model the viewpoints of the different nodes, may result in inconsistencies that are caused by the bridging rules. To deal with them, we follow a non-monotonic approach; bridging rules are expressed as *defeasible rules* (rules that may be defeated in the existence of adequate contrary evidence), and priorities between conflicting rules are determined by the level of *trust* that each node has on the other system nodes. In this way, the proposed approach manages to exploit the knowledge of every system node, and reason in a consistent and efficient manner, taking into account the viewpoint of each different node with regard to its context and cooperating peers.

The rest of the paper is structured as follows. Section 2 refers to the most prominent recent studies on reasoning in P2P data management systems and contextual reasoning. In Section 3, we present the algorithms that constitute our approach for reasoning with distributed rule theories. The conclusive section briefly describes the next steps of our work.

2   Related Work

Several recent studies have focused on developing formal models and methods for reasoning in peer-to-peer database systems. A key issue in formalizing data-oriented P2P systems is the semantic characterization of the *mappings* (bridging rules). One approach (followed in [15,16]) is the first-order logic interpretation of P2P systems. In [17], Calavanese *et al.* identifies several drawbacks with this approach, regarding modularity, generality and decidability, and proposes new semantics based on epistemic logic. A common problem of both approaches is that they do not model and thus cannot handle inconsistency. Franconi *et al.* in [18] extends the autoepistemic semantics to formalize local inconsistency. The latter approach guarantees that a locally inconsistent database base will not render the entire knowledge base inconsistent. A broader extension, proposed by Calvanese *et al.* in [19], is based on nonmonontonic epistemic logic, and enables isolating local inconsistency, while also handling peers that may provide mutually inconsistent data. The proposed query evaluation algorithm assumes that all peers share a common alphabet of constants, and does not model *trust* or *priorities* between the peers. The propositional P2P inference system proposed by Chatalic *et al.* in [20] deals with conflicts caused by mutually inconsistent information sources, by detecting them and reasoning without them. The main problem is the same, once again: To perform reasoning, the conflicts are not actually resolved using some external trust or priority information; they are rather isolated.

Relevant to our work are also some recent research studies that combine the fields of multi-context systems (MCS) and nonmonotonic reasoning. The first prominent work in this research line was conducted by Roelofsen and Serafini. They define in [21] a non-monotonic rule-based MCS framework, which contains default negation in the rules. The multi-context variant of Default Logic, introduced by Brewka *et al.* in [22] is a step further towards nonmonotonic contextual reasoning. Specifically, the authors propose to model the bridge relations between different contexts as *default rules*. The latter study has the additional advantage that is closer to implementation due to the well-studied relation between Default Logic and Logic Programming. However, the authors do not provide certain reasoning algorithms, leaving some practical issues, such as the integration of priority information, unanswered.

3   Our Approach

We propose modeling the agents of an ambient environment as nodes in a P2P system. This choice is not arbitrary. The P2P paradigm captures many critical properties of ambient settings:

1. Each different peer independently collects and processes in its own way the available context information.
2. Each peer may not have (immediate) access to all information sources.
3. The peers share their knowledge through messages with their neighboring nodes.
4. Each peer may not trust all the other peers at the same level.
5. Peers join and leave the system randomly.

Below, we define our P2P model, which captures local knowledge, mapping relations through which the nodes exchange information, and trust between the system nodes. We also define the specific reasoning problem that we deal with, and describe the reasoning algorithms that we have developed.

3.1 Definitions

We assume a peer-to-peer system P as a collection of local theories:

$$P = \{P_i\}, i = 1, 2, ..., n$$

Each peer has a proper distinct vocabulary V_{P_i} and a unique identifier i. Each local theory is a set of rules that contain only local literals (literals from the local vocabulary). These rules are of the form:

$$r_i : a_i, b_i, ...k_i \rightarrow x_i$$

where i denotes the peer identifier.

Each peer also defines mappings that associate literals from its own vocabulary (*local literals*) with literals from the vocabulary of other peers (*remote literals*). The acquaintances of peer P_i, $ACQ(P_i)$ are the set of peers that at least one of P_i's mappings involves at least one of their local literals. The mappings are rules of the form:

$$m_i : a_i, b_j, ...z_k \rightarrow x$$

The above mapping rule is defined by P_i, and associates some of its own local literals with some of the literals defined by P_j, P_k and other system nodes. Literal x may belong to whichever vocabulary of these system nodes. Finally, each peer defines a trust order T_i, which includes a subset of the system nodes.

3.2 Problem Statement

Given a peer-to-peer system P, and a query about literal x_i issued at peer P_i, find the truth value of x_i considering P_i's local theory, its mappings and the theories of the other system nodes.

We assume that the local theories are consistent, but this is not necessarily true for the case of the unified theory $T(P)$, which is the collection of the theories (local rules and mappings) of the system nodes. The inconsistencies result from interactions between local theories and are caused by mappings.

An example of such conflicts derives in the following system of theories:

P_1	P_2	P_3
$r_{11} : a_1 \rightarrow x_1$	$r_{21} : \ \rightarrow a_2$	$r_{31} : \rightarrow a_3$
$m_{11} : a_2 \rightarrow a_1$		
$m_{12} : a_3 \rightarrow \neg a_1$		

P_i's theory is locally consistent, but with the addition of the the two mapping rules (m_{11}, m_{12}), which associate the literals of P_1 with those of P_2 and P_3, a conflict about literal a_1 derives from the interaction of the three theories.

3.3 *P2P_DR* Algorithm

The algorithm follows four main steps. In the first step (lines 1-16), it uses P_i's local theory to prove x_i. If x_i or its negation, $\neg x_i$, derives from the peer's local theory, the algorithm terminates returning Yes/No respectively, without considering the peer's mappings or the theories of other peers in the system.

In the second step (lines 17-41), if neither x_i nor $\neg x_i$ derives from the local theory, the algorithm also uses P_i's mappings. It collects all the rules that support x_i. For each such rule, it checks the provability of the literals in its body. For each local/remote literal, it issues similar queries (recursive calls of the algorithm) to P_i (local literals) or to the appropriate P_i's acquaintances (remote literals). To avoid circles, before each new call, the algorithm checks if the same query has been issued before, during the same query evaluation process. At the end of this step, the algorithm builds the mapping supportive set of x_i; this contains the set of mapping (locally or remotely defined) rules that can be used to prove x_i in the absence of contradictions.

The third step (lines 42-66) involves the rules that contradict x_i. The algorithm builds the mapping conflicting set of x_i, by collecting the rules that support $\neg x_i$.

In the last step (lines 64-71), the algorithm decides about x_i by comparing the supportive and conflicting sets. To compare two mapping sets, a peer uses its trust order T_i. According to this order, one mapping rule m_k is considered to be stronger than m_l from P_i's viewpoint if P_i trusts P_k more than P_l. The strength of a mapping set is determined by the weakest rule in this set. In the followings, we denote as:

r_i^l: a local rule of P_i
r_i^m: a mapping rule of P_i
r_i^{lm}: a rule (local/mapping) of P_i
R^m: the set of all mapping rules
$R_s(x_i)$: the set of supportive rules for x_i
$R_c(x_i)$: the set of conflicting rules for x_i

When a node P_i receives a query about x_i, it runs the **P2P_DR** algorithm. The algorithm parameters are:

x_i: the queried literal
P_0: the peer that issued the query
P_i: the local node
SS_{x_i}: the set of supportive mappings for x_i (initially empty)
CS_{x_i}: the set of conflicting mappings for x_i (initially empty)
$Hist_{x_i}$: the list of pending queries of the form: $[x_1, ..., x_i]$
Ans_{x_i}: the answer returned for x_i (initially empty)

P2P_DR$(x_i, P_0, P_i, SS_{x_i}, CS_{x_i}, Hist_{x_i}, Ans_{x_i})$
1: **if** $\exists r_i^l \in R_s(x_i)$ **then**
2:     $localHist_{x_i} \leftarrow [x_i]$
3:     run $local\_alg(x_i, localHist_{x_i}, localAns_{x_i})$

4:    **if** $localAns_{x_i} = Yes$ **then**
5:      $Ans_{x_i} \leftarrow localAns_{x_i}$
6:      terminate
7:    **end if**
8: **end if**
9: **if** $\exists r_i^l \in R_c(x_i)$ **then**
10:   $localHist_{x_i} \leftarrow [x_i]$
11:   run $local\_alg(\neg x_i, localHist_{x_i}, localAns_{\neg x_i})$
12:   **if** $localAns_{\neg x_i} = Yes$ **then**
13:     $Ans_{x_i} \leftarrow \neg localAns_{\neg x_i}$
14:     terminate
15:   **end if**
16: **end if**
17: **for all** $r_i^{lm} \in R_s(x_i)$ **do**
18:   $SS_{r_i} \leftarrow \{\}$
19:   **for all** $b_t \in body(r_i^{lm})$ **do**
20:     **if** $b_t \in Hist_{x_i}$ **then**
21:      stop and check the next rule
22:     **else**
23:      $Hist_{b_t} \leftarrow Hist_{x_i} \bigcup b_t$
24:      run $P2P\_DR(b_t, P_i, P_t, SS_{b_t}, CS_{b_t}, Hist_{b_t}, Ans_{b_t})$
25:      **if** $Ans_{b_t} = No$ **then**
26:       stop and check the next rule
27:      **else**
28:       $SS_{r_i} \leftarrow SS_{r_i} \bigcup SS_{b_t}$
29:      **end if**
30:     **end if**
31:   **end for**
32:   **if** $r_i^{lm} \in R^m$ **then**
33:     $SS_{r_i} \leftarrow SS_{r_i} \bigcup r_i^{lm}$
34:   **end if**
35:   **if** $Stronger(SS_{r_i}, SS_{x_i}, T_i) = Yes$ **then**
36:     $SS_{x_i} \leftarrow SS_{r_i}$
37:   **end if**
38: **end for**
39: **if** $SS_{x_i} = \{\}$ **then**
40:   return $Ans_{x_i} = No$ and terminate
41: **end if**
42: **for all** $r_i^{lm} \in R_c(x_i)$ **do**
43:   $SS_{r_i} \leftarrow \{\}$
44:   **for all** $b_t \in body(r_i^{lm})$ **do**
45:     **if** $b_t \in Hist_{x_i}$ **then**
46:      stop and check the next rule
47:     **else**
48:      $Hist_{b_t} \leftarrow Hist_{x_i} \bigcup b_t$

49:         run $P2P\_DR(b_t, P_i, P_t, SS_{b_t}, CS_{b_t}, Hist_{b_t}, Ans_{b_t})$
50:         **if** $Ans_{b_t} = No$ **then**
51:            stop and check the next rule
52:         **else**
53:            $SS_{r_i} \leftarrow SS_{r_i} \bigcup SS_{b_t}$
54:         **end if**
55:      **end if**
56:   **end for**
57:   **if** $r_i^{lm} \in R^m$ **then**
58:      $SS_{r_i} \leftarrow SS_{r_i} \bigcup r_i^{lm}$
59:   **end if**
60:   **if** $Stronger(SS_{r_i}, CS_{x_i}, T_i) = Yes$ **then**
61:      $CS_{x_i} \leftarrow SS_{r_i}$
62:   **end if**
63: **end for**
64: **if** $CS_{x_i} = \{\}$ **then**
65:   return $Ans_{x_i} = Yes$ and SS_{x_i} and terminate
66: **end if**
67: **if** $Stronger(SS_{x_i}, CS_{x_i}, T_i) = Yes$ **then**
68:   return $Ans_{x_i} = Yes$ and SS_{x_i} and terminate
69: **else**
70:   $Ans_{x_i} = No$ and terminate
71: **end if**

The $local\_alg(x_i, localHist_{x_i}, localAns_{x_i})$ is used to determine if x_i is a consequence of P_i's local theory. The algorithm parameters are:

x_i: the queried literal

$localHist_{x_i}$: the list of pending queries in P_i of the form: $[x_i^1, ..., x_i^m]$

$localAns_{x_i}$: the local answer returned for x_i (initially No)

local_alg$(x_i, localHist_{x_i}, localAns_{x_i})$
 1: **for all** $r_i^l \in R_s(x_i)$ **do**
 2:   **if** $body(r_i^l) = \{\}$ **then**
 3:      return $localAns_{x_i} = Yes$
 4:      terminate
 5:   **else**
 6:      **for all** $b_i \in body(r_i^l)$ **do**
 7:         **if** $b_i \in localHist_{x_i}$ **then**
 8:            stop and check the next rule
 9:         **else**
10:            $localHist_{b_i} \leftarrow localHist_{x_i} \bigcup b_i$
11:            run $local\_alg(b_i, localHist_{b_i}, localAns_{b_i})$
12:         **end if**
13:      **end for**
14:      **if** for every b_i: $localAns_{b_i} = Yes$ **then**

15:          $localAns_{x_i} \leftarrow Yes$
16:          terminate
17:       **end if**
18:    **end if**
19: **end for**

The $Stronger(S, C, T_i)$ function is used by P_i to check if the S set of mappings is stronger than the C set of mappings based on P_i's trust level order, T_i.

Stronger(S, C, T_i)

1: $r_s^w \leftarrow r_s \in S$ s.t. $forall\ r_i \in S : r_s$ is not weaker than r_i (according to T_i)
2: $r_c^w \leftarrow r_c \in C$ s.t. $forall\ r_j \in C : r_c$ is not weaker than r_j (according to T_i)
3: **if** r_s^w is stronger than r_c^w **then**
4:    $Stronger = Yes$
5: **else**
6:    $Stronger = No$
7: **end if**

3.4   Algorithm Properties

The application of the proposed algorithms in real scenarios largely depends on some properties regarding its termination and complexity.

Termination. We assume that there are a finite number of nodes in the system, each of which with a finite number of literals in its vocabulary. As a consequence, there are a finite number of rules that a peer may define. If the algorithm did not terminate, it would have to make indefinite recursive calls, adding each time a new query to the history, without ever returning an answer or detecting a cycle. However, this is impossible, because: (a) the number of recursive calls is bounded by the total finite number of literals in the system; and (b) there can be a finite number of independent (with different history) algorithm calls. These are bounded by the total finite number of rules in the system. Consequently, the algorithm will eventually terminate.

Number of Messages. To reduce the complexity of the algorithm with regard to the number of messages that the system nodes have to exchange, and the computational overhead of the algorithm on each system node, we can make the following optimization: Each node is required to retain two states: (a) the state of the queries it has been requested to process, INC_Q; this contains tuples of the form (q_i, Ans_{q_i}), where q_i is the queried literal, and Ans_{q_i} is $true/false$ in the case the node has completed the computation, or $undetermined$ otherwise; and (b) the state of the queries it has requested other peers to process, OUT_Q (of the same form). Before sending a query to one of its neighbors, a node checks if the same query is in OUT_Q. If this is the case, it retrieves the answer stored in OUT_Q if this has the value $true/false$, or waits until the pending query returns a $true/false$ answer. When a new query is issued at a node, the node checks if the same query is in its INC_Q. If it is, the node returns the stored $true/false$ answer for that query if this has already been computed; otherwise, it suspends the new query until the pending query returns a $true/false$ answer. The space overhead of both states is proportional to the number of mappings that a node defines. The two states need to be updated every time a new query is issued at the system from an external source (we assume that the state of the network remains unchanged during the computation of each such query).

With these optimizations, each node will have to make at most one query for each of the remote literals that appear in the body of its mapping rules. In the worst case, that each peer has defined mappings that involve literals from all the other nodes in the system, and needs to apply all these mappings during a query evaluation, each peer will have to make $n \times n_l$ queries, where n is the number of system nodes and n_l is the maximum number of literals that a node may define. So, the total number of messages that need to be exchanged for the computation of a single query is in the worst case $n \times n \times n_l = O(n^2)$ (assuming that the number of nodes is the most critical parameter in the system).

4   Conclusion

We presented an approach for distributed reasoning in P2P settings, taking into account some special properties and constraints of context knowledge and ambient environments. The proposed reasoning algorithm models and reasons with potential conflicts that may arise during the integration of the distributed theories; to resolve these conflicts it uses trust information from the system nodes. We have already proved some desirable algorithm properties regarding its termination and complexity, and we are in the course of studying other properties, such as the computational complexity of the distributed algorithm on a single node. Other planned research directions of the same work are: (a) Study if there is an equivalent defeasible theory that derives from the unification of the distributed theories and produces the same results; (b) Extend the algorithm to support overlapping vocabularies; (c) Extend the algorithm to support defeasible local rules, and non-Boolean queries; and (d) Study applications in the Ambient Intelligence domain, where the theories may represent ontological knowledge (Horn logic subset of OWL DL), policies or regulations.

References

1. Henricksen, K., Indulska, J.: Modelling and Using Imperfect Context Information. In: Proceedings of PERCOMW 2004, Washington, DC, USA, pp. 33–37. IEEE Computer Society Press, Los Alamitos (2004)
2. Chen, H., Finin, T., Joshi, A.: Semantic Web in a Pervasive Context-Aware Architecture. Artificial Intelligence in Mobile System, 33–40 (2003)
3. Forstadius, J., Lassila, O., Seppanen, T.: RDF-based model for context-aware reasoning in rich service environment. In: PerCom 2005 Workshops, pp. 15–19 (2005)

4. Patkos, T., Bikakis, A., Antoniou, G., Plexousakis, D., Papadopouli, M.: A Semantics-based Framework for Context-Aware Services: Lessons Learned and Challenges. In: Indulska, J., Ma, J., Yang, L.T., Ungerer, T., Cao, J. (eds.) UIC 2007. LNCS, vol. 4611, pp. 839–848. Springer, Heidelberg (2007)
5. Gu, T., Pung, H.K., Zhang, D.Q.: A Middleware for Building Context-Aware Mobile Services. In: Proceedings of the IEEE Vehicular Technology Conference (VTC 2004), Milan, Italy (2004)
6. Wang, X.H., Dong, J.S., Chin, C.Y., Hettiarachchi, S.R., Zhang, D.: Semantic Space: an infrastructure for smart spaces. IEEE Pervasive Computing 3(3), 32–39 (2004)
7. Ranganathan, A., Campbell, R.H.: An infrastructure for context-awareness based on first order logic. Personal Ubiquitous Comput. 7(6), 353–364 (2003)
8. Gandon, F.L., Sadeh, N.M.: Semantic web technologies to reconcile privacy and context awareness. Journal of Web Semantics 1, 241–260 (2004)
9. Toninelli, A., Montanari, R., Kagal, L., Lassila, O.: A Semantic Context-Aware Access Control Framework for Secure Collaborations in Pervasive Computing Environments. In: Proc. of 5th International Semantic Web Conference, pp. 5–9 (2006)
10. Kofod-Petersen, A., Mikalsen, M.: Representing and Reasoning about Context in a Mobile Environment. Revue d'Intelligence Artificielle 19(3), 479–498 (2005)
11. Hatala, M., Wakkary, R., Kalantari, L.: Ontologies and rules in support of real-time ubiquitous application. Journal of Web Semantics, Special Issue on Rules and ontologies for Semantic Web 3(1), 5–22 (2005)
12. Khushraj, D., Lassila, O., Finin, T.: sTuples: Semantic Tuple Spaces. In: First Annual International Conference on Mobile and Ubiquitous Systems: Networking and Services (MobiQuitous 2004), pp. 267–277 (2004)
13. Krummenacher, R., Kopecký, J., Strang, T.: Sharing Context Information in Semantic Spaces.. In: OTM Workshops, pp. 229–232 (2005)
14. Korpipaa, P., Mantyjarvi, J., Kela, J., Keranen, H., Malm, E.-J.: Managing Context Information in Mobile Devices. IEEE Pervasive Computing 02(3), 42–51 (2003)
15. Bernstein, P.A., Giunchiglia, F., Kementsietsidis, A., Mylopoulos, J., Serafini, L., Zaihrayeu, I.: Data Management for Peer-to-Peer Computing: A Vision. In: WebDB, pp. 89–94 (2002)
16. Halevy, A.Y., Ives, Z.G., Suciu, D., Tatarinov, I.: Schema Mediation in Peer Data Management Systems. In: ICDE, p. 505 (2003)
17. Calvanese, D., De Giacomo, G., Lenzerini, M., Rosati, R.: Logical Foundations of Peer-To-Peer Data Integration, pp. 241–251. ACM Press, New York (2004)
18. Franconi, E., Kuper, G.M., Lopatenko, A., Serafini, L.: A Robust Logical and Computational Characterisation of Peer-to-Peer Database Systems. In: DBISP2P, pp. 64–76 (2003)
19. Calvanese, D., De Giacomo, G., Lembo, D., Lenzerini, M., Rosati, R.: Inconsistency Tolerance in P2P Data Integration: An Epistemic Logic Approach. In: Bierman, G., Koch, C. (eds.) DBPL 2005. LNCS, vol. 3774, pp. 90–105. Springer, Heidelberg (2005)
20. Chatalic, P., Nguyen, G.H., Rousset, M.C.: Reasoning with Inconsistencies in Propositional Peer-to-Peer Inference Systems. In: ECAI, pp. 352–356 (2006)
21. Roelofsen, F., Serafini, L.: Minimal and Absent Information in Contexts. In: IJCAI, pp. 558–563 (2005)
22. Brewka, G., Roelofsen, F., Serafini, L.: Contextual Default Reasoning. In: IJCAI, pp. 268–273 (2007)

Model-Based Default Refinement of
Partial Information within an Ambient Agent

Fiemke Both, Charlotte Gerritsen, Mark Hoogendoorn, and Jan Treur

Vrije Universiteit Amsterdam, Department of Artificial Intelligence
De Boelelaan 1081, 1081 HV Amsterdam, The Netherlands
{fboth,cg,mhoogen,treur}@cs.vu.nl
http://www.few.vu.nl/~{fboth,cg,mhoogen,treur}

Abstract. Ambient agents react on humans on the basis of partial information obtained by sensing. Appropriate types of reactions depend on in how far an ambient agent is able to interpret the available information (which is often incomplete, and hence multi-interpretable) in order to create a more complete internal image of the environment, including humans. This interpretation process, which often has multiple possible outcomes, can make use of an explicitly represented model of causal and dynamic relations. Given such a model representation, the agent needs a reasoning method to interpret the partial information available by sensing, by generating one or more possible interpretations. This paper presents a generic model-based default reasoning method that can be exploited to this end. The method allows the use of software tools to determine the different default extensions that form the possible interpretations.

1 Introduction

Ambient Intelligence [1, 2, 21] applications usually involve sensor information about the environment, including humans. As this information is often incomplete, applications that require a high level of context awareness (see also [22, 23, 24]) depend on the availability of methods to analyse such information. One way is to include computational models about environmental and human functioning in ambient agents. However, even when incomplete sensor information is refined on the basis of such models to create a more complete internal image of the environment's and human's state, still this may result in partial information that can be interpreted in different manners. Reactions of ambient agents then depend on in how far they are able to handle the available multi-interpretable information. To do this, the agent needs a reasoning method to generate one or more of the possible interpretations. Tools from the area of nonmonotonic logic can provide adequate analysis tools for reasoning processes concerning partial information. Within nonmonotonic logic approaches it is possible to formalise reasoning processes that deal with multiple possible outcomes, which can be used to model different possibilities of interpretation; see [15] for a similar perspective on the application of nonmonotonic logic tools.

This paper presents a generic model-based default reasoning method that can be exploited to this end. The method exploits causal models and allows the use of software tools to determine default extensions that form the possible interpretations, given the sensor information and the causal model. Moreover, by formally specifying default rules

M. Mühlhäuser et al. (Eds.): AmI 2007 Workshops, CCIS 11, pp. 34–43, 2008.

in an executable temporal format according to the approach put forward in [12, 14], explicit default reasoning processes can be generated.

Section 2 describes two case studies used to illustrate the approach. In Section 3 the basic concepts used are briefly introduced. Section 4 presents the approach to use default logic in conjunction with causal graphs to refine partial information by defining multiple interpretations. Finally, Section 5 is a discussion. In Appendix A[1] it is shown how multiple interpretations can be generated by controlled default reasoning processes. A number of simulation experiments to obtain reasoning traces are performed. The reasoning method provides a solid basis for conceptual and detailed design of model-based ambient agents that need such a capability.

2 Case Studies

2.1 Wristband for Elderly

As a case study, the reasoning concerning conditions that occur amongst elderly people is used. Figure 1 shows a simplified causal model for such conditions. On the left hand side five conditions are shown: awake, asleep, syncope (fainted), myocardial infarction (heart attack) and cardiac arrest. The output of the model consists of symptoms that can be measured with a wristband, which are pulse, blood pressure and body temperature. Such a causal model can help in finding out the current condition of an elderly person based on sensory information from the wristband.

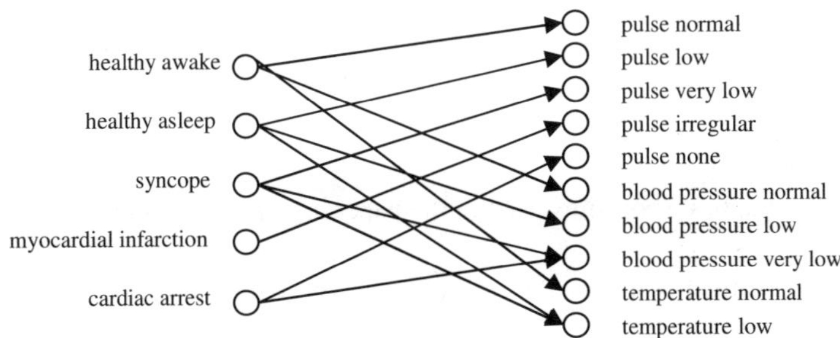

Fig. 1. Causal model for the condition of an elderly person

2.2 Crime Case

In this case study, a system is used that can help the police solve a crime using ambient intelligence facilities. A Dutch company (Sound Intelligence) developed microphones that can distinguish aggressive sounds. Consider the situation in which these microphones are distributed at crucial points in the city, similar to surveillance cameras. Furthermore, suppose in this scenario that for some persons ankle bracelets are used as a form of punishment, which can measure the level of ethanol in the person's perspiration, and indicate their position.

---

[1] http://www.few.vu.nl/~fboth/default-refinement

In this example scenario, someone is beaten up nearby a microphone. The microphone picks up the sound of the fight and records this. After an investigation, the police have three suspects. The first suspect is known to have a high level of testosterone, which often leads to aggressive behaviour. The second suspect is someone who is sensitive for alcohol (causing aggression) and wears an ankle bracelet that measures the level of ethanol in his system. He has been seen in a nearby cafe. The third suspect is diagnosed with Intermittent Explosive Disorder (IED), which is a disorder that can lead to a terrible outburst of rage after an unpleasant or stressful meeting. Witnesses saw suspect 2 in the company of someone else.

Figure 2 shows a causal model that is used for this situation that can help the police officers to figure out what information is missing and help them to plan their strategy. For example, did suspect 2 have a conflict with the person he was with? Did suspect 3 drink alcohol? Aggressive sounds are caused by persons that are aggressive, according to the model. Three possible causes for this aggressiveness are considered, as can be seen in Figure 2: someone can have a high level of testosterone, someone can just have been in a situation of conflict or someone can have a high level of alcohol.

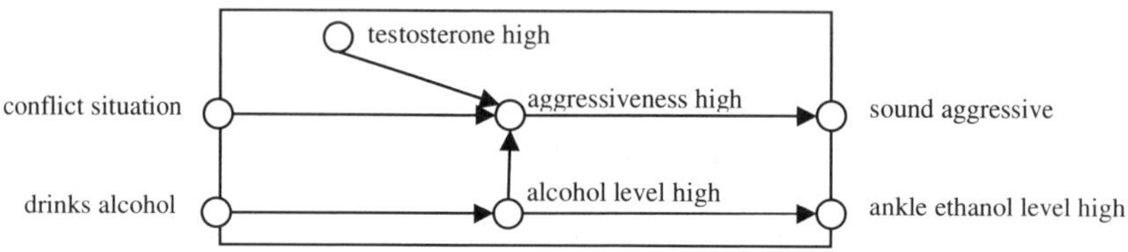

Fig. 2. Causal model for the crime case

3   Basic Concepts Used

In this section the basic concepts used in the paper are briefly introduced.

Causal models. In this paper, this dynamic perspective on reasoning is applied in combination with facts that are labelled with temporal information, and models based on causal or temporal relationships that relate such facts. To express the information involved in an agent's internal reasoning processes, the following ontology is used.

leads_to_after(I:INFO_EL, J:INFO_EL, D:REAL)	state property I leads to state property J after duration D
at(I:INFO_EL, T:TIME)	state property I holds at time T

Multiple Interpretation. Reasoning to obtain an interpretation of partial information can be formalised at an abstract generic level as follows. A particular interpretation for a given set of formulae considered as input information for the reasoning, is formalised as another set of formulae, that in one way or the other is derivable from the input information (output of the reasoning towards an interpretation). In general there are multiple possible outcomes. The collection of all possible interpretations derivable from a given set of formulae as input information (i.e., the output of the reasoning towards an interpretation) is formalised as a collection of different sets of formulae. A formalisation describing the relation between such input and output information is described at an abstract level by a multi-interpretation operator.

The input information is described by propositional formulae in a language L_1. An interpretation is a set of propositional formulae, based on a language L_2.

a) A *multi-interpretation operator* MI with input language L_1 and output language L_2 is a function MI : $P(L_1) \rightarrow P(P(L_2))$ that assigns to each set of input facts in L_1 a set of sets of formulae in L_2.

b) A multi-interpretation operator MI is *non-inclusive* if for all $X \subseteq L_1$ and $S, T \in MI(X)$, if $S \subseteq T$ then $S = T$.

c) If $L_1 \subseteq L_2$, then a multi-interpretation operator MI is *conservative* if for all $X \subseteq L_1$, $T \in MI(X)$ it holds $X \subseteq T$.

The condition of non-inclusiveness guarantees a relative maximality of the possible interpretations. Note that when MI(X) has exactly one element, this means that the set $X \subseteq L_1$ has a unique interpretation under MI. The notion of multi-interpretation operator is a generalisation of the notion of a nonmonotonic belief set operator, as introduced in [10]. The generalisation was introduced and applied to approximate classification in [15]. A reasoner may explore a number of possible interpretations, but often, at some point in time a reasoner will focus on one (or possibly a small subset) of the interpretations. This selection process is formalised as follows (see [15]).

a) A *selection operator* s is a function s : $P(P(L)) \rightarrow P(P(L))$ that assigns to each non-empty set of interpretations a nonempty subset: for all A with $\phi \neq A \subseteq P(L)$ it holds $\phi \neq s(A) \subseteq A$. A selection operator s is *single-valued* if for all non-empty A the set s(A) contains exactly one element.

b) A *selective interpretation operator* for the multi-interpretation operator MI is a function $C : P(L_1) \rightarrow P(L_2)$ that assigns one interpretation to each set of initial facts: for all $X \subseteq L_1$ it holds $C(X) \in MI(X)$.

Representation in Default Logic. The *representation problem* for a nonmonotonic logic is the question whether a given set of possible outcomes of a reasoning process can be represented by a theory in this logic. More specifically, representation theory indicates what are criteria for a set of possible outcomes, for example, given by a collection of deductively closed sets of formulae, so that this collection can occur as the set of outcomes for a theory in this nonmonotonic logic. In [18] the representation problem is solved for default logic, for the finite case. Given this context, in the current paper Default Logic is chosen to represent interpretation processes. For the empirical material analysed, default theories have been specified such that their extensions are the possible interpretations.

A *default theory* is a pair $\langle D, W \rangle$. Here W is a finite set of logical formulae (called the background theory) that formalise the facts that are known for sure, and D is a set of default rules. A default rule has the form: $\alpha : \beta / \gamma$. Here α is the precondition, it has to be satisfied before considering to believe the conclusion γ, where the β, called the justification, has to be consistent with the derived information and W. As a result γ might be believed and more default rules can be applied. However, the end result (when no more default rules can be applied) still has to be consistent with the justifications of all applied default rules. *Normal default theories* are based on defaults of the form $\alpha: \beta / \beta$. In the approach *supernormal* default rules will be used: normal default rules where α is trivial: true. Such supernormal rules are denoted by β / β or $: \beta / \beta$; they are also called prerequisite-free normal defaults. For more details on Default Logic, such as the notion of extension, see, e.g., [17, 20].

Temporal Specification of Reasoning Processes. In this paper a dynamic perspective on reasoning is taken, following, e.g. [12, 14]. In practical reasoning situations usually different lines of reasoning can be generated, each leading to a distinct set of conclusions. In logic semantics is usually expressed in terms of models that represent descriptions of conclusions about the world and in terms of entailment relations based on a specific class of this type of models. In the (sound) classical case each line of reasoning leads to a set of conclusions that are true in all of these models: each line of reasoning fits to each model. However, for non-classical reasoning methods the picture is different. For example, in default reasoning or abductive reasoning methods a variety of mutually contradictory conclusion sets may be possible. It depends on the chosen line of reasoning which one of these sets fits.

The general idea underlying the approach followed here, and inspired by [12, 14], is that a particular reasoning line can be formalised by a sequence of *information states* M_0, M_1, ... Here any M_t is a description of the (partial) information that has been derived up to time point t. From a dynamic perspective, an inference step, performed in time duration D is viewed as a transition $M_t \rightarrow M_{t+D}$ of a current information state M_t to a next information state M_{t+D}. Such a transition is usually described by application of a deduction rule or proof rule, which in the dynamic perspective on reasoning gets a temporal aspect. A particular reasoning line is formalised by a sequence $(M_t)_{t \in T}$ of subsequent information states labelled by elements of a flow of time T, which may be discrete, based on natural numbers, or continuous, based on real numbers.

An information state can be formalised by a set of statements, or as a three-valued (false, true, undefined) truth assignment to ground atoms, i.e., a partial model. In the latter case, which is followed here (as in [12, 14]), a sequence of such information states or reasoning trace can be interpreted as a partial temporal model. A transition relating a next information state to a current one can be formalised by temporal formulae the partial temporal model has to satisfy.

4 Representing Model-Based Interpretation in Default Logic

In this section it is discussed how a model-based interpretation operator can be represented in default Logic.

4.1 Default Logic for Model-Based Refinement of Partial Information

The *causal theory* CT of the agent consists of a number of statements $a \rightarrow b$ for each causal relation from a to b, with a and b atoms. Sometimes included in this set are some facts to indicate that some atoms exclude each other (for example, ¬(has_value(temperature, high) ∧ has_value(temperature, low) assuming that temperature can only be high or low), or that at least one of a set of atoms is true, (for example: has_value(pulse, high) ∨ has_value(pulse, normal) ∨ has_value(pulse, low)). A set of literals S is *coherent* with CT if S ∪ CT is consistent. The set S is called a *maximal coherent* set for CT if it is coherent, and for all sets T coherent with CT with S $\subseteq$ T it holds S = T. Let X be a set of formulae. The multi-interpretation operator $MI_{CT}(X)$ is defined by

$$MI_{CT}(X) = \{ Cn(X \cup CT \cup S) \mid S \text{ maximal coherent with CT} \}$$

This operator defines for the partial information the agent may have at some point in time (indicated by set of literals X) the set of all complete refinements of X which are coherent with the causal model. This operator has been defined above in an abstract manner, and only indicates the possible outcomes of a reasoning process, not the steps of the reasoning process itself. A next step is to obtain a representation of this operator in a well-known formalism such as default logic. Based on this default logic representation, reasoning processes can be defined that can be performed to obtain one or more of the interpretations.

The following Default Theory $\Delta_{CT}(X) = \langle W, D \rangle$ can be used to represent the multi-interpretation operator MI_{CT} (notice that this is a supernormal default theory); see also [18], Theorem 5.1:

$$W \;=\; CT \cup X$$
$$D \;=\; \{ (true: a \,/\, a) \mid a \text{ literal for an atom occurring in CT} \}$$

Here a literal is an atom or a negation of an atom. That this default theory represents MI_{CT} means that for any set X indicating partial information the set of interpretations defined by $MI_{CT}(X)$ can be obtained as the set of all extensions of the default theory $\Delta_{CT}(X)$. This representation allows to determine the interpretations by using known methods and tools to determine the extensions of a default theory. One of these methods is worked out in a tool called Smodels, based on answer set programming; cf. [19]. The use of this for the two case studies will be discussed in the next two Subsections 4.2 and 4.3. Another method to determine the extensions of a default theory is by controlled or prioritised default reasoning. This method will be illustrated in Section 5.

4.2   A Default Theory for the Wristband for Elderly Case

In order to represent the knowledge introduced in Section 2.1, the following default theory has been specified. First, the causal background theory (W = CT) is defined, based on the causal graph shown in Figure 1. Furthermore, inconsistent values are defined for the various facets (i.e. pulse, temperature, blood pressure, and condition):

    inconsistent_values(pulse, normal, low)
    inconsistent_values(condition, healthy_awake, healthy_asleep) etc.

If the value of an attribute is inconsistent with another value, then this other value is not the case: has_value(y, x1) $\wedge$ inconsistent_values(y, x1, x2) $\rightarrow \neg$ has_value(y, x2).

Besides the background theory, also the default theory Δ_{CT} has been generated from this causal theory CT. The default rules for the atoms are simply as follows:

    has_value(condition, healthy_awake) / has_value(condition, healthy_awake)
    has_value(condition, healthy_asleep) / has_value(condition, healthy_asleep)
    has_value(condition, syncope) / has_value(condition, syncope)
    has_value(condition, myocardial_infarction) / has_value(condition, myocardial_infarction)
    has_value(condition, cardiac_arrest) / has_value(condition, cardiac_arrest)
    has_value(pulse, normal) / has_value(pulse, normal)
    has_value(pulse, low) / has_value(pulse, low)
    has_value(pulse, very_low) / has_value(pulse, very_low)
    has_value(pulse, irregular) / has_value(pulse, irregular)
    has_value(pulse, none) / has_value(pulse, none)

```
has_value(blood_pressure, normal) / has_value(blood_pressure, normal)
has_value(blood_pressure, low) / has_value(blood_pressure, low)
has_value(blood_pressure, very_low) / has_value(blood_pressure, very_low)
has_value(temperature, normal) / has_value(temperature, normal)
has_value(temperature, low) / has_value(temperature, low)
```

Besides these default rules, similar defaults for the negations of these atoms are included. Using a system called Smodels [19], the extensions for the default theory specified can be calculated. Using the theory above, 30 extensions result. Hereby, in 19 out of 30 cases neither of the 5 conditions holds (i.e. awake, asleep, syncope, myocardial infarction and cardiac arrest). However, by adding strict rules which express that at least one of the conditions holds, only 11 extensions are found. The extensions that follow after adding these strict rules are shown in Table 1.

Table 1. All extensions of the default theory

#	Condition	Values	#	Condition	Values
1	healthy_awake	has_value(pulse, normal) has_value(blood_pressure, normal) has_value(temperature, normal)	7	myocardial_infarction	has_value(pulse, irregular) has_value(blood_pressure, normal) has_value(temperature, low)
2	healthy_asleep	has_value(pulse, low) has_value(blood_pressure, low) has_value(temperature, low)	8	myocardial_infarction	has_value(pulse, irregular) has_value(blood_pressure, low) has_value(temperature, low)
3	syncope	has_value(pulse, very_low) has_value(blood_pressure, very_low) has_value(temperature, low)	9	myocardial_infarction	has_value(pulse, irregular) has_value(blood_pressure, very_low) has_value(temperature, low)
4	myocardial_infarction	has_value(pulse, irregular) has_value(blood_pressure, normal) has_value(temperature, normal)	10	cardiac_arrest	has_value(pulse, none) has_value(blood_pressure, very_low) has_value(temperature, normal)
5	myocardial_infarction	has_value(pulse, irregular) has_value(blood_pressure, low) has_value(temperature, normal)	11	cardiac_arrest	has_value(pulse, none) has_value(blood_pressure, very_low) has_value(temperature, low)
6	myocardial_infarction	has_value(pulse, irregular) has_value(blood_pressure, very_low) has_value(temperature, normal)			

Partial information X may be given that includes the information that the person has a normal temperature. Such a set X can be added to the background theory W. Table 2 shows the extensions resulting when the following facts are added to W:

X = { has_value(temperature, normal), has_value(pulse, irregular) }

Finally, when set X, defined as X = { has_value(temperature, normal) , has_value(pulse, normal) , has_value(blood_pressure, normal) }, is added to W, the extension is: has_value(condition, healthy_awake), has_value(pulse, normal); has_value(blood_pressure, normal); has_value(temperature, normal).

Table 2. All extensions given the changed background theory

#	Condition	Values
1	myocardial_infarction	has_value(pulse, irregular) has_value(blood_pressure, normal) has_value(temperature, normal)
2	myocardial_infarction	has_value(pulse, irregular) has_value(blood_pressure, low) has_value(temperature, normal)
3	myocardial_infarction	has_value(pulse, irregular) has_value(blood_pressure, very_low) has_value(temperature, normal)

4.3   Crime Case Default Theory

Similar to the Elderly Wristband, the default theory Δ_{CT} for the crime case has been generated from the causal model:

```
has_value(situation, conflict) / has_value(situation, conflict)
has_value(situation, drinks_alcohol) / has_value(situation, drinks_alcohol)
has_value(testosterone, high) / has_value(testosterone, high)
has_value(sounds, aggressive) / has_value(sounds, aggressive)
has_value(ankle_ethanol_level, high) / has_value(ankle_ethanol_level, high)
has_value(aggressiveness, high) / has_value(aggressiveness, high)
has_value(alcohol_level, high) / has_value(alcohol_level, high)
not(has_value(situation, conflict) / not(has_value(situation, conflict))
not(has_value(situation, drinks_alcohol) / not(has_value(situation, drinks_alcohol))
not(has_value(testosterone, high) / not(has_value(testosterone, high))
not(has_value(sounds, aggressive) / not(has_value(sounds, aggressive))
not(has_value(ankle_ethanol_level, high) / not(has_value(ankle_ethanol_level, high))
not(has_value(aggressiveness, high) / not(has_value(aggressiveness, high))
not(has_value(alcohol_level, high) / not(has_value(alcohol_level, high))
```

Furthermore, aggressive sound has been observed, therefore the following fact is added to W: X = {has_value(sound, aggressive)}. The resulting number of extensions is 18. Hereby however, the reasoning has not been performed using a closed world assumption, whereby values can only occur in case they result from a known causal relation or in case they are input variables (i.e. the situation). In order to perform reasoning with such a closed world assumption, the following rules have been added. First, a rule expressing that in case there is only one source from which a value can be derived, then this source should have the appropriate value (in this case, this holds for all variables except for aggressiveness).

```
has_value(X1,Y1)∧leads_to(has_value(X2,Y2),has_value(X1,Y1))∧X1≠aggressiveness→has_value(X2,Y2)
```

For the aggressiveness a different set of rules is used, since only one out of three conditions needs to hold. An example of one instance of such a rule is the following:

```
has_value(aggressivness, high) ∧ not(has_value(testosterone, high) ∧ not(has_value(situation, conflict) →
has_value(alcohol_level, high)
```

Given that these rules are added, 7 extensions result using Smodels as shown in Table 3. Note that the sound is not shown since that is fixed in advance already. The last column shows to which suspect this extension is applicable. Hereby the suspect with high testosterone is marked with 1, the oversensitive alcohol suspect with 2, and the IED suspect with 3.

Table 3. Extensions given that aggressive sound has been observed

#	Situation	Testosterone	Aggressiveness	Alcohol level	Ankle Ethanol level	Suspect
1	¬conflict; ¬drinks_alcohol	high	high	¬high	¬high	1
2	conflict; ¬drinks_alcohol	high	high	¬high	¬high	1
3	conflict; ¬drinks_alcohol	¬high	high	¬high	¬high	3
4	conflict; drinks_alcohol	high	high	high	high	1
5	conflict; drinks_alcohol	¬high	high	high	high	2, 3
6	¬conflict; drinks_alcohol	¬high	high	high	high	2
7	¬conflict; drinks_alcohol	high	high	high	high	1

5 Discussion

This paper shows how a number of known techniques and tools developed within the area of nonmonotonic reasoning and AI can be applied to analyse model-based interpretation. The formal techniques exploited in the approach, are causal graphs and causal reasoning in conjunction with techniques from the nonmonotonic reasoning area such as: multi-interpretation operators as an abstract formalisation multiple interpretation and a default theory to represent this multi-interpretation operator. Model-based default refinement can be useful to obtain (on top of sensor information) a high level of context awareness; see also [22, 23, 24]. The properties and default rules presented in this paper have all been specified in a generic fashion, such that they can easily be reused for studying other cases.

More formalisms for handling causal or temporal reasoning within ambient intelligence have been proposed, see e.g. [16]. The application of nonmonotonic logic as put forward in this paper adds the possibility to specify human like reasoning in a natural way, possibly even resulting in multiple stable sets that can be the outcome of such a reasoning process.

Currently, the approach put forward is a theoretical framework, whereby case studies have been conducted on paper. Future work is to see how well such a theoretical framework can be applied in a practical setting, for example for elderly care or crime analysis. Issues such as how to extract the appropriate information needed within the system from domain experts, how useful the system can be in supporting human decision makers, and how accessible the method can be made for people not familiar with formal methods will need to be addressed.

References

1. Aarts, E., Collier, R.W., van Loenen, E., de Ruyter, B. (eds.): EUSAI 2003. LNCS, vol. 2875, p. 432. Springer, Heidelberg (2003)
2. Aarts, E., Harwig, R., Schuurmans, M.: Ambient Intelligence. In: Denning, P. (ed.) The Invisible Future, pp. 235–250. McGraw Hill, New York (2001)
3. Bosse, T., Hoogendoorn, M., Jonker, C.M., Treur, J.: A Formal Empirical Analysis Method for Human Reasoning and Interpretation. In: Lewis, R., Polk, T. (eds.) Proceedings of the 8th International Conference on Cognitive Modeling, ICCM 2007, pp. 241–246. Taylor & Francis, Abington (2007)
4. Bosse, T., Jonker, C.M., Treur, J.: Formalization and Analysis of Reasoning by Assumption. Cognitive Science Journal 30(1), 147–180 (2006)
5. Bosse, T., Jonker, C.M., van der, L., Treur, J.: A Language and Environment for Analysis of Dynamics by Simulation. International Journal of Artificial Intelligence Tools 16, 435–464 (2007)
6. Bosse, T., Treur, J.: Modelling Dynamics of Cognitive Agents by Higher-Order Potentialities. In: Stone, P., Weiss, G. (eds.) Proceedings of the Fifth International Joint Conference on Autonomous Agents and Multi-Agent Systems, AAMAS 2006, vol. 2006, pp. 117–119. ACM Press, New York (2006)

7. Bosse, T., Treur, J.: Higher-Order Potentialities and their Reducers: A Philosophical Foundation Unifying Dynamic Modelling Methods. In: Veloso, M.M. (ed.) Proceedings of the Twentieth International Joint Conference on Artificial Intelligence, IJCAI 2007, pp. 262–267. AAAI Press, Menlo Park (2007)

8. Brewka, G.: Adding priorities and specificity to default logic. In: MacNish, C., Moniz Pereira, L., Pearce, D.J. (eds.) JELIA 1994. LNCS, vol. 838, pp. 247–260. Springer, Heidelberg (1994)

9. Brewka, G., Eiter, T.: Prioritizing Default Logic: Abridged Report. In: Festschrift on the occasion of Prof.Dr. W. Bibel's 60th birthday, Kluwer, Dordrecht (1999)

10. Engelfriet, J., Herre, H., Treur, J.: Nonmonotonic Reasoning with Multiple Belief Sets. Annals of Mathematics and Artificial Intelligence 24, 225–248 (1998)

11. Engelfriet, J., Jonker, C.M., Treur, J.: Compositional Verification of Multi-Agent Systems in Temporal Multi-Epistemic Logic. Journal of Logic, Language and Information 11, 195–225 (2002)

12. Engelfriet, J., Treur, J.: Temporal Theories of Reasoning. Journal of Applied Non-Classical Logics 5, 239–261 (1995)

13. Engelfriet, J., Treur, J.: An Interpretation of Default Logic in Minimal Temporal Epistemic Logic. J. of Logic, Language and Information 7, 369–388 (1998)

14. Engelfriet, J., Treur, J.: Specification of Nonmonotonic Reasoning. Journal of Applied Non-Classical Logics 10, 7–27 (2000)

15. Engelfriet, J., Treur, J.: Multi-Interpretation Operators and Approximate Classification. Int. Journal of Approximate Reasoning 32, 43–61 (2003)

16. Galton, A.: Causal Reasoning for Alert Generation in Smart Homes. In: Augusto, J.C., Nugent, C.D. (eds.) Designing Smart Homes. LNCS (LNAI), vol. 4008, pp. 57–70. Springer, Heidelberg (2006)

17. Marek, V.W., Truszczynski, M.: Nonmonotonic Logics. Springer, Heidelberg (1993)

18. Marek, V.W., Treur, J., Truszczynski, M.: Representation Theory for Default Logic. Annals of Mathematics and AI 21, 343–358 (1997)

19. Niemelä, I., Simons, P., Syrjänen, T.: Smodels: a system for answer set programming. In: Proceedings of the 8th International Workshop on Non-Monotonic Reasoning, Breckenridge, Colorado, USA (April 2000)

20. Reiter, R.: A logic for default reasoning. Artificial Intelligence 13, 81–132 (1980)

21. Riva, G., Vatalaro, F., Davide, F., Alcañiz, M. (eds.): Ambient Intelligence. IOS Press, Amsterdam (2005)

22. Schmidt, A.: Interactive Context-Aware Systems - Interacting with Ambient Intelligence. In: Riva, G., Vatalaro, F., Davide, F., Alcañiz, M. (eds.) Ambient Intelligence, pp. 159–178. IOS Press, Amsterdam (2005)

23. Schmidt, A., Beigl, M., Gellersen, H.W.: There is more to Context than Location. Computers & Graphics Journal 23,19, 893–902 (1999)

24. Schmidt, A., Kortuem, G., Morse, D., Dey, A. (eds.): Situated Interaction and Context-Aware Computing, Personal and Ubiquitous Computing, vol. 5, pp. 1–81 (2001)

25. Tan, Y.H., Treur, J.: Constructive Default Logic and the Control of Defeasible Reasoning. In: Neumann, B. (ed.) Proc. ECAI 1992, pp. 299–303. Wiley and Sons, Chichester (1992)

CAMPUS NEWS - Artificial Intelligence Methods Combined for an Intelligent Information Network

Markus Maron, Kevin Read, and Michael Schulze

Department of Computer Science, Artificial Intelligence Research Group
University of Koblenz-Landau, Universitätsstr. 1, 56070 Koblenz
{maron,kread,schulzemich}@uni-koblenz.de

Abstract. In this paper we describe a network for distributing personalised information with the usage of artificial intelligence methods. Reception of this information should be possible with everyday mobile equipment. Intelligent filtering and spam protection aim at integrating this technology into our environment. Information on the system architecture and usage of the installation are also presented.

1 Introduction

At the start of each semester much information is presented to the freshmen students. Ranging from basic questions like the location of the registrar's office up to course-specific data, each morsel of information must be looked up in a different part of the campus. Senior students look for office opening hours, announcements for specific courses or extracurricular events. Our concept of developing a campus information system seeks to answer these questions in a personalised way, at any time, at any location. The idea is to enable the user to find and access all information that is of relevance to her. All she needs is a Bluetooth enabled mobile device, like a PDA or mobile phone. All used techniques are in themselves not new or unique, but the combination of instant messaging, Bluetooth-centric information transport and profile based information narrowcast is novel. Likewise the involved AI methods are well-known but combine to a complete and complex result. On top of that, the system based on a platform made purely for research is in the stage of evolving into a product and is even now being utilised as a public service on-campus.

This information network is only one piece of the puzzle of our view of a ambient intelligence information network. Previous steps done on the Koblenz campus: in a series of projects funded by the EU (Trial Solution) and BMBF (In2Math, [1]) we developed "Living Books" [2], personalized, intelligent teaching material, which is also available for PDAs and smart mobile phones. There is also an approach to use mobile devices for interaction during classroom teaching[1]. Altogether we find a situation on Campus, where students use their mobile device for learning and interacting and for location-based, personalized information.

---

[1] `www.mobilearn.org`

M. Mühlhäuser et al. (Eds.): AmI 2007 Workshops, CCIS 11, pp. 44–52, 2008.

Research done in the area of mobile information systems include the projects SmartWEB[3] and SmartKOM[4] , which allow queries from anywhere, at any time, utilizing natural language and speech recognition. These technologies require state-of-the-art hardware and broadband mobile network connections. Other groups researching applications on mobile personal computers for ambient intelligence have come to the same conclusion as we have, that the main attention with pervasive applications has shifted from a "use anytime, anywhere" perspective to a location-based, personalized view [5]. A lot of work is happening in this area at the moment. Using a Bluetooth mesh for positioning to send data over non-local wireless links like GSM or GPRS is one avenue to take [6]. In our approach we opted for positioning and transmission over the same channel. The local wireless link can also be skipped completely, which leads to different usage models [7]. A bit closer to our usage scenario of a intelligent university environment than these mentioned projects is the project "mobile cafeteria menu"[2], although there are neither location-based nor personalized aspects involved. Our approach is in a certain sense a reduction of all mentioned projects as we do not install software on the phone, which is a fragile process, nor do users incur additional costs.

2   Campus News – Concept

The Campus News System is based on results of the research project IASON[3], funded by the "Stiftung Rheinland-Pfalz für Innovation". Motivated by the development of powerful mobile devices and the semantic web, we defined a *Semantic Mobile Environment*. In such an environment, so-called service nodes are installed at chosen points of interest. These service nodes broadcast messages to nearby mobile users using Bluetooth wireless technology. For example a bookshop could send its latest offers, or the University restaurant could present its menu or a faculty presents the schedule of events to the students. Each message is annotated with a profile, so that end users will only receive messages that are of interest to them.

This semantic annotation is a logical concept in Description Logic (DL) [8, 9]. We also gave the users the opportunity to build their individual interest profile. The first usable prototype of the project (see [10]) was implemented in J2ME, such that the user profile and the inference engine for the personalization was stored in the mobile device.

During several tests in the University and in the City of Koblenz within the framework of the EU project Spatial Metro[4] it turned out that most mobile phones did not yet fulfill our system requirements. They could not access the Bluetooth wireless functions from Java. Apart from that we learned that the barrier to install software on mobile phones or PDAs is higher than with computers. As of today, users aren't used to application installation on these devices

---

[2] http://www.studentenwerk-dresden.de/mensen/handy.html

[3] www.uni-koblenz.de/~iason

[4] www.spatialmetro.org

and as such distrust the idea. To overcome both the technical shortcomings of mobile devices and the need for application installation, we chose to move the decision process (the "reasoning engine") from the mobile phone onto a server, thus eleminating the application. The profile of the user now needs to be entered centrally on a web page. The following describes this solution, which we call "Campus News Information System".

2.1 System Architecture

The architecture of the Campus News Information System consists of three components (as shown in figure 1): a web application as the user frontend (blue), a server application (red) in the middle and a freely scalable number of service nodes (green) for delivering the information to the mobile devices. We implemented two different kinds of frontends, one for each group of users. We need an administration interface for the users that want to offer information to the public. We call this frontend the Management Console. We also need a user interface for the recipients of the information, in our case the students. This is called the Userweb; it is depicted in figure 2.

Both Management Console and Userweb access the backend, consisting of a relational database and a server application. The database acts as a central storage for message data, profile data and service node information. Both web frontends store any user-made changes here. The server application also accesses the database, but uses this data to drive the service nodes. As soon as mobile devices are recognized by one of the service nodes, the server looks up the profiles of the corresponding users. This lookup uses a combination of several aspects of the mobile phone including its Bluetooth address to ensure that this matching between mobile phone and user is correct. Using

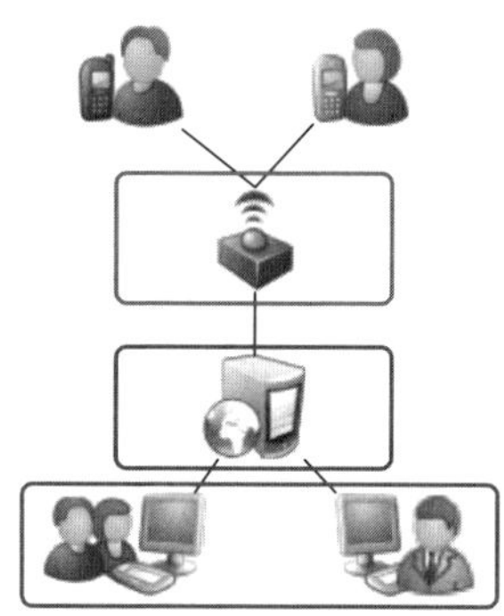

Fig. 1. System architecture

a subsumption check on the annotation of the messages and the users' profile, the server decides on which information conforms to the users' interests. In the next step a history query is made to ensure that no mobile device receives the same information twice. All relevant messages are then transferred to the service node by either wireless or wire-bound networking.

The service nodes scan for mobile devices with activated Bluetooth visibility. After handing this information to the server and receiving the messages, they attempt to transfer this data. After two successive rejections by the mobile device no further attempts will be made for a certain duration, to adapt to students that are not interested in the service.

Fig. 2. CampusNews Management Console (left) and CampusNews Userweb (right)

2.2 Content Entry

Up to now, the system allowed for content to be entered centrally by trusted administrators as described, creating a one-way flow of information. Content will only be received at the end of the flow, i.e. the mobile device, if it fits into the users' need according to a concept filter as outlined above and explained in more detail in 3.1. This has been realized for the CampusNews system and is in daily use. Our requirements for an intelligent communication utility required also peer-to-peer or community-centric communication models. This necessitated a bi-directional and decentralized flow of information, which is now being implemented.

The first step is to enable the service nodes to receive messages in a fixed form that is understood by most mobile devices. Using known aspects of the mobile phone and the Bluetooth hardware, the sender can be identified within the network. There are two ways to route the message. It could be a broadcast message in the style of an announcement, which would then be injected into the central database. Example broadcast messages could be *"The car with license plate X is parked with lights on"* or *"The course Y at 1 AM was cancelled"*. Apart from transfer via Bluetooth, this information could then be displayed on public TV screens as a news ticker or on web pages. One problem area here is to filter out unappropriate or hurtful contents, which will be discussed in 3.2.

The other possibility would be to route this message only to a certain set of recipients, thereby enabling personal messaging systems. This platform could then be used for a whole range of applications in the area of ambient intelligence, utilizing the mobile device as a messaging center that is highly portable and ubiquitous. In the context of the intelligent university environment, personal messages with grades, examination appointments and schedule changes could be sent to individuals. In this scenario, as with most peer-to-peer communcation, information would not necessarily have to be scanned for malicious content.

3   AI Methods

In this section we describe the methods of artifical intelligence which are used within the CampusNews environment. As mentioned before we are developing an information system which allows bi-directional flow of information. Each direction requires its own methods of filtering and selection to make sure that only wanted messages pass the system and reach the user.

3.1   Concept Filtering

As already mentioned we give the users the possibility to choose the topics they want to be informed about. To achieve this goal we developed a mechanism which is called concept filtering, based on DL profiles and ontologies. A similar server-side reasoning process was already used in the Living Book which is a tool for the management of personalized teaching material. For this the KRHyper [11], a full first order theorem prover based on the hyper tableau calculus was used. Inspired by the Pocket KRHyper, small version for mobile devices, of the theorem prover, we developed the algorithm for filtering the huge amount of messages which comes within the system.

The reasoning process itself consists of these steps: before transmitting a message to the user, the server has to decide whether the information fits to the users interest or not. This deduction process called matchmaking [12] is done by first order reasoning. The user's interests are called a profile. Each message is annotated by its author with a concept. Both consist of Description Logic concepts and are based upon the same terminology. We also built a small ontology for our semantic environment. The decision whether a message matches a user's profile is based on concept satisfiability and subsumption of the DL in use. The task is done by only two queries.

$$profile \sqcap annotation \not\equiv \bot \tag{1}$$

$$annotation \sqsubseteq profile \tag{2}$$

If the annotation satisfies test (1) the annotation is *compatible* with the profile. Because an unsatisfiable annotation will be subsumed by every profile, the first test prevents any unsatisfiable annotation to be considered as a match. This test avoids spam. Test (2) will give a better *match degree* for those annotations that are subsumed by at least one of the *positive* terms. We call these annotations a *match*. This second test is only performed after successfully testing satisfiability (1).

Example. The example shall illustrate the match decisions with respect to a user that is interested in lectures about philosophy and information about the vegetarian menu, but hates sports. The profile contains the interests $\exists offer.(lectures \sqcap \forall hasTopic.philosophy) \sqcup \exists offer.(menu \sqcap \forall hasDiet.vegetarian)$ and the disinterest $\exists offer.sports$.
(**Note:** a user who is requesting something is interested in offering the same thing.)

Table 1. Example messages

Message Text   Annotation
The menseria offers the delicious menu *Lasagne Bolognese* $\exists$ *offers.(meal $\sqcap$ noon)*
and for the vegatarians a salad $\exists$ *offers.(meal $\sqcap$ noon $\sqcap$ $\forall$ hasDiet.vegetarian)*
An extra curricula lecture about Descartes is offered $\exists$ *offers.(lectures $\sqcap$ $\forall$ hasTopic.philosophy)*

On her walk through the campus, the mobile user passes different service nodes and receives the messages listed in Table 1.

With this profile the messages of the lecture and the vegetarian menu are matched, but the message related to the famous menu *Lasagne Bolognese* is rejected.

3.2 Message Filtering

Broadcast messages are displayed on public TV screens or transmitted to all interested mobile users. They are entered by the admins into aforementioned "Management Console". The next step is to enable the users to enter their own messages. Appropriate channels would be either the CampusNews web interface or sending messages directly from the mobile device via Bluetooth.

The content entered by the admins is trusted content, since it is a closed and well-known user group. But messages that originated in the user base have to be filtered to ensure that hurtful or malicious content is not displayed, since the admins do not control this content. This problem is exacerbated by the fact that users feel anonymous, although the operator can track identity by means of Bluetooth metadata. These messages therefore cannot be inherently trusted. Admins need tools to classify messages as "spam" or "ham". The system should preferably be able to automatically classify messages after setting a few basic settings and manually classifying a few messages.

Many proven approaches exist for classifying email into the two categories "spam" and "ham". Some of them filter messages according to a list of keywords [13]. If one these keywords appear in the message, it is classified as spam, otherwise as ham. Other methods are based on a statistical approach. A well known method is to use Bayesian filters [14]. Another popular approach is to use decision trees [15]. Instance-based approaches are also in use [15]. When used to filter emails, the layout and email headers can also be analysed. Examples for the use of this metadata would be to categorize emails based on attached figure files or to look into the route the email took according to information in the header.

Format and mode of display for broadcast messages differ significantly from emails. Compared to the well-known form of email spam, our messages are much shorter. Our tests showed that messages should not be longer than 200 characters, otherwise they will not be readable or intelligible, spread out over many screen widths. Our message format does not include headers or layout instructions, so we cannot use this metadata to aid classification. We have a format that makes classification more difficult, but on the other hand there are less possibilities to trick the filter mechanism. All techniques that rely on header information (as with email) are not an option.

Only a few of these methods are of relevance to our project, like the search for keywords, or rather more "key phrases". The admin can edit this list of keywords. For categorization Bayesian filtering, decision trees and instance-based methods are interesting too. All these approaches have to be tested with respect to our specialized situation.

When users or certain mobile devices abuse the system, the admins can blacklist [13] these entities. There is also a whitelist [13], to specify senders that never need to be filtered.

4   Results and Outlook

Now, ten weeks after introducing the Campus News System at the University of Koblenz, we are pleased to say that the usage and acceptance by the students is very high for this short time frame. It will be interesting to see if acceptance will climb even higher in the future. The ratio of found devices to devices that received information was at 12.8% in April 2007. This ratio climbed to 47.1% in June. We consider this to be the number of Bluetooth capable devices owned by users willing to activate Bluetooth functionality, divided by the number of CampusNews adopters. We detected over 2200 different mobile devices with Bluetooth activated and served 675 of them. These 675 are comprised of 464 unregistered users that received the cafeteria menu and urgent public announcements, and 211 registered users that got news according to the profile they set. All in all we transmitted over 4078 different messages in this short time frame (see table 2). To put the numbers into perspective, the campus Koblenz has around 5000 students. Taking into account occasional visitors, more than one third of all people on-campus have actived Bluetooth and more than ten percent have received CampusNews information.

We also did a questionnaire on user wishes and opinion regarding CampusNews. We sent out a code and asked the students to enter that code on the answer sheet. On top of that we asked about mobile phone brand and model, opinion of the system in general and wishes or suggestions for future work. Of the 97 students that replied, 12 could not receive the code. Using the stated information about the mobile phone brand we got insight into the workings of Samsung and Motorola brand phones and could increase the compatibility in this area. The opinions varied from general vague acceptance of the concept up to enthusiasm. The most wanted feature was a higher density of service nodes and up-to-date information in the system for course schedule changes.

Table 2. Usage of the Campus News System

	April	May	June	since Roll-out (16/04)
found devices	1079	785	1103	2286
served devices	139	163	520	675
transmitted data	828	903	2347	4078

The next step is building a pervasive community by extending the system for reception of messages. Combined with the concept of intelligent categorization and thus personalization, this community enables ubiquitous mobile devices to became intelligent information centers.

Acknowledgments. Campus News has been carried out by the cooperative work between the University of Koblenz, Studierendenwerk Koblenz, Arbeitsgruppe Künstliche Intelligenz and wizAI Solutions GmbH and is based on the research work within the IASON project, which is funded by the "Stiftung Rheinland-Pfalz für Innovation".

References

[1] Baumgartner, P., Grabowski, B., Oevel, W., Melis, E.: In2math - Interaktive Mathematik- und Informatikgrundausbildung. Softwaretechnik-Trends 24(1), 36–45 (2004)

[2] Baumgartner, P., Furbach, U., Groß-Hardt, M., Sinner, A.: 'living book': - 'deduction', 'slicing', 'interaction'. In: CADE, pp. 284–288 (2003)

[3] Wahlster, W.: Smartweb: Getting answers on the go. In: ECAI, p. 6 (2006)

[4] Wahlster, W. (ed.): SmartKom: Foundations of Multimodal Dialogue Systems. Cognitive Technologies, vol. XVIII. Springer, Heidelberg (2006)

[5] Roussos, G., Maglavera, S., Marsh, A.: Enabling pervasive computing with smart phones. IEEE Pervasive Computing 4(2) (2005)

[6] Aalto, L., Göthlin, N., Korhonen, J., Ojala, T.: Bluetooth and wap push based location-aware mobile advertising system. In: MobiSys 2004: Proceedings of the 2nd international conference on Mobile systems, applications, and services, pp. 49–58. ACM Press, New York (2004)

[7] Ferscha, A., Vogl, S.: Pervasive web access via public communication walls. In: Pervasive 2002: Proceedings of the First International Conference on Pervasive Computing, London, UK, pp. 84–97. Springer, Heidelberg (2002)

[8] Baader, F., Calvanese, D., McGuinness, D.L., Nardi, D., Patel-Schneider, P.F (eds.) : The Description Logic Handbook: Theory, Implementation, and Applications. In: Baader, F., Calvanese, D., McGuinness, D.L., Nardi, D., Patel-Schneider, P.F. (eds.) Description Logic Handbook. Cambridge University Press, Cambridge (2003)

[9] Baader, F., Horrocks, I., Sattler, U.: Description logics as ontology languages for the semantic web (2003)

[10] Maron, M.: IASON Mobile Application - Konzept und Realisierung einer mobilen Anwendung für profilbasiertes Matchmaking von Nachrichten. Master's thesis, Universität Koblenz-Landau (2005)

[11] Baumgartner, P., Furbach, U., Gross-Hardt, M., Kleemann, T., Wernhard, C.: Krhyper inside — model based deduction in applications. In: Proc. CADE-19 Workshop on Novel Applications of Deduction Systems (2003)

[12] Kleemann, T., Sinner, A.: Description logic based matchmaking on mobile devices. In: Baumeister, J., Seipel, D. (eds.) 1st Workshop on Knowledge Engineering and Software Engineering - KESE 2005, pp. 37–48 (2005)

[13] Hebel, W.G.: Spam mail classification system. Master's thesis, University of Georgia (2001)

[14] Schüler, B.: Aggregator - a tool to bootstrap text classification. Master's thesis, Universität Koblenz-Landau (2004)

[15] Blankenhorn, K.: Spam-filterung mittels maschinellem lernen. Master's thesis, Fachhochschule Furtwangen (2002)

Searching for Temporal Patterns
in AmI Sensor Data

Romain Tavenard[1], Albert A. Salah[2], and Eric J. Pauwels[2]

[1] IRISA/ENS de Cachan, Av. du Gén. Leclerc, 35042 Rennes Cedex
[2] CWI, Kruislaan 413, 1098 SJ Amsterdam, NL

Abstract. Anticipation is a key property of human-human communication, and it is highly desirable for ambient environments to have the means of anticipating events to create a feeling of responsiveness and intelligence in the user. In a home or work environment, a great number of low-cost sensors can be deployed to detect simple events: the passing of a person, the usage of an object, the opening of a door. The methods that try to discover re-usable and interpretable patterns in temporal event data have several shortcomings. Using a testbed that we have developed for this purpose, we first contrast current approaches to the problem. We then extend the best of these approaches, the T-Pattern algorithm, with Gaussian Mixture Models, to obtain a fast and robust algorithm to find patterns in temporal data. Our algorithm can be used to anticipate future events, as well as to detect unexpected events as they occur.

1 Introduction

The success of Ambient Intelligence (AmI) depends on observing the activities of humans and responding to their behaviour patterns intelligently. In ubiquitous environments, where a wealth of sensory data is produced, mining the data for temporal patterns serves this need by discovering associations and structure, either in an offline manner to pave the way for new designs and applications, or in an online manner to ensure adaptation to the user of the AmI environment.

Two things make this task especially challenging. First of all, in a real environment, action patterns that are composed of separate events are interleaved, either by the presence of multiple users, or simply by our habit of doing multiple actions at the same time. Thus, taking an event window to predict the next event in the system will simply not work. Secondly, these patterns exist in different time scales, and the time difference between related events of a single action can have a large variation. Consequently, detecting associations with these patterns becomes a very challenging task, and many traditional pattern analysis methods are not directly applicable as we show in the next section.

In Section 2, a brief survey of the relevant literature is presented, with an emphasis on the more prominent compression-based approaches. The T-pattern method and our proposed modifications to it are presented in Section 3 and Section 4, respectively, followed by our experimental results.

M. Mühlhäuser et al. (Eds.): AmI 2007 Workshops, CCIS 11, pp. 53–62, 2008.

2   Description of the Problem and Related Work

The temporal data we would like to analyze is in form of a sequence of point events, derived from a dense network of non-intrusive and low-resolution sensors. The patterns that we hope to detect are in the form of short event sequences, with additional information about the expected time of each event in the sequence, relative to the previous event. These patterns can then serve for semantic analysis or prediction of events for responsive environments, for instance in scheduling of maintenance jobs or in arming home security systems. The challenge of the problem is the existence of multiple causes (e.g. multiple users of the environment), triggering unrelated events one after the other.

The most straightforward way to detect temporal events is by representing them spatially, where portions of the input feature are associated with increasing time indices. This approach does not work except for the simplest cases, as the absolute positions in a feature vector are not relevant at all.

A more appropriate way of representing time is to make it a part of the model. For instance in recurrent neural networks, the temporal dimension is taken into account with the help of context units [3]. However, recurrent neural networks and related approaches cannot deal with overlapping patterns, they quickly become cumbersome for larger input intervals, and they require lots of training samples.

Markov models have been recently employed to tackle simplified versions of this problem, where there are no action overlaps, and events are generated as one long sequence [6]. These models have three main disadvantages for the problem at hand. First and foremost, the first order Markovian assumption does not hold, as action patterns are construed as sequences of events, and the complete sequence is relevant for the prediction of the next event. Secondly, the estimation algorithms assume that the topology of the HMM-structure is known, which is not the case. Finally, they cannot predict patterns that have long event intervals.

A recent approach involves PCA-based methods to uncover daily human behaviour routines [2]. The data for each subject are stored in an activity matrix, whose most prominent eigenvectors (dubbed *eigenbehaviors*) are then interpreted. One obvious drawback with this method is that it requires a fixed sized activity vector. Additionally, there is no hierarchical decomposition of activities.

Finding a *dictionary* of patterns is possible with **compression-based algorithms** that treat events as "words" in a stream, and seek the patterns that lead to the best compression of the stream. These methods use the Lempel-Ziv compression algorithm, which is known to achieve Markov entropic compression, or a variant of it (e.g. Lempel-Ziv-Welch and Active Lempel-Ziv algorithms) [1].

The basic Lempel-Ziv algorithm (**LZ78**) uses an automatically updated dictionary to extract recurring "words" (patterns) in a string. The Lempel-Ziv-Welch (**LZW**) variant starts off with a pre-defined basic dictionary (in the case of sensor networks these are single sensor events) to avoid ill-detected patterns at the beginning of the stream and to introduce some continuity. The **Active LeZi** uses a sliding window of length l (length of the longest phrase in LZ table) on the stream to extract all possible sequences of size l.

LZW and Active LeZi both aim at adding continuity to LZ pattern extraction, yet they still have linear complexity, which is a beneficial feature for a real-time event detection system. On the other hand, none of the compression based methods take into account the temporal structure of the patterns, as the time delays are not modeled, and subsequently overlapping events may escape detection. For a dense, low-cost sensor network without the identification of event source, this is a major drawback as is clearly borne out by the experimental results reported below. This is the main reason why we turn our attention to *T-patterns* as discussed in the next section.

3   T-patterns

The temporal pattern detection methods mentioned in the related work section ignore the time information, and cast the problem into a simpler representation by retaining only the order of events. In neural network, HMM, and compression based approaches, the emphasis is on predicting the next event, which is not a suitable perspective for an environment with multiple overlapping event sequences.

In the *T-pattern* approach, as introduced and explored by Magnusson, symbolic time series are investigated, where each symbol represents the onset of a particular event or activity, with the principal goal of elucidating possible relationships between pairs of symbols and then building trees of temporal dependencies in a hierarchical fashion [5]. A thorough search is conducted on the training sequence for symbols of an ever-growing dictionary. As the algorithm proceeds, pairs of strongly correlated events joined into new events, and the search is resumed with the expanded dictionary.

Magnusson introduced the notion of a *critical interval* (CI): $[d_1, d_2]$ is considered to be a CI for the pair of symbols (events) (A, B) if the occurrence of A at time t entails that B is more likely to occur in the time interval $[t+d_1, t+d_2]$ than in a random interval of the same size. He then suggested to use the standard p-value to gauge how exceptional the observed frequency of the combination under scrutiny is.

More precisely, suppose the total data stream has length T with N_A and N_B occurrences of A and B, respectively. If we assume (following Magnusson [5]) as null-hypothesis that A and B are independent Poisson processes with intensity (i.e. the average number of events per unit time interval) $\lambda_A = N_A/T$, and $\lambda_B = N_B/T$, respectively. Now, assume in addition that there are N_{AB} occurrences of B in a predefined CI (of length d) trailing each A-event. Notice that under the null-hypothesis the expected number of B-events in a time interval of length d equals $\mu_B = \lambda_B d$. In particular, the probability of not observing a B-event in this CI is therefore equal to $\pi_0 = e^{-\mu_B} = e^{-\lambda_B d}$. The above-mentioned p-value is then computed as the probability of observing at least N_{AB} B-events in the CI, if we assume that A and B are independent. Hence,

$$p = P(N_{AB} \text{ B-events or more} \mid \text{A, B indep.})$$

$$= 1 - \sum_{k=0}^{N_{AB}-1} \binom{N_A}{k} (1 - \pi_0)^k \pi_0^{(N_A-k)}.$$

Magnusson suggests as a T-pattern detection scheme to test for every possible pair of symbols of the form (A, B), every possible CI, from the largest to the smallest one, until the p-value is sufficiently small, indicating significance (.05 is a typical upper bound). Note that p will be high for high values of d, which means that short intervals will be favored.

4   The Modified T-pattern Algorithm

We propose two modifications to the T-pattern algorithm to make it more resilient to spurious patterns, and to make the search for patterns more robust.

4.1   Testing Independence between Two Temporal Point Processes

The repeated significance testing of the basic T-pattern approach substantially increases the risk of false positives (suggesting spurious dependencies). Applying a Bonferroni correction would be one way to mitigate this adverse effect. In this paper, however, we put forward a more efficient way of testing this independence between A and B which is based on the following proposition.

Proposition 1. *If A and B are independent temporal point process, then*

$$T_{AB} \sim U(0, \tilde{T}_B).$$

In plain language this proposition asserts that if the A and B processes are independent, then whenever an A-event occurs between two successive B-events, it will be uniformly distributed in that interval. Due to lack of space we will not attempt to give a rigorous proof, but it is intuitively clear that non-uniformity of A within the B-interval, would allow a keen observer to improve his or her prediction of the next B-event, thus contradicting independence (for a graphical illustration of this proposition we refer to Fig.2. This therefore allows us to formulate a statistical procedure to test whether A and B are dependent: using the notation established above we compare for each event A_k the time till the next B-event to the current B-interval length:

$$U(k) = \frac{T_{AB}(k)}{\tilde{T}_B(k)} = \frac{B_{k^*} - A_k}{B_{k^*} - B_{k^*-1}}$$

which, under the assumption of independence, should be uniformly distributed between 0 and 1: $U \sim U(0, 1)$. This can be easily checked by any number of standard statistical test (e.g. Kolmogorov-Smirnov). If the null hypothesis (independence) is rejected then it makes sense to start looking for inter-event time intervals (i.e. CI's). This is taken up in the next section.

4.2   Modelling T_{AB} Times

The CI detection scheme as proposed in [5] has the drawback that only the first occurrence of B following A is considered. However, if the average occurrence rate of A is relatively high, or if the inter-event time for B is long, this could lead to fallacious associations.

For this reason, we propose to proceed differently. If the above-discussed uniformity test has rejected independence, then we look for the characteristic period by modelling the conditional probability $P(B \text{ at } t + \Delta t \,|\, A \text{ at } t)$ using Gaussian Mixture Models (GMM). More precisely, all the A-events are aligned at time zero, whereupon all subsequent B-events are plotted. If an A-event tends to induce a B-event after a delay of t time-units, this will show up in this plot as a significant peak. All the non-related B-events will contribute to a very diffuse background. For that reason, we model the B-events as a 2-component GMM. One sharp and localized peak sits on top of the critical interval, while all the other B-events give rise to a flat and broad second component. The standard variation of the sharp peak immediately suggest a value for the width of the CI.

5   Experimental Results

In order to have a simple and realistic experimental setup, we simulate simple interruption sensors in a home or office environment (See Fig.1). We have one or two users of the system generating simultaneous interruption events from a predefined event dictionary, which serves as a catalogue of prominent behaviours.

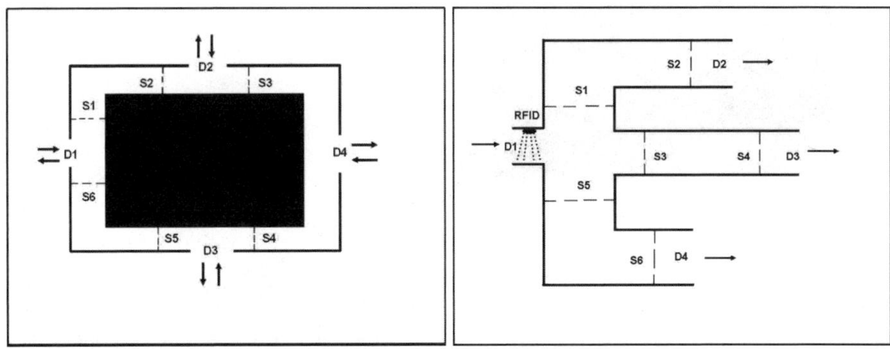

Fig. 1. Ground plan for two corridor layouts used in experiments. Left: Layout 1 shows 4 doors and 6 interruption sensors. Right: Layout 2 shows an entrance door and 3 exit doors, as well as an RFID reader and 6 binary interruption sensors.

For each configuration, we generated training and test sequences of $1,000$ symbols by simulating one or two persons walking in the corridors. We have investigated to what degree we could use the patterns discovered in the training phase as predictors for events in the second stream. The prediction is made for

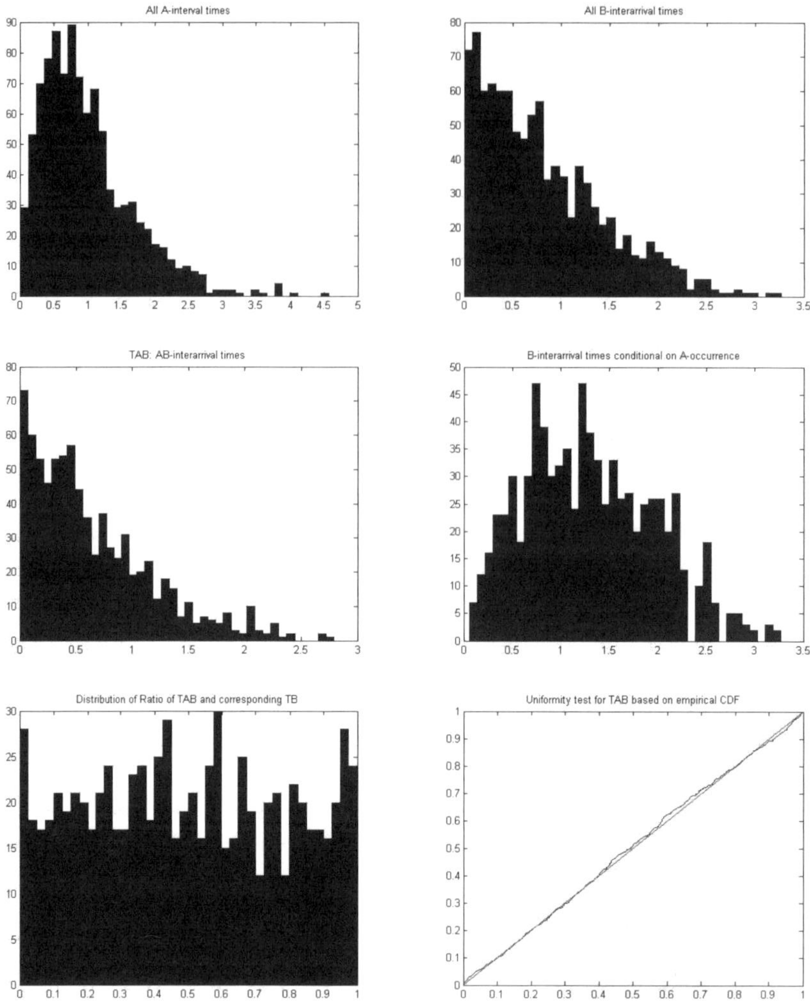

Fig. 2. Top row: Histogram for interevent times for the A (*left*) and B (*right*) process; *Middle row: left* T_{AB} distribution: time intervals between the occurrence of A and *next* B-event; *right:* Lengths of B-intervals in which a A-event occurred; notice the bias towards longer intervals (compared to histogram of all B interevent times above). *Bottom row: left:* Histogram of ratio $T_{AB}/\tilde{T}_B$, if A and B are independent, this ratio should be uniformly distributed between 0 and 1, a fact which is even more clearly borne out by its cumulative density function to the theoretically predicted one. (The *p*-value in this case was 0.61 which means that the null-hypothesis of independence is accepted.)

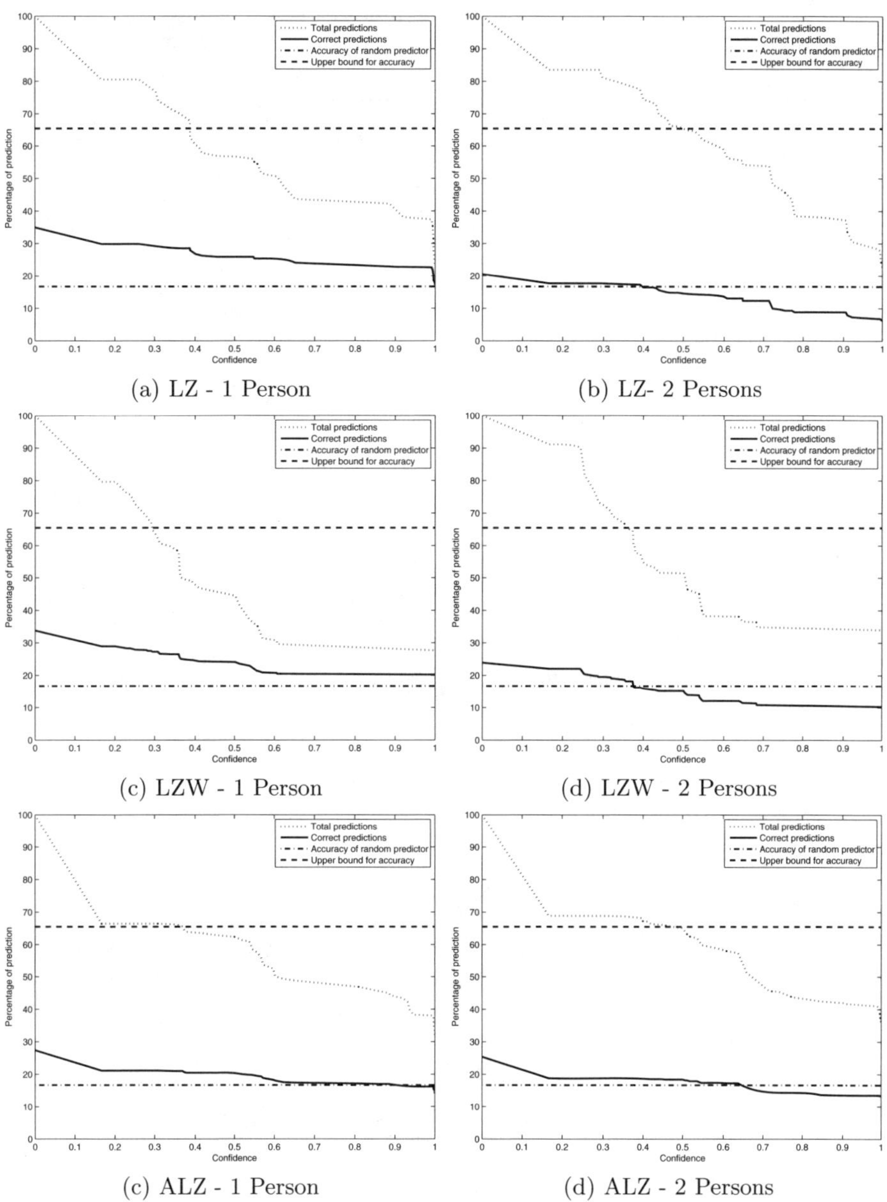

Fig. 3. Predition results for the compression based algorithms for the first layout. Detailed results for the second layout omitted for brevity.

each discrete time slot, which is more granular than predicting the next event. We have contrasted the compression based methods, T-patterns, and our modified T-pattern approach. As the first symbol emitted by each new pattern is random

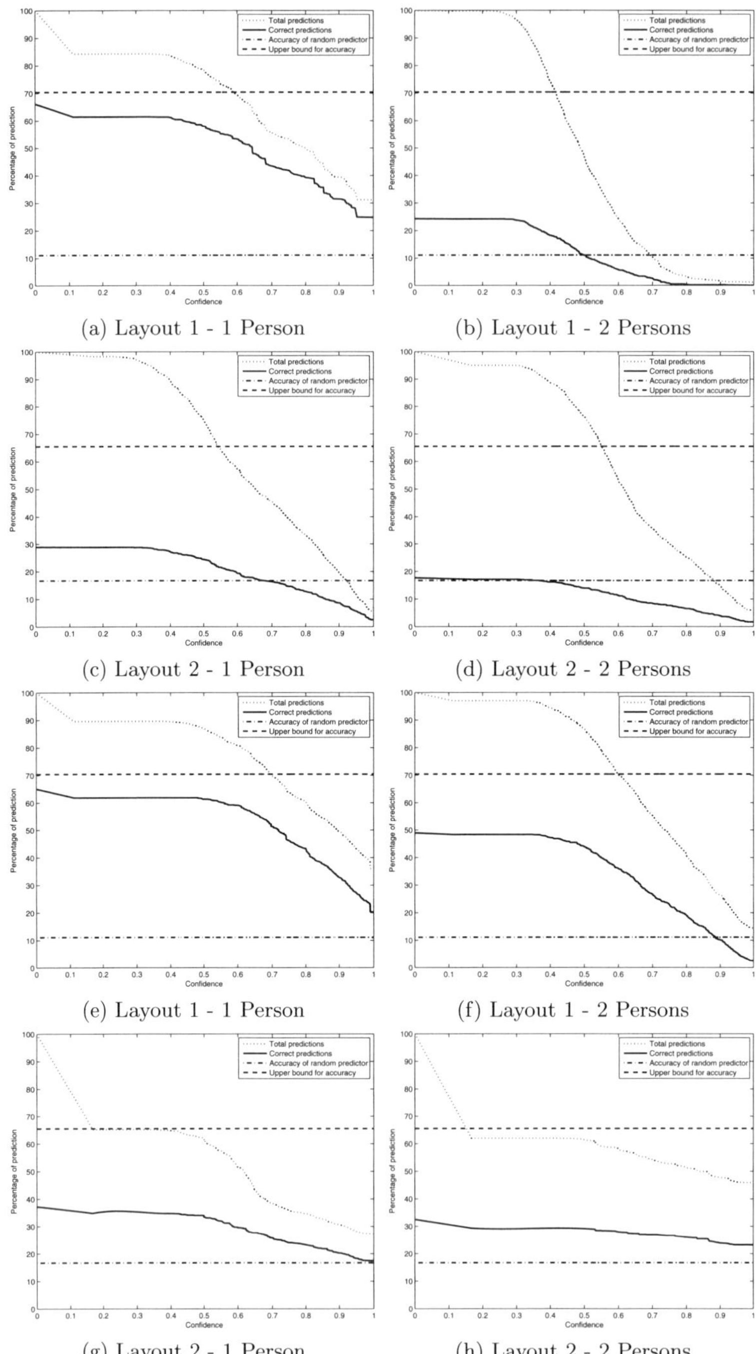

(a) Layout 1 - 1 Person   (b) Layout 1 - 2 Persons

(c) Layout 2 - 1 Person   (d) Layout 2 - 2 Persons

(e) Layout 1 - 1 Person   (f) Layout 1 - 2 Persons

(g) Layout 2 - 1 Person   (h) Layout 2 - 2 Persons

Fig. 4. Predition results for (a)-(d) the T-Pattern and (e)-(h) the modified algorithm

and therefore completely unpredictable, and as individual patterns are short, the prediction rate will have an inherent upperbound.

Fig.3 summarizes the experimental results for the different compression algorithms. In each case the x-axis represents the minimal confidence in the prediction. Confidence is high (in fact 100%) whenever the current pattern unambiguously predicts a unique symbol. If there more potential outcomes, confidence drops accordingly. The dotted line indicates the percentage of cases for which prediction is possible with the confidence specified on the x-axis. The left column show results for scenarios in which only one person is present, the right column shows results for the case when two person intermingle. The two horizontal lines indicate the upper bound for the achievable accuracy (recall that the first symbol in each pattern is unpredictable) and the accuracy of a random prediction.

The results displayed in Fig.4 show contrasts the original CI-extraction (as detailed in [5]) with T-Patterns that use the GMM modelling expounded above. It transpires that Magnusson's original scheme produces too many (spurious) T-patterns making high-confidence prediction impossible as is clear from the way the curves quickly drop to zero. This is most apparent in the 2-person scenario where the intermingling of 1-person patterns generates a large number of new combinations, a fair bit of which are erroneously identified as T-patterns. The GMM approach fares much better, even in the more difficult 2-person scenario.

6 Conclusion

Detecting temporal patterns in sensor data is useful for semantic analysis and event prediction in AmI environments. In this paper we have reviewed two methodologies for the discovery of temporal patterns. The first one collapses the sequence into a string and then uses compression-based techniques to extract repetitive "words". The second one (so-called T-patterns) takes advantage of the time dimension to find the typical delay between related events. We have proposed some improvements to the basic T-pattern methodology (referred to in this text as GMM T-patterns) that significantly improve the performance. Experiments show that T-patterns outperform the compression-based techniques, which is not really surprising as the compression discards most of the temporal information. The experiments also show that the proposed T-pattern improve-

Table 1. Percentage correct predictions at the 20% confidence level

	Layout 1		Layout 2	
	1 person	2 persons	1 person	2 persons
LZ	29.8	17.7	56.5	13.2
ALZ	21.1	18.8	66.4	19.6
LZW	28.9	22.0	60.5	15.1
T-patterns	28.8	17.1	61.5	24.2
GMM T-patterns	**34.8**	**29.3**	**61.9**	**48.3**

ments (independence testing and GMM-modelling of correlation times) yield more reliable results.

To conclude we summarize the experimental results in Table 1. It was obtained by computing for each experiment the correct prediction rate for a confidence level of 20% (this amounts to constructing a vertical line at the x-value 0.20 in each of the figures and reading of the intersection with the solid curve). The significance of the proposed improvements is obvious.

While we focus on detecting behaviour patterns, a complementary problem would be to track multiple people using low-cost sensors, for which Bayesian filtering techniques are proposed in the literature [4]. The patterns that we aim to detect can serve the tracking problem in constructing a Voronoi graph of the environment. This application is currently inspected by our group.

Acknowledgments

This work was done while R.T. was at CWI. The authors gratefully acknowledge partial support by EC's NOE MUSCLE (FP6-507752), and the Dutch BSIK/BRICKS project. We are grateful to M.S. Magnusson for providing us with additional information on T-patterns.

References

1. Cook, D.J.: Prediction algorithms for smart environments. In: Diane, J., Cook, D.J., Das, S.K. (eds.) Smart Environments: Technologies, Protocols, and Applications, p. 175. Wiley Series on Parallel and Distributed Computing, Chichester (2005)
2. Eagle, N., Pentland, A.: Eigenbehaviors: Identifying structure in routine. In: Proc. Roy. Soc. A (submission, 2006)
3. Elman, J.L.: Finding Structure in Time. Cognitive Science 14(2), 179–211 (1990)
4. Fox, D., Hightower, J., Liao, L., Schulz, D., Borriello, G.: Bayesian Filtering for Location Estimation. In: IEEE Pervasive Computing, pp. 24–33 (2003)
5. Magnusson, M.S.: Discovering hidden time patterns in behavior: T-patterns and their detection. Behav. Res. Methods Instrum. Comput. 32(1), 93–110 (2000)
6. Rao, S.P., Cook, D.J.: Predicting inhabitant action using action and task models with application to smart homes. International Journal on Artificial Intelligence Tools 13(1), 81–99 (2004)

Evaluating Ubiquitous Systems with Users
(Workshop Summary)

Christian Kray[1], Lars Bo Larsen[2], Patrick Olivier[1], Margit Biemans[3],
Arthur van Bunningen[4], Mirko Fetter[5], Tim Jay[6], Vassilis-Javed Khan[7],
Gerhard Leitner[8], Ingrid Mulder[3], Jörg Müller[9], Thomas Plötz[10],
and Irene Lopez de Vallejo[11]

[1] Newcastle University, Newcastle upon Tyne, United Kingdom
{c.kray}@ncl.ac.uk
[2] Aalborg Universitet, Aalborg, Denmark
[3] Telematica Instituut, Enschede, The Netherlands
[4] University of Twente, Enschede, The Netherlands
[5] Bauhaus-University Weimar, Weimar, Germany
[6] University of Bath, Bath, United Kingdom
[7] Eindhoven University of Technology, Eindhoven, The Netherlands
[8] Alpen-Adria University of Klagenfurt, Klagenfurt, Austria
[9] University of Münster, Münster, Germany
[10] Technische Universität Dortmund, Dortmund, Germany
[11] University College London, London, United Kingdom

Abstract. Evaluating ubiquitous systems with users can be a challenge, and the goal of this workshop was to take stock of current issues and novel approaches to address this challenge. In this paper, we report on the discussions we had during several plenary and small-group sessions. We first briefly review those evaluation methods that we identified as being used in ubiquitous computing, and then discuss several issues and research questions that emerged during the discussion. These issues include: data sources used for evaluation, comparing ubiquitous systems, interdisciplinary evaluation, multi-method evaluation, factoring in context and disengaged users.

1 Introduction

A significant number of ubiquitous systems have been built to support human users in performing a variety of tasks. These applications cover a large range of scenarios, including safety-critical medical applications, customized support in the workplace, and leisure-related applications. Users interact with these systems via implicit or explicit means, e. g. by moving about in an environment or using custom-built devices. At the same time, many ambient applications deploy sensors to gather information about the context, in which those interactions take place, and system behavior can change depending on contextual factors. All this adds up to a fairly complex situation, which poses new challenges for evaluation, potentially pushing the boundaries of traditional evaluation methods and opening up opportunities for novel approaches.

The goal of this workshop was to bring together researchers with an interest in this area to discuss the current state of the art in evaluating ubiquitous systems with real

M. Mühlhäuser et al. (Eds.): AmI 2007 Workshops, CCIS 11, pp. 63–74, 2008.

users, to identify shortcomings and benefits of traditional evaluation methods and to explore novel approaches. In order to facilitate the exchange of ideas, all but the first session were dedicated either to working in small groups or to plenary discussion. This paper tries to summarize the main issues that were identified during the discussions, and to highlight some areas, where further research is needed.

In the remainder of this paper we will first briefly summarize existing approaches to evaluation (in section 2) before discussing several issues and research questions that arise from evaluating ubiquitous computing (in section 3). While we engaged with a number of issues during the workshop, we would not want to claim to fully cover every possible aspect relating to the evaluation of ubiquitous systems. There are, however, several related events that have explored this area from different angles, which we briefly describe in section 4. In the final section of this paper, we summarize the key outcomes of the workshop and briefly discuss a number of research challenges, which will need to be addressed in the future.

2   Current Approaches to Evaluation

In principle, almost any evaluation technique used in human computer interaction (HCI) can also be applied to evaluate ubiquitous systems. However, a significant portion of ubiquitous technology is meant to weave itself invisibly into the users' life [1], so that both the users' task and their interactions with a system are defined less clearly than in traditional settings. For this reason, it is not always straightforward to apply the techniques, which are widely used in HCI (e. g. methods based on task performance), for ubiquitous systems [2]. The same can be said for some commonly used metrics in HCI, such as task completion time and error rate. Consequently, different measures have been proposed for ubiquitous applications, e. g. Scholz's and Consolvo's set of conceptual measures and associated metrics [3].

Preece et al. [4] identified four main paradigms for evaluating systems with users. *Quick and Dirty* evaluations have the benefit of delivering results fast and cheap and are used by many projects during the requirements analysis phase. *Usability tests* usually take place in a laboratory, where user performance scores such as task completion time or error rates can be easily measured. *Field studies* aim at gathering data in a natural setting. There has been an intense debate about the value of field studies compared to lab-based studies. Some authors consider it necessary to gather data on how ubiquitous systems are used in the real world [2] [5]. Others believe that in many cases the associated effort is not justified by the additional insights gained [6]. Field studies can considerably vary in terms of their duration. While some studies take place in a single day or week, some projects go as far as letting users live with the technology for months or even years to gain insights on the long term effects of technology [7] [8] [9]. *Predictive techniques* use experts, heuristics and user models to evaluate systems without incorporating users.

Evaluation techniques can also be classified according to a number of dimensions. *Formative evaluations* are employed during design iterations to inform design. *Summative evaluations* are used after the design phase has finished to compare the system to other systems or a set of predefined goals. *Introspective techniques* ask for what users think or believe, while *observation techniques* look at the actual behavior of users. *Qualitative techniques* gather data to describe behavior, establish usage scenarios or build categories, while *quantitative techniques* gather data for statistical data analysis. *Short term studies* look at the immediate effects a system has on its users, while *long term studies* aim at identifying effects that only occur after months or even years of usage. In applying any of these techniques, the degree of sophistication or fidelity of the system can vary widely. Sometimes, only user behavior without any prototype is evaluated. Most of the time, an instantiation of a ubiquitous system is part of the evaluation, and it can take the form of a paper based prototype, interface mockups, or (partially) functional prototypes.

A further way to categorize evaluation techniques is according to the way in which users are involved, i. e. whether they are being observed, whether users/experts are being asked directly, whether they are brought into a usability lab, or being modeled using a user model. Observing users can happen directly, with the experimenter directly witnessing the fact, or indirectly, where the experimenter can merely analyze artifacts that were created during the experiment. Direct observation often employs techniques from ethnography. Information can be kept using a notebook and a still camera, using audio recording and a still camera, or using video, for example [4]. Indirect observations can use (photo) diaries, guest books [10], interaction logs [5] or logs from diverse sensors [11]. Cultural probes [12] are small artifacts like still cameras or modeling clay that are given to users. Within a certain time period, users can use these artifact to capture their experiences. Systems that intent to change user behavior can be evaluated by measuring user behavior before and after they used the system. Similarly, the change of the environment around the system can be observed.

Common ways to directly gather user feedback are *questionnaires* and *interviews* [4] [13]. Interviews can be structured (i. e. they follow a rigid predefined procedure), or unstructured. Semi-structured interviews often start with pre-planned questions but then probe the interviewee for more information. *Focus groups* [14] are widely used to let users from different user groups react to each other. *Laddering* [8] is a special interviewing technique to establish users values regarding a system. *Online questionnaires* hold the potential to reach a large number of users, but it is harder to control the sample. *Experience sampling* [15] is a widely used technique to ask the user simple questions many times distributed over a certain time period. The *Day Reconstruction Method* [16] combines features of time-budget measurement and experience sampling. It is used to assess how people spend their time and how they experience the various activities and settings of their lives. *Conjoint analysis* [17] asks users to rank a number of paper based prototypes, where system features are systematically varied. Using this technique, the relative values users attribute to system features can be established. The *repertory grid* technique [18] aims at eliciting so-called personal constructs (e. g. bad-good, playful-expert-like). It can be used to identify a users perceived dimensions regarding a system. With *participatory design,* users are directly involved in the design phase, such that design and evaluation become closely entangled.

Some techniques aim at observing and asking the user at the same time. In a *contextual inquiry* [8], the interviewer takes on the role of an apprentice and the interviewee shows and explains important tasks. With the *think-aloud* technique, the user is asked to state what he currently is thinking while completing a task. Asking experts is also a widely employed evaluation technique. Heuristics [19] guide the expert along defined constructs to evaluate a system. In a usability lab, certain variables of a system can be measured, while context variables can be held constant. Usually, users are asked to solve a clearly defined task, and task completion time and error rate are measured. The real context of system usage can be reconstructed to a certain degree, and context variables can be held constant [20] [21]. If *user models* [22] are used, users are often modeled with respect to completion of a certain task. This can be done, for example, using GOMS [23] or ACT-R [24].

3   Issues and Research Questions

In the previous section we briefly listed a number of evaluation techniques that have been used in ubiquitous computing. While there certainly are a large number of options available to evaluate a ubiquitous system, it is not necessarily clear which technique is best suited for a particular system or context of use. In addition, it is not obvious whether a technique can be applied straight away or whether it needs to be adapted to accommodate the specific properties of ubiquitous computing (such as context-dependency or potentially invisible interfaces). Ideally, a framework or a set of guidelines would provide help in selecting the most appropriate evaluation methods based on specific properties of a system and the aims and objectives of the evaluation. Working towards this goal, we discussed a number of issues and questions at the workshop (see Figure 1 for an overview), which we report on in the remainder of this section.

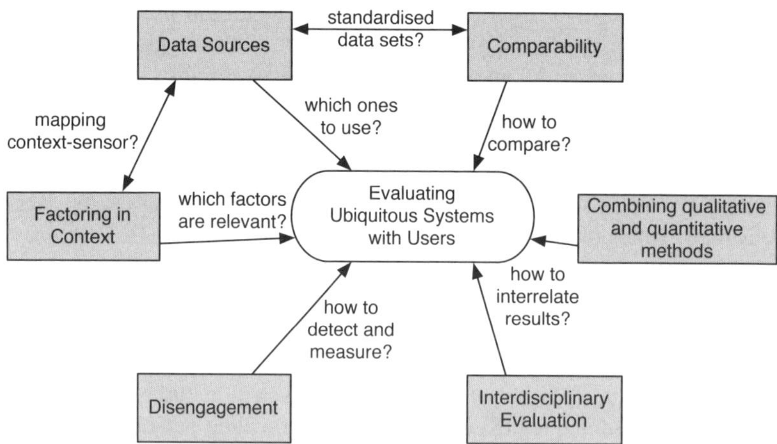

Fig. 1. Overview over issues identified during the workshop

3.1   Data Sources for Evaluation

A key ingredient for realizing ambient intelligence is the acquisition, processing and analysis of data from multiple sensor sources at a large scale. The motivation for this approach is to enable a system to become aware of its context by constantly integrating different sources of information. Compared to more traditional settings (e. g. a desktop use scenario), where oftentimes the users' tasks are very clearly defined, ubiquitous applications can be more difficult to evaluate. This is due to tasks possibly being less well defined, to the tight integration of a system with its environment, and to the complexity of the context in which it is used. For example, whereas a speech recognition system "only" needs to perform the transcription of the recorded utterances, a ubiquitous system may have to analyze the context of a particular situation in order to derive an appropriate system behavior. In the first case, a system can be evaluated by counting correctly classified words, whereas in the second case, such a measure would be insufficient. To illustrate this, consider the example of a smart conference room analyzing context using multiple sensor sources. Using a combination of both microphones and further sensors (such as active tags) the system might infer that currently a very important business meeting is being held. A reasonable system behavior might include that no disturbances occur (e. g. all telephones are muted), all attendees are kept up-to-date with relevant information only (e. g. delivery of urgent emails only) and the creation of a convenient ambience (perfect lighting conditions, constant temperature and humidity).

The more integrated a system is into an environment and the more complex its behavior can be, the more difficult it is to evaluate the system and, thus, the more data sources may have to be taken into account during the evaluation. Although all components of a ubiquitous system can (and have to) be evaluated separately[1] this usually does not give detailed insights into the effectiveness of the overall system. Oftentimes, there is no accepted quality measure which can be evaluated numerically in terms of e. g. recognition rates. In the above mentioned example (the smart meeting room), a good indicator for the effectiveness of the system would be the number of successful deals made *due to* the corresponding meetings being held in the smart conference room.

Obviously, such an effect is rather difficult to measure. Nevertheless, it seems advisable to gather as much data as possible in order to have as much information available for analysis as possible. The benefit of such an approach is that once collected the data can be analyzed in many ways. Furthermore, if data sets are made publicly available, it opens up the opportunity to run different algorithms on them and to compare their performance (see also section 3.2). In addition to the data captured by actual sensors, system logs are another good source of information. They contain a wealth of information regarding the overall behavior of the system and may also help to put the sensor data into perspective (e. g. to detect system errors that might have lead to erratic system behavior).

When combining these primary and secondary sources of information (i. e. sensor data and system logs) with feedback obtained from users (e. g. using one of the methods discussed in the previous section), it is obvious that a potentially very large body of data has to be analyzed. While this can be beneficial in a number of ways (e. g. by increasing the coverage, or by enabling cross-checking of different sources), it can also entail significant problems. The latter include dealing with contradicting data, the effort required to analyze a very large body of heterogeneous data and the lack of tools to facilitate the task.

---

[1] Examples are the recognition rate of a speech recognizer built into the system, or the robustness of video-based person identification.

Generally speaking, the evaluation of ubiquitous systems oftentimes requires the analysis of multiple data sources. Individual results need to be integrated to include both technical aspects (e. g. in terms of multi-modal sensor fusion) and socio-psychological factors. The key goal of this integration process is to fully evaluate the performance of a ubiquitous system with respect to both overall user satisfaction and the 'technical' performance of the system.

While the large amount of data being gathered can be beneficial in terms of getting a clearer picture of the context and regarding the detailed evaluation of a system, there are also some drawbacks and further implications. The data being gathered may potentially include sensitive data with respect to the security and privacy of people or places. It is hence the responsibility of the researchers collecting the information to ensure that the data is handled appropriately. Furthermore, there is the danger that the volume of data is so larger that extracting meaningful information can become very time-consuming.

3.2 Comparability

The comparability of evaluations is very important, yet problematic. The purpose of evaluations is to inform the development of future applications and systems. Later systems should be better than those they replace. That term 'better' causes problems because it implies measurability. The evaluation of two systems should enable us to say that one system is better than another, according to some set of goals.

At present, there are a number of obstacles to this. One significant problem, as can be seen from preceding sections of this paper, is the number of methods available to researchers working on ubiquitous computing. While within this paper we advocate the use of multiple methods in evaluation, it is clear that this can make it difficult to compare results of the evaluations of systems.

A second issue concerns the clarity of goals of given systems. Having the ability to compare a system or the outcome of an evaluation requires the definition of user goals that are to be reached or exceeded. However, goal definition in ubiquitous computing is inherently problematic for many ubiquitous applications due the the complications of contextual factors. However, the basic requirements on goal setting can be borrowed from usability engineering literature, for example [25]. The Usability Engineering Lifecycle differentiates between quantitative and qualitative goals. Quantitative goals usually have clearly measurable properties, such as the time to access information. By contrast qualitative goals relate to less tangible requirements such as the facilitation of high quality collaboration between users, which can best evaluated through qualitative methods such as interviews and focus groups.

Often the unambiguous definition of goals is not possible, because of the richness of the environment in which the systems are used. This is particularly true of ubiquitous computing application when the a value proposition cannot be formulated in a meaningful manner. For example, in ambient assisted living applications, the cumulative benefit of the application is the independent living of the occupants, but this is often hard to decompose into specific achievement of goals in a new smart home system. Such a system might typically observing the everyday activities of the occupants e.g. activities relating to dressing, washing and medication taking, prompting and calling for care as appropriate. However, the individual achievement of goals does not add up, in a simple manner, to the achievement of the goal of independent living. Achievement of the broader goal is itself determined by the disruption that such a system is deemed to make to a user's daily routine, the reliability and predictability of the system, and ultimately the user's (and their carers') confidence in it.

The problem of comparing two systems in ubiquitous computing can be significantly more difficult than in other domains. This is partially due the unpredictability of contextual factors and its impact on repeatability, which is a prerequisite for rigorous investigation and the comparison of systems with one another. For example, while it may be quite easy to measure whether buying a book using one website is faster than using another website, but comparing two ubiquitous systems providing adaptive navigation support depending on the context may be more difficult. The main areas for consideration at this time then, is to consider carefully how evaluations are to be compared across systems for the benefit of continued development of ubiquitous computing and to develop a shared conception of the goals that are to be achieved through this development.

3.3   Benefit of Interdisciplinary Evaluation

Interdisciplinarity is an important issue in the evaluation of ubiquitous systems. An unusually wide variety of skills and knowledge are required for this kind of research. We need an understanding of design, of software and electrical engineering, of what is possible to achieve in ubiquitous computing – along with a thorough understanding of research methods, including a knowledge of how to choose appropriate methods for a given situation. Of course, interdisciplinarity can bring its own complications.

It can be argued that thoroughly understanding evaluating ubiquitous computing in context requires cross-domain research. The increasing complexity that comes with ubiquitous technologies along with the dynamic characteristic of these technologies even furnishes more proof. Bridges across disciplines are necessary. Theoretical insights, methods, best practices, and experiences from several disciplines, such as constructivist theories, behavior sciences, educational science, computer science, electronics, ethnography, discourse, and sociology, should be combined, and should feed back to the current ubiquitous computing research. These bridges are necessary, not only between theory and practice or between social scientists and technological scientists, in order to evaluate ubiquitous systems with users. The traditional disciplinary borders must be crossed to integrate different standards and approaches as well as different evaluation methods, to enable a holistic understanding of the impact and qualities of a ubiquitous system.

3.4   Combining Quantitative and Qualitative Methods

Currently the ubiquitous computing community is mainly driven by the rapid advance of technological solutions. The mechanics of these technological solutions (network connectivity, mobile devices, sensors, programming interfaces etc.) are plentiful, accessible and inexpensive. This enables the community to easily experiment by creating prototypes. However, it is often the case that the evaluation goals of such prototypes are unclear.

There is always an anticipated value proposition of the prototype. However it might not always be possible to subsequently evaluate it in a rigorous, scientific way. We would argue that this is somehow expected since in many cases it is either difficult to deploy a prototype with many users or the purpose of the prototype is exploratory. Such prototypes are still in their early development. That fact makes it challenging for researchers to evaluate their benefits and costs since there is little knowledge about the way users would interact with such systems. Thus, a thorough understanding of the available methods to evaluate such systems is needed.

To better understand the use of ubiquitous systems and to rigorously evaluate their proposed benefits and costs, we argue that a combination of qualitative and quantitative methods is needed. Since these systems are still in development qualitative methods should be first deployed to evaluate the way people interact and fit into their lives such systems. Then, when a clearer idea of the context and the proposed benefit is established, quantitative methods are needed to rigorously evaluate that proposed benefit. In this way their potential can be generalized.

For example, an ethnographic study, diary study or interview can be used to assess the way users interact with a system. Such qualitative methods would allow the user to openly discuss about all the aspects of the interaction. In this way researchers decrease the possibility of having overlooked either a benefit or a cost that their system might bring. Having clearly established what to evaluate in the system, the use of questionnaires or a log of behavioral measures would give the means to the researcher to meticulously demonstrate the effect of the system.

3.5   Factoring in the Context

As ubiquitous technologies become more and more personal, they increasingly stay with one person at a time and are consequently used in various contexts. One way to deal with these challenges is the Living Lab concept. Living Labs move research out of laboratories into real-life contexts to stimulate innovation. The Living Lab concept is acknowledged in Europe as an open innovation instrument, and refers to a network of infrastructure and technologies as well as a network of people; it seems appropriate to study questions related to the design and evaluation of ubiquitous technologies that improve and enrich everyday life. The Living Lab approach represents a research methodology for sensing, prototyping, validating and refining complex solutions in multiple and evolving real-life contexts. The user experience focus involves areas of user interface design and ergonomics as well as user acceptance, extending to user co-design process, finally leading to service or product creation.

It might be clear that the Living Lab concept opens a wealth of possibilities to exploit the evaluation of ubiquitous technologies in context with and by real users. However, as indicated by Mulder and Kort [26]:

> there are no agreed upon generic methods for logging yet. Only system events, but these are detailed and not always complete. Often logging is implemented into the ICT product or service during implementation. This implementation is not always straightforward or even possible, when you do not have access to the source code. Many of the automated tools alone do not deliver the desired

insight, they need to be combined with common methods such as interviews and focus groups which either provide input for the automated measurements (which things should be captured and asked for during experience sampling) or provide additional information after the automated measurements (clarifications of specific experience sampling data, behaviors or contexts in which it appeared).

Moreover, there is still a need for research in methodological guidelines and tool requirements for data-analysis. In particular, analysis techniques for correlating objective behavior and subjective user experience data into relevant design context parameters.

3.6   Disengagement

The fact that pervasive and ubiquitous systems are often designed for public consumption can add some interesting issues in terms of their evaluation. As well as evaluating the usability of the system, it is necessary to understand how the system engages or fails to engage users.

Taking an example of interactive or intelligent public displays, there will be a subset of users who have engaged with the system to some extent and a subset who have not. It is clearly important, in evaluating such systems, to work towards an understanding of both of these behaviors. With regard to informing the development of future systems, it is arguably more important to understand the reasons for disengagement than it is to understand patterns of use by engaged users.

Those who engage with a system can be assumed to a certain extent to have a certain range of expectations of that system, whereas it is much more difficult to predict the expectations of those who have failed to engage. Similarly, the motivations of the engaged users, with respect to the use of a system, are relatively easy to predict, compared to the motivations of the disengaged.

There are many potential reasons for disengagement with any public system. There may be issues of investment of time and effort, coupled with difficulties to assess benefit. There may be issues of feeling that a system is likely to be too complicated or otherwise for a exclusive group - 'not for me'. There may be issues of embarrassment of self-consciousness. There are likely to be many and varied reasons amongst a population for disengagement - it is vital that these are considered an integral part of evaluation. The main goal of evaluation of such a system must be the future development of more effective, more usable systems. To this end, we need to gain an understanding of the barriers to use amongst a population of users. We need to do this through evaluation with potential users who have all the means necessary to engage with a system but choose not to.

In the case of systems designed for a workplace or an educational institution, there is a 'captive' audience or user-group. Where there is a defined user-group, access to the disengaged is possible through random or stratified sampling of the population. In these cases, the user-group has a certain level of commitment to, and investment in, the evaluation. For public systems, however, there is not necessarily a well-defined user group. Also, the (potential) user group has no commitment to, or investment in, the evaluation of such a system. They may indeed have the opposite motivation - having chosen not to engage with a system, they may want to actively avoid being questioned about it.

There are two main issues, then, to keep in mind. The first is that an understanding of disengagement is a vital part of the evaluation of public systems. The second is that some thought must be given to the development of suitable methods for gaining this understanding.

4   Related Events

This workshop and its results have to be seen in the context of a series of event aiming in the same direction. One of the early events focusing on the evaluation of ubiquitous computing, the *Workshop on Evaluation Methodologies for Ubiquitous Computing* took part during the 1st UbiComp conference in 2001 organized by Jean Scholtz et. al. [27] resulting in a first sketch of a framework for evaluation, outlining four relevant dimensions: universality, utility, usability, and ubiquity. Along these dimensions the workshop participants exemplarily identified new metrics and challenges as well as needed tools and methodologies specific to the evaluation of ubiquitous computing and so delivered a sound starting point for the definition of an overall framework.

Since then, a number of further workshops on this topic were held. In the following we want to briefly describe the two events that took place immediately before this workshop, namely the *In-Situ* workshop [28] and the *1st International Workshop on Ubiquitous Systems Evaluation (USE '07)* [29] both held in September 2007.

The In-Situ workshop focussed on tools and methodologies for evaluating user behavior and user experience particular aiming at pervasive and mobile systems. The presented approaches predominately concentrated on methods and tools for an evaluation in the wild and can be divided into two categories. The first category consists of approaches where classic methodologies and tools like Thinking-Aloud, Interviews etc. were applied - some times in new combinations - to pervasive systems in field experiments. The approaches in the second category all proposed methods in which the ubiquitous computing technology itself was used to evaluate systems, for example by analyzing and capturing the data of the various sensors in a mobile phone.

Only one week later USE '07 also brought together researchers from various fields of the Ubiquitous Computing domain, fostering the idea of creating an overall framework for the user-centered evaluation of ubiquitous systems by identifying specific techniques. During the workshop a set of challenges, needs and requirements were identified that are special to the evaluation of ubiquitous systems, e. g. the limitations regarding the reproducibility of experiments in dynamic environments, privacy issues and the question on how to compare personalized evaluations. In addition, the workshop participants identified the need for published data-sets, that make research results more comparable in the community and for extendible high-reaching benchmarks. The combination of the benefits of in-situ, virtual, and immersive were found useful as well as the evaluation of personal experiences during natural interaction with the system and deriving implicit feedback from that unlike tests that require the user to follow a script and asking for explicit feedback.

All these events advanced the state of the art with the goal to establish an overall framework for user-centered evaluation of Ubiquitous Computing systems by framing relevant dimensions, identifying specific tools and techniques, and formulating requirements and needs. Furthermore, this series of events reflects both the relevance of this topic to the community and the continued effort to tackle the problem by delivering a common set of tool, techniques and methods.

5   Conclusion and Outlook

During the discussion at the workshop, it quickly became clear that evaluating ubiquitous systems with users poses some new challenges while at the same time opening up opportunities for research. Due to the nature of ubiquitous computing – e. g. the impact of contextual factors, the tight integration into everyday life and interfaces that may be invisible – some evaluation methods do not work well or need to be adapted. We have identified several challenges relating to this issue, including the need to incorporate/control the context of use, comparing different systems that serve similar purposes and the question how to cope with disengaged users. While these are important areas that should be tackled in the future, a key problem in evaluating ubiquitous systems with users is the lack of clear guidelines for the selection of evaluation methods tailored to ubiquitous computing.

At the workshop, we discussed an interesting idea related to this problem. Since many ubiquitous systems already capture a lot of sensor data and thus information about the context, a promising way to optimize the efficacy of evaluation would be to automate the selection of particular evaluation methods based on the context. For example, a system could pick different sets of questions depending on the current context, or it could choose a method such as contextual enquiry in one case and a post-hoc interview in another case.

References

1. Weiser, M.: The computer of the 21st century. Scientific American, 94–100 (1991)
2. Abowd, G.D., Mynatt, E.D.: Charting past, present, and future research in ubiquitous computing. ACM Trans. Comput.-Hum. Interact. 7, 29–58 (2000)
3. Scholz, J., Consolvo, S.: Toward a framework for evaluating ubiquitous computing applications. IEEE Pervasive Computing 3, 82–88 (2004)
4. Preece, J., Rogers, Y., Sharp, H.: Interaction Design. Wiley, Chichester (2002)
5. Rogers, Y., Connelly, K., Tedesco, L., Hazlewood, W., Kurtz, A., Hall, R., Hursey, J., Toscos, T.: Why its worth the hassle: The value of in-situ studies when designing ubicomp, pp. 336–353 (2007)
6. Kjeldskov, J., Skov, M.B., Als, B.S., Hegh, R.T.: Is it worth the hassle? exploring the added value of evaluating the usability of context-aware mobile systems in the field, pp. 61–73 (2004)
7. Abowd, G.D., Atkeson, C.G., Bobick, A.F., Essa, I.A., Macintyre, B., Mynatt, E.D., Starner, T.E.: Living laboratories: the future computing environments group at the georgia institute of technology. In: CHI 2000: CHI 2000 extended abstracts on Human factors in computing systems, pp. 215–216. ACM Press, New York (2000)
8. Müller, J., Paczkowski, O., Krüger, A.: Situated public news and reminder displays, pp. 248–265 (2007)

9. Cheverst, K., Dix, A., Fitton, D., Rouncefield, M., Graham, C.: Exploring awareness related messaging through two situated-display-based systems. Human-Computer Interaction 22, 173–220

10. Taylor, N., Cheverst, K., Fitton, D., Race, N., Rouncefield, M., Graham, C.: Probing communities: Study of a village photo display. In: Proc. OzCHI 2007 (2007)

11. Müller, J., Krüger, A.: Learning topologies of situated public displays by observing implicit user interactions. In: Proceedings of HCI International 2007 (2007)

12. Hutchinson, H., Mackay, W., Westerlund, B., Bederson, B., Druin, A., Plaisant, C., Lafon, B.M., Conversy, S., Evans, H., Hansen, H., Roussel, N., Eiderbck, B., Lindquist, S., Sundblad, Y.: Technology probes: inspiring design for and with families (2003)

13. Breakwell, G., Fyfe-Schaw, C., Hammond, S.: Research Methods in Psychology. Sage Publications Ltd, Thousand Oaks (1995)

14. Marshall, C., Rossman, G.B.: Designing Qualitative Research. Sage Publications, Inc, Thousand Oaks (2006)

15. Consolvo, S., Walker, M.: Using the experience sampling method to evaluate ubicomp applications. IEEE Pervasive Computing 2, 24–31 (2003)

16. Kahneman, D., Krueger, A.B., Schkade, D.A., Schwarz, N., Stone, A.A.: A survey method for characterizing daily life experience: The day reconstruction method. Science 306, 1776–1780 (2004)

17. Gustafsson, A., Herrmann, A., Huber, F.: Conjoint Measurement: Methods and Applications. Springer, Heidelberg (2001)

18. Hassenzahl, M., Wessler, R.: Capturing design space from a user perspective: The repertory grid technique revisited. International Journal of Human-Computer Interaction 12, 441–459 (2001)

19. Mankoff, J., Dey, A.K., Hsieh, G., Kientz, J., Lederer, S., Ames, M.: Heuristic evaluation of ambient displays. In: CHI 2003: Proceedings of the SIGCHI conference on Human factors in computing systems, pp. 169–176. ACM Press, New York (2003)

20. Singh, P., Ha, H.N., Kuang, Z., Olivier, P., Kray, C., Blythe, P., James, P.: Immersive video as a rapid prototyping and evaluation tool for mobile and ambient applications. In: MobileHCI 2006: Proceedings of the 8th conference on Human-computer interaction with mobile devices and services, pp. 264–264. ACM Press, New York (2006)

21. Schellenbach, M.: Test methodologies for pedestrian navigation aids in old age. In: CHI 2006 Extended Abstracts on Human Factors in Computing Systems, pp. 1783–1786 (2006)

22. Jameson, A., Krüger, A.: Special double issue on user modeling in ubiquitous computing. User Modeling and User-Adapted Interaction (2005)

23. John, B.E., Kieras, D.E.: The GOMS family of user interface analysis techniques: comparison and contrast. ACM Trans. Comput.-Hum. Interact. 3, 320–351 (1996)

24. Anderson, J.R., Matessa, M., Lebiere, C.: Act-r: A theory of higher level cognition and its relation to visual attention. Human-Computer Interaction 12, 439–462 (1997)

25. Mayhew, D.J.: The Usability Engineering Lifecycle: A Practitioner's Guide to User Interface Design. Morgan Kaufmann Publishers, San Francisco (1999)

26. Mulder, I., Kort, J.: Mixed emotions, mixed methods: the role of emergent technologies to study user experience in context (in press)

27. Scholtz, J., Richter, H.: Report from ubicomp 2001 workshop: evaluation methodologies for ubiquitous computing. SIGCHI Bull.: suppl. interactions 2002, 9–9 (2002)

28. Mulder, I., ter Hofte, H., Kort, J., Vermeeren, A.: In situ workshop at mobile hci (last accessed on November 22, 2007), `http://insitu2007.freeband.nl/`

29. Neely, S., Stevenson, G., Terzis, S.: Ubiquitous systems evaluation workshop (USE 2007) (last accessed on November 22, 2007), `http://www.useworkshop.org`

Preface to MDSE4AmI 2007

Felix Flentge[1], Andreas Petter[1], and Thomas Ziegert[2]

[1] Technische Universität Darmstadt, Germany
[2] SAP Research, CEC Darmstadt, Germany

The implementation of AmI applications is a task of tremendous complexity requiring the seamless integration of heterogeneous systems in an open and flexible way while providing the means for adaptivity and context-awareness. Ubiquitous devices have to cooperate to realize smart environments, multimodal user interfaces have to adapt to the available modalities for interaction and context information has to be taken into account. Therefore, new engineering approaches are needed in order to facilitate efficient design, development and deployment of AmI applications.

Model driven approaches may be able to contribute to a solution by providing the means to build specific applications in a (semi-)automatic way from abstract models using well-defined transformations. The workshop on Model Driven Software Engineering for Ambient Intelligence Applications, held on on November 7, 2007, in the context of the European Conference on Ambient Intelligence in Darmstadt, supported this assumption. The workshop presented a stimulating mixture of talks ranging from basic research to industrial applications.

Looking at the nine papers presented at the workshop one can identify certain trends:

- Usability and inclusion of the end-user perspective
  The usability of the developed applications is an important but largely unsolved issues. There is a number of different approaches, like the inclusion of user models, the use of usability metrics or the application of usability rules. However, currently all these approaches lack from an adequate formalization and a proper integration into the development process.
- Distributed and flexible user interfaces
  Smart environments and the widespread use of mobile devices expand the possibilities for user interaction. There needs to be a shift from user interface design to interaction design to make use of all available modalities and to provide a satisfying user experience. This requires new concepts and methods for the design, the implementation and the evaluation of user interaction.
- Use of models at runtime
  In order to provide the flexibility and openness required for ambient intelligence applications there is an increasing trend to use models at runtime. However, it is difficult to find the right balance between design time modeling and runtime interpretation and it is still unclear whether runtime interpretation can really provide a general approach without the need to fine-tune for each modality and application domain.

M. Mühlhäuser et al. (Eds.): AmI 2007 Workshops, CCIS 11, pp. 75–76, 2008.

All these issues are closely interrelated. A fundamental question is how to increase the usability while maintaining flexibility and openness in ambient intelligence applications. Model based approaches have the potential to contribute to a solution and therefore we are looking forward to exploring these issues in more detail in future workshops.

We would like to thank our invited speaker Markus Lauff from SAP who gave an interesting talk about the integration of context information into mobile business applications using a model-based approach. We also appreciate the work of organizing committee of AmI 2007 and especially like to thank our workshop co-organizers Karin Coninx, Hasselt University, and Jean Vanderdonckt, Université catholique de Louvain. Last but not least we would like to express our gratitude to all Program Committee members and all authors for their contributions to make the workshop a success.

Modeling for Users

Emilio Iborra and José Iborra

AmI2 a research & development company. Murcia, Spain
`emilio.iborra@ami2.net, jose.iborra@ami2.net`

Abstract. This position paper attempts to address the need of including persons, users, as a part of software conception and design. The proposal encourages a keen understanding of the context of use. How and why will the users "use" the product? When? What are their personal goals for using it? Model Driven Engineering has proven its capacity to create software products from (UML) models, but -in our understanding-, it is not enough for specifying products that persons use and love. In order to create human-aware products, traditional analysts of functionality results incomplete. In order to complete the specification of a system a so-called user analysis is considered, complementing the traditional OO functionality and structure analysis. This paper should encourage research in such a line, extending modeling languages to include the new requirements and creating methods to incorporate them in the engineering process.

1 Introduction

Maybe because we are some of the people who have put modeling in practice by creating commercial products [1] that implement the MDA theories [2], we are one of the first to be amazed by the fact that model driven engineering technology works. MDE represents, in our opinion, one of the biggest steps in software engineering in history, but after years of practice, it has become evident that MDA is not enough: the software is created faster and more reliable, but there is no difference for final users. Our customers said to obtain "more of the same". After all, we are still creating the very same type of software.

Most users of software systems, including computer scientists, suffer from a peculiar lack of "common sense" in the design of most these systems [3]. Computer Science people in theory –and practice– are happy when the system just "works", but we seem to ignore anything about the persons that will use it. The users as persons are seldom considered at any stage of a project. This might explain why most of created functionality is rarely used, or it is used by a much reduced set of power users while most users are at a "perpetual intermediate" [4] level.

This raises a straightforward question. If a product is not going to be used, why should it be built? Computer scientists' aim should be to create software products that become really used and maybe even loved by the people using them.

Model Driven Engineering has really proven its ability to create high quality software products in a fraction of time and cost. Functionality and structure are fully included in the Object-Oriented theory that embodies the paradigm of MDE and

M. Mühlhäuser et al. (Eds.): AmI 2007 Workshops, CCIS 11, pp. 77–82, 2008.

comes as a heritage of the tradition of process analysis. UML and MDA are being used nowadays to; in essence, answer the question of WHAT has to be done?[5].

It can be said that modeling is one of the most reliable techniques to create outstanding software products. MDE, when done properly, will ensure that the product functionality has been fully understood, and that the system specification is complete: everything needed is fully described and nothing else is required [6]. Nevertheless, even functionally excellent software products happen to be little beneficial to their users, usually due to either complexity or user unfriendliness.

We consider here the need to know more about what users WANT and the ways to combine this knowledge with the knowledge of WHAT the system should do. Before facing functionality, we propose to understand the users and their context when they use the system answering some other questions about users like: WHO are they? WHEN will they use the system? WHY do they use it?

This paper is organized as follows. After the introduction, section 2 deals with the gathering of User concerns. Section 3 provides a brief insight on creating a modeling language. Section 4 presents the need of understanding the context of use. Section 5 mentions how to use the new knowledge to create a product. Section 6 describes some related work. Finally, section 7 concludes the paper by providing some suggestions on how to interpret this work.

2 Finding User Concerns

In Software Engineering, it is a commonly accepted the problem that users are unable of specifying what they want. However, it is our opinion that they know much more than they are able to say. Users are not necessarily buyers. This is a serious drawback, since buyers are quick to explain their decisions on why they want to buy a product, but users are not. If you think of yourself as a user, it is not easy to give a reason to use something you didn't buy.

In order to perform the user analysis, Cooper [4] proposes an abstraction of users he calls "personas" and a context study named "scenario". It is remarkable the abstraction of a user as a pure character in a theater-play. This imaginary user acts as a stereotype of the expected mass of real users of the system Considering the users not being real persons anymore, the analyst can separate main goals and missions of the abstracted character from accidental duties and false desires of the real user. The team of engineers conducts a brainstorming session where the hypothetical character is interviewed. The conclusions drive the definition of a set of requirements that can be considered WHY users will use the system, what parts of it will be used most.

We propose to complement the mentioned user analysis by validating the obtained results. This is done by using the results obtained in the analysis as base material for a survey directed to real users. The questions in the survey will address all and every aspect that was asked to the set of "personas". The survey will allow better understanding why the system will be use and relevant items in the context.

Finally, we use the validated user analysis to train design solutions in the sense of [7] where internal and surface representations of interfaces help artifacts to fit to their users. The proposed designs are first tested with "personas" and later to relevant users.

It is now time to address the functional requirements. We will concentrate in processes and tasks using traditional MDE techniques. These two separate activities have proven to have a positive mutual influence when the same team performs them.

3 Modeling User Concerns

MDE has proven its unprecedented capacities for reality abstraction[8]. The abstraction of concepts present in modeling suites well to the exposed challenges so far: these include mostly modeling of functional requirements. The challenge is to complement these models with more information so that user concerns were also described in them. Or will it be a better alternative creating a completely new model and later combine them?

We believe that the first option is not viable because the concepts we have found in the previous section seemed to be too distant from traditional functional analysis. When functional models are built, the analyst focus in system's processes and tasks and in the structure of the system. When performing user analysis, goals and missions of become protagonists.

However, these two sets of concepts complement each other: Tasks help users to obtain their goals; processes help organizations to obtain their missions. We suggest to let the user concerns drive the analysis; to center the debate in WHY the users do WHAT they do.

If we want to extend MDE with a new model suited to specify user concerns, we should first try to clear up what is behind the modeling effort. First, we demand for abstractions that accurately model concepts. These abstractions are the so called "semantic primitives". There is a required research effort identifying these primitives. Second, a grammar to combine these primitives into sentences with full meaning. Both elements constitute a language that can be formalized and included in a modeling methodology.

The question then lies in whether it is feasible to find these primitives and how well do they compose with traditional functional and structural primitives present in current MDE theory and practice. The challenge is finding a model to describe the outcomes of the user analysis phase introduced in the previous section. The goal will be to combine this model with the rest of MDE models to cover the functionality.

4 The Contextual Semantics

If the interaction between a person and a computer is considered as if it was a normal conversation, the context in which the conversation happens is of relevance. As in linguistics, the speakers' context determines the frame, sense and limits of the transmitted message [9]. In software engineering, this context has gone mostly unnoticed.

The analysis of the context might be too vast to be considered in generic terms. However, we propose to include the semantic present in this context as part of the analysis phase before any coding effort. We call this notion "contextual semantics".

The screen + keyboard + mouse combination is too limited to be used in most contexts. Hopefully some devices will replace them smoothly in the future so people will likely communicate with computers by gestures, words and face expressions and in many more contexts than sitting in front of a computer screen with a keyboard and a mouse.

It is easy to find many devices in the market that perform a great variety of functionalities, such as movement detection, temperature reading, image recognition or car plate reading. These features will improve the communication between computers and their users. All the mentioned devices could cooperate to understand the context in which the user demands for a particular "transaction", or better put: a "service".

It could be possible to employ patterns of small events and link them to a particular notion we could call "happening" at this point. A happening is a sequence of events with a common context. I.e. the detection of presence in the door, the opening of the door and the detection of movement in the entrance can be grouped in a happening and linked to a concrete meaning like "arrived home" [11].

The fact that you arrived home, is added to a set of detected happenings which represent the current context. E.g. in the context after the user arrived home, the user approximating to the stairs acquires a new sense for the system, which reacts by either switching on the lights or opening the curtains, as the hour, date and season of the year, belonging to the context too, may influence the conversation.

We would like to finish this section by encouraging the research community to come up with solutions in this direction.

5 Product Building and Design

How do the user and context analysis influence the final product? We will illustrate this section with a very simple example that follows what has been said in this position paper: Imagine a system like judicial case tracking. The critical task for users has a low level of complexity but with a big impact in the case of an operator mistake where a person may go to jail. If we delivered a traditional interface based on functional and structural analysis phase, we will see that there will appear may be 10 check boxes in the form to mark the inspectors' evaluation of the subject in prison. All of them are identical to the rest with codes or meaningful characters. This is what they had so far in green and black.

If we perform the user analysis, (create a set of "personas") to really understand WHO they are and what are their main concerns, we will discover that the main issue is precisely to avoid mistakes. They are very sensible to this type of dramatic mistakes. Therefore, the simple form the system shows is perceived with some fear because of the stress this form causes to their personal life.

Working in the phase of context analysis, we find out that the operation is frequently interrupted. Our inspector works in a multi-tasking environment with time pressure to fill-in quite a set of cases at the end of the journey.

In summary, what we found were: frustration because of delays in getting the information, desperation because one cannot leave home unless all the evaluations forms were filed; anger, because they are interrupted frequently; finally, fear because it is so easy to make mistakes.

The output of our traditional MDA-functional approach is clearly not enough. We should establish what the success factors are. We will consider successful any solution that effectively reduced the users' anxiety and minimized the number of mistakes.

It is evident that there is more than one solution for this. Today the output of users and context analysis cannot go any further than giving recommendations that developers apply based on... common sense?. Another approach could be to expose several prototypes to users and measure their achievements with each one. It is in this where MDE could be very effective because its prototyping capacity.

Thanks to the user analysis it was possible to understand the real nature of this particular interaction being "avoid errors" the critical point. The context analysis let us know that the filling-in of forms will be frequently interrupted and that most of the cases are done in a row, one after the other. Both of these factors lead to errors. Window switching is detectable and can be used to strengthen the mistake prevention measures. The repeating of the previous last cases can be used the same way too. Both scenarios can be modeled as happenings and being used to prevent mistakes.

6 Related Work

There are few MDE offerings in the market that address the user interface definition. Among these we distinguish two broad categories. In the first group we find those that attach interface definition to the functional models. The interface abstractions are rendered as rich attributes of the functional elements. We already enumerated the shortcomings of this approach in the previous sections.

In the second group we find the offerings that provide complete separate models that are not attached at all to the functional models. Being completely free from the constraints of functional modeling, these offerings have the ability to describe the interfaces with as much detail as desired. Unfortunately. the lack of standards causes that doing the same thing with different products requires learning a different set of modeling primitives. Almost every product proposes its own set of abstractions and its own method for describing the interfaces. The freedom also has a price to pay in the form of possible inconsistencies between interface models and functional models. This represents s a step back in MDE where consistency is warranted. In any case, these tools are seriously limited in their capacity of incorporating users and context analysis to the system specification. Therefore, the created software products continue to ignore both, users and context. There are many contributions towards understanding context, like in [10], that suggest its inclusion in analysis. These reasons make us recognize that MDE is not so revolutionary for end users. The users are right when they claim that they still get "more of the same thing".

UsiXML[11-12] is a modeling initiative that proposes an interface model which can be combined with functionality models. These interface models can be used as a base to perform the bridge between user interaction analysis and context analysis. A good reason to be optimistic is that these products include several abstraction models and methodologies to support model transformations.

7 Conclusions

Nowadays, the realistic use of MDE is restricted to functionality. It is necessary to turn to manual programming to build the interfaces. This is already difficult enough without throwing context into the picture. As a result, pretty much no one does it, and the outcome is that we engineer unfriendly and poor products.

We propose to create a new model for user analysis and combine it with the traditional MDE models. We have recently started the research effort towards to finding the semantic primitives for a specification language for user analysis. The context of interaction is very relevant and we propose to include it as part of problem's analysis. The knowledge obtained from these models will be used to create user and context aware products by creating prototypes to be tested by final users.

References

1. Olivanova, http://www.care-t.com
2. OMG, http://www.omg.org
3. Norman, D.A.: The design of everyday things. Basic Books, New York
4. ALAN Cooper: The inmates are running the asylum. SAMS publishing
5. Pastor, O.: An OO Software Production Environment Combining Conventional and Formal Methods. In: Olivé, À., Pastor, J.A. (eds.) CAiSE 1997. LNCS, vol. 1250, Springer, Heidelberg (1997)
6. Pastor, O., Ramos, I., Cerdá, J.H.C.: OASIS: DEXA 1996. In: DEXA 1996, pp. 79–90 (1996)
7. Norman, D.A.: Things that make us smart. Basic Books. Ch. 4
8. Grady Booch, http://www.booch.com
9. de la Vega García, M.E.: Lenguaje y comunicación: editor-texto-alumno. Editorial Pueblo y Educación La Habana, Cuba
10. Dei, A.K.: Dei Understanding and Using Context in Personal and Ubiquitous Computing, vol. 5, pp. 4–7 (2001)
11. Linbourg, Q., Vanderdonckt, J.: UsiXML. In: Proceedings of the 3rd annual conference on Task models and diagrams SESSION: Task analysis and diagrams for task models table. ACM International Conference Proceeding Series, vol. 86, pp. 155–163 (2004)
12. Calvary, G., Coutaz, J., Thevenin, D., Linburg, Q., Souchon, N., Bouillon, L., Florins, M., Vanderdonckt, J.: Plasticity of User interfaces: A revised Reference Framework. In: TALMODIA 2002: Proceedings of the First International Workshop on Task Models and Diagrams for User Interface Design, pp. 127–134. INFOREC Publishing House Bucharest (2002)

Usability Aware Model Driven Development of User Interfaces

Matthias Thiel[1], Andreas Petter[2], and Alexander Behring[3]

[1] NorCom Information Technology AG, Germany
`matthias.thiel@norcom.de`
[2] Telecooperation Group, TU Darmstadt, Germany
`a_petter@tk.informatik.tu-darmstadt.de`
[3] Telecooperation Group, TU Darmstadt, Germany
`behring@tk.informatik.tu-darmstadt.de`

Abstract. We propose an approach how to develop and integrate usability metrics in (multimodal) dialog systems and user interfaces with Model Driven Software Development (MDSD). It enables the developer to start early with simple metrics and allows him to refine them during the ongoing work. Additionally, we show how the resulting metrics can be used to estimate the usability in advance, so that the developer may care about critical parts of the application before testing it.

1 Introduction

The development of user interfaces by the aid of Model Driven Software Development (MDSD, e.g. [17]) technologies is a popular approach, especially when realizing web services. But in the field of multimodal user interfaces used in ambient intelligence, this approach is rarely used so far, resulting in few literature available on the topic. In this article, we want to get one step closer to automate usability evaluation by presenting an approach that allows integrating and developing usability metrics during the development process. The reason, why usability metrics should be considered to be an important aspect of the development process has been explained a lot of times [12]. Currently, the only reliable way to verify the usability is to perform user studies for the particular application. The disadvantages are high costs and that evaluation can only take place after development of the application has been almost completed [18,4]. One common approach to evaluate the usability of interactive systems is the analysis of log files for getting statistical values (e.g. timings) that are used for measuring usability or guessing the major usability problems. E.g. the approach presented in [15] derives Petri nets from log files that serve as foundations for applying usability metrics.

By introducing usability awareness into the development process analysis can be partially done automatically during development. Thus, the developer can watch usability metrics during development and may react on them as soon as problems are reported.

M. Mühlhäuser et al. (Eds.): AmI 2007 Workshops, CCIS 11, pp. 83–92, 2008.

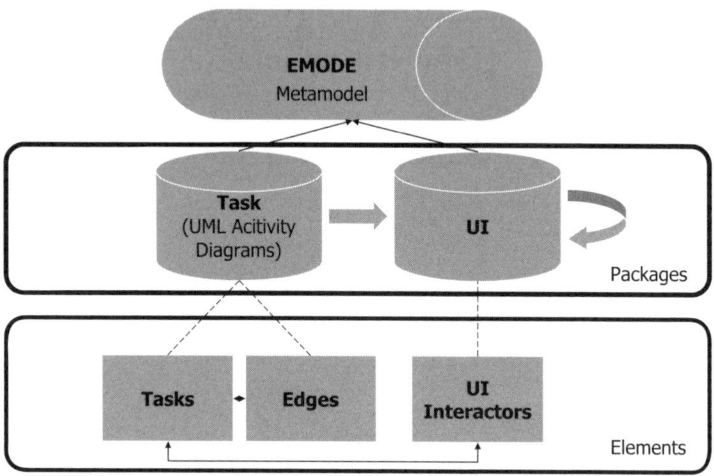

Fig. 1. EMODE Metamodel Overview

In section 2, a short overview of the meta models used is given. Models are introduced and the type of model editors which should get usability aware. In section 3, a new approach is presented for estimating usability in advance and refined in 4. Section 5 presents a small example for applying the new approach.

2   Meta Models

This section gives a brief overview about the meta models of the EMODE project [6] which we will use as an example for applying our usability metrics. An overview of the most important metamodel packages is given in figure 1. It is to be mentioned that the following definitions are not absolutely matching the EMODE meta model definition. They should just illustrate the concepts.

The meta models that are of relevance here are the task model and aui model. The main elements of the task model are tasks which can be subdivided into different types. The interesting type is the interaction task which will be associated to elements of the aui model, especially the interactor elements. An interactor element may be seen as a subtask that describes a needed information exchange between the user and the system, also called interaction step. Accomplishing the interaction steps will fulfil the associated interaction task.

3   Usability Evaluation

In this section an approach for estimating usability of interactive systems is proposed. Beginning from an abstract level metrics will be derived that are suitable to be applied on model transformations.

According to [9] a lot of the analysis methods presented in literature are to be used manually after software development has been finished. In contrast, the approach presented here tries to predict usability by investigating models before they are transformed into code.

Definition 1. *Usability analysis can either be* **post-development** *or* **predictive**. *Post-development analysis is applied after development, while predictive analysis is applied during development.*

When regarding usability, it is assumed that the user wants to reach one or more goals during the interaction with the system. Additionally, it is assumed that the goal is well-defined and reachable within the application. For getting to the desired dialog state the user has to invest some effort by performing one or more actions.

Definition 2. *Usability is inversely proportional to the user's effort in reaching his goal.*

Similar to the ideas in [5] and [14] we define:

Definition 3. *Concerning the time dimension (which is used often as a major metrics in post-development usability analysis) the user's effort for one interaction step can be structured in following phases:*

P_1 *Perception of the system output*
P_2 *Understanding the output and integrating it into the user's context*
P_3 *Inferential thinking processes for determining the next reaction*
P_4 *Uttering the next reaction*

Calculation of these efforts depends on the user and therefore it is not possible to perform them without a user model.

Definition 4. *A user model can be given* **explicitly** *by a formal model in machine readable format or* **implicitly** *by providing it within the algorithm to compute the metric.*

Potential problems of implicit user models are that they may not be argued upon, as they are not precise and consistent, and that they must be very well understood by developers and designers. However, most metrics are given without explicit user models. The reason why one would not define an explicit user model is that there is no agreement of how a meta model for a user model should look like.

Metrics are mostly based on evaluations of statistical values about usability properties derived from them. Therefore, evaluators cannot provide a user model without significant extra research and much effort would have to be invested to additionally create a user model for the metrics. Instead of proposing an elaborated user model here, it is proposed to figure out the user model iteratively by looking at the metrics involved and the needs of the applications to be developed.

3.1 Example

In the following a simple *example* is presented how to use the four phases involved and the development or integration of new metrics into the calculation of the overall usability evaluation value.

Assume the system output is: *"What is the color that the clocks should have and how many do you need?"* As noted above, the developer wants to estimate the effort that the user has to perform for reacting to this system output. For now, he will use an implicit user model for getting faster to a first draft of his metrics, which could look like this:

P_1 It is assumed that the user's effort somehow depends on the amount of words he has to perceive. Therefore we define the effort for P_1 to be $E(P_1) := m$ *(amount of words)*.

P_2 Similar to P_1 we count the concepts that the user has to map to his domain model. In this case, the concepts *color* and *clock* are candidates. For now, we ignore relationships between them.

P_3 Like most of the human computer interfaces, it is assumed that the user already knows what he wants. The system just asks for known facts, like an html form does. This means $E(P_3) := 0$.

P_4 The system could estimate the amount of words the user might need for answering. For example, the answer of the user could be: *"I need three ones in blue."*. The general formula might be $E(P_4) := m$ *(average amount of words that the user utters)*. Taking the example as average case, we get $E(P_4) = 6$. For getting a better estimation of the average case this could be retrieved (automatically) by analyzing the corresponding (speech) grammar.

After having determined the efforts for each of the four phases, the developer wants to summarize the particular efforts. However, at the current stage of development of the proposed approach this turns out to be very difficult, since metrics are not normalized and the developer needs to normalize them manually. This means that the effort for processing at P_1 is not comparable with the effort of mapping a concept to the domain model at P_2 without further research by the developer. A simple approach is to sum the weighted efforts per phase. This reduces the problem to how the weights w_i are to be estimated for calculating the total effort for each interaction step

$$\sum_{i=1}^{4} w_i \cdot E(P_i) \tag{1}$$

The determination of the weights strongly depends on the definition of the functions, because the range of values could be very different. The user model plays an important role here, if the user will have to face difficult circumstances (e.g. a noisy environment or a disability) in a phase.

Most of dialog manager components integrate the four phases into a single transition from one dialog state to the next one [3]. This may be seen as the basis on which most of the definitions of existing usability metrics are based on.

3.2   Implementation of the Framework

The current state of the art is to use style guide analyzers [7] to tell the developer which parts of the user interface have to be improved. To provide better support for usability to developers, the implementation presented here applies metrics and presents hints within the task editor for maximum visibility. The framework which is needed to integrate metrics into the development environment has already been implemented. The implementation uses the EMODE models presented in section 2, but may be applied to any other meta model, which includes a task model and a user interface model (such as [10,16]). The idea is to employ usability metrics in measures used in rules for model-to-model transformation (this is similar to, or an implementation of, the definition "usability preserved by transformation" given in [2]) or in the editor to be an aid for the developer. Currently the latter has been implemented (see figure 2).

First, each of the metrics defined are calculated and summed up as presented in the previous section. Then, each task which may be connected to a user interface component is annotated by a small rectangle with changing colours. Green rectangles symbolize that the user interfaces connected to the tasks are usable according to the implemented metrics, gradually ranging to red rectangles showing that the associated user interfaces are not as usable as the ones marked using green. As the task model is central to the development process, a centralized view is provided to the developer, who then can edit the user interfaces which are considered to be not as good (more red rectangles) as the others (more green rectangles). In lack of a standard language to describe usability

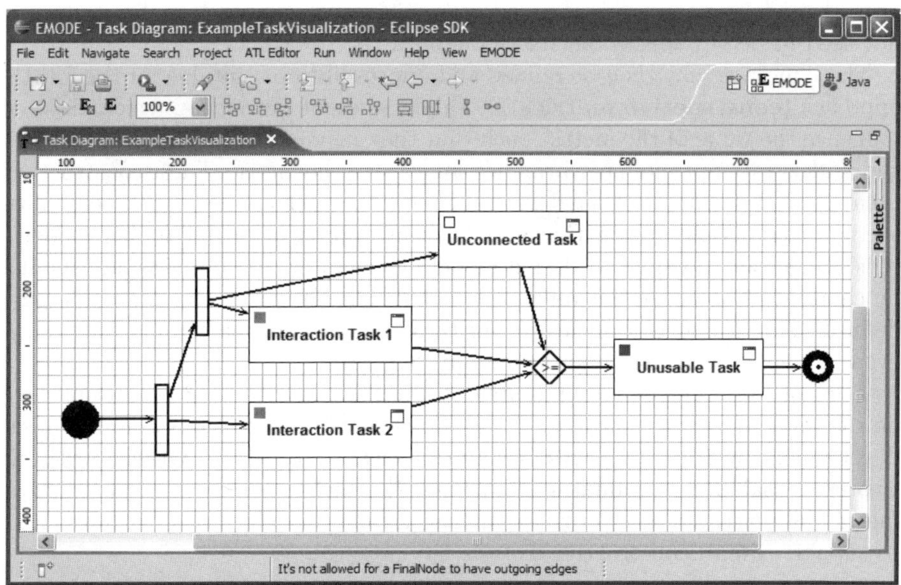

Fig. 2. Development Environment

metrics in specialized declarative or imperative languages in a flexible way, the implementation of the metrics is based on JAVA.

4   Usability Metrics During Application Development

There exist several options, how to apply usability metrics during application development. So far four types have been identified, which may be seen as to build on top of insights gained from usability studies as shown in figure 3. Each bar of the pyramid corresponds to a period during the development process.

The first approach, at the bottom of the figure, involving at least one **user study**, has been applied practically very often. After having designed a mock-up or a prototype user interface, a usability evaluation is done by asking questionnaires or logging user actions while performing tasks. Then, the whole process re-iterates as the developers improve the user interfaces using the evaluation outcome. As a second approach, a **post-development** metric (level 2 in the figure) may be derived from the knowledge gained from the user studies. Applying a post-development metric allows for usability evaluation without asking real users. This may not always be possible, as knowledge may not always be generalized from user studies in a way that it may be formalized, or the knowledge may apply to specific situations only. However, it is always possible to evaluate the usability against real users.

The third approach, which is propagated here, involves the definition of metrics on application models (**predictive metrics**, level 3). These metrics are either drawn from literature or created by analyzing previously performed user-studies, which present metrics for applications. These metrics will reduce turnaround times as tests are performed on models, such that the application does not need to be developed, but its model only.

These metrics may then be refined and improved to be suitable for the fourth approach (**constructive metrics**) by thinking about properties, which directly influence the value of the metric, such that they may be used to directly develop the models with optimum performance concerning the metric. These constructive plans prevent developers from developing models, which are not usable according to the metric. While being the most efficient approach for developing models, it is not always possible to derive model elements or attributes which should be changed to optimize the value of a metric, e.g. the predictive metric is only defined using a heuristic measure. As these metrics are algorithms, they may even be applied to model transformations, e.g. [8].

A lot of works in the research area of usability metrics have been published on the topic of user studies (e.g. [9,13]). Some works try to assess usability after development by applying post-development metrics (e.g. [15]). Other works try to predict usability by evaluating guidelines [7], which may be seen as a predictive metric. [8] presented a set of rules for transformations which has been designed to support several constructive metrics.

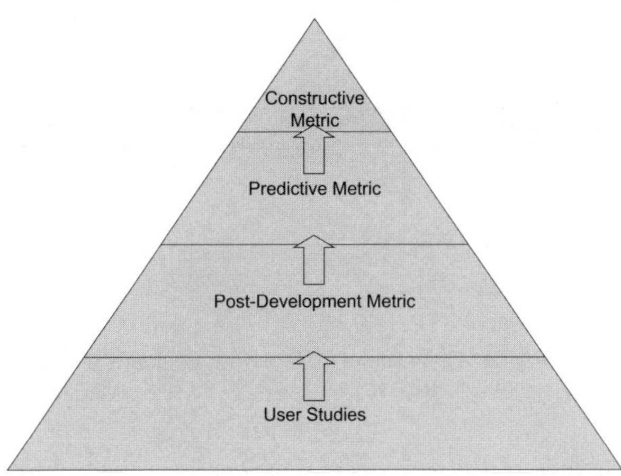

Fig. 3. Types of Metrics

In fact, usability metrics are a formalization of usability quality factors and criteria as optimization problem. We currently try to refine the factors defined in [1,19]. [1] defines quality factors like multimodality and recoverability, where multimodality means to give the user the opportunity to choose the appropriate modality at any time for providing his input. Metrics may be derived, e.g. estimating usage of the modality dependent interaction phases can serve as a foundation for predicting, what kind of set of modalities will be more usable for a given dialog situation. [19] enumerates unambiguousness as a usability attribute. An established way of ensuring this is to insert confirmation questions into the dialog. On the other hand, using too many confirmation questions is in conflict to an efficient dialog (in sense of a fast walkthrough). By estimating the user effort, it is possible to reason about the frequency of confirming facts.

5   Example Metric

In this section, it is shown how to integrate known metrics [11] into the $E(P_1)$ definition of section 3.1. The calculation is done for a particular interaction phase and uses specific knowledge about interactors or tasks. Starting from the example $E(P_1) := m$ given above, further metrics will be added step by step. m measures efforts for voice modality while the new metrics aspect ration (α) will measure efforts for visual modality.

α is the ratio of the height of a dialog box to its width. Desireable values are between 0.5 to 0.8 (ca. 0.65). Therefore, the extended formula is

$$E(P_1) := g_1(m) + g_2(\|\alpha - 0.65\|)$$ (2)

where g_i are functions for normalizing and weighting the particular efforts.

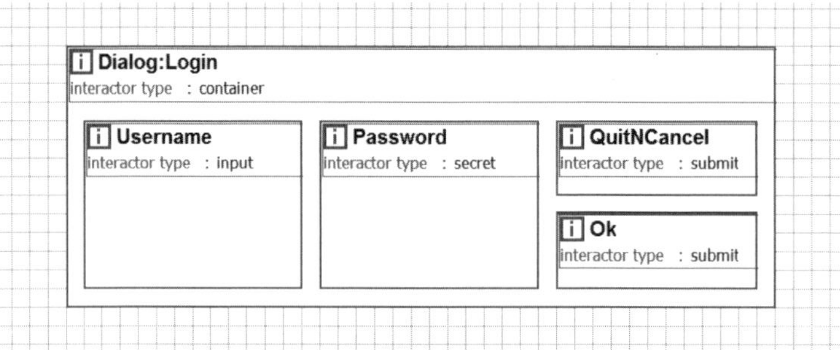

Fig. 4. Example of AUI model for login dialog

In 4, an example of the aui model diagram for a login dialog is shown. The resulting login dialog uses voice and graphical modalities. The voice modality asks for username and password with the phrase: "What is your name and password, please? ", while the graphical modality shows a usual login dialog box (in our case with the size of 300x150 pixels). The developer wants to calculate

$$E(P_1) = g_1(m)+g_2(\|\alpha-0.65\|) = g_1(7)+g_2(\|\frac{150}{300}-0.65\|) = g_1(7)+g_2(0.15) \quad (3)$$

In this case defining the normalization functions is straightforward. $g_i(x)$ may be defined by $g_i(x) = x$. The dialogue will suffer from large amounts of words being output, but is flexible towards α. However, bounds do exist. To produce high pain factors for extreme dialog box sizes (imagine a dialog box of 1000x1 pixels in size) g_2 is extended by: $x < 0.5 \vee x > 0.8 => g_2(x) = 1000$. Since this is not the case, the result is $E(P_1) = 7 + 0.15 = 7.15$.

6   Conclusion

An interaction step has been defined to be composed of four interaction phases. Using these phases an example was provided which shows how to calculate usability for interaction steps by giving metrics for each phase.

Distinguishing post-development, predictive and constructive metrics helps to select metrics for the evaluation process. The approach presented displays the outcome of predictive metrics in the task model to give the developer an overview of the usability of his application.

We feel that the approach presented seems promising to optimize the costs of developing usable interfaces. This is achieved by defining metrics and informing the developer about the usability of his user interfaces on an abstract level.

In the future we want to get more experience in defining usability metrics and especially the weighting of the different phases. The comparison of usability for different modalities will also be an issue. Additionally, model transformations should use predictive metrics for optimizing their resulting models.

References

1. Abowd, G.D., Coutaz, J., Nigay, L.: Structuring the space of interactive system properties. In: Proceedings of the IFIP TC2/WG2.7 Working Conference on Engineering for Human-Computer Interaction, pp. 113–129. North-Holland, Amsterdam (1992)
2. Abrahão, S., Iborra, E., Vanderdonckt, J.: Usability evaluation of user interfaces generated with a model-driven architecture tool. In: Law, E., Hvannberg, E., Cockton, G. (eds.) Maturing Usability: Quality in Software, Interaction and Value. HCI Series, vol. 10, pp. 3–33. Springer, Heidelberg (2007)
3. Balme, L., Demeure, A., Barralon, N., Coutaz, J., Calvary, G.: CAMELEON-RT: A Software Architecture Reference Model for Distributed, Migratable, and Plastic User Interfaces. In: Markopoulos, P., Eggen, B., Aarts, E., Crowley, J.L. (eds.) EUSAI 2004. LNCS, vol. 3295, pp. 291–302. Springer, Heidelberg (2004)
4. Beringer, N., Kartal, U., Louka, K., Schiel, F., Türk, U.: Promise - a procedure for multimodal interactive system evaluation. Technical Report 23, Ludwig-Maximilians-Universität München (May 2002)
5. Card, S., Moran, T.P., Newell, A.: The Psychology of Human-Computer Interaction. Lawrence Erbaum Associates, London (1983)
6. Dargie, W., Strunk, A., Winkler, M., Mrohs, B., Thakar, S., Enkelmann, W.: Emode - a model-based approach to develop adaptive multimodal interactive systems. In: Proceedings of the Second International Conference on Software and Data Technologies, Barcelona, Spain (July 2007), ISBN: 978-989-8111-09-8
7. Farenc, C.: ERGOVAL: une méthode de structuration des règles ergonomiques permettant l'évaluation automatique d'interfaces graphiques. PhD thesis, Université Toulouse (January 1997)
8. Florins, M.: Graceful Degradation: a Method for Designing Multiplatform Graphical User Interfaces. PhD thesis, Université catholique de Louvain (2006)
9. Ivory, M.Y., Hearst, M.A.: The state of the art in automating usability evaluation of user interfaces. ACM Comput. Surv. 33(4), 470–516 (2001)
10. Limbourg, Q.: Multi-Path Development of Multimodal Applications. PhD thesis, Université Catolique de Louvin (2004)
11. Mahajan, R., Shneiderman, B.: Visual & textual consistency checking tools for graphical user interfaces. (CS-TR-3639) (1996)
12. Nielsen, J.: Guerrilla HCI: using discount usability engineering to penetrate the intimidation barrier, pp. 245–272. Academic Press, Inc., Orlando, FL, USA (1994)
13. Nielsen, J.: How to conduct a heuristic evaluation. Internet (December 1994), `http://www.useit.com/papers/heuristic/heuristic_evaluation.html`
14. Norman, D.: The Design of Everyday Things. Currency (February 1990), ISBN 0-38526-774-6
15. Rauterberg, M.: A method of a quantitative measurement of cognitive complexity. In: Bagnara, S., van der Veer, G.C., Tauber, M.J., Antalovits, A. (eds.) Human-Computer Interaction: Tasks and Organisation, Roma, pp. 295–307. CUD (1992)
16. Sottet, J.-S., Calvary, G., Favre, J.-M.: Models at run-time for sustaining user interface plasticity. In: Proceedings of the Workshop Models at Run Time, Glasgow (October 2006)

17. Stahl, T., Völter, M.: Modellgetriebene Softwareentwicklung, 2nd edn., Dpunkt Verlag (May 2007), ISBN 3-89864-448-0
18. Walker, M.A., Litman, D.J., Kamm, C.A., Abella, A.: PARADISE: A framework for evaluating spoken dialogue agents. In: Cohen, P.R., Wahlster, W. (eds.) Proceedings of the Thirty-Fifth Annual Meeting of the Association for Computational Linguistics and Eighth Conference of the European Chapter of the Association for Computational Linguistics, Somerset, New Jersey, pp. 271–280. Association for Computational Linguistics (1997)
19. Winter, S., Wagner, S., Deissenboeck, F.: A comprehensive model of usability. In: Proc. Engineering Interactive Systems 2007, Salamanca, Spain, Springer, Heidelberg (2007)

An Agent-Based Generic Model for
Human-Like Ambience

Tibor Bosse, Mark Hoogendoorn, Michel C.A. Klein,
and Jan Treur

Vrije Universiteit Amsterdam, Department of Artificial Intelligence,
de Boelelaan 1081a, 1081 HV, the Netherlands
{tbosse,mhoogen,mcaklein,treur}@cs.vu.nl
http://www.cs.vu.nl/~{tbosse,mhoogen,mcaklein,treur}

Abstract. A reusable agent-based generic model is presented for a specific class of Ambient Intelligence applications: those cases addressing human wellbeing and functioning from a human-like understanding. The model incorporates ontologies, knowledge and dynamic models from human-directed sciences such as psychology, social science, neuroscience and biomedical sciences. The model has been formally specified, and it is shown how for specific applications it can be instantiated by application-specific elements, thus providing an executable specification that can be used for prototyping. Moreover, it is shown how dynamic properties can be formally specified and verified against generated traces.

1 Introduction

The environment in which humans operate has an important influence on their wellbeing and performance. For example, a comfortable workspace or an attentive partner may contribute to good performance or prevention of health problems. Recent developments within Ambient Intelligence provide technological possibilities to contribute to such personal care; cf. [1], [2], [22]. For example, our car may warn us when we are falling asleep while driving or when we are too drunk to drive. Such applications can be based on possibilities to acquire sensor information about humans and their functioning, but more substantial applications depend on the availability of adequate knowledge for analysis of information about human functioning. If knowledge about human functioning is represented in a formal and computational format in devices in the environment, these devices can show more human-like understanding, and (re)act accordingly by undertaking actions in a knowledgeable manner that improve the human's wellbeing and performance. As another example, the workspaces of naval officers may include systems that track their gaze and characteristics of stimuli (e.g., airplanes on a radar screen), and use this information in a computational model that is able to estimate where their attention is focussed at; cf. [8]. When it turns out that an officer neglects parts of a radar screen, such a system can either indicate this to the person (by a warning), or arrange in the background that another person or computer system takes care of this neglected part.

M. Mühlhäuser et al. (Eds.): AmI 2007 Workshops, CCIS 11, pp. 93–103, 2008.

In recent years, human-directed scientific areas such as cognitive science, psychology, neuroscience and biomedical sciences have made substantial progress in providing an increased insight in the various physical and mental aspects involved in human functioning. Although much work still remains to be done, dynamic models have been developed and formalised for a variety of such aspects and the way in which humans (try to) manage or regulate them. From a biomedical angle, examples of such aspects are (management of) heart functioning, diabetes, eating regulation disorders, and HIV-infection; e.g., [3], [17]. From a psychological and social angle, examples are emotion regulation, attention regulation, addiction management, trust management, stress management, and criminal behaviour management; e.g., [18], [5], [10], [11].

The focus of this paper is on the class of Ambient Intelligence applications as described, where the ambient software has context awareness (see, for example, [23], [24], [25]) about human behaviours and states, and (re)acts on these accordingly. For this class of applications an agent-based generic model is presented, which has been formally specified. For a specific application, this model can be instantiated by case-specific knowledge to obtain a specific model in the form of executable specifications that can be used for simulation and analysis. In addition to the naval officer case already mentioned, the generic model has been tested on a number of other Ambient Intelligence applications of the class as indicated. Three of these applications are discussed as an illustration, in Section 5. Section 2 describes the modelling approach. In Section 3 the global architecture of the generic model is presented. Section 4 shows the internal structure of an ambient agent in this model. Finally, Section 6 is a discussion.

2   Modelling Approach

This section briefly introduces the modelling approach used to specify the generic model. To specify the model conceptually and formally, the agent-oriented perspective is a suitable choice. The processes in the generic process model can be performed by different types of agents, some human, some artificial. The modelling approach used is based on the component-based agent design method DESIRE [12], and the language TTL for formal specification and verification of dynamic properties [6], [20].

Process and Information Aspects. Processes are modelled as components. A component can either be an active process, namely an agent, or a source that can be consulted or manipulated, which is a world component. In order to enable interaction between components, interaction links between such components are identified and specified. Ontologies specify interfaces for components, but also what interactions can take place between components, and the functionalities of components.

Specification Language. In order to execute and verify human-like ambience models, the expressive language TTL is used [6], [20]. This predicate logical language supports formal specification and analysis of dynamic properties, covering both qualitative and quantitative aspects. TTL is built on atoms referring to states, time points and traces. A *state* of a process for (state) ontology Ont is an assignment of truth values to the set of ground atoms in the ontology. The set of all possible states for ontology Ont is denoted by STATES(Ont). To describe sequences of states, a fixed *time frame* T is assumed which is linearly ordered. A *trace* γ over state ontology Ont and time frame T is a mapping $\gamma : T \rightarrow$ STATES(Ont), i.e., a sequence of states γ_t ($t \in$ T) in STATES(Ont). The set of *dynamic properties* DYNPROP(Ont) is the set of temporal statements that can be formulated with respect to traces based on the state ontology Ont in the following manner. Given a trace γ over state ontology Ont, the state in γ at time point t is denoted by state(γ, t). These states can be related to state properties via the formally defined satisfaction relation $\models$, comparable to the Holds-predicate in the Situation Calculus [21]: state(γ, t) $\models$ p denotes that state property p holds in trace γ at time t. Based on these statements, dynamic properties can be formulated in a sorted first-order predicate logic, using quantifiers over time and traces and the usual first-order logical connectives such as $\neg$, $\wedge$, $\vee$, $\Rightarrow$, $\forall$, $\exists$. A special software environment has been developed for TTL, featuring both a Property Editor for building and editing TTL properties and a Checking Tool that enables formal verification of such properties against a set of (simulated or empirical) traces.

Executable Format. To specify and execute simulation models, the language LEADSTO [7], an executable sublanguage of TTL, is used. The basic building blocks of this language are causal relations of the format $\alpha \twoheadrightarrow_{e, f, g, h} \beta$, which means:

if	state property α holds for a certain time interval with duration g,
then	after some delay (between e and f) state property β will hold for a certain time interval of length h.

where α and β are state properties of the form 'conjunction of literals' (where a literal is an atom or the negation of an atom), and e, f, g, h non-negative real numbers.

3   Global Structure of the Agent-Based Generic Model

For the global structure of the model, first a distinction is made between those components that are the *subject* of the system (e.g., a patient to be taken care of), and those that are *ambient*, supporting components. Moreover, from an agent-based perspective (see, for example, [11], [12]), a distinction is made between active, *agent* components (human or artificial), and passive, *world* components (e.g., part of the physical world or a database). Furthermore, within an agent a mind may be distinguished from a physical body. This provides the types of components distinguished shown in Figure 1. Here the dotted rectangles depict agents with mind and body distinguished within them, and the other geometrical shapes denote world components. Given the distinctions made between components, interactions between such components are of different types as well. Figure 1 depicts a number of possible interactions by the arrows. Table 1 shows an overview of the possible interactions.

Interaction Between Agents. Interaction between two agents may be *communication* or *bodily interaction*, for example, fighting. When within the agent a distinction is made between mind and body, communication can be modelled as information transfer between an agent's mind and another agent's mind. Whether for a given application of the generic model, within agents a mind and a body are distinguished, depends on the assumptions made about the application domain. If it is assumed that communication is independent of and cannot be affected by other processes in the

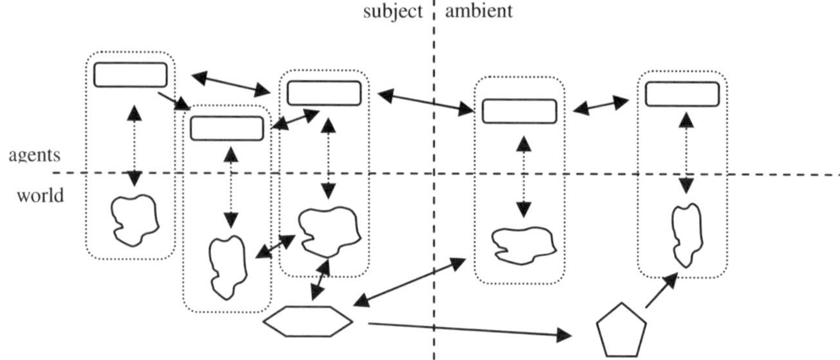

Fig. 1. Different types of components and interactions

Table 1. Different types of interaction

to from	subject agent	subject world component	ambient agent	ambient world component
subject agent	subject communication; subject body interaction	subject observation focus; subject action performance; subject body-world interaction	subject-ambient communication; subject-ambient body interaction	subject-ambient observation focus; subject-ambient action performance; subject-ambient body- world interaction
subject world component	subject observation result; subject world-body interaction	subject world component interaction	subject-ambient observation result; subject-ambient world- body interaction	subject-ambient world component interaction
ambient agent	ambient-subject communication; ambient-subject body interaction	ambient-subject observation focus; ambient-subject action performance; ambient-subject body - world interaction	ambient communication; ambient body interaction	ambient observation focus; ambient action performance; ambient body-world interaction
ambient world component	subject-ambient observation result; ambient-subject world- body interaction	ambient-subject world component interaction	ambient observation result; ambient world-body interaction	ambient world component interaction

world, then communication can most efficiently be modelled as information transfer between minds. If, in contrast, it is to be modelled how communication is affected by other processes in the world (e.g., effects on the quality of a channel or network), then it is more adequate to model communication as bodily interaction. Obviously, also in cases that it is to be modelled how agents affect each others bodies, as in fighting, the latter is the most adequate option.

Agent-World Interaction. Interaction between an agent and a world component can be either *observation* or *action* performance; cf. [11]. An action is generated by an agent, and transfers to a world component to have its effect there. An observation has two directions: the *observation focus* is generated by an agent and transfers to a world component (providing access to a certain aspect of the world), and the provision of the *observation result* is generated by the world component and transfers to the agent. Combinations of interactions are possible, such as performing an action and observing the effect of the action afterwards. When the agent's body is distinguished from its mind, interaction between agent and world can be modelled as transfer between this body and a world component. In addition, interaction between the agent's mind and its body (the vertical arrows in Figure 1) can be used to model the effect of mental processes (deciding on actions and observations to undertake) on the agent-world interaction and vice versa (incorporating observation results). Also here, whether for a given application of the generic model interaction between an agent and the world is modelled according to the first or the second option, depends on the assumptions made about the application domain. If it is assumed that performance of an intended action generated by the mind has a direct effect on the world and has no relevant effect on an agent's body, then it can most efficiently be modelled according to the first option. If, in contrast, it is to be modelled how actions and observations are also affected by other processes in the body or world, then the second option is more adequate. Also in cases that it is to be modelled how the world affects an agent body, obviously the second option is the most adequate.

The Naval Officer Example. Table 2 illustrates the different types of components and interactions for a case concerning a naval officer, as briefly explained in the introduction. The officer keeps track of incoming planes on a radar screen, and acts on those ones classified as dangerous.

Table 2. Components and interactions for a naval officer case

subject components	**subject agents**		**subject world components**
	human naval officer		radar screen with moving planes
subject interactions	**observation and action by subject agent**		
	naval officer gaze focuses on radar screen with planes, extracts information from radar screen view, naval officer acts on planes that are dangerous		
ambient components	**ambient agents**		
	dynamic task allocation agent (including an eye tracker), task-specific agent		
ambient interactions	**communication between ambient agents**		
	communication between task allocation agent and task-specific agent on task requests		
interactions between subject and ambient	**communication**	**observation and action**	
	task allocation agent communicates over-looked dangerous item to naval officer	ambient agent has observation focus on radar screen and naval officer gaze ambient agent extracts info from views	

Generic State Ontologies at the Global Level. For the information exchanged between components at the global level, generic ontologies have been specified. This has been done in a universal order-sorted predicate logic format that easily can be translated into more specific ontology languages. Table 3 provides an overview of the generic sorts and predicates used in interactions at the global level. Examples of the use of this ontology will be found in the case studies.

98   T. Bosse et al.

Generic Temporal Relations for Interaction at the Global Level. Interaction between global level components is defined by the following specifications. Note that in such specifications, for state properties the prefix input, output or internal is used. This is an indexing of the language elements to indicate that it concerns specific variants of them either present at the input, output or internally within the agent.

Action Propagation from Agent to World Component
∀X:AGENT ∀W:WORLD ∀A:ACTION   output(X)|performing_in(A, W) ∧ can_perform_in(X,A,W) —»
   input(W)|performing_in(A, W)
Observation Focus Propagation from Agent to World Component
∀X:AGENT ∀W:WORLD ∀I:INFO_EL output(X)|observation_focus_in(I, W) ∧ can_observe_in(X,I,W) —»
   input(W)|observation_focus_in(I, W)
Observation Result Propagation from World to Agent
∀X:AGENT ∀W:WORLD ∀I:INFO_EL output(W)|observation_result_from(I, W) ∧ can_observe_in(X,I,W) —»
   input(X)|observed_result_from(I, W)
Communication Propagation Between Agents
∀X,Y:AGENT ∀I:INFO_EL output(X)|communication_from_to(I,X,Y) ∧ can_communicate_with_about(X,Y,I) —»
   input(Y)|communicated_from_to(I,X,Y)

Table 3. Generic Ontology for Interaction at the Global Level

SORT	Description	
ACTION	an action	
AGENT	an agent	
INFO_EL	an information element, possibly complex (e.g., a conjunction of other info elements)	
WORLD	a world component	
Predicate		**Description**
performing_in(A:ACTION, W:WORLD)		action A is performed in W
observation_focus_in(I:INFO_EL, W:WORLD)		observation focus is I in W
observation_result_from(I:INFO_EL, W:WORLD)		observation result from W is I
communication_from_to(I:INFO_EL, X:AGENT, Y:AGENT)		information I is communicated by X to Y
communicated_from_to(I:INFO_EL,X:AGENT,Y:AGENT)		information I was communicated by X to Y
can_observe_in(X:AGENT, I:INFO_EL, W:WORLD)		agent X can observe I within world W
can_perform_in(X:AGENT, A:ACTION, W:WORLD)		agent X can perform action A within W
can_communicate_with_about(X:AGENT,Y:AGENT,I:INFO_EL)		agent X can communicate with Y about I

4   Generic Ambient Agent and World Model

This section focuses on the ambient agents within the generic model. As discussed in Section 3, ambient agents can have various types of interactions. Moreover, they are assumed to maintain knowledge about certain aspects of human functioning in the form of internally represented dynamic models, and information about the current state and history of the world and other agents. Based on this knowledge they are able to have a more in-depth understanding of the human processes, and can behave accordingly. This section presents an ambient agent model that incorporates all these.

Components within the Ambient Agent Model. In [11] the component-based Generic Agent Model (GAM) is presented, formally specified in DESIRE [12]. The process control model was combined with this agent model GAM. Within GAM the component *World Interaction Management* takes care of interaction with the world, the component *Agent Interaction Management* takes care of communication with other agents. Moreover, the component *Maintenance of World Information* maintains information about the world, and the component *Maintenance of Agent Information* maintains information about other agents. In the component *Agent Specific Task*, specific tasks can be modelled. Adopting this component-based agent model GAM, the Ambient Agent Model has been obtained as a refinement, by incorporating components of the generic process control model described above.

The component *Maintenance of Agent Information* has three subcomponents. The subcomponent *Maintenance of a Dynamic Agent Model* maintains the causal and temporal relationships for the subject agent's functioning. For example, this may model the relationship between a naval officer's gaze direction, characteristics of an object at the screen, and the attention level for this object. The subcomponent *Maintenance of an Agent State Model* maintains a snapshot of the (current) state of the agent. As an example, this may model the gaze direction, or the level of attention for a certain object at the screen. The subcomponent *Maintenance of an Agent History Model* maintains the history of the (current) state of the agent. This may for instance model the trajectory of the gaze direction, or the level of attention for a certain object at the screen over time.

Table 4. Components within the Ambient Agent Model

Maintenance of Agent Information	
maintenance of dynamic models	model relating attention state to human body state and world state
maintenance of state models *subject agent* *subject world component*	 model of attention state and gaze state of the naval officer model of state of radar screen with planes
maintenance of history models	model of gaze trajectory and attention of time
Maintenance of World Information (similar to Maintenance of Agent Information)	
Agent Specific Task	
simulation execution	update the naval officer's attention state from gaze and radar screen state
process analysis	determine whether a dangerous item is overlooked
plan determination	determine an option to address overlooked dangerous items (to warn the naval officer, or to allocate another human or ambient agent to this task)
World Interaction Management	processing received observation results of screen and gaze
Agent Interaction Management	preparing a warning to the officer preparing a request to take over a task

Similarly, the component *Maintenance of World Information* has three subcomponents for a dynamic world model, a world state model, and a world history model, respectively. Moreover, the component *Agent Specific Task* has the following three subcomponents, devoted to the agent's process control task. The subcomponent *Simulation Execution* extends the information in the agent state model based on the internally represented dynamic agent model for the subject agent's functioning. For example, this may determine the attention level from a naval officer's gaze direction, and the characteristics of an object at the screen, and his previous attention level. The subcomponent *Process Analysis* assesses the current state of the agent. For instance, this may determine that a dangerous item has a level of attention that is too low. This component may use different generic methods of assessment, among which (what-if) simulations and (model-based) diagnostic methods, based on the dynamic and state models as maintained. The subcomponent *Plan Determination* determines whether action has to be undertaken, and, if so, which ones (e.g. to determine that the dangerous item with low attention from the naval officer has to be handled by another agent).

Finally, as in the model GAM, the components *World Interaction Management* and *Agent Interaction Management* prepare (based on internally generated information) and receive (and internally forward) interaction with the world and other agents. Table 4 provides an overview of the different components within the Ambient Agent Model, illustrated for the case of the naval officer.

Generic State Ontologies within Ambient Agent and World. To express the information involved in the agent's internal processes, the ontology shown in Table 5 was specified. As an example, belief(leads_to_after(I:INFO_EL, J:INFO_EL, D:REAL)) is an expression based on this ontology which represents that the agent has the knowledge that state property I leads to state property J with a certain time delay specified by D. This can provide enhanced context awareness (in addition to information obtained by sensoring).

Table 5. Generic Ontology used within the Ambient Agent Model

Predicate	Description
belief(I:INFO_EL)	information I is believed
world_fact(I:INFO_EL)	I is a world fact
has_effect(A:ACTION, I:INFO_EL)	action A has effect I
Function to INFO_EL	**Description**
leads_to_after(I:INFO_EL, J:INFO_EL, D:REAL)	state property I leads to state property J after duration D
at(I:INFO_EL, T:TIME)	state property I holds at time T

Generic Temporal Relations within an Ambient Agent. The temporal relations for the functionality within the Ambient Agent are as follows.

Belief Generation based on Observation, Communication and Simulation
∀X:AGENT, I:INFO_EL, W:WORLD   input(X)|observed_from(I, W) ∧ internal(X)|belief(is_reliable_for(W, I))
        ⟶ internal(X)|belief(I)
∀X,Y:AGENT, I:INFO_EL   input(X)|communicated_from_ to(I,Y,X) ∧ internal(X)|belief(is_reliable_for(X, I))
        ⟶ internal(X)|belief(I)
∀X:AGENT ∀I,J:INFO_EL ∀D:REAL ∀T:TIME
    internal(X)|belief(at(I, T)) ∧ internal(X)|belief(leads_to_after(I, J, D)) ⟶ internal(X)|belief(at(J, T+D))

Here, the first rule is a generic rule for the component *World Interaction Management*. Similarly, the second rule is a generic rule for the component *Agent Interaction Management*. When the sources are assumed always reliable, the conditions on reliability can be left out of the first two rules. The last generic rule within the agent's component *Simulation Execution* specifies how a dynamic model that is explicitly represented as part of the agent's knowledge (within its component *Maintenance of Dynamic Models*) can be used to perform simulation, thus extending the agent's beliefs about the world state at different points in time. This can be considered an internally represented deductive causal reasoning method. As another option, an abductive causal reasoning method can be internally represented in a simplified form as follows.

Belief Generation based on Simple Abduction
∀X:AGENT ∀I,J:INFO_EL ∀D:REAL ∀T:TIME
    internal(X)|belief(at(J, T)) ∧ internal(X)|belief(leads_to_after(I, J, D)) ⟿ internal(X)|belief(at(I, T-D))

Generic Temporal Relations within a World. For World Components the following specifications indicate the actions' effects and how observations provide their results.

Action Execution and Observation Result Generation in the World
∀W:WORLD_COMP ∀A:ACTION ∀I:INFO_EL input(W)|performing_in(A, W) ∧ internal(W)|has_effect(A,I)
    ⟿ internal(W)|world_fact(I)
∀W:WORLD_COMP ∀I:INFO_EL input(W)|observation_focus_in(I, W) ∧ internal(W)|world_fact(I)
    ⟿ output(W)|observation_result_from(I, W)
∀W:WORLD_COMP ∀I:INFO_EL input(W)|observation_focus_in(I, W) ∧ internal(W)|world_fact(not(I))
    ⟿ output(W)|observation_result_from(not(I), W)

5   Case Studies

To test the applicability of the generic model introduced above, it has been tested in three different case studies. Case study 1 addresses an ambient driver support system, case study 2 addresses an ambient aggression handling system, and case study 3 [19] addresses an ambient system for management of medicine usage, see e.g., [17]. For all of the case studies, the generic model has been instantiated with sufficiently detailed domain-specific information to be able to perform simulations. Moreover, for each case study a formal analysis has been performed, in which relevant dynamic properties of the cases considered (such as requirements imposed on the systems) have been verified. In the future, also the IFIP properties on user interfaces for AmI applications can be tested [16]. Due to space limitations, the details of the case studies have been omitted. See, however: http://www.cs.vu.nl/~tbosse/AmI/AmI07cases.pdf.

6   Discussion

The challenge addressed in this paper is to provide a generic model that covers the class of Ambient Intelligence applications that show human-like understanding and supporting behaviour. Here human-like understanding is defined as understanding in the sense of being able to analyse and estimate what is going on in the human's mind and body (a form of mind/bodyreading). Input for these processes are observed information about the human's physiological and behavioural states and dynamic models for the human's physical and mental processes. For the mental side such a dynamic model is sometimes called a Theory of Mind (e.g., [13], [14], [15]) and may cover concepts such as emotion, attention, intention, and belief. This can be extended to integration with the human's physical processes, relating, for example, to skin conditions, heart rates, and levels of blood sugar, insulin, adrenalin, testosterone, serotonin, and specific medication taken. In this class of Ambient Intelligence applications, knowledge from human-directed disciplines is exploited, in order to take care of (and support in a knowledgeable manner) humans in their daily living, in medical, psychological and social respects. Thus, an ambience is created that uses essential knowledge from the human-directed disciplines to provide a more human-like understanding of human functioning, and from this understanding can provide adequate support. This may concern, for example, elderly people, criminals and psychiatric patients, but also humans in highly demanding tasks.

The generic model introduced in this paper is a template for the specific class of Ambient Intelligence applications as described. One of the characteristics of this class is that a high level of human-directed context awareness plays a role; see also [23], [24], [25]. The ambient software and hardware design is described in an agent-based manner at a conceptual design level and to support context awareness has generic facilities built in to represent human state models and dynamic process models, and methods for model-based simulation and analysis on the basis of such models. For a particular application, biomedical, neurological, psychological and/or social ontologies, knowledge and dynamic models about human functioning can be specified. The generic model includes slots where such application-specific content can be filled in to get an executable design for a working system. This specific content, together with the generic methods to operate on it, enables ambient agents to show human-like understanding of humans and to react on the basis of this understanding in a knowledgeable manner. The model has been positively evaluated in three case studies related to existing Ambient Intelligence applications.

References

1. Aarts, E., Collier, R.W., van Loenen, E., de Ruyter, B. (eds.): EUSAI 2003. LNCS, vol. 2875, p. 432. Springer, Heidelberg (2003)
2. Aarts, E., Harwig, R., Schuurmans, M.: Ambient Intelligence. In: Denning, P. (ed.) The Invisible Future, pp. 235–250. McGraw Hill, New York (2001)
3. Bosse, T., Delfos, M.F., Jonker, C.M., Treur, J.: Analysis of Adaptive Dynamical Systems for Eating Regulation Disorders. Simulation Journal (Transactions of the Society for Modelling and Simulation) 82, 159–171 (2006)
4. Bosse, T., van Doesburg, W., van Maanen, P.P., Treur, J.: Augmented Metacognition Addressing Dynamic Allocation of Tasks Requiring Visual Attention. In: Schmorrow, D.D., Reeves, L.M. (eds.) HCII 2007 and FAC 2007. LNCS (LNAI), vol. 4565, pp. 166–175. Springer, Heidelberg (2007)
5. Bosse, T., Gerritsen, C., Treur, J.: Integration of Biological, Psychological, and Social Aspects in Agent-Based Simulation of a Violent Psychopath. In: Shi, Y., van Albada, G.D., Dongarra, J., Sloot, P.M.A. (eds.) ICCS 2007. LNCS, vol. 4488, pp. 888–895. Springer, Heidelberg (2007)
6. Bosse, T., Jonker, C.M., van der Meij, L., Sharpanskykh, A., Treur, J.: Specification and Verification of Dynamics in Cognitive Agent Models. In: Nishida, T., et al. (eds.) Proc. of the Sixth Int. Conf. on Intelligent Agent Technology, IAT 2006, pp. 247–254. IEEE Comp. Society Press, Los Alamitos (2006)
7. Bosse, T., Jonker, C.M., van der Meij, L., Treur, J.: A Language and Environment for Analysis of Dynamics by Simulation. International Journal of Artificial Intelligence Tools 16, 435–464 (2007)
8. Bosse, T., Maanen, P.-P., van Maanen, P.-P., Treur, J.: A Cognitive Model for Visual Attention and its Application. In: Nishida, T., et al. (eds.) Proc. of the Sixth Intern. Conf. on Intelligent Agent Technology, IAT 2006, pp. 255–262. IEEE Computer Society Press, Los Alamitos (2006)
9. Bosse, T., Memon, Z.A., Treur, J.: A Two-level BDI-Agent Model for Theory of Mind and its Use in Social Manipulation. In: Olivier, P., Kray, C. (eds.) Proc. of the Artificial and Ambient Intelligence Conf., AISB 2007, Mindful Environments Track, pp. 335–342. AISB Publications (2007)

10. Bosse, T., Schut, M.C., Treur, J., Wendt, D.: Trust-Based Inter-Temporal Decision Making: Emergence of Altruism in a Simulated Society. In: Paolucci, M., Antunes, L., Norling, E. (eds.) Proc. of the Eighth International Workshop on Multi-Agent-Based Simulation, MABS 2007, pp. 103–118. Springer, Heidelberg (to be published, 2007)

11. Brazier, F.M.T., Jonker, C.M., Treur, J.: Compositional Design and Reuse of a Generic Agent Model. Applied Artificial Intelligence Journal 14, 491–538 (2000)

12. Brazier, F.M.T., Jonker, C.M., Treur, J.: Principles of Component-Based Design of Intelligent Agents. Data and Knowledge Engineering 41, 1–28 (2002)

13. Dennett, D.C.: The Intentional Stance. MIT Press, Cambridge Mass (1987)

14. Gärdenfors, P.: How Homo Became Sapiens: On The Evolution Of Thinking. Oxford University Press, Oxford (2003)

15. Goldman, A.I.: Simulating Minds: The Philosophy, Psychology and Neuroscience of Mind Reading. Oxford University Press, Oxford (2006)

16. Gram, C., Cockton, G. (eds.): Design Principles for Interactive Software. Chapman & Hall, London (1996)

17. Green, D.J.: Realtime Compliance Management Using a Wireless Realtime Pillbottle – A Report on the Pilot Study of SIMPILL. In: Proc. of the International Conference for eHealth, Telemedicine and Health, Med-e-Tel 2005, Luxemburg (2005)

18. Gross, J.J. (ed.): Handbook of emotion regulation. Guilford Press, New York (2007)

19. Hoogendoorn, M., Klein, M., Treur, J.: Formal Design and Simulation of an Ambient Multi-Agent System Model for Medicine Usage Management. In: Mühlhäuser, M., Ferscha, A., Aitenbichler, E. (eds.) AmI 2007 Workshops. CCIS, vol. 11, pp. 207–217. Springer, Heidelberg (2008)

20. Jonker, C.M., Treur, J.: Compositional Verification of Multi-Agent Systems: a Formal Analysis of Pro-activeness and Reactiveness. International Journal of Cooperative Information Systems 11, 51–92 (2002)

21. Reiter, R.: Knowledge in Action: Logical Foundations for Specifying and Implementing Dynamical Systems. MIT Press, Cambridge (2001)

22. Riva, G., Vatalaro, F., Davide, F., Alcañiz, M. (eds.): Ambient Intelligence. IOS Press, Amsterdam (2005)

23. Schmidt, A.: Interactive Context-Aware Systems - Interacting with Ambient Intelligence. In: Riva, G., Vatalaro, F., Davide, F., Alcañiz, M. (eds.) Ambient Intelligence, pp. 159–178. IOS Press, Amsterdam (2005)

24. Schmidt, A., Beigl, M., Gellersen, H.W.: There is more to Context than Location. Computers & Graphics Journal 23(19), 893–902 (1999)

25. Schmidt, A., Kortuem, G., Morse, D., Dey, A.: Situated Interaction and Context-Aware Computing. Personal and Ubiquitous Computing 5(1), 1–81 (2001)

Model-Driven Approach to the Implementation of Context-Aware Applications Using Rule Engines

Luís Ferreira Pires, Nieko Maatjes, Marten van Sinderen,
and Patrícia Dockhorn Costa

Centre for Telematics and Information Technology, University of Twente,
PO Box 217, 7500 AE Enschede, the Netherlands
{l.ferreirapires,m.j.vansinderen,p.dockhorncosta}
@ewi.utwente.nl, n.c.maatjes@alumnus.utwente.nl

Abstract. This paper aims at demonstrating that the Model-Driven Architecture (MDA) approach to transformation is suitable to cope with the abstraction gap between the specification of application rules for context-aware applications and the implementation of these rules using rule engines. This paper reports on the transformation of Event-Condition-Action (ECA) rules onto rules that can be executed by the Jess rules engine. We have applied the MDA approach to define this transformation, by specifying it in terms of mappings between elements of the ECA Domain-specific Language (ECA-DL), which is the language we developed to represent ECA rules, and the Jess metamodel. The transformation was fully specified, implemented using the Atlas Transformation Language (ATL) and tested with a simple example.

Keywords: Context-aware application, rule engines, automated transformations, model-driven architecture.

1 Introduction

Context-aware applications are capable of acquiring information about their own or their users' context without explicit user intervention. These applications can react intelligently upon changes in the user's context, and perform behaviour that is tailored to the user needs. These applications are particularly useful in domains where context changes are frequent and corresponding changes in the application behaviour cannot be managed manually by the user. Examples include tele-monitoring and tele-treatment of patients, and certain emergency and crises management services.

The context information and the specific behaviour of context-aware applications may vary for each individual user, such that particular attention must be paid to the cost-effective development of context-aware applications. Therefore, context-aware services platforms have been proposed, which facilitate the development and deployment of applications that can be tailored to each individual user [6].

Context-aware applications are meant to respond properly to various inputs and context changes (events), in terms of actions that may correspond, for example, to service invocations. An example is an application that sends an SMS notification to a friend of

M. Mühlhäuser et al. (Eds.): AmI 2007 Workshops, CCIS 11, pp. 104–112, 2008.

the application's user (action), once the user is in the neighbourhood of that friend (event). Based on the observation that the pattern of 'events that trigger actions' recurs in most context-aware applications, we have proposed to apply the Event-Control-Action (ECA) pattern to the design of context-aware platforms [5]. This allows application designers to define application behaviour in terms of Event-Condition-Action (ECA) rules[1], which are rules that match the ECA pattern and can be supported by a context-aware services platform.

In order to allow application behaviours to be specified in terms of ECA rules, we have developed the so called ECA Domain-specific Language (ECA-DL) [4, 7]. ECA-DL is close to the intuitive understanding of application developers, relieving them from the task of defining application implementation details. However, we expect that context-aware services platforms may contain a Controller component, possibly built based on expert systems, particularly rule engines [7]. In this case, the ECA rules defined at a high level of abstraction have to be translated to a form that can be understood by the rule engine embedded in the Controller component. The benefits of using rule engines to implement ECA rules in context-aware applications are their reasoning capabilities, flexibility and structure, which resembles the structure of ECA rules [3].

This paper aims at demonstrating that the Model-Driven Architecture (MDA, [9]) approach to transformation is suitable to cope with the abstraction gap between the specification of application rules for context-aware applications and the implementation of these rules using rule engines. This paper reports on the transformation of ECA rules onto rules that can be executed by the Jess engine [12]. We have applied the MDA approach to define this transformation, by specifying it in terms of mappings between elements of the ECA-DL and the Jess metamodel. The transformation was fully specified, implemented using the Atlas Transformation Language (ATL, [2]) and tested with a simple example.

The paper is further structured as follows: Section 2 gives an overview of our approach, Section 3 introduces and gives the metamodel of the ECA-DL language, Section 4 introduces Jess and gives the metamodel of the Jess language, Section 5 presents our transformation specification, and Section 6 gives our conclusions and identifies topics for further work.

2 Approach

In essence, the problem to be solved consists of translating rules expressed in ECA-DL to rules expressed using the Jess language. In principle we could have implemented this translation based on the concrete syntax (textual) elements of the language, building a compiler for ECA-DL. However, this compiler would be hard to extend and reuse, which is unfavourable for ECA-DL, which is a language still under development. Furthermore, this would have forced us to deal with the syntax and structure of the languages in the same tool.

---

[1] The ECA architectural pattern denotes a separation between Event, *Control* and Action concerns, while ECA rules are defined in terms of Events, *Conditions* and Actions. This means that the 'C' in ECA has a different meaning when applied to the pattern or the rules.

Instead, we have applied an MDA-based approach in which the transformation is specified in terms of mappings between elements of the source and target language metamodels, namely the ECA-DL and Jess language metamodels, respectively. This corresponds to layer M2 of the OMG metamodelling layering [10]. The transformation is executed at layer M1, in which an ECA-DL model is transformed to a Jess model by a transformation engine that executes the transformation specification. In this way we concentrate on the structural (conceptual) mappings between the languages, and leave the syntax issues to be handled by parsers and serialisers. Fig. 1 gives an overview of our transformation approach.

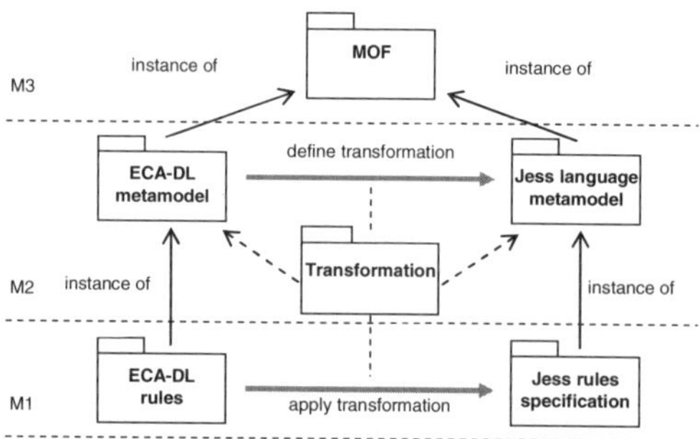

Fig. 1. Overview of our transformation approach

Our approach is structured in two phases: a preparation phase in which the metamodels and the transformation are defined, and an execution phase, in which the ECA rules in textual form are parsed and transformed to an ECA-DL model, this model is transformed to a Jess rules model, and the latter is serialised to the textual Jess language statements that can be executed by the Jess engine. In Fig.1 the preparation phase and the execution phase correspond to the M2 and M1 layers, respectively. Fig. 2 shows the execution phase in more detail.

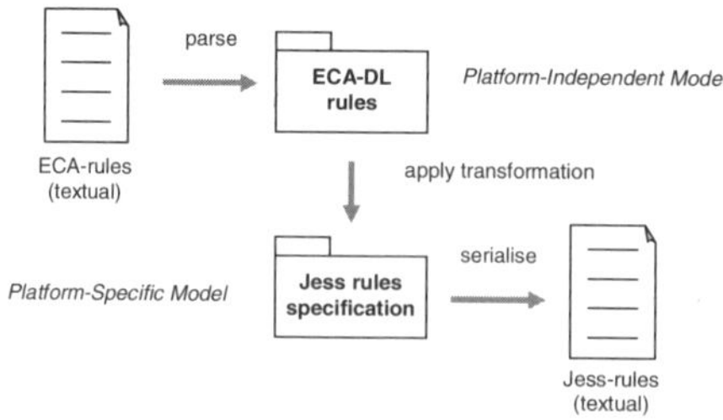

Fig. 2. Details of the execution phase

According to the MDA terminology, the ECA-DL model corresponds to a Platform-Independent Model (PIM), since it is neutral with respect to the actual concrete platform that executes the rules defined in the model. The transformation to Jess rules can be executed (semi)-automatically by a transformation engine. It results in a model that corresponds to a Platform-Specific Model (PSM), since this model is more concrete and bound to a specific implementation platform (the Jess rule engine).

3 ECA-DL

ECA Domain-specific Language (ECA-DL, [1]) is a domain-specific language defined in order to allow the specification of ECA rules. ECA-DL rules consist of three parts, namely Event, Condition and Action. Each of these parts is represented in the ECA-DL syntax as follows:

- Event: `Upon <event>`
- Condition: `When <condition>`
- Action: `Do <action>`
  where
- `<event>` defines an event, which consists of one or more state transitions. There are three possible states for a certain situation: `true`, `false` and `unknown`. A transition is denoted using functions like `EnterTrue(inOffice)` or `FalseToUnknown(lightOn)`, which can be used to indicate context changes. Multiple transitions can be combined using logical operators like `AND`, `OR` and `NOT` to create a compound transition. Only when the entire compound expression has evaluated to true, i.e., when the required transitions have happened, the event is generated and a number of actions can be triggered. Transitions can contain expressions, but they cannot contain other transitions;
- `<condition>` defines a condition that has to be fulfilled in order for the actions to be triggered. Whereas transitions occur at a certain point in time, conditions hold for certain periods. Examples of conditions are `Peter.height < Mary.height` and `isTurnedOff (computer) AND belongsTo(computer, Pete)`. Conditions are expressions and can contain other expressions;
- `<action>` denotes one or more actions to be triggered when an event takes place and the condition is satisfied. In context-aware applications, an action is often a notification. For example, a notification can be sent to a student's supervisor to notify her that the student has arrived at university. In this example, the action could be `Notify(Supervisor, "Student x has entered the building!")`.

A simple example of an ECA-DL rule to define that when Peter enters his office his computer should be automatically switched on is the following:

```
Upon EnterTrue(isInRoom(Peter, office))
When isTurnedOff(computer) AND belongsTo(computer,
Peter)
Do turnOn(computer)
```

In addition to events, conditions and actions, ECA-DL also supports the definition of scopes, selection of value collections, and rules lifetime (how often and when rules are expected to be triggered). For more detail on ECA-DL we refer to [1].

We defined the ECA-DL metamodel in three steps [8]. In the first step a simplified model was defined, including only the events, conditions and actions. In the second step, the metamodel was extended with expressions, functions and compound transitions. In the last step the complete metamodel was defined, including the scope, select and lifetime constructs.

Fig. 3 shows the complete ECA-DL metamodel we used to define the transformation.

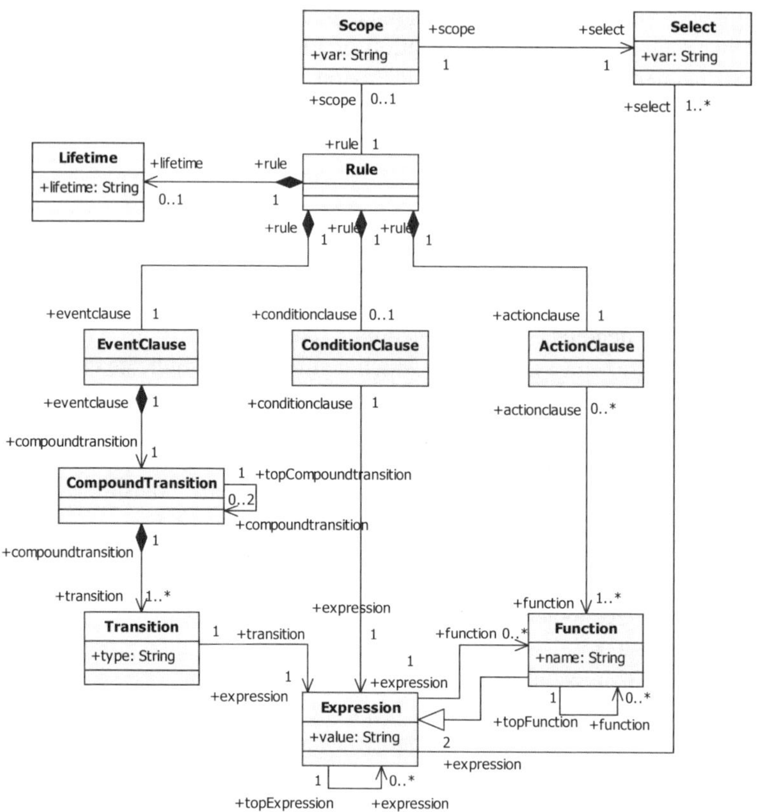

Fig. 3. Complete ECA-DL metamodel

4   Jess

Our target system is the Java Expert System Shell (Jess, [12]), which is a rule engine for Java. A rule engine (also called inference engine) is a program that tries to match rules against information and then triggers one or more actions.

A Jess program can contain two kinds of declarations, namely facts and rules. A fact contains basic information, such as, e.g. "Pete is male" or "Mary is the mother of Tom". Facts are stored in the working memory. A rule contains a simple *if-then* construct containing statements about facts, such as, e.g. "*If* Pete is male AND Pete has a child, *then* Pete is father". This information is stored in the knowledge base. The *if*-part of a rule is called Left-Hand Side (LHS), while the *then*-part is called Right-Hand Side (RHS).

When the Jess engine executes, it searches for matches between the rules and the facts. When a match is found, the rule is fired and the actions defined in the RHS of the rule are triggered. This process is repeated as long as changes occur in the working memory or knowledge base. At a given time more than one rule may match, so that other rules also have to be fired. Furthermore, the RHS of a rule can declare new facts or rules, or destroy old ones, so that new rules also have to be evaluated and may be fired.

Fig. 4 shows the Jess metamodel that we used to define our transformation.

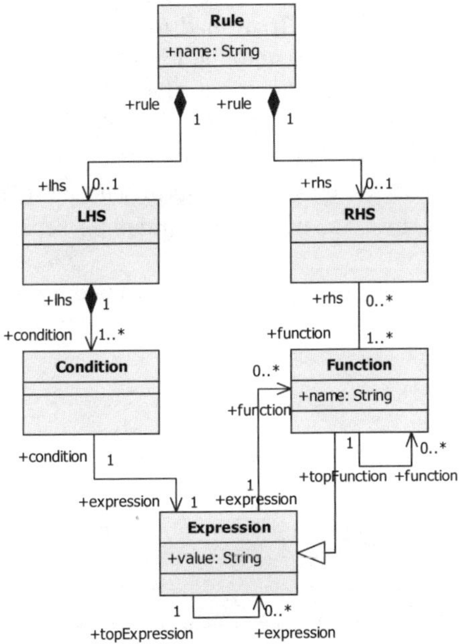

Fig. 4. Jess metamodel

In this paper we refrain from discussing the details of the Jess engine and the syntax of the Jess language. More detail on Jess can be found at [12].

5   Transformation Specification

The transformation from ECA-DL to Jess has been defined in terms of mappings from the ECA-DL metamodel elements to Jess metamodel elements. We started with the mappings for a trivial case, in which no conditions are defined. In this case, the ECA-DL rule is mapped onto one Jess rule, where the Event and the Action parts of the ECA-DL rule are mapped onto the LHS and the RHS of the Jess rule, respectively.

In case the ECA-DL rule contains a Condition part, the mapping gets more complex, since the Condition should hold when the Event occurs for the rule to be triggered. Because it is not possible to implement this behaviour using only one Jess rule, we have decided in this case to map one ECA-DL rule onto three Jess rules:

- Rule 1, which is fired when the condition holds and the event has not happened yet. This adds the fact `fact-cond-holds` to the working memory;
- Rule 2, which is fired when the event occurs and `fact-cond-holds` holds;
- Rule 3, which is fired as soon as the condition does not hold anymore. This removes `fact-cond-holds` from the working memory and prevents Rule 2 from firing.

We illustrate our mapping with the simple rule 'When Mary enters the room, and Pete is already there, act surprised'. If we had mapped both 'Mary enters the room' (event) and 'Pete is there' (condition) onto the LHS of the Jess rule, the rule would be triggered also in case Pete enters the room after Mary, which is not the original intention of the rule. Therefore, we map this rule onto three rules, namely: (1) Pete enters the room but Mary is not there yet → `fact-cond-holds`; (2) Mary enters the room and `fact-cond holds` → act surprised; and (3) Pete leaves the room → remove `fact-cond-holds`, where the symbol → separates the LHS from the RHS.

Fig. 5 shows the mapping of ECA-DL events, conditions and actions onto Jess rules.

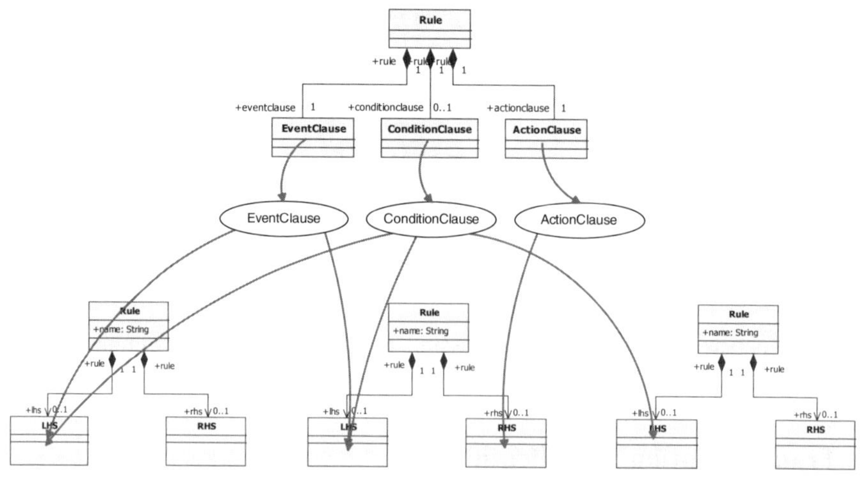

Fig. 5. Mapping for events, conditions and actions

Fig. 6 shows the additional mappings defined in the transformation specification (for the select, scope, lifetime, transition, expression and function language elements).

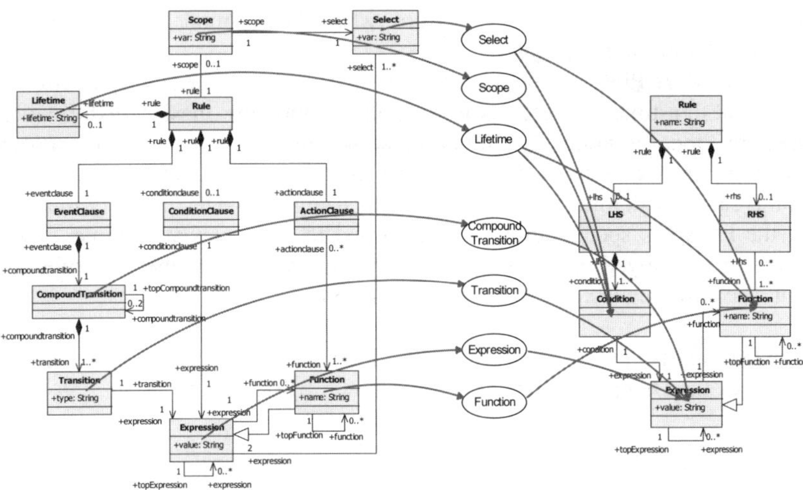

Fig. 6. Additional mappings

The complete transformation specification can be found in [8].

The transformation has been completely specified in ATL and tested with the transformation example mentioned above. The ECA-DL specification has been written directly in XMI [11], and the metamodels have been defined using the KM3 notation and translated to Ecore in order to be used in the Eclipse environment. The resulting Jess model has been generated by the ATL Development Tools (ADT, [2]) as an Ecore model.

6 Conclusions and Further Work

The structure of ECA-DL and the Jess language are similar in case no conditions are defined, so that a trivial one-to-one mapping could be defined for this case. In case conditions are used, one ECA-DL rule is mapped onto three rules, to cope with the semantics of events and conditions in a proper way. However, our mapping of ECA-DL onto Jess is not yet complete. Particularly the combination of Scope and Lifetime may have to be reconsidered. In ECA-DL, Lifetime is defined on a per-rule basis. When a rule is embedded in a Scope, the ECA-DL semantics states that each rule gets its own Lifetime. However, in our mapping, the Scope construct merges with the rule, so that the Lifetime holds for this single created rule, instead of for each rule of the original set. It is still unclear whether this limitation creates undesirable behaviours at the Jess language level. Constructs that have not yet been mapped onto Jess are the 'unknown' state in transitions, and lifetimes with time periods and frequency in combination with a period. These mappings are left for further study.

In this work we have aimed at developing an automated transformation from ECA-DL rules to Jess rules. Except for the parsing and serialisation of the ECA-DL rules and Jess models, respectively, the transformation can be performed automatically.

These steps will be facilitated in future when text-to-model and model-to-text transformation tools are available.

Although MDA PIM-to-PSM transformations have been originally devised to be applied at design-time, we see some benefits of applying these transformations at runtime, by incorporating the transformation engine (with the transformation specification) in the context-aware services platform. We envisage a situation in which the end-user defines the desired services using ECA-DL (possibly in a simpler form), the ECA-DL specification is transformed to Jess rules at runtime, and these Jess rules are deployed on the Controller component running the Jess rule engine, without discontinuing the operation of the platform.

Acknowledgments. The work is part of the Freeband A-MUSE project. Freeband is sponsored by the Dutch government under contract BSIK 03025.

References

[1] Almeida, J.P.A., Iacob, M.E., Jonkers, H., Quartel, D.A.C.: Model-Driven Development of Context-Aware Services. In: Eliassen, F., Montresor, A. (eds.) DAIS 2006. LNCS, vol. 4025, pp. 213–227. Springer, Heidelberg (2006)

[2] ATL project, `http://www.eclipse.org/m2m/atl`

[3] Daniele, L.: Towards a Rule-based Approach for Context-aware Applications. MSc Thesis, University of Twente, Enschede (2006)

[4] Dockhorn Costa, P., Ferreira Pires, L., van Sinderen, M.J., Broens, T.H.F.: Controlling Services in a Mobile Context-aware Infrastructure. In: David, K., Drögehorn, O., Haseloff, S. (eds.) Second Workshop on Context Awareness for Proactive Systems (CAPS 2006), pp. 153–166. Kassel University Press, Kassel (2006)

[5] Dockhorn Costa, P., Ferreira Pires, L., van Sinderen, M.: Architectural Patterns for Context-Aware Services Platforms. In: Mostéfaoui, S.K., Maamar, Z. (eds.) Second International Workshop on Ubiquitous Computing (IWUC 2005), pp. 3–18. INSTICC Press, Setúbal (2005)

[6] Dockhorn Costa, P., Ferreira Pires, L., van Sinderen, M.J.: Designing a Configurable Services Platform for Mobile Context-Aware Applications. International Journal of Pervasive Computing and Communications 1(1), 13–25 (2005)

[7] Etter, R., Dockhorn Costa, P., Broens, T.: A Rule-based Approach Towards Context-aware User Notification Services. In: IEEE International Conference on Pervasive Services 2006, pp. 281–284. IEEE Computer Society Press, Los Alamitos, California (2006)

[8] Maatjes, N.C.: Automated Transformations from ECA Rules to Jess. MSc Thesis, University of Twente, Enschede (2007)

[9] Object Management Group: MDA Guide, V1.0.1 (2003)

[10] Object Management Group: UML 2.0 Infrastructure Specification (2003)

[11] Object Management Group: Meta Object Facility (MOF) 2.0 XMI Mapping Specification (2005)

[12] Sandia National Laboratories: Jess: the Rule Engine for the Java Platform, `http://herzberg.ca.sandia.gov/jess/`

Multimodal User Interaction in Smart Environments: Delivering Distributed User Interfaces

Marco Blumendorf, Sebastian Feuerstack, and Sahin Albayrak

DAI-Labor, Technische Universität Berlin
Ernst-Reuter Platz 7, D-10587 Berlin, Germany
{Marco.Blumendorf,Sebastian.Feuerstack,
Sahin.Albayrak}@dai-labor.de

Abstract. The ongoing utilization of computer technologies in all areas of life leads to the development of smart environments comprising numerous networked devices and resources. Interacting in and with such environments requires new interaction paradigms, abstracting from single interaction devices to utilize the environment as interaction space. Using a networked set of interaction resources allows supporting multiple modalities and new interaction techniques, but also requires the consideration of the set of devices and the adaptation to this set at runtime. While the generation of user interfaces based on UI models, although still challenging, has been widely researched, the runtime processing and delivery of the derivable user interfaces has gained less attention. Delivering distributed user interfaces while maintaining their interdependencies and keeping them synchronized is not a trivial problem. In this paper we present an approach to realize a runtime environment, capable of distributing user interfaces to a varying set of devices to support multimodal interaction based on a user interface model and the management of interaction resources.

Keywords: multimodal distributed user interfaces, model-based user interfaces, human-computer interaction, smart environments.

1 Introduction

The integration of multiple computer-based appliances in people's homes and the convergence of home electronic and computer systems lead to networks of powerful devices, comprising multiple connected Interaction Resources (IRs) [7] (i.e. screen, speaker, microphone or mouse) that provide access to services and applications. Microphones, cameras, accelerometers and specialized instruments as well as e.g. screens and speakers make multimodal user input perceivable for the system and present multimedial system output to the user. While the generation of user interfaces based on UI models has been widely researched, the runtime interpretation and delivery of the derived user interfaces for such highly distributed environments has gained less attention yet.

Problems arising from utilizing distributed interaction in smart environments are the development of multimodal user interfaces distributed across various interaction resources as well as the delivery of the parts of the user interface and their synch-

M. Mühlhäuser et al. (Eds.): AmI 2007 Workshops, CCIS 11, pp. 113–120, 2008.

ronization across loosely coupled collections of interaction resources in smart environments.

This paper presents an approach, addressing these challenges by the development of a runtime system for the interpretation of model-based multimodal user interfaces. The system combines an interpretation engine for user interface models with a channel-based user interface delivery mechanism. Based on previous work presented in [2] we develop a definition of interaction channels and describe the implementation of the approach, focussing on the integration into our model-based runtime system. After describing the state of the art in the next section, we introduce the idea of interaction channels and describe their utilization for the delivery of user interfaces. In section 5 we give a brief overview of the implementation of our model-based runtime system followed by the conclusion and outlook.

2   Related Work

The basic process of interaction between human and computer can be described as the bidirectional exchange of information between the (digital) computer and the (analog) human user - both with an internal representation - via a physical medium (light, sound or kinetic energy) [9]. To access the physical medium, an *interaction resource* is required allowing perceiving or affecting the medium. [7] defines an interaction resource as "atomic input or output channel" to the user, thus addressing only one modality. Such an *atomic channel* can be described from two points of view: From the human perspective it represents the human sense (vision, hearing, smell, taste, and touch) and motory system used to perceive or affect the physical medium. From the system perspective it connects the interaction resource and thus the physical medium to the system internals.

The term *"channel"* has thereby been used in different contexts and there is no common understanding of the term yet. While [1] uses the term "communication channel" to refer to mouse, keyboard or voice as input and visual, audio or haptic as output, [3, 4] uses the term "presentation channel" to classify the input and output format (HTML/WML). Braun and Mülhäuser utilize the idea of multiple channels to connect several devices grouped in a federation to an interactive system [5]. Nigay et al. [10] define a *communication channel* as the "temporal, virtual, or physical link that makes the exchange of information possible between communicating entities" and based on this multimodality as the "capacity of the system to communicate with a user along different types of communication channels and to extract and convey meaning automatically".

3   Interaction Channels

In this work, we want to introduce the term "Interaction Channel" to identify the complete chain, mediating between the system and the human user (Figure 1). Considering that user and system both have an internal representation of their

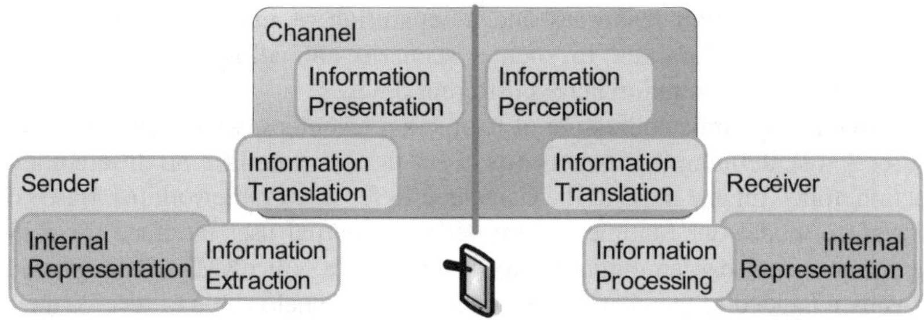

Fig. 1. Channels mediate between the internal representation of the system and the user

knowledge there is an urgent need to mediate and translate between the two. While the systems internal representation is defined by an application model allowing the derivation of resource specific user interfaces, the user maintains a mental model in her head and perceives the state of the system via her senses, mediated by interaction resources. Each channel can be split in a sender- and a receiver-part, with an interaction resource connecting the two sides. Which side is system or user switches depending on the direction of the information flow (input vs. output). Information flow between the two sides requires the following steps: First the sender extracts the information to convey and decides how to communicate by selecting an appropriate channel. Afterwards the information is translated into a channel-specific format and finally presented via an interaction resource. The presented information is perceived by the receiver and translated into an understandable format. The translated information is processed and incorporated into the receiver's internal representation. Applying this approach to the idea of a runtime system creating, delivering and synchronizing user interfaces by interpreting a UI model leads to the need for an implementation of the channel concept on the system side.

4   Delivering User Interfaces

Focusing on the system view of an interaction channel, the channel provides access to the interaction resource properties and also takes care of the delivery of the derived UI and its synchronization with the state of the system. Delivery of UI parts to different interaction resources and the synchronization of the different parts is especially important when considering distributed UIs in smart environments. Utilizing the concept of interaction channels on the system side allows the free combination of multiple resources and their utilization in new and unconventional ways (e.g. the direct control of a large display via a PDA or the creation of a GUI controllable via voice input and mouse gestures). Dynamically assembling sets of resources used for interaction allows the user to combine various input and output modalities according to her specific needs during interaction. Similar to assembling a device like e.g. a PDA, the user first picks the different resources e.g. display, touchpanel, keyboard and stylus pen to define the environment. Afterwards interaction channels established to these resources allow the communication and make the resources available for the use with the interactive system. The independent addressing of interaction resources and a separation of input and output resources becomes especially important in such a scenario and allows addressing multiple modalities through distribution across different devices.

To enable the dynamic addressing of interaction resources, we utilize a user interface model [6, 8, 12], defining the various aspects of the user interface on different levels of abstraction, following the ideas of the Cameleon Reference Framework [6]. Based on this user interface model our runtime system derives a partial user interface for a specific interaction resource, e.g. an output UI for a screen or a VoiceXML UI for voice input, which is then handed to the channel. An interaction channel is able to receive the partial user interface, derive the final user interfaces and deliver it to the interaction resource. It also maintains a connection to each interaction resource, providing the basic mechanisms required to push information like a UI to present to the resource. Once the user interface has been delivered, the channel is responsible for the delivery of updates triggered by changes to the state of the application to the user interface and for receiving and interpreting user input. The propagation of state changes allows the synchronization of multiple user interfaces according to the state of the internal UI model of the system. As soon as the model is changed an update message is created and delivered to the channel, altering the partial UI the channel maintains. This alteration is then also communicated to the final user interface and also alters its presentation (or, in case of an input user interface, the processable inputs for example).

In case of a partial input user interface addressing an input interaction resource the UI also provides information about how to map the input received from the interaction resource to the format of the internal representation of the system. Input events received from an interaction resource are interpreted by the interaction channel based on the partial input UI and mapped to the internal format of the system. This allows the manipulation of the user interface model by such input events, which then again can trigger update events altering the final user interfaces.

Based on the described concept we implemented the delivery mechanism of the Multi-Access Service Platform described in the next section.

5 The Multi-access Service Platform

Our implementation of the concepts described above is based on the runtime interpretation of a user interface model. Different other approaches follow the idea of utilizing the user interface model at runtime [8] or utilizing similar concepts as our interaction channels to deliver user interfaces [11]. In contrast to other approaches we focus on the utilization of models at runtime to derive partial user interfaces, which can be distributed to various interaction resources connected via interaction channels. The combination of model and delivery allows a stronger integration of model and final UI and the synchronization of distributed UIs based on the underlying common user interface model.

In our current implementation, the task model, described in the CTT notation [13], defines the workflow of the application and a domain model defines the objects manipulated by the defined tasks and thus the internal state of the application. Each leaf task references objects defined in the domain model as well as a user interface description allowing the creation of partial user interfaces for each task. User interface

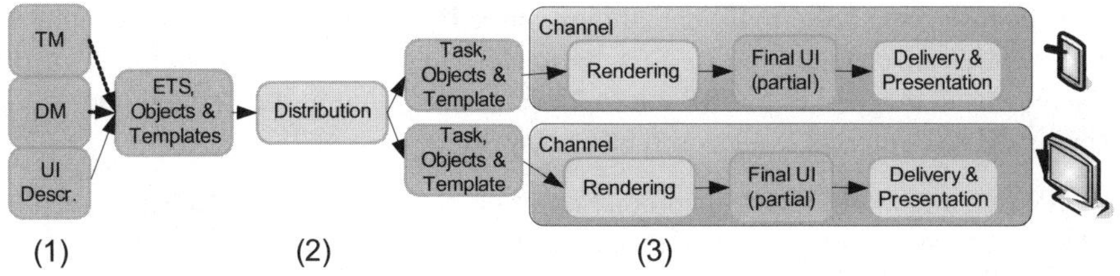

Fig. 2. Basic MASP Architecture and information flow during UI derivation and delivery

descriptions are currently realized as velocity templates[1] allowing the creation of user interfaces in various output formats, based on the objects referenced in the related task. Figure 2 (1) shows the parts of the model.

During the user interface creation process in a first step the Enabled Task Set (ETS) is derived from the task model and the related objects and user interface descriptions are loaded. According to the set of available interaction channels the set of tasks is distributed to the channels. [Figure 2 (2)] For our current applications we are supporting multiple templates to support the multiple types of interaction resources and initially deliver all output tasks to all output channels that templates have been defined for and all input tasks to all input channels respectively. However, we also support the manipulation of the distribution by the user by sending single tasks to different channels and implemented a simple algorithm to calculate the distribution of related tasks based on the "distance" of two tasks, the processed objects and the type of the tasks (input or output task). The distance thereby denotes the number of parent tasks that have to be passed when moving through the hierarchy from one task to the other. The closer the tasks, the more likely they are directly related and should be presented together, especially if they also work on the same objects.

Figure 2 (3) shows the connected channels. Whenever a channel receives the request to deliver a partial user interface to the connected resource, the velocity templates are rendered, producing final user interfaces based on the passed objects defined in the related task. The result of the rendering process is then delivered to the interaction resource, presenting the UI to the user. Interaction resources can thereby be manually registered, by calling a URL or be discovered using UPnP. Technologies like CC/PP also allow the description of the resource specifics, which is currently not directly supported in our implementation.

Interaction with this system takes place in two ways. On the one hand changes to the system model are communicated as UI updates via the channel and alter the presented UI. The annotation of the related objects in the task tree allows the relation of objects to templates as well as the implementation of an observing mechanism for the domain model, ensuring that each UI element, referencing a domain object is updated as soon as the domain object changes. On the other hand, user input is processed via interaction mappings. Interaction mappings for each interaction task describe the relation of the receivable input to the user interface model. In the current implementation these user interaction is communicated via the event types described

---

[1] http://velocity.apache.org/

in [2] (FocusEvent, SelectionEvent, InputEvent). However, to provide a meaning to these events, and enable them to alter the underlying application model, any of the above events is mapped to MASP internal events according to the defined interaction mapping. MASP internal events currently comprise:

- DSWrite, allows the direct manipulation of objects stored in the domain model. A DSWrite event therefore contains a query to the object, which has the form ObjectID(.FieldID)*.
- TaskDone, allows indicating that the user has finished performing a task, which results in marking a task as done.

Based on a given partial UI description an interaction channel is able to create a mapping between the interaction events and the model manipulation events.

In our implementation we currently support the creation of HTML and VoiceXML code for *output user interfaces* and HTML, VoiceXML and XML-based gesture descriptions for *input user interfaces*. In both cases (input and output) the execution of the template creates a code snippet (a <div> tag in case of HTML and a <form> tag in case of VoiceXML). For HTML, using Javascript, initially deployed to the browser when the channel is established, allows adding <div> tags to the displayed web page initially or replacing existing <div> whenever information in the model changes. The layout is in this case defined by Cascading Style Sheets (css) allowing the definition of the properties of the <div> tags, e.g. the position. The position can either be determined by the interface developer or be calculated by a layouting algorithm, which allows the dynamic positioning of the elements when distributing the UI. An input channel allows the processing of input by delivering Javascript code executed by the browser that creates the related events. Currently the relation of the input to the output presented e.g. "pressing a button" is done by the browser. In a next step we move that processing to the server, to be able to e.g. relate mouse coordinates to button positions on server side, which allows more advanced user interaction like simple mouse gestures or the increasing of the active area of a button without increasing the button size, to ease touchscreen interaction.

The described implementation allows the creation of multimodal user interfaces distributed across multiple interaction resources. Resources currently supported are screens, mouse and keyboard – in this case we use a web browser as an integration platform providing access to the resources via Javascript functions – as well as voice input and output – in this case we use a VoiceGenie voice server – and gesture based input. Gesture based input is realized via a small device we build, that allows the interpretation of simple gestures detected by an accelerometer.

6 Conclusion and Future Work

This paper introduced the Multi-Access Service Platform and an approach to support the delivery of user interfaces to sets of interaction resources to allow the flexible combination of multiple diverse interaction resources. This approach on the one hand allows the creation of multimodal user interfaces for smart environments and on the other hand provides the basis for more advanced user interfaces, capable of dynamically addressing the users' needs. However, during our work we discovered that the dynamic incorporation of multiple interaction resources requires strong user interface models allowing the derivation of multiple different user interfaces. Experimenting with user interfaces separating input and output also made clear, that there is a strong relation between input and output. While the output describes application specific information it also provides the reference point for the user input. This makes it necessary to on the one hand guide the user by communicating input capabilities, provide help systems and supportive output like e.g. a screen keyboard for free text entry via mouse and on the other hand also provide direct input feedback like e.g. the mouse pointer, whenever a user provides (partial) input.

Working on the MASP and several prototypes utilizing the implemented features, it also turned out that the anticipated very flexible interaction in smart environments requires new interaction technologies as well as new paradigms for human-computer interaction. Shifting the human attention away from a single device, towards a whole system of connected interaction resources allows a much more flexible interaction and the utilization of various instruments other than mouse and keyboard to address special needs. However, the creation of such flexible systems requires highly flexible user interfaces, adapting to the users need and environment. This requires a focus shift away from designing user interfaces towards the design of interaction instead. Interaction with smart environments requires interaction concepts, patterns and methodologies not widely researched yet. Our hope is to be able to formalize such interaction concepts into widgets and interaction pattern allowing the flexible creation of easy to understand interaction and the automatic adaptation to the device specifics in the future.

The work described in this paper is part of the Service Centric Home[2] project sponsored by the German Federal Ministry of Economics and Technology. The MASP and a Virtual Cook application developed using the technology is deployed as part of the Ambient Living Testbed which has been set up as part of the project as well. The Ambient Living Testbed consists of a kitchen a living room and an office and provides infrastructure for the development and test of smart home services and the realization of usability studies. Earlier studies with a basic prototype of the system already showed positive feedback for multimodal interaction in smart home environments and underlined the need for the integration of different interaction devices in smart home environments. Currently we are developing several prototypes to integrate multiple interaction resources and allow more flexible interaction in our smart environment. We are very positive that the following experiments will again show positive feedback for the developments.

References

[1] Abowd, G., Coutaz, J., Nigay, L.: Structuring the space of interactive system properties. In: Engineering for Human-Computer Interaction. IFIP Transactions, vol. A-18, pp. 113–129 (1992)

[2] Blumendorf, M., Feuerstack, S., Albayrak, S.: Event-based synchronization of model-based multimodal user interfaces. In: LNCS MoDELS 2006 workshop proceedings: MDDAUI 2006 (2006)

---

[2] www.sercho.de

[3] Book, M., Gruhn, V.: Modeling web-based dialog flows for automatic dialog control. In: ASE 2004: Proceedings of the 19th IEEE international conference on Automated software engineering, pp. 100–109 (2004)

[4] Book, M., Gruhn, V., Lehmann, M.: Automatic dialog mask generation for device-independent web applications. In: ICWE 2006: Proceedings of the 6th international conference on Web engineering (2006)

[5] Braun, E., Mühlhauser, M.: Automatically generating user interfaces for device federations. In: ISM 2005: Proceedings of the Seventh IEEE International Symposium on Multimedia (2005)

[6] Calvary, G., Coutaz, J., Thevenin, D., Limbourg, Q., Bouillon, L., Vanderdonckt, J.: A unifying reference framework for multi-target user interfaces. Interacting with Computers 15(3), 289–308 (2003)

[7] Clerckx, T., Vandervelpen, C., Coninx, K.: Task-based design and runtime support for multimodal user interface distribution. In: Proceedings of Engineering Interactive Systems (2007)

[8] Coninx, K., Luyten, K., Vandervelpen, C., Van den Bergh, J., Creemers, B.: Dynamically generating interfaces for mobile computing devices and embedded systems. In: Chittaro, L. (ed.) Mobile HCI 2003. LNCS, vol. 2795, Springer, Heidelberg (2003)

[9] Coomans, M., Timmermans, H.: Towards a taxonomy of virtual reality user interfaces. In: IV 1997: Proceedings of the IEEE Conference on Information Visualisation (1997)

[10] Nigay, L., Coutaz, J., Salber, D.: The msm framework: A design space for multi-sensori-motor systems. In: EMO 2001. LNCS, vol. 753 (1993)

[11] Elting, C., Rapp, S., Möhler, G., Strube, M.: Architecture and implementation of multimodal plug and play. In: ICMI 2003: Proceedings of the 5th international conference on Multimodal interfaces (2003)

[12] Mori, G., Paternò, F., Santoro, C.: Design and development of multidevice user interfaces through multiple logical descriptions. IEEE Trans. Softw. Eng. 30(8), 507–520 (2004)

[13] Paternò, F.: Model-Based Design and Evaluation of Interactive Applications. Applied Computing. Springer, Heidelberg (1999)

Distributed User Interfaces in Ambient Environment

Jean Vanderdonckt[1], Hildeberto Mendonca[1], and José Pascual Molina Massó[1,2]

[1] Belgian Laboratory of Computer-Human Interaction (BCHI)
Louvain School of Management (LSM), Université catholique de Louvain
Place des Doyens, 1 – B-1348 Louvain-la-Neuve (Belgium)
`{vanderdonckt,mendonca,molina}@isys.ucl.ac.be`
[2] Laboratory of User Interaction & Software Engineering (LOUISE)
Inst. de Investigación en Informática de Albacete (I3A), Universidad de Castilla-La Mancha
Campus universitario s/n – S-02071 Albacete (Spain)
`jpmolina@dsi.uclm.es`

Abstract. Before developing an Ambient Intelligence (AmI) application, it is often required to examine how its user interface will be distributed across the various interaction surfaces of its physical environment and which types of services these user interfaces will provide to end-users. For this purpose, a virtual reality rendering engine has been developed that renders a user interface model in a physical environment expressed by an environment model and a service model which enables designers to prototype the definition and the distribution of such user interfaces. After the modeling phase, the user interface is rendered in a virtual reality scene that may be subject to prototyping thanks to the model rendering engine. Any suggestion for modification applied on the underlying models (i.e., user interface, environment, and service) is propagated in the virtual reality scene. Depending on the interaction surface where a particular user interface is rendered, some adaptation rules may be performed expressed in terms of model-to-model transformations.

Keywords: context-aware adaptation, distributed user interfaces (DUI), environment model, intelligent user interfaces, interaction surface, physical environment, service model, user interface prototyping.

1 Introduction

A preliminary problem that arises when designing and developing Ambient Intelligence (AmI) applications, but not the only one, consists in determining how portions of its User Interface (UI) will be distributed in a physical environment (e.g., an augmented room, a home, a virtual laboratory) [5,6] and which shape this UI will take (i.e., digital, physical, or mixed) [9]. Once this distribution is more or less determined, it is the responsibility of designers to identify which interaction surfaces [4] will build the ambient environment and which capabilities they will be equipped with [7]. This lead to the notion of Distributed User Interfaces (DUIs), which is a particular type of UI whose portions are distributed and executed in time and space in a particular physical environment.

When the development cost of a DUI turns out to be too high for considering alternative designs, it is likely that this exploration will be abandoned soon or limited

M. Mühlhäuser et al. (Eds.): AmI 2007 Workshops, CCIS 11, pp. 121–130, 2008.

largely limited. A rapid and cheap prototyping technique may be then preferred. In addition, the usability issues raised by distributing a UI across one or several locations [7] are serious, although the benefits have been empirically demonstrated [11]: the display size has a positive effect of task completion time, tasks are better performed in multi-displays environment, to name a few.

Therefore, we believe that rapid prototyping of DUIs in AmI remains a key issue: not only rapid prototyping could be used as a vehicle for developing and demonstrating visions of innovative DUIs, but also they could help showing various distribution configurations before going to full implementation. However, rapid prototyping is also a challenging problem since the design space involves multiple dimensions: the physical environment itself, the DUI, the interaction surfaces, and the capabilities offered by these interaction surfaces. In order to address this problem more specifically, this paper provides a context model decomposed into three facets (i.e., user, computing platform, and physical environment). The environment is itself linked to interaction surfaces and their capabilities expressed as a service model.

The remainder of this paper is structured as follows: some related work is reported in Section 2, the models used in our approach are defined in Section 3. Section 4 will exemplify this model with some application in an augmented room. Section 5 will sum up the benefits of the models provided and some future avenues for this work.

2   Related Work

Some advanced researches share some similarities with the work described in this paper or provided initial material from which an extension has been introduced. Only the ones closest to this work are reported.

DYNAMO-AID [3] provides a distribution manager which distributes the sub-tasks of a task model to various computing platforms in the same physical environment, thus fostering a task-based approach for distributing UIs across locations of the physical environment. In contrast, the approach of this paper does not rely on a task model but rather gives the freedom and the responsibility to designers to distribute UIs in the environment by providing them with the appropriate mechanisms. In addition, there is no genuine model of interaction surfaces coupled with services described in a model.

The MIGRATION project [1] distributes UIs across web-based platforms of a cluster and provides a service-oriented approach for ensuring migration of these portions across the elements of the cluster. Again, this could be expanded with a model of interaction surfaces and services if more services are desired.

In Everywhere [10], DUIs could be rendered on various interaction surfaces such as large screens, white-boards, wall displays as well as personal surfaces. Only digital interfaces are considered as opposed to 3DSim [8], where only hardware interfaces are supported because it is the tool goal to prototype physical interfaces in a physical environment, thus also providing some sort of rapid prototyping. The material development of the physical UI is conducted after the prototype is validated.

VAQUITA [2] consists of a tool for reverse engineering an existing web page and redisplay it for another platform whose model has been previously defined. Per se, this tool is not a tool for supporting DUIs, but for retargeting a UI to another platform, according to the paradigm of multiple channel UIs [12,13,14].

In this paper, the environment model is produced as a virtual reality scene, thus allowing the rendering of both software (e.g., widgets) and hardware (e.g., physical buttons) objects, but this is achieved mainly for rapid prototyping purposes only. It is obvious that it cannot produce a physical UI, but the models used to prototype them could be passed to the development team afterwards. The tool provides basic operations such as copy a UI from one surface to another one, whether they belong to a computing platform or not, duplicate, and migrate.

The approach described in this paper is different from the above important pieces of work in that it explicitly relies on a physical environment model decomposed into surfaces, some of them being interactive some others not. These surfaces are then attached to a service model characterizing the capabilities they can offer to the UI rendering engine in virtual reality. The DUI could be physical, digital, or mixed.

3   Modeling Context of Use, Physical Environment, and Services

Figure 1 reproduces the meta-model of the various models exploited by the rendering engine and their relationships. The constituent models are then explained successively in the following respective sub-sections.

3.1   The Context of Use and the Physical Environment

The *Context of use* describes all the entities that may influence how the user's task is carried out with the UI [5]. It takes into account three relevant aspects, each aspect having its own associated attributes contained in a separate model: *user stereotype* (e.g., system experience, task experience, task motivation), *computing platform* (e.g., mobile platform, desktop, laptop, wall screen), and *physical environment* (e.g., office conditions such as lighting, level of noise). The physical context is here represented as a virtual reality scene, this is why we adopted a simplified representation inspired from X3D (see http://www.web3d.org/x3d/) where such as scene is composed of *surfaces* (i.e., any type of plane with its size, position, angle, etc.). This physical environment is populated by surfaces which could be connected together to form a topology of the scene (e.g., a floor, some walls and a ceiling to form an augmented lab), but also with *shapes* (i.e., any type of volume which could represent a scene object, such as a chair, a desk, cupboards). Defined as a sub-type of surface, the concept of *interaction surface*, firstly introduced in [4], is hereby referred to as any physical surface which can be "acted on or observed" so as to support user interaction with a system, whether visible or embedded. For instance, an interaction surface could be digital (e.g., a screen, a monitor, a wall display) or physical (e.g., a table equipped with camera tracking techniques, a pad with projection). The definition of physical (e.g., weight, size, material, solidity/fluidity/nebulosity) and modality attributes is in [4].

Each computing platform could be located precisely with respect to an environment surface and could hold none, one or many hardware platforms, which are declared as a general form of output (e.g., a display, a monitor, a screen). Each such platform is of course an interaction surface which could be acted on (by using pointers) and/or observed (by looking at the screen). Each interaction surface is defined by its shape, which is the area sensible to interaction. Hardware platforms are therefore considered as rectangular-shaped interaction surfaces. One could imagine probably other

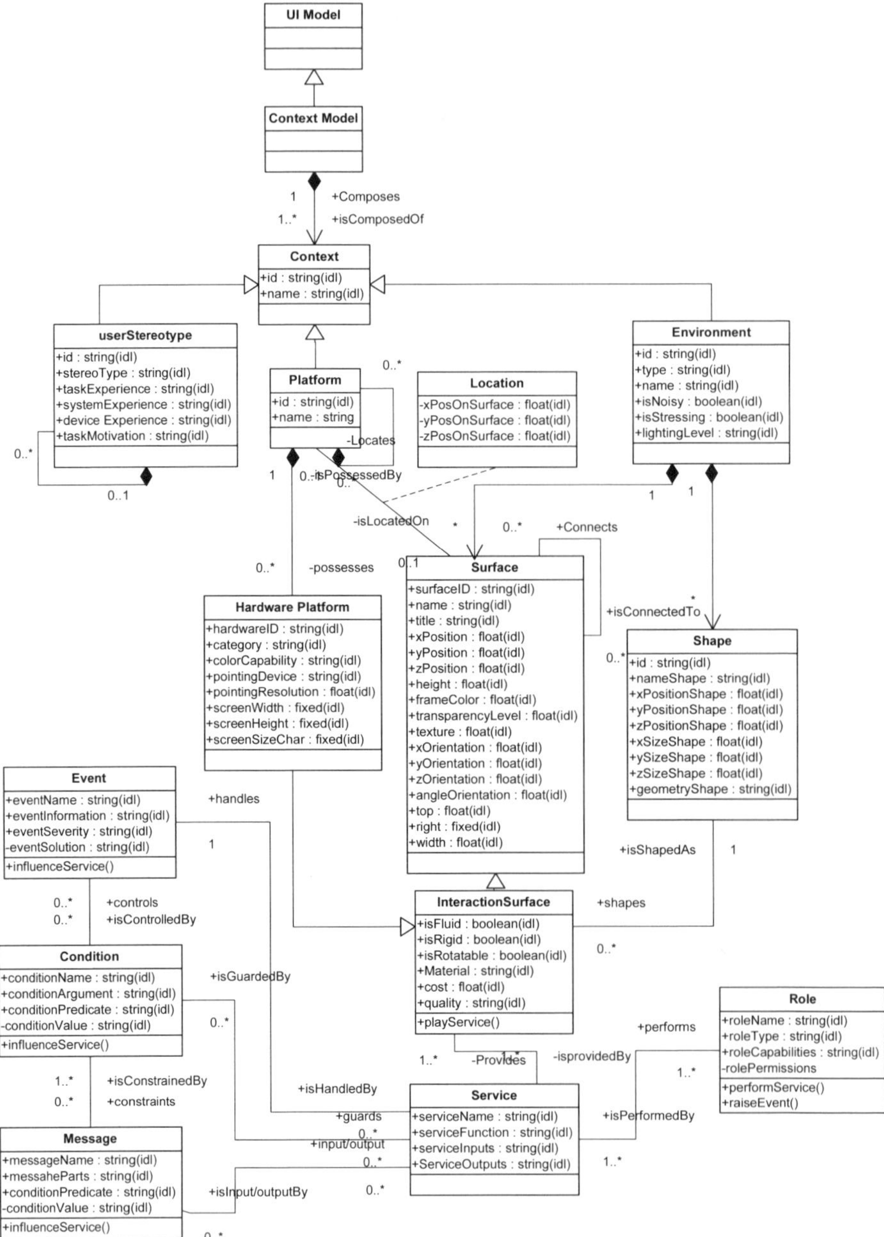

Fig. 1. The meta-model used for rendering a user interface in an ambient environment

shapes like a circle or an oval, but in our implementation, only convex surfaces are supported. The interaction surface type depicts the level of physicality of the surface used to render the DUI. A computer monitor and a public display are considered as digital surfaces, as opposed to projection surfaces that are considered as physical ones. This distinction will impact the rendering of an object as a widget for a digital surface or as a physical device for a physical surface.

3.2 The Services

The service model is a meta-model comprising of five concepts useful for service modeling, calling, and composition inspired from the service model of [9]. This meta-model is based on generic service composition constructs derived after a thorough study of the current standards such as Business Process Execution Language (BPEL – http://en.wikipedia.org/wiki/BPEL) and Business Process Modeling Language (BP ML – www.bpmi.org). Based on this study and on requirements for DUIs [1], the following classes have been identified:

- *Service*: This abstract class represents a well-defined business function similar to basic activities such as those found in BPML. It contains four attributes: unique name, function, inputs, and outputs. An instance of this class can be defined as follows: Service: (name="cuiRendering", function="concreteUserInterfaceRendering", inputs="cuiModel, contextModel", outputs="cuiModel.instance"). This example shows a service named "cuiRendering" that is meant for rendering a particular concrete UI. It requires several input parameters to carry out this task, such as, for instance, the UI model and the context model in which the UI should be rendered. The output parameter of this class includes the handle to the UI instance created in this context. Note that this service may exploit several sub-models such as the platform model to render properly the UI whose model is provided.
- *Event*: This abstract class describes occurrences during the process of service execution and composition. These can be both of a normal and exceptional nature (e.g., a serviced executed in case of an abnormal status). An instance of this class can be defined as follows: Event: (name="widgetRenderingError", context= "concreteUserInterfaceRendering", severity="unrecoverable", information="renderingStatus", solution="abandonExecution"). This example illustrates an event class called "widgetRenderingError". If the attribute "Severity" in this event class is set to "unrecoverable", then the execution needs to be abandoned. To signal the occurrence of "widgetRenderingError", a "widgetStatus" message must be sent to indicate that a particular widget cannot be rendered on a particular platform. For instance, the check box does not exist in WML 2.0, thus raising a rendering error. This is recoverable though and possible solutions could be indicated: an empty bow could be rendered instead or another service could be called, e.g. to replace the failing widget by a list box with the two opposite values.
- *Condition*: This class constrains the behavior of the service and possible compositions by controlling event occurrences, guarding activities and enforcing preconditions, post-conditions and integrity constraints. For this purpose, a condition class has four attributes, name, argument, predicate, value. A typical postcondition for "cuiRendering" could be that "a CUI has been rendered and could be manipulated by its handle". A typical precondition for "cuiRendering" could be that the platform model exhibits a resolution that is large enough to accommodate the rendering of a particular UI, i.e. not too large.
- *Message*: This abstract class represents a container of information (like properties in BPEL). Messages are used and generated by services as input and output, respectively. They are also used to signal events, and can be correlated to other

messages to express data dependencies. They have attributes such as name and parts.

- *Role*: This class provides an abstract description for a party participating in the service execution or composition. Roles are responsible for performing services and raising events. An instance of this class can be: Role: (name="renderingEngine", type="renderer", capabilities="(cuiRendering, cuiStoring, cuiRetrieving)", permissions="(cuiRenderingAllowed)"). The previous example describes "renderingEngine" as being of the type "renderer", both capable and authorized to render UI, to store a currently being rendered UI and to retrieve its status during execution. Note that the cuiRendering is executed prior to cuiStoring and cuiRetrieving.

To support the various services involved in Fig. 1, a rendering engine called VUI-Toolkit has been developed above the UsiXML (www.usixml.org) and expanded with the service model of Fig. 1 so as to render a concrete UI as a final UI in a virtual world. First, the environment model gives rise to a virtual world com-posed on surfaces, some of them being interactive. In particular, computing platforms could be located on some of these surfaces or considered as an interaction surface per se. Second, the toolkit abstracts objects belonging to Web3D languages (e.g., VRML, VRML97, X3D which are typically used in modeling virtual reality worlds and scenes). The next section exemplifies how this toolkit could be used to support the execution of an individual service, then the composition of several services taken together.

4   Executing, Composing Services for Distributed User Interfaces

4.1   User Interface Rendering

The *cuiRendering* service is responsible for rendering a UI or a portion of a UI on an interactive surface in the physical environment. For this purpose, the service is invoked with appropriate parameters such as the UI model, the environment model in which the rendering should occur and the interactive surface in it. Figure 2 reproduces a UI rendering of a simple Internet radio UI on a laptop in an augmented room.

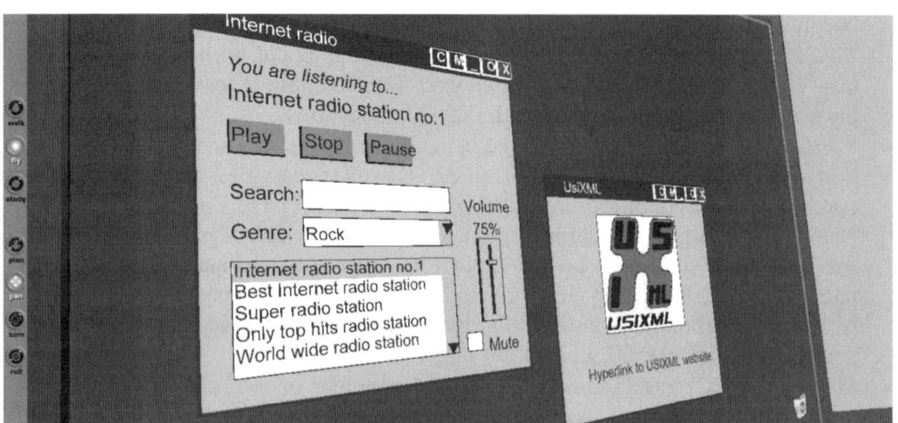

Fig. 2. Example of a user interface rendering

4.2   User Interface Migration

The *cuiMigration* service is responsible for migrating a UI or a portion of a UI from a source interactive surface in the physical environment to a target one. For this purpose, a composition of services is executed in the following sequence: *cuiStoring* for storing the current values of the UI widgets (e.g., their default values, their current values, the current behavior), *cuiUnrendering* to undisplay the UI from the interactive surface of concern, *cuiRetrieving* to retrieve an existing UI model instantiated through its handle, and *cuiRendering* to render it on another interactive surface. Figure 3 reproduces some steps during the migration. A message is first produced to indicate the beginning of a migration and when a new interactive surface is designated, an event triggers the composition of services on the appropriate surface. In the current implementation, single windows can be migrated as a portion of a UI, but not individual window elements.

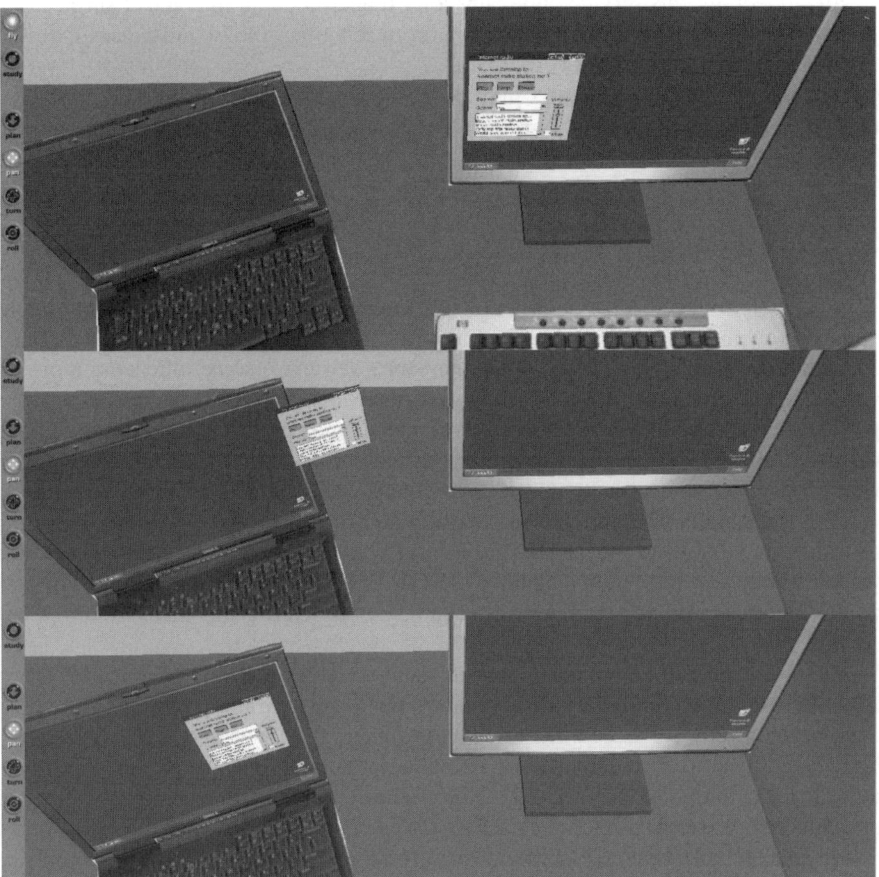

Fig. 3. Example of a user interface migration

4.3 User Interface Adaptation

The *cuiMigration* service is responsible for adapting a UI or a portion of a UI to a particular platform. This service is invoked when the target interactive surface is not able to render the required UI due to space constraints.

4.4 Other User Interface Services

In AmI, other types of services are particularly useful such as, but not limited to:

- *uiPhysicalization*: this service is responsible for rendering a UI on a target interaction surface that is physical such as a projected screen or a physical device. For this purpose, different rendering functions select appropriate widgets or physical widgets depending on the type of interaction surface used.
- *uiDigitization* is the inverse process, that is a service responsible for converting a physical UI rendered on a physical interactive surface onto a digital one (screen).
- *uiDuplicating*: this service duplicates a UI rendered on an interactive surface onto another one, thus creating a duplicate. From this time, the two instances live their own life and are no longer coordinated.
- *uiCopying*: this service creates multiple copies of a singled rendered UI
- *uiSwitching*: this service is responsible for switching two UI between two interactive surface.

5 Conclusion

This paper introduced a service model for rendering DUIs in AmI as a support for rapid prototyping of DUIs by manipulation in a virtual reality scene. Some services are rather traditional (e.g., copy, duplicate, store, retrieve), some others are more advanced (e.g., adaptation, migration). The main advantage of the structure in terms of services is that functions can be precisely modeled and can be composed in a rigorous way, that is, a new service can be created as the composition of already existing services, thus creating a climate that is favorable for expanding the set of existing services. For example, when an interface is migrated from a PC to a PDA, it may simply be transferred thanks to the *cuiMigration* service and followed by a *cuiRendering* service or it may also trigger an adaptation service (e.g., *cuiAdaptation*). If one wishes to do this automatically, the three services can be composed together so as to form a new service.

The prototype can be obtained as soon as an underlying model is created. Then, it could be used in any software development method where the prototyping stage occurs. In the future, we would like to develop functions as web services so that everybody could benefit from them. In the virtual environment, one can explore alternative designs by calling services related to the desired operation. In this way, a designer may redistribute the DUI elements across the interactive surfaces of the environment and investigate different assembling or manifestation of the DUI elements as physical and/or digital objects. However, it is the manual operation what triggers the services, as there is no algorithm for distributing UI pieces on interaction surfaces. Besides, even though transition between digital and physical worlds is easy in this virtual environment, rendering is currently limited by widgets provided by VUIToolkit.

The present work does not implement composition of services, neither dynamic discovery of services (as in [1,6,9]), but sets the pave towards this direction. There should be no reason why these services could not be invoked at run-time instead of design-time, but their implementation should be updated accordingly. Composition should be based on messages, but also on quality of services, e.g., find the closest surface that could render a given UI. Thus, further extension of this work could also include modeling quality of services provided by interaction surfaces, which may start from existing models, such as Q-WSDL, WSLA or DAML-QoS, to name a few.

Acknowledgments. We gratefully acknowledge the support of the SIMILAR network of excellence (http://www.similar.cc), the European research task force creating human-machine interfaces similar to human-human communication of the European Sixth Framework Programme (FP6-2002-IST1-507609). This research is fully funded by SIMILAR.

References

1. Bandelloni, R., Paterno, F., Salvador, Z.: Dynamic discovery and monitoring in migratory in-teractive services. In: Proc. of the 4th Annual IEEE Int. Conf. Pervasive Computing and Com-munications Workshops PERCOMW 2006, March 13-17, 2006, IEEE Computer Society Press, Los Alamitos (2006)
2. Bouillon, L., Vanderdonckt, J.: Retargeting Web Pages to other Computing Platforms with VAQUITA. In: Proc. of IEEE Working Conf. on Reverse Engineering WCRE 2002, October 28 -November 1, 2002, pp. 339–348. IEEE Computer Society Press, Los Alamitos (2002)
3. Clerckx, T., Vandervelpen, C., Luyten, K., Coninx, K.: A Task Driven User Interface Archi-tecture for Ambient Intelligent Environments. In: Proc. of 10th ACM Int. Conf. on Intelligent User Interfaces IUI 2006, Sydney, January 29 -February 1, 2006, pp. 309–311. ACM Press, New York (2006)
4. Coutaz, J., Lachenal, C., Dupuy-Chessa, S.: Ontology for Multi-surface Interaction. In: Proc. of 9th IFIP TC 13 Int. Conf. on Human-Computer Interaction INTERACT 2003, Zurich, September 1-5, 2003, pp. 447–454. IOS Press, Amsterdam (2003)
5. Dey, A.K., Salber, D., Abowd, G.D.: A Conceptual Framework and a Toolkit for Supporting the Rapid Prototyping of Context-Aware Applications. Human-Computer Interaction Journal 16(2-4), 97–166 (2001)
6. Ghorbel, M., Mokhtari, M., Renouard, S.: A Distributed Approach for Assistive Service Provi-sion in Pervasive Environment. In: Proc. of 4th Int. workshop on Wireless mobile applications and services on WLAN hotspots WMASH 2006, Los Angeles, September 29, 2006, pp. 91–100. ACM Press, New York (2006)
7. Giaglis, G.M., Kourouthanassis, P., Tsamakos, A.: Towards a Classification Framework for Mobile Location Services. In: Mennecke, B.E., Strader, T.J. (eds.) Mobile commerce: technology, theory, and applications, pp. 67–85. IGI Publishing, Hershey (2003)
8. Nazari Shirehjini, A.A., Klar, F., Kirste, T.: 3DSim: Rapid Prototyping Ambient Intelligence. In: Proc. of the 2005 Joint Conf. on Smart objects and ambient intelligence: innovative context-aware services: usages and technologies sOc-EUSAI 2005, Grenoble, October 2005. ACM Int. Conf. Proc. Series, vol. 121, pp. 303–307 (2005)

9. Orriëns, B., Yang, J., Papazoglou, M.P.: Model Driven Service Composition. In: Orlowska, M.E., Weerawarana, S., Papazoglou, M.P., Yang, J. (eds.) ICSOC 2003. LNCS, vol. 2910, pp. 75–90. Springer, Heidelberg (2003)
10. Pinhanez, C.: The Everywhere Displays Projector: A Device to Create Ubiquitous Graphical Interfaces. In: Abowd, G.D., Brumitt, B., Shafer, S. (eds.) UbiComp 2001. LNCS, vol. 2201, pp. 315–331. Springer, Heidelberg (2001)
11. Tan, D.S., Czerwinski, M.: Effects of Visual Separation and Physical Discontinuities when Dis-tributing Information across Multiple Displays. In: Proc. of 9th IFIP TC 13 Int. Conf. on Human-Computer Interaction INTERACT 2003, Zurich, September 1-5, 2003, pp. 9–16. IOS Press, Amsterdam (2003)
12. Vanderdonckt, J., Puerta, A.R.: Computer-Aided Design of User Interfaces II. In: Proc. of 3rd Int. Conf. of Computer-Aided Design of User Interfaces CADUI 1999, Louvain-la-Neuve, October 21-23, 1999. Information Systems Series, pp. 21–23. Kluwer Academics, Dordrecht (1999)
13. Wolff, A., Forbrig, P., Reichart, D.: Tool Support for Model-Based Generation of Advanced User Interfaces. In: Proc. of the MoDELS 2005 Workshop on Model Driven Development of Ad-vanced User Interfaces MDDAUI 2005, Montego Bay, CEUR Workshop Proceedings, vol. 159 (October 2, 2005)
14. Ziegert, T., Lauff, M., Heuser, L.: Device Independent Web Applications – The Author Once – Display Everywhere Approach. In: Koch, N., Fraternali, P., Wirsing, M. (eds.) ICWE 2004. LNCS, vol. 3140, pp. 244–255. Springer, Heidelberg (2004)

Supporting Ambient Environments by Extended Task Models

Maik Wurdel*, Christoph Burghardt*, and Peter Forbrig

Department of Computer Science, University of Rostock,
Albert Einstein Str. 21, 18055 Rostock, Germany
{maik.wurdel,christoph.burghardt,peter.forbrig}@.uni-rostock.de

Abstract. Task models are able to specify the behavior of actors in ambient environments in a compact and readable form. Their original notations have to be extended to meet the requirements in this context. The corresponding tool support has to be flexible in terms of integrating domain concepts rapidly. We propose a model-based approach for tool support of task model editors. By doing so, new modeling concepts can be introduced easily. Thus task models can be extended and provide a basis for analysis and high level design for a wide spread of domains. We fortify our approach by an example in the domain of AmI.

Keywords: Task model, AmI, model-based development, Markov model.

1 Introduction

Requirements engineering can be supported by specifying the behavior of actors by use cases, sequence diagrams, activity diagrams and task models. To model the behavior in an adequate manner the fundamentals of the domain have to be taken into account as well as the tasks users are able to perform using the envisioned software system.

Based on our experience with task models we discovered that task models need to incorporate the concepts of the domain as well as the corresponding tool support. In [1] an extension of task models was presented that allows a transformation into Markov models, which are widely used in Ambient Intelligence (AmI). They have the disadvantage of very large specifications. Task models are able to specify the same information more compact. The transformation algorithm allows to generate an initial version of a Markov model from a task model that can be adapted in further development. In order to achieve high flexibility in terms of adaptability we propose the application of model-driven development (MDD) to design tool support for task models and other models as well.

The structure of the remainder of this paper is as follows. Section 2 elaborates on requirements engineering and the importance of domain concepts within this phase of development. Section 3 briefly reviews task modeling approaches and

---

* Supported by a grant of the German Research Foundation (DFG), Graduate School 1424, Multimodal Smart Appliance Ensembles for Mobile Applications (MuSAMA).

M. Mühlhäuser et al. (Eds.): AmI 2007 Workshops, CCIS 11, pp. 131–138, 2008.

examines previously made extensions of task models. In section 4 we propose our approach of developing task modeling environments, followed by section 5 which fortifies this approach by an example for AmI. Finally in section 6 we draw the conclusion and give an outlook to future research avenues.

2   Requirements Engineering and the Domain of Concern

Developing software in an engineering like approach is based on the elicitation and documentation of requirements. Requirements engineering denotes the task of eliciting the system and user requirements during analysis phase of software engineering [2]. User requirements are defined as a rather abstract form of requirements using natural language and diagrams (e.g UML [3]) whereas system requirements are more detailed descriptions of the offered services and can be considered as contract between stakeholder and software developer. System requirements are usually derived from user requirements by gradual refinement.

To capture software requirements the problem domain has to be analyzed according to the envisioned functions of the software system. This process can not be carried out by the developer on its own, but needs close cooperation with the domain experts. Thus created artifacts, such as analysis models and requirements documents, have to be understandable for the stakeholder as well as formal enough to start development. Extracted requirements have to reflect the concepts and terminology of the domain [2], because using this terminology fosters stakeholders understanding of the artifacts and paying regard to the domain concepts is crucial for the feasibility of the development since these concepts express the special constraints and fundamentals of the application domain. The subset of the domain concepts which are regarded as important for the envisioned software systems are denoted as the *Domain of Concern*. Retaining this subset during requirements elicitation is needed to develop the system in an adequate manner.

In what follows we elaborate on model notations, in particular task models, that provide capabilities of capturing user interface (UI) requirements.

3   Utilization of Task Models

Task models are a common accepted tool to capture requirements during analysis phase of interactive system development. They describe which activities have to be carried out to achieve a certain user goal. Several notations with different focus were introduced to model the tasks and activities including there interrelation, such as GOMS, GTA, CTT, TKS or HTA [4,5,6,7,8]. Even though these notations differ in level of granularity, attributes and expressiveness they all share the same tenet: tasks are arranged hierarchically whereas tasks are decomposed into sub-tasks until an atomic level, the action, is reached. The most common notation, ConcurTaskTree (CTT), introduced by Paternó [6] uses hierarchical task trees and temporal dependencies to specify the possible execution order of actions to accomplish a certain goal. Nodes of the tree correspond to different task types and temporal relationships are represented by arcs between sibling tasks. In Fig. 1 a coarse-grained task model for a simplified digital library application is given as CTT specification.

In the analysis stage during the development of interactive systems task models contribute to a thorough understanding of how users achieve certain goals using the envisioned application. The designed models can be used as basis for stakeholder discussions and be revised based on the feedback of the domain experts. Thus development cycles can be triggered without designing costly prototypes by animating task models or generating abstract prototypes automatically from task models.

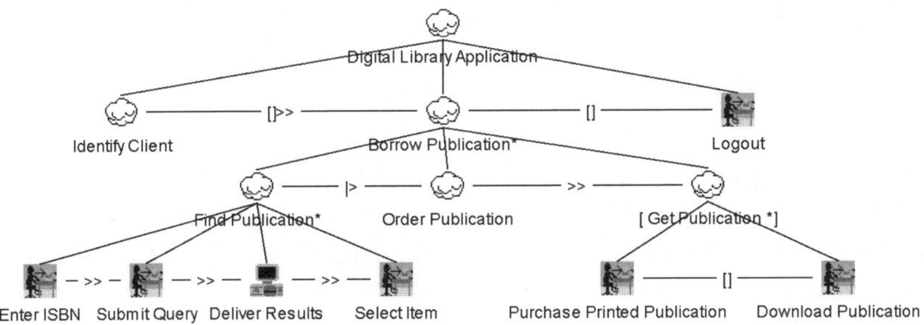

Fig. 1. Coarse-Grained Example of a Task Model

In recent years task modeling has been gained much attention especially in the research field of model-based UI development ([9,10,11,12]) where task models were introduced as design tool to specify the abstract user system interaction. Most model-based UI development processes use task models as initial design artifact to blueprint how a certain goal is achieved using the envisioned software system. Beside the research field of model-based UI development task analysis and modeling through hierarchical task models, such as CTT, has been adopted to ease the design of software systems in other domains as well [1,13,14].

We argue that task modeling can be employed for the development of software systems in general which exhibit a high degree of interaction with the user. Note that pro-active assistance in AmI can be considered as a form of interaction as well. Thus task models build a general foundation for user-centered design independent from the domain of concern, however the domain concepts have to be taken into account. Hence extensions of the meta-model are often necessary to incorporate the domain concepts in task models. In Table 1 different types of extensions are illustrated.

Note that extensions can be made on different levels: syntactically and/or semantically. Syntactical enhancements introduce new modeling elements whereas semantical extensions adapt the underlying meaning of existing model elements.

Table 1. Dimensions of Domain Enhancements

Type	Description	Examples
Task Type	New nodes are introduced which extended the set of CTT node types.	Decision Node for Context of Use integration [9,15], Cooperative Task of CCTT [6]
Operator Set	New operators are introduced, restrictions of usage are eased or new constraints are proposed.	Temporal dependencies between arbitrary tasks [16], Comprehensive operators to enable cooperative task models [17], Adaptation of the information exchange operators using input/output ports [18]
Attributes	New attributes are assigned to tasks or operators.	Priority of task execution [1], Platform dependencies of tasks [10], Enabling condition for context-sensitive tasks [9,15]

4   Using MDD to Support Task Modeling

Task modeling environments, like Teresa [11], TaoSpec [12] or CTTE [11] help software designers using task models during development by computer supported creation and manipulation of models, but these tools are not able to cope with pragmatical extensions of task models. MDD seems to be suitable to develop modeling environments which have to be flexible in terms of extending the subject of modeling and incorporating the domain of concern.

MDD is a development paradigm which employs a set of declarative models that describe the system from different viewpoints. Model transformations link these models by using one or more models as input and derive an output model. Transformations are performed several times until the lowest level of abstraction is reached, such as code-level or any other executable specification. The advantages of MDD are, beside others, the raised level of abstraction, the underlying concept of separation of concerns and the concealment of technical details which are encoded in the transformation.

Our task modeling environment is based on the Eclipse platform [19] and several frameworks for MDD. We are using a UML-CASE Tool (Rational Rose) to specify our meta models, e.g. the task model, in terms of class diagrams and generate model and editor code as Eclipse plug-in (using ecore-models and the EMF [19]). This code includes the model classes, serialization, a tree-based editor to manipulate the model and a wizard to create new model files. Afterwards the editor can be adapted using Java and the Eclipse API. New modeling concept can be introduced easily by means of adapting the meta-model and regenerate the modeling environment. Manually changed code of the generated editor can be retained using Java Annotations.

In the next section we elaborate on a domain specific extension of the CTT task model for AmI. Further on this extended task model is employed to generate a domain specific model, the Markov model.

5   Task Models and Dynamic Bayesian Networks

With the advent of ubiquitous computing intention recognition of users has become an interesting research field. It examines, among others, the possibility of inferring the intention of users while acting in a ubiquitous environment to achieve appropriate computer supported pro-active assistance. Graphical probabilistic models, such as Dynamic Bayesian Networks (DBN), are one way to accomplish this task.

In the first part of this section we define graphical probabilistic models and examine their employment for intention recognition. Afterwards our model-based approach of deriving Markov models from annotated task models is presented. We exemplify this process with a basic Markov model.

5.1   Introducing Markov Models

A Bayesian Network (BN) is a probabilistic graphical model that specifies the relations between a finite set of discrete random variables. Formally spoken, a Bayesian Network (BN) is a directed acyclic graph $G = (V, E)$. V is the set of finite vertexes and E denotes the finite set of directed edges. Each node in a BN represents a random variable Q with a conditional probability distribution. Edges describe the dependencies of random variables whereas a directed edge from node A to B denotes that the state of B conditionally depends on the state A. DBNs are time-sliced based and in each time slice the possible state of the system is defined in terms of a BN, but conditionally dependencies can occur between variables of different time slices. This is used to express that the value of a variable at time slice t can depend on a variable at time slice $t - 1$.

The conditional probability distribution of the random variable Q in its simplest form is a discrete distribution with a number of states. The state transition probabilities are stored in a conditional probability table (CPT), a matrix.

For the sake of brevity, we omit the details about how to perform inference and filtering with these models and the interested reader is referred to specific literature [20].

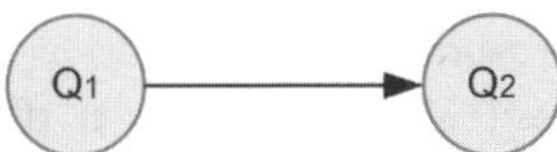

Fig. 2. Simple Markov Model

The simplest form of a DBN is the Markov model (Fig. 2). This type of model is characterized by the Markov property which embodies that the state of the variable Q in the current time slice depends only on the previous time slice. The transition probabilities from one to the next states are stored in a matrix. In the next chapter we illustrate the use of such a model for intention analysis in a meeting environment and how to ease the development process with task models.

5.2 Employing Task Models for the Generation of Markov Models

We exemplify our approach by modeling the possible behavior of a team performing a meeting. The agenda is defined in terms of a task model. The example, taken from [1], is depicted in Fig. 3. Three persons want to give a talk (task A, B, C). A discussion (task D) is scheduled afterwards. The aim of the intention analysis is to find out the right sequence, the meeting is taking place.

To utilize task models in the domain of intention analysis, they need to be extended to comprise the CPTs. The priority attribute is used to give the designer a way to store these transition probabilities. The automatically derived Markov model is depicted in Fig. 4. The numbers assigned to the directed edges are the state transition probabilities which are calculated according to the conditional probability. For further information, refer to [1].

As already pointed out Markov models are characterized by the Markov property which embodies that the state in the current time slice depends only on the previous time slice. This is not common in real-world situations. For the intention analysis it is important whether A, B or C gives the talk first during the execution of the meeting. Still, this fact can be captured in Markov models, but the number of states rises exponentially to track which tasks were executed beforehand.

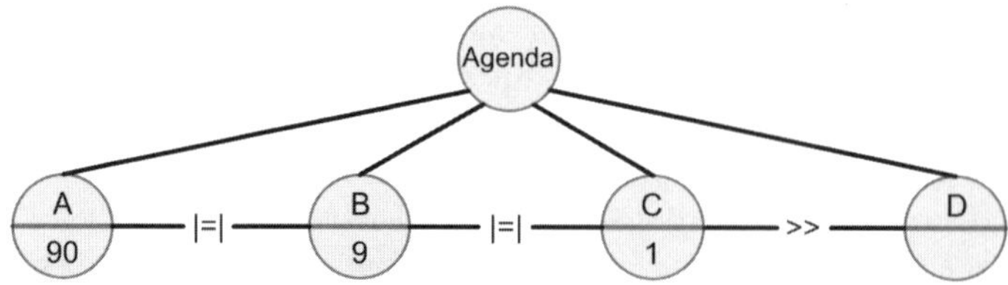

Fig. 3. Meeting Agenda Task Model

The tasks A, B, C in the task model can be executed in any order (denoted by the order independence operator $|=|$). A state in the corresponding Markov model represents already presented talks whereas the execution order is not considered. This causes $n! + 1$ states whereas n denotes the number of order independent talks. Additionally one state for the execution of D plus an initial state are added. Thus 9 states are created.

Note that the number of generated states strongly depends on the temporal operators used to connect tasks. The state explosion arises because of the order independence operator (for choice and concurrent applies the same) whereas other operators do not cause this problem (e.g. enabling), but human behavior is often not that well defined and certain.

The simple example, consisting of 4 tasks in the task model evolves into 9 states (Fig. 4) in the Markov model. The number of states grows exponential in more realistic and comprehensive examples. Designing the Markov model from scratch is therefore a more tedious and error-prone task. Consequently starting

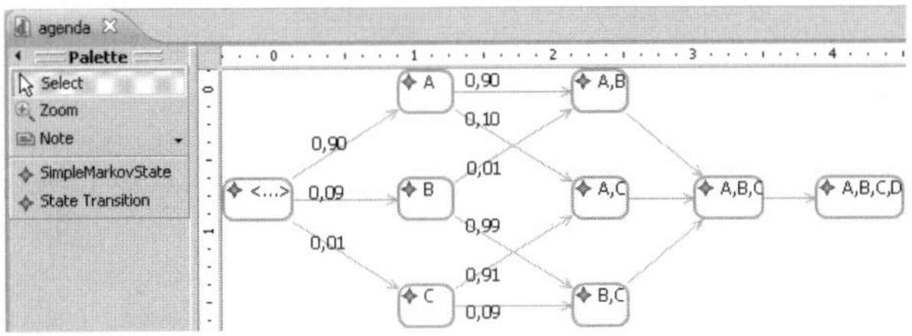

Fig. 4. Markov Model of Meeting Performance

to model on a higher level of abstraction and generate the probabilistic model seems to be more suitable to tackle the intention analysis. Thus the initial design is shifted from Markov models with CPTs to task models. Subsequent adaptation of the generated Markov model can be performed by the designer.

The priority attribute of a task reflects the domain of concern in this scenario. In order to achieve a convenient tool support this extension was integrated in our task modeling environment by adding a task attribute to the meta model and regenerating the editor. Moreover we defined a meta model for Markov models, generated an editor and specified a transformation of task models to Markov models which are visualized by means of a graphical editor including rich graphical manipulations of the model (Fig. 4) specified using the GMF [19].

6   Conclusion and Future Research

In this paper we have shown that integrating the concepts of the domain into task modeling is highly important to model the tasks and their relation to the domain in an adequate manner. Thus we have presented an approach for developing task modeling environments which is able to cope with extensions in order to integrate new modeling concepts easily. Our task modeling environment is developed following the proposed approach and we already applied other changes to the modeling environment and regenerated it [15].

We have given an example of a domain specific extension of task models to derive Markov models which are used in our SmartLab. Furthermore we defined the Markov model in the same vein as the task model and implemented the transformation algorithm. We were able to shift the design to a higher level of abstraction and reduced the complexity of the initial design which can be adapted in subsequent development steps.

Based on this experience we believe that task models are instrumental for other domains as well where high level descriptions of tasks and action are needed. This hypothesis has to examined in future research. Another future research avenue would be to employ task models to specify the behavior of each team member as well and infer the intention of the team based on the agenda model and individual actor models. Further on we are still in progress of investigating if changes in the Markov model can be mapped backward into the task model to achieve a round-trip engineering process.

References

1. Giersich, M., Forbrig, P., Fuchs, G., Kirste, T., Reichart, D., Schumann, H.: Towards an Integrated Approach for Task Modeling and Human Behavior Recognition. In: Jacko, J.A. (ed.) HCI 2007. LNCS, vol. 4550, pp. 1109–1118. Springer, Heidelberg (2007)
2. Sommerville, I.: Software Engineering: International Computer Science, 8th edn. Addison-Wesley Longman Publishing Co., Inc., Boston, MA, USA (2006)
3. UML: Unified modeling language (Accessed July 10, 2007), available at, http://www.uml.org/
4. Card, S.K., Newell, A., Moran, T.P.: The psychology of human-computer interaction. L. Erlbaum Associates, Mahwah (1983)
5. van der Veer, G., Lenting, B., Bergevoet, B.: Gta: Groupware task analysis - modeling complexity. Acta Psychologica 91, 297–332 (1996)
6. Paterno, F.: Model-Based Design and Evaluation of Interactive Applications. Springer-Verlag, London, UK (1999)
7. Johnson, P., Johnson, H., Hamilton, F.: Getting the knowledge into hci: Theoretical and practical aspects of task knowledge structures. Cognitive Task Analysis (2000)
8. Annett, J., Duncan, K.D.: Task analysis and training design. Journal of Occupational Psychology 41, 211–221 (1967)
9. Luyten, K., Vandervelpen, C., Coninx, K.: Task modeling for ambient intelligent environments: design support for situated task executions. In: 4th International Workshop of TAMODIA, pp. 87–94. ACM Press, New York (2005)
10. Seffah, A., Forbrig, P.: Multiple User Interfaces: Towards a Task-Driven and Patterns-Oriented Design Model. In: Forbrig, P., Limbourg, Q., Urban, B., Vanderdonckt, J. (eds.) DSV-IS 2002. LNCS, vol. 2545, pp. 118–132. Springer, Heidelberg (2002)
11. Mori, G., Paterno, F., Santoro, C.: Design and development of multidevice user interfaces through multiple logical descriptions. IEEE Trans. Softw. Eng. 30(8), 507–520 (2004)
12. Dittmar, A., Forbrig, P., Heftberger, S., Stary, C.: Tool support for task modelling - a constructive exploration. In: Proc. EHCI-DSVIS 2004 (2004)
13. Trapp, M., Schmettow, M.: Consistency in use through model based user interface development. In: The Many Faces of Consistency in Cross-Platform Design (2006)
14. Eisenstein, J., Rich, C.: Agents and guis from task models. In: IUI 2002, pp. 47–54. ACM Press, New York (2002)
15. Wurdel, M., Forbrig, P., Radhakrishnan, T., Sinnig, D.: Patterns for Task- and Dialog-Modeling. In: Jacko, J.A. (ed.) HCI 2007. LNCS, vol. 4550, pp. 1226–1235. Springer, Heidelberg (2007)
16. Forbrig, P., Dittmar, A., Müller, A.: Adaptive Task Modelling: From Formal Models to XML Representations. In: Multiple User Interfaces, pp. 169–192. John Wiley & Sons, Chichester (2004)
17. Sinnig, D., Wurdel, M., Forbrig, P., Chalin, P., Khendek, F.: Practical extensions for task models. In: 6th International Workshop of TAMODIA (2007) (Forthcoming)
18. Klug, T., Kangasharju, J.: Executable task models. In: 4th International Workshop of TAMODIA, pp. 119–122. ACM Press, New York (2005)
19. Eclipse (accessed August 10, 2007), available at http://www.eclipse.org/
20. Murphy, K.: Dynamic Bayesian Networks: Representation, Inference and Learning. PhD thesis (2002)

Prototyping of Multimodal Interactions for Smart Environments Based on Task Models

Sebastian Feuerstack, Marco Blumendorf, and Sahin Albayrak

DAI-Labor
Technische Universität Berlin
Secretary TEL 14, Ernst-Reuter Platz 7
D-10587 Berlin, Germany
{Sebastian.Feuerstack,Marco.Blumendorf,Sahin.Albayrak}
@dai-labor.de

Abstract. Smart environments offer interconnected sensors, devices, and appliances that can be considered for interaction to substantially extend the potentially available modality mix. This promises a more natural and situation aware human computer interaction. Technical challenges and differences in interaction principles for distinct modalities restrict multimodal systems to specialized systems that support specific situations only. To overcome these limitations enabling an easier integration of new modalities to enhance interaction in smart environments, we propose a task-based notation that can be interpreted at runtime. The notation supports evolutionary prototyping of new interaction styles for already existing interactive systems. We eliminate the gap between design- and runtime, since support for additional modalities can be prototyped at runtime to an already existing interactive system.

1 Introduction

The change from single computing systems towards smart environments connecting complex networks of devices leads to new requirements for applications and human-computer interaction. A smart environment extends the amount of potential interaction devices from a small amount of isolated utilized devices like for instance a PDA or a smart phone to combinations of devices that enable addressing a mixture of modalities. Together with various interconnected sensors that make the environment aware of the user, interactions can be embedded in the environment: Not a specific device, but the whole environment can be used as the interface.

Whereas model-based approaches introduce various abstractions to design interactive systems, each enabling a comprehensive view of the whole application, they are currently focused on analysis- and design support. Thus, these approaches require the developer to consider all combinations of devices, which the interactive system should be able to adapt to during the development process. Each new mix of devices and modalities requires going through most of these design models again to compile a new user interface.

This paper presents our approach to prototype multimodal interactions in smart environments. It extends an approach that we have presented earlier [3] by supporting

M. Mühlhäuser et al. (Eds.): AmI 2007 Workshops, CCIS 11, pp. 139–146, 2008.

prototyping of additional modalities that have not been considered during development of the application. Realizing such an approach requires two problems to be solved:

- A *notation* that is comprehensive enough to be interpreted at runtime while also providing the application designer with an overview of the whole application, because adding new multimodal interactions often affects the complete interaction flow of the application. The notation should support prototyping of new interactions without changing the original application.
- *Runtime interpretation of the user interface model with support for model synchronization*: The runtime environment must reflect commonly used design time models describing several abstract views of an interactive application and has to support mappings to the runtime environment to eliminate the gap between design and runtime. Every modification to the models that is done during prototyping has to be instantly propagated to be synchronized with all other models.

This paper focuses on the notation that we can interpret in our runtime environment that we have successfully implemented. Instead of presenting the runtime architecture in greater detail we concentrate on examples to discuss the most important aspect, the synchronization requirements for such a runtime environment. The paper is structured as follows: The next section starts with discussing the actual requirements and issues for prototyping multimodal applications in smart environments. Based on this discussion we propose a task model notation that enables a model-based evolutionary prototyping at runtime and specially addresses synchronization problems that occur when prototyping new forms of interactions to a running interactive application. To evaluate our approach we describe the Smart Home Energy Assistant (SHEA) that we have implemented with our model-based runtime environment (MASP[1]) [3] and enhance the SHEA with a new interaction device, a gesture and orientation aware remote control to illustrate our approach. Section 3 discusses the related work that has been considered. Finally, section 4 concludes the paper with a short evaluation of our approach and outlines future work.

2   A Task Modeling Notation Supporting Smart Environments

The runtime interpretation of task models requires a notation that specifies the interactive system detailed enough to be executed without further information. Thus it requires integrating static concepts with a temporal description. We found the ConcurTaskTree (CTT) notation [10] a good starting point as it allows a user-centric design enabling a step by step abstract to concrete modeling using task trees, which eases prototyping. The notation also allows focusing on the user's goals by defining sequences of tasks using a LOTUS-based temporal specification.

However, to interpret CTT-based task trees generating user interfaces for smart environments at runtime, some changes to CTT are required:

---

[1] MASP - Multi-Access Service Platform.

- CTT abstracts from the functional core of the system, as for analyzing interactive systems it is focused to the interaction with the user. In smart environments continuously acquired sensor data or the physical control of appliances can influence the interaction with the user by triggering or disabling user interaction tasks.
- CTT allows specifying objects that are required for task performance but does not provide the possibility to explicitly model the object usage by including it into its graphical notation. From a designer's perspective an explicitly modeled object usage enables consistency and feasibility checks of the concept distribution. In smart environments tasks can be extensively distributed and the object usage enables to identify those tasks that are relevant for continuous updates of sensor data or synchronizes tasks that are interconnected by referring to the same domain objects.
- The notation is mainly targeted to model interactions that are independent from any modality. Modeling modality specific interactions is limited to hide tasks for devices with limited capabilities. Whereas CTT abstracts from how a tasks is performed by a specific device, decision nodes [2] can be used to design device specific task realizations. To our knowledge modeling interactions involving simultaneous usage of more than one device using the task model is not possible by using decision nodes, since decision nodes describe a choice and are not addressing simultaneous usage of more than one modality. Further on interdependencies between the used devices to implement complementary or redundant relations [8] between the modalities cannot be addressed.

In the following sections we describe how we are addressing these issues by introducing changes to the CTT notation to support modeling multimodal interaction in smart environments. First we describe the way to refer to the functional core of an interactive system by changing the task types; secondly we enhance the notation to explicitly annotate the domain concepts as well as the object flow through the task tree. Finally we introduce our approach to prototype the simultaneous usage of modalities using interconnected task trees.

2.1 Referencing the Functional Core from a Task Tree

Different to CTT we distinguish two types of interaction tasks: output interaction tasks (OIT) and input interaction tasks (IIT). While OITs require no human intervention but present information to the user until they become disabled by another task, IITs require human intervention like data input. Additionally to this understanding of interaction tasks we use a different interpretation of "application tasks" since modeling the information exchange with the backend system is crucial to be able to use the task tree definition for the user interface creation at runtime. To enable a loose coupling of the smart environments infrastructure to the user interface and an easier inclusion of backend services, we define application tasks as solely executed by the application without user's intervention, not offering a presentation to the user.

2.2 Annotating Domain Concepts and Modeling the Object Flow

Utilizing task trees as the workflow definition of a user interface at runtime also requires a stronger and more detailed connection of task and domain concepts. Such a connection on the one hand allows the identification of inaccurate domain abstractions not conforming to the task abstraction as well as the review of the distribution of concepts over the whole task tree and on the other hand provides the basis to derive meaningful user interfaces based on the task tree definition. While CTT already allows the annotation of objects and the marking of an LOTUS operator as "information passing" [9], this approach does not completely reflect the requirements to model interactive systems embedded into smart environments. Such systems require modeling of the object flow throughout the complete task tree, which considers the object synchronization not only between two tasks but between all tasks that are enabled and are using the same domain concepts. Following the approach of Klug et al. [5] we annotate the required objects as well as the access type directly to each task of the task tree allowing a fine grained modeling of the object flow.

An abridged version of the task model of the SHEA application we have implemented is depicted in figure 1. The application discovers all appliances, which we have installed in our ambient test-bed and presents an overview of all appliances. By selecting an appliance the user can control and inspect past energy consumptions as well as extrapolations of future consumptions by issuing voice commands or using a wall-mounted touch display. Like depicted in figure 1, the access type is limited to read (R), modify (M) or create (C) operations. Introducing the declaration (D) of each object before the first usage also allows the definition of a scope for each object. Similar to a programming language each object has to be declared before it can be created and only can be modified or read after it has been successfully created. Under each task's name, we annotate the domain objects type in square brackets (by referencing a class name) together with the domain object name, whose attributes can be accessed by using a dot followed by the attribute name.

During interpretation of the task tree at runtime the domain object annotation is used to synchronize the enabled tasks objects, which are actually performed. Thus, if one task modifies a domain object and another task that is enabled concurrently has read access to the same domain object, the task receives the object's modifications instantly. Further on, the declaration of objects enables the runtime environment to keep track of objects and to remove objects that are no longer required as the user continues the interaction.

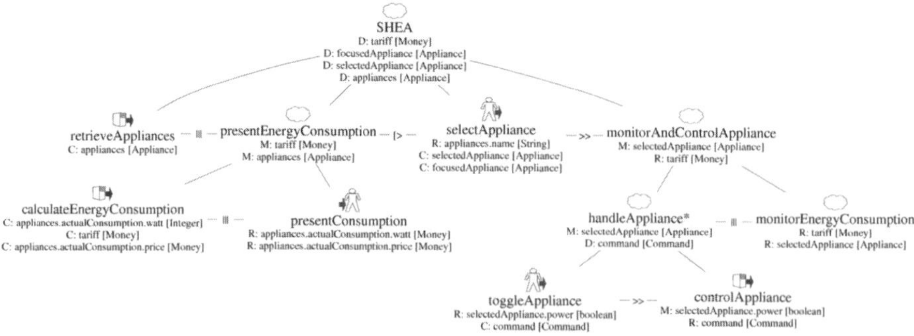

Fig. 1. Abridged task tree of the SHEA application

Inaccurate domain abstractions that do not conform to the task abstraction can be identified easily by checking the cluttering and granularity of the object annotations. Furthermore basic automatic consistency checks (i.e. create before modify and read) across multiple subtasks are possible, because declarations as well as all defined operations are also summarized in the next higher level of abstraction. The designer can further partition and detail domain concepts in sub-trees together with the tasks performing on the concepts. This ensures that the resulting interactive application is not switching between several concepts too often, which make the application complicated to use, since it raises the cognitive workload of the user. If the same concepts are spread over the whole tree remodeling the task tree should be considered, regarding two aspects. On the one hand the conceptual abstractions should be reviewed and it should be checked, whether these concepts can be detailed conforming to the associated task abstractions. On the other hand the domain object distribution should be solved by moving tasks that are performing on the same domain objects together into the same sub-tree.

2.3   Interconnecting Tasks and Objects to Prototype the Simultaneous Usage of Modalities

Prototyping of additional interaction capabilities for an already existing interactive application is done by designing a new modality specific task tree. This tree addresses the specific tasks that are describing a new way of interaction that the additional interaction device should support. Modality specific trees are interpreted in parallel to the application task tree and are related to the application task tree by referring to some of the application task tree's objects and tasks.

Figure 2 depicts a modality specific task tree we have prototyped for the SHEA application that describes a remote control that is aware of the direction it points to and is able to detect gestures that are interpreted as appliance control commands. The remote requires the user to point to an appliance first, and then waits that the user presses the remote's button, which starts the gesture detection and initiates a command for the selected appliance that is issued after the button has been released by the user.

The modality specific tree can be interconnected by the designer with the application tree using two synchronization methods: On the one hand domain objects of the application task tree can be synchronized with the modality specific task tree. This is specified by annotating the same domain objects names to the modality specific task tree. For instance, to interconnect the object that the remote is pointing to (see figure 2: *focusedAppliance*) with a presentation of the focus in the SHEA task tree (in the *selectAppliance* task of figure 1). Further on, all discovered appliances (stored by the appliances domain object) as well as the actual selected appliance (*selectedAppliance* object) get synchronized between the remote and the SHEA application.

On the other hand tasks of the modality specific tree can be connected to tasks of the application task tree. In our example we use task synchronization when the user has to choose the application he wants to control (in the *selectAppliance* task). Since both trees are started simultaneously, the first task that the user is required to perform in the SHEA application is to select an appliance to monitor its energy consumption

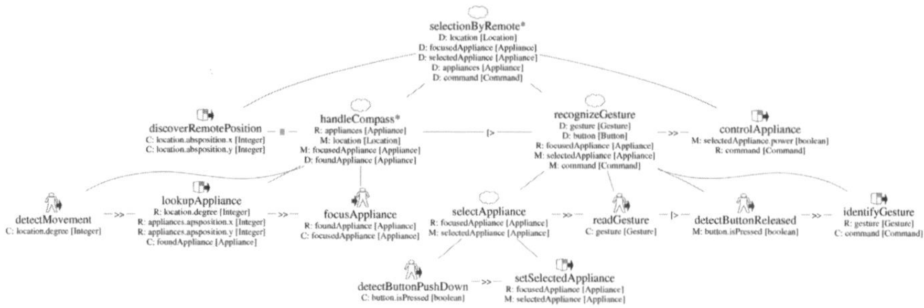

Fig. 2. A modality specific task tree that describes a remote with support for gesture and orientation detection to control interactive applications

history. Following the design of the application task tree this has to be done by choosing one appliance of a list of appliances. Using the remote the user just needs to point to the appliance (*handleCompass*) and press the remote's button to select it to perform the *selectAppliance* task. We interconnect both *selectAppliance* tasks using a directional connection, which is only enabled if the connected application task's trees task is enabled and does not require changes to the application task tree. The remote can be used independently but if both trees are in the same state, requiring the user to select an appliances both *selectAppliance* tasks can be either performed by using the remote or the touch display originally supported by the application task tree.

In our current implementation we have implemented support for interconnecting IIT and support every temporal operator of the CTT notation for interconnected tasks. Interconnecting application tasks is supported as well (see *controlAppliance* task in both figures) but only describes that a call to the functional core has to be done once only. The modality specific tree should follow the basic interaction flow of the application task tree since this eases the complete integration of the prototyped interaction with the new modality into the application later on. Following a prototyping approach, not the whole application is required to be supported by the modality specific task tree. Thus, in the beginning only parts can be covered by the new modality and can be continuously evolved during the prototyping process.

The order of all interconnected tasks must remain the same for both, the application task tree and the modality specific task tree. In our actual implementation the remote of figure 2 cannot be designed to support initiating the control command before selecting an appliance, since this will break the design of the SHEA application. But requiring the same fixed sequence of interconnected tasks for all modality specific trees has the benefit, that the modality specific task tree can be merged with the application task tree after the prototyping process has been finished.

3   Related Work

Research in the area of model-based user interface development mainly concentrates on the creation of models and tools suitable to design models and then derive final user interfaces from these models following a transformational approach following the ideas of the CAMELEON reference framework [1]. Current prototyping approaches following a model-based development process support high- as well as low fidelity prototyping [12] but are limited to design time or are focusing on simulation of the targeted environment using virtual reality technologies [4].

Pribeanu et al. [11] have identified three ways to relate context-sensitive parts to context-insensitive parts of task trees: Firstly, by following a monolithic approach by specifying both parts in one tree. Secondly, by following a separation approach both trees can be connected using decision nodes. Finally, by following a graph-oriented approach that uses general arcs to connect both trees. Clerckx et al. [2] follow the separation approach introducing decision tasks as a modified CTT notation to support context-sensitive user interfaces. In the separation approach continuous context switching at any time on behalf of the user is limited to happen only before a separation task. After a decision has been taken the user or the system, context switching without adding special mappings is not possible and ends up in context switching problems [7]. This is why we rely on separate task trees that are linked to the main applications task tree to prototype various contexts of thus follow a graph-oriented approach. Lewandowski et al. [6] propose an approach for task model assembling based on tree algebra operators to automatically merge task trees. Their composition mechanism can be used to merge the modality-independent application tree with the prototyped modality specific task trees to derive a monolithic task tree.

4 Conclusion and Future Work

Supporting multimodal interaction in smart environments requires extended methods to model applications and their user interfaces. In this paper we present an approach to support the prototyping of additional modalities to already running interactive systems based on a modified Concurrent Task Tree notation. The notation explicitly includes the annotation of domain concepts to make the task designer aware of concept distribution and supports modeling actions triggered by context changes through the use of application tasks. We are currently working on formalizing and improving our notation by supporting the tree concatenation approach [6] to merge a successfully prototyped modality back to the main application task tree. In addition we are currently experimenting with prototyping a combined gaze direction and voice control for the SHEA application to further improve our user interfaces runtime environment for smart environments (MASP) in our Ambient Living Test-bed, set up as part of the Service Centric Home[2] project at the DAI-Labor of the Technische Universität Berlin.

References

1. Calvary, G., et al.: A unifying reference framework for multi-target user interfaces. Interacting with Computers 15(3), 289–308 (2003)
2. Clerckx, T., den Bergh, J.V., Coninx, K.: Modeling Multi-Level Context Influence on the User Interface, pp. 57–61 (2006)

---

[2] http://www.sercho.de

 3. Feuerstack, S., Blumendorf, M., Albayrak, S.: Bridging the Gap between Model and Design of User Interfaces. In: Proccedings of Informatik 2006, Dresden, pp. 131–137 (2006)
 4. Gonzalez, J.M., Vanderdonckt, J., Arteaga, J.M.: A Method for Developing 3D User Interfaces of Information Systems. In: Proc. of 6th Int. Conf. on Computer-Aided Design of User Interfaces CADUI 2006, Bucharest, June 6-8, 2006, ch. 7, pp. 85–100. Springer, Berlin (2006)
 5. Klug, T., Kangasharju, J.: Executable task models. In: Proceedings of the 4th international Workshop on Task Models and Diagrams. TAMODIA 2005, pp. 119–122. ACM Press, New York (2005)
 6. Lewandowski, A., Lepreux, S., Bourguin, G.: Tasks models merging for high-level component composition. In: Proc. of HCI International (2007)
 7. Luyten, K., Vandervelpen, C., den Bergh, J.V.: Coninx: Context-sensitive User Interfaces for Ambient Environments: Design, Development and Deployment. In: Mobile Computing and Ambient Intelligence: The Challenge of Multimedia (2005)
 8. Nigay, L., Coutaz, J.: Multifeature Systems: The CARE Properties and Their Impact on Software Design Intelligence and Multimodality in Multimedia Interfaces (1997)
 9. Mori, G., Paternò, F., Santoro, C.: Design and Development of Multi-Device User Interfaces through Multiple Logical Descriptions. IEEE Transactions on Software Engineering (2004)
10. Paterno, F.: Model-based Design and Evaluation of Interactive Applications. Springer, Berlin (1999)
11. Pribeanu, C., Limbourg, Q., Vanderdonckt, J.: Task Modelling for Context-Sensitive User Interfaces. In: Johnson, C. (ed.) DSV-IS 2001. LNCS, vol. 2220, Springer, Heidelberg (2001)
12. Sottet, J., Calvary, G., Favre, J., Coutaz, J., Demeure, A.: Towards Mappings and Models Transformations for Consistency of Plastic User Interfaces. In: Proceedings of CHI 2006 Workshop The Many Faces of Consistency in Cross-Platform Design (2006)

Challenges to the Model-Driven Generation of User Interfaces at Runtime for Ambient Intelligent Systems

Sebastian Adam[1], Kai Breiner[2], Kizito S. Mukasa[1], and Marcus Trapp[2]

[1] Fraunhofer IESE, Fraunhofer-Platz. 1,
D-67663 Kaiserslautern, Germany
{sebastian.adam,kizito.mukasa}@iese.fraunhofer.de
[2] University of Kaiserslautern, Software Engineering Research Group,
D-67663 Kaiserslautern, Germany
{breiner,marcus.trapp}@informatik.uni-kl.de

Abstract. Context-awareness, personalization and adaptation are among salient features of Ambient Intelligent (AmI) Systems. The User Interfaces (UI) in AmI environments should therefore also be dynamic at runtime. Developing such UIs is challenging since many aspects have to be considered. Most existing approaches follow Model-driven Engineering (MDE) as a solution. However, they only address design time issues. We successfully applied MDE for runtime generation of UI in the BelAmI[1] project but encountered challenges that we presented in this paper. Possible solutions have also been discussed.

Keywords: Model-driven User Interfaces, Ambient Intelligence, Ubiquitous Computing, Adaptive User Interfaces, Usability Patterns

1 Introduction

An Ambient Intelligence (AmI) refers to electronic environments that are sensitive and responsive to the presence of people. In the AmI word devices operate collectively using information and intelligence that is hidden in the network connecting the devices [1]. Specifically, the AmI environment can be characterized by the existence of many gadgets and services, interoperability that yields new (not even envisioned) functionality, growing number of user interface (UI) platforms, ubiquity and mobility. Nevertheless users should control and interact with the environment in a natural and personalized way regardless of the interaction device used. Thus adaptability of the UI to its users and their varying devices, interactive services and environmental contexts at runtime is one of the important features of interactive applications in AmI-Environments.

Model-driven engineering suggests the usage of different models for system und UI-related aspects and promises an efficient handling of system variants. For example there might be a user model, a task model, an environment model, a presentation model, dialog model etc [16]. When all aspects are known at design time, bringing the models together for the generation of the UI is not much problematic. However, AmI-Systems can dynamically change at runtime: new previously unknown services can be

---

[1] BelAmI is a bilateral AmI project between Germany and Hungary (see acknowledgement).

M. Mühlhäuser et al. (Eds.): AmI 2007 Workshops, CCIS 11, pp. 147–155, 2008.

registered or/and existing ones can be removed from the system dynamically. Therefore, the UI must also adapt to the changing functionality of the underlying system and under the consideration of the current user with regard to usability issues. This leads to new challenges when applying the model-driven approach at runtime.

So far, several approaches have been addressing model-driven generation of user interfaces for predefined systems (see [7] for an extensive survey). For example, the work published by Luyten et al. in 2005 [8] addresses issues of context sensitive UIs for AmI-Environments based on model-based user interface development methodology. In another work, an XML-based language for describing runtime user interfaces was introduced [9]. Missing in these works is among others the explicit handling of usability aspects which we see as essential for the generation of usable UIs. In this paper, we suggest a solution for this and present the major challenges related to MDE for AmI.

The remainder of this paper is structured as follows. In section 2, we present our approach for UI generation at runtime in AmI-Systems. By implementing the approach, we encountered the challenges depicted in section 3. This section also contains our first ideas for solution. The paper closes with a section on conclusion and future work.

2 Our UI Generation Approach at Runtime for AmI-Systems

In order to successfully obtain usable UI at runtime, we defined an approach that makes use of models, transformation rules and usability rules. In this way, we were able to capture UI-information, transformation knowledge and usability knowledge as described in the following sections.

It should be noted that the scope of our research lies in the internal procedures of UI design and how to deal with variability in the users and environments state. Therefore, issues like determining the user's experience and mood are beyond the scope of this paper.

2.1 User Interface Modeling

In the model-driven approach, different models are required to capture system and UI aspects. For this purpose, we built our approach upon UsiXML [7]. Based on the four basic levels of abstractions defined in the Cameleon reference framework [3] and by defining a transformation language based on graph grammars, UsiXML appeared to best suit user interface modeling for AmI-Systems. The abstraction levels are used to capture variation of system functionality, users, tasks, environment etc. In user interaction design *task models* are favored to capture the functionality in a technology independent way. To capture the domain knowledge and usage environment, the *domain model* and the *context model* are used respectively. The domain model provides a static view of the conceptual domain objects dealt with and the context model carries various parameters that influence the user interaction (e.g. user capabilities, environmental factors). The latter comes from external sources in the AmI-System at runtime (e.g. sensors, profiles). All these models are found at the top level. Following this level is the *abstract user interface (AUI)* model. here, the UI is defined in the modality independent way. This includes for example, the dialogue flow and dependencies between UI elements. From AUI models a third model layer, the *concrete user interface* (CUI) model, is generated. Elements at this level are modality dependent. Thus there exists a family of models, one for each modality, while toolkit independence is still maintained. The CUI is then transformed into the executable UI implementation with toolkit specific elements (e.g. JSP). The four abstraction levels are shown in Figure 1.

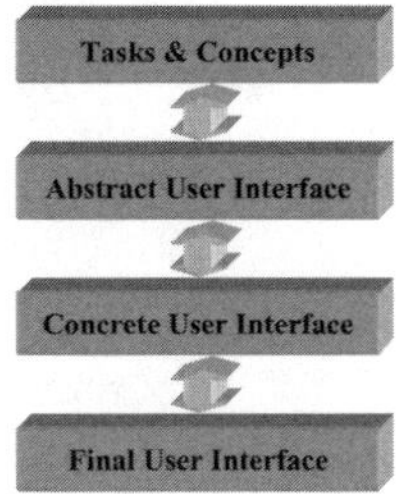

Fig. 1. The four basic levels of the Cameleon reference framework [3]

UsiXML is also a valuable UI specification approach for several other reasons: First it possesses a clear separation of concerns and thus maps well to "intellectual" UI design processes. For example it maps well to UI abstraction levels defined in TORE, the Task and Object-Oriented Requirements approach defined at Fraunhofer IESE [14]. Moreover, the model layers of UsiXML are well aligned with the Model-driven architecture [22] and the transformation rules used are specified by *attributed graph grammar* (AGG) that comes with its own execution engine [6].

2.2 Transformation Rules

Model transformation rules define the automatic generation of models between the abstraction levels. In order to achieve acceptable usability of the generated user interface, formalized usability rules should also be included. User interaction patterns [23, 18] as well as ergonomic guidelines [11] are known to support the design of usable interfaces [4]. Especially for the format of patterns we have developed a method for stepwise formalization into transformation rules. An empirical investigation has showed that formalized patterns enhance the usability of generated user interfaces [2].

2.3 The Usability Engine

To manage the transformation process between the levels of abstraction mentioned earlier (see Figure 1) as well as to manage the usability knowledge, we developed a separate component – the *Usability Engine* – . This component is integrated in the service-oriented infrastructure. It retrieves input data from other services, generates the corresponding UI and sends it to any UI rendering service available. The UI was then deployed on a web-server. Figure 2 shows the architecture with the UI based on Java Server Pages and Struts [19]. The system in our Ambient Assisted Living Lab was developed using the Dynamic Adaptive System Infrastructure (DAiSI) middleware, a middleware platform for dynamic integration of services as well as their reconfiguration during runtime [24]. It consists of Dynaptive Component Model, which defines how a component for dynamic adaptation has to be structured.

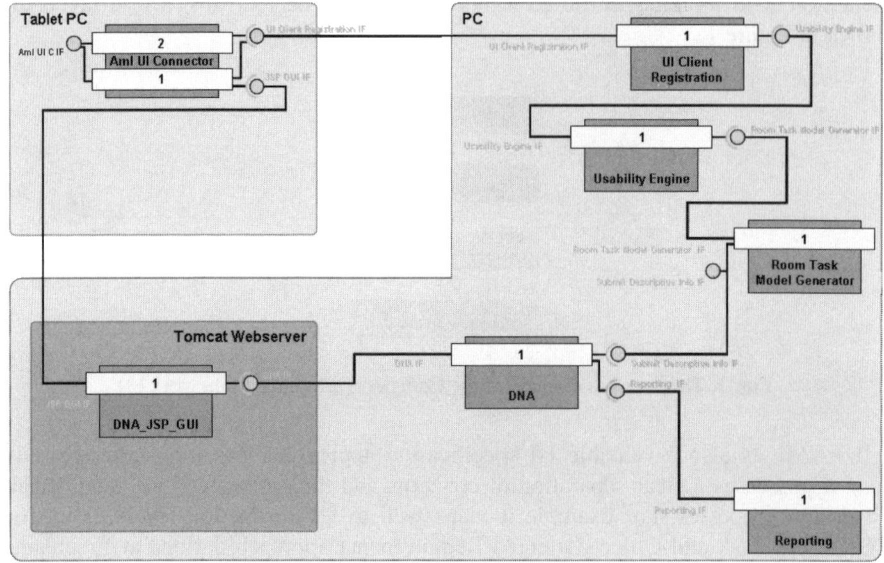

Fig. 2. High level Architecture of our demonstrator application

Now let us give a short introduction of the Dynaptive Component Model. Figure 3 shows the "AmI UI Connector" Component. It consists of several parts: The blue box (*AmI UI Connector*) represents the component itself. Each component may support several configurations depicted by yellow bars (*1st best Configuration, 2nd best Configuration*). Each of these component configurations is specified by component service interfaces, which it requires depicted by the red semi-circles (*UI Client Registration IF, JSP GUI IF*) and the component service interfaces which it provides depicted by green circles (*AmI UI C IF*)

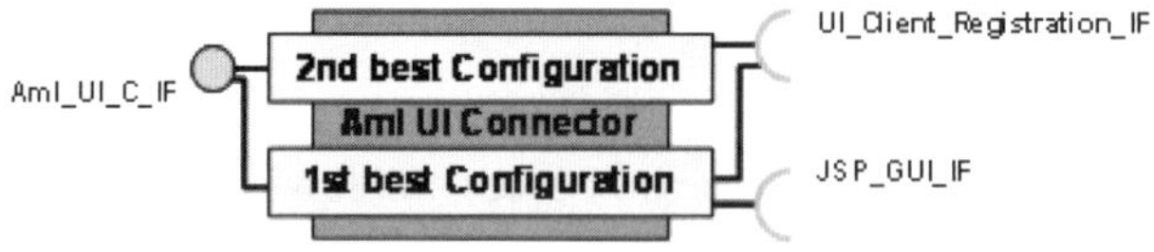

Fig. 3. An Example DAiSI Component

The generated UI was running on a Sony Vaio UMP as a client (s. Figure 4).

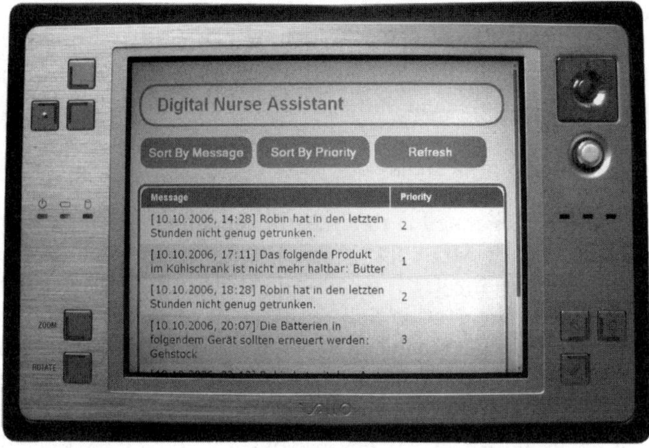

Fig. 4. A Sony Vaio UMP as a client device

3 Challenges and Possible Solutions

We implemented model driven UI generation in the BelAmI project (see Acknowledgement). The high level architecture of the application based on the DAiSI Architecture which follows the Service Oriented (SOA) is shown in Figure 2. It was implemented as a demonstrator in the Ambient Assisted Living Lab (AALL) of the Fraunhofer IESE [12]. The client device is represented by the Tablet PC (UMPC). The server is a PC that hosts the rest of the services including the registration, the usability engine, the room task generator, the web server, the reporting service and the digital nursing assistant (DNA). The latter is responsible for supporting the care giving persons during their visit to the care-taker (most likely elderly) for example by reporting the amount of medication or fluid taken by the care-taker during their absence or simply by reporting, if there are adulterated food in the kitchen or refrigerator.

By using this architecture we were able to investigate possible scenarios, formalization of ergonomic rules and architectural aspects in a (vertical) prototype. The following sections describe the challenges that we identified.

3.1 Interfacing Services

In Ambient Intelligence systems, the functionality is typically provided by services connected by a service oriented middleware. The common task and domain models used in MB-UID approaches assume that a task can be directly mapped to a canonical domain data operation. However, services and their interfaces are not equivalent to tasks and their manipulation of domain objects. Each operation performable on a domain object must thus be mapped to the real interfaces of a service that implement the required functionality. The syntax of these callbacks varies depending on the used middleware. But the domain model can also used for choosing appropriate widgets for representing objects. Therefore its syntax should also be related to the widgets, which might differ from that of the callbacks.

Our suggestion is to have a domain model, which holds information on data and objects in a canonical way and another model, which is platform-specific (e.g. IDL syntax). Every element of the domain model, which is manipulated by a task, has then to be "implemented" by an element of the platform-specific model.

3.2 Modeling Notations and Tools

While the UI should be generated at runtime, the modeling activities are performed at design time. In the chosen MD-UID approach two service specific models are required: the task model in the CTT notation [15] describes the decomposition and logical-temporal flow of interaction and the domain model (a simplified class diagram) that represents the conceptual data to be presented and modified in the UI. Each model has a different notation and requires a different tool. For example the TERESA tool for the task model as CTT [17] and any UML-based tool for the domain model. This means that the designers have to use separate, non-integrated tools for the different models. Combining these models later on can also lead to inconsistencies. In our case, we used the AGG editor [6] for combining the models and defining transformation rules as suggested in [7]. For more complex models, this tool is clearly insufficient due to several usability issues and lack of even basic management functionality. Unfortunately, this lack of reliable tool support is a general problem within MB-UID environments [10].

Efforts to combine the models in one tool can be seen in [13]. Also Eclipse based plug-ins can provide a solution. For example the Tiger project [5] is developing a framework for generating specialized visual editors for Eclipse, which promises enhanced usability and functionality.

3.3 Transformation Engine Requirements

As mentioned above, we choose the AGG engine for attributed graph grammars for executing transformation rules as suggested in [7]. This is indeed a very powerful mechanism for model transformation and is appropriate for visual editing of models (despite the shortcomings in the graphical editor, see section 3.2). Unfortunately, the AGG engine is designed close to the theoretical foundations of graph theory and thus not optimized for performance. A full transformation of very simple UI models with the complete rule set takes beyond a minute of execution time. This might not be problematic with design time generation, but for productive runtime environments, it leads to unacceptable response times. Additionally, the management of a very large number of transformation rules seems to be problematic, especially if these rules are competing. A transformation engine with similar expressiveness and much faster execution performance is required.

3.4 Formalization of Usability Rules

Automatically generated UIs have been suffering from being of low quality, even if the generation does not take place at runtime [16]. With UI generation at runtime, the situation even becomes worse, since no human inspections or manual refinements are possible. To solve this problem, we formalized the ergonomic rules (see 2.2). However, we experienced that it is difficult and tedious to formalize ergonomic rules, especially the non trivial ones. Some reasons for this are:

- It is not possible to formalize the whole knowledge possessed by a designer in models.
- Even simple rules can easily conflict.
- To make rules applicable for a wide variety of situations, often many special cases have to be treated separately, hence making it difficult to crosscheck conflicting rules.

Moreover as the number of rules increases, the performance for the generation decreases, since more resources are needed. While a response time of several seconds does not matter at design time, this can be unacceptable at runtime.

On the other hand there are some attributes and features of a (graphical) user interface that can be well generated, e.g. the optimal control or display widget for a specific object type. Moreover, modern UI toolkits have well designed complex widgets, which just need to be selected in the transformation path. Some of these, but by far not all, are already elements in the current UsiXML specification [21].

For AmI-Environments (e.g. our demonstrators) the solution could be to shorten the transformation path to the abstract or even concrete specification level. This will significantly reduce the number of rules and enables us to "handcraft" slick user interface layouts at design time. Also we might choose target UI platforms that provide a rich set of complex widgets, (e.g. ActiveX, SWT). Thus "selecting" instead of "constructing" widgets.

3.5 Handling of Platform Diversity

Model-driven approaches promise to significantly reduce development effort, when there are many target platforms. This is advantageous when multiple software products or product versions can be generated for a variety of platforms. But this also requires a distinct transformer for each final target platform to be considered. In the case of interactive distributed systems, two final platforms exist: (1) The *infrastructure* (or middleware), which connects services and handles remote execution, events and messages and (2) the *user interface toolkit or description language*. Accordingly, two families of platform-specific transformers have to be developed to keep the promise of platform independence. A mere research project might not be capable of carrying this overhead, which makes it difficult to empirically prove that model driven UI generation works and reduces effort in the long term.

This problem can be significantly mitigated, when third party components can be used for handling the platform diversity. For the UI platforms, we recently started to cooperate with a vendor of a middleware for mobile services. If this succeeds, we will be able to generate UIs for thousands of different mobile devices.

3.6 UI Specification of Dynamic Services

The vision of Ambient Intelligence is not only to transparently provide services within an environment, but also combining existing services to provide new ones. For instance, a data storage (service) and a phone (service) could be combined to provide an answering machine (service). This vision leads to several challenges. Regarding the user interface design, one challenge is how the user interaction for that new service should be specified. In the given example, the resulting answering machine (service) is quite different from the two separate services. Therefore the specification of its user interaction can not be obtained by combining the specifications of the two. We suspect that there exists no technical solution to infer the UI specification. Instead, we suggest that the interplay of services (such as dependency and composition) should be specified. We think of this specification as a standardized domain-specific model containing all implemented and envisioned services – elemental as well as combined services. This domain service model should be maintained by an independent standardization consortium. Industrial producers might then develop components and describe their capabilities according to the domain service model. We already ran some simple examples, where the service capabilities are specified as fragments of a domain task model [20].

4 Conclusion and Future Work

Our recent research is about encountering the new requirements for UIs in AmI environments with a model-based generation approach. While this idea is still striking in theory, we experienced several practical challenges and obstacles. These include technical problems like lack of proper tools and engines as well as handling the diversity of platforms. Very problematic was the formalization and management of ergonomic rules as well for proper usability. While technical challenges could be solved by for example taking another tool or shortening the transformation path, formalization of non trivial usability rules is still a big challenge. This will be the focus of our next work package in the project.

Acknowledgments. The work presented in this paper was (partially) carried out in the BelAmI project, funded by German Federal Ministry of Education and Research (BMBF), Fraunhofer-Gesellschaft and the Ministry for Science, Education, Research and Culture (MWWFK) of Rheinland-Pfalz.

References

1. Aarts, E., Encarnacao, J.: Into Ambient Intelligence. In: True Visions - The Emergence of Ambient Intelligence, pp. 1–16. Springer, Heidelberg (2006)
2. Apfelbacher, F.: Formalisierung von ergonomischen Regeln zur Verbesserung der Benutzerfreundlichkeit von adaptiven Benutzungsschnittstellen. TU Kaiserslautern, Kaiserslautern, master thesis (2006)
3. Calvary, G., Coutaz, J., Thevenin, D., Limbourg, Q., Bouillon, L., Vanderdonckt, J.: A Unifying Reference Framework for Multi-Target User Interfaces. In: Interacting with Computers, vol. 15(3), Elsevier, Amsterdam (2003)
4. Cowley, N.L.O., Wesson, J.L.: An Experiment to Measure the Usefulness of Patterns in the Interaction Design Process. In: Costabile, M.F., Paternó, F. (eds.) INTERACT 2005. LNCS, vol. 3585, pp. 1142–1145. Springer, Heidelberg (2005)

5. Ehrig, K., Ermel, C., Hänsgen, S., Taentzer, G.: Generation of visual editors as eclipse plug-ins. In: Proceedings of the 20th IEEE/ACM international Conference on Automated Software Engineering, Long Beach, CA, USA (2005)
6. Ermel, C., Schultzke, T.: The Agg Environment: A Short Manual, TU Berlin, Berlin (2007), http://tfs.cs.tu-berlin.de/agg/ShortManual.ps
7. Limbourg, Q.: Multi-Path Development of User Interfaces. Université catholique de Louvain, Louvain, PhD (2004)
8. Luyten, K., Coninx, K.: An XML-Based Runtime User Interface Description Language for Mobile Computing Devices. In: Johnson, C. (ed.) DSV-IS 2001. LNCS, vol. 2220, pp. 17–29. Springer, Heidelberg (2001)
9. Luyten, K., Vandervelpen, C., Van den Bergh, J., Coninx, K.: Context-sensitive User Interfaces for Ambient Intelligent Environments: Design, Development and Deployment. In: Mobile Computing and Ambient Intelligence: The Challenge of Multimedia 2005. Dagstuhl Seminar Proceedings, nr. 05181, IBFI, Dagstuhl, Germany (2005)
10. Molina, P.J.: A Review to Model-Based User Interface Development Technology. In: Proceedings of IUI 2004, ACM Press, New York (2004)
11. NASA. Man-Systems Integration Standards (August 13, 2007), http://msis.jsc.nasa.gov/default.htm
12. Nehmer, J., Becker, M., Karshmer, A., Lamm, R.: Living assistance systems: an ambient intelligence approach. In: Proceeding of the ICSE 2006, pp. 43–50. ACM Press, New York (2006)
13. Nóbrega, L., Nunes, N.D., Coelho, H.: Mapping ConcurTaskTrees into UML 2.0. In: Gilroy, S.W., Harrison, M.D. (eds.) DSV-IS 2005. LNCS, vol. 3941, pp. 237–248. Springer, Heidelberg (2006)
14. Paech, B., Kohler, K.: Task-driven Requirements in object-oriented Development. In: Perspectives on Requirements Engineering, pp. 45–68. Kluwer Academic, Dordrecht (2003)
15. Paternò, F., Mancini, C., Meniconi, S.: ConcurTaskTrees: A Diagrammatic Notation for Specifying Task Models. In: Proceedings of the INTERACT 1997, pp. 362–369. Chapman & Hall, Sydney (1997)
16. Szekely, P.: Retrospective and Challenges for Model-Based Interface Development. In: Proceedings of DSV-IS96, pp. 1–27. Springer, Heidelberg (1996)
17. TERESA (August 13, 2007), http://giove.cnuce.cnr.it/teresa.html
18. Tidwell, J.: Designing Interfaces: Patterns for Effective Interaction Design. O'Reilly, Sebastopol (2005)
19. The Apache Foundation, Apache Struts (August 13, 2007), http://www.struts.apache.org
20. Trapp, M., Schmettow, M.: Consistency in use through Model based User Interface Development. In: Proceedings of CEUR Workshop, Montreal, vol. 198, pp. 66–71 (2006)
21. UsiXML Documentation (August 13, 2007), http://www.usixml.org
22. Vanderdonckt, J.: A MDA-Compliant Environment for Developing User Interfaces of Information Systems. In: Pastor, Ó., Falcão e Cunha, J. (eds.) CAiSE 2005. LNCS, vol. 3520, pp. 16–31. Springer, Heidelberg (2005)
23. van Welie, M.: Patterns in interaction design (August 13, 2007), http://www.welie.com/
24. Anastasopoulos, M., Klus, K.H.J., Niebuhr, D., Werkman, E.: DoAmI - A Middleware Platform facilitating (Re-)configuration in Ubiquitous Systems. International Workshop on System Support for Ubiquitous Computing (UbiSys) at the 8th International Conference of Ubiquitous Computing (Ubicomp), New Port Beach, California, USA (2006)

Smart Products: Building Blocks of Ambient Intelligence

Fernando Lyardet[1,2] and Erwin Aitenbichler[2]

[1] SAP Research Darmstadt, Germany
[2] Telecooperation Group, Department of Computer Science, TU Darmstadt, Germany
{fernando,erwin}@tk.informatik.tu-darmstadt.de

The first edition of AmI-Blocks'07 workshop took place on 7th of November 2007 in Darmstadt, in conjunction with the European Conference on Ambient Intelligence (AmI-07). The focus of the workshop was to bring together experts of diverse areas such as Ubiquitous Computing, Product Engineering, Cognitive Science, Human Computer Interaction, Economics, and Artificial Intelligence, with the specific goal of helping shape a vision of creating living and working environments out of Smart Products. The topic chosen to focus the workshop's discussions was: *"Smart Products: Building Blocks of Ambient Intelligence"*. This focus reflects a growing trend of research that understands the creation of future technology-assisted living and working spaces, as the result of the collaborations between devices and services gradually being deployed, one product at a time.

Ambient Intelligence foundations lie on the increasing technological advances in embedding computational power, information and sensing capabilities into everyday objects and environments. However, in spite of the current availability of technology, there is a notorious absence of large scale settings. This absence raises questions about the complexity and effort required with current approaches to building such intelligent living and working spaces. We believe that future ambient intelligent infrastructures should be able to configure themselves and grow from the available, purposeful objects (be it software services or consumer appliances) in order to become effective in the real world.

In this workshop we refer to these purposeful objects as *"Smart Products"*, that are real-world objects, devices or software services bundled with knowledge about themselves and their capabilities. These properties make Smart Products not only *intelligible* to users, but also *smart* to interpret user's actions and adapt accordingly. By naming these objects *Smart Products* we convey not only the notion of technology available "off-the-shelves", but also the notion of componentized software services and hardware objects required to assemble new, innovative end-user components. Therefore, Smart Products share some key properties: the ability to have multiple uses, be deployed independently, and network with other objects to augment their individual and collective capabilities.

The papers presented at the workshop showed concrete examples of how knowledge-enriched smart products together with ontological inference could positively impact end consumers and business throughout their life cycle, and what kinds of security and technological platforms are being developed today to enable large deployment settings.

M. Mühlhäuser et al. (Eds.): AmI 2007 Workshops, CCIS 11, pp. 156–157, 2008.

The workshop was divided in two sessions, with a notable keynote given by Prof. Max Mühlhäuser who outlined the overall vision of Smart Products and motivated the discussions held later in the afternoon.

We wish to thank our keynote speaker Prof. Max Mühlhäuser for his participation, and also special thanks to the Program Committee members for supporting this workshop:

- Michael Beigl, Braunschweig University of Technology, Germany
- Elgar Fleisch, University of St. Gallen, Switzerland
- Sylvain Giroux, Université de Sherbrooke, Canada
- Stephan Haller, SAP Research (St. Gallen), Switzerland
- Sumi Helal, University of Florida, USA
- Tomas Herndl, Infineon Technologies Austria AG, Austria
- Gerd Kortuem, Lancaster University, United Kingdom
- Max Mühlhäuser, Darmstadt University of Technology, Germany
- Thomas Odenwald, SAP Research (Palo Alto), USA
- Karnouskos Stamatis, SAP Research (Karlsruhe), Germany
- Martin Strohbach, NEC Europe Ltd., Germany
- Frédéric Thiesse, University of St. Gallen, Switzerland
- Simon Vogl, Research Studios Austria, Austria
- Harald Vogt, SAP Research (Karlsruhe), Germany

Smart Products: An Introduction

Max Mühlhäuser

Technische Universität Darmstadt, Hochschulstr. 10, D-64289 Darmstadt, Germany
`max@informatik.tu-darmstadt.de`

Abstract. Sophisticated commercial products and product assemblies can greatly benefit from novel IT-based approaches to the conditioning of these products
and of 'product knowledge', leading to what we call Smart Products. The paper
motivates the need for such novel approaches, introduces important relevant
challenges and research domains, and provides an early definition of Smart
Products.

Keywords: Smart Products, product data, context awareness, human interaction, agent based communication.

1 Introduction and Motivation

This paper presents key statements made at the invited introduction to the AMI '07
workshop on Smart Products.

The current chapter outlines the need for considerable advancements in the way information, information technology (IT), and products are combined. This is done by
taking cars as an example and by comparing past, present, and future issues with
respect to two key requirements relevant for (smart) products.

Simplicity: In the past, ease-of-use of cars was "almost built in" (in comparison to the
present) in the sense that cars had very limited functionality. Steering wheel, gear-
shift, and pedals directly exposed the key product features to the user. At present, cars
are equipped with a wealth of functionality. Only some of this new functionality can
be realized without any need for active user participation (ESP, ABS etc.), the rest
cannot operate satisfactorily without means for the user to take influence (air condition, radio, electronoic seat positioning, ...). Almost all these features are accessible
via computers[1]. Efforts were made for assuring as little interaction as possible and for
greatly improving the usability; further R&D focused on maintaining the user's feeling of "being in control" in cases were "wheels & levers" expose car functions via
computers and not directly any more (cf. power steering, power gears etc.).

As to the future, it has become evident that mastering the "simplicity paradox" will
be deterministic for product success: huge efforts towards better usability are foiled
by ever more feature laden products, 'imposed' by the need to differentiate products
from their competitors.

It is important to emphasize that product 'users' are by no means limited to the typical customers. Over the lifetime of a product, the quest for a high degree of usability

---

[1] This term is used In the large sense throughout the paper, including microcontrollers etc.

M. Mühlhäuser et al. (Eds.): AmI 2007 Workshops, CCIS 11, pp. 158–164, 2008.

and simplicity equally regards the manufacturing process (cf. shop floor workers), maintenance (cf. repair technicians), and the actual use (cf. different categories of passengers) – and reaches even further, e.g., to the design step in the beginning and resale or recycling at the end. Given the increasing sophistication and ever shorter innovation cycles (which increase the 'learning' needs for manufacturing and service workers), simplicity can be identified as a crucial lifecycle-covering need.

Openness: Car production in the past was dominated by the power of the manufacturer. In the early days, everything was 'produced under one roof'; soon, car manufacturers started to build networks with suppliers, but these networks were initially dominated by the final-product vendor and remained stable over the life time of the model. Today, openness has increased in many ways, in particular the following two: (i) suppliers build trusts aiming at increased independence from car manufactures; on the other hand, manufacturers seek independence from supplier for enabling faster changes in the supply chain, e..g, in case of quality, quantity (production capacity etc.), or price disagreement; (ii) the number and variety of optional parts has dramatically increased, both with respect to the choices at the time of order and with respect to additional equipment introduced during the product lifetime (entertainment systems, mobile phone dockings, special supply parts like racing seats).

In the future, openness will further increase for two major reasons: (i) personalization of cars will remain an important differentiator for vendors and will be driven to even more custom made cars; at the same time, stock production is not a viable option any more if 'no two cars are identical' – which is in turn an optimization opportunity since a production process for 'cooked-to-order' cars minimizes capital lockup and facilitates the above-mentioned strive for more flexible manufacturer–supplier relations (ii) ever more IT equipment is added to cars after sales and exchanged during the product life time (navigation, phone, entertainment, air condition, etc.). To this end, improved openness helps 'implanted' products to leverage off functionality available at the 'car as a docking station', like high quality sound systems, speed dependent operations, etc.

But not only will the car be an 'environment' in which 'smaller' products are embedded: the car itself will become ever more tightly embedded into its environment, as current research on car-to-car and car-to-infrastructure research indicates.

A vast majority of the innovations made in the automobile sector are linked to computers; as a consequence, modern cars contain some seventy computers or more. In this context, it is obvious that advancements in simplicity and openness must be related to computers and information technology, too.

It must be noted that the example of cars used up to now can be replaced by many other examples from the area of *tangible products* (cf. telecommunications, consumer electronics, manufacturing etc.), *software products,* and the *services sector* (both public and private).

2   A Quest for Integrated Research

From the arguments and definitions provided so far, we can derive that a considerable improvement in the **simplicity** and **openness** of products has the potential to facilitate technological and economic advancement[2] – and can thus be considered a key technology for the industrialized and emerging countries. We advocate such an improvement and propose to apply information technology (IT) as the key enabler. On a high level of abstraction, this proposal is grounded on two arguments:

1. IT is *the* overall motor for improved product sophistication; many facets of 'smartness' can be directly linked to areas of IT research and development.

2. The advent of 'ubiquitous computing' (aka pervasive computing, aka ambient intelligence) enables 'real world awareness' in IT solutions: sensors and smart labels (such as RFID tags), wearable and embedded computers connect the statuses, events, and 'constellations' of the real world (here: products and their users and environment) to software in real time without the need for human input. This technological advancement of recent years may be considered a prerequisite for IT-based Smart Products.

Looking at a slightly deeper level of detail, two important major research directions may be identified. They will be related below to pertinent *existing* research domains.

Simplicity: considerably improved product-to-user (p2u) interaction. Information technology must be applied in novel ways for improving the simplicity of interaction between products and their users (of different categories, across the lifecycle, see above). Two major goals must be pursued to this end:

1. The "smartness" of products must be improved, turning them into more adequate interaction peers for humans. With respect to the simplicity paradox i.e. growing number and sophistication of features, improved smartness must help to *hide* irrelevant features (based on improved and dynamically adapted 'knowledge' about which features are actually important and which not) and to *assist* the user with respect to actually relevant features. A number of pertinent approaches were developed in recent years; unfortunately, they were cultivated in different disciplines (AI, HCI, Cognitive Psychology, Software Engineering, Ubiquitous Computing) with different emphasis and published under a variety of headings, such as context awareness, adaptive and proactive user interfaces, adaptive user models, sentient computing, and self-explanation. For an introduction, the reader may consult [6] and [13].

2. The state of the art in mobile multimodal user interfaces must be exploited and advanced. In interacting with products, users will often have to concentrate on attention-demanding primary tasks, be it operation of the product itself (e.g., operating a tool which is about to explain itself to the user as she applies it) or be it a different activity (e.g., driving a car while adjusting the 'air condition Smart Product'). Under such conditions, hands-and-eyes interaction is rarely as adequate any more as it was for desktop PC work. As a consequence, mouth-and-ear (primarily: speech based) interaction has to be cultivated further. Moreover, available and appropriate interaction modalities and devices must be dynamically federated in order to achieve optimal interaction, cf. [10]; to this end, Smart Products must cooperate with interaction devices available

---

[2] Further properties are crucial for this success, in particular reliability/robustness and security, but lie beyond the scope of this introduction.

in the environment (cf. p2p interaction below). As to speech based interaction, a lot of emphasis has been put on the core technology i.e. speech recognition and speech synthesis in the past. Since unconstraint natural language human-machine dialog remains far from being at par with human-to-human dialog, the preferable approach taken 'atop' core speech recognition varies. Choices range from 'simple' grammar based approaches (which can reach an astonishing level of usability [11]) via statistical language models and conversational interfaces (cf. [4], [7]) to the use of controlled natural language [12]. Resource constraints of embedded systems (demanding distributed solutions) and environmental noise aggravate the problem space. In light of this, further research as well as agreement about a canonical approach to Smart Product p2u interaction must be regarded as one of the biggest challenges.

Openness: considerably improved product-to-produvct (p2p) interaction. The above-mentioned issue of federated interaction devices indicates that improved p2p interaction (here: device federation) helps to improve Smart Products (here: p2u interaction). More generally speaking, it is fair to say that in a given situation, the actual usefulness and pertinence of a product can only be exploited in the context of its environment. Thereby, 'environment' may refer to three different levels of scope: (i) the encompassing environment (for a car in use: streets, gasoline/parking infrastructure etc.; note the very different environment for a car under construction or a car under repair); (ii) the peer products (in the car example: peer vehicles, traffic lights, toll stations etc.); (iii) dynamically embedded devices (e.g., an mp3 player or GPS receiver brought in by a passenger).

Many publications about smart environments rely *implicitly* on the assumption that such environments be designed to a large degree 'top down' with someone having a holistic view on the overarching purpose of the smart environment, its components, and their interworking. This implicit assumption is debatable for most realistic scenarios in which everyday products are applied, be it in industry or for private use. One can easily show that in reality, the degree of top-down on-purpose design varies considerably (roughly speaking, there is a declining slope, e.g., from production plants to office buildings to private transportation). Support for complementary bottom-up support is beneficial in each case and mandatory for truly open cases like homes and private transport. In other words, smart environments can greatly benefit from a considerable degree of self-organization. Two important areas of research must be considered here again;

1. From the IT perspective, Smart Products can be conceived as 'services'; this way, they can leverage off intensive research on 'service composition' and sub-issues like service (self-)description and discovery, orchestration and choreography. As a basis for vendor independent interworking, intensive research on semantic service composition can be 'tapped' for Smart Products. The most intensive research in these areas concerns Web services and semantic Web services [2]). These emerging service-oriented approaches must be adapted and extended for use with Smart Products (e.g., by reflecting the concept of active knowledge mentioned below).

2. Beyond service composition as investigated in 'mainstream' (semantic Web) service oriented software research, Smart Products need to exploit more far-reaching self organization approaches. One important research direction in this respect concerns the application of AI planning algorithms for rather descriptive, goal oriented (as opposed to prescriptive i.e. workflow oriented) composition. Extensions of the Semantic Web Services domain in this respect have already been attempted (see [9] for an example). Another important issue concerns the need to automatically identify, distill, and re-use important patterns of product use and of 'product assembly' use. To this end, machine learning and apttern recognition algorithms appear to be promising, especially if context awareness is applied in order to 'feed' machine learning with automatic observations of 'scenes' in which users, products, and their interactions are reliably described (cf. [8] for a patent on an approach to entertainment products). It must be mentioned that self organization (in the sense of self-diagnosis and self-healing) is also an important approach to improved reliability, but as mentioned, this issue is beyond scope here.

P2u and p2p interaction can greatly benefit from an effort to harmonize the modeling and realization of both. In particular, such an effort can lead to a concept for easily exchanging humans by products and vice versa in a given environment. On one hand, one can imagine an ensemble of Smart Products with an entry level of sophistication deployed at affordable cost. As demands (and budget) grow, human involvement may be lowered by introducing additional components (products) which automate formerly manual activities. Therefore, an easy replacement of users by products should be cared for. On the other hand, in case of a defect in one of the Smart Products assembled in a smart environment, manual intervention – for securing overall operation – can be facilitated if a human can easily step in as a replacement for the defective component. Also, repair can be facilitated if humans can mimic the p2p interaction with the defective component itself.

3   Defining Smart Products

A concise definition of Smart Products should be established and widely agreed if a corresponding new research field and community shall emerge. The present paper attempts a first step towards this end.

Definitions for Smart Environments may be taken into account as a first reference, since Smart Products have to be considered in the context of their (typically smart) environment as argued above. Such a definition can be found in [3]: "A Smart Environment is a small world where all kinds of smart devices are continuously working to make inhabitants' lives more comfortable". In [5], the same authors 'redefine' the term as follows: "A Smart Environment is one that is able to acquire and apply knowledge about an environment and to adapt to its inhabitants in order t improve their experience in that environment". It is interesting that the knowledge aspect has obviously been recognized as a key issue – a fact which backs the 'active knowledge' approach to Smart Products taken by the Telecooperation group, see below.

Referring back to the very origins of Smart Environments and Ubiquitous Computing, i.e. to Mark Weiser's ground breaking work, one may remember characteristics that he attributed to future smart environments: "richly and invisibly interwoven with ... sensors, actuators, displays, and computational elements, seamlessly embedded in everyday objects of our lives, connected through a continuous network". In this respect, Smart Products can be viewed as those augmented everyday objects. However, given the considerations from the first two chapters, it is easy to see that the level of sophistication described can only be achieved if smartness is carefully designed-in with products in a product design process, where the actual product and the corresponding smartness are co-constructed; later in the lifecycle, knowledge held by the Smart Product has to consist of both 'constructed' and 'accumulated' parts. Another important finding from the first chapters was the need to cater for different categories of users and environments in the course of the product lifecycle. All these considerations should be reflected in a definition along with the primary aim to improve both p2u and p2p interaction. Altogether, this leads to the following 'early' definition:

> "A Smart Product is an entity (tangible object, software, or service) designed and made for self-organized embedding into different (smart) environments in the course of its lifecycle, providing improved simplicity and openness through improved p2u and p2p interaction by means of context-awareness, semantic self-description, proactive behavior, multimodal natural interfaces, AI planning, and machine learning."

At this point, a short reference shall be made to the specific approach taken at the Telecooperation group. We emphasize the concept of **active knowledge** as a design-center for Smart Products in our research. The term 'active' refers to the ability to autonomously interact with the user. This contrasts the passive nature of most product 'knowledge' that is digitally available to date: one may think of engineering drawings, PLM (product lifecycle management) data, user manuals, and the like. Such passive knowledge is only used today if it 'happens to be' found and accessed by users or processes; moreover, it is bound to a predefined modality. Active knowledge, in contrast, can trigger p2u and p2p interaction based on perceived needs (occurring events, interaction needs 'computed' by the product as part of its smartness, etc.); modalities can be chosen and combined as appropriate. Informally speaking, active knowledge enables p2u interaction where the product "talks, guides, proposes, and understands"; it also enables p2p interaction and thereby the realization of the self-organization properties discussed. At a coarse view, it appears useful to distinguish three classes of Smart Product knowledge:

1. About *itself* i.e. its features and functions, dependencies, product history etc.
2. About its potential and actual *environments*, in particular perceived possibilities to adapt to and cooperate with these environments and their constituents
3. About its *users*, based on elaborate user models that take into account dynamically changing user knowledge (learning/forgetting) and distinguish the different user categories reflected in the lifecycle plus each individual user herself.

This short reference to own work shall be sufficient for the scope of this introductory paper, for a next level of detail the reader may refer to [1].

4 Summary and Conclusion

As an introductory contribution to the AMI workshop on Smart Products, the paper provided a motivation, definition, and quest for integrated research. On one hand, it became evident that quite a number of disciplines and research fields must be integrated towards widespread use of Smart Products. On the other hand, considerable advancements achieved in these fields in recent years give rise to the hope that the integration, adaptation, and furthering of these results can lead to highly sophisticated yet widely useable Smart Products in a not so distant future. This conclusion may encourage interested researchers to develop the area of *Smart Products* into a highly recognized and active new research community.

References

1. Aitenbichler, E., Lyardet, F., Austaller, G., Kangasharju, J., Mühlhäuser, M.: Engineering Intuitive and Self-Explanatory Smart Products. In: Proc. 22nd Annual ACM Symp. Applied Computing, pp. 1632–1637. ACM Press, New York (2007)
2. Cardoso, J.: Semantic Web Services: Theory, Tools and Applications. IGI Publishers (2007)
3. Cook, D., Das, S.: Smart Environments: Technology, Protocols, Application. Wiley, Chichester (2004)
4. Cohen, M., Giangola, J., Balogh, J.: Voice User Interface Design. Addison-Wesley, Reading (2004)
5. Das, S., Cook, D.: Designing Smart Environments: A Paradigm Based on Learning and Prediction. In: Shorey, R., Ananda, A., Chan, M.C., Ooi, W.T. (eds.) Mobile, Wireless, and Sensor Networks: Technology, Applications, and Future Directions, pp. 337–358. Wiley, Chichester (2006)
6. Delisle, S., Moulin, B.: User Interfaces and Help Systems: From Helplessness to Intelligent Assistance. Artificial Intelligence Review 18, 117–157 (2002)
7. Harris, R.: Voice Interaction Design: Crafting the New Conversational Speech Systems. Morgan Kaufmann, San Francisco (2004)
8. Hoffberg, S., Hoffberg-Borghesani, L.: Ergonomic man-machine interface incorporating adaptive pattern recognition; US Patent No. 7136710 (2006)
9. Klusch, M., Renner, K.-U.: Fast Dynamic Re-planning of Composite OWL-S Services. In: Proc. IEEE/WIC/ACM International Conferences on Web Intelligence and Intelligent Agent Technology – Workshops, pp. 134–137 (2006)
10. Paternò, F., Giammarino, F.: Authoring interfaces with combined use of graphics and voice for both stationary and mobile devices. In: Proceedings of the Working Conference on Advanced Visual interfaces AVI 2006, pp. 329–335. ACM, New York (2006)
11. Pieraccini, R., Huerta, J.: Where do we Go from Here? Research and Commercial Spoken Dialog Systems. In: 6th SIGdial Workshop on Discourse and Dialogue, Lisbon (2005)
12. Schwitter, R., Tilbrook, M.: Controlled Natural Language meets the Semantic Web. In: Proc. Australasian Language Technology Workshop, pp. 55–62 (2004)
13. Wu, M., Friday, A., Blair, G., et al.: Novel Component Middleware for Building Dependable Sentient Computing Applications. In: ECOOP 2004 Workshop on Component-oriented approaches to Context-aware Systems, Oslo, Norway (June 2004)

Reasoning on Smart Products in Consumer Good Domains

Wolfgang Maass, Andreas Filler, and Sabine Janzen

Research Center Intelligent Media,
Hochschule Furtwangen University,
Robert-Gerwig-Platz 1, 78120 Furtwangen, Germany
{wolfgang.maass,andreas.filler,sabine.janzen}@hs-furtwangen.de

Abstract. Ambient intelligence technologies rapidly change product capabilities but also the way how users interact with physical products. This product-centered stance requires an *instance-centered Product Life Cycle* (iPLC) view which perceives products as autonomous actors performing in physical situations which leads to the concept of smart products. Smart products adapt to situations on the basis of internal representations. We present a generic extensible data model, called *Smart Product Description Objects* (SPDO), whose semantics are described by formal and machine-readable ontologies. SPDO instantiations are computational counterparts of physical product instances. We exemplify the use of SPDO by inferring similarity sets of products within a fashion domain.

Keywords: ambient intelligence, product life cycle, product reasoning.

1   Introduction

Electronic and wireless point of sale solutions start to revolutionize the interaction between customers, retailers and producers in consumer good industries. Recommendation agents increasingly help customers to make educated buying decisions, to better understand customer needs but also to exert influence [1]. At the same time, robotic intelligence has made enormous leaps forward and is now expected to realize commercial solutions till 2015 [1]. In short, those kind of technologies will rapidly and thoroughly change the design of products. Step by step, products will become interactive (as already accepted in cars), adaptive to contexts and users, and pro-active, i.e., products will gain capabilities of a problem solver that is self-acting in tangible and intangible environments.

For the realization of this vision, wireless information and communication technologies are embedded into any kind of physical object. This allows embedding of communication capabilities based on sound, smell, gestures, language, physical interactions, and actuators that enable objects to move.

Under the umbrella of Ambient Intelligence, several attempts have been made to leverage these capablities by innovative product types, such as at the Philips

---

[1] e.g., RIKEN's robotics program in Japan or MIC's smart robots in Korea.

M. Mühlhäuser et al. (Eds.): AmI 2007 Workshops, CCIS 11, pp. 165–173, 2008.

Research Laboratories, Fraunhofer Assisted Living, or the MIT project Oxygen. As a melting pot of several disciplines, Ambient Intelligence integrates knowledge and methods from product design, artificial intelligence, economics, electro-engineering, robotics, computer linguistics, cognitive science and many more. Examples for prototypes are Philips' iCat, and MIT's Leonardo. Simple commercial applications can already be found in electronic point of sales (ePOS) systems, such as Paxar's "magicmirror".

Because ambient intelligent technologies aim at better adaptation of products to user needs and contexts on various levels, it becomes apparent that a producer-centered design approach is of little help and needs to be replaced by user-centered design approaches that advocate incremental and interactive development of new designs in cooperation with various communities, such as cooperative, participatory and contextual design approaches.

From an economic perspective it is premature to identify the overall potential of Ambient Intelligence technologies for products in general. Therefore we will analyze on a more focused level how those technologies can be utilized by users. In this article, we will focus on an integrated foundational model for Smart Products with a special focus on consumer goods and application to sales situations, w.o.l.g. for other good categories and other product interaction situations. First, we will discuss generic situations in which smart products can be used before we derive requirements that are used for a generic computational model for smart products, called *Smart Product Description Object* (SPDO). Then we show within a fashion domain an example of basic reasoning capabilities on SPDO by entailing similar products. Finally, we bring up open issues and directions of our future work.

2   The Concept of a Product

2.1   Definition

A product is generally defined by taking a performance view which perceives a product as a good or service that a business offers to its customers to satisfy wants or needs. More general, products are perceived as problem solutions that establish producer-product and product-user interfaces [2]. Hence, products are intermediaries that transmit functionalities, communications, and knowledge exchanges by application and integration of different design cultures [2].

Products are characterised according to their complexity which is usually defined by the number of *attributes* that describe a product, the number of substitutes, or the *number of steps* involved in the use of the product (for an overview cf. [1]). E-commerce literature defines product complexity along three dimensions: number of product attributes, variability of each product attribute, and interdependence of product attributes.

A product can deliver its performance if its interfaces are understood by users. This leads to a working definition: *a product is a tangible or intangible entity that transfers capabilities from producers to users via defined interfaces with the goal to utilize the establishing of situations that are congruent with goals derived from user needs and user intentions.*

2.2 Instance-Centered Product Life Cycle

The life cycle of a product type is often structured according to the quantitative development of sales [3]: development, introduction, growth, maturity, and decline. From the viewpoint of a single product an *instance-centered product life cycle* (iPLC) is structured by eight situations (on the basis of [3], cf. fig 1). We found by application to various domains that iPLC is better suited for the analysis of situations in which product instances interact with their environments than category-driven PLC models. In iPLC three situations (sales, support and disposal) integrate product-centered interactions between producers and users.

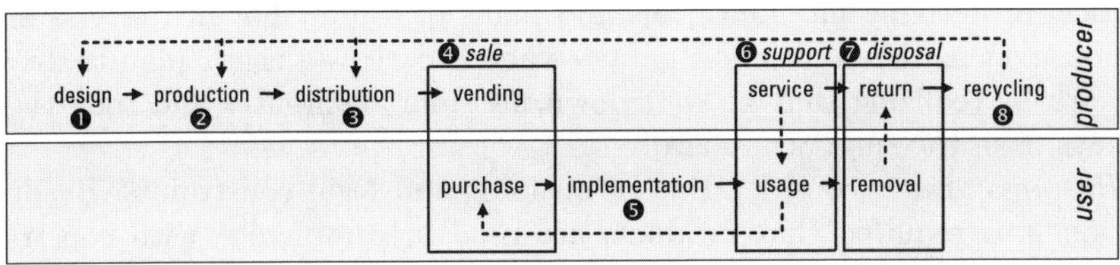

Fig. 1. Instance-centered Product Life Cycle (iPLC) model

A basic requirement for smart products is that they provide extended capabilities to adapt to iPLC situations. In the following we use the sales situation to exemplify the concept of a smart product.

3 Smart Products

3.1 Characteristics of Smart Products

A main requirement for smart products is the capability to adapt to situations and in particular to users and other products. Hence, smart products exhibit various degrees of behavior relative to situations which places smart products on a continuum between passive and static products and autonomous smart robotics. By adopting a symbolic stance, behavior requires representations of situations which can be used to derive goals, plans, and execution of appropriate activities.

We pose that the representation of smart products is required to encompass the capabilities and attributes by the product itself and information about situations on different logical levels, such as organisation, business, law and physical contexts [4,5]. Fully implemented smart products are required to exhibit the following characteristics [4,5]:

1. *Situated*: recognition and processing of situational and community contexts. A smart product maintains internal representations of physical environments and in particular of role-taking entities. For instance, smart products derive that a particular situation is a sales situation with other products and particular actors taking buyer and seller roles.

2. *Personalized*: tailoring to producer and user needs and affects. Beside temporal-spatial information smart products also keep track of anticipated and perceived needs and affects of certain actors. For instance, in usage situations a smart dryer has learned that a particular user always wants to dry her hair with medium heat.

3. *Adaptive*: change according to buyers and consumers responses and tasks in a particular situation. For instance, a smart light in a kitchen might dim when it realizes that a user has switched on the TV in the living room.

4. *Pro-active*: attempt to anticipate user plans and intentions. Adaptiveness is defined on activity level while pro-activity requires the integration of activities for deriving intented goals and plans of a user. For instance, a smart house opens the door of the garage when it derives a user's plan to drive to work by realizing that he shut down his smart computer and took the car keys from the smart cupboard.

5. *Business-aware*: consideration of business and legal constraints. By definition it is required that products are used in compliance with constraints that are defined in contracts. For instance, a smart coffee machine might be restricted to produce 20 coffee cups per day but might allow the production of additional coffee on a pay-per-item basis.

6. *Network capable*: ability to communicate and bundle (product bundling) with other products or product sets. For instance, a computer establishes a product bundle because it determined that a laser printer of another brand is compatible with it and that a bundling strategy exists between both companies.

These characteristics span a vector space for the class of smart products. For realization of smart products by computational infrastructures we adopt a design approach by which digital representations are carried by smart products with the goal that any kind of computational entity that is able to process these representations can fully or partially interact with a smart product. Another design goal is that any behavior of smart products is grounded in appropriate representations which has a trade-off relationship to the third design goal which requires that smart product should only carry representations which provide benefits to users. In short: "No interaction without representation" and "No representation without utilization". The second design principle is easy to prove while the third principle is semi-decidable.

Next we discuss design principles for computational models of smart products from which a generic model is derived.

3.2   A Computational Model for Smart Products

Because of the complexity of products in general we assume that different product categories have different requirements for describing product attributes in more or less detail and variety. As typical for web-based systems we adopt an extensible data model called *Smart Product Description Object* (SPDO) which leads to variable semantics based on formal ontologies. The SPDO model consists of five facets [4]: (1) product description, (2) presentation description, (3) community description, (4) business description, and (5) trust&security description. In our SPDO reference implementation we use the foundational ontologies DOLCE [6] and DnS [7] with additional domain-specific core conceptualizations for semantic descriptions of SPDO instantiations. Figure 2 visualizes an excerpt of a simplified SPDO model with focus on the product description facet for a fashion domain. In DOLCE/DnS, SPDO is an *information object realization* that explicates a *conceptualization*.

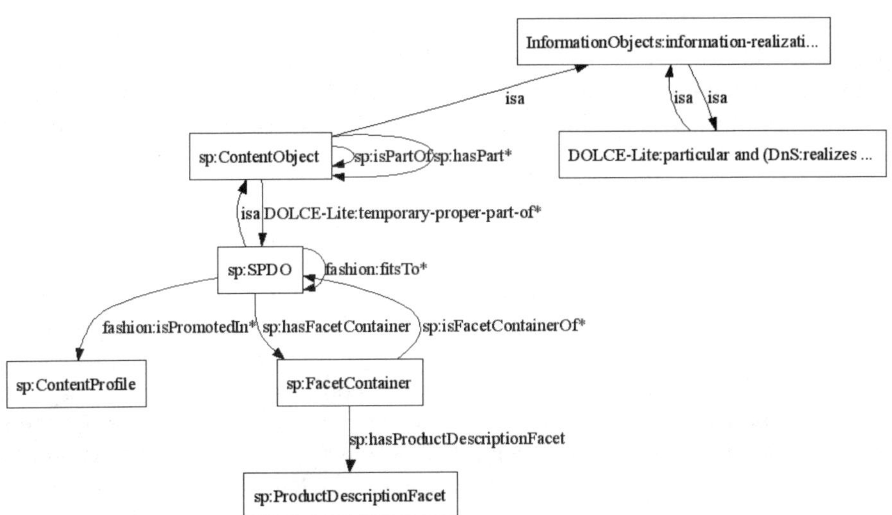

Fig. 2. SPDO extract with product description facet

SPDO instantiations are processed by the Tip 'n Tell middleware [4]. A request on a product in focus is sent via a SPARQL-based request protocol to a SPDO broker that manages product information by the semantic representation format OWL. This broker collects requested product information from web services that are referenced by the product ID in the product description facet of a SPDO. The SPDO broker integrates product information from different sources into SPDO representations and sends it to a dynamic product interface of the smart product in focus for communication with users. In the following we describe how SPDO models are used for reasoning purposes. This is exemplified by a fashion shopping scenario.

4   A Fashion Shopping Example

Sales situations from a customer perspective can be structured by five stages defined by the diffusion theory: knowledge, persuasion, decision, implementation, and confirmation [8]. We focus on the first phase (knowledge) in which a customer gathers and evaluates information about a product. When a customer approaches a dress she might want to ask various questions, such as "Who has produced this dress?", "Which handbag fits to it?" or "Do I get a discount when I take this dress with a particular necklace?". In this scenario all fashion products are equipped with RFID tags and are described by associated SPDO instantiations stored on a web service. A product in focus is identified by a costumer's pointing gesture so that the RFID reader of this mobile device (here: a Cathexis IDBlue RFID Pen) can read the dress' identification number. This gesture is interpreted as a communication request which initiates a sales situation between customer and product by starting a natural language based sales dialogue [5]. After reading the product identification number, the SPDO broker retrieves the SPDO data model for this product from a web service and sends it to the natural language processor which uses it as the local knowledge base [5].

In the following we use requests on product information that relate to other products and in particular information about similar products to exemplify the use of the SPDO model.

4.1   Deduction of Smart Product Similarity Sets

The determination of relevant product features for similarity testing is domain dependent. Assertive data is represented by SPDO models of smart products. Rule knowledge is represented by standardized web-based rule languages, in particular SWRL. Let us assume that two fashion products are similar if both have color of a particular color class, e.g., red color class and their size differs by not more than one dress size, e.g., dress size 39 and 40 are similar. Products are fashion products if they have a fashion size. The following simple rule in rule language SWRL [2] will determine all fashion products that are similar.

$PropoProdDescr^3(?a1) \land isPropProdDescrOf(?a1, ?pfd1) \land$
$isProdDescrFacetOf(?pfd1, ?fc1) \land isFacetContOf(?fc1, ?spdo1) \land$
$hasMaterial(?a1, ?b1) \land hasColor(?b1, ?c1) \land abox : hasClass(?c1, ?d1) \land$
$tbox : isDirectSubClassOf(?toCompare1, fashion : Color) \land$
$tbox : isSubClassOf(?d1, ?toCompare1) \land PropProdDescr(?a2) \land$
$isPropProdDescrOf(?a2, ?pfd21) \land isProdDescrFacetOf(?pfd2, ?fc2) \land$
$isFacetContainerOf(?fc2, ?spdo2) \land hasMaterial(?a2, ?b2) \land$
$hasColor(?b2, ?c2) \land abox : hasClass(?c2, ?d2) \land$
$tbox : isDirectSubClassOf(?toCompare2, fashion : Color) \land$
$tbox : isSubClassOf(?d2, ?toCompare2) \land$

---

[2] http://www.w3.org/Submission/SWRL/
[3] Some properties are abbreviated; properties without namespace have namespace *smartproduct*.

$tbox : sameAs(?toCompare1, ?toCompare2) \wedge hasDim(?a1, ?e1) \wedge$
$fashion : size(?e1, ?s1) \wedge hasDimension(?a2, ?e2) \wedge fashion : size(?e2, ?s2) \wedge$
$swrlb : subtract(?sd, ?s1, ?s2) \wedge swrlb : abs(?d, ?sd) \wedge$
$swrlb : divide(?dresult, ?d, 2) \wedge swrlb : lessThanOrEqual(?dresult, 1) \wedge$
$differentFrom(?spdo1, ?spdo2)$
$\rightarrow fashion : fitsTo(?spdo1, ?spdo2) \wedge fashion : fitsTo(?spdo2, ?spdo1)$

With this mechanism product descriptions from various product information services are dynamically integrated into similarity sets which are presented on request or pro-actively. In our application scenario a customer uses a question-and-answer-based Natural Language query interface on his mobile device which allows him to ask for similar or compatible products and for external content on this particular product [5].

5   Related Work

Under the umbrella of tangible user interfaces [9] several shopping assistant systems have been recently developed. The Mobile ShoppingAssistent (MSA) [10] supports dialogs between users and products while focusing on multimodal communication. Earlier systems, such as MyGrocer [11] and [12], venture the integration of physical objects and digital representations. A broad field is the dynamic construction of spaces in which annotated entities and users interact. One of the first systems have been E-Tag [13] and CoolTown [14]. Recently this approach has been extended by ELOPE [15]. Speakeasy [16] investigates how patterns can support users to reduce the complexity of interactions. Furthermore, computational systems that allow annotation of physical objects increasingly become more powerful. In Smart-Its it is investigated whether this allows new methods for new product designs processes [17]. Another approach is the idea of Invisible Media [18] which are able to augment objects around the buyer and support him by voice-based user-system dialog. A similar approach for the interaction between users and single augmented objects has been followed in the Reachmedia project [19] that investigates the touch based interaction with objects based on command represented by gestures. Similarly, Cooperative Artefacts provide a communication and interaction framework [20]. Strohbach et al. investigated the use of reasoning mechanisms for evaluating compatibilities of dangerous goods in physical situations. These approaches use proprietary non-web-based knowledge representations and ad-hoc product ontologies.

6   Summary and Future Work

Starting with simple data models and tiny semantic representations we have fully developed SPDO to a generic semantic data model for describing smart products. We have tested and extended this model in various domains, such as shopping, consumer electronic and toys.

The run-time environment Tip 'n Tell makes heavy use of latest semantic web technologies, such as OWL-DL and SWRL. Our current SPDO realisation has been implemented within various domains but suffers from insufficiencies of underlying technologies. For instance, on language level OWL-DL and SWRL/Jess have no concept for named properties which leads to inefficient formal representations. On technical level there is no integration of SWRL into the Jena2 middleware which we use as the basis for Tip 'n Tell. Another technical issue is the use of RFID-based systems. In general, the integration with Tip 'n Tell and SPDO works very robust but problems arise if different tag types and protocols are used which might be cured by finalized standards.

Currently we work on extended domain models with elaborated rule models. A key issue is the relation between SPDO instantiations and rule sets and how rules can be automatically activated by SPDO instances according to situational changes.

References

1. Bo, X., Benbasat, I.: E-commerce product recommendation agents: Use, characteristics, and impact. MIS Quarterly 31(1), 137–209 (2007)
2. Schmid, B.: Inszenierung von Produkten im E-Business. In: Wunderlich, W., Spoun, S. (eds.) Medienkultur im digitalen Wandel, pp. 91–113. Haupt, Bern (2002)
3. Suomala, P.: The life cycle dimension of new product development performance measurement. International Journal of Innovation Management 8(2), 193–221 (2004)
4. Maass, W., Filler, A.: Towards an infrastructure for semantically annotated physical products. In: Hochberger, C., Liskowsky, R. (eds.) Informatik 2006. Lecture Notes in Informatics, vol. P-94, pp. 544–549. Springer, Berlin (2006)
5. Maass, W., Janzen, S.: Dynamic product interfaces: A key element for ambient shopping environments. In: 20th Bled eConference, Bled, Slovenia (2007)
6. Masolo, C., Borgo, S., Guarino, N., Oltramari, A.: The wonderweb library of foundational ontologies. Technical Report D17, WonderWeb (2003)
7. Gangemi, A., Borgo, S., Catenacci, C., Lehmann, J.: Task taxonomies for knowledge content. Technical Report D07, METOKIS Deliverable (2004)
8. Rogers, E.M.: Diffusion of innovations, 5th edn. Free Press, New York (2003)
9. Ullmer, B., Ishi, H.: Emerging frameworks for tangible user interfaces. In: Carroll, J.M. (ed.) Human-Computer Interaction in the New Millenium, pp. 579–601. Addison-Wesley, Reading (2001)
10. Wasinger, R., Wahlster, W.: The anthropomorphized product shelf: Symmetric multimodal human-environment interaction. In: Aarts, E., Encarnaçao, J. (eds.) True Visions: The Emergence of Ambient Intelligence, Springer, Heidelberg, Berlin, New York (2006)
11. Kourouthanassis, P., Spinellis, D., Roussos, G., Giaglis, G.M.: Intelligent cokes and diapers: Mygrocer ubiquitous computing environment. In: First International Mobile Business Conference, pp. 150–172 (2002)
12. Fox, A., Johanson, B., Hanrahan, P., Winograd, T.: Integrating information appliances into an interactive workspace. IEEE Computer Graphics and Applications 20(3), 54–65 (2000)
13. Want, R., Fishkin, K.P., Gujar, A., Harrison, B.L.: Bridging physical and virtual worlds with electronic tags. In: CHI 1999: Proceedings of the SIGCHI conference on Human factors in computing systems, pp. 370–377. ACM Press, New York (1999)

14. Kindberg, T., Barton, J., Morgan, J., Becker, G., Caswell, D., Debaty, P., Gopal, G., Frid, M., Krishnan, V., Morris, H., Schettino, J., Serra, B., Spasojevic, M.: People, places, things: Web presence for the real world. In: WMCSA 2000: Proceedings of the Third IEEE Workshop on Mobile Computing Systems and Applications (WMCSA 2000), Washington, DC, USA, p. 19. IEEE Computer Society, Los Alamitos (2000)
15. Pering, T., Ballagas, R., Want, R.: Spontaneous marriages of mobile devices and interactive spaces. Commun. ACM 48(9), 53–59 (2005)
16. Edwards, W., Newman, M., Sedivy, J., Smith, T., Balfanz, D., Smetters, D., Wong, H., Izadi, S.: Using speakeasy for ad hoc peer-to-peer collaboration. In: CSCW 2002: Proceedings of the 2002 ACM conference on Computer supported cooperative work, pp. 256–265. ACM Press, New York (2002)
17. Gellersen, H., Kortuem, G., Schmidt, A., Beigl, M.: Physical prototyping with smart-its. Pervasive Computing 3(3), 12–18 (2004)
18. Merrill, D., Maes, P.: Invisible media: Attention-sensitive informational augmentation for physical objects. In: Proc. of the Seventh International Conference on Ubiquitous Computing, Tokyo, Japan (2005)
19. Feldman, A., Taoa, E.M., Sadi, S., Maes, P., Schmandt, C.: Reachmedia: On-the-move interaction with everyday objects. In: ISWC 2005, pp. 52–59. IEEE, Los Alamitos (2005)
20. Strohbach, M., Gellersen, H.W., Kortuem, G., Kray, C.: Cooperative artefacts: Assessing real world situations with embedded technology. In: Sixth International Conference on Ubiquitous Computing (UbiComp) (2004)

Proof of Possession:
Using RFID for Large-Scale Authorization Management

Eberhard Grummt[1,2] and Ralf Ackermann[1]

[1] SAP Research, CEC Dresden
{eberhard.oliver.grummt,ralf.ackermann}@sap.com
[2] Technische Universität Dresden

Abstract. In inter-organizational supply chains, sharing of distributed, item-related information gathered using RFID can enable novel applications. Access control (AC) is needed to selectively disclose information to authorized participants. Given the large amount of data and the number of participants, common AC approaches would require extensive manual efforts. These efforts can be reduced significantly by the ability to prove physical possession of items to other companies. We examine how such Proofs of Possession can be designed. Based on two promising approaches, we introduce the concept of a Possession Service that may become a key factor in addressing the AC challenges in future supply chains.

1 Introduction

Using physical items to perform access control is a proven approach to enhance security. With the proliferation of the "Internet of Things" [3], billions of physical items with the ability to digitally carry identifying information will be linked to information stored in networked databases. In commercial scenarios such as RFID-enabled supply chains, both the data on the items and in the databases is potentially confidential, as it can contain mission-critical information like vendor-buyer-relationships or quantities. It seems self-evident to leverage the physical items themselves to manage access to their digital representations. Since the flow of an RFID-tagged item through a supply chain implies business relationships, periods of physical possession and their chronological order can be leveraged to infer access rights to item-related information. We name this approach *Possession-centric Access Management (PCAM)*. In contrast to tokens traditionally used in access control scenarios, basic RFID tags employed in supply chain management (SCM) are not permanently bound to a specific person or organization, but travel from company to company. They often do not contain secrets and are seldom tamper-proof. These properties pose hurdles to the realization of the PCAM approach. Still, it is attractive considering the amount of information that is automatically acquired in RFID-enabled supply chains and needs to be securely shared between companies to enable novel applications [2,1,13]. We argue that the ability to *prove* current or past physical possession of an item can form a sound basis for authorization decisions.

Based on a problem statement in Section 2, we systematize how such *Proofs of Possession* (PoPs) can be constructed and managed, discussing several approaches' differences regarding reliability and infrastructural requirements (Section 3). In Section 4,

M. Mühlhäuser et al. (Eds.): AmI 2007 Workshops, CCIS 11, pp. 174–182, 2008.

we introduce the novel concept of a *Possession Service* that can enable organizations to evidence whether other organizations were in possession of an item of interest or not. We present related work in Section 5 and conclude with a summary in Section 6.

2   Problem Statement

We investigate how physical access to RFID-tagged items at chosen points in time can be proved to remote parties while and after a company possessed them.

2.1   Definitions

Let $C = \{c_1, c_2, \ldots, c_n\}$ be a set of companies that successively handle an Item $i \in I$. With $T = \{t_1, t_2, \ldots\}$ being the ordered set of all values in a discrete time system, the relation *Possession* is defined as $Poss \subseteq C \times I \times T$, where a tuple (c, i, t) is in $Poss$ when a company c possessed item i at time t, i.e. $(c, i, t) \in Poss \Leftrightarrow c\ possessed\ i\ at\ t$. We define the relation *Possession Period* as $PossPer \subseteq C \times I \times T \times T$ with $(c, i, t_{start}, t_{end}) \in PossPer \Leftrightarrow \forall t \in T \exists (c, i, t) \in Poss, t_{start} \leq t \leq t_{end}$.

A *Proof of Possession (PoP)* is defined as information that enables others to verify, with a certain probability, if a company c really is or was in possession of an item of interest i at a chosen point in time t or during an interval (t_{start}, t_{end}).

A *Claim of Possession (CoP)* is a statement made by a company that it possesses or possessed an item i at t or during (t_{start}, t_{end}). We denote claimed possessions as elements of the relations $Poss'$ and $PossPer'$.

We distinguish between *Possession Time*, comprising time values at which actual possessions exists, and *Validation Time*, referring to the time when PoPs are evaluated by participants. A *Verification Service* (VS) is an abstract concept for a networked service operated by a party that is trusted by all $c \in C$, e.g. to calculate and store PoPs, manage secret keys, certificates, or transactional information. The concrete meaning and tasks of a VS is explained in the context of the several approaches and may differ slightly.

2.2   Use Case

As an item i travels through a supply chain, each $c \in C$ gathers and stores information related to i, the aggregation of which represents the item's history. The involved companies (i.e. the route of the item) are not completely known beforehand. All companies agreed on a generic policy that permits any company that possessed a specific item to access the related information stored at any of the other companies. Thus, the access control decision includes determining if the requester has ever possessed the item or not. Fig. 1 illustrates a scenario where i has passed through n companies, each of which operates a database containing information about i. c_n wants to access information related to i stored at c_1. c_1 does not know the route i took, in particular it does not know c_n. However, c_1 can rely on a PoP to grant c_n access. Note that c_n "found" c_1 in the first place by using a *discovery service*, which again might have performed access control based on a PoP. These initial steps are not depicted.

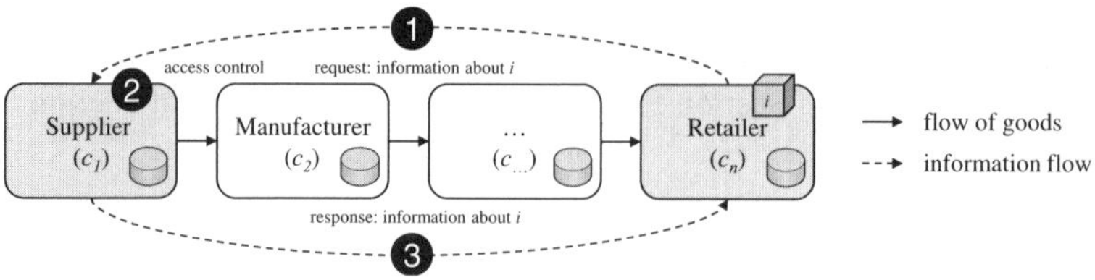

Fig. 1. The Access Decision Problem: how can c_1 decide if the request from c_n is legitimate?

2.3 Challenges and Evaluation Criteria

The main challenge is to maximize the probabilities with which a PoP is correct and with which a wrong CoP is identified. We consider that participants might issue wrong CoPs. A malicious company c could manipulate values for i or t. As we assume that every company $c \in C$ can be identified reliably, spoofing of identity is not addressed in this paper. When designing a system facilitating PoPs, the following high-level criteria need to be considered:

C1: it should be difficult to "prove" non-existent possession. We further distinguish
  C1a: it should be difficult *before* a company had actual possession and
  C1b: it should be difficult *after* a company has had actual possession
C2: it should be hard to repudiate possession

The difficulty of the operations needed to construct an invalid CoP that is accepted as a PoP can be measured in computational and monetary resources, in the amount of colluders needed, and in the amount of a priori information an attacker needs. Additional requirements and criteria strongly depend on the application domain and can therefore not be stated in detail here. Tag costs, infrastructure dependencies, and trust in participants and third parties are a few examples.

3 Methods for Constructing Proofs of Possession

3.1 Method Alternatives

In the simplest case, one could treat a CoP as a PoP, meaning one would need to trust the issuing company not to make any false statements. If such a PoP was used in access control, access would be granted to anyone who claims "I am authorized", which is obviously not a satisfactory solution.

Manual signature. A similar approach is to have each company $c \in C$ digitally sign their CoPs using software under their control, i.e. $PoP = CoP + Sig_c(CoP)$. This way, assuming a reliable public key infrastructure (PKI), c could at least be sanctioned for issuing wrong PoPs. Yet, none of the criteria C1 and C2 are met.
Signature by trusted reader. The signing process can be done by a "trusted" RFID reader r whose signature key $k_s(r)$ is not known to c and is physically protected against extraction. The public signature verification key $k_v(r)$ needs to be logically

bound to c, for example using a directory and certificates issued by a trusted third party (TTP). The integrity of the reader and possibly its location may be certified by a TTP, too. If the tags can be cloned or emulated, false PoPs can still be generated without tampering the reader hardware.

Linking and reasoning on supply chain transactions. This approach is based on the fact that an item can only be at one location at any point in time and is successively handled by companies, each of which usually knows its predecessor and its successor. A company c_m can issue a CoP at Possession Time of the form $possper'(c_m, i, t_{received}, t_{sent})$ along with c_{m-1} and c_{m+1} to identify its predecessor and its successor. If the majority of participants tells the truth, wrong CoPs can be identified as logic discrepancies. The PoP can be calculated by an instance that has access to all the CoPs submitted by the participants. Ideally, this instance could reconstruct the *Possession Chain* defined as $PossChain(i) = \bigcup_{c \in C}((c, i, t_{start}, t_{end}) \in PossPer)$ for every item $i \in I$.

Tags with static secrets. If a tag contains a static secret that can only be determined by companies possessing the item, a proof of knowledge of this secret can be used as PoP meeting C1a, but not C1b. At creation time of the tag, the secret could be shared with a VS that can later on perform the verification of CoPs by comparing the stored and the submitted secrets. Alternatives are using *zero-knowledge proofs* to prevent the VS from learning anything about the secret, and using the secret as a signature key. The latter approach would need a PKI for individual tags.

Tags with secret generator. Instead of using a static secret, a tag could continuously generate unpredictable "secrets", for example by signing or encrypting the tag's id together with the current timestamp using the tag's secret key $k_s(i)$. This approach requires actively powered, physically shielded tags with clocks. At Possession Time, a company c would send a signed CoP $poss'(c, i, t)$ along with $check = \{(i, t)\}_{k_s(i)}$ to a VS. The VS would then verify c's signature and if $check$ was really calculated by i. The latter can be realized using both symmetric and asymmetric cryptography.

Tag constellations. Simple RFID tags expected to be dominant in SCM contain an Electronic Product Code (EPC) which is not secret and therefore not suited as a PoP. But a *set* of EPCs (called a *constellation*) can be considered a secret if its distribution of EPCs is sufficiently chaotic. This secret can be used as described in *Using tags with static secret numbers* and even be changed by repackaging items.

Chosen, temporarily valid secrets. To avoid the need of expensive secret generators, a tag's secret could be altered *manually* at every transition of i from c_m to c_{m+1}. c_m could choose a secret s_m and share it with the VS and with c_{m+1}. c_{m+1} acknowledges s_m to the VS and chooses a new secret s_{m+1} which it again shares with the VS and with c_{m+2}, and so on. The VS keeps a list of secrets and their validity intervals. Instead of overwriting the secret on the tag, each company could slightly alter it, for example by inserting some random bits at random positions. So some kind of fingerprint of every company remains on the tag.

3.2 Storage Alternatives

Proof-on-Tag. Means that the PoPs are stored directly in the memory of the tag attached to i. Data protection against outsiders becomes mainly a concern of physical protection of the tags. However, a hostile participant in the supply chain has the whole range of attack possibilities such as probing, cloning, destruction, and removal. Especially where no permanent network connectivity is available, PoT has advantages. PoT requires more complex tags, providing an increased amount of (re-)writable memory and possibly means to perform access control. In order to access the PoPs, physical access to the respective tag is needed.

Proof-on-Network. Means that PoPs are stored on a remote networked server. We discussed several methods in Section 3.1 that rely on such a server. Most importantly, using this approach the PoPs can be accessed from any location with a network connection. The tag hardware requirements are lower. However, the server needs to be trusted, forms a single point of failure, and thus an attractive target for attackers. Companies will depend on its availability and the network infrastructure.

Hybrid Approaches. Can be used to combine the benefits from both of the aforementioned approaches. As we pointed out, the ability to write onto tags is a viable means to prove possession and to transfer small amounts of data directly bound to objects between and only between the companies that exchange goods. An auxiliary networked service trusted by all supply chain participants can increase security and availability of the possession information.

3.3 Evaluation

As a first step towards evaluating the different approaches, we reviewed them using the criteria introduced in 2.3 and the complexity of the required tags. The results are shown in Tab. 1.

Table 1. Evaluation of the approaches

Approach	Tag reqs.	C1a	C1b	C2
Manual signature	low	no	no	no
Signature by trusted reader	low	no	no	no
Linking and reasoning on SC Trans.	low	yes	yes	yes
Tags with static secrets	medium	yes	no	no
Tags with secret generator	high	yes	yes	no
Tag constellations	low	yes	yes*	no
Chosen, temporarily valid secrets	low or medium	yes	yes	no

"Low" tag requirements mean that simple tags like EPC Gen 2 Class 1 tags can be used. "Medium" means that rewritable memory or other features not available in the aforementioned class of tags are required, while "high" requirements imply complex computational functionality or active power supply. "low or medium" in the last row refers to the fact that the secrets can either be stored on the tags (leading to medium requirements) or be transferred between the companies using a network connection. (*) Note that to meet C1b, repackaging is neccessary.

4 Towards a Secure Possession Service

In this section, we describe early work on a networked *Possession Service* (PS) and associated protocols enabling to reliably answer questions of the general form $poss'(c, i, t) \in Poss \rightarrow \{true, false\}$. Based on our evaluation, we identified *linking and reasoning on supply chain transactions* and *chosen, temporarily valid secrets* as the two most promising approaches we strive to combine. They both do not need sophisticated tags and meet the criteria C1a and C1b. To meet C2, i.e. making it difficult for c_m to repudiate possession, using information submitted by other companies such as c_{m-1} and c_{m+1} is about the only viable approach because an illicitly behaving c_m could simply not submit any CoP at all. Fig. 2 depicts the two main ideas: companies choose a new secret when an item arrives (s_1 and s_2) while the PS maintains an internal representation of the Possession Chain together with the secrets.

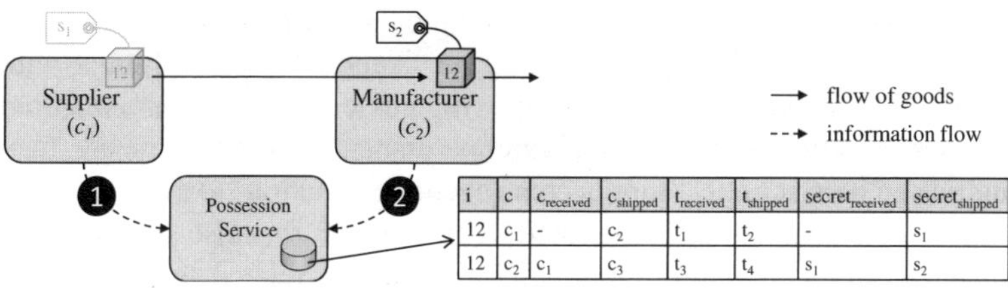

i	c	$c_{received}$	$c_{shipped}$	$t_{received}$	$t_{shipped}$	$secret_{received}$	$secret_{shipped}$
12	c_1	-	c_2	t_1	t_2	-	s_1
12	c_2	c_1	c_3	t_3	t_4	s_1	s_2

Fig. 2. Interaction between Possession Service and companies

The two main functional requirements are (i) calculating and storing PoPs based on CoPs issued by companies handling an item at Possession Time, and (ii) evaluating and answering CoPs at Validation Time. In the following overview, we present first requirements and insights regarding the different components of the envisioned Possession Service.

Query Interface (QI). Using this interface, legitimate requesters can answer the following questions: (a) did c possess i at all? (b) is c currently possessing i? (c) when did c possess i?

Capture Interface (CI). This interfaces's main purpose is to receive supply chain events such as CoPs and different security tokens submitted by individual companies. They are then passed to the *Possession Chain Reconstruction Component*.

Access Control (AC). Access to both the QI and the CI needs to be controlled as mission-critical information can be obtained using the QI and integrity can be compromised using the CI. AC can either itself be based on the PCAM, or employ explicit assignment of rights using Access Control Lists (ACLs) or Role-based Access Control (RBAC). The query interface might also be limited so companies can only request certificates attesting *own* possessions. These certificate can in turn be used to gain access to other companies' information systems.

Possession Chain Reconstruction Component. This component uses information received via the CI to decide whether it is correct or not and to integrate it into an internal representation of an item's Possession Chain. Depending on the information submitted by the individual companies, knowledge of secrets and spacial and temporal reasoning can be employed.

We want to decouple the Possession Service from any actual access control decisions to information systems. What kind of rights (read, write, delete etc.) a company c_l grants to c_m under which kind of possession relation (past or present) shall be up to the individual companies.

5   Related Work

Using physical items, and especially RFID for controlling access to physical resources is not new [10]. In the context of RFID and security, current literature focuses on reader/tag authentication and secure communication [9,7].

RSA's *SecurID* and related technologies employ small tokens generating one time passwords that can be verified by a remote server. Combining this technique with RFID could yield a very secure mechanism for proving possession. The *Authenticated RFID model* [8] uses signatures of the manufacturer permanently stored on the tag. Each company handling an item submits "supply chain event information" to a networked service. It is signed by PKI-enabled "Authenticated RFID readers" that also support verification of the manufacturer's signature. Optionally, timestamps related to the events can be written onto the tag to enable further plausibility checks.

The approach of linking and reasoning on supply chain transactions is currently discussed in the area of anti-counterfeiting [11], especially in the pharmaceutical industry. It however relies on the assumption that all involved parties submit correct information to a central service. In the same context, Ilic et al. [6] propose that companies establish temporary 1:1-"ownership"-links between physical items and their networked electronic pedigree records. These links can be used to infer and delegate access rights. The key idea is that only one company at a time is allowed to establish such a link, which is supposed to correspond to physical possession. The authors however do not discuss how actual possession can be proved to the pedigree record service provider and how the "links" can be maintained in detail.

The data structures in a PS are similar to those expected to be found in discovery services. While in the EPCglobal Architecture Framework [12], discovery services are not yet specified, early approaches can be found in [5]. In contrast to discovery services in other application areas, access control is crucial because of the sensitive nature of data, both regarding read and write access [4]. To our best knowledge, this problem has not been studied in detail before. A reliable proof of possession would be a suitable criteria to decide if a party is granted write access to a discovery service or not.

6   Summary and Future Work

If reliable proofs for the past and present possession of items can be generated and shared between supply chain participants, access control to item-related data can be simplified because less manual setup of access rights would be needed. In reality, policies would not be as simple as "temporary physical access $\Rightarrow$ unlimited data access", so temporal constraints as well as exceptions, for example to hide suppliers from wholesalers, would be needed.

PoPs with RFID tags can be constructed either *using item-specific information from a single source* or *combining item-specific information from different sources*. *Item-specific information* can be secrets on the tag which may be static, dynamically generated, or manually chosen. Leaving digital "traces" on the item, maybe using watermarking techniques, is a promising approach made possible by (re-)writable RFID-tags.

Information from different sources can be combined to increase resilience against minorities of misbehaving companies. Regarding our evaluation criteria, C1a is generally easier to achieve than C1b. If a tag contains a secret s that every company can only read out when possessing the tagged item, and companies do not disclose s to others, than knowledge of s proves possession.

PoPs can be generated by individual companies to prove possession to other companies. Alternatively, an external service can be used by a group of participants to assist in constructing, storing and querying PoPs. The main problem with such a service is that it has to be trusted not to disclose any of the information it gathers about business relationships between the companies that use the service. The same issue applies in the context of discovery services for individual items.

In our future work, we will examine how these limitations can be addressed by distributing the Possession Service and protecting its data so only minimal trust needs to be put into single instances. Case studies need to be examined in order to evaluate to what extent PCAM can be used in practical settings and what its advantages are against manually setting and delegating access rights. We are also concerned with the question how access control agreements that leverage PoPs can be negotiated, verified and enforced in dynamic groups of supply chain partners.

References

1. Bose, I., Pal, R.: Auto-ID: managing anything, anywhere, anytime in the supply chain. Commun. ACM 48(8), 100–106 (2005)
2. Delen, D., Hardgrave, B.C., Sharda, R.: RFID for Better Supply-Chain Management through Enhanced Information Visibility. Productions and Operations Management Journal (2007)
3. Fleisch, E., Mattern, F. (eds.): Das Internet der Dinge: Ubiquitous Computing und RFID in der Praxis, June 2005. Springer, Heidelberg (2005)
4. Grummt, E., Müller, M., Ackermann, R.: Access Control: Challenges and Approaches in the Internet of Things. In: Proceedings of the IADIS International Conference WWW/Internet 2007, Vila Real, Portuga, October 2007, vol. 2, pp. 89–93. IADIS Press (2007)
5. Harrison, M., Moran, H., Brusey, J., McFarlane, D.: PML Server Developments. In: White paper, Auto-ID Centre, University of Cambridge, Mill Lane, Cambridge, CB2 1RX, United Kingdom (June 2003)

6. Ilic, A., Michahelles, F., Fleisch, E.: The Dual Ownership Model: Using Organizational Relationships for Access Control in Safety Supply Chains. In: Advanced Information Networking and Applications Workshops (AINAW 2007), Niagara Falls, Ontario, Canada, May 2007, vol. 2, pp. 459–466 (2007)
7. Juels, A.: RFID Security and Privacy: A Research Survey. IEEE Journal on Selected Areas in Communication 24(2), 381–394 (2006)
8. Pearson, J.: Securing the Pharmaceutical Supply Chain with RFID and Public-key infrastructure (PKI) Technologies. White Paper RFIDPH01. Texas Instruments Radio Frequency Identification Systems (June 2005)
9. Peris-Lopez, P., Hernandez-Castro, J.C., Estevez-Tapiador, J., Ribagorda, A.: RFID Systems: A Survey on Security Threats and Proposed Solutions. In: Cuenca, P., Orozco-Barbosa, L. (eds.) PWC 2006. LNCS, vol. 4217, pp. 159–170. Springer, Heidelberg (2006)
10. Rieback, M.R., Crispo, B., Tanenbaum, A.S.: The Evolution of RFID Security. IEEE Pervasive Computing 5(1), 62–69 (2006)
11. Staake, T., Thiesse, F., Fleisch, E.: Extending the EPC Network – The Potential of RFID in Anti-Counterfeiting. In: SAC 2005, pp. 1607–1612. ACM Press, New York (2005)
12. Traub, K., Allgair, G., Barthel, H., Burstein, L., Garrett, J., Hogan, B., Rodrigues, B., Sarma, S., Schmidt, J., Schramek, C., Stewart, R., Suen, K.: The EPCglobal Architecture Framework – EPCglobal Final Version of (July 1, 2005), `http://www.epcglobalinc.org/standards/Final-epcglobal-arch-20050701.pdf`
13. Wamba, S.F., Lefebvre, L.A., Lefebvre, E.: Enabling Intelligent B-to-B eCommerce Supply Chain Management Using RFID and the EPC Network: A Case Study in the Retail Industry. In: ICEC 2006, pp. 281–288. ACM Press, New York (2006)

U-TOPIA: A Ubiquitous Environment with a Wearable Platform, UFC and Its Security Infrastructure, pKASSO

Kyu Ho Park, Ki-Woong Park, Jupyung Lee, Jong-Woon Yoo,
Seung-Ho Lim, and Hyun-Jin Choi

Computer Engineering Research Laboratory,
School of Electrical Engineering and Computer Science,
Korea Advanced Institute of Science and Technology
{kpark,woongbak,jplee,jwyoo,shlim,hjchoi}@core.kaist.ac.kr

Abstract. U-TOPIA, introduced in this paper, is an advanced ubiquitous computing environment mainly focusing on a university campus. Research in U-TOPIA spans various components each of which is essential to realize U-TOPIA: from user device hardware/software, user interface, communication technology, indoor/outdoor testbed, middleware to practical applications and security infrastructure. We designed and implemented a wearable platform from the scratch and make use of it as a main user device inside U-TOPIA. In addition to this, as a new user interface, we developed a wireless gesture recognition device, called i-Throw to communicate with U-TOPIA in an intuitive manner. For data communication and location tracking in U-TOPIA, campus-wide indoor and outdoor testbed was deployed. To keep up with secure and dynamic U-TOPIA environment, a new security infrastructure,called pKASSO, and extensible middleware, μ-ware, was developed. Finally, as a practical application for U-TOPIA, we implemented a ubiquitous testbed room where multiple users interact with various ubiquitous devices or other users securely in a user-friendly manner. Integrating these components all together, we show that U-TOPIA can be a realistic role model to improve current paradigm of ubiquitous computing environment one step forward within a few years.

1   Introduction

Ubiquitous and pervasive computing have had a wide ranging influence in the ideas of how the future would look like. Ubiquitous computing, already described in the early 1990 by Mark Weiser, can be seen today in various forms [1,2,3,4]. In recent years, the rapid progress of ubiquitous and pervasive computing technology, fueled by either a government-led or a company-led efforts to encourage the research, has led to the emergence of various 'smart' places powered by ubiquitous computing technology, ranging from smart room and smart campus to smart city.

M. Mühlhäuser et al. (Eds.): AmI 2007 Workshops, CCIS 11, pp. 183–193, 2008.

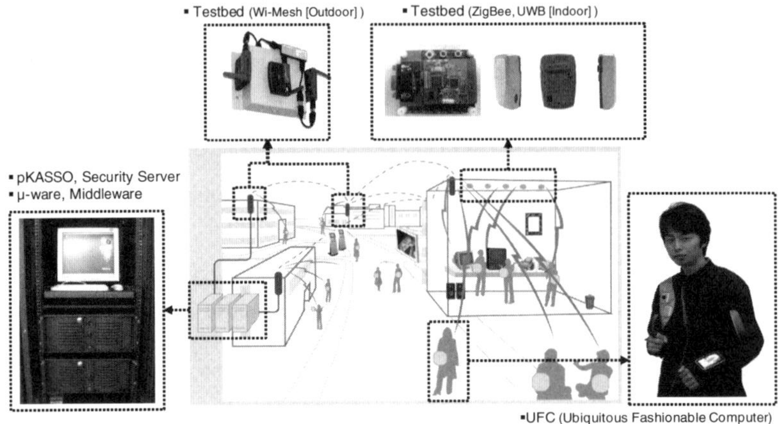

Fig. 1. Overall Architecture of U-TOPIA

In 2005, our team launched a government-funded project aimed at realizing a campus-wide advanced ubiquitous computing environment until the end of 2007. The ubiquitous computing environment was named as *U-TOPIA*, where 'U' stands for 'ubiquitous' and 'TOPIA' stands for 'place' in Greek. In order to realize U-TOPIA, we developed a wearable computer that allows people to exploit ubiquitous computing environment in a user-friendly manner and security infrastructure for secure ubiquitous services based on our testbed and middleware called μ-ware. The most important contribution of U-TOPIA can be summarized as follows;

- **UFC:** A wearable computer with modularity and extensibility is implemented based on ARM9 processor and embedded LINUX. Our hardware platform is called Ubiquitous Fashionable Computer (UFC), which is named based on our special emphasis on its wearability, aesthetic design and close interaction with ubiquitous environment.
- **i-Throw:** A new human computer interface called i-Throw is invented to throw/get information in one's UFC to the other UFC(s) or Objects when a throwing/getting action is taken by his hands.
- **μ-ware:** It is composed of light-weight service discovery protocol, distributed information sharing, context manager and instance service loader, all of which are useful to manage dynamic data and to develop new application that utilizes various ubiquitous resources.
- **pKASSO:** A new PKI-based security mechanism and security infrastructure, pKASSO, is devised for secure and seamless transaction between UFC and U-TOPIA where various devices frequently interact with each other or a surrounding infrastructure.

In addition to this, for data communication and location tracking in U-TOPIA, campus-wide indoor and outdoor testbed was installed. These efforts are closely related with realizing U-TOPIA in our campus.

2   U-TOPIA Internal

Overall architecture of U-TOPIA is described in Fig. 1. U-TOPIA consists of various components each of which is essential to realize U-TOPIA: from wearable platform (UFC), user interface (i-Throw), middleware (μ-ware) and security server (pKASSO) to practical and secure applications, and indoor/outdoor testbed. We have tried to push each research field a step forward to meet the ambitious goal, realizing a campus-wide advanced ubiquitous computing environment.

2.1   Indoor and Outdoor Testbed

Since U-TOPIA aims for a campus-wide environment, it is essential to build a large-scale testbed inside which various services can be operated. Two important components of a target testbed are a communication infrastructure and a location-tracking infrastructure.

Communication infrastructure lays the groundwork for ubiquitous computing. Communication inside U-TOPIA is made possible by wireless mesh network that is installed inside our campus. Location-tracking infrastructure is necessary for a location-based service. In outdoor environment, we made use of widely-used GPS information to track the location of moving objects. In indoor environment, we basically used ZigBee signal strength-based location tracking mechanism. To do this, we installed enough number of ZigBee sensor nodes inside two selected buildings inside U-TOPIA. During the measurement, however, we found that the resolution of location sensing using this mechanism was not sufficient for our target application. Thus, we also utilized UWB-based location tracking device[13] whose typical accuracy is 6 inches(15cm). Due to the high cost of this solution, UWB-based location tracking device have installed in only two rooms inside U-TOPIA.

2.2   Middleware, μ-Ware

In U-TOPIA, we assume a situation where thousands of users move here and there, interact with each other or ubiquitous computing environment, share information with authorized other users, access to diverse devices for diverse purposes, run various location-based applications. In this situation, an extensible middleware framework is necessary to keep up with highly variable dynamic environment. We have been working with middleware team and they developed a extensible middleware, called μ-ware[11]. μ-ware is composed of light-weight service discovery protocol, distributed information sharing, context manager and instance service loader, all of which are useful to manage dynamic data and develop new application utilizing various ubiquitous resources.

2.3   Wearable Platform, UFC

In U-TOPIA, a hardware platform is necessary to provide a user with plentiful ubiquitous computing resources. The hardware platform should be light-weight,

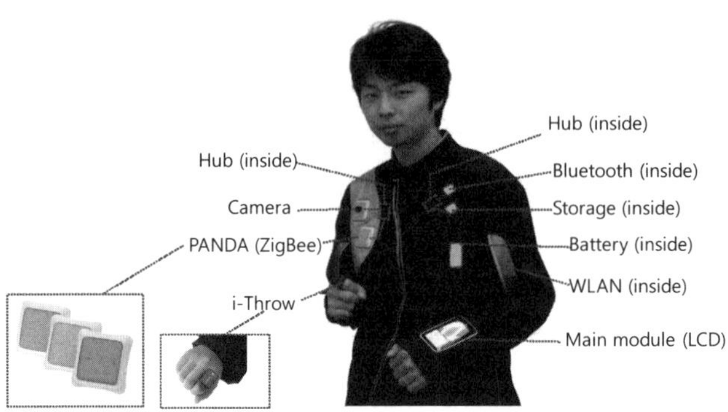

Fig. 2. UFC Platform Design and Implementation

easy to carry, easy to use and it should have aesthetic appearance and social acceptance. We chose to design and implement a wearable platform from the scratch and make use of it as a main user device inside U-TOPIA. Our wearable platform, in contrast to either laptop PC or handheld device, allows a user to carry the computing device in a comfortable and natural manner, because clothes have been already a essential component of our daily lives. Large surface area of clothes can be utilized for various purposes and thus, I/O interface does not have to be located in only a small-sized computing device. Moreover, the wearable platform makes it easier to measure and gather bio signal data such as temperature and heart rate by integrating body-attached sensors and computing devices upon a same clothes interface.

The implemented UFC platform is shown in Fig. 2. UFC modules are distributed on a garment, considering the distribution of weight and aesthetic design. Moreover, each UFC module can be attached and detached easily on a garment, allowing users to construct one's own UFC platform. Since we utilized a standard USB protocol to communicate between the main module and various UFC modules, due to the hotswap capability of USB devices, each UFC module can be attached and detached while the system is running.

The success of wearable computer relies on not only wearability, but also the aesthetic appearance and social acceptance. We tried to find the solution to fulfill the requirements by repeating the prototyping bodystorming progresses. We defined the target users as young university students and drew design concepts by analyzing their activities in everyday life and fashion trend. In addition, we have made effort for each part of the UFC platform to look like familiar fashionable components: for example, an attachable/detachable module is comparable to a button of clothing and an i-Throw device is comparable to a ring. Also, PANDA can be worn as a form of a necklace.

2.4   User Interface, i-Throw

In U-TOPIA, since plentiful resources locate outside a user, rather than inside a user device, a brand-new user interface is required to manipulate various outside

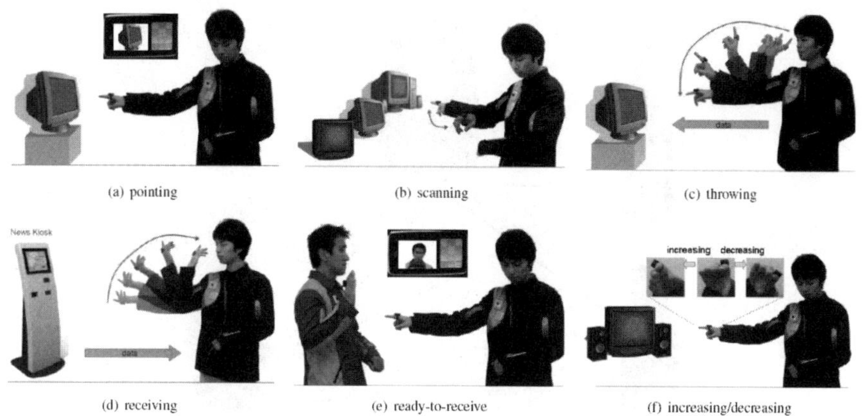

Fig. 3. Gesture Sets of i-Throw

resources in a user-friendly manner. To meet this requirement, we developed a wireless gesture recognition device, called i-Throw. Using this device, a user can express one's intention easily by using one's spatial movement and hand gesture. It is small enough to be worn on one's finger like a ring and has a three-axis accelerometer and a three-axis magneto-resistive sensor for recognizing a gesture and the direction of the finger. It also has a ZigBee transceiver for transmitting the recognized gesture information to the UFC platform.

The gesture recognition consists of two stages: *feature extraction* stage and *testing* stage. The feature extraction stage is a preprocessing stage to find reference features of each gesture. A feature f is represented by a four dimensional vector as follows:

$$f = (A_{THx}, A_{THy}, A_{THz}, T_H), \tag{1}$$

where A_{THx}, A_{THy} and A_{THz} are the acceleration thresholds of each axis and T_H is time duration threshold. In the feature extraction stage, we should find appropriate thresholds for each possible input gesture. Due to the limitation of space, we omit the detailed explanation of the feature extraction stage. In the testing stage, i-Throw device compares the output of the accelerometer with each reference feature for over T_H seconds. If one of the features is matched, then i-Throw transmits the recognized gesture to the UFC platform via ZigBee interface. The gesture recognition algorithm is designed to be simple enough to run on a micro-controller inside the i-Throw by extracting the minimum set of required features and using threshold-based simple features. We summarized and illustrated the gesture sets that the i-Throw recognizes in Fig. 3. Other possible gestures, scrolling up/down and canceling, are intentionally omitted here. Every time a UFC user points to a device, the UFC platform displays the selected target device upon its screen. This feedback information helps the UFC user find the correct target device. Similarly, a scanning gesture allows the user to investigate controllable devices inside the room. This scanning operation is

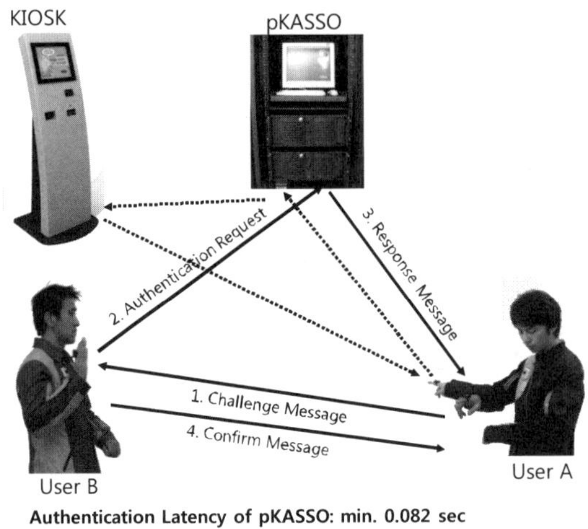

Fig. 4. Authentication flow description with pKASSO

similar to the operation of moving a mouse pointer across several icons in a typical PC desktop environment. 'Ready-to-receive' gesture is necessary for a UFC user to express one's intention to receive other UFC users' objects. When one user makes a pointing or scanning gesture, only limited users who makes the 'ready-to-receive' gesture can be selected.

2.5   Security Infrastructure, pKASSO

In order to provide a full-fledged security solution especially tailored for U-TOPIA, wherein numerous devices and sensors with severe resource-constraints interact with each other, we developed an computationally efficient PKI-based security infrastructure, pKASSO enhanced with single sign-on and delegation technology. It enables a cost-effective but uncompromisingly secure development of UFC. The delegation mechanism of pKASSO makes it possible to offloads complex cryptography operations from UFC to server-side so that it significantly improves authentication latency as well. According to the performance evaluation, the authentication latency (Avg. 0.082sec) is much shorter than a contact type smart card (Avg. 4.31sec) and a conventional PKI-based authentication latency (Avg. 5.01sec) [5]. Overall process of authentication based on pKASSO is illustrated in Fig.4.

1. User A sends a challenge message to user B who wants to communicate with user A.
2. User B generates an authentication request message (two symmetric key operations) and sends it to pKASSO. and it performs transactions for verification and authentication on behalf of user B.

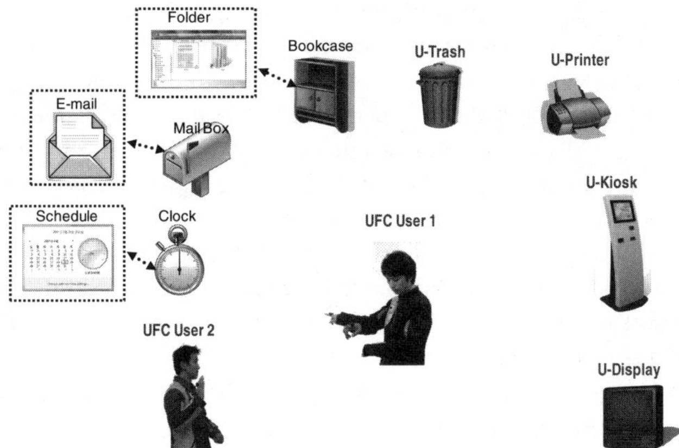

Fig. 5. The Concept of the Ubiquitous Testbed Room

3. pKASSO makes a response message and transmits it to user A.
4. The authentication is completed with the arrival of a confirming message from user B.

3 Target Application: User-Friendly Interaction with U-TOPIA

As mentioned in Section 2.4, we took 'user-friendly interaction with ubiquitous devices using i-Throw' as a target application. To execute this application, we have implemented a ubiquitous testbed room where multiple UFC users interact with various ubiquitous devices or other UFC users. Fig. 5 illustrates the concept of the ubiquitous testbed room which present a practical application that runs upon the UFC platform and the ubiquitous devices in testbed, which makes it possible to exchange the various objects and control ubiquitous devices very easily.

3.1 Motivation

Due to its small form factor, most portable devices, including our UFC platform, have only small-sized display and limited input devices. The UFC platform has 2.5" LCD display and 12 input buttons, which are definitely insufficient to monitor the status of a UFC main module and various peripheral modules, control the modules, and send a user's intention to the UFC platform.

This problem is exacerbated when a UFC user tries to control various ubiquitous devices using one's UFC platform: as the number of controllable ubiquitous devices increases, it becomes more inconvenient to find one among them and exchange information with it, due to the small-sized display and limited input devices of the UFC platform.

We attempt to resolve this problem by making full use of spatial resources inside the testbed room: given that various ubiquitous devices are spatially distributed inside the testbed room, a UFC user can express one's intention easily by using one's spatial movement and gesture. For example, let us assume that one UFC user takes a picture and intends to put it on a public display so that other people can see the picture he takes. From the perspective of the user, the most natural way of reflecting one's intention on the environment is pointing his finger at the public display and throwing one's picture at the public display. If this kind of a user-friendly spatial gesture interface is supported, the limitation of the I/O resources of the UFC platform can be overcome by fully utilizing abundant spatial resources.

For the UFC platform to support such a practical and secure interface, the following components are necessary:

- **gesture recognition device** recognizes the target device that a UFC user is pointing at and the gesture such as 'throwing' and 'receiving'.
- **location tracking device** keeps track of a UFC user's location. This is necessary because finding the target device that a UFC user is pointing at is dependent on the absolute location of the UFC user. We utilized UWB-based location tracking device[13] whose typical accuracy is 6 inches(15cm).
- **location server** gathers and manages the location information of both UFC users and ubiquitous devices. When one UFC user points at a specific device, the recognized gesture information is sent to the location server and it finally decides what the target device is.
- **Mutual Authentication and secure key distribution**: In order to provide secure and seamless transaction between UFC and U-TOPIA where various devices frequently interact with each other or a surrounding infrastructure, pKASSO is deployed.
- **Application that runs upon UFC platform** infers a UFC user's intention based on a gesture, a target device and previous operations and conducts a corresponding operation.

3.2   Detection of Target Device

Our target detection algorithm is based on Cone selection which is used in virtual computing environments[9]. A cone is cast from i-Throw and a set of devices that intersect with it are chosen. Additionally, we have modified that typical cone selection algorithm to vary the area of the cone adaptively to improve the overall target detection accuracy. To do this, the orientation of i-Throw and the position of the UFC user and devices should be known. The location information is gathered and managed by *virtual map* of μ-ware. The *virtual map* contains interactive objects around a user in a specific ubiquitous environment and supports several services as follows:

- **Interactive Object Registration:** For fast spatial queries, the repository of *virtual map* maintains a current snapshot of the interactive objects.

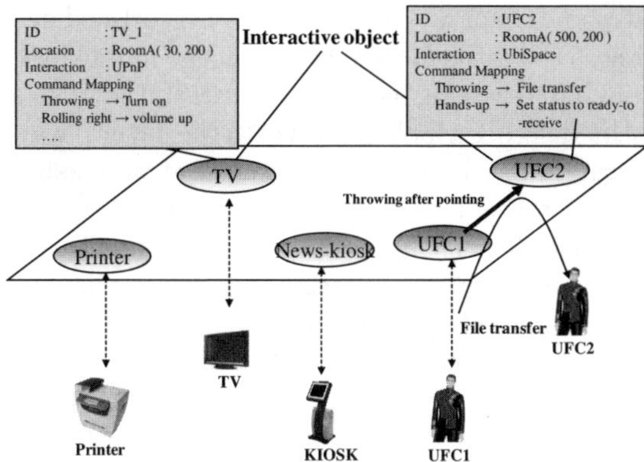

Fig. 6. Virtual map and interactive objects

- **Interactive Object Discovery:** When UFC detects logical address change, the virtual map repository is resolved by logical address key.
- **Target Selection in a Virtual Map:** UFC can see the target in the given boundary space with objects with priorities.

The scope of the virtual map is automatically adjusted upon user's location(inside building or outdoors). In the virtual map, each interactive object is tagged with geographic information and attributes to interact with. An interactive object is an abstraction unit of physical object on the virtual map. Interactive object contains location, and service attributes to interact with. Figure6 shows the virtual map and interactive objects. In Figure 6, the UFC1 has information about UFC2's location, interaction method, and the command configuration that assigns throwing motion as transferring a file. And the orientation of i-Throw can be obtained by combining the accelerometer and magnetic sensor outputs. The accelerometer is used for tilt compensation. By using the orientation and position information, target detection can be performed properly.

We define the target device sets which consist of possible target devices in the ubiquitous testbed and the characteristics of each one, which are summarized in Table 1. Among these devices, the *news kiosk* automatically gathers recent news

Table 1. Target Device Sets

Target device	Supported objects	Flow of objects
U-Display	News, Photo	Input, Output
U-Kiosk	News	Output
U-printer	News,Photo	Input
U-trash	News,Photo,music	Input
Clock, Mail, Bookcase	Supported Application	Input, Output
UFC	news,photo,music	Input, Output

from internet web sites and displays each one, that is refreshed every 10 seconds. When one UFC user sees the interesting news upon the news kiosk, he or she can obtain the news by making 'receiving' gesture towards the news kiosk. The *u-trash* functions as a symbol of 'deleting a file'. Similarly to the natural way of using an actual trash, throwing something that is useless anymore at the trash, if one UFC user makes a throwing gesture towards the u-trash, the current object will be deleted automatically. The u-trash device is different from other devices in that it is not an electric device; it acts only as a marker standing for a particular operation and thus actual operation is not conducted inside it. This example gives us insight as to how to fully utilize spatial resources inside the room. If various markers whose symbolic meaning can be easily interpreted are added inside the room and each corresponding operation is efficiently conducted, the spatial gesture interface allows UFC users to conduct various operations in a user-friendly manner.

4   Conclusion

U-TOPIA, introduced in this paper, is a campus-wide advanced ubiquitous computing environment. We summarized five essential components to realize U-TOPIA paradigm in our campus: indoor/outdoor testbed, middleware (μ-ware), wearable platform (UFC), user interface (i-Throw), security infrastructure (pKASSO). Since 2005, we have tried to push each research field a step forward to meet the ambitious goal, realizing a campus-wide advanced ubiquitous computing environment. Specifically, we designed and implemented a wearable platform from the scratch and make use of it as a main user device inside U-TOPIA. In addition to this, as a new user interface, we developed a wireless gesture recognition device, called i-Throw. To keep up with secure and dynamic U-TOPIA environment, a new security infrastructure,called pKASSO, and extensible middleware, μ-ware, was developed.

In addition to this, for data communication and location tracking in U-TOPIA, campus-wide indoor and outdoor testbed was installed. Finally, as a practical application for U-TOPIA, we implemented a ubiquitous testbed room where multiple users interact with various ubiquitous devices or other users in a user-friendly manner. All these efforts are closely related with realizing U-TOPIA in our campus. We believe that U-TOPIA can be a realistic role model to improve current paradigm of ubiquitous computing environment within a few years. As a future work, we will attempt to apply our indoor application to outdoor testbed, so that a user can extract suitable information from outdoor components, such as building, billboard, large display and vehicles.

References

1. Mann, S.: Wearable computing as means for personal empowerment. In: Proc. 3rd Int. Conf. on Wearable Computing (May 1998)
2. Pentland, A.: Wearable intelligence. Proc. Scientific American 1, 276 (1998)

3. Starner, T.: The challenges of wearable computing: Part 1. In: Proc. IEEE Micro, July 2001, pp. 44–52 (2001)
4. Weiser, M.: The computer for the 21st century. In: Proc. Scientific American, September 1991, vol. 3, pp. 66–75 (1991)
5. Park, K.W., Seok, H.C., Park, K.H.: pKASSO: Towards Seamless Authentication providing Non-Repudiation on Resource-Constrained Devices. In: Proc. 21st IEEE Symposium on Pervasive Computing and Ad Hoc Communications, May 2007, vol. 2, pp. 105–112 (2007)
6. Lee, J., Lim, S.H., Yoo, J.W., Park, K.W., Choi, H.J., Park, K.H.: A Ubiquitous Fashionable Computer with an i-Throw Device on a Location-Based Service Environment. In: Proc. 21st IEEE Symposium on Pervasive Computing and Ad Hoc Communications, May 2007, vol. 2, pp. 59–65 (2007)
7. IEEE802.15.2 Specification, Coexistence of Wireless Personal Area Networks with Wireless Devices Operating in Unlicensed Frequency Bands (August 28, 2003)
8. Back, M., Lahlow, S., Ballagas, R., Letsithichai, S., Inagaki, M., Horikira, K., Huang, J.: Usable Ubiquitous Computing in Next-genration Conference Rooms: Design, Evaluation, and Architecture. In: Proc. UbiComp 2006 Workshop, September (2006)
9. Liang, J., Green, M.: JDCAD: A Highly Interactive 3D Modeling System. Proc. Computers & Graphics 4, 499–506 (1994)
10. Kang, M., Chong, J., Hyun, H., Kim, S., Jung, B., Sung, D.: Adaptive Interference-Aware Multi-Channel Clustering Algorithm in a ZigBee Network in the presence of WLAN Interference. In: Proc. IEEE International Symposium on Wireless Pervasive Computing, Puerto Rice (February 2007)
11. Song, Y., Moon, S., Shim, G., Park, D.: μ-ware: A Middleware Framework for Wearable Computer and Ubiquitous Computing Environment. In: Proc. 5th Conference on Pervasive Computing & Communications(PerCom 2007) (March 2007)
12. UPnP Forum, UPnP Device Architecture 1.0, Version 1.0.1 (December 2003)
13. Ubisense, http://www.ubisense.net
14. KAIST UFC Project, http://core.kaist.ac.kr/UFC

Ambient Assisted Living Systems –
Notes on a Plenary Discussion

Martin Becker[1], Martin Floeck[2], and Thomas Fuhrmann[3]

[1] Fraunhofer IESE, Kaiserslautern
[2] Technical University of Kaiserslautern
[3] Thomas Fuhrmann, University of Karlsruhe and Technical University of Munich

The joint workshop on Ambient Assisted Living Systems was held in Darmstadt on 10th November 2007. It consisted of a plenary talk by Gregory Abowd from the Georgia Institute of Technology, a keynote by Hartmut Strese from VDI/VDE-IT, a track on the progress in the EU project MonAMI, and a scientific track presenting eight peer reviewed papers on various topics in ambient assisted living (AAL). The workshop was concluded by a joint discussion about the future of AAL. Here, we report on the outcome of this discussion. The views and ideas put forth in the following summary are the joint contributions of all the participants in that discussion whom we hereby want to express our thanks.

The discussion outcome can be structured into issues relating to AAL applications and services on the one hand, and technological challenges on the other. We begin with the service oriented aspects:

Security and safety are important topics in all kinds of computer based solutions. With AAL systems they are even more important because technical laymen are expected to trust those systems – and sometimes trust their lives to those systems. Thus the dependability of AAL should be in the focus of all future developments in AAL. Moreover, with AAL we need to discuss not only the security and safety of the system itself, but also the way these systems bring additional security and safety to our everyday lives. In particular, many AAL systems will be designed to protect the homes and lives of their inhabitants.

In this respect, **emergency detection and prevention** are among the key applications for AAL systems. The monitoring of vital data is probably the foremost point here – and one of the simpler tasks. Other obvious applications such as the reliable detection of a fallen or helpless person have been found astonishingly difficult by many participants in the discussion. This is even more the case for more complicated tasks such as the prediction of an upcoming disease based on the monitored vital data in an AAL system. Monitoring the daily medication might be an important first step. According to several projects, such an application might be comparatively simple and will already have a significant impact on the health of the persons living in an AAL environment.

Even though many ongoing projects focus on elderly or impaired people, quite a few proposals in the discussion addressed a wider audience of users. Various kinds of **memory aids** such as automated calendars and reminders, personal records and activity tracking can be useful to everybody. Quizzes and other brain exercises additionally have

M. Mühlhäuser et al. (Eds.): AmI 2007 Workshops, CCIS 11, pp. 194–196, 2008.

fun and **edutainment** aspects. The communicative aspect of such systems can also satisfy some of the social needs of the inhabitants. More generally, AAL systems could support many household chores such as cooking including the management of the respective groceries.

Furthermore, AAL can also be envisaged to create **new branches of service businesses**, for example, the management and maintenance of intelligent homes. In general, the AAL business might become more a service and franchise oriented sort of business rather than a business that sells devices to end-users.

Besides the application and service oriented view described so far, the participants discussed the technology and process aspects that need to be addressed on the way to successfully realize this AAL potential.

Cheap, universal sensors for all kinds of physical parameters were seen as foremost challenge in AAL technology. Many AAL applications need unobtrusive sensors for easy long term monitoring of the respective physical parameters such as vital data and object handling. The sensors' price point should allow the inexpensive deployment of a large number of such sensors. They should be easy to install and be operational (almost) without prior configuration. The sensors' capabilities and deployment profile should be sufficiently general to allow usage in a large number of applications. To this end, their interfaces should also be open to allow various applications to benefit from these sensors. Here, existing standards like IEEE 1451 might help to quickly build up a sufficiently large set of interoperable sensors. Considering the legal aspects it is important to be aware of the differences in national legislation. In any case, the discussion's participants pointed out that it is important to make the systems transparent enough to always be able to track malfunctions to the respectively responsible component.

Furthermore, **resource efficiency** especially in terms of energy is important. Clearly, energy harvesting is up to now still impractical for most real applications. Notable exceptions are self-powered switches and similar devices that can benefit from a person exerting a force on the device. Meanwhile it is more important to indicate the power status of the devices, for example, to help the support staff in replacing batteries in time.

The **reliable recognition of a large number of activities** is seen as a challenge. Context interpreters provide partial solutions, but systems that are scalable, self-learning, and easy to administer are still missing. Especially, a system for recognizing the inhabitants' mood was seen as a valuable milestone in AAL. It requires extensible, intelligent reasoning and needs to be self-adaptive to individual preferences and habits. Moreover, it would be a helpful component to detect various disorders such as depression or worsening dementia. As a first step, researchers will need a sufficiently large corpus of statistical data on which they can train the algorithms and systems. These shall be able to find interesting data in the data bases and learn about the normal and potentially peculiar behaviour of human beings. It is however important to consider the privacy aspects in the design of these systems.

In general, successful AAL solutions were envisaged to provide an **interrelation between applications and technology**. Thereby, the output of one system can serve as input to others. In other words, successful AAL requires semantic interoperability. Here, the discussion participants saw a lack of joint concepts of the AAL stakeholders.

Regarding the process of AAL research, many participants stated that is was important to focus on the real needs of the respective target group, for example, elderly or impaired people. This requires, for example, an interactive brainstorming between psychologists, computer scientists, sociologists, and lawyers. AAL systems should be designed to be interesting to use, not stigmatising, and they should be generation compatible. This can be achieved by early and continuous user involvement.

We hope that our workshop and the joint discussion have contributed to direct the future AAL research to successful goals and challenges so that the society can best benefit from the research community's efforts.

Attitudes and Requirements of Elderly People Towards Assisted Living Solutions

Jonas Grauel and Annette Spellerberg

Research Area of Urban Sociology, University of Kaiserslautern
grauel@rhrk.uni-kl.de, spellerb@rhrk.uni-kl.de

Abstract. In this paper, the most important results of the social research within the Project "Assisted Living" [1] at the Technical University of Kaiserslautern, are discussed: First we present impressions of elderly people who tested a newly developed user interface for touch screen Computers. Second, experiences of elderly people who use assistive devices in their everyday life are illustrated. Third, results of a standardised survey on acceptance of home automation technology are presented: The overall willingness to use new technical devices among the elderly is higher than often expected. Still, Ambient Assisted Living (AAL) for elderly people still faces some challenges: Costs and installation efforts are still very high, the most urgent needs and wants of elderly people should be emphasized more strongly for AAL to evolve into successful products on the market.

1 Introduction

Independent living at home is important for everybody, but especially for elderly people. 93 % of the 65-year-olds and older in Germany live in normal private flats and houses, only 7 % live in institutions or special forms of housing for elderly people [1]. Most elderly people wish to stay in their self-chosen-environment as long as possible even if they experience a growing loss in quality of life. Because of demographical and social changes, the importance of independent living at home will increase further in the future: In the EU-25, the percentage of 65-year-olds and older will increase from 16 % in 2005 to 25 % in 2030 [2]. At the same time, the personal basis of the family as the traditional system of care for the elderly is ceasing because of divorces, childless marriages and increasing flexibility demands of the labour market. These changes enforce to find new

---

[1] The Project "Assisted Living" is conducted by the Institute of Automatic Control (Prof. Dr. Lothar Litz and Dipl.-Ing. Martin Floeck) and the Research Area of Urban Sociology (Prof. Dr. Annette Spellerberg and Dipl.-Soz. Jonas Grauel) at the Technical University of Kaiserslautern from 1/2006—12/2008. The project is funded by the Ministry of Finance of Rhineland-Palatinate and the housing societies Bau AG Kaiserslautern, Wohnbau Mainz GmbH, Gemeinschaftliche Siedlungs-Gesellschaft Neuwied mbH and Gemeinnuetzige Baugenossenschaft Speyer eG. We would like to thank our partners for their kind support.

M. Mühlhäuser et al. (Eds.): AmI 2007 Workshops, CCIS 11, pp. 197–206, 2008.

social and technical solutions enabling seniors to live independently as long as possible.

Ambient Assisted Living is seen as a promising contribution to this aim. But until now it is not clear which technological concepts and which single devices are of use for elderly people and are accepted at the same time. Apart from pilot projects AAL-technology is not prevalent in senior households. Housing companies and scientists who conducted pilot projects often experience disappointments, because the needs of elderly people are not considered adequately.

Therefore, it is the aim of the project "Assisted Living" to directly involve the target group into the development process of an Ambient Assisted Living system. In Kaiserslautern, Speyer, Mainz and Neuwied, facilities for senior citizens are newly constructed or modernised. Technical solutions from the field of home automation will be used to assist elderly people in the areas of comfort, safety, security and also health. All four subprojects are accompanied by social research. In the forefield, studies about technical acceptance of elderly people were carried through. Once the tenants move into the newly built facilities, they are interviewed before and after using new technical devices to gather feedback about how technology helps in their everyday life. By bringing in the user perspective, potential improvements can be pointed out.

The aim of this paper is to present the most important outcomes of our social research up to date. First, we would like to shortly describe the technical concept (chapter 2) and present first impressions of elderly people who tested PAUL (Personal Assistant Unit for Living), a newly developed user interface for touch screen computers (chapter 3). In chapter 4, we will illustrate first experiences of elderly people who use assistive devices in their everyday life. Finally, we will take a broader perspective and present results concerning overall technology attitudes and acceptance of assisted living devices of the elderly. In the conclusion, we suggest some new pathways AAL-projects should take.

2   Concept of the Project "Assisted Living" in Kaiserslautern

The technical concept is described on the example of the subproject in Kaiserslautern, since it is the technically most advanced. A facility with 20 barrier free apartments is completed in November 2007. All apartments are equipped with an EIB/KNX-Bus, several sensors to detect activity of the tenant (e.g. motion detectors, indication of water usage) and a touchscreen tablet-PC called PAUL (Personal Assistant Unit for Living). Furthermore, there is a door camera, which shows the picture of visitors in front of the building door. When leaving the apartment, a light indicates open windows and a switch offers the possibility to turn off certain plugs (e.g. the oven plug).

With this equipment, multiple functions in the areas of comfort, safety, security can be covered, and it is also aspired to cover health. Comfort means e.g. remote-controlled shutters. Also, PAUL offers the possibility to contact the family or neighbours via a communication system and an alarm clock. Other functions like TV, Internet and memory training games will be implemented later on. The plug switch and the open window indication enhance safety while the door camera offers protection against tricksters. While these functions can be easily covered by common home automation devices, often special devices are needed for monitoring a person's health status, e.g. wrist watches for monitoring the pulse, the blood pressure and so on. In this project, it is desired to also use the information provided by the home automation sensors to monitor the health status of the tenant. Activities like movements, the usage of PAUL, light switches and water are registrated and the data is collected on the tablet-PC. Once a day the data will be transferred to the Technical University. All tenants agreed to this procedure in signing a contract. This data is necessary to develop algorithms to detect behavioral patterns. Over time, a typical profile of daily activities can be generated for each person. On the basis of these daily profiles, PAUL will be able to trace changes in behavioral patterns over a long time, e.g. if the activity of a person becomes less. Also, it is desired to detect instant critical situations like downfalls. If a downfall is detected, PAUL can give a call to neighbours, relatives or an emergency centre, asking for help. Because no vital data can be registrated via ambient sensors, it will be not possible to detect critical situations like heart attacks which require help very urgently. For a more detailed description of this approach see [3].

All the described functions can be operated via PAUL's touchscreen. The aim of the user interface (Fig.1) is to make the handling as easy as possible for elderly

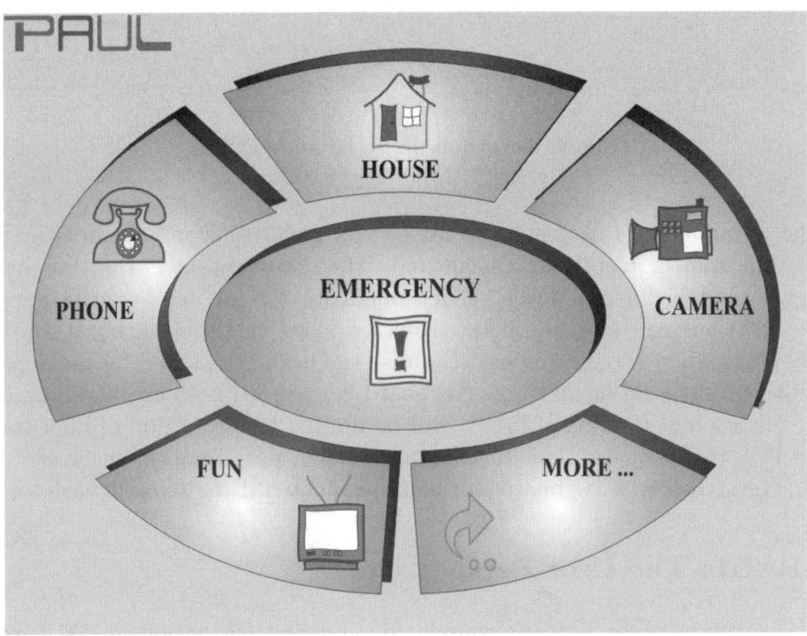

Fig. 1. The main menu of PAUL's user interface

people. A common way to control home automation is to have a map of the flat
and symbols for shutters, lights etc. In contrast, we decided to use a menu with
up to three layers. By pressing a button in the main menu, the next layer, e.g.
"House" is reached (Fig.2). Here, a room can be selected which leads to another
submenu. Additionally, in this menu all lights and shutters in the flat can be
operated at once.

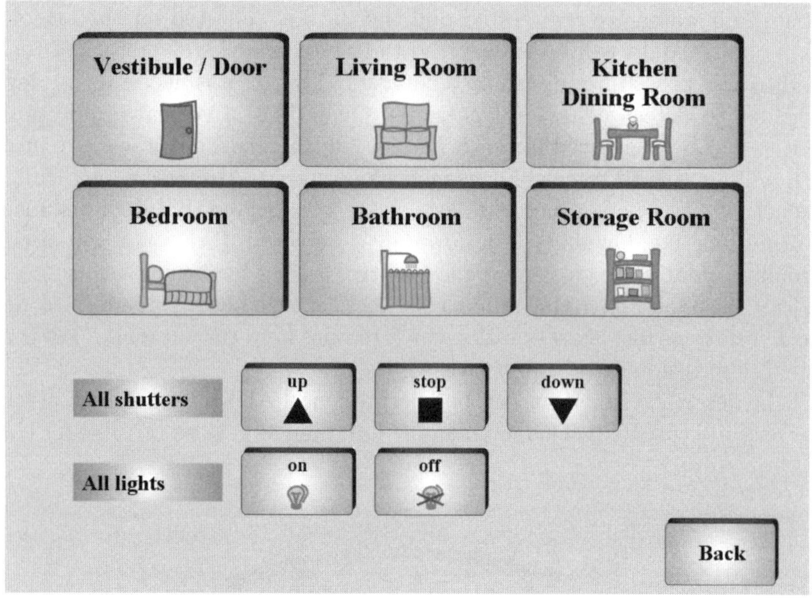

Fig. 2. The submenu for house functions

The advantage of this design is that very large buttons and symbols are possible, thus good perceptibility is ensured. The disadvantage is that one has to
navigate though different levels, which might be difficult for forgetful persons.
Some functions can also be operated via switches on the wall, e.g. turning of
safety plugs when leaving the flat. Because the usability should be as simple as
possible, no external or on-screen-keyboard is used. To keep the handling intuitive, the internet options of PAUL will be limited to a selection of information
pages like weather, bus plan, theatre and cinema programmes, newsticker and
so on. Nevertheless, a keyboard can be implemented if the tenants wish for it.

3   PAUL: The User Perspective

In May 2007, a model flat was completed, so a first evaluation of PAUL could
take place. Questions were: How do the testers manage to handle the touch
screen? Are they able to intuitively find the desired functions? Are the symbols

clear enough? Is the font readable? etc. Eight persons were interviewed for this purpose. The interviewees were between 60 and 76 years old, seven women and one man. It has to be assumed that the test persons are very committed and have an above-average technical competence for their age since five out of eight are active computer users. The testers were "normally aging" persons, so no statements can be made about how the control of PAUL works with dementia or MS patients. Therefore, PAUL has to be tested further with persons who are less competent in using modern technology and have different impairments or diseases. Many more results will be available after the facility in Kaiserslautern will be inhabitated and there are regular users. The testers were asked to solve several tasks, for example to control the light, turn on the TV or play a piece of music. Afterwards, they were questioned about their impressions.

On the positive side, the results of this first evaluation indicate that the user interface is well designed, possible improvements affect only details. The symbols were judged to be intuitive to understand and nice to look at, the fonts were assessed readable, also colours and contrast between symbols, buttons and background was judged as good (Fig.1 and 2). Seven out of eight persons managed to fulfil the given tasks without bigger problems. Four persons intuitively found their way through the menu without any explanation by the interviewers. They also tried different functions autonomously, even if those were not included in the tasks. Three persons initially needed to overcome their reservations against using a touch screen, but finally also managed to fulfil the tasks without problems. One test person did not manage to fulfil some of the tasks, during which she had to switch through several screens. This points out that the interface might be too complicated for forgetful persons.

But the tests indicated also some problems still to be solved: First, in the current state PAUL is not an appropriate device to send emergency calls. The emergency button is only displayed on the entrance screen. If this screen isn't shown in case of emergency, the user would have to return to the main menu to send a call, which might not be possible in a critical situation. For an easy emergency call function, we think it is necessary to have an extra device with just one button. This is difficult to realise within the concept of an interface with several screens. One solution might be a portable button that is linked wirelessly with PAUL to call for help.

Second, there is a conflict between PAUL's portability and using it for monitoring health. Because the risk of a power-breakdown can not be accounted for, it would be advisable to fixate PAUL in one place because the battery lasts only for a few hours. On the other hand, PAUL is a multifunctional device and a fixed installation might devalue some features of PAUL, depending on which place is chosen. From our testers, four persons preferred to have PAUL in the living room because that is where they are during day time. One woman would prefer PAUL in the bedroom because she thinks she would need the emergency call function mostly at night. Three persons could not decide because they think some functions like the door camera and the phone would be needed in the living room while other functions like the TV or the alarm clock would be more useful in the bedroom. In Kaiserslautern, a compromise was made to solve this conflict: The apartments will be equipped with two power stations, one in the bedroom and in the combined kitchen and living room area. PAUL can be carried from one station to the other. Doing so it should be ensured that some functions are not devalued and the risk of a power-breakdown is at least minimized. Generally, it would be preferable to separate the touchscreen control unit and the computer that collects and interprets the data. This way, portability and constant power supply could be ensured.

Asked for additional features, the majority said they would like to hear radio with PAUL. This function was not thought of before, so this is a good example that technology should be developed in close contact with the target group.

4   Experiences with Assisted Living Devices in Everyday Use

In Neuwied, 63 barrier-free apartments for seniors with lower incomes were constructed. They are pre-equipped with an EIB/KNX Bus System. PAUL is not included, but can be integrated easily if a tenant decides to buy one later. Still, the apartments offer a higher technical standard than normal flats: There are electrical shutters for comfort. For safety reasons it is possible to turn off oven and iron plugs when leaving the flat. To tenants in the basement, open windows are indicated. The security concept consists of a combination of interphone, spy holes in different heights and a door bell with different ring tones for the house door and the apartment door. An extra interphone next to the bed makes it possible to open the front door without getting up. To cover health issues, there is a standard home emergency call.

The tenants moved into the apartments in July 2006. Five months later, we interviewed 41 persons from 34 out of 57 apartments occupied at that time personally. The aim was to examine the experience and satisfaction with the technology installed and to find out about further needs of assistance.

The overall satisfaction with the apartments in Neuwied was high: 37 out of 41 said to be content or very content. Mentioned reasons for complete satisfaction were the barrier free accessibility of the flats, the good location close to the inner city and the sound insulation. Also the general satisfaction with the technical equipment of the flats was high. The underfloor heating and the electric shutters were seen to enhance comfort. The emergency call and the interphone system were judged positively because they gave the tenants a feeling of security. Nevertheless, not all devices were assessed helpful:

The LED to indicate open windows is not regarded by four out of five persons since they leave windows open intentionally. Also, some tenants feared that the LED would waste energy. Only one woman used the light as a help for remembrance. Several respondents made negative experiences with the switch to turn off plugs when leaving the apartment. Some complained that clocks on ovens and video recorders have to be reprogrammed. Others said that their freezer defrosted. For these reasons, some tenants pasted tape over the switch so it could not be used anymore. Even if those problems were solved, the switch was considered needless because no necessity to turn off plugs during absence was seen. Based on these experiences, some improvements were made in the Kaiserslautern subproject: Here, the plugs have two different colours, red and grey. Only the red ones are turned off by a switch at the apartment door. This way, the tenants know where to connect devices that should be or should not be turned off. Also, an automaton that recognizes if the the tenant(s) are absent or not is tested. In the future, it could be used to turn off and on the red plugs automatically, so safety is given even if the person forgets to switch off the plugs.

The second focus of the study concerned the performing of 16 everyday tasks. 18 out of 41 persons were free of restrictions, but 17 persons stated to have difficulties performing up to six household tasks and six had problems with more than ten tasks. The biggest difficulties were expressed for exhausting tasks like cleaning windows and grounds, putting up curtains, vacuum-cleaning and making the bed. Most of the persons with problems had private help by their partners or relatives. Persons left without help wished for private rather than professional help. When we asked for interest in additional technical assistance, the response was retained. While the Neuwied tenants would be provided with the PAUL software for free because the facility is in the pilot project, they would have to pay the touchscreen PC, which costs around 2500 €. The average monthly household income was of the interviewees 1030 € , which is less than average for western german tenants. [2] Thus, the financial possibilities for buying PAUL are limited. Also, most interviewees already considered the technological equipment of their apartments optimal for their need. At the same time their most urgent needs (help with household tasks) and wants (personal contact) are of a non-technical nature. Therefore, no need in additional technical improvements was seen.

5   Overall Acceptance of AAL-Technology

In May 2006, 383 over 60-year-olds from the city of Mainz were polled via a postal questionnaire. The participants in this survey were asked about their attitudes towards technology, their acceptance of 18 home automation devices and their willingness to pay for the installation and use of home automation. The aim of the study was to explain differences in acceptance between subgroups of the elderly. Three results are important in this context, for detailed results of the study see [4]:

First, it can be stated that there is a big open-mindedness towards technology among the elderly. In a cluster analysis of leisure types, we found a group of 13 % of the polled tenants who actively use computer and internet at least on a weekly or even a daily basis. The respondents were also asked to give their opinion about eight statements which express personal and general attitudes towards

---

[2] The average income of western german tenants over 60 years old is 1070 €, while flat or home owners in this age category have an average income of 1350 € (own calculations on the basis of the representative social survey ALLBUS 2004).

technology (e.g. "Technology makes life more convenient", "I am interested in computers"). On this basis, types of attitudes were built via cluster analysis. 60 % of the respondents were attributed to types of attitude which can be characterized by a high personal interest in technology in general, in computers as a single key technology and a self-ascribed high ability to handle everyday technology. The other 40 % expressed little interest and unease with handling technology.

Second, we asked if the respondents could imagine the use of home automation devices. Figure 1 shows that the willingness to use the tested home automation devices is high, at least for some applications.

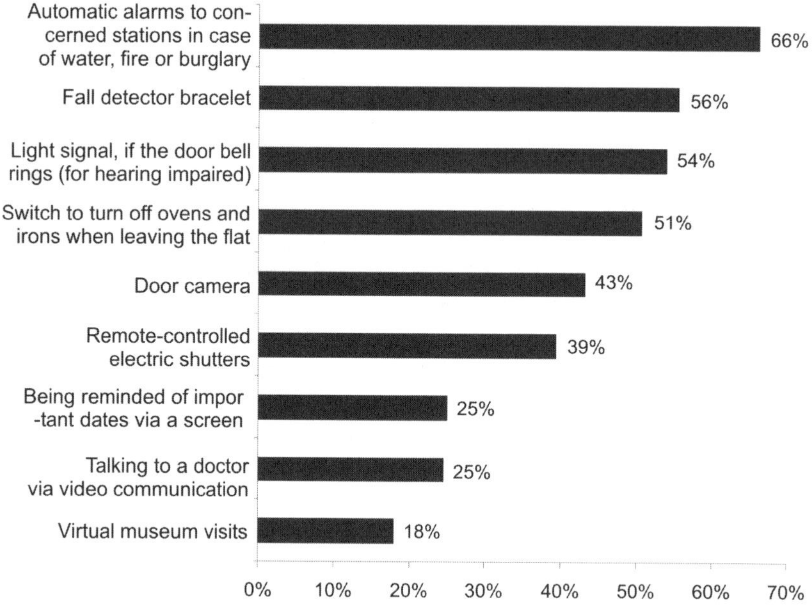

Fig. 3. Willingness to use selected Assisted Living devices

66 % of the respondents could imagine to use automatic alarms to the concerned stations in case of fire, water damage or burglary. Other devices with a high acceptance of over 50 % are a downfall detector bracelet; a light signal for hearing impaired, if the door bell rings; intelligent clothing which sends alarm calls in case of sanitary emergency; automatic heating regulation and a button which switches off potential sources of danger like ovens or irons when leaving the flat. Standard home automation devices like door cameras, electric shutters, automated windows and remote-controlled light reach an average acceptance of 37 % to 44 %. We assume that many respondents see these applications as mere comfort and thus as not absolutely necessary. The share of potential users for applications of video-communication like talking to a doctor (25 %), memory training or virtual museum visits (18 % each) is relatively low. This can be

explained by the lack of computer experience of the elderly: Respondents with computer experience show a much higher acceptance of monitor-based services than respondents who never used a computer.

Third, 35 % of the respondents said they would be willing to pay for the installation and 31 % for monthly costs of home automation. These values are high concerning the fact, that many of the tested applications are unknown to the respondents and it is hard for them to evaluate the potential use.

These very positive numbers confirm the results of other studies about the acceptance of AAL-technology [5,6]. Nevertheless, the positive attitudes towards technology expressed by seniors should not be overestimated. The stated willingness to use cannot be transcribed one to one into a market potential for the tested applications. Meyer et al. state that seniors often are retentive in effectively using technology even though they have very positive attitudes [7]. Seniors often judge the use of AAL-technology positively for "the others", while a use in their own household is not desired.

6   Conclusion

As we pointed out, the majority of the elderly show positive attitudes towards technology and high rates of respondents can imagine using assisted living devices in the future. Still, there is little request for additional technology when people have to pay for it themselves.

On the positive side, the described home automation concept offers many useful features that can be controlled by a single device like PAUL. Like the first tests showed, it is easy to use for "normally aging" persons. Compared to standard emergency call systems, the strengths of the concept are to offer technological assistance in the areas of comfort, safety and security. Also, the use of ambient technology is desirable because it is less stigmatizing than devices that have to be worn on the body.

On the other hand, there are some challenges to face: First of all, most urgent needs and wants of elderly people often concern traditional housework and personal contact. These factors should not be ignored in any AAL-concept. In the pilot project in Kaiserslautern, this is solved by initiating a community building process. But a concept for accompanying services still needs to be developed for a home automation approach ready to enter the market. Second, on the technical side, monitoring health status via sensors still has to prove to be reliable. Third, the financial restrictions of elderly people have to be taken into account: About one third are willing and able to pay, but in average only about 30 € per month [4,8]. Considering this, the costs of an EIB/KNX-Bus are too high and a cheaper solution for crosslinking devices seems necessary. For PAUL, a leasing model should be developed to reach monthly costs that are affordable for the elderly. Fourth, also the effort for installing an EIB-bus in the existing housing stock is too high. Elderly people are often afraid of changes and rarely accept structural alteration works. Therefore the described concept will only work in newly constructed apartments. For older housing stocks, wireless solutions should be tested.

If these challenges are successfully taken, a home automation solution might find broad acceptance by the target group and become a realistic alternative to the solutions available today. To reach this acceptance it will be necessary to continue developing technology and accompanying service packages in close contact with the target group.

References

1. Oswald, F.: Wohnbedingungen und Wohnbeduerfnisse im Alter. In: Schlag, B., Megel, K. (eds.) Mobilitaet und gesellschaftliche Partizipation im Alter, pp. 97–115. Kohlhammer Verlag, Stuttgart (2002)
2. European Commission (ed.) Europe in figures. Eurostat yearbook 2006-07. Online ressource (2007) (access on July 30, 2007), `http://epp.eurostat.ec.europa.eu/cache/ITY_OFFPUB/KS-CD-06-001/EN/KS-CD-06-001-EN.PDF`
3. Brinkmann, M., Floeck, M., Litz, L.: Concept and Design of an AAL Home Monitoring Sys-tem based on a Personal Computerized Assistive Unit. AmI-07, Darmstadt (October 11, 2007)
4. Grauel, J., Spellerberg, A.: Acceptance of new housing technologies for an autonomous living at high age explanation by social structure variables, technological competence and attitudes towards technology. Journal of Social Policy Research 2(53), 191–215 (2007)
5. BIS, Berliner Institut fuer Sozialforschung; DZFA, Deutsches Zentrum fuer Alternsforschung (eds.): Technik im Alltag von Senioren. Arbeitsbericht zu vertiefenden Auswertungen der sentha-Repraesentativerhebung. Heidelberg (2002)
6. BIS, Berliner Institut fuer Sozialforschung (ed.): Smart Home Smart Aging. Akzeptanz und Anforderungen der Generation 50+. Vierter Smart Home Survey des BIS. Berlin (2003)
7. Meyer, S., Schulze, E., Helten, F., Fischer, B.: Vernetztes Wohnen. Die Informatisierung des Alltagslebens, Edition Sigma, Berlin, p. 249 (2001)
8. Forschungsgesellschaft fuer Gerontologie; Institut Arbeit und Technik; Ruhr-Universitaet Bochum (eds.): Wohnen im Alter. Seniorenwirtschaft in Deutschland. Dortmund (2006) (access on July 30, 2007)., Online ressource, `http://www.inwis.de/htm/start/images/wus_trendreport.pdf`

Formal Design and Simulation of an Ambient Multi-agent System Model for Medicine Usage Management

Mark Hoogendoorn, Michel C.A. Klein, and Jan Treur

Vrije Universiteit Amsterdam, Department of Artificial Intelligence
De Boelelaan 1081a, 1081 HV Amsterdam, The Netherlands
{mhoogen,michel.klein,treur}@cs.vu.nl

Abstract. A formally specified multi-agent-based model for medicine usage management is presented and formally analysed. The model incorporates an intelligent ambient agent model that has an explicit representation of a dynamic system model to estimate the medicine level in the patient's body by simulation, and is able to analyse whether the patient intends to take the medicine too early or too late.

1   Introduction

The fast developing area of Ambient Intelligence [2, 1, 13] is an interesting application area for agent-based methods. In this paper a formally analysed ambient multi-agent system model for the domain of medicine usage management is presented. The main problem addressed in this health domain is to achieve in a non-intrusive, human-like manner that patients for whom it is crucial that they take medicine regularly, indeed do so. Examples of specific relevant groups include independently living elderly people, psychiatric patients or HIV-infected persons. One of the earlier solutions reported in the literature provides the sending of automatically generated SMS reminder messages to a patient's cell phone at the relevant times; e.g., [14]. A disadvantage of this approach is that patients are disturbed often, even if they do take the medicine at the right times themselves, and that after some time a number of patients start to ignore the messages. More sophisticated approaches make use of a recently developed automated medicine box that has a sensor that can detect whether a medicine is taken from the box, and can communicate this to a server; cf. SIMpill [8]. This paper explores and analyses possibilities to use automated devices such as an automated medicine box, servers and cell phones as non-human agents, in addition to human agents such as the patient and a supervising doctor. The aim is to obtain a form of medicine usage management that on the one hand achieves that the patient maintains the right amount of medicine, whereas the human factors are also incorporated in an adequate manner, e.g. that a patient is only disturbed if it is really required, thus providing a human-like ambience.

The ambient multi-agent system model for medicine usage management as discussed was formally specified in an executable manner and formally verified using dedicated tools. The system hasn't been actually deployed in a real life situation. The model developed can be used as a blueprint for specific applications in the domain of

M. Mühlhäuser et al. (Eds.): AmI 2007 Workshops, CCIS 11, pp. 207–217, 2008.

medicine usage management. The model incorporates an intelligent ambient agent model that has an explicit representation of a dynamic system model to estimate the concentration of the medicine in the patient's body by simulation, and is able to analyse whether the patient intends to take medicine too early or too late. For actual deployment, the model might have to be extended with other aspects of the patient, e.g. his physical activity and his food consumption, which all has impacts on the drug doses.

In this paper, Section 2 describes the modelling approach. In Section 3 the multi-agent system is introduced, whereas Section 4 presents the specification at the multi-agent system level. The specification of the ambient agent is presented in Section 5. Furthermore, Section 6 presents simulation results, and finally, Section 7 is a discussion.

2   Modelling Approach

This section briefly introduces the modelling approach used to specify the multi-agent model. Two different aspects are addressed. First of all, the process aspects, and secondly, the information and functionality aspects. Thereafter, the language used for execution of a model and the specification and verification of dynamic properties is briefly introduced.

2.1   Process and Information/Functionality Aspects

Processes are modelled as components in the generic model. A component can either be an active process, namely an *agent*, or a source that can be consulted, which is a *world component*. In order to enable interaction between components, *interaction links* between such components can be specified. From the perspective of information, *interfaces* of components are specified by *ontologies*. Using ontologies, the *functionalities* of components in order to perform the tasks of the component can be specified as well.

2.2   Specification Languages

In order to execute and verify multi-agent models, an expressive language is needed. To this end, the language called TTL is used [10, 3]. This predicate logical language supports formal specification and analysis of dynamic properties, covering both qualitative and quantitative aspects. TTL is built on atoms referring to states, time points and traces. A *state* of a process for (state) ontology Ont is an assignment of truth values to the set of ground atoms in the ontology. The set of all possible states for ontology Ont is denoted by STATES(Ont). To describe sequences of states, a fixed *time frame* T is assumed which is linearly ordered. A *trace* γ over state ontology Ont and time frame T is a mapping $\gamma : T \rightarrow$ STATES(Ont), i.e., a sequence of states γ_t ($t \in$ T) in STATES(Ont). The set of *dynamic properties* DYNPROP(Ont) is the set of temporal statements that can be formulated with respect to traces based on the state ontology Ont in the following manner. Given a trace γ over state ontology Ont, the state in γ at time point t is denoted by state(γ, t). These states can be related to state properties via the formally defined satisfaction relation |=, comparable to the Holds-predicate in the Situation Calculus: state(γ, t) |= p denotes that state property p holds in trace γ at time t. Based on these statements, dynamic properties can be formulated in a formal manner in a sorted first-order predicate logic, using quantifiers over time and traces and the usual first-order logical connectives such as $\neg$, $\wedge$, $\vee$, $\Rightarrow$ $\forall$, $\exists$. A special software environment has been developed for TTL, featuring both a Property Editor for building and editing TTL properties and a Checking Tool that enables formal verification of such properties against a set of (simulated or empirical) traces.

To logically specify simulation models and to execute these models in order to get simulation traces, the language LEADSTO, an executable subset of TTL, is used; cf. [4]. The basic building blocks of this language are temporal (or causal) relations of the format $\alpha \twoheadrightarrow_{e, f, g, h} \beta$, which means:

> If   state property α holds for a certain time interval with duration g,
> then   after some delay (between e and f) state property β will hold
>   for a certain time interval of length h.

with α and β state properties of the form 'conjunction of literals' (where a literal is an atom or the negation of an atom), and e, f, g, h non-negative real numbers.

3   Overview of the Multi-agent System

Figure 1 presents an overview of the entire system as considered. Two world components are present in this system: the medicine box, and the patient database; the other components are agents. The top right corner shows the patient, who interacts with the medicine box, and communicates with the patient cell phone. The (ambient) Medicine Box Agent monitors whether medicine is taken from the box, and the position thereof in the box. In case, for example, the patient intends to take the medicine too soon after the previous dose, it finds out that the medicine should not be taken at the moment (i.e., the sum of the estimated current medicine level plus a new dose is too high), and communicates a warning to the patient by a beep. Furthermore, all information obtained by this agent is passed on to the (ambient) Usage Support Agent. All information about medicine usage is stored in the patient database by this agent. If the patient tried to take the medicine too early, a warning SMS with a short explanation is communicated to the cell phone of the patient, in addition to the beep sound already communicated by the Medicine Box Agent.

On the other hand, in case the Usage Support Agent finds out that the medicine is not taken early enough (i.e., the medicine concentration is estimated too low for the patient and no medicine was taken yet), it can take measures as well. First of all, it can warn the patient by communicating an SMS to the patient cell phone. This is done soon after the patient should have taken the medicine. In case the

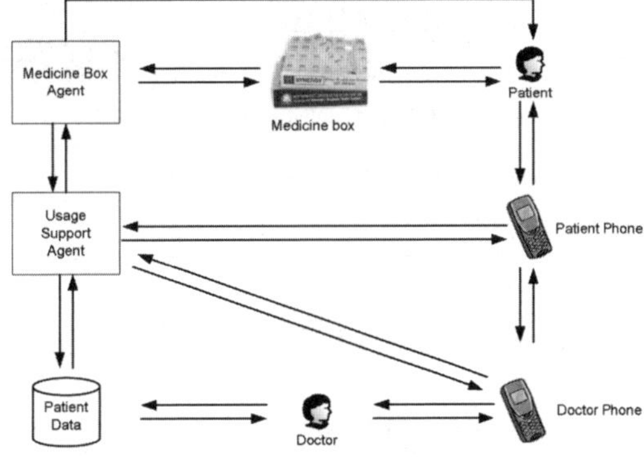

Fig. 1. Multi-Agent System: Overview

patient still does not take medicine (for example after a number of hours), the agent can communicate an SMS to the cell phone of the appropriate doctor. The doctor can look into the patient database to see the medicine usage, and in case the doctor feels it is necessary to discuss the state of affairs with the patient, he or she can contact the patient via a call using the doctor cell phone to the patient cell phone.

4   Specification of the Multi-agent Level

In order for the various components shown in Figure 1 to interact in an appropriate manner, generic temporal rules at the global level are specified that model the interaction between the various components. First of all, Table 1 shows the ontology needed to express such rules. Using the ontology, the following generic temporal rules were specified.

Action Propagation from Agent to World
$\forall$X:AGENT $\forall$W:WORLD $\forall$A:ACTION
output(X)|performing_in(A, W) $\wedge$ can_perform_in(X,A,W) $\longrightarrow\!\!\!\!\rightarrow$ input(W)|performing(A)
Observation Focus Propagation: from Agent to World
$\forall$X:AGENT $\forall$W:WORLD $\forall$I:INFO_EL
output(X)|observation_focus_in(I, W) $\wedge$ can_observe_in(X,I,W) $\longrightarrow\!\!\!\!\rightarrow$ input(W)|observation_focus(I)
Observation Result Propagation from World to Agent
$\forall$X:AGENT $\forall$W:WORLD $\forall$I:INFO_EL

output(W)|observation_result_from(I, W) $\wedge$ can_observe_in(X,I,W) $\longrightarrow\!\!\!\!\rightarrow$ input(X)|observed_result_from(I, W)
Communication Propagation Between Agents
$\forall$X,Y:AGENT $\forall$I:INFO_EL
output(X)|communication_from_to(I,X,Y) $\wedge$ can_communicate_with_about(X,Y,I)
        $\longrightarrow\!\!\!\!\rightarrow$ input(Y)|communicated_from_to(I,X,Y)

Table 1. Ontology for Interaction at the Global Level

SORT	Description
ACTION	an action
AGENT	an agent
INFO_EL	an information element, possibly complex (e.g., a conjunction of other info elements)
WORLD	a world component

Predicate	Description
performing_in(A:ACTION, W:WORLD)	action A is performed in W
observation_focus_in(I:INFO_EL, W:WORLD)	observation focus is I in W
observation_result_from(I:INFO_EL, W:WORLD)	observation result from W is I
observed_result_from(I:INFO_EL, W:WORLD)	the observed result from W is I
communication_from_to(I:INFO_EL, X:AGENT, Y:AGENT)	information I is communicated by X to Y
communicated_from_to(I:INFO_EL,X:AGENT,Y:AGENT)	information I was communicated by X to Y
can_observe_in(X:AGENT, I:INFO_EL, W:WORLD)	agent X can observe I within world component W
can_perform_in(X:AGENT, A:ACTION, W:WORLD)	agent X can perform action A within world component W
can_communicate_with_about(X:AGENT, Y:AGENT, I:INFO_EL)	agent X can communicate with agent Y about info element I

5   Specification of the Ambient Agents

The Ambient Agent Model used is based on a combination of the Generic Agent Model GAM described in [5], and the generic process control model in [11]. To express the agent's internal states and processes, the ontology shown in Table 2 was specified.

Table 2. Ontology Used within the Ambient Agent Model

Predicate	Description
belief(I:INFO_EL)	information I is believed
world_fact(I:INFO_EL)	I is a world fact
has_effect(A:ACTION, I:INFO_EL)	action A has effect I
Function to INFO_EL	**Description**
leads_to_after(I:INFO_EL, J:INFO_EL, D:REAL)	state property I leads to state property J after duration D
at(I:INFO_EL, T:TIME)	state property I holds at time T
critical_situation(I:INFO_EL)	the situation concerning I is critical

An example of an expression that can be made by combining elements from this ontology is belief(leads_to_after(I:INFO_EL, J:INFO_EL, D:REAL)) which represents that the agent has the knowledge that state property I leads to state property J with a certain time delay specified by D. Using this ontology, the functionality of the agent has been specified by generic and domain-specific temporal rules.

5.1 Generic Temporal Rules

The functionality within the Ambient Agent Model has the following generic specifications.

```
∀X:AGENT, I:INFO_EL, W:WORLD
    input(X)|observed_result_from(I, W) ∧ internal(X)|belief(is_reliable_for(W, I))  ⟶⟶ internal(X)|belief(I)
∀X,Y:AGENT, I:INFO_EL
    input(X)|communicated_from_ to(I,Y,X) ∧ internal(X)|belief(is_reliable_for(X, I))  ⟶⟶ internal(X)|belief(I)
∀X:AGENT ∀I,J:INFO_EL ∀D:REAL ∀T:TIME
    internal(X)|belief(at(I,T)) ∧ internal(X)|belief(leads_to_after(I, J, D))  ⟶⟶ internal(X)|belief(at(J, T+D))
```

When the sources are assumed always reliable, the conditions on reliability can be left out. The last rule specifies how a dynamic model that is represented as part of the agent's knowledge can be used by the agent to perform simulation, thus extending its beliefs about the world at different points in time.

For the world components the following generic formal specifications indicate how actions get their effects and how observations provide their results:

```
∀W:WORLD_COMP ∀A:ACTION ∀I:INFO_EL
    input(W)|performing_in(A, W) ∧ internal(W)|has_effect(A,I)  ⟶⟶ internal(W)|world_fact(I)

∀W:WORLD_COMP ∀I:INFO_EL
input(W)|observation_focus_in(I, W) ∧ internal(W)|world_fact(I)
    ⟶⟶ output(W)|observation_result_from(I, W)

∀W:WORLD_COMP ∀I:INFO_EL
input(W)|observation_focus_in(I, W) ∧ internal(W)|world_fact(not(I))
    ⟶⟶ output(W)|observation_result_from(not(I), W)
```

5.2 Domain-Specific Temporal Rules

Domain-specific rules are both shown for the Medicine Box Agent and the Usage Support Agent.

Medicine Box Agent. The Medicine Box Agent has functionality concerning communication to both the patient and the Usage Support Agent. First of all, the observed usage of medicine is communicated to the Usage Support Agent in case the medicine is not taken too early, as specified in MBA1.

MBA1: Medicine usage communication
If the Medicine Box Agent has a belief that the patient has taken medicine from a certain position in the box, and that the particular position contains a certain type of medicine M, and taking the medicine does not result in a too high medicine concentration of medicine M within the patient, then the usage of this type of medicine is communicated to the Usage Support Agent. Formally:

```
internal(medicine_box_agent)|belief(medicine_taken_from_position(x_y_coordinate(X,Y))) ∧
internal(medicine_box_agent)|belief(medicine_at_location(x_y_coordinate(X, Y), M)) ∧
internal(medicine_box_agent)|belief(medicine_level(M, C)) ∧
max_medicine_level(maxB) ∧ dose(P) ∧ C + P ≤ maxB
→→0,0,1,1 output(medicine_box_agent)|communication_from_to(
                medicine_used(M), medicine_box_agent, usage_support_agent)
```

In case medicine is taken out of the box too early, a warning is communicated by a beep and the information is forwarded to the Usage Support Agent (MBA2 and MBA3).

MBA2: Too early medicine usage prevention
If the Medicine Box Agent has the belief that the patient has taken medicine from a certain position in the box, that this position contains a certain type of medicine M, and taking the medicine results in a too high medicine concentration of medicine M within the patient, then a warning beep is communicated to the patient.

```
internal(medicine_box_agent)|belief(medicine_taken_from_position(x_y_coordinate(X,Y))) ∧
internal(medicine_box_agent)|belief( medicine_at_location(x_y_coordinate(X, Y), M)) ∧
internal(medicine_box_agent)|belief(medicine_level(M, C)) ∧
max_medicine_level(maxB) ∧ dose(P) ∧ C + P > maxB
→→0,0,1,1 output(medicine_box_agent)|communication_from_to(
                sound_beep, medicine_box_agent, patient)
```

MBA3: Early medicine usage communication
If the Medicine Box Agent has a belief that the patient was taking medicine from a certain position in the box, and that the particular position contains a certain type of medicine M, and taking the medicine would result in a too high concentration of medicine M within the patient, then this is communicated to the Usage Support Agent.

```
internal(medicine_box_agent)|belief(medicine_taken_from_position(x_y_coordinate(X,Y))) ∧
internal(medicine_box_agent)|belief(medicine_at_location(x_y_coordinate(X, Y), M)) ∧
internal(medicine_box_agent)|belief(medicine_level(M, C)) ∧
max_medicine_level(maxB) ∧ dose(P) ∧ C + P > maxB
→→0,0,1,1 output(medicine_box_agent)|communication_from_to(
                too_early_intake_intention, medicine_box_agent, usage_support_agent)
```

Usage Support Agent. The Usage Support Agent's functionality is described by three sets of temporal rules. First, the agent maintains a dynamic model for the concentration of medicine in the patient over time in the form of a belief about a *leads to* relation.

USA1: Maintain dynamic model
The Usage Support Agent believes that if the medicine level for medicine M is C, and the usage effect of the medicine is E, then after duration D the medicine level of medicine M is C+E minus G*(C+E)*D with G the decay value.

```
internal(usage_support_agent)|belief(leadsto_to_after(
        medicine_level(M, C) ∧ usage_effect(M, E) ∧ decay(M, G),
        medicine_level(M, (C+E) - G*(C+E)*D), D)
```

In order to reason about the usage information, this information is interpreted (USA2), and stored in the database (USA3).

USA2: Interpret usage
If the agent has a belief concerning usage of medicine M and the current time is T, then a belief is generated that this is the last usage of medicine M, and the intention is generated to store this in the patient database.

```
internal(usage_support_agent)|belief(medicine_used(M)) ∧
internal(usage_support_agent)|belief(current_time(T))

→»0,0,1,1
internal(usage_support_agent)|belief(last_recorded_usage(M, T) ∧
internal(usage_support_agent)|intention(store_usage(M, T))
```

USA3: Store usage in database
If the agent has the intention to store the medicine usage in the patient database, then the agent performs this action.

```
internal(usage_support_agent)|intention(store_usage(M, T))
→»0,0,1,1   output(usage_support_agent)|performing_in(store_usage(M, T), patient_database)
```

Finally, temporal rules were specified for taking the appropriate measures. Three types of measures are possible. First, in case of early intake, a warning SMS is communicated (USA4). Second, in case the patient is too late with taking medicine, a different SMS is communicated, suggesting to take the medicine (USA5). Finally, when the patient does not respond to such SMSs, the doctor is informed by SMS (USA6).

USA4: Send early warning SMS
If the agent has the belief that an intention was shown by the patient to take medicine too early, then an SMS is communicated to the patient cell phone that the medicine should be put back in the box, and the patient should wait for a new SMS before taking more medicine.

```
internal(usage_support_agent)|belief(too_early_intake_intention)
→»0,0,1,1
output(usage_support_agent)|communication_from_to(put_medicine_back_and_wait_for_signal,
                        usage_support_agent, patient_cell_phone)
```

USA5: SMS to patient when medicine not taken on time
If the agent has the belief that the level of medicine M is C at the current time point, and the level is considered to be too low, and the last message has been communicated before the last usage, and at the current time point no more medicine will be absorbed by the patient due to previous intake, then an SMS is sent to the patient cell phone to take the medicine M.

```
internal(usage_support_agent)|belief(current_time(T3)) ∧
internal(usage_support_agent)|belief(at(medicine_level(M, C), T3)) ∧
min_medicine_level(minB) ∧ C < minB ∧
internal(usage_support_agent)|belief(last_recorded_usage(M, T)) ∧
internal(usage_support_agent)|belief(last_recorded_patient_message_sent(M, T2)) ∧
T2 < T ∧ usage_effect_duration(UED) ∧ T3 > T + UED

→»0,0,1,1 output(usage_support_agent)|communication_from_to(
    sms_take_medicine(M), usage_support_agent, patient_cell_phone)
```

USA6: SMS to doctor when no patient response to SMS
If the agent has the belief that the last SMS to the patient has been communicated at time T, and the last SMS to the doctor has been communicated before this time point, and furthermore, the last recorded usage is before the time point at which the SMS has been sent to the patient, and finally, the current time is later than time T plus a certain delay parameter for informing the doctor, then an SMS is communicated to the cell phone of the doctor that the patient has not taken medicine M.

```
internal(usage_support_agent)|belief(last_recorded_patient_message_sent(M, T)) ∧
internal(usage_support_agent)|belief(last_recorded_doctor_message_sent(M, T0)) ∧
internal(usage_support_agent)|belief(last_recorded_usage(M, T2)) ∧
internal(usage_support_agent)|belief(current_time(T3)) ∧
T0 < T ∧ T2 < T ∧ max_delay_after_warning(DAW) ∧ T3 > T + DAW
  ↠₀,₀,₁,₁ output(usage_support_agent)|communication_from_to(sms_not_taken_medicine(M),
          usage_support_agent, doctor_cell_phone)
```

6 Simulation Results

In order to show how the above presented system functions, the system has been implemented in a dedicated software environment that can execute such specifications [4]. To enable creation of simulations, a patient model is used that simulates the behaviour of the patient in a stochastic manner. The model specifies four possible behaviours of the patient, each with its own probability: (1) too early intake, (2) correct intake (on time), (3) responding to an SMS warning that medicine should be taken, and (4) responding to a doctor request by phone. Based upon such probabilities, the entire behaviour of the patient regarding medicine usage can be simulated. In the following simulations, values of respectively 0.1, 0.8, 0.9 and 1.0 have been used.

Figure 2 shows the medicine level over time in an example of a simulation trace as estimated by the agent based on its dynamic model. Here the x-axis represents time whereas the y-axis represents the medicine level. Note that in this case, the minimum level of medicine within the patient is set to 0.35 whereas the maximum level is 1.5. These numbers are based on the medicine half-life value, that can vary per type of medicine. In the trace in Figure 2, it can be seen that the patient initially takes medicine at the appropriate time, this is done by performing an action:

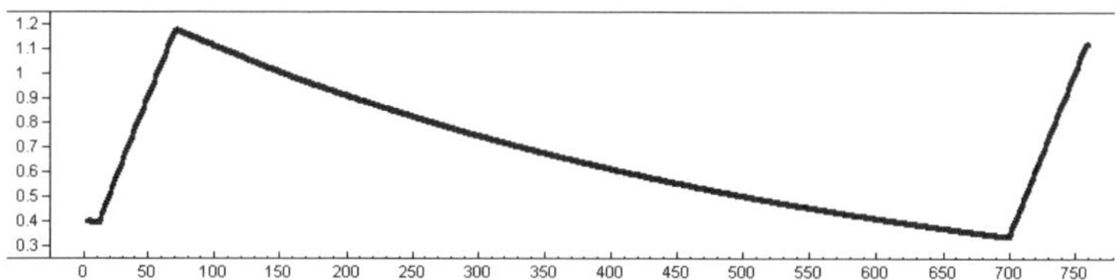

Fig. 2. Medicine level over time

```
output(patient)|performing_in(take_medicine_from_position(x_y_coordination(1,1)), medicine_box)
```
This information is stored in the patient database:
```
input(patient_database)|performing_in(store_usage(recorded_usage(hiv_slowers, 8)), patient_database)
```

Resulting from this medicine usage, the medicine level increases, as can be seen in Figure 3. In this simulation, the medicine takes 60 minutes to be fully absorbed by the patient. Just 240 minutes after taking this medicine, the patient again takes a pill from the medicine box. This is however too early, and as a result, the Medicine Box Agent communicates a warning beep, which is received by the patient:

```
input(patient)|communicated_from_to( sound_beep, medicine_box_agent, patient)
```

The patient does not take the medicine, and waits for an SMS, as the patient is instructed to do. The SMS is received a little while later, stating that the patient should wait with taking the medicine until a new message is sent.

```
input(patient)|communicated_from_to(put_medicine_back_and_wait_for_signal,
        patient_cell_phone, patient)
```

The patient awaits this message, which is sent after the medicine level is considered to be low enough such that medicine can be taken. The Usage Support Agent therefore communicates an SMS to the patient cell phone:

```
output(usage_support_agent)|communication_from_to(sms_take_medicine(hiv_slowers),
        usage_support_agent, patient_cell_phone)
```

This message is received by the patient:

```
input(patient)|communicated_from_to( sms_take_medicine(hiv_slowers), patient_cell_phone, patient)
```

The patient does however not respond to the SMS, and does not take its medicine. The usage support agent responds after 60 minutes, and sends an SMS to the doctor of the patient:

```
input(doctor)|communicated_from_to(sms_not_taken_medicine(hiv_slowers), usage_support_agent, doctor)
```

The doctor immediately calls the patient, and makes sure the patient understands that it is essential to take the medicine immediately. As a result, the patient takes the medicine:

```
output(patient)|performing_in(take_medicine_from_position(x_y_coordination(1,1)), medicine_box)
```

As can be seen in Figure 2, during the entire simulation the patient medicine level never exceeds the maximum level (1.5), and never goes below the minimum required level (0.35).

An example graph of the medicine level of a patient not using the support system presented in this section is shown in Figure 3. Note that this is a simulation over a longer time period (3000 minutes). As can be seen, the intake interval fluctuates a lot and the medicine level does not always stay above the desired level of 0.35.

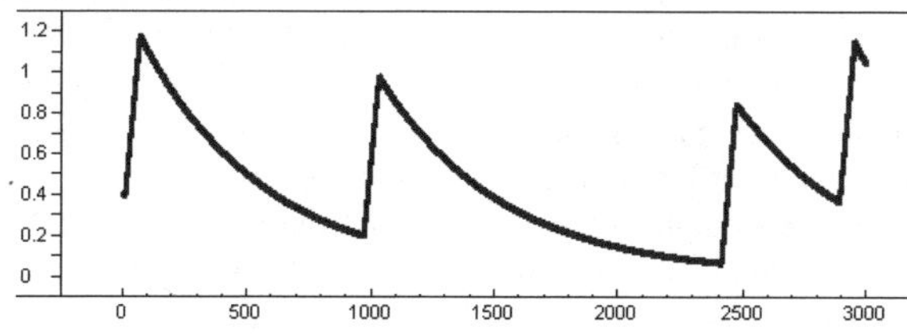

Fig. 3. Medicine level without support system

7   Discussion

In this paper, a multi-agent system model was presented that supports the users of medicine in taking their medicine at the appropriate time. The system has been specified using a formal modelling approach which enables the specification of both quantitative as well as qualitative aspects [10, 3]. To specify the model, both generic and domain specific temporal rules have been used, enabling reuse of the presented model. Evaluation of the model has been conducted by means of simulation runs using a stochastic model for patients. For a demonstration of how such results can be automatically verified, see [9].

The presented multi-agent system model fits well in the recent developments in Ambient Intelligence [1, 2, 13]. Furthermore, it also shows that multi-agent system technology can be of great benefit in health care applications, as also acknowledged in [12]. More approaches to support medicine usage of patients have been developed. Both in [12] as well as [7] models are presented that do not simply always send an SMS that medicine should be taken such as proposed by [14]. Both approaches only send SMS messages in case the patient does not adhere to the prescribed usage. The model presented in this paper however adds an additional dimension to such a support system, namely the explicit representation and simulation of the estimated medicine level inside the patient. Having such an explicit model enables the support agent to optimally support the patient. Evaluating the system using actual users is future work.

References

1. Aarts, E., Collier, R., van Loenen, E., de Ruyter, B. (eds.): Ambient Intelligence. EUSAI 2003. LNCS, vol. 2875, p. 432. Springer, Heidelberg (2003)
2. Aarts, E., Harwig, R., Schuurmans, M.: Ambient Intelligence. In: Denning, P. (ed.) The Invisible Future, pp. 235–250. McGraw-Hill, New York (2001)
3. Bosse, T., Jonker, C.M., van der Meij, L., Sharpanskykh, A., Treur, J.: Specification and Verification of Dynamics in Cognitive Agent Models. In: Nishida, T., et al. (eds.) Proceedings of the Sixth International Conference on Intelligent Agent Technology, IAT 2006, pp. 247–254. IEEE Computer Society Press, Los Alamitos (2006)
4. Bosse, T., Jonker, C.M., van der Meij, L., Treur, J.: A Language and Environment for Analysis of Dynamics by Simulation. International Journal of Artificial Intelligence Tools, vol. 16, pp. 435–464 (2007)
5. Brazier, F.M.T., Jonker, C.M., Treur, J.: Compositional Design and Reuse of a Generic Agent Model. Applied Artificial Intelligence Journal 14, 491–538 (2000)
6. Brazier, F.M.T., Jonker, C.M., Treur, J.: Principles of Component-Based Design of Intelligent Agents. Data and Knowledge Engineering 41, 1–28 (2002)
7. Floerkemeier, C., Siegemund, F.: Improving the Effectiveness of Medical Treatment with Pervasive Computing Technologies. Workshop on Ubiquitous Computing for Pervasive Healthcare Applications at Ubicomp 2003, Seattle (October 2003)
8. Green, D.J.: Realtime Compliance Management Using a Wireless Realtime Pillbottle – A Report on the Pilot Study of SIMPILL. In: Proc. of the International Conference for eHealth, Telemedicine and Health, Med-e-Tel 2005, Luxemburg (2005)

9. Hoogendoorn, M., Klein, M., Memon, Z., Treur, J.: Formal Analysis of Intelligent Agents for Model-Based Medicine Usage Management. In: Azevedo, L., Londral, A.R. (eds.) Proceedings of the International Conference on Health Informatics, HEALTHINF 2008, pp. 148–155. INSTICC Press (2008)

10. Jonker, C.M., Treur, J.: Compositional Verification of Multi-Agent Systems: a Formal Analysis of Pro-activeness and Reactiveness. International Journal of Cooperative Information Systems 11, 51–92 (2002a)

11. Jonker, C.M., Treur, J.: A Compositional Process Control Model and its Application to Biochemical Processes. Applied Artificial Intelligence Journal 16, 51–71 (2002b)

12. Moreno, A., Nealon, J.L. (eds.): Applications of Software Agent Technology in Health Care Domain. Birkhäuser, Basel (2004)

13. Riva, G., Vatalaro, F., Davide, F., Alcañiz, M. (eds.): Ambient Intelligence. IOS Press, Amsterdam (2005)

14. Safren, S.A., Hendriksen, E.S., Desousa, N., Boswell, S.L., Mayer, K.H.: Use of an on-line pager system to increase adherence to antiretroviral medications. In: AIDS CARE, vol. 15, pp. 787–793 (2003)

Concept and Design of an AAL Home Monitoring System Based on a Personal Computerized Assistive Unit

Matthias Brinkmann, Martin Floeck, and Lothar Litz

Institute of Automatic Control, University of Kaiserslautern,
67633 Kaiserslautern, Germany
`brinkma@rhrk.uni-kl.de, {floeck,litz}@eit.uni-kl.de`

Abstract. An ambient assisted living (AAL) approach based on standard home automation devices is presented. The aim of this AAL project is to enable senior citizens to live independently as long as possible. Two basic principles have been observed during the development of the AAL environment: first, in order to make the project a success it is crucial to consider both the needs and the wants of seniors. Second, health monitoring issues are important but the project will only be successful if it comes as a package with additional benefits (comfort, entertainment, safety, and communication). To provide these extra functionalities, the tablet PC-based PAUL – the Personal Assistant Unit for Living – has been developed. The HCI has been specifically designed for high ease of use and intuitive interaction. Moreover, PAUL also monitors the activities of daily living (ADL) and can generate alarms. The algorithms and automata used for this purpose are described in this paper.

Keywords: Assisted Living, Home Automation, Assistive Technology, Elder Care, Senior Housing, Housing for the Elderly, Activities of Daily Living.

1 Introduction

Due to the increased expectancy of life today, a diminishing work force will have to care for an increasing number of elder people. This development shows that there is an urgent need for new technologies which will help senior citizens to maintain their independent life styles and a high quality of life. At the same time, these technologies will ease the work of nursing services and homes.

Numerous research groups worldwide are working on new ideas to create a safe and comfortable environment for seniors staying in their accustomed homes. Amongst others, the Health "Smart" Home (HSH) in France [1], the Citizen Health System (CHS) in Greece [2], the Welfare Techno House in Japan [3], the Smarthouse in the US [4], or a project at the University of Québec à Montréal [5] are only a few to be mentioned.

However, most of these projects only focus on monitoring activities of daily living (ADL) to detect medical emergencies. In contrast to that, aspects facilitating the acceptance of a monitoring system only play a secondary role. Thus, our approach focusses on both the needs *and* the wants of persons who will use our system called PAUL (Personal Assistant Unit for Living). Distinguishing needs and wants is crucial,

M. Mühlhäuser et al. (Eds.): AmI 2007 Workshops, CCIS 11, pp. 218–227, 2008.

since there is a strong difference between what the elder persons want and what others, i.e. their family, doctors, or scientists, believe they need. The former certainly do not want a stigmatizing home care system always reminding them of how frail and needy they are. Thus, PAUL is designed in such a way that it is an infotainment kiosk on the one hand, giving it the air of a modern gadget, while, on the other hand, providing safety and security for the user and peace of mind for their loved ones.

In order to fulfill these tasks, the ADL are continuously monitored while at the same time, comfort and safety are increased. On top of that, we aim at improving the means of communication, e.g. by offering video and VOIP telephony. PAUL (Fig. 1) covers all these functions. Information on safety (e.g. statuses about windows, doors, and roller blinds) and comfort issues (e.g. remote control of roller blinds or door opener) are provided. Furthermore, various multimedia features are made available to the user (e.g. TV, radio, Internet, music player). In addition, PAUL also continuously monitors activities in the flat, analyses potential health risks, and – should the situation require it – alerts either the user himself/herself or predetermined support personnel.

In order to assess the developed assisted living technology under real conditions, an assisted living project comprising 20 apartments is currently being conducted in Kaiserslautern, Germany [6, 7].

2 Technical Concept

2.1 PAUL

PAUL is a laptop-like tablet-PC based assistant unit for living. But there is neither keyboard nor mouse – PAUL is operated via a touch screen of 12". Inside, there is the same hardware as in a "classical" laptop: an Intel Centrino processor, 256 MB of RAM and a 40 GB hard drive. During normal operation, PAUL is mounted inside the flats in a docking station to ensure continuous power supply and reduce the risk of damage to the unit. Each of the apartments in the Kaiserslautern field trial is equipped with approximately 30 sensors and switches[1]: motion detectors, window and door sensors, a water flow sensor, digital light and roller blind switches, etc. As unobtrusively as possible, they provide data about the inhabitant's activities of daily living (ADL) and also the state of the apartment. The tasks of PAUL are collecting and interpreting data and thus increasing the resident's comfort and safety. During the development of the GUI, much effort was devoted to creating an easy-to-use interface. All functions of PAUL are designed to be self-explanatory. In order to achieve this, buttons combining text and symbols are used for the different options. In order to facilitate the cognition of the various elements on the screen, different colors have been used: All icons to be touched are green with a shadow and a faded centre, resembling a "real" button, while areas with informational nature only are grey without a shadow. According to [8], patterned backgrounds might distract elderly people. Thus, a single-colored background was chosen for PAUL. In order to further ease the use of PAUL, the organization of the different menus is simple and

---

[1] Since switches in a bus system transmit information to a controller (i.e. PAUL), they can be considered *sensors* of ADL as well.

straightforward. To make the layout of the various screens look consistent, e.g. the "back" button, taking the user up one level in the menu, is always in the same position: the bottom right corner of the screen. All buttons and icons are even large enough to be used by people with vision impairment or with a tremor. In order to assess the acceptance of PAUL by seniors, tests with persons aged over 60 are currently being conducted [11].

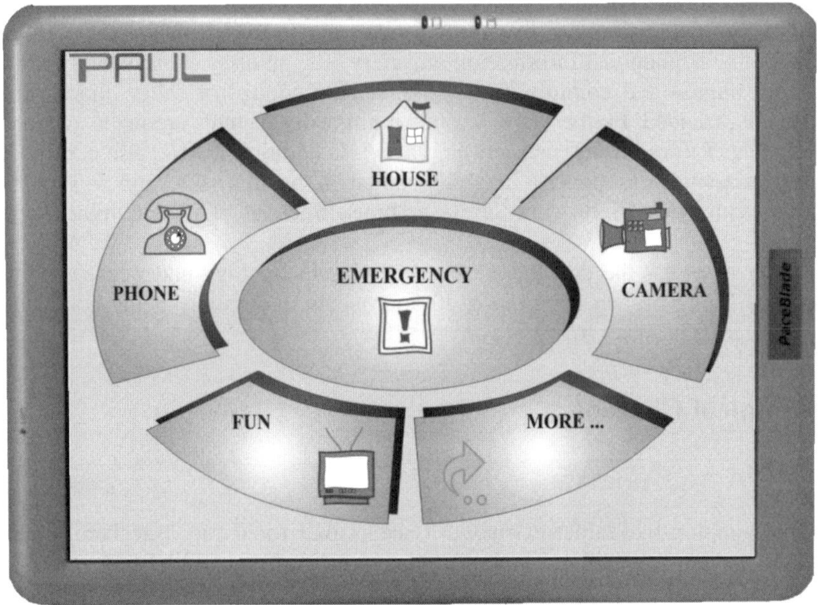

Fig. 1. A picture of PAUL and the start page of the GUI

2.2 Data Processing

Different tasks have to be fulfilled by PAUL to gain useful final information from the raw sensor data (Fig. 2). This data first needs to be transformed into standardized primary information. This is done in the sensor data transformation layer: depending on the hardware installed (i.e. sensors) proprietary data formats are used. For instance, the movement detectors used in our case do not retrigger continuously if there is continuous movement in the monitored area. Instead, they only send a start and stop telegram when movement begins and ceases, respectively. Thus, the task of the transformation layer is to generate uniform primary data of a specified format that PAUL knows how to deal with. However, this primary data still does not provide any information on the state of the apartment or the tenant's state of health. The primary data solely serves as input for automata, fuzzy systems, statistical analysis, and algorithms for the identification of activity patterns of the inhabitant.

In step two, secondary information is derived from primary data using automata. These automata are defined using expert knowledge. Parts of this knowledge can for instance be obtained by evaluating sample data. Details of this process are described in section 3.2 and 3.3. The data generated by the automata contains information about the state of the apartment but still none concerning the state of health of the inhabitants. However, in a highly non-deterministic environment, strictly rule-based approaches might require a huge number of additional rules for handling exceptions to the initial rules. If extremely complex situations shall be tracked, additional methods such as self-learning algorithms or the use of classifiers might also be promising approaches.

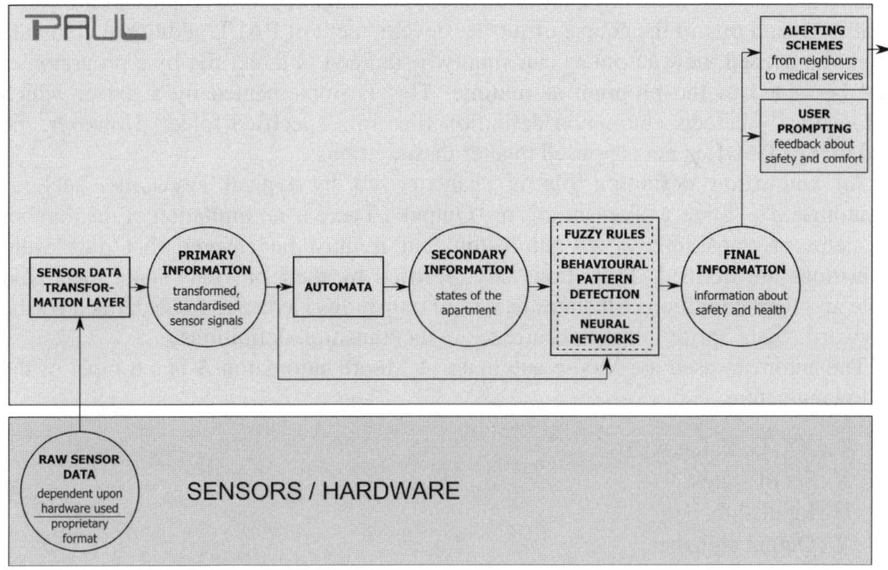

Fig. 2. Data acquisition, processing, and effects of final information

In step three, final information, i.e. information about the health status, will be generated. This final information will be based on primary and secondary information. The algorithms used in this process include fuzzy rules and pattern recognition. If there are unexpected changes in the activity patterns (i.e. ADL), they need to be classified in terms of severity. For example, feasible classifications could be "normal behavior", "low activity", or "extremely low activity". If the latter occurs, a case of emergency might be existent so that an alarm is raised. This is step four, done subsequently to the data processing. Details concerning the alerting scheme are given in section 3.4.

3   Monitoring System

3.1   Information Handling

Basic state information for the monitoring task is a person's presence in the apartment. To gain this information the data of three motion detectors and two sensors observing the state of the front door are processed. The sensors communicate via an

EIB/KNX-system, which is a standardized system for home automation [9]. All sensors are modeled by event-triggered automata. Events are created by a server acting as an interface between the EIB/KNX-network and PAUL every time one of the motion detectors or of the door sensors fires. The automata are implemented as parts of the software run on PAUL.

3.2 Principles of Automata Representation on PAUL

Due to the fact that there are a lot of different automata needed to represent the entire apartment and that in the course of further development of PAUL additional automata might be needed, new automata can simply be defined in a text file by a programmer and be added to the program at runtime. This is implemented by a parser which automatically detects automaton definition files in a specified folder. However, the end user of PAUL is not supposed to alter these settings.

An automaton definition file is characterized by typical keywords, such as "Automaton", "State", "Transition", or "Output". There is no limitation of the number of states or transitions in an automaton, but it must be ensured that only valid transitions are defined. Transitions are specified by their previous state, their next state and their condition. All states named in transitions have also to be defined by the keyword "State" prior to their occurrence in the transition definitions.

The automata used are Moore automata. A Moore automaton $\mathbf{A}$ is a 6-tupel of the following nature:

$$A = (X, U, Y, f, g, x_0)$$
$$X : \text{Set of states,}$$
$$U : \text{Input alphabet,}$$
$$Y : \text{Output alphabet,}$$
$$f : X \times U \to X : \text{Transition function,}$$
$$g : X \to y \in Y : \text{Output function,}$$
$$x_0 : \text{Initial state.}$$

To eventually solve the problems – also that one of the inhabitant's presence monitoring – a combination of the aforementioned basic automata is needed. This combination is implemented using a parallel composition [10] of two automata A_1 and A_2. It is defined as follows:

$$A_1 \| A_2 = (X_1 \times X_2, U_1 \cup U_2, Y_1 \times Y_2, f, g, (x_{01}, x_{02}))$$

where:

$$f((x_1, x_2), e) = \begin{cases} (f_1(x_1, e), f_2(x_2, e)) & \text{if } f_1(x_1, e) \text{ and} \\ & \quad f_2(x_2, e) \text{ are defined} \\ (f_1(x_1, e), x_2) & \text{if only } f_1(x_1, e) \text{ is defined} \\ (x_1, f_2(x_2, e)) & \text{if only } f_2(x_2, e) \text{ is defined} \\ \text{undefined} & \text{otherwise} \end{cases}$$

Parallel composition is an operation which combines the interpretation of events by several different automata within one single automaton. The resulting automaton has $X_1 \times X_2$ states, which means that for each possible combination of two states of the two original automata a new state is created. Since the new automaton accepts every event of the two original automata, its input alphabet is defined by $U_1 \cup U_2$. The resulting output alphabet and the new output function can be obtained in the same way as the set union of the original alphabets.

The transition function $f((x_1,x_2),e)$ yields the subsequently following state upon occurrence of event e. It is analyzed which state combination is the result of event e by observing the reaction of the basic automata. If the event affects both automata, they will both change their actual states. Thus, the transition function $f((x_1,x_2),e)$ leads to the combination of those two states. If the event solely affects a single automaton (e.g. A_1) only this automaton will change its state. Hence, the resulting state in $A_1\|A_2$ is a combination of the new state of A_1 and the persistent state of A_2.

3.3 Automata Composition for the Inhabitant's Presence Problem

The inhabitant's presence detection uses three motion detectors and two sensors monitoring the state of the front door (open/closed, unlocked/locked). These signals are used in different automata which can be merged as shown below.

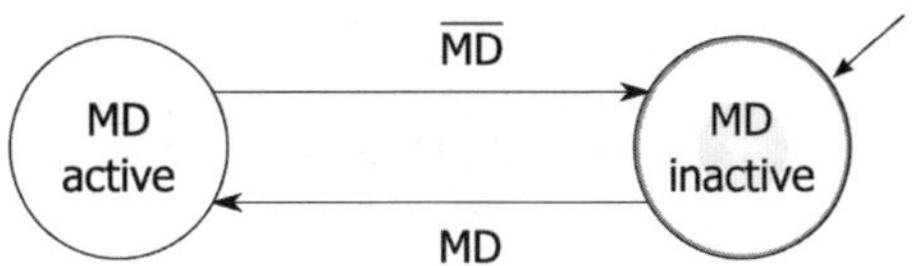

Fig. 3. Motion detector model

The model of the motion detector (Fig. 3) includes two states "*motion detector active*" (*MD active*), "*motion detector inactive*" (*MD inactive*) and the transitions "*motion detected*" (*MD*) and "*no motion detected*" ($\overline{MD}$). The installed motion detectors are configured as follows: They send a telegram immediately when motion is detected. This telegram is interpreted as the event *MD*. No further telegrams are sent until there has been no motion detected for a time span of approx. 10 seconds. After the elapse of this time span of no motion, the sensor sends a stop telegram which is interpreted as the event $\overline{MD}$.

The combined model comprising three motion detectors (Fig. 4) is created with parallel composition as explained above. Again, each single motion detector has two states: "*active*" and "*inactive*". The active motion detectors in each state are highlighted. Thus, the combined model includes $2^3 = 8$ states. To each state with at least one active motion detector the output "*occupied*" has been assigned. To the one single state without any active motion detector, the output "*empty*" has been assigned.

The model can be split into four sections:

– Section 1: All motion detectors are active;
– Section 2: Two of three motion detectors are active;
– Section 3: One of three motion detectors is active;
– Section 4: No motion detector is active.

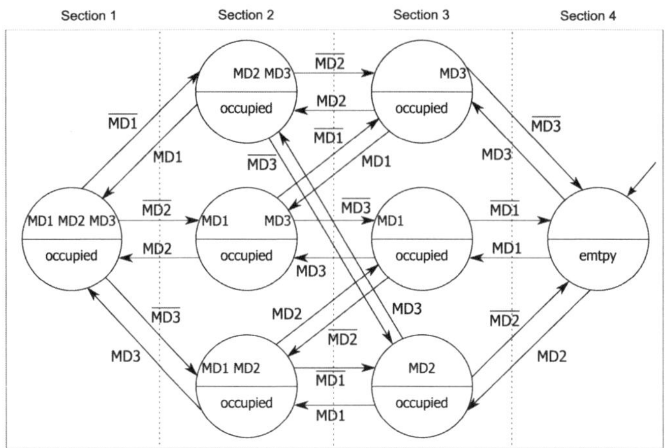

Fig. 4. Combined model of three motion detectors

To design the model for the monitoring system, the transitions between section 3 and section 4 are the most interesting ones. For purposes of clarity, all states having the same output *"occupied"* in the combined model of the three motion detectors are pooled into a single state *"occupied"* in the model shown in Fig. 5.

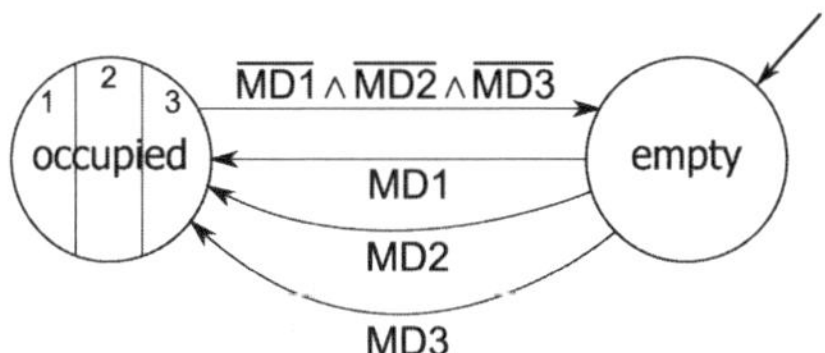

Fig. 5. Pooled model of three motion detectors

The state *"occupied"* is a pool of seven states. The numbers symbolize the sections as defined in Fig. 4: The transition from *"occupied"* to *"empty"* is legal if the actual state is a state of section 3 and the last active motion detector sends the telegram *"no motion detected"* ($\overline{MD1}$, $\overline{MD2}$ or $\overline{MD3}$). Depending on which motion detector sends the telegram *"motion detected"* (*MD1, MD2 or MD3*), the transition from *"empty"* to *"occupied"* connects to the adequate state in section 3.

The fact that the output (i.e. *"occupied"* vs. *"empty"*) not only depends on the state of one motion detector but on the state of all motion detectors increases the robustness of the model. A change in the output is only possible if the actual state is one of the states in section 3 or 4. For future work it will be important to know which state was the active one before the output *"empty"* is created. Knowledge about the last active motion detector allows conclusions about the position of the inhabitant inside the flat.

In order to further increase the robustness of the information about whether the apartment is occupied or not, data about the use of the front door is required. Thus, the door was equipped with two different sensors: a reed switch to monitor whether the door is closed (*door_closed*) or open (*door_open*) and a deadbolt sensor indicating whether the closed door is unlocked (*door_unlocked*) or locked (*door_locked*). Fig. 6 shows the automaton model of the door.

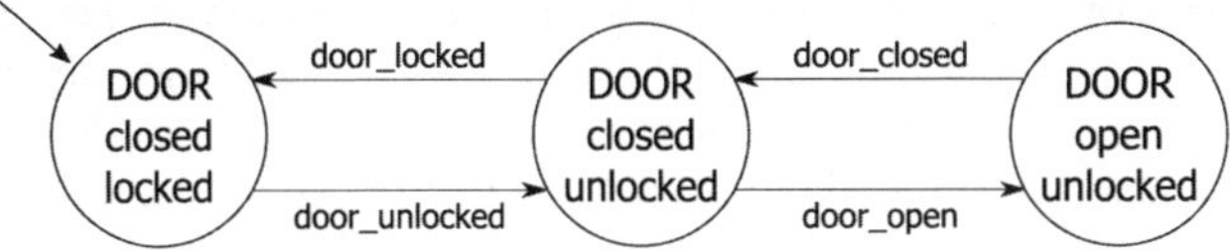

Fig. 6. Automaton model of the front door

The next step was to apply the parallel composition to merge the model of the door (Fig. 6) and the combined motion detector model (Fig. 4). The resulting automaton model is depicted in Fig. 7. Changing between *"open occupied"* and *"closed occupied"* or *"closed occupied"* and *"locked occupied"*, respectively, is possible under all conditions.

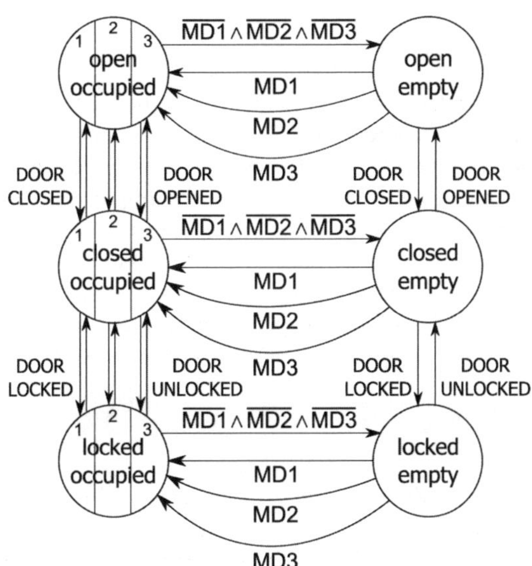

Fig. 7. Model of the monitoring system

However, due to the fact that the automaton includes all transitions from the basic automata, but not all of them are legal without further rules, some amendments are required: Since the inhabitant cannot leave the flat without opening the front door, it might be assumed that there should not be any transitions from *"occupied"* to *"empty"* or vice versa while the door is closed. Nevertheless, since the motion detectors need about 10 seconds to switch from *"active"* to *"inactive"* after the last motion had been detected, there is a possibility for the automaton to enter a faulty state when the inhabitant leaves the flat. This problem stems from the delay of the status change of the movement detectors which can not be avoided because of hardware restrictions. There are two conceivable scenarios: one might be the sequence of a person unlocking and opening the door, leaving the apartment and locking the door again from outside taking less than 10 seconds. In this case, our system will not be able to determine whether the person has actually left the apartment or just opened and closed the door again from inside because the motion detectors have not yet sent their stop telegram. Another scenario might be that there are two or more persons in the apartment of whom only one is moving around. If this person leaves the apartment, PAUL will assume that the apartment is uninhabited.

Thus, the transitions leading from *"occupied"* to *"empty"* ($\overline{MD1}, \overline{MD2}$, or $\overline{MD3}$) while the door is closed or locked are not removed but additional rules are applied to them. First, within a time span of 10 seconds after closing the front door, the automaton will switch to the *"empty"* state if movement ceases inside the apartment. Second, if the system has switched to the *"empty"* state and 10 seconds have already elapsed, it will still switch back to *"occupied"* if it detects more than a certain number of typical user interactions per time unit inside the apartment. Requiring a certain number of sensor responses per time unit prevents misinterpretation of unexpected (faulty) sensor signals (e.g. erroneous detection of motion due to shadows of clouds passing by).

3.4 Emergency Alerts

The states of all implemented automata models and other sensor data are continuously monitored for potential alarm situations. These alarm situations have to be defined in text files which can be created and loaded at runtime. In addition to the alarm situation defined, a graded alerting scheme will be implemented. On the one hand, this means that there can be alarms of different priority. On the other hand, it also means that depending on the severity of the alarm situation, different measures will be taken. I.e. in case of a low alarm priority, the system will first try to contact the resident directly. If he/she does not respond, the system will run through a list of possible contacts, ultimately calling an emergency medical service.

4 Outlook

The automata-based monitoring system will be integrated into the next version of PAUL. This future version will be deployed to the assisted living facility in Kaiserslautern to residents who agree to participating in a field test of the new algorithms. The outcome of this field test will be evaluated both in terms of technical and social aspects, i.e. reliability of the monitoring algorithms and also the acceptance of the monitoring technology by the residents concerned.

The results of this field test will help to improve and refine the algorithms used. Furthermore, they will help to ameliorate the advanced automatic alerting scheme based on automated rating of the safety and health level of the residents.

Acknowledgements

This work was granted by the Ministry of Treasury of Rhineland-Palatinate, Germany and housing societies in Kaiserslautern, Mainz, Neuwied, and Speyer.

References

1. Rialle, V., Duchene, F., Noury, N., Bajolle, L., Demongeot, J.: Health Smarthome: Information technology for patients at home. Telemedicine Journal And E-Health 8(4), 395–409 (2002)
2. Maglaveras, N., Chouvarda, I., Koutkias, V., Gogou, G., Lekka, I., Goulis, D., Avramidis, A., Karvounis, C., Louridas, G., Balas, E.: The Citizen Health System (CHS): A Modular Medical Contact Center Providing Quality Telemedicine Services. IEEE Transactions on Information Technology In Biomedicine 9(3), 353–362 (2005)
3. Kawarada, A., Takagi, T., Tsukada, A., Sasaki, K., Ishijima, M., Tamura, T., Togawa, T., Yamakoshi, K.: Evaluation of automated health monitoring system at the Welfare Techno House Engineering in Medicine and Biology Society. In: Proceedings of the 20th Annual International Conference of the IEEE, October 29- November 1, 1998, vol. 4(4), pp. 1984–1987 (1998)
4. Alwan, M., Leachtenauer, J., Dalal, S., Kell, S., Turner, B., Mack, D., Felder, R.: Validation of rule-based inference of selected independent activities of daily living. Telemedicine Journal And E-Health 11(5), 594–599 (2005)
5. Descheneaux, C., Latfi, F., Lefebvre, B.: Activity Recognition In A Smart Environment. In: Proceedings of the 2nd International Conference on Technology and Aging (ICTA), Toronto, Canada (2007)
6. University of Kaiserslautern: Website of the Research Group Assisted Living (In German), http://www.assistedliving.de
7. Litz, L., Gross, M.: Covering Assisted Living Key Areas based on Home Automation Sensors in Networking, Sensing and Control. In: Proceedings of the IEEE International Conference On.Networking, Sensing, and Control, London, UK (2007)
8. National Institute on Aging, U.S. and National Library of Medicine, U.S. : Making Your Web Site Senior Friendly: A Checklist (2002), http://www.nlm.nih.gov/pubs/checklist.pdf
9. http://www.eiba.com
10. Cassandras, C.G., Lafortune, S.: Introduction to Discrete Event System. Kluwer Academic Publishers, Dordrecht (1999)
11. Grauel, J., Spellerberg, A.: Akzeptanz neuer Wohntechniken für ein selbstständiges Leben im Alter – Erklärung anhand sozialstruktureller Merkmale. Technikkompetenz und Technikeinstellungen, Zeitschrift für Sozialreform 53(2), 191–215 (2007)

Detecting Activities for Assisted Living

Dorothy Monekosso and Paolo Remagnino

CISM, Kingston University,
Kingston upon Thames, London, UK
{n.monekosso,p.remagnino}@kingston.ac.uk

Abstract. The objective is to detect activities taking place in a home for the purpose of creating models of behavior for the occupant. An array of sensors captures the status of appliances used in the home. Models for the occupant's activities are built from the captured data using unsupervised learning techniques. Predictive models can be used in a number of ways: to enhance user experience, to maximize resource usage efficiency, for safety and for security. This work focuses on supporting independent living and enhancing quality of life for older persons. The goal is for the system to distinguish between normal and anomalous behavior. In this paper, we present the results of unsupervised classification techniques applied to the problem of modeling activity.

1 Introduction

This paper describes a system designed for detecting the activities of one occupant of a home. Activities are captured by an array of sensors embedded in the environment in such a way as to unobtrusively record daily activities. The objective of the work described here is to discover patterns in the data leading to differentiation of activities. The next step will be to discover patterns in sequences of activities described as behaviors. Predictive models can be used in a number of ways: to enhance user experience, to maximize resource usage efficiency e.g. energy consumption, to enhance safety and security. This work focuses on prolonging independent living and enhancing quality of life of older persons. To this end, the final system must be capable of distinguishing between normal and abnormal activity. The steps are to detect activities, categorize these activities, detect trends and patterns in the activities and detect abnormal behaviors. This paper describes the detection of activities. With improved health care and living standards, an increasing number of people are living well into their old age. A challenge for society is to provide appropriate care allowing older persons to maintain the level of autonomy they want whilst ensuring an enhanced quality of life. In a study conducted by Giuliani et al [1], it was found against the stereotype of technology aversion by the elderly who would in fact be prepared to use it if they perceived benefits. In the study described in this paper, a home was equipped with a number of sensors and actuators. The sensors employed are small in size to facilitate embedding and are non-visual to promote acceptance by users. In the next Section, 2, published work related to

M. Mühlhäuser et al. (Eds.): AmI 2007 Workshops, CCIS 11, pp. 228–237, 2008.

the proposed system will be discussed. In Section 3 the methodology is described followed by a description of the experimental set up in Section 4. In Section 5 the results are presented and discussed in Section 6. The paper concludes in Section 7.

2   Related Work

In recent years, there have been significant advances in the field of intelligent environments. The advances were made possible in part by progress in sensor and device technologies, network and computer technologies. A number of research projects and a smaller number of fielded projects addressing issues of intelligent environments have been published. These include Microsoft's EasyLiving project [2] , the Intelligent Dormitory iDORM [3], the Interactive Room iROOM [4], the HyperMedia Studio [5], The MavHome project [6] to name a few and fielded applications such as CARE [7]. Technology is gradually gaining acceptance as a means to complement caregivers and to assist persons with reduced physical or cognitive capacity in their day to day living. A review of published works, fielded systems and the state of the art in assistive technologies can be found in Pollack [8]. There are a number of ways in which an intelligent environment can be employed: to assist an individual in daily activities, to facilitate and complement the caregiver or to assess the occupant. Recent advances in technology have made it possible to embed sensors into an environment. The sensors range from arrays of relatively simple sensors that record on/off status, temperature, lighting, and RFID to more complex sensors to record sound and images. From these embedded sensors, various environmental attributes can be detected and activity inferred. The physical or cognitive status of the occupant can be inferred from the activity. A number of researchers are currently working on the problem of modeling occupant behavior based on input from multimodal sensor arrays. Supervised and unsupervised learning algorithms have been applied to learning a model of activity. In supervised model learning, Muehlenbrock et al [9] and Tapia et al [10] use Nave Bayes classification to identify activities. In the latter case, the data is supplied by a large number of very simple binary valued sensors while in the former case the data source consists of PDA, keyboard, and telephone usage information. Brdiczka et al [11] employ Bayesian classifier and Support Vector Machine to classify activities based on video data. An example of activity learning based on speech data is described in Brdiczka et al [12]. A drawback of supervised learning is the need for a teacher to provide answers. This may take the form of annotated data. Typically the sensors will produce a very large amount of data that must be annotated. Unsupervised learning has the advantage of not requiring a teacher. Doctor et al model activity in the the iDorm unsupervised; employing fuzzy rule learning [13] while Rivera-Illingworth [14] employ neural networks. Mozer, in the ACHE project [15], employs reinforcement learning to learn models of behavior from observations for the purpose of predicting low level actuator status. In the MavHome project [16], [17], and [18] predictive models are built based on Hidden Markov Models techniques. As with the ACHE project, the aim is to predict low level activity such as on/off switching. By contrast, the work presented in this paper aims to predict high level activity i.e. the occupant's behavior.

3 Methodology

The aim is to build a model to allow prediction of the next activity given the current activity and in so doing detect anomalous behavior. The first step is to differentiate between activities. The activities in the experiment are cooking, working, watching TV, etc... In previous work, supervised classification was investigated for detecting activities. However it is not always possible to annotate data and so unsupervised learning techniques are investigated here. Four classification algorithms were applied to the problem of building models of activities. The techniques investigated are all unsupervised learning techniques. The performance of the various classifiers was assessed by cross-validation against an annotated dataset. The classification algorithms are all well established algorithms and include partitioning methods (Kmeans, KMedoids, and EM - a probabilistic method) and a hierarchical agglomerative method. A brief overview of the similarities and differences [19] is given here. Agglomerative clustering is a hierarchical method. It starts with singleton clusters and recursively merges the clusters until the stopping criterion is satisfied. Partitioning methods differ on the method by which the iterative relocation of points is performed. In probabilistic partitioning methods, the cluster is identified with a model that consists of a mixture of distributions. The aim is to find the parameters of these distributions that maximize the log-likelihood. Rather than calculating pair-wise similarities or distance as in hierarchical methods, partitioning methods such as KMeans and KMedoids use a single point to represent a cluster. In this way time complexity is improved with a linear objective function. The KMedoid point is selected based on the location of the larger fraction of points and thus is less sensitive to outliers. In KMeans, the representative point is the centroid and thus is more sensitive to outliers. The KMeans is better suited to numeric data while the KMedoid can be used with non-numeric data. Advantages of the hierarchical methods over the partitioning methods are 1) the flexibility in terms of the granularity and 2) the use of any form of similarity or distance metric however the stopping criteria can be vague if not number of clusters. In partitioning methods, intermediate clusters are revisited for improvements while most hierarchical algorithms make no attempt at improving intermediate clusters. Partitioning methods generally suffer from time complexity.

4 Experimental Set Up and Data Collection

In this section, the experimental setup and the data collection from the sensors are described. The array comprises temperature sensors, motion detectors, pressure mat, window and door status (open or closed), light level, light status (on, off and brightness level), smoke detector and RFID readers. Appliances are under control and their status sensed by sensors. The nature of sensor output varied from binary valued data to continuous range. The sensors are located throughout a home, each room having at least one motion detector, one temperature sensor, one light level detector and two lighting status (on, off and light level setting) sensors. It is intended to use the RFID system in future works to disambiguate between users (occupant) of the home. RFID was not used in the experiment. In all data were captured by 47 sensors. For the purpose of the experiment, closed loop feedback control is disabled so that the users operate directly all actuators that control temperature, door, windows, and lighting. The control points (e.g. switches) are located at the same positions as would be standard controls i.e. the actuator control belonging to the experiment are located where one would expect to find them in a normal home so as not to skew the behavior and hence data collection and analysis. The reason for maintaining manual control is that users are monitored to allow a model of their behavior to be built. The monitoring took place over several periods each lasting a week; data logging was continuous, taking place night and day. The house data were collected and analyzed using the algorithm described in Section 3.

There are various sources of error that add noise to the data collected. These are mainly due to intermittent failure of equipment to measure and/or record activity that trigger the sensors and are relatively rare. The sources of error are:

1. Failure of equipment to record an action for example a sensor failing to trigger. This was considered the most frequent and likely error,.
2. Failure of equipment to take an action due to radio signal interference.
3. Random activation due to noise on mains or radio signal interference.
4. Sensor activation shorter than the sampling time during data processing. This happens particularly with motion detectors that trigger for a specific length of time.

The impact of these errors is discussed next. Error 2 has no impact on data mining; the problem is user inconvenience as the action must be repeated for example the user must activate a switch a second time. Error types 1 and 3 are problematic; the result is potentially inaccurate data point (1) or missing data point (3). An example of this is a light recorded as on when it is in reality off or vice versa. These types of problems show up as a persisting ON/OFF beyond the expected duration. Data filtering can easily identity such cases. Graphical representations of the data very easily show outliers that can be further investigated. Note that errors in these two classes are relatively infrequent. Error type 4 results in missing data because the sensor ON time is shorter than the data processing sampling time. This problem is minimized by reducing the sampling time. Heuristics can be used to automate the data cleansing; in addition the heuristics can be inferred from the data. These heuristics relate to temporal characteristics of sensor activity; examples are average ON/OFF times of sensors, exploiting the repetitive characteristics of activities. The activities to distinguish are listed in Table 1 with the percentage of instances in the data set.

Table 1. List of activities and percentage of instances in the dataset

Activity ID	Description	% instances
0	NO-ACTIVITY	50
1	BED TIME	3
2	ABLUTION	16
3	COOKING	6
4	EATING	6
5	RELAX-TV	1
6	ENTRANCE-EXIT	8
7	WORK	6

5   Experimental Results

The results of unsupervised classification are presented in this section. Prior to modeling, the raw sensor data is converted to a vector time series. Each vector is of dimension n where n is the number of sensors. Following formatting, outliers within were investigated.

5.1   Data Pre-processing: Formatting and Class Annotation

The objective was to produce sequences that represent snapshots of the sensor status at discrete time steps. The sequences were then used to build a model of the activity. Each sensor represents a dimension; there are 47 sensors. Sensors are either binary-valued or analogue and scaled to give an output range of 0 to 1. The data were collected over a period of weeks. The raw data format is a time stamp followed by a sensor ID, name/description and status. A typical record is *[15/02/2007 06:20:55 22855.7 0 BathMotionDetect 0]*. During pre-processing, an additional attribute indicating period of the day was included. The day is divided into six periods. The data set contains a total of 3267 examples.

5.2   Data Filtering

Data filtering may be used to identify outliers and discard these if thought to be the consequence of equipment failure. Data filtering was performed manually and automatically for comparison. Manual data filtering involved graphical representations to identify outliers. The automated method makes use of two or more classification algorithms to generate an initial classification and remove instances that were misclassified (by all classifiers) from the data set prior to the modeling [20]. In the experiments only manual filtering of data was employed however no significant improvements were achieved with filtered data compared to the raw data. Pre-processed data is displayed as histograms showing the frequency of occurrence of sensor active state. Examples are shown in Fig. 1. The data were grouped into six classes corresponding to different times of the day.

The time periods are 0-4, 4-8, 8-13, 12-16, 16-20, and 20-24. With some knowledge of the patterns of behavior of the occupant, outliers were investigated and removed from the data set if the outlier could be explained by any one of the error sources described above. In Fig. 1(a), given prior knowledge of the expected activities and most likely time of day for the activities, the histogram shows no outlier. In contrast, Fig. 1(b) the histogram shows an unexpected outlier. It can be seen that a light sensor (purple, ceiling light) is active during all six periods. Investigation of the raw data indicated that the sensor status was incorrectly recorded indicating it was active for an extended period of time during which it was known not to be active.

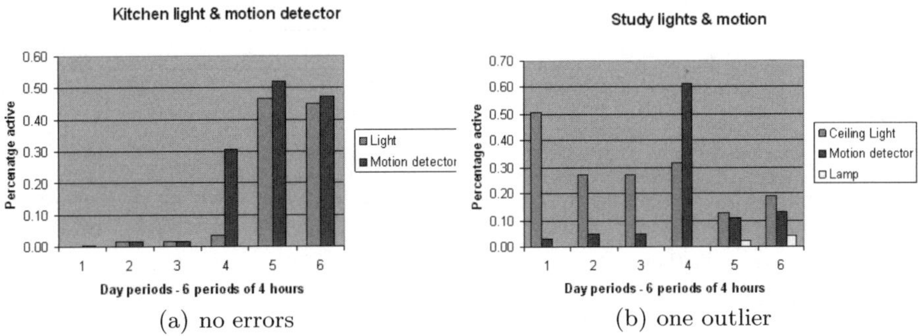

(a) no errors   (b) one outlier

Fig. 1. Graphical representation for data cleansing

5.3   Models - Unsupervised Classification

The raw data set consists of a time series of n-dimension vectors (one dimension per sensor). Prior to applying the clustering algorithms, useless attributes were removed. The selection criterion for removal was 1) nominal attributes having the same value for more than p percent of all examples and 2) numerical attributes which standard deviation is less or equal to a given deviation threshold. Applying these criteria to the data, 3 attributes were removed. The Kmeans, KMedoids, EM and Agglomerative algorithms were applied to the data and evaluated against the annotated classes (activities). The classification accuracies are shown in Table 2. The Kappa statistic gives an indication of whether the agreement between the prediction and the real value exceeds that expected by chance. Based on Landis and Koch [21], the agreement is moderate for Kmeans, Kmedoids, EM and Agglomerative.

Activity-Cluster Associations. The activities cross-validated against the annotated data are shown in Table 3. The sensitivity is the relative number of examples correctly classified as positive among all positive examples. The class sensitivity averaged over 20 runs is shown in Table 3.

Table 2. Classification rates and kappa values

	%Accuracy	Kappa
KMeans	73.4	0.595
KMedoids	66.73	0.436
EM	71.23	0.558
Agglomerative	65.90	0.457

Table 3. Comparison of activity classification sensitivity

	Class Sensitivity (%)			
Activity	KMeans	KMedoids	EM	Agglomerative
A0	98.79	99.88	97.33	92.05
A1	0.00	0.00	0.00	0.00
A2	94.32	52.08	64.20	87.88
A3	60.40	53.47	0.00	0.00
A4	66.96	67.41	66.07	68.75
A5	0.00	0.00	0.00	0.00
A6	0.00	0.00	84.59	6.45
A7	0.00	0.00	0.00	0.00

6 Discussion

All algorithms fail to classify activities A1, A5, and A7. The poor sensitivity for
activity 5 is explained by the relatively small number of instances in the training
set (Table 1). The number of examples for a1 represents only 1% of the total
data set. According to Jain et al [22], the minimum amount of training examples
required is at least 10 times the vector dimension. In this specific case this means
approximately 200 or 6% of the total examples. From activity A6, it can be inferred that the EM algorithm is better suited as expected to deal with noisy data.
The main sensor that caters for A6 was prone to false triggering from movement at
a neighboring location. By contrast from activity A3 (and to a degree A2), it can
be inferred that KMeans is better suited when the data is scarce but less noisy. It is
known from the experimental set up that data relating to A2 and A3 are less noisy
than A6. The nature of activity A7 was such that it occurred in parallel with other
activities. This meant that even hand annotation was difficult with knowledge of
the inhabitant behavior. The system has difficulty with modeling multiple simultaneous activities. The simple error rates (accuracy) in Tables 2 and 3 would
be adequate assuming that all errors have equal importance. The application is
behavior modeling for the purpose of detecting abnormal behavior and alerting
a caregiver. In this context a false negative is more serious than a false positive.
The latter represents a nuisance while the former could be life threatening. In addition, for this particular application, certain activities may be considered to have

greater value in indicating the health status of the inhabitant of the house. For example the activity Cooking has more diagnostic value than say TV/Relaxation. Another disadvantage of the simple rates is that it is dependent on the instance distribution. The confusion matrix provides more information. It lists the correct classification against the prediction for each class i.e. activity in this case as shown in Table 4 for the KMeans classifier. In the case of the KMeans, looking along the diagonal, incorrect associations are made for two of the activities (A3 and A6) and no association for another two (A5 and A7). The impact of this is assessed when modeling behaviors.

Table 4. Confusion matrix for the Kmeans classifier

	True class (%)							
	A0	A1	A2	A3	A4	A5	A6	A7
A0	835	1	32	0	1	23	2	7
A1	2	76	10	28	1	8	3	0
A2	0	0	146	13	19	1	27	35
A3	0	0	0	0	0	0	50	0
A4	0	0	0	0	148	0	4	0
A5	0	0	0	0	0	0	0	0
A6	1	0	5	81	19	0	58	0
A7	0	0	0	0	0	0	0	0

A perceived drawback of supervised learning in the context of an intelligent environment is the necessity for the occupant to be trained to use to system at least for the duration of the computational model learning. This would be particularly unhelpful in this context. In addition, as discussed in Mozer [15], there is a tendency for the user to attempt to 'enforce' regular habits which would skew the data. This works attempts to overcome the problem by the use of very simple unobtrusive sensors. The selection criterion for the sensors and actuators and placement of these within the environment is to mimic existing technology. For example the light switches resemble and operate in the same manner as ordinary light switches.

For assisted living application, the accuracy of the system must be improved to bring all activities to a detection accuracy equivalent to at least activity A2 before proceeding to the next step of behavior modeling. A careful re-design of the experimental setup to minimize noise and further collection of data would significantly improve the results. In addition, the system has difficulty with modeling multiple simultaneous activities. This is problem that must be investigated.

7   Conclusion

In this paper, classification of activities based on data gathered from multiple simple sensors installed in a home was performed employing unsupervised classification techniques. The aim was to identify activities based on information such as lights status, motion detectors, and pressure mat status and create a model of daily activity that will help in detecting anomalous behavior. Experimental results indicate that supervised learning is effective at classifying the activities however annotating data can be time consuming and would be difficult as the number of sensors and number of activities increased. The present results show that unsupervised classification as expected performs less well than supervised learning. However unsupervised classification is necessary as in some circumstances it may not be possible to observe inhabitants for annotation. In such cases unsupervised learning is the only solution.

References

1. Giuliani, M.V., Scopelliti, M., Fornara, F.: Elderly People at Home: Technological Help in Everyday Activities. In: Proc. of the 14th IEEE Int. Conf. on Robot and Human Interactive Communication, pp. 365–370 (2006)
2. Brumitt, B., Meyers, B., Krumm, J., Kern, A., Shafer, S.: EasyLiving: Technologies for Intelligent Environments. In: Thomas, P., Gellersen, H.-W. (eds.) HUC 2000. LNCS, vol. 1927, pp. 12–29. Springer, Heidelberg (2000)
3. The iDorm project home page: Intelligent Inhabited Environments Group, Department of Computer Science, University of Essex, Essex University, UK (September 20, 2007), http://iieg.essex.ac.uk/idorm.htm
4. The iRoom project home page: Stanford Interactive Workspaces Project Overview (September 20, 2007), http://iwork.stanford.edu/
5. The HyperMedia studio project home page: UCLA HyperMedia Studio (September 20, 2007), http://hypermedia.ucla.edu/
6. The MavHome project home page: University of Texas, Arlington (September 20, 2007), http://cygnus.uta.edu/mavhome/
7. The Elite Care project home page: Elite Care Corporation, Milwaukie, OR, USA (September 20, 2007), http://www.elitecare.com/technology
8. Pollack, M.E.: Intelligent technology for an aging population: The use of AI to assist elders with cognitive impairment. AI Magazine 26(2), 9–24 (2005)
9. Mühlenbrock, M., Brdiczka, O., Snowdon, D., Meunier, J.-L.: Learning to detect user activity and availability from a variety of sensor data. In: Proc. of the 2nd IEEE Conf. on Pervasive Computing and Communications, pp. 13–22 (2006)
10. Tapia, E.M., Intille, S.S., Larson, K.: Activity Recognition in the Home Using Simple and Ubiquitous Sensors. In: Ferscha, A., Mattern, F. (eds.) PERVASIVE 2004. LNCS, vol. 3001, pp. 158–175. Springer, Heidelberg (2004)
11. Brdiczka, O., Reignier, P., Crowley, J.: Detecting Individual Activities from Video in a Smart Home. In: Proc. of the 11th Int. Conf. on Artificial Intell. Knowledge-Based and Intelligent Information and Engineering Systems, pp. 195–203 (2007)
12. Brdiczka, O., Vaufreydaz, D., Maisonnasse, J., Reignier, P.: Unsupervised Segmentation of Meeting Configurations and Activities using Speech Activity Detection. In: Proc. of the 3rd IFIP Conf. on Artificial Intell. Applications and Innovations, pp. 195–203 (2006)
13. Doctor, F., Hagras, H., Callaghan, V.: An Intelligent Fuzzy Agent Approach for Realising Ambient Intelligence in Intelligent Inhabited Environments. IEEE Tran. on Systems, Man and Cybernetics 35, 55–65 (2004)

14. Rivera-Illingworth, F., Callaghan, V., Hagras, H.A.: Neural Network Agent Based Approach to Activity Detection, in AmI Environments. In: IEE Int. Workshop on Intel. Environments, pp. 92–99 (2005)
15. Mozer, M.C.: Lessons from an adaptive house. In: Cook, D., Das, R. (eds.) Smart environments: Technologies, protocols, and applications, pp. 273–294. J. Wiley & Sons, Chichester (2004)
16. Cook, D., Das, S.: Prediction Algorithms for Smart Environments. In: Cook, D., Das, R. (eds.) Smart Environments: Technology, Protocols and Applications, pp. 175–192. J. Wiley & Sons, Chichester (2004)
17. Das, S., Cook, D.J.: Designing and Modeling Smart Environments. In: Int. Symposium on a World of Wireless, Mobile and Multimedia Networks (WoWMoM 2006), pp. 490–494 (2006)
18. Rao, S., Cook, D.J.: Predicting Inhabitant Actions Using Action and Task Models with Application to Smart Homes. Int. J. of Artificial Intel. Tools 13(1), 81–100 (2004)
19. Berkhin, P.: Survey of Clustering Data Mining Techniques. Accrue Software (July 10, 2002), `http://www.ee.ucr.edu/~barth/EE242/clustering-survey.pdf`
20. Witten, I.H., Frank, E.: Data Mining: Practical Machine Learning Tools and Techniques, 2nd edn. Morgan Kaufmann, San Francisco (2005)
21. Landis, J.R., Koch, G.G.: An Application of Hierarchical Kappa-type Statistics in the Assessment of Majority Agreement among Multiple Observers. Biometrics 33(2), 363–374 (1977)
22. Jain, A.K., Duin, R.P.W., Mao, J.: Statistical pattern recognition: A review. IEEE Tran. on Pattern Analysis and Machine Intelligence 22(1), 4–37 (2000)

BERNIE – Consultant for Nutrition and Intelligent Shopping

Michael Hellenschmidt[1] and Felix Kamieth[2]

[1] Fraunhofer Institute for Computer Graphics Research IGD,
Fraunhoferstr. 5, 64283 Darmstadt, Germany
`michael.hellenschmidt@igd.fraunhofer.de`
[2] Technische Universität Darmstadt
64289 Darmstadt, Germany
`felix.kamieth@stud.tu-darmstadt.de`

Abstract. The paper presents the BERNIE prototype that realizes health assistance within super markets based on RFID technology. By storing the list of ingredients of each individual good, BERNIE is able to support shoppers in an unobtrusive and anonymous fashion. The paper ends with the description of the quantitative results of a 7-days field trial that was conducted at the CeBIT 2007 exhibition.

1 Introduction

Health becomes an issue of ever growing importance within an ageing society. Both health maintenance and the elderly society itself will raise new challenges for information technology and assistive applications [3]. One major part of staying healthy is obviously the maintenance of a healthy diet. This begins already in the super-market when people run their errands. For example you may be on a special diet or you have been told by your doctor that certain ingredients are not conductive to health and you have to avoid them in the future. You are then forced to read the labels on the goods and have to be aware of different notations of ingredients you might have to avoid. But it gets even worse, since not all the ingredients are displayed on the labels. So it's not even possible to feel confident that you avoid certain ingredients without prior study. The problem, however, increases when you consider allergies or other food incompatibilities. In this case, eating food with ingredients you are not supposed to eat can lead to unpleasant symptoms and may in some case even be life-threatening. Having to check everything you buy is a major inconvenience especially for people who have just developed an allergy as these things are often poorly documented, especially if the allergy is a rare condition.

Imagine you have invited someone else for dinner and that person tells you about his allergies. Maybe an allergy you might never have ever heard of. After all, you may cause a risk to your visitor's health. How convenient would it be to have a guide by your side that assist you in making the right choices whenever you go shopping. You would just go shopping as usual, without long and tiresome prior study and your assistant would immediately tell you if what you have just put into your shopping cart is an allowed

M. Mühlhäuser et al. (Eds.): AmI 2007 Workshops, CCIS 11, pp. 238–245, 2008.

Fig. 1. BERNIE as a shopping cart equipped with an RFID-antenna, a laptop and a RFID-reader that is hidden beneath the cover plate

food or if it contains ingredients that are undesired or even harmful with regards to your personal health conditions.

In this paper we describe BERNIE[1], an assistance system based on Radio Frequency Identification (RFID) that provides this kind of service. The system was first demonstrated at the CeBIT 2007 exhibition in Hannover, Germany. Given that products are already supported with RFID-Tags – which they will be for automatic price calculation in the future – we put additional information about the products' ingredients on the tags. Our system suggests equipping each shopping cart with an application system, which reads the information on the tags with an RFID-antenna/reader combination, checks it with the customer's preferences and then gives a warning to the user to prevent him from buying undesired or forbidden foods. The warning is given by visual means as opposed to auditory signals to allow for privacy during the shopping experience. Since only the goods' information is saved on the tags, the customer also doesn't have to worry about revealing his personal data, which is an often-raised concern whenever RFID-technology is used, since his data will remain secure within this closed system of tag and shopping cart and not be sent to a central server where it could be saved and matched with other personal data. This provides a useful extension to ordinary RFID-Tag solutions which allow for automatic price calculation at the check-out, and thereby leverages the existing technology to provide the customer with additional services. The remainder of this paper is organized as follows: Section 2 covers the technical requirements to be met to establish a system which realizes the scenario above. Section 3 describes how this system was realized while section 4 gives some details about our experiences with field trials on the CeBIT 2007 exhibition. Section 5 illustrates the scientific context of our application and names other projects and initiatives that are dealing with the realisation of assistance in daily life. Finally a summary of our work and an outlook on future work is given.

---

[1] BERNIE is a german acronym for "Consultant for Nutrition and Intelligent Shopping".

2 Scenario Considerations

An unobstrusive interaction is the major requirement to make our system accepted and usable. Here, the user shouldn't be disturbed in his usual shopping experience. He should move his cart around and put products inside just as he normally would without having to change any of his behaviour, which could be seen as a hindrance that spoils the shopping experience and will decrease acceptance rates and therefore the viability of the system. Consequently the system should guide the user without him having to do any major alterations in his shopping customs. To make this possible, it is necessary to read the product data in a long-distance fashion while the customer is shopping. One needs to know the ingredients of the product the moment the customer puts it into his cart. The product information is thus best saved on the product itself and then read as it is placed inside the shopping cart. Also, the customer should not be required to do anything special to make the information read. So any technology that requires contact for information transmission, be it physical or just visual is out of the question to guarantee user acceptance. What is then needed is non-contact transfer of information at a distance from the product to the assistance-system whenever the user puts a product into his shopping-cart. The logical solution to this problem is the usage of RFID-Tags. RFID-Tags can be read without physical or visual contact. All that is needed is to write the information about the contained ingredients onto the tags and an RFID-antenna whose field covers the interior of the shopping cart. Applying this the information is read without any additional effort on the user's part[2].

3 Realisation

We implemented the system by equipping a shopping cart with the necessary RFID technology, namely an antenna, a reader and a laptop to process the data and display the result to the user (see figure 1). Additionally we labelled about 50 products with RFID-tags. The products were chosen from an ordinary shopping list, e.g. milk, soup, chocolate, cereals, beer, apple juice, or spaghetti. Both antenna and tags operated at 868 MHz, which is the current EPC standard frequency when using ultra high frequency (UHF) technology. The antenna can be identified as the white box inside the shopping cart in figure 1. The antenna's field was calibrated so that it contained the entire shopping cart, that additionally possesses some shielding effects that screens the cart's outside from the stimulating RFID signal. The Sirit INfinity 510 UHF reader [2] is hidden inside the box at the bottom of the cart. It takes the raw information received from the antenna and interprets it to describe if a tag has entered the antenna's field, if it's a tag that hasn't been inside the field before, or if a tag has left the field. It also records the tag's EPC code and sends the gathered information to the laptop where it is then processed. The tags are self-adhesive labels with an EPC Class 1 Gen2 UHF Chip which are placed on the products. Consequently, the EPC code was used to identify the product and to gain additional information about the product itself. The ingredients

---

[2] We assume that every good will be equipped with RFID-Tags in the future at least for logistic purposes. Thus the additional usage of information stored on RFID-Tags will be possible in a very cost-efficient fashion.

we took into account for our first prototype were: animal products (to support vegetarians), gluten, lactose (to assist allergic persons) and alcohol (in order to guard recovering alcoholics).

The product information was encoded bitwise. Each bit of information represented a specific ingredient, which was either inside the product (1) or not (0). Since our system supported 4 ingredients, we needed 4 bit or one hexadecimal number to codify the entire information needed on the tag. Observing this hex-number gave you all the information about which ingredients the product contained and which it didn't (cp. table 1).

Table 1. Bitwise codification of goods' ingredients lists (examples)

Product	Animal Products	Gluten	Lactose	Alcohol	Hex-Nr.
Spaghetti	0	1	0	0	4
Bread	0	1	1	0	6
Pudding	1	1	0	0	C
Beer	0	1	0	1	5
...					

One remark with respect to the information storage on the RFID-tags: The tags we used were passive tags in conformity with the EPC Class 1 Gen2. No additional memory on the tags was available. Thus we replaced the already stored EPC code by a number that allows both the identification of individual RFID-tags without ambiguity (needed by the RFID-antenna and RFID-reader) and the readout of the product's ingredients list[3]. This chosen approach provides two important features with respect to the user's anonymity and the underlying application infrastructure:

1. the shopping cart represents a close system: There is no wireless connection to an external/central database necessary that has to identify a product number in order to make available additional product information.
2. shopping experience takes place in a complete anonymous fashion: Thus no information about the chosen product (in order to gain any ingredients list) is revealed, the shopper can be confident that no one (not even super market personnel) will be informed about his allergics or illnesses.

This encoded information about the product's ingredients was then compared to the conditions the user has chosen using the interface – the moment the user places the product into the trolley. Figure 2 illustrates the graphical user interface that is presented

---

[3] In fact we replaced the last 4 bits of each tag's EPC code by the hex-number that represents the product's ingredients, listed the resulting new EPC numbers and avoided to have a number twice. This was done manually while programming the tags and the application. W.l.o.g. we assume to have tags that provide additional memory for future prototypes. Thus the uniqueness of each EPC code could be guaranteed without manual interfering.

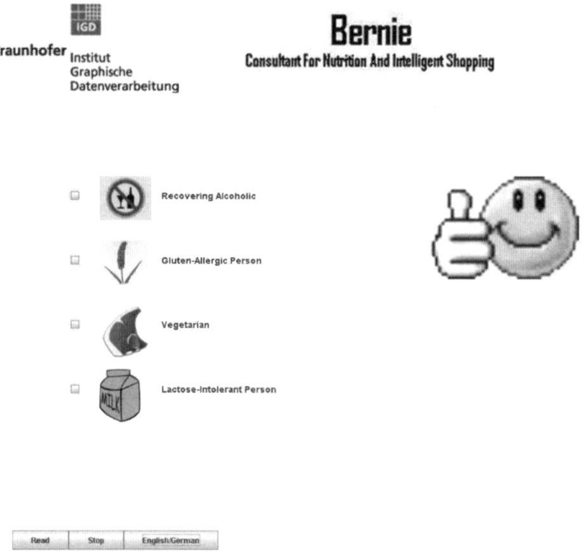

Fig. 2. The graphical user interface of BERNIE. On the left the user adjusts his allergics resp. preferences. On the right the tolerance of each good's ingredients is displayed by an abstract face.

to the shopper by means of a laptop on the trolley. Here the user can enter his preferences resp. indicate the ingredients that should be avoided. Thereby the indication of multiple options are possible. Consequently a shopper could be (a person that is) a recovering alcoholic as well as a vegetarian for instance. As soon as the customer puts a product into the cart that is in contrast to the condition(s) that are chosen a visual alarm is given. In order to realize the alarm in an effective (that is: understandable) and non-threatening manner, an image is then displayed that shows a frowning smiley with thumbs down.

4   Field Trial Experiences

We presented BERNIE on the CeBIT 2007 exhibition in Hannover, Germany, this year (see figure 3). The CeBIT 2007 exhibition was visited by more than 480,000 visitors from all over the world (from which 379,000 of them were professionals)[4]. Consequently we had the chance to demonstrate BERNIE and its assistive functions to at least one hundred people a day.

   Although we did not carry out a qualitative study, some quantitative results – with respect to user acceptance and technical obstacles – could be summarized:

   – User Acceptance: the idea of health assistance in a real daily life scenario – especially supported by unobtrusive interaction – was appreciated and went down

---

[4] Numbers from the official CeBIT website http://www.cebit.de

Fig. 3. Demonstration of BERNIE prototype to various exhibition visitors at CeBIT 2007

well by the a vast majority of the visitors (summarizing the visitor's reactions we estimate an acceptance rate of more than 90 per cent)[5]. Especially the users liked to have a clear and concise interface that does not disturb them from their actual tasks (going shopping). Having additional sound or voice output was deprecated. The users were afraid to cause attentiveness and to give up their anonymity against other customers or members of the super market staff.

– Allergics: although we assumed that we had considered the most relevant allergies (gluten and lactose) we learned a lot about other diseases and handicaps. Very often mentioned were: nut allergy, sesame allergy, legume allergy (especially peanuts[6] or beans), or seafood and shellfish allergy.

– Reliability: reading the tags does not work in a robust manner when they are placed near metal or water. So a tag placed on a metal can or a water bottle can not be read consistently unless one has put a buffer between the tag and the product. Also, shielded by several bottles or cans, the tags behind this barrier are beyond the reach of the antenna's field, which creates a problem for user convenience and a challenge for further scientific study. Another limiting factor is the orientation of the tag – placed on the good – and the antenna. A 90 degree orientation makes reading of tag information almost impossible (more information about RFID limitations e.g. [5,6]).

One discussion point – that was raised very often – should not be concealed here: Most exhibition visitors liked to know some technical details, especially how the assistant (visible on the laptop) knows about the good that was placed into the trolley at last. After explaining the details and mentioning the term RFID some people were upset because of

---

[5] Here, a lot of exhibition visitors made remarks like "Very good idea!", "Is this already on the market?", or "Finally. It was high time (for such a development)!".

[6] Peanuts belong to the class of legumes (not nuts).

the usage of RFID technology. There were afraid of revealing their individual personal data and of losing their anonymity[7]. But in fact it is vice versa: Anonymity would have been given up when using another technology as RFID, e.g. bar codes. Here we would have been forced to contact an external data base and thus reveal the individual customer's preferences. Obviously there is an unascertained fear of especially this kind of technology.

5 Scientific Background

The BERNIE prototype follows the main Ambient Intelligence ideas to assist people in their daily life in an unobtrusive and non distractive manner [1]. This application is not meant to broaden the horizon of RFID or to develop new innovative technologies for radio frequency identification. Here, the reader could refer to well-known events, e.g. the initiatives of Europe's Information Society [7], or conferences [8]. BERNIE is mainly meant for establishing assistance in daily life[8] based on the application of still existing basic technologies. Other projects resp. initiatives that represent this kind of approach are for instance the usage of personal souvenirs for viewing holiday photos [9], the diet-aware dining table [10] or recommender systems for movies [11,12] to name only a few.

6 Conclusion and Future Work

This article presents a system for assisting the user while going shopping. This is achieved in an unobtrusive manner by applying an RFID-equipped trolley that is controlled by an application that is able to interpret the ingredients list of the goods in accordance to the user's individual preferences (resp. diseases). By applying RFID-tags, each good is able to provide information about its own ingredients. This we achieved by encoding the good's individual ingredients list that is stored on the good's tag. Doing this, we achieved both shopping in an anonymous fashion and support for allergics and other customer groups. A very important class of consumers are diabetics. Nevertheless, it is often not unambiguous whether a food is suitable for diabetics or not. For most goods the principle of exclusion cannot be applied. This is, because most diabetics are allowed to consume the majority of offered food – but it depends on quantity resp. on the composition (and often on the daily history of each individual patient).

Consequently our future work has to concentrate on both the support of further customer groups and the evaluation (and enhanced application) of the RFID-technology. Here, we try to learn more about mechanisms to support diabetics in order to specify concrete algorithms for this kind of disease, we also experiment with high-frequency RFID technology (13,56 MHz) in order to evaluate possibilities for minimizing potential shielding effects of goods containing water resp. packagings that contain metal or aluminium.

---

[7] In fact we have chosen RFID technology both to achieve unobtrusive interaction mechanisms and to obtain customers anonymity.

[8] In agreement with "stop thinking of doing everything for everyone, start realisizing something for someone" (heard at the Pervasive 2006 conference in Dublin, Ireland, from a panellist).

References

1. Aarts, E., Encarnação, J.L.: Into Ambient Intelligence. In: Aarts, E., Encarnação, J.L. (eds.) True Versions: The Emergence of Ambient Intelligence, vol. 1, pp. 1–16. Springer, Heidelberg (2006)
2. Sirit Inc. (2007), `http://www.sirit.com/`
3. ISTAG Report on Shaping Europe's Future Through ICT, European Commission (March 2006), `http://cordis.europa.eu/ist/istag.htm`
4. Svendsen, B., et al. (eds.): ISTAG Report on Experience and Application Research – Involving Users in the Development of Ambient Intelligence. European Commission (September 2004), `http://cordis.europa.eu/ist/istag.htm`
5. Lahiri, S.: RFID Sourcebook, August 31, 2005, p. 304. IBM Press (2005) ISBN-10: 0-13-185137-3
6. Tobolski, J.: RFID: An Introduction and the Realities. In: Proceedings of the Pervasive 2006 Workshop Pervasive Technology Applied - Real-World Experiences with RFID and Sensor Networks, Dublin, Ireland, May 7 (2006)
7. Europe's Information Society, Towards an RFID Policy for Europe (2007), `http://ec.europa.eu/information_society/policy/rfid/index_en.htm`
8. IEEE International Conference on RFID 2007 Gaylord Texan Resort, Grapevine, Texas, USA (March 26-28, 2007), `http://www.ieee-rfid.org/2007/`
9. Van den Hoven, E., Eggen B.: Personal souvenirs as Ambient Intelligent Objects. In: Proceedings of the 2005 joint Conference on Smart objects and Ambient Intelligence, Grenoble, France, pp. 123–128 (2005)
10. Chang, K.-h., Liu, S.-y., Chu, H.-h., Hsu, J., Chen, C., Lin, T.-y., Chen, C.-y., Huang, P.: Diet-Aware Dining Table: Observing dietary behaviors over tabletop surface. In: Proceedings of the International conference on Pervasive Computing (PERVASIVE 2006), pp. 366–382, Dublin Ireland (May 2006)
11. Masthoff, J.: Group modeling: Selecting a sequence of television items to suit a group of viewers. In: User Modeling and User Adapted Interaction, vol. 14, pp. 37–85. Springer, Heidelberg (2004)
12. Nitschke, J., Hellenschmidt, M.: Design and Evaluation of Adaptive Assistance for the Selection of Movies. In: Proceedings of IMC Workshop: Assistance, Mobility and Applications, Stuttgart, pp. 129–135. Fraunhofer IRB Verlag (2003)

Ambient Assisted Living in Rural Areas: Vision and Pilot Application

Ferenc Havasi and Ákos Kiss

University of Szeged, Department of Software Engineering
Árpád tér 2., H-6720 Szeged, Hungary
{havasi,akiss}@inf.u-szeged.hu

Abstract. Rural areas cover 90% of the EU's territory and half of the Europeans live in these areas. It is of high priority to ensure the full participation right of these people in the information society, which means considering them during the newest developments (such as AAL) as well. In this paper, we envision a PDA-centered medical sensor system setup that is suitable for the AAL homecare scenario and identify a problem that can easily arise in rural areas. Additionally, we intruduce a pilot application that can act as the seed of the envisioned system and gives an answer to the identified problems.

1   Introduction

Rural areas cover 90% of the (enlarged) EU's territory and approximately half of the Europeans live in these rural and remote areas. It is of high priority to ensure the full participation right of these people in the information society, which means considering them during the newest developments (such as AAL) as well. However, rural and remote areas can impose additional problems to those experienced in urban environments.

First, let us consider the general problems of AAL. We can say that ambient assisted living and ambient assisted home care is at our doorstep. Several mobile medical sensors are already available: mobile ECG devices, pulse oxymeters, blood pressure monitors, glucometers, etc. are produced by various vendors. Still, these sensors cannot reach the aims of AAL alone. To be able to *intelligently assist* our lives, these devices should overcome some of their major deficiencies: first, these devices are usually short of *resources* (memory and computational power), and secondly, the vital data gathered by the sensors are not processed in an *integrated* manner, i.e., the devices work without knowing the data sensed by each other. However, the seemingly trivial solution, i.e., to extend the sensors with more resources may not be a viable one because of several constraints on usability such as size, weight or energy consumption.

We propose a construction which offers a solution for the above mentioned problems but does not hinder usability and uses already available devices thus making AAL able to cross the doorstep. In our vision, the centre of ambient assisted living is a personal digital assistant – quite simmilarly as PDAs or

M. Mühlhäuser et al. (Eds.): AmI 2007 Workshops, CCIS 11, pp. 246–252, 2008.

smartphones start to play a central role in our normal lives. PDAs are small, mobile and they are equipped with sufficient resources to process and integrate data coming from several sources. And last but not least, they are able to connect (wirelessly) to sensors.

And what about the problems of the rural and remote areas? In this paper we focus on one: providing cost effective internet coverage for scarcely inhabited areas is not an easy task. Wired internet connections, GPRS-based mobile connections, or full WiFi coverage provided by hotspots might all turn out to be too expensive in such scenarios. Thus, we propose to use the PDAs as active members of an ad-hoc wireless mesh network where the internet connectivity is provided by a gateway and the ad-hoc network together, without the need of additional fixed components.

In this paper, we intruduce a pilot application that can act as the seed of the envisioned system. We connected a mobile ECG device to the Nokia N800 Internet Tablet using Bluetooth technology and extended the capabilities of the sensor by exploiting the resources of the PDA. As the N800 runs on an open source platform, the extension of the current system with additional sensors becomes easy. Additionally, we adapted a network layer application for the N800 which makes it able to act as an active device of an ad-hoc network.

The rest of the paper is organized as follows: Section 2 describes the hardware components of our pilot application in detail, Section 3 gives the details of the AAL functionality implemented in the application, and in Section 4 we give some information on the network layer designed for rural areas. Finally, in Section 6 we conclude our work and give directions for future work.

2   System Components

In our pilot project, codenamed SmartECG [1], we used the CardioBlue mobile ECG event recorder manufactured by Meditech Ltd., which is a typical representative of the currently available mobile (medical) sensors. The device is able to record 1-5 ECG channels, either automatically in regular intervals or at the patients request, but it can store only 60 minutes of recorded data in its internal memory. Moreover, while its 16-bits core running at 8MHz consumes extremely low power, it is not suitable for complex signal processing purposes. Fortunately, CardioBlue is equipped with a Bluetooth interface which both allows the configuration of the device and grants access to the sensed ECG data, even in real time. This feauture opens the possibility to extend the functionality of this highly resource-constrained device.

It turned out that the Nokia N800 Internet Tablet (and its predecessor, the Nokia 770) is an ideal tool for this extension. It has an easy to use user interface (large and high-resolution touch screen display), sufficient computational power and data storage for performing complex tasks (32-bits ARM core clocked at 320MHz, 128MB RAM, and 256MB flash memory), standard wireless interfaces that allow connectivity to other devices (Bluetooth and WiFi), and an easily extensible software environment (Linux operating system and Maemo desktop

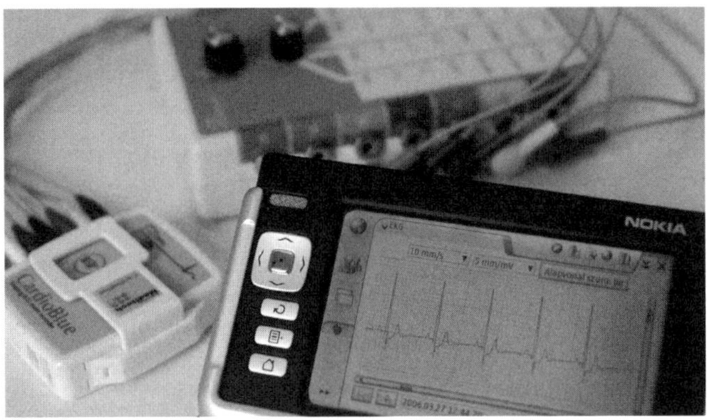

Fig. 1. The system setup: A Nokia Internet Tablet, a CardioBlue mobile ECG device, and an "artificial patient"

environment both being open source). And besides (or against) its strengths, the Tablet remains a leightweight and portable device.

Thus, with these two devices (see Fig. 1) we can demonstrate that AAL is not the future, but it can already be made a part of our lives today with the help of the available tools.

3   The SmartECG Application

When designing the functionality extension of CardioBlue, we had two application areas in mind: the PDA can be useful in the clinical domain and, naturally, in the homecare scenario. Thus, the SmartECG application that runs on the N800 has two operation modes: the "doctor" and the "patient" modes.

3.1   Doctor Mode

The doctor mode offers full access to the CardioBlue device. In this mode, the PDA can be used to configure the ECG device to periodically make records, it can download the data that is stored in the memory of the device, and it is able to display the downloaded (multichannel) ECG graphs (see Fig. 2).

What is more important and useful in a clinical scenario however, in doctor mode, the SmartECG application is capable of maintaining a live connection with the CardioBlue device and accessing the ECG data in real time. Moreover, we implemented the feature of transferring the ECG data to a remote computer through the internet (using the PDA's WiFi interface), and developed a multiplatform client application (running on both Windows and Linux), which is capable of receiving and displaying the real-time ECG data. This feature, when used together with a VoIP application (a GoogleTalk-compatible client comes preinstalled with N800) makes the consultation between remote-located members of a medical group (nurses, doctors, and/or experts) possible.

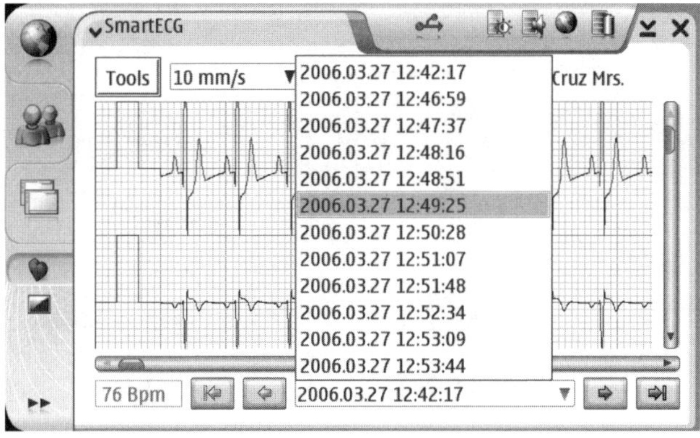

Fig. 2. Browsing through downloaded ECG data in doctor mode

3.2   Patient Mode

The patient mode is specifically designed for a homecare scenario. In this mode, the user interface is intentionally very simple, consisting of only three large buttons that fill the whole screen (see Fig. 3a). This allows even elderly people with sight deterioration to activate the required functionality.

These functionalities are the following: the ECG data stored in the built-in memory of the CardioBlue can be downloaded to the Internet Tablet thus freeing up valuable space in the ECG device. Additionally, when connected to the internet, the already downloaded ECG records can be sent to the doctor via e-mail. And finally, if the patient has to remove the electrodes at home and then wants to place them back (e.g., because of bathing), then SmartECG can provide help by displaying the correct placement of electrodes (see Fig. 3b).

Besides pressing one of the three buttons and thus activating the above described functionalities the patient has nothing to fiddle with the application. All the operational parameters, even the e-mail address where the ECG records are sent, are preconfigured by the doctor, which makes the use of the application simple enough to be useful in a homecare situation.

4   Network Layer

The prototype application that was described in the previous section can work in two different wireless network environments. Naturally, it can connect to traditional WiFi hotspots, thus making use of the coverage that is becoming more widely used in urban areas, even in private homes. More and more medical institutes and hospitals deploy internal wireless networks, which offers new opportunities for the clinical application of the system.

For those who live in rural, remote and scarcely inhabited areas, the application offers an alternative solution [2]. The Internet Tablet can be equipped with

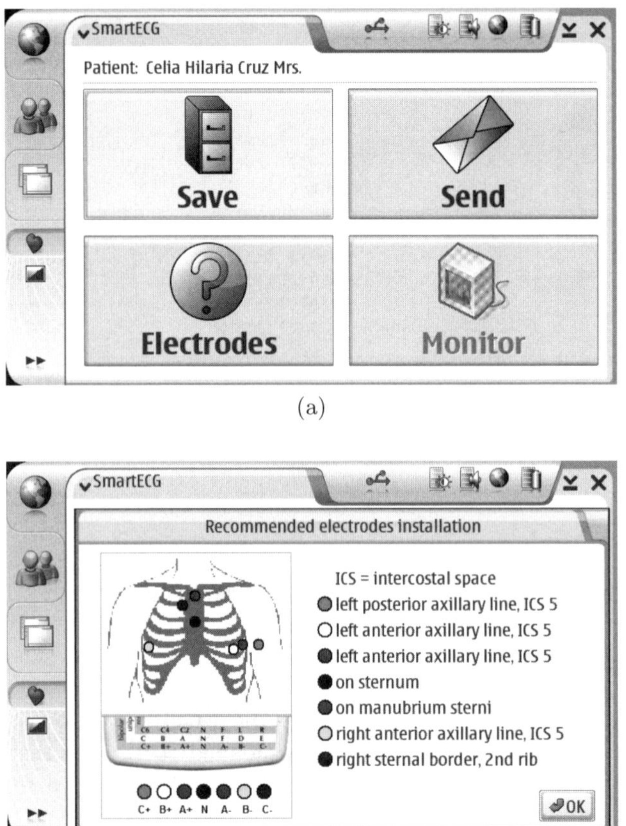

(a)

(b)

Fig. 3. Patient mode: (a) the functionality accessible to patients, (b) help to replace the electrodes in a correct way

an ad-hoc wireless mesh network layer, which makes the PDA capable of being an active device in the wireless network and transferring data (ECG records, among others) over it. This eliminates the need for statically deployed wireless devices (except for one gateway node, which connects the ad-hoc network to the rest of the internet) and offers a cost effective solution for the AAL applications to connect to the internet when required.

5   Related Work

Homecare systems have been researched for several years. There are already a few commercial solutions available. However, several existing solutions rely on call centers and transmit their data through phone lines.

The first established system is well@home, which uses wired sensors to acquire vital data and transmits them via a built-in modem. For wireless systems, a popular approach is the Body Area Network to gather sensor data and the use of a Mobile Base Unit for temporary data storage and data transfer. Often, the latter unit is a smartphone that uses GSM to transmit the data. MobiHealth [3] is a representative of such BAN-based monitoring systems. The Citizens' Healthcare System [4] and several other ECG home devices use the microphones of phones to send the collected data in the form of acoustical signals to the clicnic. The WiPaM [5], Motiva [6], TOPCARE [7], CardioScout [8] and Bluetooth ECG [9] projects use a Home Care Unit to gather data via Bluetooth and then transmit them to a healthcare provider using normal phone or data lines.

Compared to the above systems, our solution merges the best features of them. In our system, the PDA has enough computational power to integrate and process the gathered data like a home unit but it is lightweight enough to be portable like a mobile unit. It needs no wiring either for the sensors nor for the connection to the outside world. And finally, it uses digital data transfer over the internet instead of an analogue one over phone lines.

6   Conclusion and Future Plans

In this paper, we envisioned a PDA-centered medical sensor system setup that is suitable for the AAL homecare scenario. Additionally, we identified a problem (lack of internet access) that can easily arise in rural areas. Then we introduced a pilot application, which is a manifestation of the envisioned system, consisting of a Bluetooth-capable mobile ECG device, an open source platform-based PDA, and a software running on the PDA that extends the ECG device with AAL functionalities. Moreover, the PDA has been equipped with a network layer that can provide internet access even in rural areas in a cost efficient way.

For the future, there are several plans for enhancing the current application. First, we plan to add more medical sensors to the system, and then the application is going to be extended with medical intelligence that integrates the acquired data and takes all of them into account during decision making. Additionally, we plan to cooperate with organizations of rural settlements and Rural Living Labs, thus ensuring the field testing of the application and its enhancement based on the feedbacks. Finally, we are looking for application possibilities of the system not only in the homecare scenario but in other AAL areas as well.

Acknowledgement. This work was supported by the Hungarian National Office for Research and Technology within the frameworks of the Péter Pázmány Program (no. RET-07/2005) and the Bilateral German-Hungarian Collaboration Project on Ambient Intelligence Systems (BelAmI), and by the European Commission through the Collaboration@Rural project (FP6-IST 034921).

References

1. Department of Software Engineering, University of Szeged: SmartECG project,
   `http://www.inf.u-szeged.hu/smartecg`
2. Department of Software Engineering, University of Szeged: MCC project,
   `http://www.inf.u-szeged.hu/$\sim$bilickiv/mcc`
3. Konstantas, D., Jones, V., Herzog, R.: MobiHealth - innovative 2.5 / 3g mobile
   services and applications for healthcare. In: Proceedings of the 11th IST Mobile and
   Wireless Telecommunications Summit 2002, Thessaloniki, Greece (June 2002)
4. Maglaveras, N., Chouvarda, I., Koutkias, V.G., Gogou, G., Lekka, I., Goulis, D.,
   Avramidis, A., Karvounis, C., Louridas, G., Balas, E.A.: The Citizen Health System
   (CHS): a modular medical contact center providing quality telemedicine services.
   IEEE Trans Inf Technol Biomed 9(3), 353–362 (2005)
5. RDSM nv: WiPaM: a wireless patient monitoring platform,
   `http://www.rdsm.eu/telemedicine/wipam.html`
6. Koninklijke Philips Electronics N.V.: Motiva interactive healthcare platform, `http://`
   `www.medical.philips.com/main/products/telemonitoring/products/motiva`
7. Millan, J., Park, S.-E., Kiefer, S., Meyer, J.-U.: TOPCARE – implementation of
   a telematic homecare platform in cooperative health care provider networks. In:
   Proceedings of the Second Joint EMBS/BMES Conference, 2002, Hialeah, Florida,
   USA, October 2002, vol. 3, pp. 1869–1870 (2002)
8. Jansen, D., Paulat, K., Eichner, C., Frank, H.: 24 h EKG-rekorder mit bluetooth-
   funkschnittstelle für telemedizinische anwendungen. horizonte 24, 24–27 (2004)
9. Institut für Technik der Informationsverarbeitung, Universität Karlsruhe: Bluetooth
   ECG – mobile capturing of ECG-measurements,
   `http://www.itiv.uni-karlsruhe.de/opencms/workgroups/MST_Optik/`
   `vitalsensorik/ekg.html`

Predictions for Epidemiologic Indicators of Age-Related Diseases and Implications for the Development of Health-Enabling Technologies

Michael Marschollek[1], Klaus-H. Wolf[1], Oliver J. Bott[2], Juergen Howe[3],
and Reinhold Haux[1]

[1] Peter L. Reichertz Institute for Medical Informatics (PLRI)
University of Braunschweig – Institute of Technology and Hannover Medical School
Muehlenpfordtstrasse 23, 38106 Braunschweig
Michael.Marschollek@plri.de
Klaus-Hendrik.Wolf@plri.de
Reinhold.Haux@plri.de
[2] University of Applied Sciences and Arts
Faculty for Media, Information and Design
Expo Plaza 12, 30539 Hannover
oliver.bott@fh-hannover.de
[3] Institute for Gerontopsychology
University of Braunschweig – Institute of Technology
Bueltenweg 74/75, 38106 Braunschweig
j.howe@tu-braunschweig.de

Abstract. The steady increase in life expectancy in our modern industrialized societies will not only lead to a significant change in demographics, but also in epidemiologic factors. This paper reviews current predictions for epidemiologic indicators and derives implications for the development of future health-enabling technologies. Methods: A literature search in PubMed/MEDLINE was conducted and several statistical data bases were used to obtain up-to-date prediction data on health in the elderly population. Results: Prevalence rates for the leading diseases such as cardiovascular diseases, diabetes mellitus and cancers will remain almost constant in the next decades, but incidence rates will rise markedly because of the increase in the elderly population. For neuropsychiatric diseases such as dementias and depression an increased impact is expected. Conclusion: One focus for the development of health-enabling technologies is and will remain on monitoring, especially cardiovascular parameters. More research needs to be conducted to tap the full technological potential of preventive measures, e.g. for the prevention of social isolation and the promotion of a healthy lifestyle.

Keywords: epidemiology, prevalence, mortality, home care, sensors, health information systems.

1 Introduction and Motivation

Advances in medicine and hygiene have led to a substantial increase in life expectancy in the last 200 years. The demographics of industrialized, but also those of developing

M. Mühlhäuser et al. (Eds.): AmI 2007 Workshops, CCIS 11, pp. 253–260, 2008.

countries, are changing dramatically. This is sometimes referred to as the 'age wave'. In Germany, the population aged between 65 and 80 years will rise from 12.1 million in 2005 to an estimated 12.6 million in 2020 and to 16.7 million in 2035 [1]. Whereas the proportion of this group of people will again decrease from then on (2050: 12.8 m), the population aged above 80 years will rise substantially and constantly from 3.6 million in 2005 to 6.3 million in 2030 and 10.0 million in 2050 [1].

This change in demographics will have an impact on health costs as especially the very old require a substantial share of funds. In Germany e.g., the total average per capita health costs in 2004 were 2,730 euros. The costs increase with advancing age: the 15-65-year-old persons required 1,980 euros, the 65-85-year-olds 5,950 euros and the over 85-year-olds 14,750 euros [2]. One possible measure to get a grip on this problem can be – apart from intensified prevention programs – the use of health-enabling technologies that allow for telemonitoring and telecare along with individual decision support systems. In order to evaluate the future need – and thus market opportunities – for different health-enabling technology solutions, it is of paramount importance to take a closer look from a medical point of view at the predictions for future diseases and disability conditions that will affect the elderly population so that the development of solutions can be directed accordingly.

The aim of this paper therefore is

- to review and summarize current predictions on future changes in epidemiological indicators of diseases and conditions (prevalence, incidence, costs, causes of death and level of impairment) with special regard to those affecting the elderly population (section 3), and
- to discuss implications for the future development of health-enabling technologies (section 4).

2 Methods

The results presented were obtained by conducting a literature search in PubMed/ MEDLINE on March 20th 2007, using the search term *((prevalence) OR (incidence)) AND ((prediction) OR (prognosis)) AND (future) AND ((disease) OR (condition)) AND ((elderly) OR (age-related)) AND (review)*. The search yielded 212 abstracts which were subsequently reviewed, and cross-references were examined. Apart from this, several databases of statistical institutions, especially those of the World Health Organization (WHO Statistical Information System, *WHOSIS*) and the German Federal Statistical Office (*GENESIS*), were used to obtain up-to-date epidemiologic data that were analyzed and visualized. Complying with rules for good scientific practice (e.g. [3]), all literature review data recorded by the authors as the basis for this publication have been stored. Copies of the files can be requested from the authors.

3 Results

Most of the studies identified are concerned with prognoses for the prevalence or morbidity of specific chronic diseases and conditions, e.g. diabetes [4] or heart failure

[5]. Often the data are specific for certain populations, so that generalizations are not viable (e.g. [6]).

3.1 Prevalence, Incidence and Costs

WHO's WHOSIS data base does not contain explicit predictions for the future prevalence of age-related diseases, but for high-income countries these can be generalized from predictions conducted with data from the US *Medicare* System. Goldman et al. [7] have developed a model for future health care costs based on 10,881 data sets of the *Medicare Current Beneficiary Surveys* (MCBS) from the years 1992-1998. The estimated disease prevalence of the five leading diseases in the age group 65+ along with the mean annual costs is shown in Table 1.

Table 1. Prevalence and annual costs of the five leading diseases (US Medicare data) in the 65+ year-group in 1998 and 2030 [7]

rank	disease or injury	prevalence in %		avg. costs in 1998 in $
		1998	2030	
1	arthritis	57.3	68.4	5,160
2	hypertension	55.8	58.8	5,764
3	heart disease (cardiovascular disease)	38.2	40.1	7,268
4	diabetes mellitus	16.0	18.4	8,079
5	cancer (malignant neoplasms)	17.7	16.4	6,775

The data show that prevalence rates for the leading diseases are rising slowly, with the exception of malignant neoplasms. The authors conclude that, although prevalence will not change dramatically, total costs will rise significantly, from $176 billion in 2000 to $360 billion in 2030, due to the rising incidence caused by the growth of the elderly population. The most expensive disease is diabetes mellitus, causing a number of complications such as diabetic nephropathy, cerebral, cardial and peripheral vascular disease, loss of vision due to cataracts, etc.

3.2 Level of Impairment and Causes of Death

The most comprehensive data sets containing global data on different diseases and conditions and for different population subsets are kept by WHO. An often-cited and influential study, the *Global Burden of Disease* (GBD) Study was published by Murray and Lopez in 1997 [8] and later revised [9]. The GBD Project of the WHO followed and new adjusted predictions up to the year 2030 have been published recently by Mathers and Loncar [10] along with the original data.

Tables 2 and 3 show the ranked predicted causes of death in 2030 for the global population and that of the high-income countries, respectively [10]. Ischaemic heart disease and cerebrovascular disease are top-ranked in both lists and originate from the same underlying pathological process – arteriosclerosis. HIV infections respectively AIDS will become the most important infective cause of death, with a much higher prevalence in low-income countries (ranked 2nd). Airway cancers and chronic obstructive pulmonary disease (COPD) are closely associated with smoking, which is also a leading risk factor for arteriosclerosis. The prevalence of diabetes mellitus will also rise, causing a step-up in world-wide ranks from 11th (2002) to 7th (2030).

Table 2. Rank prediction of causes for world-wide mortality for the year 2030 [10]

rank	disease or injury	% of deaths
1	ischaemic heart disease	13.4
2	cerebrovascular disease	10.6
3	HIV/AIDS	8.9
4	chronic obstructive pulmonary disease (COPD)	7.8
5	lower respiratory infections	3.5

Table 3. Rank prediction of causes for mortality in high-income countries for the year 2030 [10]

rank	disease or injury	% of deaths
1	ischaemic heart disease	15.8
2	cerebrovascular disease	9.0
3	tracheal, bronchial and lung cancers	5.1
4	diabetes mellitus	4.8
5	chronic obstructive pulmonary disease (COPD)	4.1

The cause-of-death statistics show but one facet of the whole picture, because they do not include metrics that account for the cost of a disease, the reduction in the individual's quality of life or the period of suffering. To overcome this restraint, WHO has introduced the metric of 'disability-adjusted life years' (*DALYs*), which is defined as the sum of life years lost because of premature death and the years lost to disability [11]. One DALY means the loss of one year of unrestricted health and is related to the burden of a disease and – to a certain degree – to its costs. Figure 1 shows the WHO DALY predictions for the seven most limiting diseases and conditions (cardiovascular, neuropsychiatric, malignant, respiratory, digestive, sense organ, and diabetes mellitus) in the age group 70+ (*baseline* scenario [10]). All these diseases have growing DALY measures with cardiovascular diseases in the lead. There is also a marked rise in malignant diseases and especially in neuropsychiatric conditions, among which dementias and unipolar depressive disorders are the most prominent ones.

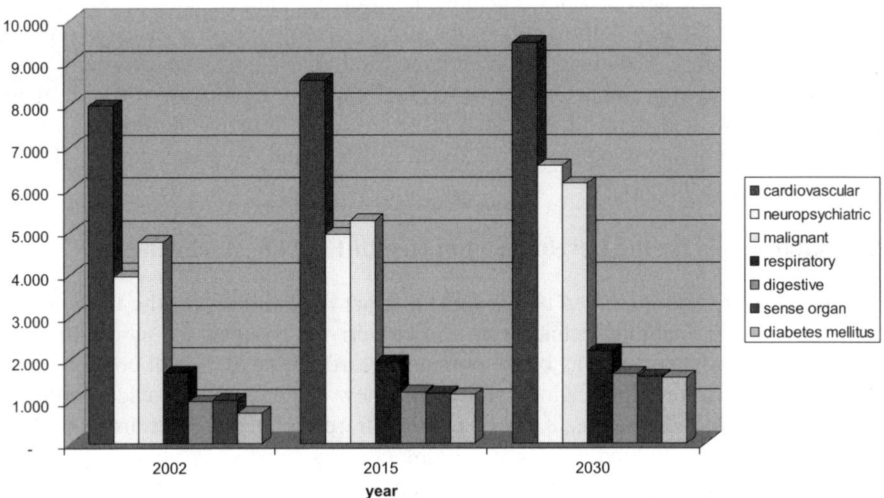

Fig. 1. DALY predictions for the age group 70+ in high-income countries for the seven diseases/ groups with the highest predictions for 2030 (baseline predictions from WHO data sets [10], DALY = disability adjusted life years)

4 Discussion

4.1 Epidemiologic Indicators

The marked demographical change that modern societies have to face within the next 40 years will bring about a significant change in epidemiological indicators. Although the prevalence rates of the leading diseases will not rise dramatically in high-income countries [7], their incidence will rise as the population group of the very old (80+ years) – who are most often affected – will nearly triple. Apart from that, comorbidity is a problem that primarily affects persons in advanced age: The *Berlin Aging Study* [12] revealed that – in the population group of persons aged 70+ – the prevalence of five or more somatic diseases at the same time is about 88%.

The mortality rates shown in Tables 2 and 3 and especially the DALY predictions of the WHO indicate that the most relevant diseases as far as the socio-economic impact is concerned are those of the cardiovascular system (ischaemic heart disease, hypertension, general vascular disease), followed by neuropsychiatric disorders, malignant neoplasms, and diabetes mellitus, which is less prevalent, but very costly. Cardiovascular diseases and diabetes mellitus share common risk factors (e.g. obesity, hypertriglyceridaemia, hypercholesterolaemia and hypertension) and interact with each other. Preventive measures could reduce morbidity significantly, e.g. if arteriosclerosis could be reduced e.g. by healthier nutrition and more physical exercise [13]. Malignant neoplasms can also partly be attributed to civilizational influences, but are less accessible to preventive measures as they come along naturally with advancing age. Communicable diaseases such as AIDS are not very common in industrialized countries, but are a major problem in many developing countries and expected to spread further in the next decades if health education does not catch on.

A remarkable finding is the grade of the rise of neuropsychiatric diseases (cf. Figure 1), most notably Alzheimer's dementia and unipolar depressive disorders. These conditions have a high impact on the individual's quality of life, are difficult or impossible to treat, and demand extensive efforts in care. Among the reasons for the high numbers of depressive patients are social isolation and the disintegration of traditional family structures [14].

4.2 Implications for the Development of Health-Enabling Technologies

Based on the predictions stated above some distinct implications for the future development of health-enabling technologies can be derived. Systems for monitoring cardiovascular parameters such as blood pressure, heart rate or ECG will continue to be in the focus of future applications along with new systems that provide additional information on blood contents, e.g. using near-infrared reflectance spectroscopy [15], or on the condition of blood vessels, e.g. by monitoring pulse-wave velocity [16, 17].

The DALY predictions (cf. Figure 1) emphasize the need for technologies to address the problems that come along with neuropsychiatric diseases. Apart from assistive systems for persons suffering from dementia, e.g. tracking systems [18], there is an urgent need for solutions for patients with bipolar diseases. Upcoming episodes of depression may be identified by monitoring daily activity routines and by detecting changes over time, so that countermeasures (e.g. changes in medication dosage) can be taken timely. Furthermore, modern communication technology, e.g. videophones, can be effectively employed to overcome social isolation [19] and to contact health care providers [20], provided that the user interfaces are adapted to the users' specific needs. Ease of use is one critical factor for acceptance or refusal, as e.g. demonstrated in [21]. Several frameworks and models can be employed to evaluate user acceptance [22], e.g. the *technology acceptance model* (TAM) by Davis and Bagozzi [23, 24], which also provides a template test procedure.

Apart from applications for monitoring the ill, there is an obvious need for proactive technology that helps to prevent diseases respectively their progress in the first place. Solutions for promoting healthier lifestyles and nutrition [25, 26] by giving individual feedback on behavior have a high potential for development [27]. Yet only few groups concentrate on designing feedback tools that incorporate knowledge from the field of behavioural psychology, e.g. to overcome denial mechanisms, and are able adapt themselves with regard to the user's emotional status [28].

Finally, health-enabling technologies need to be embedded in existing health information system architectures in order to avoid *information* or *data islands*. Knowledge about the individual patient, e.g. taken from her or his electronic health record (EHR), is essential to on the one hand analyze and interpret complex data, and on the other hand re-use it. Therefore the use of standards for data representation (e.g. HL7 Clinical Document Architecture [29]) and device communication (e.g. ISO/IEEE 11073 [30]) will be mandatory. Furthermore, a reference model for a flexible and sustainable home care architecture [31-33] is necessary to guide the development of a collaborative home care platform.

5 Conclusion

The demographic figures show that within the next 40-50 years there will be a significant increase in the number of elderly persons, especially of those aged 80 years and older. As this group has the highest numbers in disease prevalence and associated health costs there is a growing need for improved prevention and monitoring. Health-enabling technologies [34] have the potential to support both, as they permit continuous monitoring, e.g. of the cardiovascular system, and provide mechanisms for an individual feedback to promote healthier living. Apart from cardiovascular diseases especially neuropsychiatric conditions are on the rise and challenge future application builders to develop new methods that support treatment and care of the persons affected.

References

1. Federal Statistical Office of Germany: 11. Koordinierte Bevölkerungsvorausberechnung - Annahmen und Ergebnisse. Vol. 2007. Press office, Wiesbaden (2006)
2. Federal Statistical Office of Germany: Gesundheit - Ausgaben, Krankheitskosten und Personal 2004. Vol. 2007. Press office, Wiesbaden (2004)
3. Deutsche Forschungsgemeinschaft: Proposals for Safeguarding Good Scientific Practice 1998. Vol. 2006. Wiley-VCH, Weinheim (1998)
4. Janka, H.U., Michaelis, D.: Epidemiology of diabetes mellitus: prevalence, incidence, pathogenesis, and prognosis. Z Arztl Fortbild Qualitatssich 96, 159–165 (2002)
5. Schocken, D.D.: Epidemiology and risk factors for heart failure in the elderly. Clin. Geriatr. Med. 16, 407–418 (2000)
6. Noda, H., Iso, H., Sairenchi, T., Irie, F., Fukasawa, N., Toriyama, Y., Ota, H., Nose, T.: Prediction of stroke, coronary heart disease, cardiovascular disease, cancer, and total death based on results of annual health checkups. Nippon Koshu Eisei Zasshi 53, 265–276 (2006)
7. Goldman, D.P., Shekelle, P.G., Bhattacharya, J., Hurd, M., Joyce, G.F., Lakdawalla, D.N., Matsui, D.H., Newberry, S.J., Panis, C.W.A., Shang, B.: Health Status and Medical Treatment of the Future Elderly - Final Report. RAND Corporation (2004)
8. Murray, C.J., Lopez, A.D.: Alternative projections of mortality and disability by cause 1990-2020: Global Burden of Disease Study. Lancet 349, 1498–1504 (1997)
9. Murray, C.J., Lopez, A.D.: On the comparable quantification of health risks: lessons from the Global Burden of Disease Study. Epidemiology 10 (1999) 594-605
10. Mathers, C.D., Loncar, D.: Projections of global mortality and burden of disease from 2002 to 2030. PLoS Med 3, e442 (2006)
11. Murray, C.J., Salomon, J.A., Mathers, C.D., Lopez, A.D.: Summary measures of population health: concepts, ethics, measurement and applications, WHO, Geneva (2002)
12. Steinhagen-Thiessen, E., Borchelt, M.: Morbidität, Medikation und Funktionalität im Alter Morbidity, medication and functional status in the elderly. In: Mayer, K.U., Baltes, P.B. (eds.) Die Berliner Altersstudie The Berlin Aging Study, pp. 151–184. Akademie Verlag, Berlin (1996)
13. Aldahl, M., Kjaer, M., Joergensen, T.: Associations between overall physical activity level and cardiovascular risk factors in an adult population. Eur. J. Epidemiol. 22, 369–378 (2007)
14. Anderson, D.N.: Treating depression in old age: the reasons to be positive. Age Ageing 30, 13–17 (2001)
15. Soller, B.R., Favreau, J., Idwasi, P.O.: Investigation of electrolyte measurement in diluted whole blood using spectroscopic and chemometric methods. Appl. Spectrosc. 57, 146–151 (2003)

16. Kubo, T., Miyata, M., Minagoe, S., Setoyama, S., Maruyama, I., Tei, C.: A simple oscillometric technique for determining new indices of arterial distensibility. Hypertens. Res. 25, 351–358 (2002)
17. Naidu, M.U., Reddy, B.M., Yashmaina, S., Patnaik, A.N., Rani, P.U.: Validity and reproducibility of arterial pulse wave velocity measurement using new device with oscillometric technique: a pilot study. Biomed Eng Online 4, 49 (2005)
18. Lin, C.C., Chiu, M.J., Hsiao, C.C., Lee, R.G., Tsai, Y.S.: Wireless health care service system for elderly with dementia. IEEE Trans. Inf. Technol. Biomed. 10, 696–704 (2006)
19. Hensel, B.K., Oliver, D.P., Demiris, G., Willis, L.: A telehealth case study of videophone use between family members. In: AMIA Annu Symp. Proc., p. 948 (2006)
20. Mix, S., Borchelt, M., Nieczaj, R., Trilhof, G., Steinhagen-Thiessen, E.: Telematics in geriatrics–potentials, problems and application experiences. Z Gerontol Geriatr. 33, 195–204 (2000)
21. Day, M., Demiris, G., Oliver, D.P., Courtney, K., Hensel, B.: Exploring underutilization of videophones in hospice settings. Telemed J. E Health 13, 25–31 (2007)
22. Venkatesh, V., Morris, M.G., Davis, G.B., Davis, F.D.: User acceptance of information technology: Toward a unified view. MIS Quarterly 27, 425–478 (2003)
23. Bagozzi, R., Davis, F., Warshaw, P.: Development and Test of a Theory of Technological Learning and Usage. Human Relations 45, 686 (1992)
24. Davis, F.: A technology acceptance model for empirically testing new end-user information systems: Theory and results. Sloan School of Management. Massachusetts Institute of Technology, Cambridge (1985)
25. Amft, O., Kusserow, M., Troester, G.: Identification of temporal structures in chewing sounds. In: Proceedings of the IEEE International Conference on Bioinformatics and Biomedicine (BIBM 2007), San Jose, CA (2007)
26. Amft, O., Kusserow, M., Troester, G.: Probabilistic parsing of dietary activity events. In: Proceedings of the International Workshop on Wearable and Implantable Body Sensor Networks (BSN 2007), pp. 242–247 (2007)
27. Intille, S.S.: A new research challenge: persuasive technology to motivate healthy aging. IEEE Trans. Inf. Technol. Biomed. 8, 235–237 (2004)
28. Lisetti, C., LeRouge, C.: Affective computing in tele-home health. In: Proceedings of the 37th Annual Hawaii International Conference on System Sciences, p. 148 (2004)
29. Dolin, R.H., Alschuler, L., Boyer, S., Beebe, C., Behlen, F.M., Biron, P.V., Shabo Shvo, A.: HL7 Clinical Document Architecture, Release 2. J. Am. Med. Inform. Assoc. 13, 30–39 (2006)
30. Yao, J., Warren, S.: Applying the ISO/IEEE 11073 standards to wearable home health monitoring systems. J. Clin. Monit. Comput. 19, 427–436 (2005)
31. Bott, O.J., Marschollek, M., Wolf, K.H., Haux, R.: Towards New Scopes: Sensor Enhanced Regional Health Information Systems - Part 1: Architectural Challenges. Methods Inf. Med. 46, 476–483 (2007)
32. Marschollek, M., Wolf, K.H., Bott, O.J., Geisler, M., Plischke, M., Ludwig, W., Hornberger, A., Haux, R.: Sustainable ubiquitous home health care - Architectural considerations and first practical experiences. In: Kuhn, K.A., Warren, J.R., Leong, T.Y. (eds.) MEDINFO 2007, vol. 129, pp. 8–12. IOS Press, Brisbane (2007)
33. Bott, O.J., Marschollek, M., Bergmann, J., Wolf, K.H., Tegtbur, U., Haux, R.: Sensor-enhanced health information system architectures for home and telecare: concept and prototype. In: Hein, A., Thoben, W., Appelrath, H.J., Jensch, P. (eds.) European Conference on eHealth 2007, vol. P-118, pp. 193–203. GI, Oldenburg (2007)
34. Haux, R.: Individualization, globalization and health - about sustainable information technologies and the aim of medical informatics. Int. J. Med. Inform. 75, 795–808 (2006)

First International Workshop on Human Aspects in Ambient Intelligence: Preface

Tibor Bosse[1], Cristiano Castelfranchi[2], Mark Neerincx[3], Fariba Sadri[4], and Jan Treur[1]

[1] Vrije Universiteit Amsterdam, Department of Artificial Intelligence,
de Boelelaan 1081a, 1081 HV Amsterdam, the Netherlands
{tbosse,treur}@cs.vu.nl
[2] Institute of Cognitive Sciences and Technologies, National Research Council,
viale Marx 15, 00137 Roma, Italy
cristiano.castelfranchi@istc.cnr.it
[3] Delft University of Technology, Man-Machine Interaction Group,
Mekelweg 4, 2628 CD Delft, the Netherlands
M.A.Neerincx@ewi.tudelft.nl
[4] Imperial College of Science, Technology and Medicine, Department of Computing,
180 Queen's Gate, SW7 2BZ London, England
fs@doc.ic.ac.uk

The workshop on Human Aspects in Ambient Intelligence addresses multidisciplinary aspects of Ambient Intelligence with human-directed disciplines such as psychology, social science, neuroscience and biomedical sciences. The aim is to get modellers and researchers together, working in these disciplines, or on cross connections of Ambient Intelligence with such a discipline. The focus is on the use of knowledge from these disciplines in Ambient Intelligence applications, in order to take care of and support in a knowledgeable manner humans in their daily living in medical, psychological and social respects.

The workshop aims at getting modellers in the psychological, neurological, social or biomedical disciplines interested in Ambient Intelligence as a high-potential application area for their models. For example, particular problem specifications may be offered that can be addressed by the human-directed sciences. From the other side, the workshop aims at making researchers in Computer Science, and Artificial and Ambient Intelligence more aware of the possibilities to incorporate more substantial knowledge from the psychological, neurological, social and biomedical disciplines in Ambient Intelligence architectures and applications. Learning more about available knowledge and computational models for human-related processes, may serve as input for more advanced applications.

By being a member of the programme committee, the following researchers have contributed to the successful organisation of this workshop: Gerhard Andersson, Juan Carlos Augusto, Tibor Bosse, Antonio Camurri, Nick Cassimatis, Cristiano Castelfranchi, James L. Crowley, Pim Cuijpers, Henk Elffers, Rino Falcone, Dirk Heylen, Ingrid Heynderickx, Anthony Jameson, Paul Lukowicz, Isaac Marks, Silvia Miksch, Scott Moss, Mark Neerincx, Fariba Sadri, Matthias Scheutz, Elizabeth Sklar, Ron Sun, Jan Treur, Robert L. West.

M. Mühlhäuser et al. (Eds.): AmI 2007 Workshops, CCIS 11, pp. 261, 2008.
© Springer-Verlag Berlin Heidelberg 2008

On Human Aspects in Ambient Intelligence

Jan Treur

Agent Systems Research Group
Department of Artificial Intelligence, Vrije Universiteit Amsterdam
De Boelelaan 1081, 1081 HV Amsterdam, The Netherlands
treur@cs.vu.nl
http://www.few.vu.nl/~treur

Abstract. This paper briefly outlines the scientific area that addresses Ambient Intelligence applications in which not only sensor data, but also knowledge from the human-directed sciences such as biomedical science, neuroscience, and psychological and social sciences is incorporated. This knowledge enables the environment to perform more in-depth, human-like analyses of the functioning of the observed humans, and to come up with better informed actions. It is discussed which ingredients are important to realise this view, and how frameworks can be developed to combine them to obtain the intended type of systems: reflective coupled human-environment systems. Finally, further perspectives are discussed for Ambient Intelligence applications based on these reflective coupled human-environment systems.

1 Introduction

Ambient Intelligence provides possibilities to contribute to more personal care; e.g., (Aarts, Harwig, Schuurmans, 2001; Aarts, Collier, Loenen, Ruyter, 2003; Riva, Vatalaro, Davide, Alcañiz, 2005) . Acquisition of sensor information about humans and their functioning is an important factor, but without adequate knowledge for analysis of this information, the scope of such applications is limited. However, devices in the environment possessing such knowledge can show a more human-like understanding and base personal care on this understanding. For example, this may concern elderly people, patients depending on regular medicin usage, surveillance, penitentiary care, psychotherapeutical/selfhelp communities, but also, for example, humans in highly demanding tasks such as warfare officers, air traffic controllers, crisis and disaster managers, and humans in space missions; e.g., (Green, 2005; Itti and Koch, 2001).

Within human-directed scientific areas, such as cognitive science, psychology, neuroscience and biomedical sciences, models have been and are being developed for a variety of aspects of human functioning. If such models of human processes are represented in a formal and computational format, and incorporated in the human environment in devices that monitor the physical and mental state of the human, then such devices are able to perform a more in-depth analysis of the human's functioning. This can result in an environment that may more effffectively affect the state of humans by undertaking in a knowledgeable manner actions that improve their wellbeing and performance. For example, the workspaces of naval officers may include systems that, among others, track their

M. Mühlhäuser et al. (Eds.): AmI 2007 Workshops, CCIS 11, pp. 262–267, 2008.

eye movements and characteristics of incoming stimuli (e.g., airplanes on a radar screen), and use this information in a computational model that is able to estimate where their attention is focussed at. When it turns out that an officer neglects parts of a radar screen, such a system can either indicate this to the person, or arrange on the background that another person or computer system takes care of this neglected part. In applications of this type, an ambience is created that has a better understanding of humans, based on computationally formalised knowledge from the human-directed disciplines.

2 Multidisciplinarity: The Ingredients

The area as sketched is essentially multidisciplinary. It combines aspects of Ambient Intelligence with knowledge from human-directed disciplines such as psychology, social science, neuroscience and biomedical sciences. Further development will depend on cooperation between researchers from these disciplines or working on cross connections of Ambient Intelligence with the human-directed disciplines. The focus is on the use of knowledge from these disciplines in Ambient Intelligence applications, in order to take care in a more sophisticated manner of humans in their daily living in medical, psychological and social respects. For example, modellers in the psychological, neurological, social or biomedical disciplines interested in Ambient Intelligence as a high-potential application area for their models, can get inspiration for problem areas to be addressed for further developments in their disciplines. From the other side, researchers in Computer Science, and Artificial and Ambient Intelligence may become more aware of the possibilities to incorporate more substantial knowledge from the psychological, neurological, social and biomedical disciplines in Ambient Intelligence architectures and applications, and may offer problem specifications that can be addressed by the human-directed sciences.

In more detail, content from the domain of human-directed sciences, among others, can be taken from areas such as medical physiology, health sciences, neuroscience, cognitive psychology, clinical psychology, psychopathology, sociology, criminology, and exercise and sport sciences. From the domain of Artificial Intelligence, useful contributions can be found in areas such as agent modelling, knowledge and task modelling, and cognitive and social modelling and simulation. Finally, from the Computer Science domain, relevant areas are distributed systems, sensor systems, human-centred software engineering, user modelling, and human-computer interaction.

3 Frameworks to Combine the Ingredients

One of the challenges is to provide frameworks that cover the class of Ambient Intelligence applications showing human-like understanding and supporting behaviour. Here human-like understanding is defined as understanding in the sense of being able to analyse and estimate what is going on in the human's mind (a form of mindreading) and in his or her body (a form of bodyreading). Input for these processes are observed information about the human's state over time, and dynamic models for the human's physical and mental processes. For the mental side such a dynamic model is sometimes called a Theory of Mind (e.g., Baron-Cohen, 1995; Dennett, 1987; Gärdenfors, 2003; Goldman, 2006) and may cover, for example, emotion, attention, intention, and belief. Similarly for the human's physical processes, such a model relates, for example, to skin conditions, heart rates, and levels of blood sugar, insulin, adrenalin, testosterone, serotonin, and specific medicines taken. Note that different types of models are needed: physiological, neurological, cognitive, emotional, social, as well as models of the physical and artificial environment.

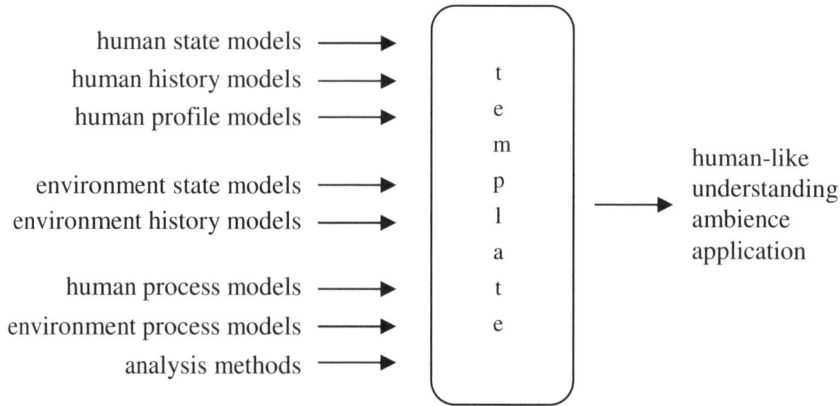

Fig. 1. Framework to combine the ingredients

A framework can be used as a template for the specific class of Ambient Intelligence applications as described. The structure of such an ambient software and hardware design can be described in an agent-based manner at a conceptual design level and can be given generic facilities built in to represent the following (see also Figure 1):

- human state and history models
- environment state and history models
- profiles and characteristics models of humans
- ontologies and knowledge from biomedical, neurological, psychological and/or social disciplines
- dynamic process models about human functioning
- dynamic environment process models
- methods for analysis on the basis of such models

Examples of such analysis methods are voice and skin analysis with respect to emotional states, gesture analysis, heart rate analysis. The template can include slots where the application-specific content can be filled to get an executable design for a working system. This specific content together with the generic methods to operate on it, provides a reflective coupled human-environment system, based on a tight cooperation between a human and an ambient system to show human-like understanding of humans and to react from this understanding in a knowledgeable manner.

4 Perspectives of Reflective Coupled Human-Environment Systems

Ambient Intelligence applications in general can be viewed as coupled human-environment systems, where 'coupled' means mutually interacting. For the specific type of applications considered here, however, the coupling takes two different forms; see also Figure 2.

- On the one hand the coupling takes place as interaction between human and environment, as in any Ambient Intelligence application:
  o the environment gets information generated by the human as input, and
  o the human gets information generated by the environment as input.
- In addition, coupling at a more deep, reflective level takes place due to the fact that
  o the environment has and maintains knowledge about the functioning of the human, the environment and their interaction, and
  o the human has and maintains knowledge about functioning of him or herself, the environment, and their interaction

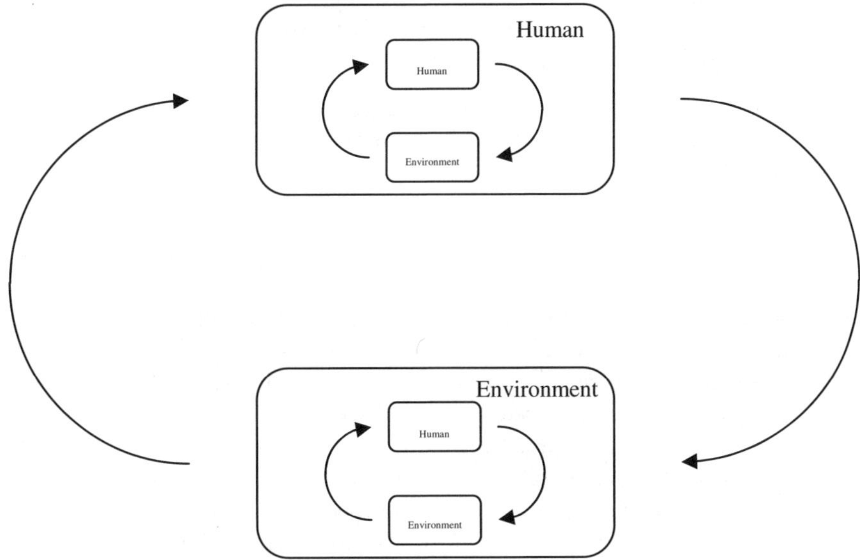

Fig. 2. Reflective coupled human-environment systems

So, in such a more specific human-environment system, being coupled does not only mean that the human and its environment interact, but also that they have knowledge, understanding and awareness of each other, themselves and their interaction. This entails two types of awareness:

- *Human awareness*:   awareness by the human about the human and environmental processes and their interaction
- *Technological awareness*:   awareness by the environment about the human and environmental processes and their interaction

By(human and technological) learning, adaptation and development processes for both the human and the environment these awarenesses can also grow over time.

Such reflective coupled human-environment systems can have a positive impact at different aggregation levels, from individual via an organisation within society to the society as a whole:

- *Individual level*
    o more effective functioning
    o stimulating healthy functioning and preventing health problems to occur
    o support of learning and development
- *Organisation level*
    o efficient functioning organisation by wellfunctioning members
    o learning and adaptation of the organisation
- *Society level*:
    o limiting costs for illness and inability to work
    o efficient management of environment

Some more specific examples of today's societal challenges, to which reflective coupled human-environment systems can contribute, are elderly care, health management, crime and security.

5 Conclusion

The scientific area that addresses Ambient Intelligence applications in which knowledge from the human-directed sciences is incorporated, has a high potential to provide nontrivial Ambient Intelligence applications based on human-like understanding. Such understanding can result in better informed actions and will feel more natural for humans. Important additional ingredients to realise this view are provided by areas in Computer Science, Artificial Intelligence and Cognitive Science; among others: agent modelling, knowledge and task modelling, user modelling, and cognitive modelling. Furthermore integrative frameworks can be developed to combine the ingredients. The resulting human-environment systems are coupled not only by their mutual interaction, but also in a reflective manner in the sense that both the human and the ambient system have and/or develop a model of the interactive processes of the human and the environment. These reflective coupled human-environment systems are an interesting type of systems to be studied scientifically, and provide a solid foundation for human-like Ambient Intelligence applications with significant benefits for individuals, organisations, and the society as a whole.

Acknowledgements

The author is grateful to a number of colleagues that in discussions have deepened insight in the area, among whom Tibor Bosse, Frank van Harmelen, Mark Hoogendoorn, Johan Hoorn, Michel Klein, Peter-Paul van Maanen, Andre Spijkervet, Maarten van Steen, Gerrit van der Veer, and Chris Verhoef.

References

1. Aarts, E., Collier, R., van Loenen, E., de Ruyter, B.: Ambient Intelligence. In: EUSAI 2003. LNCS, vol. 2875, p. 432. Springer Verlag, Heidelberg (2003)
2. Aarts, E., Harwig, R., Schuurmans, M.: Ambient Intelligence. In: Denning, P. (ed.) The Invisible Future, pp. 235–250. McGraw Hill, New York (2001)
3. Baron-Cohen, S.: Mindblindness. MIT Press, Cambridge (1995)
4. Dennett, D.C.: The Intentional Stance. MIT Press, Cambridge Mass (1987)
5. Gärdenfors, P.: How Homo Became Sapiens: On The Evolution Of Thinking. Oxford University Press, Oxford (2003)
6. Goldman, A.I.: Simulating Minds: The Philosophy, Psychology and Neuroscience of Mind Reading. Oxford University Press, Oxford (2006)
7. Green, D.J.: Realtime Compliance Management Using a Wireless Realtime Pillbottle – A Report on the Pilot Study of SIMPILL. In: Proc. of the International Conference for eHealth, Telemedicine and Health, Med-e-Tel 2005, Luxemburg (2005)
8. Itti, L., Koch, C.: Computational Modeling of Visual Attention. Nature Reviews Neuroscience 2(3), 194–203 (2001)
9. Riva, G., Vatalaro, F., Davide, F., Alcañiz, M. (eds.): Ambient Intelligence. IOS Press, Amsterdam 2001 (2005)

The Use of Brain-Computer Interfacing in Ambient Intelligence

Gangadhar Garipelli[1,2], Ferran Galán[1,3], Ricardo Chavarriaga[1],
Pierre W. Ferrez[1,2], Eileen Lew[1,2], and José del R. Millán[1,2]

[1] IDIAP Research Institute, Martigny, Switzerland
`Gangadhar.Garipelli@idiap.ch`
[2] Ecole Polytechnique Fédérale de Lausanne, Lausanne, Switzerland
[3] University of Barcelona, Barcelona, Spain

Abstract. This paper is aimed to introduce IDIAP Brain Computer Interface (IBCI) research that successfully applied Ambience Intelligence (AmI) principles in designing intelligent brain-machine interactions. We proceed through IBCI applications describing how machines can decode and react to the human mental commands, cognitive and emotive states. We show how effective human-machine interaction for brain computer interfacing (BCI) can be achieved through, 1) asynchronous and spontaneous BCI, 2) shared control between the human and machine, 3) online learning and 4) the use of cognitive state recognition. Identifying common principles in BCI research and ambiance intelligence (AmI) research, we discuss IBCI applications. With the current studies on recognition of human cognitive states, we argue for the possibility of designing empathic environments or devices that have a better human like understanding directly from brain signals.

1 Motivation

Brain Computer Interfacing (BCI) or Brain Machine Interfacing (BMI) refers to interaction with devices, where user's intentions represented as several brain states are deciphered and translated into actions without requiring any physical action [44] [25] [21]. There is a growing interest in the use of brain signals for communicating and operating devices, which is facilitated by the advances in the the measurement technologies in the past decades. As BCI bypasses the classical neuromuscular communication channels, this technology is intended to use for rehabilitation of tetraplegic or paraplegic patients to improve their communication, mobility and independence. The BCI research also opens up new possibilities in natural interaction for able-bodied people (e.g., for space applications, where environment is inherently hostile and dangerous for astronauts, who could greatly benefit from direct mental teleoperation of external semi-automatic manipulators [26], and for entertainment applications like multimedia gaming [20]). Typical applications of BCI are communication aids such as spelling devices [5] [31] [25] and mobility aids such as wheelchair [41]. In the current paper, we introduce the design of IDIAP BCI (IBCI) towards intelligent interaction and

M. Mühlhäuser et al. (Eds.): AmI 2007 Workshops, CCIS 11, pp. 268–285, 2008.

empathic devices and show how its key features are consistant with Ambient Intelligence (AmI) design principles.

The vision of AmI is designing digital environments in which the electronics devices are sensitive to people's needs, personalized to their requirements, anticipatory of their behavior and responsive to their presence. The main goals of AmI based interaction are, 1) understanding human function and sensory information, 2) analysis of sensory information, 3) design of human-like-reasoning devices and intelligent interaction. The BCI research brings a new sensing modality for tracking neurophysiological information related human's cognitive and emotive sates. The brain computer interaction can be seen also as a new mode of interaction similar to speech and vision based interaction, but with mental commands directly from the brain signals. So the general principles of interaction for destining AmI are also valid for the design of interaction with BCI.

Since we are interested in designing interactions between intelligent systems (human user and intelligent machine), it is natural to derive ideas from human-human communication. These ideas offer a starting point for a quest for new forms of interaction. According to Schmidt [39], for interaction, the context information is important. In particular, the key components are,

- *Shared knowledge*: In communication between intelligent systems, a common knowledge is essential for understanding each other. This common knowledge is extensive and is usually not explicitly mentioned. In most cases, this common knowledge includes world or environment model.
- *Communication error recovery*: Communication between intelligent systems may not be error free, many conversations include short term misunderstandings and ambiguities. But the misunderstandings are often detected by monitoring the response of the communication partner. In case of misinterpretation the dialogs are repeated and corrected.
- *Surrounding situation and context*: Communication and interaction between intelligent systems will happen in a specific situation. Inclusion of contextual information (e.g., a model of environment) provides common ground with implicit conventions.

In the current paper, we review IBCI applications that incorporated the principles for interaction. In particular, the interaction of IBCI-system is designed with the following components, *1) shared knowledge between the robot and user.* The ongoing work on recognition of human anticipatory behavior described in section 4 is based on this principle. For example, consider a scenario of an intelligent robotic wheelchair facing a dining table in a hall of several tables. From the robot-controller's point of view, the table is an obstacle and it can't decide by it self whether to dock to it or to avoid it. But it is the user who decides to dock to it if he wants to take brakefast. The user *anticipates* for the docking event to happen if he wishes to dock. The shared knowledge allows the robot to make corresponding actions (e.g., docking, or avoiding the obstacle) upon the recognition of anticipation related brain activity of the user. The shared knowledge, i.e., robot's detection of a table and user's anticipation of events allows to achieve the desired goal. *2) communication error recovery through feedback and the detection of error related brain activity.* We have implemented these two mechanisms in our applications that allow the user to correct his commands from the feedback of recognized commands by classifiers (described in 3) as well as the robot to change its commands up on the recognition of error related brain activity (described in 4) and *3) context filtering of illogical mental commands inferred by the interface.* For a brain actuated robot application (described in section 3.1), the filtering is achieved by using a finate state machine that translated the mental commands into device commands according to the environmental context. In the case of a brain actuated wheelchair application (described in section 3.2), the filtering is achieved by combining the probabilities inferred by the classifier for mental commands with that of context-based-filter of the robotic wheel chair.

In the next section we review the state of art of BCI research along with the methods that lead to the success of IBCI. In section 3, we review IBCI applications that implement the key principles introduced above. In section 4, we show the possibility of designing empathic devices with the recognition of user's cognitive states directly from brain signals. Finally in section 5 we discuss conclusions and future directions of research.

2   BCI Research and IBCI System

A schematic of a BCI system is shown in Figure 1. Brain electrical activity is acquired using electrodes (either implanted inside the brain or externally on the scalp). From the recorded signals, features (e.g., amplitudes of evoked potentials, or sensory motor cortex rhythms) that reflect user's intent, are extracted using signal processing methods. These features are then translated into device commands (e.g., using neural networks) which are then issued to systems like, virtual-keyboards, mobile robots, robotic wheelchairs and computer games. *Feedback* from these systems is given to the user using various modalities (e.g., visual, auditory etc.).

BCI is broadly classified into three categories based on invasiveness of the recording technique as 1) invasive, 2) partially invasive and 3) non-invasive BCI [22]. For an invasive BCI, the electrodes are implanted directly into the grey matter of the brain during neurosurgery. As they rest in the grey matter, it can produce the highest quality signals of BCI devices but are prone to scar-tissue build-up, causing the signal to become weaker or even lost as the body reacts to a foreign object in the brain [19]. Partially invasive BCI [10] uses electrodes implanted inside the skull but resting outside the brain rather than amidst the grey matter (e.g., Electrocorticography, ECoG). They produce better resolution than non-invasive electrodes and have lower risk of forming scar-tissue in the brain than fully invasive electrodes. Finally, Electroencephalograph (EEG), Magnetoencephalography (MEG) and functional magnetic resonance imaging (fMRI) have both been used successfully in non-invasive BCI. Among all the EEG is the most used signal acquisition method mainly due to its fine temporal resolution, ease of use, portability and low set-up cost. Since the current paper is based on non-invasive IBCI system, we review feature extraction and classification stages of EEG based BCI.

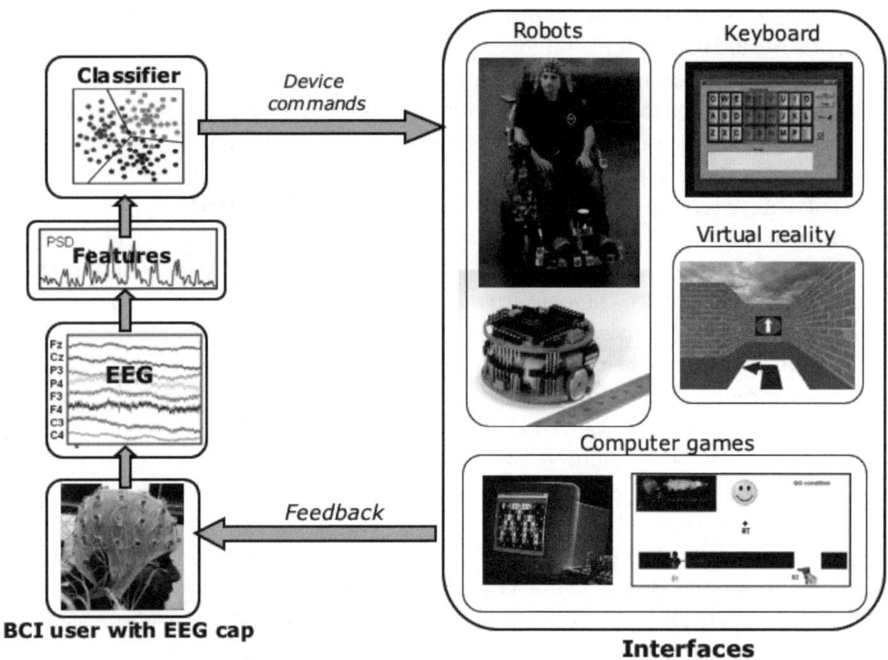

Fig. 1. Operation of a brain computer interfacing (BCI) system

Based on the operation, non-invasive BCI systems can be classified into two types, 1) system driven, 2) user driven. The system driven BCI uses EEG waveforms that are generated automatically in response to external stimulus (e.g., visual, auditory stimulus from the interfacing machine), called evoked potentials (EP). One example is the P300 signal, which is a potential evoked by an awaited infrequent event that appears at centro-parietal locations along the mid line of the scalp. It is a positive wave peaking around 300 ms after task-relevant stimuli [36]. Traditionally, P300 has been used in BCI research to develop virtual keyboards [2] [9] with a typing speed of five letters per minute, but recently this same potential has also been the basis for brain-actuated control of a virtual reality system [4] and of a wheelchair [36]. Steady-state visual evoked potentials (SSVEP) are another example of evoked potentials that are induced by a visual stimulus repeated at a rate higher than 6 Hz [40]. Most SSVEP-based BCI system depend on muscular control of gaze direction for their operation, whereas all other kinds of BCI systems do not depend on the brain's normal output pathways of peripheral nerves and muscles [15] [24] [40]. The main drawback of system driven BCI is that, since the subject's response is locked to the stimulus, he cannot generate mental commands at any time he wants.

On contrast the user-driven BCI is based on self modulation of EEG rhythms by the user, i.e. spontaneous brain activity. for instance, self modulation by imagination of movements can result in changes in EEG rhythm in central region of the scalp overlying the sensorimotor cortex [3] [8] [33] [45]. These rhythms are the basis of several BCI systems [3] [8] in which imagination of hand movement gives rise to an amplitude suppression in the α-band (8-12 Hz) and β-band (13-28 Hz) [1] rhythms over the contralateral primary hand motor cortical area [33]. Wolpaw and co-workers [43] [45] used continuous changes in the amplitudes of these rhythms to move a cursor in a computer screen. Alternatively, some researchers measure slow cortical potentials (SCP) whose negative amplitudes are related to the over-all preparatory excitation level of a given cortical network, the more negative the more active over the top of the scalp at electrode-Cz [5] [18]. Attentional modulation seems to constitute the cognitive strategy in the physiological regulation of SCP. The team lead by Birbaumer has widely shown that healthy subjects as well as severely paralyzed patients can learn to self-control their SCPs through oper-ant conditioning to move an object on a computer screen in a BCI referred to as *Thought Translation Device* (TTD) [17].

EEG-based BCIs are limited by a low channel capacity. Most of the current systems have a channel capacity below 0.5 bits/s [43]. One of the main reasons for such a low bandwidth is that they are based on *synchronous protocols* , where EEG is time-locked to externally paced cues repeated every 4-10 s and the response of the BCI is the average decision over this period (system driven BCI) [5] [31] [34] [37] [43]. The system dribven BCI is not natural for the user since his response is always time-locked to externally placed cues generated by the system. The user can't not decide by him self whenever he want to make a decision. On the contrary, the IBCI group utilizes more flexible *asynchronous protocols* where the subject makes self-paced decisions (user-driven) on when to stop performing a mental task and start immediately the next one [27] [30] [29]. In such asynchronous protocols, the subject can voluntarily change the mental task (e.g., imagination hand movement. See figure 2(b) for scalp topographies of EEG activity during these mental tasks in α band) being executed at any moment without waiting for external cues (this approach is grounded in a number of neurocognitive studies that have found that different mental tasks such as mental rotation of geometric figures [46], arithmetic operations [7], or language [32] activate local cortical areas to a different extent). The time of response of an asynchronous IBCI can be below 1 second (responds every 0.5 second) [30]. The rapid responses of asynchronous BCIs, together with their performance, give a theoretical channel capacity between 1 and 1.5 bits/s.

Coming to the feature extraction, IBCI team analyzes continuous variations of EEG rhythms over several frequency bands. The user specific EEG-features extracted using Canonical Variate Analysis (CVA) for multi-class problems [13]. This technique maximizes the separability between the patterns generated by ex-ecuting the different mental tasks. For the classification of these features, IBCI team typically uses Gaussian classifiers which are a modified Gaussian Mixture

---

[1] EEG activity is typically described in terms of rhythmic activity. The rhythmic activity is divided into several frequency bands (e.g., α band from 8 to 12 Hz. Suppression in this band power is usually observed in sensory motor areas while the user performing mental imagination.)

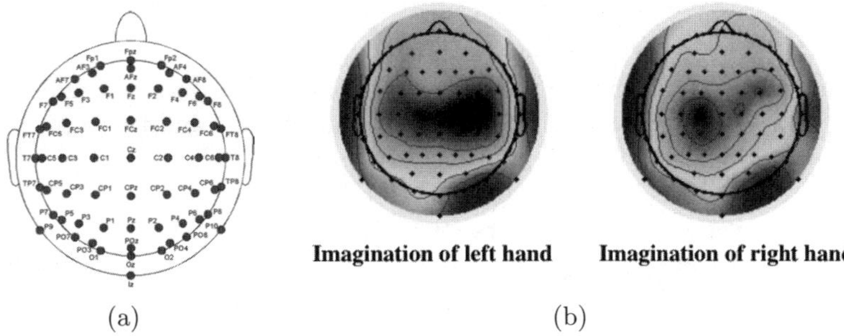

(a)   (b)

Fig. 2. (a) Top view of electrode positions according to the international 10-20 system. (c) Event related de-synchronization: decreased α-band (12Hz) power contralaterally to the imagination of hand. Dark regions correspond to lower power.

Model (GMM) [28] [29]. The output of the classifier is posterior probability that can be used to label specific classes and an 'unknown' class. It is worth noting that the use of statistical rejection criteria helps to deal with an important aspect of a BCI, namely idle states where the user is not involved in any particular mental task. These classifiers has been shown to perform better than support vector machines (SVMs), temporal processing neural networks (NNs) [16], committees of multi later perceptrons (MLPs), learning vector quantization and incremental radial basis networks [28] (for more details on the Gaussian classifier, refer [28], for a review of classification engines for BCI in general, refer Lotte et al [23]).

To sum up, the key principles behind the feature extraction and classification parts of IBCI system are, 1) using task induced EEG rhythms over cortical areas as features of mental commands, 2) canonical feature extraction for multi-class problems, 3) statistical classifier with rejection criteria and 4) asynchronous and spontaneous operation. Current research of IBCI group also focuses on adding 'cognitive states recognition' to 'mental command recognition' to improve its performance. The recognition of cognitive states can be used for implementing the principles of intelligent interaction like, shared knowledge and error recovery as described in section 1. The details of recognition of the cognitive states are described in section 4. In the next section, we discuss the design of brain actuated interaction to drive a mobile robot and a robotic wheelchair in natural environments.

3   IBCI Applications

In this section we present the current applications of IBCI system for controlling a mobile robot and a robotic wheelchair through intelligent interaction in the light of AmI with the following key components, 1) shared control, 2) error control through detection of error related potentials, 3) inclusion of contextual information.

3.1 Brain-Actuated Robots

Recently, IBCI group has shown for the first time that asynchronous analysis of EEG signals is sufficient for humans to continuously control a mobile robot (i.e. Khepera) along non-trivial trajectories requiring fast and frequent switches between mental tasks [30]. Human users learned to mentally drive the robot between rooms in a house-like environment (see Figure 3(a)). Furthermore, mental control was only marginally worse than manual control on the same task. A key element of this brain-actuated robot is shared control between two intelligent agents (i.e., the human user and the robot). The user only gives high-level mental commands (e.g., *turn left, turn right, forward*) that the robot performs autonomously. Another critical feature is that a BCI asynchronous operation, allowing the user to issue mental commands at any moment.

In order to endow the system with flexible, robust control, there is no one-to-one mapping of user's mental commands and robot's actions. Instead, we combine environmental information gathered from robot's on-board sensors with mental commands to take appropriate actions according to the context (i.e. shared control). This combination is implemented by a Finite State Automation (FSA) [30]. The transitions between different behaviors are determined by the 3 mental commands, 6 perceptual states of the environment (based on the robots sensory readings: *left wall, right wall, wall or obstacle in front, left obstacle, right obstacle,* and *free space*) and a few internal memory variables. These perceptual states are determined by using a neural network classifier that takes input from the sensory readings [30]. The memory variables keep contextual information required to implement correctly the different behaviors. Figure 3(b) shows a fragment of the FSA (for full description, see [30]). As shown in the figure, if the robot is performing the behavior forward and perceives a wall to the left, it switches automatically to the behavior follow left wall. The transition to the behavior-forward is necessary, for example, in the case where the robot is approaching an open door and the user wants the robot not to enter into the room.

A final element is the use of an appropriate feedback indicating the current mental state recognized by the embedded classifier. This is done by means of three lights (red, blue, green) on top of the robot that corresponds to the three mental commands (turn right, turn left, move forward). Thus, if the robot is following the left wall and is approaching an open door, a blue feedback indicates that the robot will turn left to continue following the left wall (and, so, it will enter into the room). On the contrary, a green feedback indicates that the robot will move forward along the corridor when facing the doorway and will not enter into the room. This simple feedback allows users to correct the robot trajectory in case of errors in the recognition of the mental states or errors in the execution of the desired behavior (due to the limitations of the robot sensors).

The figure 3(c) shows a typical trajectory of brain actuated robot. After 5 and 3 days of initial training with the interface, the users achieved a satisfactory level of performance (correct recognition was above 65% while the errors were below 7% - the remaining were 'unknown' response) (see Figure 3(d)).

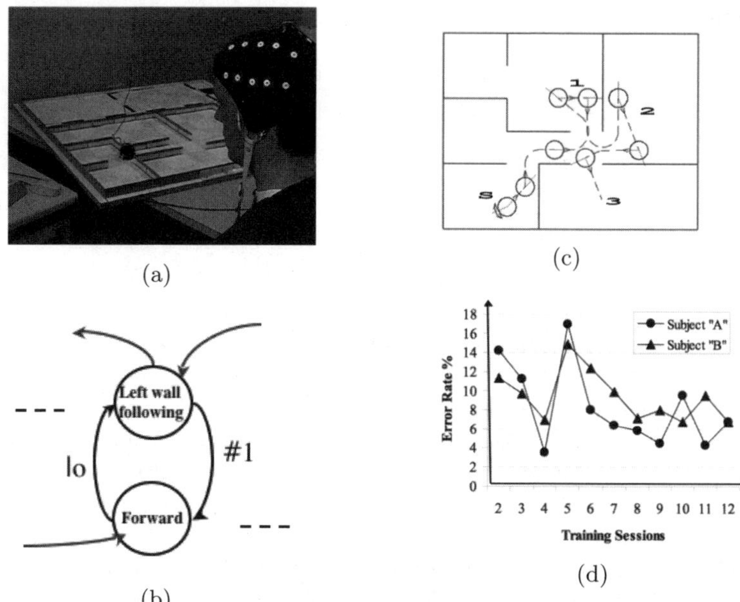

Fig. 3. Brain actuated robot control: (a) a user driving brain actuated robot (b) a fragment of Finate State Automaton (FSA) used for the shared control. Transitions between the 6 behaviors were determined by 3 mental states (#1: turn left, #2: turn right, #3: go forward), 6 perceptual states (lo: leftwall, ol:right wall, ö: wall or obstacle in front), and some memory variables.) (c) Experimental platform and a typical trajectory followed by the robot under the mental control. The robot started in bottom left room and then visited three other rooms, (d) error rate (percentage of false positives)(adopted from [30]).

Table 1. Time in seconds for three different trials in controlling first mentally and then manually by two users

Trial	User-A		User-B	
	Mental-control	manual-control	Mental-control	Manual-control
1	149	124	219	156
2	183	135	189	155
3	191	129	175	117
Average	174	129	194	143

Table 3.1 gives the time in seconds necessary to generate the desired trajectories in three different trials for the two participants comparing mental control and mannual control. Remarkably, trial duration for mental control was comparable with mannual control. On average, brain-actuated control of the robot takes only 35% longer than manual control for both the participants. The figure

Table 2. Comparison of bit-rate of online classification with static initial classifier

Session #	Static initial classifier	Online classification
1	0.29	1.44
2	0.20	1.41
3	0.14	1.34
4	0.18	1.34
Average	0.20 ± .06	1.38±0.05

3(d) shows the performance curve two users. First, a clear improvement can be observed during the first day (sessions 2 to 4), with an excellent performance. Second, the performance degrades at the beginning of second day (session 5) but recovers at the end. This shows difficulty of generalizing from one day to the next due to natural variability of brain signals. This variability can be compensated by incorporating online-learning as discussed in following paragraphs.

The variability of EEG signal within a session and from session to session is due to several factors including the background activity, fatigue and concentration levels, and intentional change of subject's strategy. This means that the classifier designed with past data might not perform well for the present or future data. To deal with this problem, IBCI applies adaptive algorithms that are constantly tuned to the subject. These techniques improve the performance of the BCI system allowing the subject to learn to use BCI more effectively. We first build classifier with the past data and then, as new EEG is obtained during the use of the BCI, we use it for updating the classifier (for more details, refer [1] [6]).

The studies on online learning are performed on offline data collected during brain-actuated robot control. The improvements in terms of the bit-rate comparing static initial and adaptive classifier are shown in table 3.1 (bit rate is channel capacity as explained in [29]). The online classification rates are much higher than the static classifiers. Moreover, the classifiers obtained at the end of each session (i.e. that were modified online throughout the experiment) outperforms the initial classifier.

From the above brain-actuated robot application, and consistent with the AmI principles, we conclude that, 1) fusing of knowledge of the human user and intelligent robot allows for effective human-computer interaction; 2) apart from using shared knowledge and contextual information, the error recovery (achieved by using feedback in the present case) is also important for successful control; 3) online adaption of the intelligent system will improve the interaction performance.

3.2   Brain Actuated Wheelchair

The recent studies of the IBCI in collaboration with KV Leuven under the framework of the European project MAIA (http://www.maia-project.org) aim at the

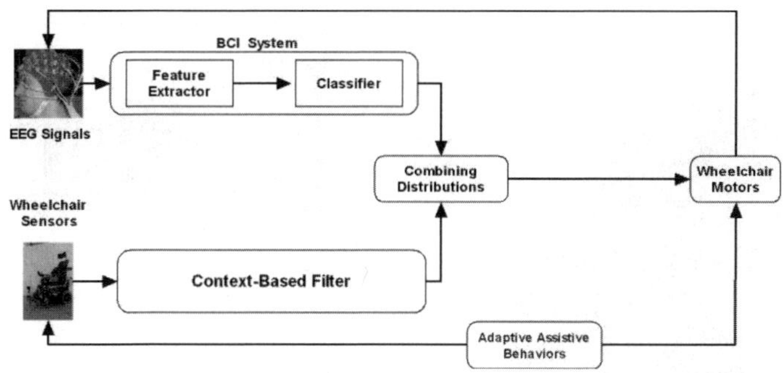

Fig. 4. A schematic of shared control system

development of a brain-actuated wheelchair that can provide mobility directly through mental control. An autonomous controller embedded in the wheelchair could serve help paralyzed patient for navigation. However, the subject might lose the feeling of continuous control with such a controller. The loss of independence is undesirable and therefore, shared control between the user and the controller is more suitable [35]. IBCI's design for such a system has three basic elements [35] [41], 1) adaptive shared controller that fuses the human and wheelchair decisions in a Bayesian way for better steering commands , 2) context information from the model of environment for filtering out unlikely decisions taken by the classifier and 3) assistive behaviors (collision avoidance (A0) obstacle avoidance(A1), and orientation recovery (A2)) based on the model of environment (e.g., openings in a corridor). See Figure 4 for the architecture of shared control of brain-actuated wheelchair.

Similar to the brain-actuated robot control, user can steer the wheelchair by issuing three discrete mental commands. The induced EEG rhythms (power spectrum density computed over one second in a selected subset of electrodes and frequency bands [14]) due to these mental commands are classified by a statistical Gaussian classifier whose outputs are posterior probabilities for the device commands (*move forward, turn left* and *turn right*). The asynchronous BCI system responds every 0.5 seconds by sending these probability distribution of the three mental commands to the shared controller which are then translated into steering commands (i.e., translational (ν) and rotational (ω) velocity). Instead of directly executing the user's steering commands, the shared control system takes environmental situation into account which is registered through a laser scanner. With this knowledge, the controller triggers one of the assistive behaviors using a *winner-takes-all* method (e.g., if the user steers too close to an obstacle, an avoidance behavior of the shared control is activated to prevent collision). Studies with the adaptive shared control are illustrated in figure 5(b). Without A2, the subject makes unnecessary loops while navigating (refer to [35]). The average elapsed time and average distance travelled (refer to [35] and [41]) also reduced significantly in navigating towards the goal.

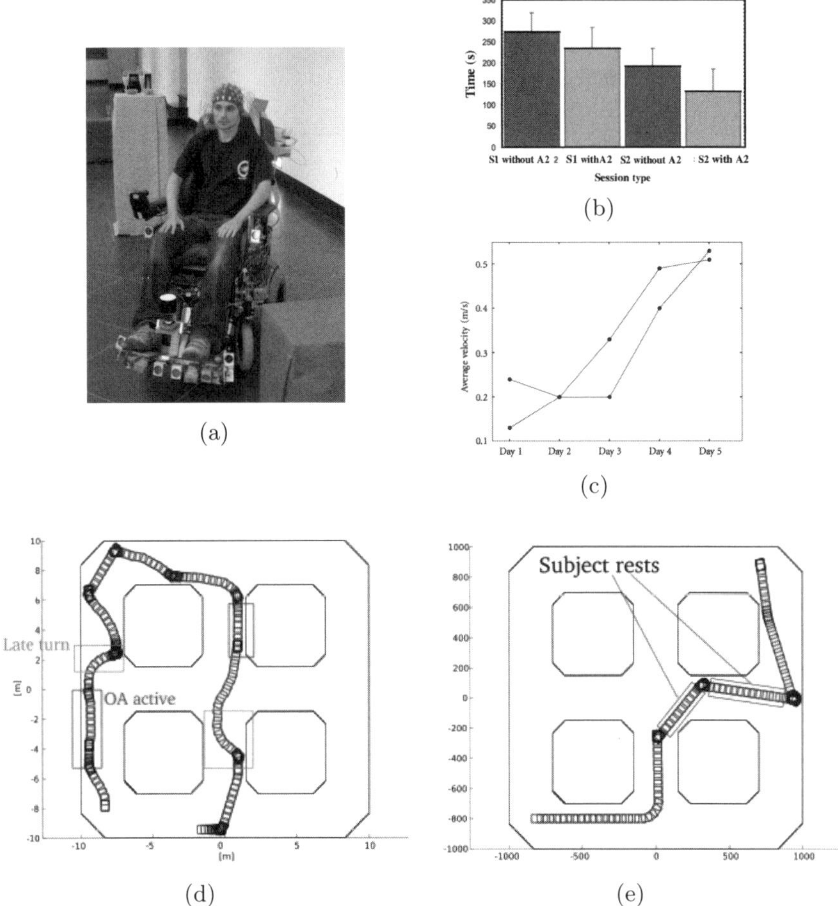

Fig. 5. (a) The subject wearing an electroencephalogram (EEG) sensor cap maneuvering the robotic wheelchair through a natural indoor environment. The visible are the sensors of the robotic platform: a laser range scanner in front and sonar sensors are visible at the lower part of the wheelchair, (b) Average navigation time with and without orientation recovery (A2) for sessions 1 and 2. (c) Average of velocity during five training days. The lower line represents the performance without context filter and the upper one represents the average velocity when the context filter is active. (d) Wheelchair trajectory in a different environment without context filtering. (e) A trajectory of a session with context filtering (the figure reproduced from [41]).

Since the mental command recognition is not perfect we need to correct them using environmental context. This is archived by adding a context filter to adaptive shared controller. The controller estimates the environmental context for detecting illogical steering signals. The context filtering in three steps. First, the context estimation is performed by defining a general, a-priory known model of the user intention (e.g., smooth and efficient forward navigation through the environment) on one hand and a constant automatic estimation of the environmental situation on the other hand. The situations were modelled as the number and location of *openings* (i.e. wide, open spaces through which user might safely navigate). Second, each opening represents a general direction in which the user might opt to continue his travel. With the knowledge of current situation, a probability distribution concerning the possible user actions were built. Third, the intelligent controller combines the probability distributions of the statistical classifier of BCI system and probability distribution generated from the environmental knowledge, so as to get a better estimation of the user's local steering intent.

The performance of the context filtering is also tested in terms of velocity of maneuvering (see figure 5(c)). Inspire of the fact that the user's driving skills improve gradually, both with and without context filtering, activation of this feature allow the user to steer faster in early stages of training. Figure 5(d) shows a trajectory performed without context filtering. We can see that there are many-nearby collisions (collisions won't happen due to A1), resulting in a rather jaggered path. Enabling context filter results in smoother trajectories, although near-collisions still occur (see figure 5(e)). More results on context filtering are described in [41].

4 Cognitive State Recognition: Towards Empathic Devices

Cognition is a mental process of knowing, including aspects such as awareness, perception, reasoning, and judgment. An *empathic agent* is a cognizant that comprehends needs, feelings, problems and views of humans and responds to them. Recently, IBCI group started investigating on the use of brain signals related to cognitive process for boosting the IBCI performance. By implementing recognition of cognitive states, the IBCI becomes a basic empathic agent. In particular the group is investigating on using "user's awareness of machine's error" and "human anticipatory states".

4.1 Decoding Human Awareness of Machine Error

BCIs are prone to errors in the recognition of user's intent from his mental commands. As in the human-human interaction, an elegant way of improving the BCI performance is to use a verification procedure directly based on presence of error related potentials (ErrP) in the brain activity. ErrP is a potential elicited after presenting the feedback of an error as response which is clearly detected in FCz and Cz electrode (see figures 6(a) and 6(b)). Several studies show the presence of this potential in typical choice reaction tasks when the subject makes mistake by himself. At IDIAP, in the context of BCI, we have shown that ErrPs are elicited even when error is made by the interface during the recognition of subject's intension. Ferrez and Millán termed this type of ErrP as *interaction-ErrP* [11] [12], as it is elicited by the presentation of feedback indicating incorrect response of simulated BCI.

Furthermore, we are interested in how ErrP can be used to improve the performance of a BCI. As shown in the Figure 6(c), after translating the subject's intention form his mental command, into control command for the robot, the BCI provides a feedback of it, which will be executed only if no ErrP follows the feedback (see figure 6(c)). In this new interaction method, the challenge is to recognize the ErrP on single trials. After characterization of these potentials, we have developed classification technique that archive successful recognition of these potentials (up to 80% correct classification of ErrP and up to 83% of correct trials [11]). In addition, this type of interaction improves the bit-rate of the BCI system by 28% for three-class problem and by 72% for two-class problem(see [11] for more detailed results).

4.2 Decoding Human Anticipation

Animals have the ability to anticipate to upcoming events given a predictive model. In particular, in humans, the EEG correlates of anticipation are well known, and one of such signal is Contingent Negative Variation (CNV). CNV is an increasing negative shift of the cortical electrical potential associated with anticipated response to an external stimulus. It is therefore interpreted as both an expectation related potential and anticipation related potential [38] [42]. Recognition of CNV can be used for implementing *shared knowledge* of the human user and a semi-autonomous system in making final decisions. For example, a robotic wheelchair facing a dining-table can not decide by itself whether to dock to it or to avoid it (i.e., obstacle avoidance behavior). But, the presence or absence of anticipation related potentials in the subject's EEG will allow the wheelchair to make a final decision. The question that we are addressing in this section is that, "Is it possible for machines to predict human anticipation to particular events?".

We study changes in the CNV depending on the task-dependent relevance of external stimulus (S1) in a classical Go/NoGo CNV paradigm. In "Go" condition, the subject is instructed to anticipate to imperative stimulus (S2) and press a key on its arrival and in "NoGo" condition, the subject instructed to do nothing. On-line recognition of such changes provides information that can be used by the semi-autonomous system in situations when it is not able to make reliable decisions. Grand averages of potentials recorded in CNV Go/NoGo paradigm is shown in figure 6(d). These potentials are classified using a simple Linear Discriminant Analysis (LDA) classifier. The results show that the anticipatory potentials can be classified up to an accuracy of 70% at least 0.5 sec before the subject presses a key.

The recognition of ErrP and anticipatory signals from the EEG introduces empathic capabilities in the BCI system. Thus, we show the feasibility of designing empathic devices that can predict human actions, judgements and needs directly brain signals. Further, the implementation of other emotive states recognition,

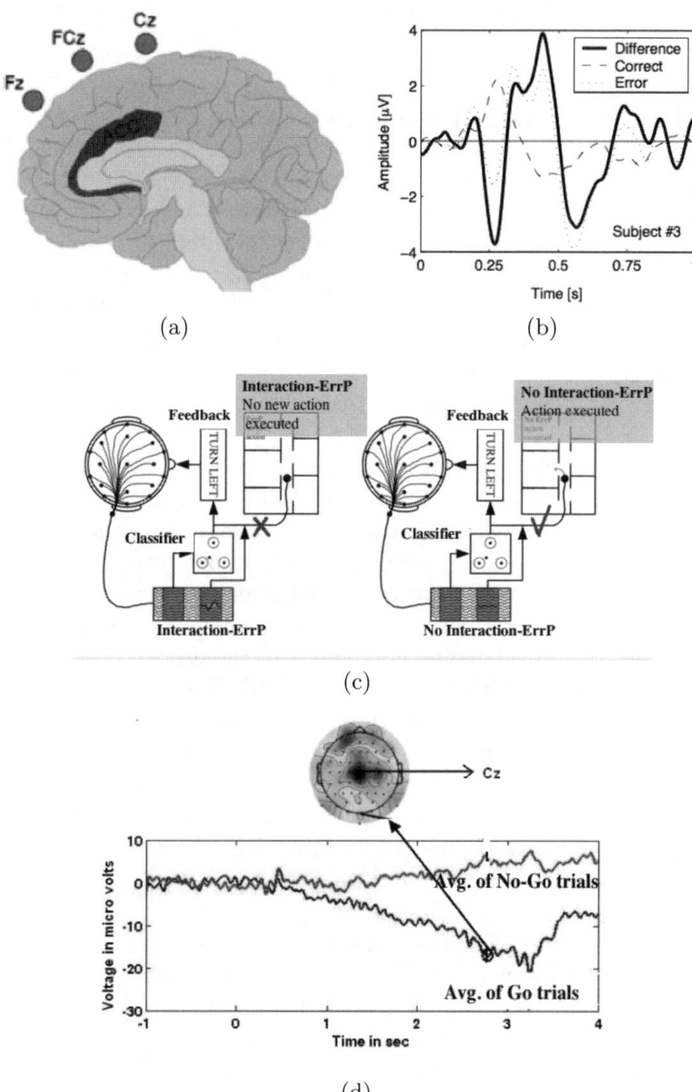

Fig. 6. (a) Position of Fz, FCz and Cz electrodes with respect to Anterior Cingulate Cortex (ACC) which is the origin of ErrP (b) Average of the difference (error-minus correct) between the potentials of error and correct trials at Cz electrode. (c) BCI based on 'Interaction ErrP'. The BCI user receives visual feedback of indicating the output of the classification engine before the actual execution of the associated command(e.g., "turn-left"). If the feedback elicits an ErrP, this command is simply ignored and the robot will stay executing the previous command (right). Otherwise, the command is sent to the robot (left). (d) Contingent Negative Variation with a classical Go/NoGo task (see text).

such as attention, alarms, frustration and confusion will improve empathic capabilities of our BCI system.

5   Conclusions and Future Work

In this paper we have introduced several applications of the IDIAP BCI (IBCI). In particular this paper shows how these applications successfully integrate design principles from human-centered approaches for intelligent interaction in the domain of Brain Computer interfaces. Namely, we have shown how the described IBCI systems are endowed with 1) Shared knowledge, 2) communication error recovery and 3) contextual information. These principles are consistant with from AmI design criteria and allows for the robust performance of the IBCI systems by showing strong evidence of the potential synergy between AmI and BCI research.

Sharing the knowledge between the human user and robot perception of environment is achieved by using FSA for the brain-actuated control of a robot. In the case of brain-actuated wheelchair, it is achieved by combining the probability distributions inferred by the Gaussian classifier from the user's mental commands with those inferred from the environment by the wheelchair sensors. We have shown two possible methods for communication recovery, 1) by giving a feedback of the recognized mental commands to the user so that he can change his mental commands in case of error, and 2) with the use of interaction-ErrP. We have also shown that context filtering of illogical mental commands inferred by the interface improves the driving performance of the wheelchair. The recent work of IBCI team shows a way to improve empathic capabilities of a machine by using human cognitive state recognition (e.g., recognition of ErrPs and anticipation related potentials). These capabilities can be improved by recognizing other cognitive and emotive states such as attentional level, frustration, alarm, and confusion.

In summary, IBCI research shows the feasibility of developing systems that have an enhanced comprehension of human's cognitive and emotive states establishing boosted intelligent human-machine interactions. The synergy between AmI and BCI research will permit to develop empathic systems and environments, providing tools for making human-machine interaction more resemblance to human-human interactions.

Acknowledgements

This work was supported in part by the Swiss National Science Foundation through the National Centre of Research on "Interactive Multimodal Information Management (IM2)", European IST Programme FET Project FP6-003758, and FP6-IST-027140. This paper only reflects the author's views and founding agencies are not liable for any use that may be made of the information contained herein. We thank 'Division PMA team' of Katholieke Universiteit, Leuven, for it's collaboration on brain-actuated-wheelchair application.

References

1. Buttfield, A., Ferrez, P.W., del Millán, J.R.: Towards a robust BCI: Error potentials and online learning. IEEE Trans. on Neural Systems and Rehabilitation Engineering 14(2), 164–168 (2006)
2. Allison, B.Z., Pineda, J.A.: ERPs evoked by different matrix sizes: implications for a brain computer interface (bci) system. IEEE Trans Neural Syst. Rehabil Eng. 11(2), 110–113 (2003)
3. Babiloni, F., Cincotti, F., Lazzarini, L., del Millán, J.R., Mouriño, J., Varsta, M., Heikkonen, J., Bianchi, L., Marciani, M.G.: Linear classification of low-resolution EEG patterns produced by imagined hand movements. IEEE Trans Rehabil Eng. 8(2), 186–188 (2000)
4. Bayliss, J.D.: Use of the evoked potential P300 component for control in a virtual apartment. IEEE Trans Neural Syst. Rehabil Eng. 11(2), 113–116 (2003)
5. Birbaumer, N., Ghanayim, N., Hinterberger, T., Iversen, I., Kotchoubey, B., Kübler, A., Perelmouter, J., Taub, E., Flor, H.: A spelling device for the paralysed. Nature 398(6725), 297–298 (1999)
6. Buttfield, A., del Millán, J.R.: Online classifier adaptation in brain-computer interfaces. IDIAP-RR 16, IDIAP (2006)
7. Chochon, F., Cohen, L., van de Moortele, P.F., Dehaene, S.: Differential contributions of the left and right inferior parietal lobules to number processing. J. Cogn. Neurosci. 11(6), 617–630 (1999)
8. Dornhege, G., Blankertz, B., Curio, G., Müller, K.R.: Boosting bit rates in noninvasive eeg single-trial classifications by feature combination and multiclass paradigms. IEEE Trans Biomed. Eng. 51(6), 993–1002 (2004)
9. Farwell, L.A., Donchin, E.: Talking off the top of your head: toward a mental prosthesis utilizing event-related brain potentials. Electroencephalogr. Clin Neurophysiol. 70(6), 510–523 (1988)
10. Felton, E.A., Wilson, J.A., Williams, J.C., Garell, P.C.: Electrocorticographically controlled brain-computer interfaces using motor and sensory imagery in patients with temporary subdural electrode implants. report of four cases. J Neurosurg. 106(3), 495–500 (2007)
11. Ferrez, P.W., del Millán, J.R.: You are wrong!—automatic detection of interaction errors from brain waves. In: Proceedings of the 19th International Joint Conference on Artificial Intelligence, Edinburgh, UK (August 2005)
12. Ferrez, P.W., del Millán, J.R.: Error-related EEG potentials in brain-computer interfaces. In: Dornhege, G., Millán, J.d.R., Hinterberger, T., McFarland, D., Müller, K.-R. (eds.) Towards Brain-Computer Interfacing, MIT Press, Cambridge (2007)
13. Galán, F., Ferrez, P.W., Oliva, F., Guàrdia, J., del Millán, J.R.: Feature extraction for multiclass BCI using canonical variates analysis. In: IEEE International Symposium on Intelligent Signal Processing, Alcalá de Henares (2007)
14. Galán, F., Nuttin, M., Lew, E., Ferrez, P.W., Vanacker, G., Philips, J., Brussel, H.V., del Millán, J.R.: An asynchronous and non-invasive brain-actuated wheelchair. In: In 13th International Symposium on Robotics Research, Hiroshima, Japan (2007)
15. Gao, X., Xu, D., Cheng, M., Gao, S.: A BCI-based environmental controller for the motion-disabled. IEEE Trans. Neural. Syst. Rehabil. Eng. 11(2), 137–140 (2003)
16. Hauser, A., Sottas, P.E.,, J.: Temporal processing of brain activity foe the recognition of EEG patterns. In: Proceedings 12th Int. Conf. on Artificial Neural Networks, pp. 1125–1130 (2002)

17. Hinterberger, T., Neumann, N., Pham, M., Kübler, A., Grether, A., Hofmayer, N., Wilhelm, B., Flor, H., Birbaumer, N.: A multimodal brain-based feedback and communication system. Exp. Brain Res. 154(4), 521–526 (2004)
18. Hinterberger, T., Schmidt, S., Neumann, N., Mellinger, J., Blankertz, B., Curio, G., Birbaumer, N.: Brain-computer communication and slow cortical potentials. IEEE Trans Biomed Eng. 51(6), 1011–1018 (2004)
19. Kennedy, P.R., Bakay, R.A.: Restoration of neural output from a paralysed patient by a direct brain connection. Neuroreport 9, 1707–1711 (1998)
20. Krepki, R., Blankert, B., Curio, G., Müller, K.R.: The Berlin brain-computer interface (BBCI) towards a new communication channel for online control in gaming applications. Multimedia Tools and Applications, 73–90 (February 2007)
21. Kübler, A., Müller, K.R.: An introduction to brain computer interfacing in Towards Brain-Computer Interfacing. MIT Press, Cambridge (2007)
22. Lebedev, M.A., Nicolelis, M.A.: Brain-machine interfaces: past, present and future. Trends Neurosci. 29, 536–546 (2006)
23. Lotte, F., Congedo, M., Lcuyer, A., Lamarche, F., Arnaldi, B.: A review of classification algorithms for eeg-based brain-computer interfaces. J. Neural Eng. 4(2), R1–R13 (2007)
24. Middendorf, M., McMillan, G., Calhoun, G., Jones, K.S.: Brain-computer interfaces based on the steady-state visual-evoked response. IEEE Trans. Rchabil. Eng. 8(2), 211–214 (2000)
25. del Millán, J.R.: Brain-computer interfaces. In: Arbib, M.A. (ed.) The Handbook of Brain Theory and Neural Networks, 2nd edn., The MIT Press, Cambridge (2002)
26. del Millán, J.R., Ferrez, P.W., Buttfield, A.: Non-invasive brain-machine interfaces. ESA report on studies on feasibility of non-invasive brain-machine interfaces (2006), www.esa.int/gsp/ACT/bio/BMI.htm
27. del Millán, J.R., Mouriño, J.: Asynchronous BCI and local neural classifiers: An overview of the Adaptive Brain Interface project. IEEE Trans. on Neural Systems and Rehabilitation Engineering, Special Issue on Brain-Computer Interface Technology 11(2), 159–161 (2003)
28. del Millán, J.R., Mouriño, J., Franzé, M., Cincotti, F., Varsta, M., Heikkonen, J., Babiloni, F.: A local neural classifier for the recognition of EEG patterns associated to mental tasks. IEEE Trans Neural Networks 13(3), 678–686 (2002)
29. del Millán, J.R., Renkens, F., Mouriño, J., Gerstner, W.: Non-invasive brain-actuated control of a mobile robot by human EEG. IEEE Trans. Biomed Eng. 51(6), 1026–1033 (2004)
30. del Millán, J.R., Renkens, F., Mourino, J., Wulfram, G.: Brain-actuated interaction. Artif. Intell. 159(1-2), 241–259 (2004)
31. Obermaier, B., Müller, G.R., Pfurtscheller, G.: "Virtual keyboard" controlled by spontaneous EEG activity. IEEE Trans. Neural Syst. Rehabil. Eng. 11(4), 422–426 (2003)
32. Petersen, S.E., Fox, P.T., Posner, M.I., Mintun, M., Raichle, M.E.: Positron emission tomographic studies of the cortical anatomy of single-word processing. Nature 331(6157), 585–589 (1988)
33. Pfurtscheller, G., Neuper, C.: Motor imagery activates primary sensorimotor area in humans. Neurosci. Lett. 239(2-3), 65–68 (1997)
34. Pfurtscheller, G., Neuper, C.: Motor imagery and direct brain-computer communication. In: IEEE, vol. 89, pp. 1123–1134 (2001)
35. Philips, J., del Millán, J.R., Vanacker, G., Lew, E., Galán, F.: Adaptive shared control of a brain-actuated simulated wheelchair. In: IEEE 10th International Conference on Rehabilitation Robotics (2007)

36. Rebsamen, B., Burdet, E., Teo, C.L., Zeng, Q., Guan, C., Ang, M., Laugier, C.: A brain control wheelchair with a P300 based bci and a path following controller. In: Proc. 1st IEEE/RAS-EMBS Int. Conf. Biomedical Robotics and Biomechatronics (2006)
37. Roberts, S.J., Penny, W.D.: Real-time brain-computer interfacing: a preliminary study using bayesian learning. Med. Biol. Eng. Comput. 38(1), 56–61 (2000)
38. Rosen, R.: Anticipatory systems. Pergamon Press, Oxford (1985)
39. Schmidt, A.: Interactive Context-Aware Systems Interacting with Ambient Intelligence, pp. 159–178. IOS Press, Amsterdam (2006)
40. Sutter, E.E.: The brain response interface: communication through visually-induced electrical brain responses. J. Microcomput. Appl. 15, 31–45 (1992)
41. Vanacker, G., del Millán, J.R., Lew, E., Ferrez, P., Galán, F., Philips, J., Brussel, H.V., Nuttin, M.: Context-based filtering for assisted brain-actuated wheelchair driving. Computational Intelligence and Neuroscience (2007)
42. Walter, W.G., Cooper, R., Aldridge, V.J., McCallum, W.C., Winter, A.L.: Contingent negative variation: An electric sign of sensorimotor association and expectancy in the human brain. Nature 203, 380–384 (1964)
43. Wolpaw, J.R.: Brain-computer interfaces (BCIs) for communication and control: a mini-review. Suppl. Clin. Neurophysiol. 57, 607–613 (2004)
44. Wolpaw, J.R., Birbaumer, N., McFarland, D.J., Pfurtscheller, G., Vaughan, T.M.: Brain-computer interfaces for communication and control. Clin. Neurophysiol. 113(6), 767–791 (2002)
45. Wolpaw, J.R., McFarland, D.L., Vaughan, T.M.: Brain-Computer Interface Research at the Wadsworth Center. IEEE Trans. Rehab. Eng. 8, 222–226 (2000)
46. Yoshino, A., Inoue, M., Suzuki, A.: A topographic electrophysiologic study of mental rotation. Brain Res. Cogn. Brain Res. 9(2), 121–124 (2000)

Design and Validation of HABTA:
Human Attention-Based Task Allocator

Peter-Paul van Maanen[1,2], Lisette de Koning[1], and Kees van Dongen[1]

[1] TNO Human Factors, P.O. Box 23, 3769 ZG Soesterberg, The Netherlands
{peter-paul.vanmaanen,lisette.dekoning,kees.vandongen}@tno.nl
[2] Vrije Universiteit Amsterdam, De Boelelaan 1081a,
1081 HV Amsterdam, The Netherlands

Abstract. This paper addresses the development of an adaptive cooperative agent in a domain that suffers from human error in the allocation of attention. The design is discussed of a component of this adaptive agent, called Human Attention-Based Task Allocator (HABTA), capable of managing agent and human attention. The HABTA-component reallocates the human's and agent's focus of attention to tasks or objects based on an estimation of the current human allocation of attention and by comparison of this estimation with certain normative rules. The main contribution of the present paper is the description of the combined approach of design and validation for the development of such components. Two complementary experiments of validation of HABTA are described. The first experiment validates the model of human attention that is incorporated in HABTA, comparing estimations of the model with those of humans. The second experiment validates the HABTA-component itself, measuring its effect in terms of human-agent team performance, trust, and reliance. Finally, some intermediary results of the first experiment are shown, using human data in the domain of naval warfare.

1   Introduction

Several challenges can be identified for work on future naval platforms. Information volumes for navigation, system monitoring, and tactical tasks will increase as the complexity of the internal and external environment also increases [1]. The trend of reduced manning is expected to continue as a result of economic pressures and humans will be responsible for more tasks, tasks with increased load, and tasks with which they will have less experience. Problems with attention allocation are more likely to occur when more has to be done with less. To avoid these attention allocation problems, in this paper it is proposed that humans are supported by cooperative agents capable of managing their own and the human's allocation of attention. It is expected that these attention managers have a significant positive impact: when attentional switches between tasks or objects are often solicited, where the human's lack of experience with the environment makes it harder for them to select the appropriate attentional focus, or where an inappropriate selection of attentional focus may cause serious damage.

M. Mühlhäuser et al. (Eds.): AmI 2007 Workshops, CCIS 11, pp. 286–300, 2008.

In domains like air traffic control (ATC) or naval tactical picture compilation these properties are found, even when the people involved are experienced.

The present study discusses the design and validation of a component of an adaptive agent, called *Human Attention-Based Task Allocator (HABTA)*, capable of managing agent and human attention. This component is based on two cognitive models: one that describes the current allocation of a humans attention and one that prescribes the way his attention should be allocated. If there is a discrepancy between the output of the two models, HABTA reallocates the tasks between the human and the agent, for instance depending on certain rules the human and agent agreed upon. Models of attention or situation awareness have already been developed and used to predict faults in attention allocation (e.g., the SEEV model [2]), but less is known about how they can be used to initiate agent adaptation, or automatic task reallocation more specifically. Furthermore, since in many domains (like ATC) it is the tasks altogether rather than mere visual stimuli that eventually require allocation of attention, the design and validation discussed in this paper is more focused on cognitive rather than visual attention. Off course the mentioned tasks also require visual attention, but all the time. Still other applied models mainly focus on visual attention. Finally, the applicability of a HABTA-based agent has not yet been investigated either.

This paper consists of the following sections. In Section 2 the psychological background of human error in the allocation of attention in the domain of naval warfare is shortly described. The understanding of these errors is important for the management of attention allocation. In Section 3 the design requirements of an agent-component *Human Attention-Based Task Allocator (HABTA)* are given. These requirements enable the agent to support the human-agent team by managing attention allocation of the human and the agent.

The main contribution of the present paper is the description of the combined approach of design and validation for the development of applied cooperative agent-components. In Section 4, two complementary methods of experimental validation against the in Section 3 stated design requirements are described. The first experiment validates the model of human attention that is incorporated in a HABTA-component. The validity of the model is determined by comparison of the model's and human's estimation of human attention allocation. The second experiment validates the HABTA-component itself, measuring its effect in terms of human-agent team performance, trust, and reliance. In Section 5 intermediary results of a pilot study are shown as a means to discuss the first experiment described in Section 4, using human data in the domain of naval warfare. In Section 6 the paper ends with concluding remarks and ideas for future research.

2   Human Error in the Allocation of Attention

As is mentioned in the introduction, the domain chosen in this research is naval warfare. One of the important tasks in naval warfare is the continuous compilation of a tactical picture of the situation (see for a description in more detail [3]). In a picture compilation task operators have to classify contacts that are represented on a radar display. The contacts can be classified as hostile, neutral or friendly, based on certain identification criteria (idcrits). Tactical picture compilation is known for its problems in the allocation of attention. To be able to identify contacts, contacts have to be monitored over time. This requires attention, but resources of attention are limited. When a task demands a lot of attention, less attentional resources are available for other tasks (e.g., [4,5]. In general, two kinds of problems with human attention allocation can be distinguished: underallocation of attention and overallocation of attention.

Underallocation of attention means that tasks or objects that need attention do not receive enough attention from the operator. *Overallocation* of attention is the opposite: tasks or objects that do not need attention do receive attention. Overallocation of attention to one set of tasks may result in underattention to other tasks. Both under- and overallocation of attention can lead to errors. Experience, training, and interface design can improve these limitations, but only to a certain level. Efforts have been done, for example, to fuse tactical information on displays [6]. To be able to investigate whether a support system for attention allocation, like HABTA, can overcome these limitations of attention, it is important to understand these types of errors and more specifically in the domain of naval warfare. In Section 2.1 and 2.2, examples of errors of under- and overallocation when performing a tactical picture compilation task and their possible causes are described.

2.1   Underallocation of Attention

Underallocation of attention means that some objects or tasks receive less attention than they need according to certain normative rules for the task to be performed. Underallocation of attention occurs because of limited resources of attention or because of an incorrect assessment of the task.

When performing a tactical picture compilation task, operators have to monitor a radar screen where the surrounding contacts are represented as icons. The contacts on the screen have to be classified as neutral, hostile or friendly based on observed criteria. This is a complex task and it is essential that attention is allocated to the right objects. Inexperienced operators often allocate too little attention to contacts that they have previously classified as neutral [7]. When the behavior of these contacts changes to that of a hostile contact, this may not be observed because of underallocation of attention to those contacts. One reason for this could be that identity changes are not expected by the operator due to the fact that people are too confident in their identified contacts. Another reason might be that changes in relevant behavior of contacts are not salient enough to be observed without paying direct attention to those objects. Underallocation of attention to objects may also occur because of a lack of anticipatory thinking. This is the cognitive ability to prepare in time for problems and opportunities. In a picture compilation task, classification of contacts that are expected to come close to the own ship have priority over those that are not expected to come close. The reason for this is that there is less need to identify contacts when the own ship is out of sensor and weapon range of those contacts. Therefore, inexperienced operators often direct their attention only to objects in the direction the ship is currently heading. When unexpected course change is needed because of emerging threats, the ship is sometimes headed toward an area with contacts that are not yet classified [7].

2.2 Overallocation of Attention

Apart from underallocation, overallocation of human attention is also a common problem. Overallocation of attention means that some objects receive more attention than needed according to certain normative rules. Overallocation of attention can occur for example, when operators overestimate the importance of a set of objects or tasks, while underestimating the importance of other objects or tasks. This occurs for example, when some contacts act like distractors and perform salient behavior. Comparable to visual search tasks where objects with salient features generate a pop-out effect (e.g., [8]), those contacts directly attract the attention of the operator (bottom-up). Especially inexperienced operators overrate those salient cues and allocate too much attention to those contacts [7]. Another possibility is that irrelevant behavior of objects is highly salient due to the manner information is presented on the interface. For instance, when a contact's behavior is unexpected, but not threatening, attention is unnecessarily drawn to this contact. In this case, the correct and quick application of identification rules will result in neutral identity and resources become available for the identification of other contacts.

3 Design Requirements

The goal of the efforts described is to come to a generic methodology for developing a component for an agent that supports humans with the appropriate allocation of attention in a domain that suffers from human error in the allocation of attention. As mentioned in Section 2, human attention allocation is prone to two types of errors with several possibilities as causes, such as inexperience and information overload.

In this section the design requirements of an agent-component is described that enables agents to determine whether objects or tasks that are required to receive attention indeed do receive attention, either by the human or the agent, and to intervene accordingly. The component is called an *Human Attention-Based Task Allocator (HABTA)*-component, since it *bases* its decisions to intervene on estimations of *human attention* and intervenes by *reallocating tasks* to either human or agent. It is expected that the combined task performance of the human-agent team will be optimized when the agent consists of such a HABTA-component. This work builds forth on earlier work. In [9] some of the possibilities are already discussed of dynamically triggering task allocation for tasks requiring visual attention, and in [10,11] the real-time estimation of human attentional processes in the domain of naval warfare is already discussed.

Properly stated design requirements are important for the design of effective agent-systems for a certain purpose and for validating whether the design meets the requirements for that purpose. A HABTA-component has four design requirements, which are the following:

1. It should have a descriptive model, meaning an accurate model of what objects or tasks in the task environment receive the human's attention,
2. It should have a prescriptive or normative model, meaning an accurate model of what objects require attention for optimal task performance,
3. It should be able to reliably determine whether actual attention allocation differs too much from the required attention allocation,
4. It should be able to support by redirecting attention or by taking over tasks such that task performance is improved.

In Fig. 1 the design overview of a HABTA-component is shown that corresponds to the above design requirements. The setting in this particular overview is a naval officer behind an advanced future integrated command and control workstation and compiling a tactical picture of the situation. If the agent cooperatively assists the officer, than the agent should have a descriptive (Requirement 1) and normative model (Requirement 2). When the operator allocates his attention to certain objects or tasks that also require to receive attention, the outcome of both models should be comparable. This means that output of the models should not differ more than a certain threshold. The output of the two models in the example shown in Fig. 1 are clearly different: in the left image, the operator is attending to different objects and corresponding tasks than the

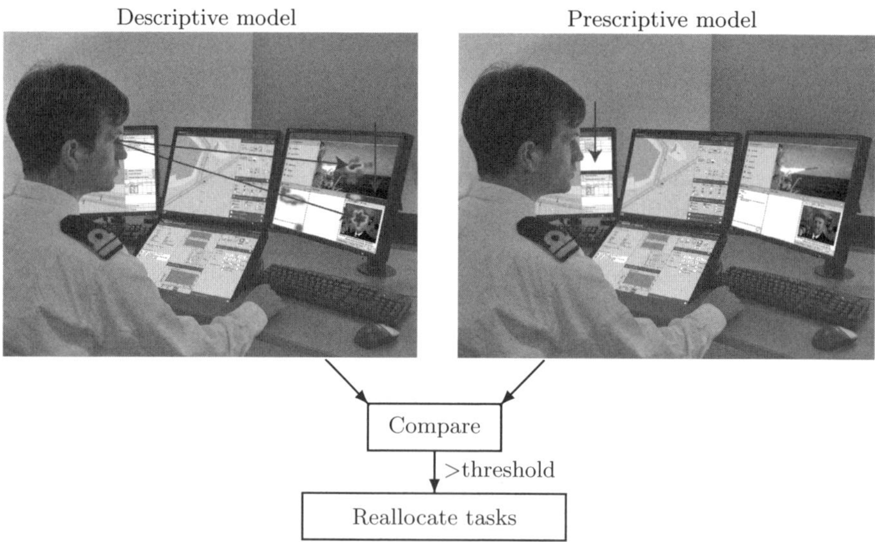

Fig. 1. Design overview of a HABTA-component for a future integrated command and control environment. The discrepancies between the output of the descriptive and prescriptive model result in a reallocation of tasks. The workstation shown in the pictures is the Basic-T [12].

right image indicates as being required (see arrows). Because of this discrepancy, which the HABTA-component should be able to determine (Requirement 3), an adaptive reaction by the agent is triggered (Requirement 4). This means that, for instance, the agent either will draw attention to the proper region or task through the workstation, or it will allocate its own attention to this region and starts executing the tasks related to that region, for the given situation.

To prevent that HABTA-based support results in automation surprises, the human-agent team should be able to make and adjust agreements about how they work as a team. It may be, for example, that the human does not want to be disturbed, and the agent is supposed to allocate tasks solely to itself. This option requires a higher form of autonomous task execution by the agent. The other possibility is that the human wants to stay in control as much as possible and therefore only wants to be alerted by the agent to attend to a certain region or execute a certain task. The choice of the agent's autonomy or assertiveness can also depend on a certain estimate of the urgency for reallocating tasks. In the case of tactical picture compilation, human and agent should agree on whether the agent is allowed to take over identification tasks for contacts that are overlooked or not.

On the one hand, the human may be preferred to be dealing with an arbitrary region or task, because the human may have certain relevant background knowledge the agent does not have. But on the other hand, the human is not preferred to be allocated to all objects or tasks at once, because, in a complex scenario, he has limited attentional resources. Hence humans cannot be in complete control, given the fact that both human and agent need each other. Optimal performance is only reached when human and agent work together as a team. Human-agent team work is expected to be effective when the right support is provided at the right time and in the right way. An obvious goal, but there are some potential obstacles in achieving it. Descriptive and prescriptive (normative) models of attention allocation may be inaccurate. Objects that require or receive attention may not be in the output of the descriptive or normative models, respectively. Similarly, objects that do not require or receive attention may be in the output of the models. The agent may conclude that descriptive and normative models differ when they do not, and vice versa. The system may be assertive and wrong, or withholding but right. Attention may be redirected to the wrong region or the wrong set of objects, or tasks are taken over by the agent that should be taken over by the human. Because of the complexity of these consequences of the above design requirements, both the validity of the model and the effectiveness of the agent's HABTA-component should be investigated and iteratively improved. This procedure of investigation and improvement is described in Section 4.

4   Validation

As described in Section 3, HABTA-components require a descriptive and prescriptive model of attention to support attention allocation of humans in complex tasks. Before HABTA-components can be used to support humans, they have to be validated. Validation is the process of determining the degree to which a model is an accurate description of certain real world phenomena from the perspective of the intended use of the model. Again referring to Section 3, for the intended use mentioned in this paper, this means that HABTA-components have to meet the design requirements (1–4) in Section 3.

In the near future two experiments will be carried out to validate a HABTA-component. In Experiment 1 the descriptive model will be validated (Requirement 1). This experiment aims at determining the sensitivity (d') of the model by comparing it with data retrieved from human subjects executing a complex task that causes problems with attention allocation. Based on the results of the experiment, the d' of the model can be improved by optimizing it off-line against a random part of the same data. It is expected that higher d' results in better support based on the HABTA-component. If the d' of the descriptive model is not high enough, the HABTA-component will consequently support at the wrong moments and for the wrong reasons, which obviously leads to lower performance, trust, and acceptance. In Experiment 2 the applicability of the (improved) descriptive model for attention allocation support is tested (Requirements 2–4). It will be investigated if the support of an agent with the HABTA-component leads to better performance than without HABTA-component.

The remainder of this section is composed of three parts. In Section 4.1 the task that will be used in the above mentioned experiments is described in more detail. After that, the specific experimental design and measurements of the experiments are described in Sections 4.2 and 4.3, respectively. Both experiments still have to be carried out. Preliminary results from a pilot of Experiment 1 will be described in Section 5.

4.1 Task Description

The task used in both experiments is a simple version of the identification task described in [13] that has to be executed in order to buildup a tactical picture of the situation. In Fig. 2 a snapshot of the interface of the task environment is shown.[1] The goal is to identify the five most threatening contacts (ships). In order to do this, participants have to monitor a radar display where contacts in the surrounding areas are displayed. To determine if a contact is a possible threat, different criteria have to be used. These criteria are the identification criteria (idcrits) that are also used in naval warfare, but are simplified in order to let naive participants learn them more easily. These simplified criteria are the speed, heading, distance of a contact to the own ship, and whether the contact is in a sea lane or not. If a participant concludes that a ship is a possible threat or not, he can change the color of the contacts by clicking with the left mouse button on the contact. Contacts can be identified as either a threat (red), possible threat (yellow), or no threat (green). It is not necessary that all contacts are identified. Only the five most threatening have to be identified as a threat (marked as red). The other types of identification (possible threat and no threat) are used

---

[1] A full color variant of Fig. 2 can be found at [14].

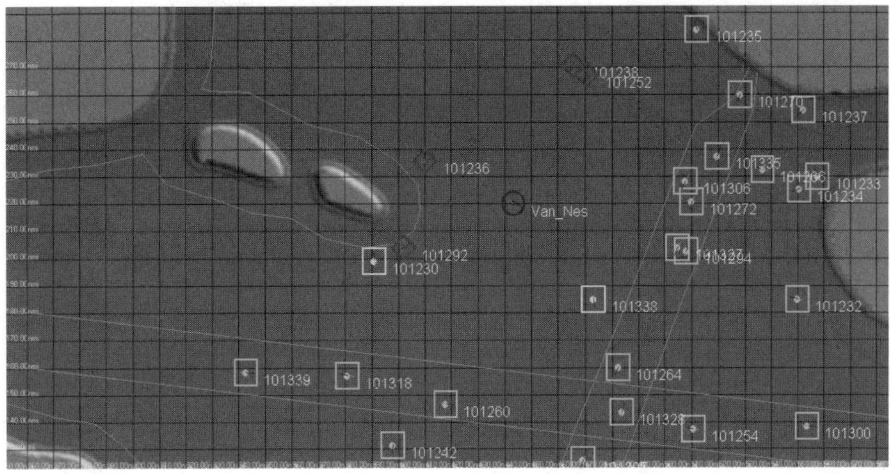

Fig. 2. The interface of the used simplified task environment based on [13]. The long lanes are sea lanes. The circle labeled with "Van_Nes" represents the own ship.

to assist the participant in his task. When a contact is marked as green, this means no direct attention is needed. When a contact is marked as yellow, this contact has to be checked regularly to decide if the contact is still no threat. The task has to be performed as accurately as possible. Contacts that are wrongfully identified as a threat will result in a lower score. Performance is determined by the accurateness, averaged over time, of the contacts that are identified as the five most threatening contacts during the task. Behavior of each contact can change during the task and therefore the soundness of classifications (which is not communicated to the participant) may change over time. For instance, a contact can suddenly come closer to the own ship, get out of a sea lane, speedup, or change its heading.

For Experiment 2 (see Section 4.3) the task is extended to one that includes the support of the HABTA-based agent. The support agent is capable of doing the same as the operator, except with limited background knowledge and therefore limited performance per object. In order to simulate this aspect, for each participant, the measured average performance per contact in Experiment 1 is used in order to set the performance of the agent. The agent can be given a list of objects provided by the its HABTA-component and compile a tactical picture related to those objects.

Apart from the primary task mentioned sofar, in both experiments a secondary task is used in order to control for the attentional resources. This secondary task is a gauge task that has to be monitored constantly. The secondary task is shown on a different screen and requires action on various occaasions depending on the value the gauge is indicating. The primary and secondary task performances are equally important in order to have the gauge task be effective.

4.2   Experiment 1: Validation of the Descriptive Model

In Experiment 1 participants perform the task as described in the previous section without support of the agent. The same scenarios will be used for all participants. Before the actual task starts, the task will be explained thoroughly to the participants. The task will be illustrated by using different examples to be sure that the participants understand the task and how to decide if a contact is a threat based on the different criteria. All participants have to perform a test to check if they sufficiently understood the rules of classifying the contacts. If they do not perform well, i.e. their score is below 80%, they receive extra instructions and another test. Also the possible second test has to be performed with a success rate of above or equal to 80%. Then they have to perform a practice trial in which they have to apply the learned rules. After this they get instructions of how to behave during the experimental interventions while they are executing their task. This is practiced as well for several times, after which the actual experiment begins. This introduction is necessary because we do not want the participants to perform badly because of a lack of understanding of the rules or experience with the experimental interface.

During the task, different variables are measured to determine the d' of the model and to be able to iteratively improve the model afterwards. The following variables will be measured: eye movements, performance of the primary and secondary task, mental workload, and at different points in time participants have to mark contacts that received attention according to the themselves. The performances and mental workload measures are used as a baseline for comparing the performances and mental workload of the task with and without using the HABTA-component (see Experiment 2). In order to measure the variables, at random moments (varying from 2–6 minutes) the scenario is frozen. There are two experimental sessions, one with an easy and one with a difficult scenario of half an hour. It is expected that the difficult scenario would also lead to a poorer performance of the model, because in those cases the participant's allocation of attention is less dynamic. During a freeze, the participants have to click on the contacts to which, in their opinion, they had allocated their attention to from 3 seconds before the scenario was frozen. The participants also have to motivate why those contacts are selected. Directly after the participant has selected the contacts, mental workload is measured during the same freezes. For this, the mental workload scale from [15] is used (BSMI). On a scale from 0 (not at all strenuous) to 150 (very strenuous) the mental workload of the task has to be indicated. Performance and eye movements of the participants are measured during the task, by calculation according to the rules described in Section 4.1 and by eye-tracker recording, respectively. The patterns of the eye movements (what objects are looked at through time) are compared with the contacts that received attention before the freezes, according to the participant. This is done to be sure that the participants were able to select the objects that received their attention. Those contacts that got a considerate amount of gaze fixations, are expected to have received attention.[2] If the participants do not mention those contacts, it is expected that they are not good at selecting the proper contacts.

After the experiment is performed, the contacts selected by the participants during the freezes are matched with the output of the model in a simulation. The calculation of d' provides information about the sensitivity of the model, i.e. whether the model is able to accurately describe the participant's dynamics of attention allocation. Information about performances, workload, and the description of the participants why contacts are selected, is expected to be valuable for determining in what cases the percentage true positives (hits) is high and percentage false positives (false alarms) is low, which in turn can be used to improve the sensitivity of the model.

4.3   Experiment 2: Validation of the HABTA-Based Support

In Experiment 2 the applicability of the model for supporting attention allocation is tested. The same task as in Experiment 1 has to be performed, except this time the participant is supported by the agent of which the HABTA-component is part of. When there is a discrepancy between the descriptive and prescriptive model, higher than a certain threshold (see Fig. 1), the agent will support the human by either performing the task for the participant or by drawing attention to the contact that should receive attention. Different variables are measured to determine the excess value of the HABTA-based support. Performances and mental workload are measured in the same way as in Experiment 1. Furthermore, trust and acceptance are measured at the end of the scenario. In order to determine the effectiveness of an agent, it is important to measure trust and acceptance of that agent and to investigate what factors influence trust and acceptance. Trust and acceptance indicate whether people will actually use the agent. For instance, it says something about whether people will follow the advice of the agent, in the case the agent provides advice. Validated questionnaires are adjusted (only when necessary) to be able to measure trust and acceptance in adaptive systems. The trust questionnaire is based on the questionnaire of [16]. An example of a question on this questionnaire is: "Is the agent reliable enough?". The acceptance questionnaire is based on the questionnaire of [17] and [18]. An example of a question on this questionnaire is: "Is the support of the agent useful for me?". The trust and acceptance scores are expected to provide more insight in the results of the experiment. If trust in and acceptance of the agent is low, people will not follow any suggestions made by the agent.

The performance and mental workload without a HABTA-based agent will be compared with those with a HABTA-based agent, using the results of Experiment 1 as a baseline. This is one of the reasons that the same participants are used as in Experiment 1. The other reason is that the measured performance in Experiment 1 is used for setting the performance of the agent. For Experiment 2, it is expected that performance is higher and mental workload is lower when supported with HABTA.

---

[2] Note that this does not hold vice versa, which would otherwise mean that attention in complex scenarios is easily described using solely fixation data.

5   Intermediary Results

In this section preliminary results of the experiments described in Section 4 are shown based on a pilot study for Experiment 1, using one arbitrary participant. The actual experiment will be performed with more participants. The pilot is primarily meant to explore the applicability of the experimental method of Experiment 1 to the given task. It is also meant as an illustration of the form and dynamics of the participant's and model's estimation of human allocation of attention. Finally, it is used as a basis for a better understanding of the possibilities of HABTA-based support, which is important for a proper preparation and performing of Experiment 2. This is because this type of support is required in the experimental setup of Experiment 2.

In the pilot study, the participant was required to execute the identification task and to select contacts during the freezes. In contrast with the procedure during the actual experiment, no questions concerning the participant's cognitive workload or motivation for the selected contacts were asked. In Fig. 2 the interface right before a freeze is shown. During a freeze both the participant and the model had to indicate their estimation of what contacts the attention of the participant was allocated to. In the situation presented in Fig.2, the participant selected contacts 101238, 101252, 101236, 101338, 101230, 101292, 101294, and 101327. Between every two freezes certain events can cause the participant to change the allocation of his attention to other attention demanding regions. The preceding course of events of the situation in Fig.2 clearly caused the participant to attend to the contacts close to his own ship "Van_Nes". If the model made a proper estimation of the participant's allocation of attention, the selected contacts by the participant would resemble those selected by the model. Consequently, the performance of the model is best determined by means of the calculation of the overall overlap of the participant's and model's selection of contacts. This calculation is explained below.

There are four possible outcomes when comparing the participant's and model's selection of contacts, namely, a Hit, False Alarm, Correct Rejection, and Miss. The counts of these outcomes can be set out in a 2×2 confusion matrix. Tab. 1 is such a confusion matrix, where T and F are the total amount of the participant's selected and not selected contacts, respectively, and T' and F' are the total amount of the model's selected and not selected contacts, respectively.

The ratios of all the possible outcomes are represented by H, FA, CR, and M, respectively. A higher H and CR, and a lower FA and M, leads to a more appropriate estimation by the model. This is the case because the selected contacts by the model then have a higher resemblance with those selected by the participant. Furthermore, a higher T' leads to a higher H, but, unfortunately, also to a higher FA. Something similar holds for F'. The value of T' therefore should depend on the trade-off between the costs and benefits of these different outcomes.

In Fig. 3 the output of the model for the situation presented in Fig. 2 is shown. If the estimated attention on the z-axis, called Attention Value (AV), is higher than a certain threshold, which is in this case set to .035, the contact is selected

Table 1. Confusion matrix of the participant's and model's estimation of the allocation of attention

		Participant		total
		t	f	
Model	t'	Hits	False Alarms	T'
	f'	Misses	Correct Rejections	F'
	total	T	F	

and otherwise it is not. The different values of AV are normally distributed over the (x, y)-plane. The threshold is dependent on the total amount of contacts the participant is expected to allocate attention to [10]. The AV-distribution in Fig. 3 results in the selection of contacts 101235, 101238, 101252, 101236, 101292, 101230, 101338, and 101260. Using this selection and the selected contacts by the participant, for each contact, the particular outcome can be determined.

For each freeze, if one counts the number of the different outcomes, a confusion matrix can be constructed and the respective ratios can be calculated. For Fig. 3, for example, these ratios are $H = \frac{6}{8} = 0.750$, $FA = \frac{2}{19} = 0.105$, $CR = \frac{17}{19} = 0.895$, and $M = \frac{2}{8} = 0.250$, respectively.

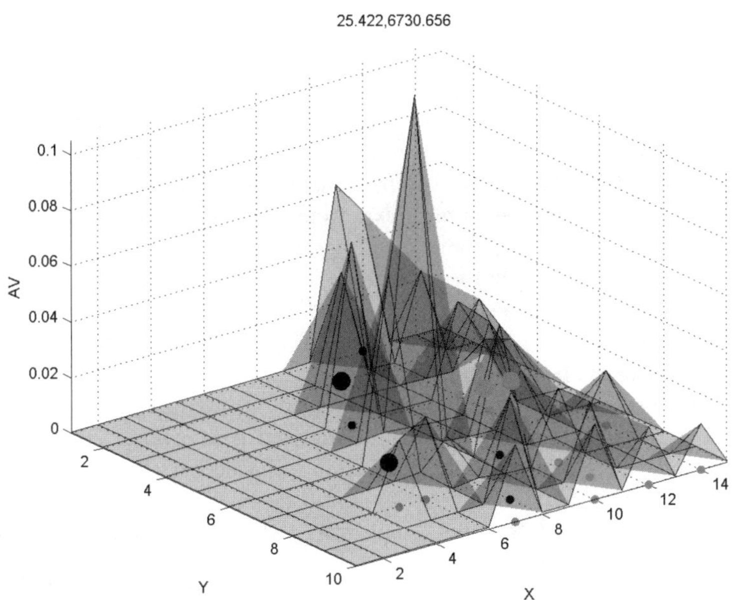

Fig. 3. The output of the model for the situation shown in Fig. 2. The black dots are the selected contacts by the model. Bigger dots mean that there are more contacts on the respective coordinates.

To study the performance of models Receiver-Operating Characteristics (ROC) graphs are commonly used. A ROC-space is defined by FA as the x- and H as the y-axis, which depicts relative trade-offs between the costs and benefits of the model. Every (FA, H)-pair of each confusion matrix represents one point in the ROC-space. Since the model is intended to estimate the participant's allocation of attention for each freeze and participant, this means that for N participants and M freezes, there are NM points in the ROC-space.

Once all points have been scatter plotted in the ROC-space, a fit of an isosensitivity curve leads to an estimate of the d' of the model. Isosensitivity corresponds to:

$$d' = z(H) - z(FA)$$

where d' is constant along the curve and $z(x)$ is the z-score of x.[3] Larger absolute values of d' mean that the model is more specific and sensitive to the participant's estimation (and thus has a higher performance). If d' is near or below zero, this indicates the model's performance is equal to or below chance, respectively. If there does not exist a proper fit of a isosensitivity curve, the area under the curve (AUC) can also be used as a model validity estimate. In non-parametric statistics the ROC-graph is determined by the data and not by a predefined curve. If the different values of H and FA appear to be normally distributed, the d' can be obtained from a z-table. In this case, the (FA, H)-pair from Fig. 3 results in $d' = 1.927$. Which is a fairly good score.

6   Conclusion and Discussion

This paper describes the development of an adaptive cooperative agent to support humans while performing tasks where errors in the allocation of attention occur. In general, human attention allocation is prone to two types of errors: over- and underallocation of attention. Several factors may cause over- or underallocation of attention, such as inexperience and information overload. The design is discussed of a component of an agent, called Human Attention-Based Task Allocator (HABTA), that is capable of detecting human error in the allocation of attention and acts accordingly by reallocating tasks between the human and the agent. In this way the HABTA-based agent manages human and agent attention, causing the performance of the human-agent team to increase. The development of such an agent requires extensive and iterative research. The agent's internal structure, i.e. the models describing and prescribing human attention allocation and the support mechanism that is based on those models, has to be validated. In this paper, two experimental designs are described to validate the internal of the agent. The first experiment aims at validating the model of

---

[3] The z-score reveals how many units of the standard deviation a case is above or below the mean:

$$z(x_i) = \frac{x_i - \mu_x}{\sigma_x}$$

where μ_x is the mean, σ_x the standard deviation of the variable x, and x_i a raw score.

human attention allocation (descriptive model) and the second experiment aims at validating the HABTA-component as a whole, incorporating a prescriptive model and support mechanism.

The results from the pilot of the first experiment presented in this paper have proven to be useful, but the actual experiments still have to be performed. Therefore, future research will focus on the performance and analysis of these experiments. It is expected that the accuracy of the model can be increased hereafter, however 100% accurateness will not be attainable. The results of the first experiment will show if the variables indeed provide enough information to improve the accurateness of the model.

With respect to the second experiment, one might argue to add another variant of support, such as one that is configurated by the participant itself. The participant will then do the same as HABTA does, which might result in him being a fair competitor for HABTA. In this way the effectiveness of HABTA-based support can be studied more convincingly, comparing human-agent performance when either the participant or the agent is managing attention allocation. Deciding on this will be subject in the near future.

If the agent does not support the human at the right time and in the right way, this might influence trust and acceptance of the agent. It is interesting to investigate whether an observable and adjustable internal structure of the agent improves trust and acceptance of the system (see for instance [19] in these proceedings). This also needs further research.

In this paper the development and validation of a normative model (prescriptive model) is not described. Validation of this model is important, as it is also a crucial part of the HABTA-component. Errors in this model will lead to support at the wrong time and this will influence performance, trust, and acceptance. Further research is needed in order to develop and validate normative models.

Finally, in general, agent-components have more value when they can be easily adjusted for other applications. It is therefore interesting to see whether HABTA-based support can be applied in other domains as well.

Acknowledgments

This research was funded by the Dutch Ministry of Defense under progr. nr. V524. The authors would like to thank Annerieke Heuvelink, Harmen Lafeber, Jan Treur, Kim Kranenborg, Marc Grootjen, Tibor Bosse, Tjerk de Greef, and Willem van Doesburg for their contribution and helpful comments.

References

1. Grootjen, M., Neerincx, M.A.: Operator load management during task execution in process control. In: Human Factors Impact on Ship Design (2005)
2. Wickens, C., McCarley, J., Alexander, A., Thomas, L., Ambinder, M., Zheng, S.: Attention-situation awareness (A-SA) model of pilot error. Technical Report AHFD-04-15/NASA-04-5, University of Illinois Human Factors Division (2005)

3. Chalmers, B.A., Webb, R.D.G., Keeble, R.: Modeling shipboard tactical picture compilation. In: Proceedings of the Fifth International Conference on Information Fusion, Sunnyvale, CA, vol. 2, pp. 1292–1299. International Society of Information Fusion (2002)
4. Kahneman, D.: Attention and effort. Prentice Hall, Englewoods Cliffs (1973)
5. Wickens, C.D.: Processing resources in attention. Varieties of attention (1984)
6. Steinberg, A.: Standardisation in data fusion. In: Proceedings of Eurofusion 1999: International Conference on Data Fusion, UK, Stratford-Upon-Avon, pp. 269–277 (1999)
7. Verkuijlen, R.P.M., Muller, T.J.: Action speed tactical trainer review. Technical report, TNO Human Factors (2007)
8. Treisman, A.: The perception of features and objects. Attention: Awareness, selection, and control (1993)
9. Treur, J., Bosse, T., van Maanen, P.-P., van Doesburg, W.: Augmented Metacognition Addressing Dynamic Allocation of Tasks Requiring Visual Attention. In: Schmorrow, D.D., Reeves, L.M. (eds.) HCII 2007 and FAC 2007. LNCS (LNAI), vol. 4565, pp. 166–175. Springer, Heidelberg (2007)
10. Bosse, T., van Maanen, P.-P., Treur, J.: A cognitive model for visual attention and its application. In: Nishida, T. (ed.) Proceedings of the 2006 IEEE/WIC/ACM International Conference on Intelligent Agent Technology (IAT 2006), pp. 255–262. IEEE Computer Society Press, Los Alamitos (2006)
11. Bosse, T., van Maanen, P.-P., Treur, J.: Temporal differentiation of attentional processes. In: Vosniadou, S., Kayser, D. (eds.) Proceedings of the Second European Cognitive Science Conference (EuroCogSci 2007), pp. 842–847. IEEE Computer Society Press, Los Alamitos (2007)
12. Arciszewski, H., Delft, J.v.: Automated crew support in the command centre of a naval vessel. In: Proceedings of the 10th International Command and Control Research and Technology Symposium (2005)
13. Heuvelink, A., Both, F.: Boa: A cognitive tactical picture compilation agent. In: Proceedings of the 2007 IEEE/WIC/ACM International Conference on Intelligent Agent Technology (IAT 2007). IEEE Computer Society Press, Los Alamitos (forthcoming, 2007)
14. http://www.few.vu.nl/~pp/public/vanmaanendekoningvandongen-AmI07.pdf
15. Zijlstra, F.R.H., van Doorn, L.: The Construction of a Scale to Measure Perceived Effort. Department of Philosophy and Social Sciences, Delft University of Technology, Delft, The Netherlands (1985)
16. Madson, M., Gregor, S.: Measuring human-computer trust. In: Proceedings of the Australasian Conference on Information Systems (2000)
17. Venkatesh, V., Morris, M.G., Davis, G.B., Davis, F.D.: User acceptance of information technology: Toward a unified view. MIS Quarterly 27(3), 425–478 (2003)
18. Davis, F.D.: Perceived usefulness, perceived ease of use, and user acceptance of information technology. MIS Quarterly 13(3), 319–340 (1989)
19. Mioch, T., Harbers, M., van Doesburg, W.A., van den Bosch, K.: Enhancing human understanding through intelligent explanations. In: Proceedings of the First International Workshop on Human Aspects in Ambient Intelligence, Springer, Heidelberg (2007)

Affective Human Factors Design with Ambient Intelligence

Jianxin (Roger) Jiao, Qianli Xu, and Jun Du

School of Mechanical & Aerospace Engineering,
Nanyang Technological University, Singapore
{mjiao,qlxu,dujun}@ntu.edu.sg

Abstract. The need to include customer's affective needs in product design presents a new direction beyond tradtional human factors and ergonomics. While the human-product interactions have been extensively studied, the interactions of these elements with the ambience have been largely ignored. This gives rise to a nascent research perspective called affective human factors design, which aims at addressing human's emotional responses and aspirations and to achieve aesthetic appreciation and pleasurable experience through human-product-ambience interactions. This paper presents a framework of affective human factors design with ambient intelligence to achieve the extensive interactions among these elements. Ambient intelligence establishes a multidisciplinary technology core that incorporates affective design, human factors and ergonomics, product development, and specific application sectors. A few application scenarios reveal the most important characteristics and emerging trends in this research area.

Keywords: affective design, human factors, ambient intelligence.

1 Introduction

The interaction between human factors and design is a common theme in the literature and a constant challenge in the practical working-out of human use issues in the design of products and systems. It is suggested that the discourse has moved on from the goal of merely attaining system usability [1]. The 'new' human factors must further support designs that address peoples' emotional responses and aspirations, whereas usability alone still demands a great deal of attention in both research and practice. Consideration of these needs has generally fallen within the designer's sphere of activities, through the designer's holistic contribution to the aesthetic and functional dimensions of human-product interactions. They have thus tended to be interpreted and explored through creative, subjective design processes rather than through the application of analytical, objectively determined methods. Such a rationale of product design represents a nascent research perspective, namely affective human factors design.

Affective human factors design originates from the field of human-computer interaction and more specifically from the developing area of affective computing. It used to address the delivering of affective interfaces capable of eliciting certain emotional experiences from users. Similarly, affective product design attempts to define the

M. Mühlhäuser et al. (Eds.): AmI 2007 Workshops, CCIS 11, pp. 301–313, 2008.

subjective emotional relationships between consumers and products, and to explore the affective properties that products intend to communicate through their physical attributes. It aims to deliver artifacts capable of eliciting maximum physiopsychological pleasure that consumers may obtain through all of their senses.

The fulfillment of affective design necessities a new dimension beyond the traditional human-product interactions, namely the ambience. Accordingly, a coherent consideration of the interactions between product, human, and ambience suggests to be more profound for the discipline of affective human factors. Such a consideration is in line with the wisdom of product ecosystems [2], which essentially entails a scenario of affective design of the entire system with customer experience in the loop (Fig. 1). Products can interact with its ambience and such an interaction influences the customer's perceptions due to the particular context created. Hence, affect is a combination of two elements, namely customer perception and customer experience. Accordingly, the aim of affective design is to address human's emotional responses and aspirations, and to achieve aesthetic appreciation and pleasurable experience through human-product-ambience interactions.

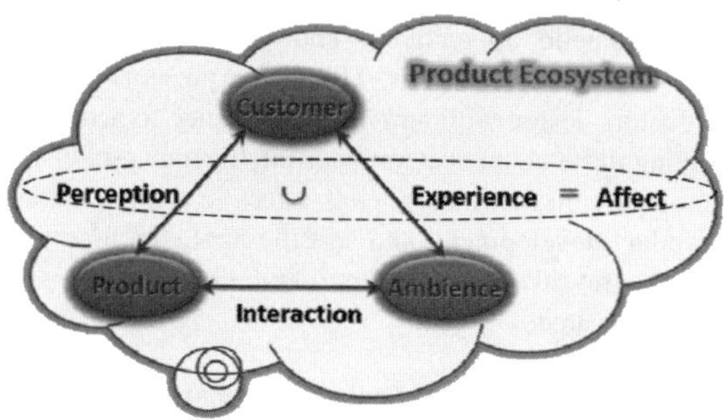

Fig. 1. Interactions between human, product, and ambience in a product ecosystem

However, it remains a challenging task to model and evaluate product ecosystems with considerations of affective human factors. Above all, the construction of a product ecosystem requires extensive human-product-ambience interactions, which could not be realized without advanced product technologies and enhanced analytical methods. In this respect, ambient intelligence suggests itself to be a promising solution to product ecosystem design. It takes the integration provided by ubiquitous and pervasive computing one step further to realize context-aware environments that are sensitive and responsive to the presence of people [3].

Considering the challenges of affective human factors design and the opportunities provided by ambient intelligence, this paper aims at developing a comprehensive solution framework of affective design with ambient intelligence by incorporating human factors and ergonomics, information and communication technologies, engineering design, product innovation, and social and psychological sciences. Section 2 presents the overall structure of the framework. The major technical issues and the proposed solution strategies are discussed in Section 3, together with application examples for illustrating the rationale. Summary and possible research directions are discussed in the last section.

2   A Framework of Affective Human Factors Design

The key issue of affective human factors design with ambient intelligence manifests itself through the development and utilization of electronic intelligent environments that are sensitive and responsive to the presence of people. This research explores the potential of applying ambient intelligence technologies for the enhancement of acquisition, analysis, and fulfillment of affective customer needs. In particular, the proposed framework is geared towards the following goals: (1) examine the feasibility and potential of ambient intelligence concept and establish the frame of references in the respective affective human factors design domains; (2) identify fundamental issues and formulate a technological roadmap of affective human factors design research.

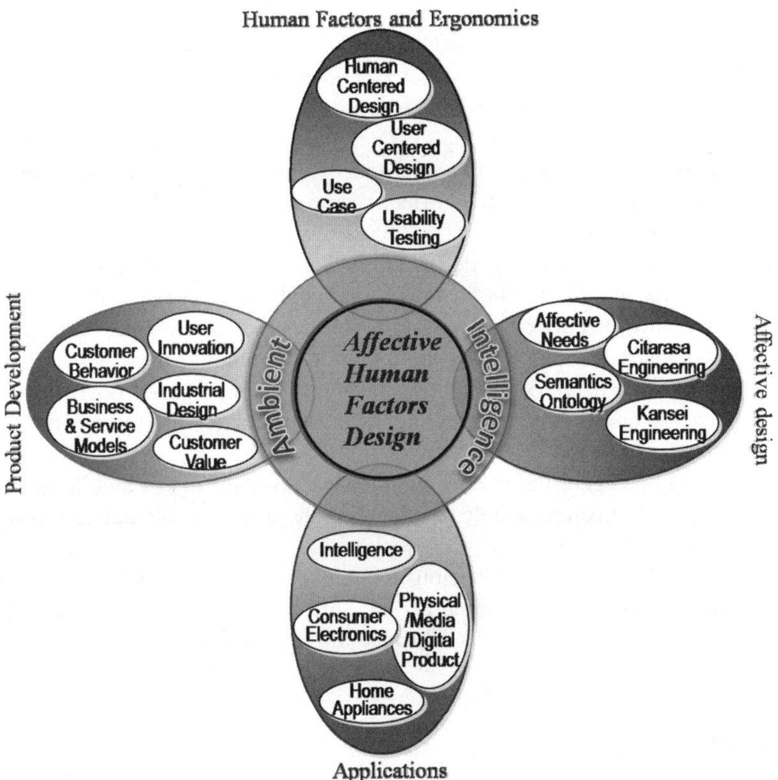

Fig. 2. Framework of the affective human factors design with ambient intelligence

Towards this end, a comprehensive technical framework is proposed, as shown in Fig. 2. This framework features a technology core of ambient intelligence in support of affective human factors design. It expands in four domain areas, including affective design, human factors and ergonomics, product development, and the specific application sectors. Among them, affective design and human factors and ergonomics define the problem context and the fundamental requirements of product ecosystem design. Product development accommodates the traditional engineering considerations in design and production. The application sectors provide various scenarios with respect to the particular requirements. Innovative solutions to affective human factors design may be developed by taking useful ingredients from these multiple disciplines.

3 Fundamental Issues

3.1 Ambient Intelligence

The strength of an ambient intelligence environment is to support affective design with context-aware adaptive applications. With ambient intelligence embedded in the product ecosystem, the behaviors and reactions of the customers can be captured in real time without interrupting the customers' normal activities. In this regard, a multi-layer ambient intelligence architecture is proposed as shown in Fig. 3. Different layers serve to link low-level details (hardware layers) with high-level view (software layers). The major responsibilities of each layer are discusses next.

- The bottom level layer is composed of domestic devices that comprise diverse virtual reality-enabled affective use cases such as home appliances in a living room or kitchen.
- A control device layer is defined to add a computing unit at the domestic device layer in order to obtain a particular application of pervasive computing.
- The control network hardware layer allows the interconnection among control devices, and thus satisfying ubiquitous communication.
- The control network abstraction layer is designed based on fuzzy markup language and is used to integrate different standards used to realize the control network layer.
- The ad hoc agent-based core middleware layer resorts to mobile agent technologies and is responsible of allocating the limited computation resources to numerous devices.
- At the top service level, various techniques, such as virtual reality, use case, data mining, mobile commerce, etc., are used to improve the elicitation of customers' affective needs and mapping of these needs to affective design elements.

3.2 Affective Design

A general roadmap can be established in terms of a series of affective mapping processes, including affective needs elicitation, analysis, and fulfillment. A few major issues and solution strategies are discussed next.

3.2.1 Affective Needs

As mentioned earlier, affect refers to customer's psychological response to the perceptual design details (e.g. styling) of the product [12]. Affect is a basis for the formation of human values and human judgment. For this reason, it might be argued that

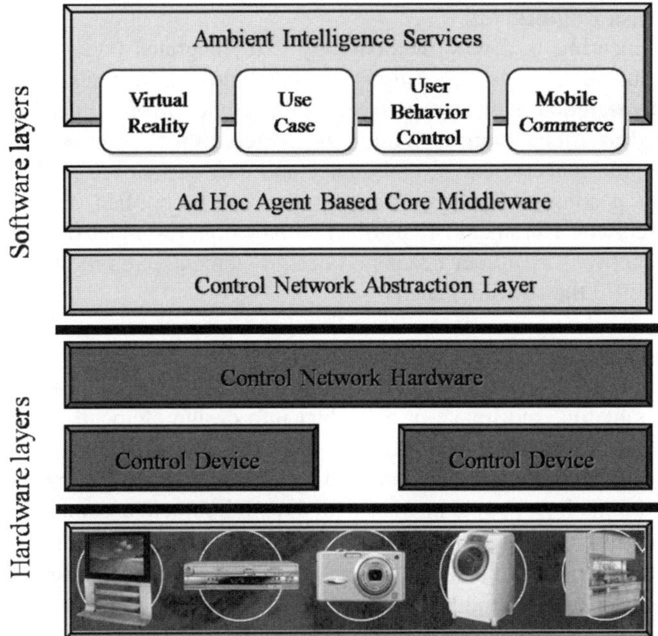

Fig. 3. A multi-layer ambient intelligence environment for affective design

Models of product design that do not consider affect are essentially weakened [13]. However, it has been difficult for customers to articulate the affective needs, and hence for designers to understand these needs. Such difficulties could be alleviated by well-defined semantic ontology and various analytical techniques, such as data mining [17] and conjoint analysis [10].

3.2.2 Semantic Ontology

The purpose of semantic ontology is to describe the affective needs that are communicable among customers and designers from different sectors using a limited number of terminologies that are as small as possible but comprehensive enough to cover the majority aspects of affective design. Each type of product ecosystem is supported by a set of affective terminology/taxonomy based on different customer requirements with respect to the particular product systems (e.g., automobile, living room, shopping mall, etc.). The development of semantics starts with customer survey, preferably carried out in an ambient intelligence-enabled environment. Next, semantic scales can be constructed for product ecosystem evaluation, which involves the collection of a large number of descriptive words for the product ecosystem, and the clustering of the words that are similar in meaning into categories [14]. From each category, one or several words are chosen to represent the category and be used on a semantic scale in order to evaluate the product ecosystem. Finally, the semantic scale assessment can be interpreted by domain experts to delineate the usage of the terminologies.

3.2.3 Citarasa Engineering

Citarasa engineering is a new methodology that integrates cognition and affect in uncovering customer needs [15]. *Cita* is a Malay word that denotes intent, hope, aspiration, and expectation that are cognitively-linked, while *rasa* indicates taste and feels that is related to affect/emotion. While affect refers to feeling responds, cognition is used to interpret, make sense of, and understand user experience [16]. Citarasa engineering hosts a combination of techniques that will be applied in the elicitation of customer needs, measurement of customer satisfaction, the identification of mapping relationship between customer needs and design elements, and the design of product portfolio to fulfill the customer needs.

3.2.4 Kansei Engineering

Developed in Japan from the 1970s, Kansei engineering is a technology for translating a consumer's feeling and image of a product into design elements [7]. Kansei in the Japanese language contrasts with Chisei. It is the subjective feeling and aesthetic aspect of customers' mindset, as opposed to Chisei's rational knowledge set. Both together determine how people interact with the environment around them.

While Kansei words excel in describing affective needs, the mapping relationships between Kansei words and design elements are often not clearly available throughout the innovation process of industrial design. Designers are often not aware of the underlying coupling and interrelationships among various design elements in regard to the achievement of customers' affective satisfaction. It is necessary to discern customer needs and product specifications, and as a result the mapping problem in between is the key issue in 'design for customers'. This leads to that affective design involves not only general fields of engineering design and industrial design, but also a number of issues related to the system-wide operations.

3.3 Human Factors and Ergonomics

Human factors and ergonomics have traditionally concerned with cause and effect relations between products and human performance, as measured by responses to tasks or by physical pain. With considerations of affective needs, it is expanding its remit to include emotional relations with the phrase 'cause and affect', in contrast to effect [19]. Research in this area requires extensive investigation of human-product interactions.

3.3.1 Human- or User-Centered Design

Human- or user-centered design process for interactive systems stands for the title of ISO 13407/1999. It supports managers of hardware and software design projects, and reflects realization of the importance of users in human-computer interface design [4]. As shown in Fig. 4, it advocates specifying the context of use for an identified need, translating that to requirements, producing and evaluating design solutions, and iterating until a satisfactory solution is attained. It implies a process but does not offer the methods for use within it. Its context is purely focused usability ergonomics; but it could likewise be applied to tackle affective issues.

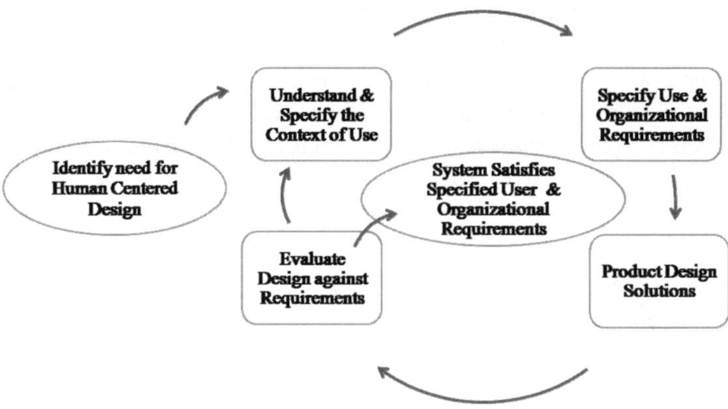

Fig. 4. Human/User-center design processes for affective design

3.3.2 Use Case

A use case is a popular technique for capturing functional requirements of systems. It allows description of sequences of events that, taken together, lead to a system doing something useful [5]. Each use case provides one or more scenarios that convey how the system should interact with the users (called actors) to achieve a specific business goal or function. Use case actors may be end users or other systems. Within the context of affective design, use cases are employed to build up testing scenarios for probing a user's tangible and intangible requirements via interacting with the product and its operating environment.

3.3.3 Usability Testing

Usability testing is a useful tool of measuring how well people can use a product and interact with the environment. Usability testing generally involves a controlled experiment to determine to what extent the users respond in terms of time, accuracy, recall, and emotional response. The results of the first test can be treated as a baseline or control measurement, whilst all subsequent tests can be compared with the baseline to justify improvement [6].

3.4 Product Development

Affective human factors design generally involves two stages: to understand customers' affective needs and subsequently to fulfill these needs in terms of product and system design, as shown in Fig. 5. While existing methods are mostly devoted to the first stage, the translation of affective needs into the product and system is even more challenging a task. In most cases, it is very hard to capture the customers' affective needs due to their linguistic origins. Since subjective impressions are difficult to translate into verbal descriptions, affective needs are relatively short-lasting emotional states and tend to be imprecise and ambiguous. Sometimes, without any technical experience, the customers do not know what they really want until their preferences are violated. In practice, customers, marketing folks and designers always employ different sets of context to express their understanding of affect information. Differences in semantics and terminology impair the coherence of transferring affective needs effectively from customers to designers. Furthermore, the sender-receiver problem which may arise during the communication process between customers and designers is a further reason leading to the misconception of customer affective needs.

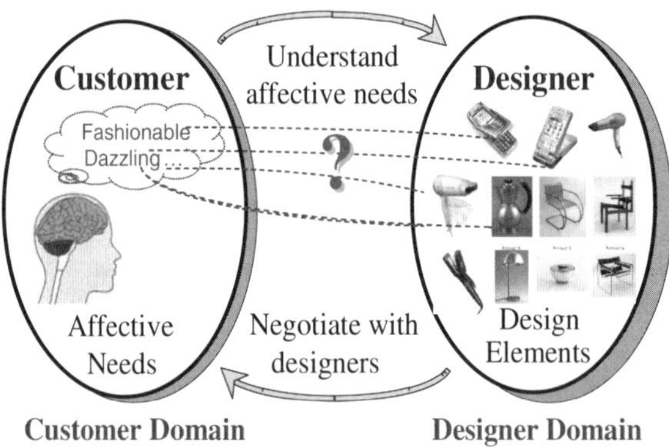

Fig. 5. The domain mapping process underlying affective product development

Inherently, affective human factors are subjective and mostly perception-based. To support affective design, these affective needs must be able to be manipulated during product design, that is, quantifiably in analytical forms. To rectify such deficiency in traditional human factors and ergonomics methods, it is necessary to adopt well established techniques of customer modeling and analysis from the business field, such as marketing research and product positioning. More specifically, discrete choice models will be applied to analyze customer behaviors and interactions with the product [8]. To alleviate difficulties in measure affect, utility theories [9] and conjoint analysis [10] are introduced to quantify customer-perceived value of affective design.

Another important area of understanding customers is user innovation, which has received limited attention in the current practice of affective design. User innovation refers to innovations developed by consumers and end users, rather than manufacturers. Von Hippel has discovered that most products and services are actually developed by users, who then give ideas to manufacturers [11]. This is because products are developed to meet the widest possible need. When individual users face problems that the majority of consumers do not, they have no choice but to develop their own modifications to existing products, or entirely new products, to solve their issues. Often, user innovations will share their ideas with manufacturers in hopes of having them produce the product – a process called free revealing. Built upon the popular lead user method, this project will further develop business and service models, incorporating with human-product-ambience interactions.

3.5 Application Scenarios

While affective design generally refers to the broad affective aspects of human factors, this research targets solid research programs by scrutinizing a concrete problem context. Considering the emerging trend of industries moving to mass customization and personalization, this research addresses the important situation of product customization and user personalization [18]. Consumer electronics products are deemed to be most indicative for this trend, and thus become one focus of this study. Vehicle design has many ingredients of customer affective needs. As a useful startup, this research investigates the interior design of the living compartment of a truck cab. Other commercial applications may be manifested through, for example, cabin comfortableness of passengers/patrons and attendants, such as an airplane, train, yacht, subway, exhibition hall, shopping mall, and alike.

3.5.1 iHome

An example of application scenario is developed by Philips Homelab, namely iHome, in which 'i' refers to the 'my' factor and an 'intelligent' sense of customization involving both the product and the ambience (http://www.research.philips.com/technologies/misc/homelab/). As shown in Fig. 6, examples of iHome may be the affective design of home appliances within a kitchen, living room, or restroom. Each of these scenarios can be constructed as virtual reality-enabled use cases in an ambient intelligence environment, through which various aspects of affective design can be explored. Within an iHome ambient intelligence environment, an affective design application is enacted as a coherent service system, including hardware and software, along with physical, media, or digital products. Various system-wide solutions can be further examined with respect to many business and service concerns.

3.5.2 Truck Cab

The interior design of truck cockpits involves both the product and the ambience through human interactions. In an effort to elicited customer affective needs, a mixed-reality environment has been installed with surveillance systems embedded (Fig. 7). The mixed-reality environment is used to simulate and rapidly reconstruct the actual truck cab environment at low cost. The surveillance system is used to capture customer response without interrupting the customer experience.

Based on the system, a number of affective descriptors are elicited and categorized, forming the vehicle affective needs ontology, an excerpt of which is shown in Table 1. The elements for constructing the truck cab ecosystem are defined as customizable design elements to be included in different versions of the actual products. Typical design elements are listed in Table 2. These results will be used in the ongoing project for defining the mapping relationship between customers' affective needs and design elements, as well as product configuration design considering producer production capabilities.

Fig. 6. Affective design with ambient intelligence application scenario: iHome

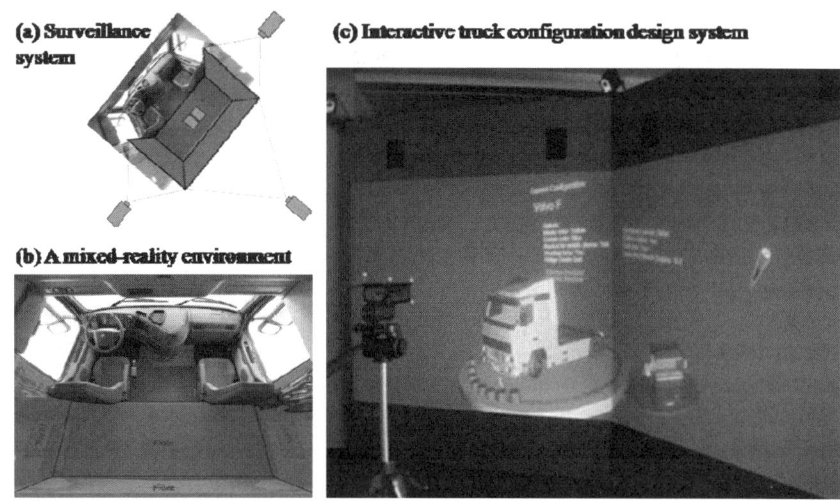

Fig. 7. Ambient intelligence environment of truck cab

Table 1. Definition of affective needs of truck cab

Affective needs	Definition	Affective needs	Definition
Durable	durable	Soft	soft
	long-lasting		silky
	hard-wearing		tender
	…		…
Solid	solid	Spacious	ample
	firm		wide
	hard		not-cramped
	…		…

Table 2. Design elements for truck cab ecosystem

Code	Description	Figure	Code	Description	Figure
Y1	Interior color_blue		Y6	Panel for switches	
Y2	Interior color_yellow		Y7	Bracket for mobile phone	
Y3	Interior color_grey		Y8	Reading lamp	
Y4	Curtain color_blue		Y9	Fridge under bed	
Y5	Curtain color_yellow		Y10	Fridge in rear shelf	

4 Summary

The proposed framework approaches affective design from an interdisciplinary perspective. To overcome the limitations of existing methods, the affective design with ambient intelligence framework orchestras relevant solutions from such fields as human factors and ergonomics, information and communication technologies, product innovation, industrial design, as well as business and management. Affective human factors have been traditionally dealt with in human factors and ergonomics with focus on the human-product interactions only. This research identifies an important dimension, namely interactions with the ambience, which has received very limited attention. In this regard, human-product-ambience interactions become the main theme of affective design, and in turn the main challenge is how to bring the environment dimension into the affective design horizon. Realizing the unique strength and potential of ubiquitous and pervasive computing, this research proposes to incorporate ambience intelligence into the affective design process, and thus enables the modeling of product ecosystems. Therefore, the proposed framework enriches the affective design problem context itself.

Main technical challenges are associated with the need of an ambient intelligence environment to support affective design. A few typical features to be realized in such an environment include:

Embedded: Since many devices are plugged into the network, the resulting system consists of multiple devices, computing equipment, and software systems that must interact with one another. Some of the devices are simple sensors, while others may be actuators owning a crunch of control activities within an ambient intelligence environment (e.g., central heating, security systems, lightning systems, washing machines, refrigerators, etc.). The strong heterogeneity makes difficult a uniformed policy-based management among diverse user interactions and services.

Context aware: A fundamental role of ambient intelligence is the capability of context sensing. This central concept of context awareness represents the possibility for the ambient intelligence system of biasing itself and its reactions to the environment. This means knowledge of many statically- and dynamically-changing parameters in relation to consciousness. In particular, affective design involves intensive user-centered contextual data, which necessitates the exploitation of relationships between the human concept of consciousness and the ambient intelligence idea of context.

Personalized: An ambient intelligence environment is supposed to be designed for people instead of generic users. This means that the system should be flexible enough to tailor itself to meet individual human needs. This is because affective design always involves highly customized products and personalized environments.

Adaptive: The affective design with ambient intelligence system, being sensible to the user's feedback, is capable to modify the corresponding actions have been or will be performed. This is consistent with the mass customization situation, where customers always want to make informed decisions of their own.

References

1. Jordan, P.W.: Designing Pleasurable Products: An Introduction to the New Human Factors. Taylor and Francis, London (2000)
2. MacQueen, M.: Ecosystem Thinking Needed for Product Design., `http://macqueen.com/`
3. Ducatel, K., Bogdanowicz, M., Scapolo, F., Leijten, J., Burgelman, J.-C.: Scenarios for Ambient Intelligence in 2010. ISTAG Report, European Commission (2001)
4. Beyer, H., Holtzblatt, K.: Contextual Design: Defining Customer-Centered Systems. Morgan Kaufmann, San Francisco (1998)
5. Bittner, K., Spence, I.: Use Case Modeling. Addison Wesley Professional, Reading (2002)
6. Virzi, R.A.: Refining the Test Phase of Usability Evaluation: How Many Subjects is Enough? Human Factors 34(4), 457–468 (1992)
7. Nagamachi, M.: Introduction of Kansei Engineering. Japan Standard Association, Tokyo (1996)
8. Train, K.: Discrete Choice Methods with Simulation. Cambridge University Press, Cambridge (2003)
9. Edwards, W.: Utility Theories: Measurements and Applications. Kluwer Academic Publishers, Dordrecht (1992)
10. Green, P., Carroll, J., Goldberg, S.: A General Approach to Product Design Optimization via Conjoint Analysis. Journal of Marketing 43, 17–35 (1981)
11. Von Hippel, E.: Democratizing Innovation. MIT Press, Cambridge (2005)
12. Demirbilek, O., Sener, B.: Product Design, Semantics and Emotional Response. Ergonomics 46(13/14), 1346–1360 (2003)
13. Helander, M.G., Tham, M.P.: Hedonomics-Affective Human Factors Design. Ergonomics 46(13/14), 1269–1272 (2003)
14. Karlsson, B., Aronsson, N., Svensson, K.: Using Semantic Environment Description as a Tool to Evaluate Car Interiors. Ergonomics 46(13/14), 1408–1422 (2003)

15. Helander, M.G., Khalid, H.M., Peng, H.: Citarasa Engineering for CATER System. In: Proc. Int. Conf. on Work with Computer Systems. Stockholm, Sweden, May 2007, pp. 21–24 (2007)
16. Khalid, H.M., Helander, M.G.: Customer Emotional Needs in Product Design. Concurrent Engineering 14(3), 197–206 (2006)
17. Jiao, J., Zhang, Y., Helander, M.: A Kansei Mining System for Affective Design. Expert Systems with Applications 30, 658–673 (2006)
18. Jiao, J., Ma, Q., Tseng, M.M.: Towards High Value-added Products and Services: Mass Customization and Beyond. Technovation 23, 809–821 (2003)
19. Talbot, J.: New Interactions: the Role of Affective Human Factors in Design. Ergonomics Australia 19, 21–25 (2005)

Smart Home Technology for the Elderly: Perceptions of Multidisciplinary Stakeholders

Anne-mie Sponselee[1], Ben Schouten[1], Don Bouwhuis[2], and Charles Willems[3]

[1] Fontys University of Applied Sciences, Hulsterweg 2-6, P.O.Box 141,
5900 AC Venlo, the Netherlands
{a.sponselee,ben.schouten}@fontys.nl
[2] Eindhoven University of Technology, Den Dolech 2, 5612 AZ Eindhoven,
the Netherlands
d.g.bouwhuis@tue.nl
[3] iRv/Vilans, Zandbergsweg 111, 6432 CC Hoensbroek, the Netherlands
ch.willems@irv.nl

Abstract. The "implementation" and use of smart home technology to lengthen independent living of non-instutionalized elderly have not always been flawless. The purpose of this study is to show that problems with smart home technology can be partially ascribed to differences in perception of the stakeholders involved. The perceptual worlds of caregivers, care receivers, and designers vary due to differences in background and experiences. To decrease the perceptual differences between the stakeholders, we propose an analysis of the expected and experienced effects of smart home technology for each group. For designers the effects will involve effective goals, caregivers are mainly interested in effects on workload and quality of care, while care receivers are influenced by usability effects. Making each stakeholder aware of the experienced and expected effects of the other stakeholders may broaden their perspectives and may lead to more successful implementations of smart home technology, and technology in general.

Keywords: smart home technology, perception, technology acceptance.

1 Introduction

The most important developments in society for smart home technology are the socialization of care, extramuralization, and ageing [1]. Socialization of care means that people in need of care are no longer concentrated in large-scale institutions, but are returned a full-fledged place within society. Instead of concentrating on people's disabilities, one looks at a person's possibilities. Supporting aging adults to stay in their homes independently for a longer period of time concedes to the wishes and needs of many people in need of care, aiming for an improvement of quality of living and daily life. Extramuralization leads to less intramural residential facilities, remarkably more small-scale extramural facilities, but also to (re)new(ed) organization of services and an increased use of technological resources. Additionally, ageing plays an important role. The fact

M. Mühlhäuser et al. (Eds.): AmI 2007 Workshops, CCIS 11, pp. 314–326, 2008.

that the amount of elderly people is growing, and people become older as well, leads to an enormous increase of care demand. The demand for houses for the elderly, for care, and for services will therefore grow in the coming years, while a shortage in care personnel is expected. The use of smart home technology to support independent living is hereby inevitable [2].

2 Multidisciplinary Stakeholders

Introducing smart home technology in care settings involves more than a technological innovation. It comprises of new processes and organisational changes. These changes all have to occur within regulations and financial rules that are most likely not adjusted to the use of technology. The stakeholders involved in the process of implementing smart home technology in extramural care setting therefore consist of: designers, care receivers, caregivers, care institutions, service providers, housing corporations, insurance companies, and the government. The perceptual worlds of these stakeholders vary due to differences in background and experiences, which lead to different interpretations on how smart home technology can be helpful in supporting independent living of elderly people.

In this paper we focus on the perception of the caregiver, the care receiver, and the designer. Problems in the interaction between the user or end-user and the technology can partially be ascribed to the design, which indicates the importance of considering both the care receiver's perception and the designer's perception. The caregiver, however, is also expected to be a user of smart home technology, and as the care processes also have to be taken into account, we consider the caregiver as third stakeholder.

2.1 The Care Receiver

Care receivers, in our case elderly people, are often considered as technofobic. Although this perspective does not apply to all elderly people, and is remonstrated by several studies (e.g. [3,4]), we believe elderly care receivers are less keen on new technologies than young people are and show lower technology usage rates [5]. One of the reasons for this technofobic perspective might be "self preservation". Elderly people have to deal with more and more limitations due to the ageing process, which make them more vulnerable and dependent than before. As older adults have less experience with computers and other (new) technologies [5], they are confronted with their (cognitive) limitations when they have to work with it, which makes them more afraid of making mistakes. Their (computer) anxiety results in unutilised chances to live and function independently [5], or to be enabled and empowered by technological possibilities [6]. Elderly people may therefore seem peevish and conservative, as they do not want their current life to be influenced too much by external factors.

An older person appears to become less technofobic when he or she knows and understands the usefulness of the technology [7]. Unfortunately, older adults often do not realise what advantages technology can bring them [5, 6]. Proper guidance and information when new (smart home) technology is introduced and used is therefore important to let the older care receiver get a positive view on the technology, and realise the possible benefits of it.

2.2 The Caregiver

Although most caregivers are younger than the care receivers, caregivers are also known for their technophobia. This reluctance towards technology can partially be explained by the caring character of caregivers. People who choose for care delivery or nursing as a professional occupation often prefer working with people who need them. Giving away personal contact, through a technology intervention, raises an aversion. Even in situations where technology replaces physical presence by virtual presence, like telecare, the caregiver gets the feeling he or she has to renounce that which is experienced as "caring". Caregivers also experience a reduction in time spent with clients as a direct decrease in quality of care [8]. According to caregivers' perception, technological developments that are cost-cutting - and are developed for that purpose - result in a loss of quality of care. Raappana et al. [8] state that technology and care service are commonly not felt as being connected, which results in unwillingness by caregivers to use technology, and difficulties when new technologies are introduced. This perception may be due to a lack of abilities and skills among caregivers, which leads to feelings of incapability, with decreased work motivation and distress as a result. Fortunately, caregivers are willing to see utilisation of a safety system as part of their professional care skills - unlike the use of a personal computer as such - and describe technology as a positive change in the (quality of) work [8].

Even though the study by Raappana et al. shows that safety technology is viewed as useful, the implementation of smart home technology results in extra work for caregivers. The caregivers' unfamiliarity with the technology, the lack of skills among care substitutes, along with an increased number of false alarms, result in time-consuming efforts for caregivers. This indicates the importance of professional training to reduce both the expected and the experienced extra workload of the caregivers. Another concern of caregivers is that they expect elderly people to become even more lonely when technology is introduced into the care process. However, screen-to-screen contact may increase social contacts among elderly and between elderly and the community or their relatives. This emphasises the importance of proper guidance and training for caregivers when smart home technology is introduced. The use of (care)technology should actually become part of care education, in which both usage and implications of smart home technology are taught. Besides, by means of good orientation on useful technologies most negative effects that caregivers experience can be eliminated.

The idea that all care workers are reluctant towards using technology needs some nuances. In a study among care workers by Lyons et al. [9] administrators appear to judge computers much more positively than physicians and nurses do, not surprisingly as computers were first introduced in the administration work field. Physicians, however, declare to be unmotivated to learn how to use computers, while nurses feel insecure and perceive the computer as a barrier between themselves and their clients. Especially the differences between managers and the nursing staff is of importance, as decisions - on the use of technology - are mostly taken by managers, without much consultation with those people who have to work with it later.

2.3   The Designer

The designer, on the other hand, is nothing but technofobic. This, at the same time, is his weakest point. For a technician it is hard to imagine the perceptual world of a technofobic user. The focus of the designer is mainly on the functionality of the technology, achieving the effective goals. The advantage of this focus is that the designer is well-aware of the benefits that the technology can bring. However, due to an often experienced vocabulary difference between the designer and the users and end-users (e.g. [10]), the designer may not be able to convince the technofobic (end)users of the usefulness and the benefits that smart home technology can have.

3   Perceptual Differences on Prevention and Privacy between Caregivers and Care Receivers

Prior to the implementation of smart home technology in care processes, a decision is made on the proper technologies which the care receiver needs. These decisions, however, are often made by the managers, based on recommendations by technicians, and have resulted in choices that were not in accordance with the actual needs of the care receiver [11, 12]. The reasons for the perceptual differences are explained here.

As mentioned before, caregivers are known for their caring character. In their perception, the care receiver is most important, but this also means that no risks will be taken. This protective view, possibly also due to a need for controllability, may in some cases result in situation that are too safe, in which elderly people are insufficiently stimulated to undertake actions by themselves and thus stay independent. Elderly people who move to a care facility often show a great regression in their functioning and their abilities, due to the increased support in comparison with the home situation. One of the goals of the caregivers should therefore be: continuation and stimulation of the independence and autonomy of the care receiver. Becker [13] refers to this inevitable change as "making care humane". He considers caregivers as the "suppliers of human luck". The protective mentality of caregivers also results in the protection of privacy of the care receivers. Caregivers are well-aware of the fact that people who are in need of care always have to deal with a loss of privacy. Protecting the remaining part of their privacy is one of the main issues for caregivers. Several studies, however, have shown that people in need of care are willing to lose some privacy if they get more independence or quality of life in return [14, 15].

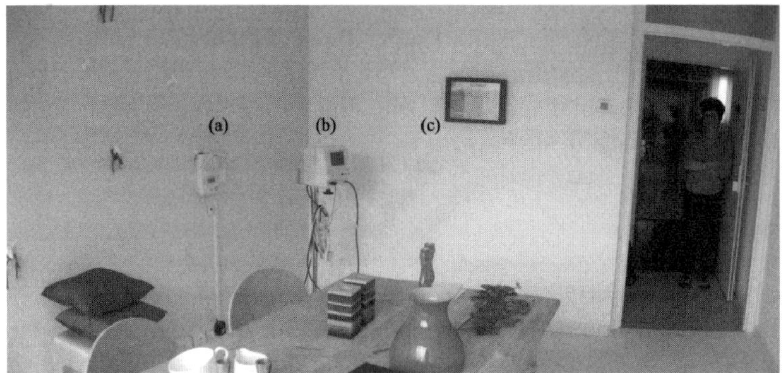

Fig. 1. Demonstration room with smart home technology: (a) Alarm unit; (b) Telemedicine monitoring system; (c) Touch screen with electronic patient file

In the study by Kearns et al. [14] the perspectives of 6 focus groups, including elderly nursing home residents, volunteer caregivers, care staff, medical surgical staff, and engineers, were combined to find requirements of elopement management systems. Although all focus groups agreed on the use of a non-stigmatizing device to attach to a wanderer (an inconspicuous device should, for instance, resemble a necklace or a watch), there was a different perception on the use of an implanted "tracking chip". The elderly focus group was less reluctant towards using an implanted chip than expected. When privacy and ethics were brought up by the researcher, it was quickly diminished as secondary. Apparently safety and independence are more important to elderly people than privacy. Kearns et al. refer to this as the liberating role of technology.

In a study by Willems [15] both elderly people and caregivers were asked to interpret the smart home technology available in a demonstration facility. One of the rooms of the demonstration facility is depicted in Fig. 1. The study showed that caregivers are more focussed on safety and security technology that may prevent harm and injuries, while elderly people are more eager to agree on care technology. Although the elderly subjects found an alarm unit useful for safety issues, they did not believe it would be necessary for them. This finding can be explained by the negative stigmatizing association that seems to overrule the positive safety effect of an alarm unit. On the other hand, elderly people are willing to hand in some of their privacy in order to facilitate the care giving process. Caregivers only agreed on the technology when they were sure the care receivers fully accepted the technology.

There is clearly a different interpretation between caregivers and care receivers in how smart home technology can be helpful supporting independent living of elderly people. While "implantables" seem accepted by the elderly, caregivers as well as researchers [16] believe that even more common technology applications likethe use of cameras for remote monitoring of people with mental disabilities is ethically not acceptable. Caregivers should realise that in situations where cameras are used to increase the safety and independence of the mentally disabled, care receivers will probably agree on the use of cameras despite the loss of privacy. The lack of concern about privacy might be ascribed to technological and social developments, such as cell phone networks, cameras in public spaces, blogs and home videos on the world wide web, and reality television shows like "Big Brother". Privacy is becoming a global good, and in some situations less relevant than safety.

Another explanation for the different perceptions between caregivers and care receivers, may be the fact that caregivers have certain habits that do not always correspond to the clients' needs [17]. As the care giving process often does not involve technology use, caregivers may react quite reluctant towards the implementation of smart home technology, and its accompanying procedures. This preference for care giving in the way people are accustomed to irrespective of care receivers' needs, does also apply to situations in which technology is used. Patient lifts, for instance, are often used in situations where clients actually do not need a lift yet [18]. Apparently caregivers accept those technologies they are accustomed to in care giving situations. These technologies, however, are often prescribed by protocols in which the labour conditions are set, which are rigidly applied to all situations (independent of client needs). Caregivers should better deviate from routines and make use of only those technologies, including new ones, that serve the needs of the care receiver. To implement smart home technology properly, caregivers have to become aware of their habits by analysing their perceptions and their way of acting.

Studies on technology perceptions of caregivers and care receivers are important to understand the acceptance of smart home technology, although these perceptions may change over time, due to experience. In the study by Willems [15] the answers were given in foresight: respondents were asked to reply on a situation which they were not yet familiar with. Answers may therefore be different than if respondents are living in a smart home, or have to work with the technology in a care setting. A passive alarm, for example, a basic functionality in many smart homes in the Dutch "Vitaal Grijs" program, appeared not to be as effective as expected before implementation [19]. On the basis of (negative) user experiences the functionality was disabled or removed in most houses. This indicates a difference between expected benefit and experienced benefit. But also questions like "willingness to pay for", as in the study by Willems [15], may result in responses different than can be expected on the basis of actual purchases and use. In case of an active alarm unit, elderly people are reluctant towards buying the technology, as initial costs are relatively high while benefits are unknown. After (effective) use people appear to judge this technology and its costs positively, as the usefulness becomes obvious (see [20] on the role of usefulness in technology acceptance).

4   Perceptual Differences on Requirements between Designers and Care Receivers

A design engineer of smart home technology for older care receivers should be able to understand the needs and wishes of the users. The designer, however, has to deal

Fig. 2. The room controller allows you to control lighting, room temperature, and television, for example. This room controller is negatively evaluated by both care receivers and caregivers, mainly due to poor legibility [15].

with a potentially technofobic user but also with an older user. The process of aging brings along many limitations or disabilities that are difficult to imagine for a non-limited and non-disabled designer. During a symposium [21] this gap was described as: "young males have to design technology for old females". Although the emphasis should not be so much on the gender difference, the age difference is truly a relevant factor [22]. As described earlier, aging often brings along changes in vision, hearing, attention, and memory. Additionally, physical disabilities due to rheumatoid arthritis or paralyses due to a Cardiovascular Accident (CVA) happen more and more often. Designing technology considering an average adolescent would not be very useful in this case, as an adolescent differs strongly from an elderly person on these physical factors. In case of sound-signals, for example, the designer must be aware of the fact that elderly people can not or hardly hear sounds of 2000Hz and above. Also, no robust actions should be needed for handling the devices, and no difficult procedures should be required. Buttons have to be larger, symbols or texts should be well-legible, and thus larger, due to decreased vision. An example of such designer/user gap is found in Fig. 2 that shows a room controller with poor usability. The design of the interface does not correspond with the abilities and expectations of the (elderly) user. The LCD screen, for example, is difficult to read, due to bad illumination and low contrasts. The use of both sides of the device as buttons is not in correspondence with intuitive use, which is important particularly for elderly users, as they have difficulties learning new skills. Depending on the limitations of the end-user, the design requirements should be altered, in favor of the user (see for example [23] on design principles for elderly). Although all design principles may be relevant when designing for the older care receiver, the consequences of their limitations for the design obviously depend on the intended functionality, and should therefore be considered separately for each technological design.

A solution to the difficulties elder care receivers experience when using (smart home) technology may be found in "inclusive design", "design for all", or "universal design". Designers of technology for the elderly have been requested for inclusive design by gerontologists for quite some time [24, 25]. Inclusive design implies that older and disabled people are part of the potential user groups in all product development processes. The design for older (and disabled) people, however, requires special attention for their needs and abilities. We may question whether designing for "all", including the elderly and the disabled, is useful and appealing to a young non-limited person. We believe it is more important that the designer of new technology takes into account those needs and wishes of the user he is designing for. This design process, however, should not only focus on the technological usability specifications, as Nielsen proposes in his user-centered design [26]. As in scenario-based models [27, 28], the technology should be viewed from different approaches. However, it should concern an iterative process in which not only the expectations people have of the technology and its interaction with their environment are taken into account, but also their eventual experiences with the technology. We expect best results when the design process involves all relevant stakeholders, at several stages of the process.

5   Perceptual Differences on Functionality between Designers and Caregivers and Relatives

The design engineer, or technician, clearly believes in the functionality of the technology. The other stakeholders, in most cases, rely on the designer's knowledge and promises. This may result, however, in expectations that are too high. The study by Raappana et al. [8], for example, shows that relatives and caring family members were satisfied with the technology, as they had the feeling that the safety of their relative was secured. One of the problems caregivers saw in the interaction between caring family members and the technology, is that they relied more on the technology that was actually possible. Relatives should be informed that the technologies cannot replace all health monitoring, while technicians should be honest about the (im)possibilities of technology [10].

Another barrier designers experience with caregivers is the so called *not invented here syndrome* [18,29]. The fact that the technology is not solely designed for care purposes, or that is designed for another care institution is often used as a reason not to accept the technology in the care professional's own organization. Care institutions however should better be open to knowledge of, and experience with technologies used in other places in order to learn from it and make better (smart home system) decisions.

6   Analyses of Multidisciplinary Stakeholders' Perceptions

To decrease the perceptual differences between the stakeholders, we propose an analysis of the expected and experienced effects (E-E Analysis) of smart home technology in care situations for each group. This means we are not only aiming at effects in relation to "effectiveness" - is the technology doing what it is supposed to do? - but also effects on the relationship between caregiver and care receiver, effects on the well-being of the client, on the nature of care giving, and matters like privacy, safety, security, and many more [18].

We are not only dealing with a gap between perceptions of various stakeholders, but also a difference between technological possibilities, related expectations, and the eventual use of the technology. The expectations and the actual use, including the subjective evaluations of the use, differ along the stakeholders and should be taken into account for successful implementation of smart home technology. This is why the analysis should include the expected and experienced effects of smart home technology of each stakeholder. The survey of these effects on all levels requires a multidisciplinary vision on this issue.

For the E-E analysis of effects the attribute-consequence-value *(A-C-V) model* [30] can be used, to get to higher and lower level effects. Attributes relate to aspects of the product or service, like functionality and design, on a very basic level. Consequences concern the functional and psychological effects of the technology, e.g. technology acceptance, while values resemble higher order merits, such as goals. The next step is to survey these attributes, consequences and values for each stakeholder involved. It is important to analyze the different layers of the technology, ranging from the functionality of the system to the behavior of people. While the designer may only be looking at the functionality, and whether or not the technology functions right, the user is interested in lower level effects, like the usability of the interface or the effect of the environment on the technology and vice versa.

To increase the acceptance and use of smart home technology, the technology should fit into the daily routines of users and end-users. The designer must be aware that his design determines how the technology intervenes with the orderliness of life-supporting everyday activities. The design of the technology may have an impact on timeliness, reliability, dependability, safety, and security [6]. Cheverst et al. propose a full user needs assessment, to analyze how the (end)user interacts with the technology from a psychological, emotional, physical, and social perspective. Also broader social and ethical effects of the technology should be identified and taken into account by the designer. As long as there are difficulties with the acceptance of smart home technology, the designer must consider an iterative design process [31], in which problem specification, matching the system to the real world, and the evaluation are an ongoing process [6]. The analysis of the effects should thus include a user-technology interaction assessment on a daily routine scale.

The E-E analysis thus displays possible mismatches between stakeholders as well as between expected and experienced effects. The implementation of a passive alarm, as mentioned earlier [19], is a good example of these differences between stakeholders and expectations and experiences. Care receivers expected great usefulness of a passive alarm, as it would give them feelings of safety and security. Their experiences after implementation, however, were feelings of insecurity and unreliability due to a high amount of false alarms. A false alarm is generated when elderly people forget to turn the switch in their house to indicate whether people are home or not. The - misplaced - expectation of the design engineer and the caregivers was that care receivers would be able to learn this new routine. By taking all of the effects into account in an iterative smart home design process, the design would better not contain a switch that needs action by an elderly user. A more valuable and less preferred solution that was chosen in the "Vitaal Grijs" project, however, was to disable or remove the technology [19].

The E-E analysis can not only be made by taken into account the expected effects on each stakeholder, but also by actually including the (end)users in the design process. Several studies have focussed on involving caregivers or elderly care receivers in the designing process [22]. In specially built user centers, user experiences can be tested beforehand, in the prototyping phase [32,33]. Another method occasionally applied is the use of drama [34]. These time-consuming processes, however, become less urgent when designers are aware of the perceptual world of caregivers and care receivers.

Analyzing the expected and experienced effects of smart home technology for each stakeholder involved, leads to better insight into human-technology interactions, which will result in better choices in the design process and system development. The possibility that the technology will not be accepted by the (end)users decreases, which will cut down expenses. At the end, the analysis may lead to the development of standardization in smart home technology. The downside of the analysis are the extra work and initial costs involved, although this will be compensated by the increase in technology acceptance. As the benefits of the investment are unclear until later, the return of investments appears negative at first. This is also the reason why care organisations are quit reluctant towards large-scale implementation of smart home technology. The initial costs of the technology and the organisational changes are relatively high, while the benefits (reduction in workload and costs) only become obvious after even more investments (increased workload). Additionally, we may also question whether elderly care receivers as well as caregivers actually know what is best for them. The latter implies that a multidisciplinary view, by combining all stakeholders' perceptions is crucial for effective smart home technology implementation.

7   Discussion

To decrease the perceptual differences between the stakeholders, we proposed an analysis of the expected and experienced effects of smart home technology (E-E Analysis) in care situations for each group. For designers the effects will involve effective goals, caregivers are mainly interested in effects on workload and quality of care, while care receivers are influenced by usability effects. It is not the case that technological possibilities are insufficient to solve the problems with smart home technology in care situations. Actually, on a technological level even more is possible than is yet applied in so called "smart" technology. Maybe the problem lays more or less in the functionalities of smart home technology that do not correspond to the actual needs of the care receivers or caregivers. Even though many researchers have stated that user requirements should be taken more into account in smart home projects, much technology development is driven by technological possibilities (technology push). The actual users obviously need to get involved in the development and implementation process of smart home technology. By involving the care receiver and the caregiver in the process, the designer may gain more insight into the true perceptions of the stakeholders he or she is designing for. As a result, the list of functional requirements for a smart home system or a smart home project must consist of more than just technological functionalities, and should comprise all stakeholders' attributes, consequences, and values. Finally, stakeholders should not only be aware of the expected effects, but also of the actual experienced effects, which may influence the list of requirements.

References

1. Provincie Utrecht: Wonen-Welzijn-Zorg: Behoefteontwikkeling en Aanbod in Gemeenten, 2003-2020 Housing-Welfare-Care: Supply and Demand Development in Communities, 2003-2020. Companen, Arnhem (2003)
2. Raad voor de Volksgezondheid en Zorg: Arbeidsmarkt en Zorgvraag Labour Market and Care Demand: Advies Uitgebracht door de Raad voor de Volksgezondheid en Zorg aan de Minister en Staatssecretaris van Volksgezondheid, Welzijn en Sport. RVZ, Raad voor de Volksgezondheid & Zorg, Den Haag (2006)
3. Rogers, W., Cabrera, E., Walker, N., Gilbert, D., Fisk, A.: A Survey of Automatic Teller Machine Usage across the Adult Life Span. Human Factors: The Journal of the Human Factors and Ergonomics Society 38, 156–166 (1996)
4. Dyck, J., Smithers, J.: Age Differences in Computer Anxiety: the Role of Computer Experience, Gender and Education. Journal of Educational Computing research 10, 239–248 (1994)
5. Czaja, S., Charness, N., Fisk, A., Hertzog, C., Nair, S., Rogers, W., Sharit, J.: Factors Predicting the Use of Technology: Finding from the Center for Research and Education on Aging and Technology Enhancement (CREATE). Psychology and Aging 21, 333–352 (2006)
6. Cheverst, K., Clarke, K., Dewsbury, G., Hemmings, T., Hughes, J., Rouncefield, M.: Design with Care: Technology, Disability and the Home. In: Harper, R. (ed.) Inside the Smart Home, pp. 163–179. Springer, London (2003)
7. Eyck, A.: Domotica in Senioren Woningen. Zijn Ouderen Bereid deze Nieuwe Voorzieningen te Accepteren en Zijn ze ook in Staat om ze te Gebruiken? [Smart Home Technology in Adapted Homes. Are Elderly Prepared to Accept these New Facilities and are They Able to Use Them?] Maastricht University, Maastricht (2004)
8. Raappana, A., Rauma, M., Melkas, H.: Impact of safety alarm systems on care personnel. Gerontechnology 6, 112–117 (2007)
9. Lyons, S., Tripp-Reimer, T., Sorofman, B., DeWitt, J., BootsMiller, B., Vaughn, T., Doebbeling, B.: VA QUERI Informatics Paper: Information Technology for Clinical Guideline Implementation: Perceptions of Multidisciplinary Stakeholders. Journal of the American Medical Informatics Association 12, 64–71 (2005)

10. Nouws, H., Sanders, L.: Monitoring Toekomst Thuis. Eerste Tussenrapportage: Leerervaringen Voorbereidingsfase [Monitoring Future Home. The First Interim Report: Experiences of the Preparation Phase]. De Vijfde Dimensie, Amersfoort (2007)
11. Smart Homes: Evaluatieonderzoek Woonzorgcomplex "Rozenhof II" te Velden en Woonzorgcomplex "De Waag" te Arcen [Smart Homes: Evaluation Research Sheltered Housing "Rozenhof II" in Velden and Sheltered Housing "De Waag" in Arcen]. Smart Homes, Eersel (2004)
12. van de Leeuw, J.: Veilig en Comfortabel Wonen met Domotica. Beschrijving en Analyse van Vraaggestuurde Domoticaprojecten in de Ouderenhuisvesting [Safe and Comfortable Living with Smart Home Technology. Description and Analysis of Demand Driven Smart Home Projects in Housing for the Elderly]. IWZ, Utrecht (2005)
13. Becker, H.: Hans Becker, Bestuursvoorzitter Humanitas: Leverancier van Geluk [Hans Becker, Chairman of Humanitas: Supplier of Luck]. Zorg + Welzijn Magazine 3 (2006)
14. Kearns, W., Rosenberg, D., West, L., Applegarth, S.: Attitudes and Expectations of Technologies to Manage Wandering Behavior in Persons with Dementia. Gerontechnology 6, 89–101 (2007)
15. Willems, C.: Evaluatie van de Demonstratiefaciliteit Domotica [Evaluation of the Demonstration Facility Domotics]. Gerealiseerd door De Erkenkamp. iRv, Hoensbroek (2007)
16. van Berlo, A.: Ethics in Domotics. Gerontechnology 3, 170 (2005)
17. Bussemaker, J.: Zorg voor Ouderen: Om de Kwaliteit van het Bestaan [Care for the Elderly: For the Quality of Life]. Ministerie van VWS, pp. 1–9 (2007)
18. Soede, M., de Witte, L.: Inaugurale Redes. Uitgesproken bij de Installatie als Lectoren Technologie in de Zorg aan de Hogeschool Zuyd, [Inaugural Speeches. Delivered at the Appointment as Lecturers Technology in Care at the Hogeschool Zuyd. Technologie in de Zorg / Hogeschool Zuyd], Heerlen (2007)
19. Bosch, A., van Daal, P., Dorrestein, A.: Thuis met Domotica. De Ervaringen van Ouderen in Zes Brabantse Domoticaprojecten. [Home with Domotics. The Experiences of Elderly People in Six Regional Projects] PON, Tilburg (2002)
20. Melenhorst, A.-S.: Adopting Communication Technology in Later Life. The Decisive Role of Benefits. J.F. Schouten School for User-System Interaction Research, Technische Universiteit Eindhoven, Eindhoven (2002)
21. Verweij, R.: Symposium ter Gelegenheid van de Inaugurele Rede van [Symposium on the Occasion of the Inaugural Speech of] dr. L. de Witte en dr. M. Soede, dd, Hogeschool Zuyd, Maastricht (June 21, 2007)
22. Hawthorn, D.: Enhancing the Contributions of Older People in Interface Design. Gerontechnology 5, 4–15 (2006)
23. Fisk, A., Rogers, W., Charness, N., Czaja, S., Sharit, J.: Designing for Older Adults: Principles and Creative Human Factors Approaches. CRC Press, Boca Raton (2004)
24. Newell, A.: Older People as a Focus for Inclusive Design. Gerontechnology 4, 190–199 (2006)
25. Whitney, G., Keith, S.: Active Ageing through Universal Design. Gerontechnology 5, 125–128 (2006)
26. Nielsen, J.: Usability Engineering. Morgan Kaufmann, San Diego (1993)

27. Rosson, M., Carroll, J.: Scenario-based Design. In: Jacko, J., Sears, A. (eds.) The Human-Computer Interaction Handbook: Fundamentals, Evolving Technologies and Emerging Applications, pp. 1032–1050. Lawrence Erlbaum Associates, Inc., Mahwah (2002)
28. Marzano, S.: The Culture of Ambient Intelligence. In: Aarts, E., Encarnaçäo, J. (eds.) True Visions. The Emergence of Ambient Intelligence, pp. 35–52. Springer, Berlin, Heidelberg (2006)
29. Kittz, It Cares, I&C Services Nederland: ICT in de Care 2004-2006. Ministerie van VWS, Woerden/Groningen, pp. 1–26 (2004)
30. Chiu, C.-M.: Applying Means-End Chain Theory to Eliciting System Requirements and Understanding Users Perceptual Orientations. Information & Management 42, 455–468 (2005)
31. Clarkson, P., Keates, S.: A Practical Inclusive Design Approach. In: Proceedings of INCLUDE 2001, London, pp. 72–73 (2001)
32. Dewsbury, G., Dickinson, A.: Enabling and Applying Person-Centred Design for Older Adults. Gerontechnology 5, 56–57 (2006)
33. de Ruyter, B., Aarts, E., Markopoulos, P., IJsselsteijn, W.: Ambient Intelligence Research in HomeLab: Engineering the User Experience. In: Weber, W., Rabaey, J., Aarts, E. (eds.) Ambient Intelligence, pp. 49–62. Springer, Berlin, Heidelberg (2005)
34. McKenna, S., Marquis-Faulkes, F., Newell, A., Gregor, P.: Requirements Gathering Using Drama for Computer Vision-Based Monitoring in Supportive Home Environments. Gerontechnology 5, 29–45 (2006)

Enhancing Human Understanding through Intelligent Explanations

Tina Mioch[1,2], Maaike Harbers[1,2], Willem A. van Doesburg[2],
and Karel van den Bosch[2]

[1] Institute of Information and Computing Sciences, Utrecht University,
P.O.Box 80.089, 3508 TB Utrecht, The Netherlands
[2] TNO Defence, Security & Safety, Kampweg 5, 3796 DE Soesterberg,
The Netherlands
{tina.mioch,maaike.harbers, willem.vandoesburg,karel.vandenbosch}@tno.nl
http://www.tno.nl

Abstract. Ambient systems that explain their actions promote the user's
understanding as they give the user more insight in the effects of their
behavior on the environment. In order to provide individualized intelligent explanations, we need not only to evaluate a user's observable behavior, but we also need to make sense of the underlying beliefs, intentions
and strategies. In this paper we argue for the need of intelligent explanations, identify the requirements of such explanations, propose a method to
achieve generation of intelligent explanations, and report on a prototype in
the training of naval situation assessment and decision making. We discuss
the implications of intelligent explanations in training and set the agenda
for future research.

Keywords: Explanations, simulation-based training, intelligent tutoring systems, cognitive modeling, feedback, learning.

1 Introduction

Human well-being and performance are highly affected by the environment in
which a person operates. People are always trying to improve their conditions,
from increasing the temperature when it is cold to developing more and more advanced computer systems to aid them in their daily work. A recent development
in the enhancement of environments is the incorporation of mechanisms that
show some understanding of humans. Such mechanisms use sensors to acquire
information about human functioning and analyze this information to adapt
to human needs. An environment containing systems with these mechanisms is
called intelligent.

Some of the applications exposing such ambient intelligence require interaction
between the human user and the system. For example, decision-support systems
have to communicate their advice to the person who is in charge of making
a decision, and tutoring agents need to convey instructions and feedback to a
student. Human-system interaction has two sides: the system or agent has to

M. Mühlhäuser et al. (Eds.): AmI 2007 Workshops, CCIS 11, pp. 327–337, 2008.

transmit information to the human, but it also has to understand the human. An agent reminding elderly or disabled people to take their medicine not only has to convey this message, it must also be able to understand when someone says he or she has already taken the medicine. One of the requirements of good human-system interaction is that the human understands and accepts a system's message. The quality of interaction between the human and the system is an important factor in the endeavor to improve human comfort and performance.

We claim that one of the factors contributing to the quality of human-system interaction is intelligent explanation. Providing explanations along with presented information is not something new. Various explanation components have been developed in recent decades for software systems, such as intelligent tutoring systems, decision-support systems and expert systems [8,4,9,12]. It is supposed that the more these explanations are tailored to the specific needs of the user, the better the user is served. A system could make distinctions between users on the basis of their knowledge, speed of learning, most efficient learning method, preferences, etc. Most of the existing explaining components do not take features of the specific user into account, but treat all users in the same way.

In this paper we will clarify that in order to improve the effectiveness of explanations, systems should be equipped with capacities that refer to the users' mistakes, performance, beliefs, knowledge, intents and the like in their explanations. First we will take a closer look at agent explanation in ambient systems: what are the requirements to make an explanation useful, and what type of explanations can be distinguished? Then we will discuss how such an explanation mechanism can be implemented in a feedback system of a simulation-based training environment.

2   Intelligent Explanations

Most people take the information on a digital clock for granted; there is no need for further explanation about the current time. However, a user is not always sufficiently informed by such basic information. Even though a system may be correct in stating 'It is time to buy a new computer', this announcement might raise some questions. He or she wants to know why the computer believes this; is the computer too outdated for its purpose, or is the computer broken? If so, it would be interesting to know what part is not functioning and whether there are possibilities to update or repair the computer. This example shows that in some cases it is not sufficient if a system just presents its conclusion. An accompanying useful explanation will make more sense to the human user and it will increase both the human's understanding and acceptance of the system [20,21].

Explanations exist in many forms. Furthermore, one single event can be explained in different ways. One explanation is not by definition better then another; the desired explanation depends on the context in which it is given. For example, a possible answer to the question 'Why did the apple fall?' is 'Because I dropped it'. In some situations however, the explanations 'Because I stumbled' or 'Because he pushed me' would be more useful. A whole other type of explanation of why the apple fell is 'Because of the gravitation force'. Dependent on the context, people need a particular type of explanation. An explanation system should be able to estimate the information need of the user and provide an explanation accordingly.

Another difficulty to overcome in providing explanations is *timing* [20]. In some applications it is obvious that each time new information is presented it should be accompanied by an explanation. For instance in diagnosis systems, every given diagnosis should be accompanied by an explanation of how the system came to this result. In contrast, in systems that constantly provide new information, there are no predefined moments in which explanations should be given. For instance, a navigation system has to decide for itself when the user needs new instructions. So in a complex and open environment, an explanation system should be able to determine when and how often the user needs explanations.

Furthermore it is desirable that explanations are adapted to the receiver, as not all people are the same and thus might need different explanations. Whereas novices tend to need extensive explanations, experts generally prefer explanations in which the to them obvious steps are skipped [17]. Besides level of expertise, other human factors such as knowledge, intents and emotions could be taken into account. An explanation commenting on an assumed strategy of a student could be: 'Because you performed action a_1, I think your plan must be P. This is not a good strategy because you do not have enough resources to perform action a_3, which is also part of plan P'. An explanation involving emotions is: 'The other agents acted this way, because your angry words scared them'. Hence, intelligent explanations should be adapted to the user's perspective to enhance understanding and learning.

3   Related Work

In the past twenty years, much research has been done on intelligent tutoring systems (ITS) [14,13,4], which are systems that teach students how to solve a problem or execute a task by giving explanations. Such systems have been successfully designed for the training of well-structured skills and tasks (e.g. LISP programming [11] or algebra [10]), which are relatively closed, involve little indeterminacy, and do not involve real-time planning. For the training of real world tasks, these conditions do not always apply [1]. Real world tasks are often complex, dynamic and open in the sense that outcomes of actions may be unpredictable. These features make it difficult to design training, because it is usually not possible to represent the domain by a small number of rules. Moreover, the space of possible actions is large. For instance, the military uses simulation-based training systems to train tactical command and control [2]. In such training, the student responds in real-time to simulated problems, so the system needs to be able to evaluate whether the actions taken are correct and whether they have been executed at the right time. A complicating characteristic of evaluating tactical performance is that there is often no single 'right' way to accomplish a task, but that there exists more than one good solution for a problem, depending on the context [3]. In addition, a training system should not only evaluate a student's behavior, but, in case of errors, it should also take cognitive processes underlying that behavior into account. The result should be suitable for inferring the student's strategy. The demands on context-sensitivity and performance diagnosis make it hard to generate appropriate feedback.

In recent years, the challenge of developing and providing explanations in open, complex and dynamic environments has been accepted by the international research community [7,15,5] and first steps forward have been made. Livak, Heffernan and Moyer [7] developed a prototype that uses a cognitive model to provide both tutoring and computer generated forces capabilities. The actions of the student are evaluated by comparing the student's behavior to the ideal behavior of an expert. If the student deviates from the behavior that the expert model demonstrates, feedback is returned to the student. The feedback that is given is a low-level explanation of why the particular action at that moment was not correct. The explanations only refer to a particular action, and no reference to consequences of actions are given. Furthermore, the tutoring agent does not maintain a model of the user to take his beliefs and intentions into account. As a consequence, the tutoring agent is not capable of adjusting its feedback to the specific knowledge and intentions of the student.

Other research focuses on the debriefing phase of the training by letting the simulation entities explain their reasons for executing particular actions to the student. Examples of this approach are the explanation system *Debrief* [8] and the *XAI system* [9]. Debrief is used to generate explanations for the individual agent's actions in the debriefing phase of the simulation, together with information about what factors were critical for taking that action. The XAI System allows the student to further investigate what happened during the exercise. In order to generate explanations, the software agents log important actions annotated with abstract information about underlying reasons of the actions as well as their consequences. Both Debrief and XAI explain the reasoning behind the executed actions on demand, expecting the student to ask the relevant questions. No assessment of the student is made, so no directed feedback can be given to the student. In addition, the explanations are directly related to knowledge about the task, giving a low-level reason for a particular action. For example, for the task of clearing a room, an agent might answer the question 'Why did you throw a grenade into a room?' by stating that 'A grenade suppresses enemies that are in the room'. It would be more informative for the student to give an explanation on a higher conceptual level, including e.g. beliefs and intentions of the agent. Such an explanation would for example be 'I believed that the enemy was in the room. My goal is to clear all rooms. By throwing grenades into the room, I intended to suppress the enemy'.

As can be seen, research on explanations has been recognized as being important in training simulations to enhance the student's learning experience. However, a lot of research is still required. Questions that still need answering are for example how to obtain insight into the cognitive processes of the student, and how to support students in acquiring an understanding of the relationships between their behavior and the consequences in the environment. To achieve understanding, explanations must be given about processes in the environment. However, as stated above, explanations in simulation-based training systems are often not profound enough to achieve this result.

4   Types of Feedback

When building simulation-based training systems, three types of feedback can be distinguished. They differ in the types of information that they take into account and the sophistication of explanations they give:

Result-based feedback: Feedback is based only on observable student behavior. Correct results, formulated by domain experts, are hard-coded into the scenario, and feedback is generated by comparing the student behavior with the correct behavior. The feedback states only whether the student has completed the task successfully, and if not, what the correct behavior should have been.

Model-based feedback: Feedback is not only based on explicit student behavior, but also on contextual knowledge of the simulation environment and explicit task knowledge. Using the different kinds of information, the feedback is generated by reasoning about an internal model.

Cognition-based feedback: As with model-based feedback, feedback is based on explicit student behavior, knowledge about the simulation environment and task knowledge. In addition, a user model is developed that makes it possible to infer cognitive strategies of the student to facilitate even better feedback.

We will illustrate how the types of feedback differ from each other in the context of a navy task, namely the tactical picture compilation task. Developing a

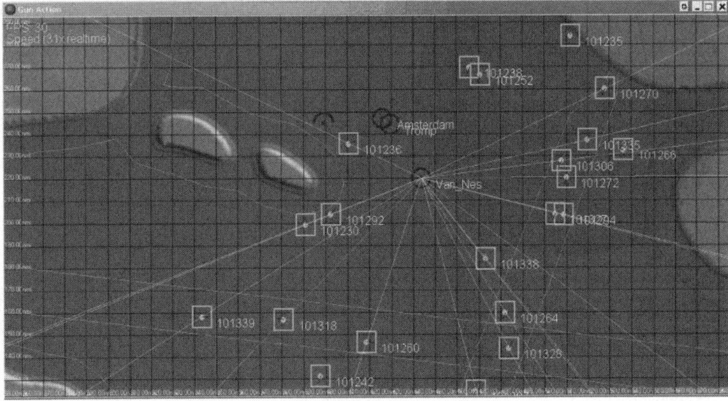

Fig. 1. Screenshot of our training scenario. The squares indicate radar tracks, the circles represent tracks of own forces.

tactical picture of the environment is an essential part of any military mission. In the tactical picture compilation task, the tracks in a radar picture have to be classified into categories such as the type of vessel, and the probable intention of the vessels has to be determined. An illustration of a situation in which a student has to develop a tactical picture can be seen in Fig. 1. Assuming that the student has to decide at a particular point in time which track poses the largest threat to the ship, the following examples of explanations illustrate the types of feedback that the system might give.

Result-based explanation. *Your answer is incorrect: You have chosen track 101304 as the most threatening track. It should have been track 101112.*

Model-based explanation. *The expert disagrees with your answer: You have chosen track 101304 as the most threatening track. However, its speed is not very high. Additionally, there are a number of ships that are moving at the same speed AND are closer to you. The expert thinks the most threatening track is 101112.*

Cognition-based explanation. *The expert disagrees with your answer: You have chosen track 101304 as the most threatening track. However, its speed is not very high. Additionally, there are a number of ships that are moving at the same speed AND are closer to you. The expert considers 101112 to be the most threatening track.*
You have assessed tracks coming from the harbors, probably because you might suspect the enemy to reside in the harbor. However, a good strategy is to start investigating close to your vessel and progress outward. We have not seen you do this in the scenarios you have played thus far. This tip should help you protect your ship by preventing enemy vessels to get too close unseen.

These examples illustrate that generating model-based explanations are the minimum requirement for *intelligent* explanations. Cognition-based explanations are the most sophisticated and would be the type of explanations from which a student learns the most. For that reason, our goal is to build a training system that generates cognition-based explanations.

5   Intelligent Tutoring Agent for the Royal Netherlands Navy

For the Royal Netherlands Navy we investigate the possibility of developing an agent that fulfills the task of an instructor in a training simulation. We focus on the functionality of evaluating student performance and deliver this evaluation along with an explanation. The task that is chosen is a modification of the tactical picture compilation task as described in Sect. 4. In the modified task, the student is presented with a radar picture at a particular point in time, showing a number of radar tracks. The student has to gather and integrate information on these tracks to form a mental tactical picture of the situation. Then the student has to decide which track poses the largest threat to his own ship. Time does not play a role as the picture is static and represents a situation at a particular point in time. Factors in this task that have to be taken into account are for example the speed of vessels, distance from own ship, whether they adhere to shipping lanes and whether they are inbound.

We are developing a training system that uses cognition-based explanations. To meet this objective, the following method is introduced. To generate feedback, an expert agent is executed, as are agents that deviate in some aspect from the expert, representing typical mistakes of students. These deficient agents intentionally fail to take one or more particular factors of the task environment into account, or are deficient in another way. It is assumed that errors of the student are the result of incorrect beliefs or an incorrect strategy. The assessment the student makes of the situation after examining the screenshot is compared to the assessment of the expert and the deficient agents. Four outcomes of the comparison can be differentiated.

First, the assessment of the student might not correspond to either the expert's assessment or to any of the deficient agents' assessments. In that case, the student did not complete the task satisfactorily nor did he make a typical mistake represented by any of the deficient agents. An explanation is then generated that explains why the assessment of the expert is preferable to the assessment of the student based on the comparison between the two performances and on task knowledge. This includes for example knowledge about the environment and knowledge about the importance of different relevant factors.

Second, the assessment of the student corresponds to the assessment of the expert agent, and to none of the assessments of the deficient agents. In this case, it is assumed that the student has solved the task satisfactorily, and accordingly, positive feedback is returned. As the environment is open, it is of course possible that the student's assessment to the problem is correct, but that the student has just been lucky, without the assessment being based on correct beliefs and a correct process of obtaining the assessment. However, over several trials of the training simulation, the incorrect strategy of the student will eventually fail and the student will then receive a feedback that shows that his beliefs are wrong.

Third, the student's assessment might correspond to the assessment of one particular deficient agent, without matching the expert agent or any other deficient agent. As it is assumed that the deficiency of the agent corresponds to the beliefs or strategies of the student, a diagnosis of the student's state of mind can be made and an explanation be generated. The explanation that is returned corresponds to the deficiency of the agent.

Fourth, it is possible that the student's assessment corresponds to several assessments, either of several deficient agents, or one or more deficient agents and the expert agent. This is possible because there are often many possible ways to arrive at the same assessment. Then, the response alone is not sufficient for deciding what feedback is appropriate. We need information about the processes that resulted in the selection of that response and which beliefs and strategies the student used to obtain his response. If we can do this validly, then we can return feedback containing an appropriate explanation. In this case, the user model is of importance, because it gives extra background information about the process that led to the assessment. On the basis of the inferred beliefs and strategies of the student, it is possible to choose the most corresponding of the matching assessments and return the appropriate explanation.

Our prototype does not yet take performance over time into account. In reality, the history of the situation should be used in situation assessment. For example, an apparently non threatening radar track (taking only properties such as, speed, distance, bearing and adherence to shipping lanes into account) may in fact be highly suspect because it has recently varied its speed and has intermittently crossed the shipping lane. A student that is sensitive to this information correctly assesses this track as threatening. A system that cannot use such information may then, erroneously, 'correct' the student and thus fault the student for his judgment even though the student actually outperforms the expert model. Such problems are typical for evaluating performance in complex, dynamic and open tasks. To overcome these problems, it is more useful not to evaluate the assessments of a student but the cognitive strategies that have led to the assessment.

A problem is that cognitive strategies are not observable. We are faced with the problem to construct a user model containing hypotheses about the strategies of the student without the ability to observe these strategies. We choose to overcome this problem by arranging the training simulation in such a way that the user is forced to provide some information about his strategy. We achieve this by allowing the student access to all information that is available in the actual operational environment, but only on explicit request of the student. For example, by initially hiding the shipping lanes and allowing these to be seen for a short period of time we gain evidence that the student is checking adherence to shipping lanes. By observing the pattern of behavior while the student is executing the task, we can build a hypothesis of the strategy that the student employs. Moreover, we can test the hypothesis by selecting a subsequent scenario and predicting the steps that the student will take. If the hypothesis is confirmed, we can then confidently proceed in providing feedback on the strategy level rather than on the performance level. In addition, it enables us to select those scenarios that practice the particular aspect which the student finds difficult. Because the user model is taken into account, the feedback is based on the perceived process of decision-making of the student, which includes an interpretation of the student's actions. By giving an explanation that has relevance to the student's actions and underlying beliefs, acceptance and understanding of the feedback are endorsed.

6   Discussion

In this paper we argued for the importance of intelligent explanations in human-system interaction. We clarified why explanations should be user-specific and what aspects should be taken into account in order to achieve this. There are different ways to generate model-based or cognition-based feedback; we use a method of modeling the user, an expert agent and deficient agents. The behavior of the user is compared to that of the agents. We argue that the results of such comparisons in combination with the user model yield insights about the user which make it possible to provide explanations fit to the particular user.

As mentioned before, we are currently implementing our method of explanation generation in a training system for the Royal Netherlands Navy. Once the system is ready, we will evaluate whether the explanations generated by the proposed method will improve the users' performances. We aim to extend the method to other situations and to apply it to more complex versions of the task, for example involving a time component, and to other tasks than tactical picture compilation. Therefore the expert model, the user model and the deficient agents need to be adapted to the new demands. Despite these changes and modifications, the core mechanism of the approach remains the same. So if the explanations are satisfying in the simple case, we are confident that the system is able to generate intelligent explanations in more complex versions of the task and other tasks as well.

A system providing the desired intelligent explanations referring to knowledge, plans, intentions and the like will yield many advantages. First, good explanations will help the user in his or her learning process, because they will improve conceptual understanding [18]. Besides this advantage while learning the task, good explanations prolong the duration of an acquired skill [16]. A practical advantage is the reduction of training costs. When systems are able to generate human-like explanations, fewer instructors are needed to complete training and this will save costs. The usual weighing between costs and quality no longer has to be made. Finally, because students are no longer dependent on the presence of a trainer, they are more flexible and can train a task whenever they want.

In future research, it could be investigated how expert and deficient agents can be modeled more efficiently. Especially a practical way of modeling deficient agents is useful, because in complex tasks many of them are needed. For this, the behavior of real students can be used. Also the relation between different deficiencies could be examined: what behavior does a user with a combination of different deficiencies show and how is this reflected in the modeled deficient agents? Further, more attention could be paid to the presentation of explanations: which way of presenting leads to the highest performance? It could also be investigated for what type of tasks the intelligent explanations turn out to be the most useful.

Acknowledgements. This research has been supported by the GATE project, funded by the Netherlands Organization for Scientific Research (NWO) and the Netherlands ICT Research and Innovation Authority (ICT Regie) and by the research programs "Cognitive Modelling" (V524) and "Integrated Training and Instruction" (V406), funded by the Netherlands defence organisation.

References

1. Zachary, W., Cannon-Bowers, J., Bilazarian, P., Krecker, D., Lardieri, P., Burns, J.: The Advanced Embedded Training System (AETS): An Intelligent Embedded Tutoring System for Tactical Team Training. International Journal of Artificial Intelligence in Education, 257–277 (1999)

2. van Doesburg, W.A., van den Bosch, K.: Cognitive Model Supported Tactical Training Simulation. In: Proceedings of the Fourteenth Conference on Behavior Representation in Modeling and Simulation (BRIMS). Universal City, CA, pp. 313–319 (2005)
3. Hutchins, S.G., Kemple, W.G., Porter, G.R., Sovereign, M.G.: Evaluating Human Performance in Command and Control Environments. In: Proceedings of the 1999 Command and Control Research and Technology Symposium, Newport, RI, pp. 50–52 (1999)
4. Murray, T.: Authoring Intelligent Tutoring Systems: An Analysis of the State of the Art. International Journal of Artificial Intelligence in Education 10, 98–129 (1999)
5. Ntuen, C.A., Balogun, O., Boyle, E., Turner, A.: Supporting Command and Control Training Functions in the Emergency Management Domain Using Cognitive Systems Engineering. Ergonomics 49, 1415–1436 (2006)
6. Murray, W.R.: Intelligent Tutoring Systems for Commercial Games: The Virtual Combat Training Center Tutor and Simulation. AIIDE, 66–71 (2006)
7. Livak, T., Heffernan, N.T., Moyer, D.: Using Cognitive Models for Computer Generated Forces and Human Tutoring. In: 13th Annual Conference on Behavior Representation in Modeling and Simulation(BRIMS), Simulation Interoperability Standards Organization, Arlington, VA (2004)
8. Lewis Johnson, W.: Agents that Learn to Explain Themselves. In: Proceedings of the Twelfth National Conference on Artifcial Intelligence, Seattle, Washington, United States, American Association for Artificial Intelligence, vol. 2, pp. 1257–1263 (1994)
9. Gomboc, D., Solomon, S., Core, M.G., Lane, H.C., van Lent, M.: Design Recommendations to Support Automated Explanation and Tutoring. In: Proceedings of the Fourteenth Conference on Behavior Representation in Modeling and Simulation (2005)
10. Koedinger, K.R., Anderson, J.R.: Illustrating Principled Design: The Early Evolution of a Cognitive Tutor for Algebra Symbolization. Interactive Learning Environments 5, 161–180 (1998)
11. Anderson, J.R., Conrad, F.G., Corbett, A.T.: Skill Acquisition and the LISP Tutor. Cognitive Science 13, 467–506 (1989)
12. Core, M.G., Traum, T., Lane, H.C., Swartout, W., Gratch, J., van Lent, M.: Teaching Negotiation Skills Through Practice and Reflection with Virtual Humans. Simulation 82(11), 685–701 (2006)
13. Psotka, J., Massey, D., Mutter, S. (eds.): Intelligent Tutoring Systems: Lessons Learned. Lawrence Erlbaum Associates, Hillsdale, NJ (1988)
14. Polson, M.C., Richardson, J.J.: Foundations of Intelligent Tutoring Systems. Lawrence Erlbaum Associates, Inc., Mahwah (1988)
15. Jensen, R., Nolan, M., Chen, D.Y.: Automatic Causal Explanation Analysis in Combined Arms Training AAR. In: Proceedings of the Interservice / Industry Training, Simulation, and Educational Conference (I/ITSEC) (2005)
16. van den Bosch, K.: Durable Competence in Procedural Tasks Through Appropriate Instruction and Training. In: Harris, D. (ed.) Engineering Psychology and Cognitive Ergonomics, Aldershot, Ashgate, vol. 3, pp. 431–438 (1999)
17. Ramberg, R.: Construing and Testing Explanations in a Complex Domain. Computers in Human Behavior 12(1), 29–47 (1996)
18. Teichert, M.A., Stacy, A.M.: Promoting Understanding of Chemical Bonding and Spontaneity through Student Explanation and Integration of Ideas. Journal of Research in Science Teaching 39(6), 464–496 (2002)

19. Morrison, P., Barlow, M.: Child's Play? Coercing a COTS Game into a Military Experimentation Tool. In: Proceedings of SimTecT 2004, Canberra, pp. 72–77 (2004)
20. Nakatsu, R.T.: Explanatory Power of Intelligent Systems: A Research Framework. In: Proceedings of the IFIP International Conference on Decision Support Systems, Prato, Italy, pp. 568–577 (2004)
21. Herlocker, J.L.: Position Statement - Explanations in Recommender Systems. In: Proceedings of the CHI 1999 Workshop, Pittsburgh, USA (1999)

Towards Natural Interaction by Enabling Technologies: A Near Field Communication Approach

Jose Bravo[1], Ramon Hervas[1], Salvador W. Nava[2], Gabriel Chavira[2],
and Carlos Sanchez[3]

[1] Castilla-La Mancha University, Paseo de la Universidad, 13071 Ciudad Real, Spain
`{jose.bravo,ramon.hlucas}@uclm.es`
[2] Autonomous University of Tamaulipas, Tampico-Madero, Mexico
`{snava,gchavira}@uat.edu.mx`
[3] CCNT: Calidad Concertada Nuevas Tecnologas, 28037 Madrid, Spain
`carlos.barba@ccnt-spain.com`

Abstract. The recent NFC technology is not only valid for payment and ticketing, a new interaction form is also available. With the only action being to put a mobile phone close to another NFC device (reader, tag or mobile phone) it is possible to get a contactless communication supported by a server or not. Some services such as open doors, location, access, presence, and so on, can be performed with a simple touch. In this work we analyze the interaction through the adaptability of two technologies: RFID and NFC. Challenges in models have been considered. In addition, we are trying to put in practice the idea of tagging context and the awareness only with a single interaction by touch. For that, we consider the benefits to adapting NFC technology as a good approach to model contexts.

1   Introduction

Ubiquitous Computing paradigm and, most recently, Ambient Intelligence (AmI), are the visions in which technology becomes invisible, embedded, present whenever we need it, enabled by simple interactions, attuned to all our senses and adaptive to users and contexts [1]. A further definition of AmI is as "an exciting new paradigm of information technology, in which people are empowered through a digital environment that is aware of their presence and context sensitive, adaptive and responsive to their needs, habits, gestures and emotions."

These visions promote the goals of: 1) embedding technology into everyday objects, 2) attaining effortless and closer interaction and finally 3) supporting a means for getting needed information anywhere and at anytime. This is our particular idea about Ubiquitous Computing, Natural Interfaces and Ubiquitous Communication. With them, the idea of creating intelligent environments requires unobtrusive hardware, wireless communications, massively distributed devices, natural interfaces and security. To attain this vision it is fundamental to analyze some definitions of the context. A. Dey defines this concept as "any information

M. Mühlhäuser et al. (Eds.): AmI 2007 Workshops, CCIS 11, pp. 338–351, 2008.

that can be used to characterize the situation of an entity. An entity is a person, place, or object that is considered relevant to the interaction between a user and an application, including the user and application themselves." [2]. Also, this author defines context awareness as the "context to provide relevant information and/or services to the user, where relevancy depends on the user's task".

In order to design context aware applications it is necessary to observe certain types of context-aware information as being more relevant than others [3]. The user profile and situation, that is, the identity-awareness (IAw), are essential. The relative location of people is location-awareness (LAw). Time-awareness (TAw) is another main type of context-awareness that should be taken into account. The task which the user carries out and everything he wants to do is transformed into Activity-awareness (AAw). Finally, Objective-Awareness (OAw) looks at why the user wants to carry out a task in a certain place. All these types of awareness answer the five basic questions ("Who", "Where", "What", "When" and "Why") which provide the guidelines for context modeling. This kind of information allows us to adapt or build the needed technology to disperse throughout the environment and to model the human behavioral support.

Once the context and its important features are defined, it is time to study new interaction forms proposing the approach to the user by means of more natural interfaces. On this point, Albrecht Schmidt proposes the Implicit Human Computer Interaction (iHCI) concept [4][5]. He defines it as "the interaction of a human with the environment and with artifacts, which is aimed to accomplish a goal. Within this process the system acquires implicit input from the user and may present implicit output to the user". Schmidt defines implicit input as user perceptions interacting with the physical environment, allowing the system to anticipate the user by offering implicit outputs. In this sense the user can concentrate on the task, not on the tool as Ubiquitous Computing Paradigm proposes. As a next step this author defines Embedded Interaction in two terms: Embedding technologies into artifacts, devices and environments and embedding interactions in the user activities (task or actions) [6].

This paper addresses the identification process as an implicit and embedded input to the system, perceiving the user's identity, his profile and other kinds of dynamic data. Then, a new technology and the context adaptability, the Near Field Communication technology (NFC), are presented. With it, proposed changes of the architecture, the model, the visualization of information and the interaction are exposed.

Under the next heading, we present the identification technologies as inputs, RFID and NFC, both with their corresponding models. In the following section, a way of tagging context and interaction by touching can be seen. The paper finishes with related works and conclusions.

2   Identification Technologies

With the ideas of context and their mentioned characteristics, we have considered some awareness features through two different technologies. We propose these approaches by the identification process. It is a specialized input to by means of identification process. This means that we have the knowledge about the user profile, the context information and the task. In the next section, we show RFID and NFC technologies with models that we propose while keeping in mind the aforementioned w's.

2.1 RFID (Radiofrequency Identification)

To create context-aware applications it is necessary to adapt sensorial capabilities to provide implicit inputs to the system in order to achieve natural interfaces closer to the users. With this the proactive aspect of the system is guaranteed. In RFID systems there are basically two elements:

Tags or transponders. Which consist of a microchip that stores data, and an antenna (coupling element), that are packaged in such a way that they can be installed in an object. They also have a unique series number.

Readers or interrogators. Have one or more antennas, which emit radio waves and receive signals back from the tag. The "interrogation" signal activates all the tags that are within its reach.

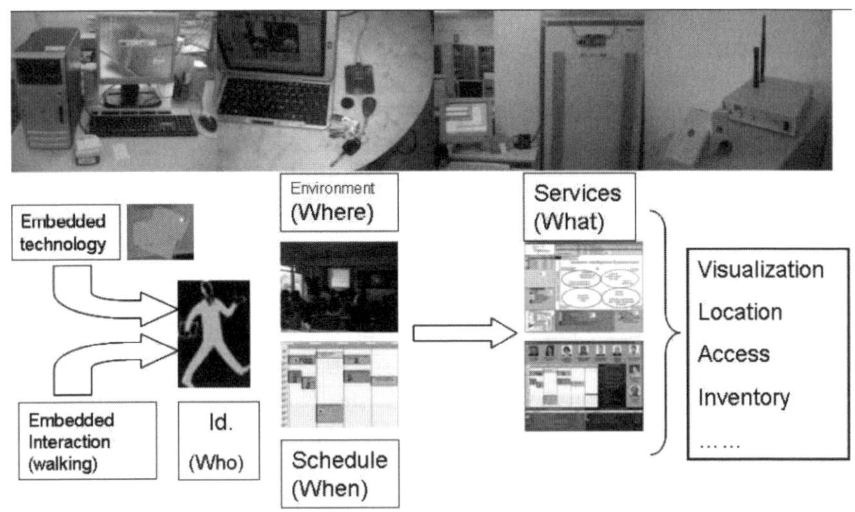

Fig. 1. RFID set and the "who" model

RFID systems are classified as active and according to the kind of tag used. In this work we use only active tags: they are those that have their own power supply (battery) with a reach of up to 100 m.

Readers have a frequency of operation and are usually divided into three basic ranges: Low (125Khz.), High (13.56 MHz), which is the standard one, and Ultra High Frequency (UHF).

At the top of Figure 1, some types of RFID devices that we have placed in different contexts can be seen. The first one on the left presents a contact reader which is an antenna with a reach of only 10 cm. A model of the tag is also shown. With it, a project in a hospital context has been developed. The second one is another contact RFID set only for identification. We have developed access control for an office, classroom and research laboratory. These systems are ideal for individual use. The next one is a reader and an antenna with a read-and-write capability reaching over 75 cm. This has been specially designed to be placed on doors, or near displays. It can read several labels simultaneously, when identifying people entering the room. Finally, we use another kind of RFID set, offering more distance be-tween reader and tags (up to 88 meters) working with UHF. The bottom of Figure 1 shows the model for this kind of sensorial specialized input. Embedding technology into daily objects and embedding interaction into daily actions, we perceive the context-awareness by the "who", "when" and "where" aspect obtaining "what". Typical services by identification are Access, Location, Inventory and so on, but we are interested in the Visualization service. With it, we try to offer information to the user in some parts of a mosaic. This way requires no user interaction according with the Ubiquitous Computing idea about not intrusion.

2.2 NFC (Near Field Communication)

It is obvious that we need a great variety of devices placed in the environment around us with wireless connection capabilities. Therefore, a new short-range wireless connectivity technology "Near Field Communications" (NFC), has appeared. Philips and Sony developed this technology in 2002. It is a combination of RFID and interconnection technologies.

NFC uses a high frequency band of up to 13.56 MHz, with a data transmission speed of 424 Kbits/s and a reach of 10 cm. It was deliberately designed to be compatible with the RFID tags operating in this band (ISO 14443), but incompatible with the standards of EPC global [10] . In 2002, international ECMA published the open standard 340 "NFC Interface and Protocol", which was adopted by ISO/IEC with the number 18092 one year later.

NFC systems consist of two elements:

Initiator. As its name indicates it begins and controls the information exchange (called reader in RFID); and

Target. The device that responds to the requirement of the initiator (called tag in RFID)

In an NFC system, there are two modes of operation: Active and Passive. In the active one, both devices generate their own field of radio frequency to transmit data (peer to peer). In the passive one, only one of these devices generates the radiofrequency field, while the other is used to load modulation for data transfers.

It is important to mention that, although the NFC protocol can be installed in any electronic device, our interest will be centered on NFC-enabled cell phones.

In this case, the model changes absolutely. While in the RFID one, the model combines the "who", "when" and "where" aspects, now there are some distinctions. The "when" aspect is not needed because is the user who decides when the action begins. In addition, another important feature is that users store the information needed to obtain services in their mobile phone. So, we can talk about a mode from a function of "who" and "what" (information) applying "where" to obtain "what" (services). This information in "what" is varied: pres-entation, note to comment, file to upload, etc.

3   Contextual Tags

When distributing context information throughout a building it is important to think about the specific place for every tag. A classification of everyone's position is needed to get services. So, the idea of context proposed by some authors has been considered when adapting input technologies.

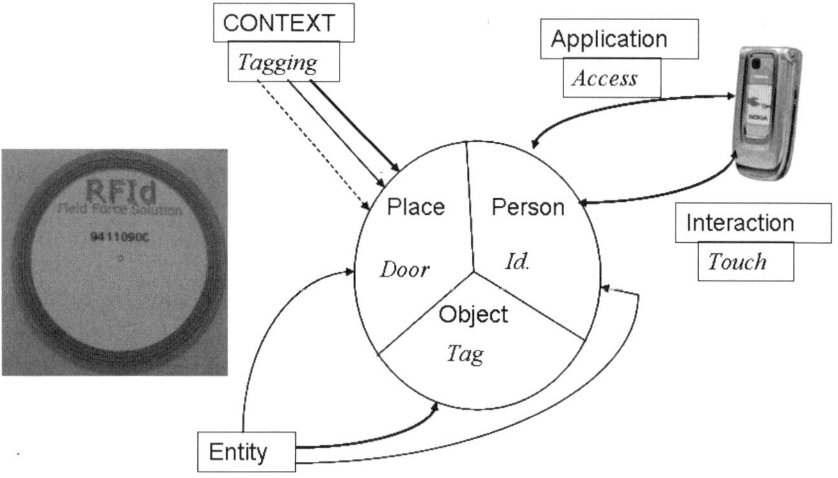

Fig. 2. Example of tagging context

Keeping in mind the definition of context by Dey, we propose a tag structure. Every tag contains information according to this definition and the three important parts of the context: the object (tag and mobile phones), the user and the place. Figure 2 shows an example of tagging a particular place: the door. Here, the information is distributed labeling the exact place (MAmI Lab door), the objects are mobile phones and, finally, the user that is identified by mobile phones. In a second step, the concept of context awareness by tagged context is accomplished. We seek to translate the context awareness capabilities with only the interaction of two devices. In this sense, we convert the implicit interaction offered by the RFID technology and users wearing tags, to another kind of interaction by touch. It is obvious that the first one is more natural, however, there are some important advantages to using the NFC technology:

The action dependability. It is included in the user action by putting a mobile phone near a context tag. The change of the model is expected. The "when" aspect is not needed. The user decides when with a simple touch. This fact saves on awareness capabilities by including them into the explicit user interaction.

The cost. It is more expensive to place RFID antennas and readers.

The readings/writing. With NFC the process is mobile and more flexible. With RFID it is located in fixed points.

Storage. There is more capacity with mobile phones (over two gigabytes in SD cards).

The server. In NFC some actions can be managed by the mobile phone. With RFID the server is always needed.

Privacy. The individual information is on the mobile phone. This fact is an important requirement for privacy aspects.

Security. The distance of readings and writing are about two or three cm. This fact could be considered a disadvantage because the RFID distance is from a few centimeters to hundreds of meters. However, security is easier to control over short distances.

3.1 NFC Architecture

With NFC technology, the information of context is included in tags. Therefore, we can place a group of these around a building in some places: door, board and PC display. The architecture is shown in Figure 3. The mobile phone can interact with the information contained on every tag (about 1Kb). With it and the capabilities of the mobile phone, process, communication and storage, it is possible to offer a context-awareness in these places. Moreover, three more connections are present: phone and phone, phone and reader, tag and reader.

With NFC technology, some services can gather without server connection. For example, we can open a door to allow people to send the correspondent signal to the open door device by Bluetooth. In addition, other services are possible: location, note to comment and visualization, but all of them need a server to be processed. Finally, other services, such as storage in tag notices for people looking for you if you are absent from your office, are possible.

All the applications are managed by the JSR 257 in a 6131 Nokia phone and the JSR 82 for Bluetooth.

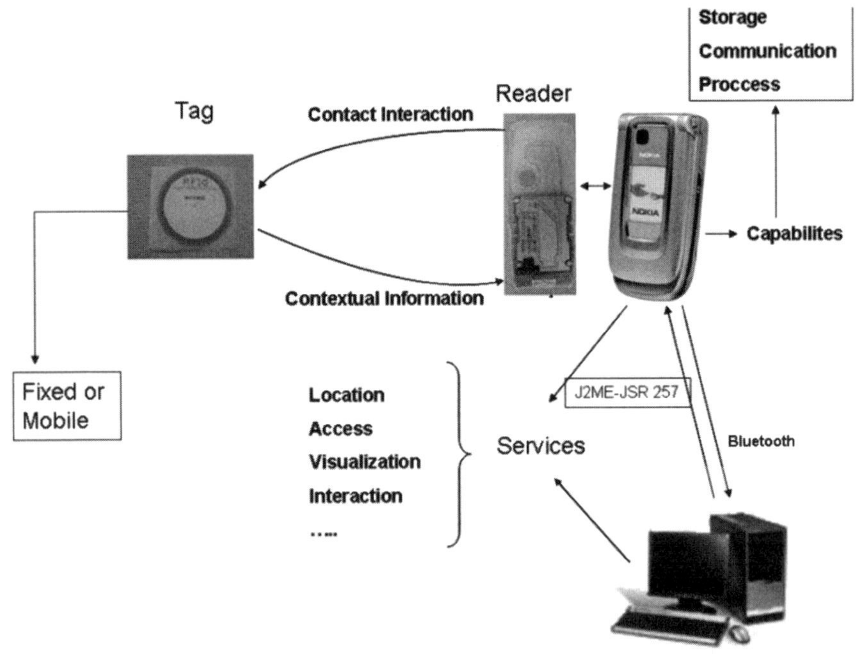

Fig. 3. NFC architecture

4   Tagging Context and Places

Our first approach for tagging context is studied in an academic environment. We selected two spaces: a research lab and a professor's office. To do so, we arranged the tag structure in three places: the door, the board and the PC display. In them, it is possible to promote interaction with a simple tag and multiple services can be gathered: location, visualization, downloading information and so on.

Figure 4 shows a distribution of information at the mentioned places. All of them have the context identification. This information is crucial in order to check the security interaction by touch. Services on the door are varied: location, access, notices about people looking at you, etc. are achievable. In addition, unexpected situations are provided. For instance, lay down the mobile phone on silent if it is necessary. Furthermore, the user can recover the normal sound status when entering another environment. Therefore, this kind of interaction in a contactless action is embedded, meaning, awareness by contact.

An important service for us is visualization of information. In order to achieve a single interaction, we have placed a set of tags next to the board. One of these is the control tag to identify people allowed to use the visualization device. In addition, it is possible to initiate interaction with the board, show contents and interact with others tags. With them, it is possible to manage the information shown (select, scrolling, etc.), entering and retrieving documents or notes to

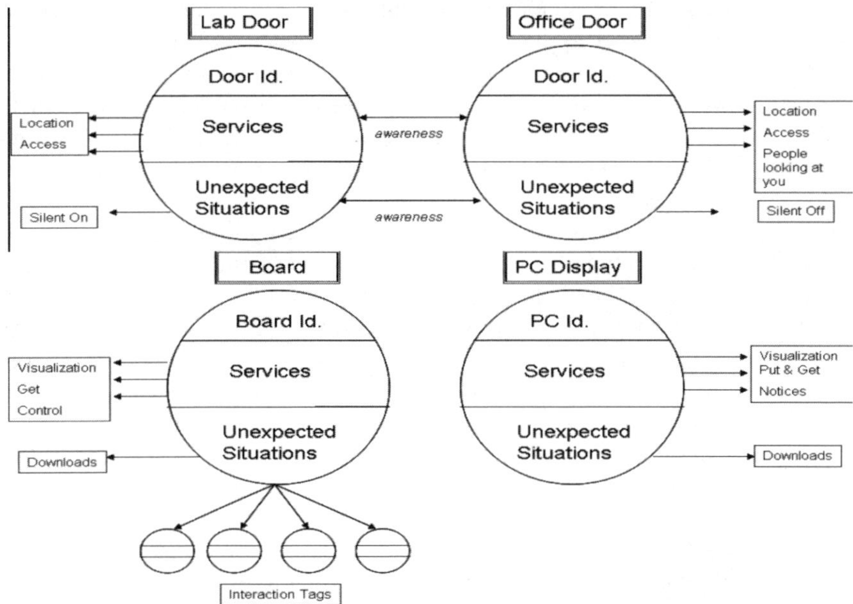

Fig. 4. Information in tags

comment on. This functionality is similar to a pen-drive. With in and out boxes, it is possible to manage information particularized for every user easily. The PC display offers similar services. In addition, notices informing if the user is not in near the PC, are considered.

4.1 Context-Awareness by Tagging and Touching

As we mentioned before, context-awareness is possible through the contactless user actions by means a simple touch. Therefore, we can talk about embedding interaction in the user actions by means of the information stored in tags. In order to do so, it is first necessary to have an application included into the mobile phone. This generic application solves the download process the first time that people interact with this context. Then, the user only has to touch different tags to execute every process. All interactions, with the proper information in tag and phone, make it possible to safe match both.

A tasks classification on context for tagging is expected:

- Find the place for tags.
- Look for needed information.
- Classify the profile Id., Services and Unexpected Situation (Awareness).
- Develop applications.
- Interaction Features (Automatic running applications, discover nearly computers, download, etc.).

People that usually interact with the context can access needed services, but others need to download applications to interact with it. For this reason, we have developed a "start point" application. It contains a process to download needed applications by touching. To do so, it is necessary for people from the organization to authorize other users. This happens by simply putting two mobile phones near each other and inserting an authorization code giving consent. Finally, every application has to reduce the time for readings. For this reason, we introduce a formalism allowing every application to obtain all the data at the first user tag contact. It is possible through the every tag structure according with the profile context and place.

Another important feature is the possibility to call up applications on the mobile phone contacting tags. This fact reinforces our idea of only a touch being needed. In addition, communication capability, meaning Bluetooth service, are activated automatically when calling application, thus saving phone battery.

It is worth highlighting the effect of the change of interaction that comes about by touching. With traditional RFID technology, interaction is closer to the user because it only requires wearing a tag and placing readers and antennas throughout the building. This case promotes complete control by the server, however. We all know that our daily routine is unpredictable and for this reason, the task responsibility for tasks could be managed by the user- this is possible with NFC technology. With just a simple contact, it is possible to decide when the task can be managed. This fact saves in modeling effort and bears in mind many kinds of everyday interruptions or unexpected situations. Besides all this, other characteristics have to be considered. While in the RFID case the server is defined, in the second one (NFC), the idea of server could "disappear" for some services. That means that every mobile phone should discover a nearly computer for supporting the required service. This fact allows us to get context reaction in places where there is no server. For instance, when I go to a colleague's office, the location service can be managed through his/her computer. It is just the discovering process between mobile phone and the computer that has to be handled. The download service can be administered, too. The idea of disperse information in tags thorough the context, could be an interesting one, bearing in mind aspects such as infrastructure and server re-sponsibilities.

In the next point, we present an approach of interaction with the visualization service that we called "Visualization Mosaic".

5   Tagging Board Interaction

By tagging boards and PC displays users can obtain visualization services to support their daily activities. We propose boards and displays with a "control tag", i. e. a tag that allows specific users to take control of the display/board. The contextual information stored in a tag determines the display behavior according the user profile. Additional tags are placed on the public displays in order to make the interaction with visualization services possible.

When a user or a set of users are placed in front of a display, the traditional human-computer interaction is not suitable because it requires frequent user interventions in order to indicate every action to the computer. Consequently, it is important to reach a more natural interaction making it implicit versus the traditional explicit dialogue with the computer.

First of all, we need to describe ViMos, an architecture that applies context-awareness providing adapted information to the user through embedded devices in the environment [7] [8] [9].

A mosaic of information is a set of information pieces that form a user interface. Initially we have a whole set of information pieces. A match between the situation and the context model makes the selection of the best pieces possible. Each piece has several associated characteristics (e.g. Optimum size, elasticity, etc.). These characteristics make the final generation process of the mosaic possible.

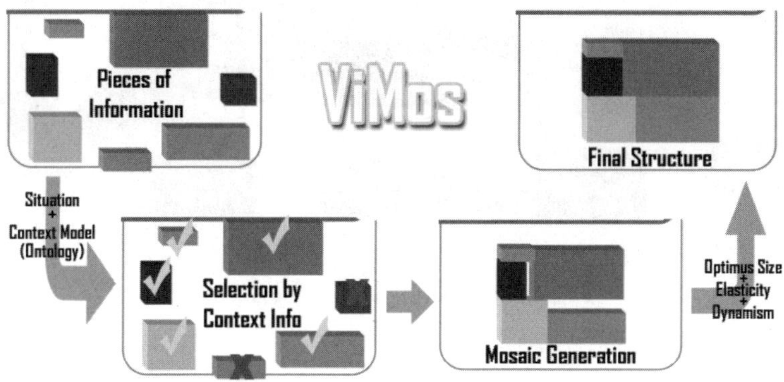

Fig. 5. ViMos Architecture

The generation of information mosaics is carried out by adapting the user interface according to the situation. In this way, we can improve the dynamism, the adaptability and the content quality.

The initial schema of interaction with ViMos was an implicit interaction. The visualization services were offered using the inferred information by a context model (represented by an ontology describing parts of the real world encompassing ViMos) and sensor information (e. g. user presence obtained by RFID antennas). However, there were several limitations, mainly when unexpired situations appeared or in the case of a user needing to navigate among the different parts of the mosaic.

By touching interaction, we can reduce the infrastructure requirements. Whenever a user takes the control of a display, implicit process is activated, such as localization and identification process. The display recognizes the user offering personal visualization services (schedule, timetable, documents in process, etc.). The main visualization services are about collaborative tasks.

In our particular context, the research lab, we have placed two virtual boards. The first one shows important information for the research group. It can be seen in Figure 6. On the right hand side of the board there are some tags for interaction with the mosaic. The second one is the works in progress for supporting collaborative tasks and discussion about new proposals.

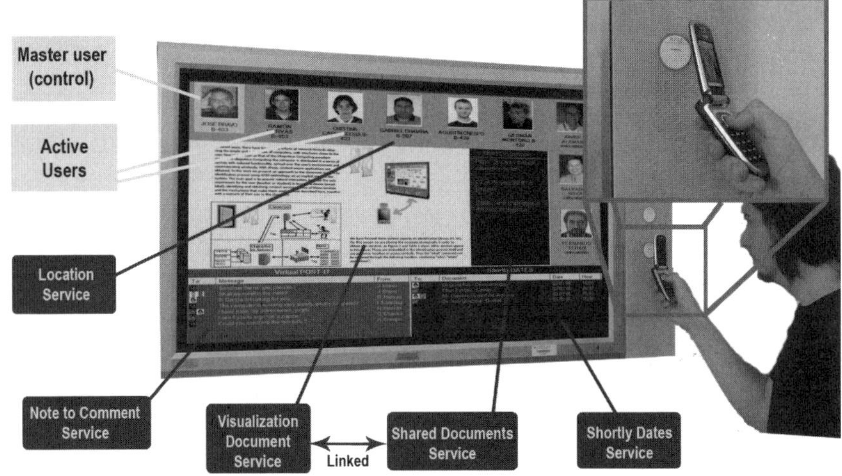

Fig. 6. Interacting with ViMos

The mosaic may be in two states. (a) When there are users in the room but nobody is near the display. ViMos should show information in order to support individual work as well as group work. (b) If one or more users are closer to the display, ViMos should show information on common work of these users. This situation requires previous planning. It offers information about member location, the group schedule, to-do lists, etc. The rest of the mosaic contains specific information regarding the research group, e.g. academic event deadlines, news, notices, member's messages and shared documents. All information changes according to the situation.

The user can take control of the visualization device simply by putting the mobile phone near the control tag. In addition, other users can interact with it. There are some important aspects to consider in order including the varied functionality for tags, visualization services by means of user profile or the interaction control. In Table 1 an example of functionalities can be seen

6   Related Works

Although NFC technology is recent, there are some interesting papers for discussion. Anokwa [10] presents an NFC model. With it, when a mobile device scans

Table 1. Example of tag funcionalities

Active Service	Take control?	Interaction Tag 1	Interaction Tag 2	Interaction Tag 3	Interaction Tag 4	Control Tag
Any	Yes	Next service	Previous service	Activate service		Get control
Any	No					Get control
Shared document	Yes	Next page	Previous page	Next document	Previous document	Get control
Shared document	No	Get document				Get control
Note to comment	Yes	Next set of comments	Previous set of comments	Expand comment	Clear comment	Get control
Note to comment	No	Get note	Get all user notes			Get control
Presentation	Yes	Next slide	Previous slide	Beginning	End	Get control
Presentation	No	Get presentation				Get control

an item, the item returns the relevant information needed to describe itself. In Kostakos [11] users with mobile phones encrypt and exchange address book information. An interesting tool for practice can be seen in Toumisto [12]. In it an emulator for supporting touching, pointing and scanning is presented. This is used to study the feasibility and usability of the context of physical browsing. In order to support a visual for touch interaction a graphics language is needed. Timo Arnall defines his particular graphic language for touch-based interactions [13].

Public displays have different physical characteristics than PCs. Consequently new interaction paradigms are necessary. This is a well-known challenge and several works have researched this problem. A large number of projects emphasize the use of large interactive/tangible displays (e g. the interactive workspace project [14]). Another trend is interaction using notebook computers or PDS and techniques like pick-and-drop, i. e. to allow a user to pick up a digital object from one screen, and drop it in a different place, typically a different computer screen or public display [15] . In general, Vogl established taxonomy of methods for user input to large displays. A good method for obtaining input to the systems comes from the devices that identify and locate people. Want and Hopper locate individuals by means of active badges which transmit signals that are picked up by sensors situated in the building [16]. IBM developed the Blueboard experiment with a display and RFID tag for the user's collaboration [17]. A similar project is IntelliBadge [18] developed for the academic conference context. There are several works on interaction with public displays by mobile devices [19] [20] . However, mobile devices have limitations in their input and output capabilities [21] . NFC can take the advantages of mobile devices and can become a valid technology to interact with devices in the environment, such as displays and boards

7 Conclusions

We have adapted a new technology that is supported by devices well known by users and offering some advantages over the traditional RFID. The idea of changing the implicit or embedded interaction that supposes to wear a tag, in front of, the explicit interaction by touch, produces a series of benefits in contexts: architecture, costs, mobile capabilities, and so on. Our proposal of tagging context reduces the awareness responsibility of the system by means of a single interaction. Tag structures, context profile and services make it easy to interact with the context. In addition, the system allows new services to be implemented as needs appear. This conclusion is possible due the decentralization of services, produced at the time that the user chooses and with the program included in a mobile phone, supported by a server or not.

Acknowledgments

This work has been financed by a 2005-2006 SERVIDOR project (PBI-05-034) from the Junta de Comunidades de Castilla-La Mancha and the Ministerio de Ciencia y Tecnologa in the Mosaic Learning project 2005-2007 (TSI2005-08225-C07-07).

References

1. ISTAG, Scenarios for Ambient Intelligence in 2010 (February 2001), http://www.cordis.lu/ist/istag.htm
2. Dey, A.: Understanding and Using Context. Personal and Ubiquitous Computing 5(1), 4–7 (2001)
3. Brooks, K.: The Context Quintet: narrative elements applied to Context Awareness. In: Human Computer Interaction International Proceedings. Crete, Greece, Erlbaum Associates, Inc. (2003)
4. Schmidt, A.: Implicit Human Computer Interaction Through Context. Personal Technologies Volume 4(2&3), 191–199 (2000)
5. Schmidt, A.: Interactive Context-Aware Systems. Intering with Ambient Intelligence. In: Riva, G., Vatalaro, F., Davide, F., Alcañiz, M. (eds.) Ambient Intelligence (2005)
6. Schmidt, A., Kranz, M., Holleis, P.: Interacting with the Ubiquitous Computing - Towards Embedding Interaction. In: Smart Objects & Ambient Intel-ligence (sOc-EuSAI 2005), Grenoble, Francia (2005)
7. Bravo, J., Hervas, R., Chavira, G.: Ubiquitous computing at classroom: An approach through identification process. Journal of Universal Computer. Special Issue on Computers and Education: Research and Experiences in eLearning Technology 11(9), 1494–1504 (2005)

8. Bravo, J., Hervas, R., Chavira, G., Nava, S., Sanz, J.: Display based services through identification: An approach in a conference context. In: Ubiquitous Computing & Ambient Intelligence (UCAmI 2005), Thomson, pp. 3–10 (2005), ISBN:84-9732-442-0

9. Bravo, J., Hervas, R., Chavira, G., Nava, S.: Modeling Contexts by RFID Sensor Fusion. In: 3rd Workshop on Context Modeling and Reasoning (CoMoRea 2006), Pisa (Italy) (2006)

10. Anokwa, Y., Borriello, G., Pering, T., Want, R.: A User Interaction Model for NFC Enabled Applications. In: PERTED Worshop at Per-com (2007)

11. Kostakos, V., O'Neill, E., Shahi, A.: Building Common Ground for Face to Face Interactions by Sharing Mobile Device Context. In: Hazas, M., Krumm, J., Strang, T. (eds.) LoCA 2006. LNCS, vol. 3987, pp. 222–238. Springer, Heidelberg (2006)

12. Tuomisto, T., Välkkynen, P., Ylisaukko-oja, A.: RFID Tag Reader System Emulator to Support Touching, Pointing and Scanning. In: Proceedings of Mobile Interaction with the Real World (MIRW 2006) (2006)

13. Arnall, T.: A graphic language for touch-based interactions. In: Proceedings of Mobile Interaction with the Real World MIRW (2006)

14. Johanson, B., Fox, A., Winograd, T.: The Interactive Workspace Project: Experiences with Ubiquitous Computing Rooms. Pervasive Computing 2(1), 71–78 (2002)

15. Vogl, S.: Coordination of Users and Services via Wall Interfaces. PhD Thesis. Johannes Kepler. University Linz (2002)

16. Want, R., Hopper, A.: The Active Badge Location System. ACM Transactions on Information Systems 10(1), 91–102 (1992)

17. Russell, D.M., Trimble, J.P., Dieberger, A.: The use patterns of large, interactive display surfaces: Case studies of media design and use for BlueBoard and MERBoard. In: Proceedings of the 37th Hawaii International Conference on System Sciences (2004)

18. Cox, D., Kindratenko, V., Pointer, D.: Proc. of 1st Interna-tional Workshop on Ubiquitous Systems for Supporting Social Interaction and Face-to-Face Communication in Public Spaces, 5th Annual Conference on Ubiquitous Computing, Seattle, WA, October 12- 4, 2003, pp. 41–47 (2003)

19. Huang, E., Mynatt, E.: Semipublic displays for small, colocated groups. In: Proceedings of the conference on Human factors in computing systems, Ft. Lauderdale, Florida, USA (2003)

20. Aizawa, K., Kakami, K., Nakahira, K.: Ubiquitous Displays for Cellular Phone Based Personal Information Environments. In: IEEE Pacific Rim Conference on Multimedia (PCM 2002) (2002)

21. Rukzio, E., Schmidt, A., Hussmann, H.: An Analysis of the Usage of Mobile Phones for Personalized Interactions with Ubiquitous Public Displays. In: Workshop on Ubiquitous Display Environments in conjunction with UbiComp, Nottingham, UK (2004)

Model-Based Reasoning Methods
within an Ambient Intelligent Agent Model

Tibor Bosse, Fiemke Both, Charlotte Gerritsen, Mark Hoogendoorn, and Jan Treur

Vrije Universiteit Amsterdam, Department of Artificial Intelligence
De Boelelaan 1081, 1081 HV Amsterdam, The Netherlands
{tbosse,fboth,cg,mhoogen,treur}@few.vu.nl
http://www.few.vu.nl/~{tbosse,fboth,cg,mhoogen,treur}

Abstract. Ambient agents react on humans on the basis of their information obtained by sensoring and their knowledge about human functioning. Appropriate types of reactions depend on in how far an ambient agent understands the human. On the one hand, such an understanding requires that the agent has knowledge to a certain depth about the human's physiological and mental processes in the form of an explicitly represented model of the causal and dynamic relations describing these processes. On the other hand, given such a model representation, the agent needs reasoning methods to derive conclusions from the model and the information available by sensoring. This paper presents a number of such model-based reasoning methods. They have been formally specified in an executable temporal format, which allows for simulation of reasoning traces and automated verification in a dedicated software environment. A number of such simulation experiments and their formal analysis are described.

1 Introduction

Recent developments within Ambient Intelligence provide technological possibilities to contribute to personal care; cf. [1, 2, 18]. Such applications can be based on possibilities to acquire sensor information about humans and their functioning, but more substantial applications depend on the availability of adequate knowledge for analysis of information about human functioning. If knowledge about human functioning is explicitly represented in the form of computational models in ambient agents, these agents can show more understanding, and (re)act accordingly by undertaking actions in a knowledgeable manner that improve the human's wellbeing and performance. In recent years, human-directed scientific areas such as cognitive science, psychology, neuroscience and biomedical sciences have made substantial progress in providing an increased insight in the various physical and mental aspects involved in human functioning. Although much work still remains to be done, dynamic models have been developed and formalised for a variety of such aspects and the way in which humans (try to) manage or regulate them. From a biomedical angle, examples of such aspects are (management of) heart functioning, diabetes, eating regulation disorders, and HIV-infection; e.g., [5, 15]. From a psychological and social angle, examples are emotion regulation, attention regulation, addiction management, trust management,

M. Mühlhäuser et al. (Eds.): AmI 2007 Workshops, CCIS 11, pp. 352–370, 2008.

stress management, and criminal behaviour management; e.g., [6, 11, 16]. Such models can be the basis for dedicated model-based reasoning methods that allow an agent to derive relevant conclusions from these models and available sensor information.

This paper addresses the design of ambient agents that have knowledge about human behaviours and states over time in the form of explicitly represented models of the causal and dynamical relations involved. First it is shown how such models can be formally represented in a logical format that also integrates numerical aspects; cf. [9]. Next a number of logical reasoning methods are presented that are based on such models. These reasoning methods are represented in a temporal logical format according to the approach put forward in [14]. A number of simulation experiments to obtain reasoning traces are described. These traces have been formally analysed by a dedicated verification tool. The types of reasoning methods addressed cover a variety of phenomena such as causal and numerical simulation, qualitative reasoning and simulation, abductive reasoning [17], and explanation generation. The reasoning methods provide a conceptual and logical foundation for these phenomena. Moreover, they provide a solid basis for conceptual and detailed design of model-based ambient agents that need such capabilities.

Section 2 describes the formal modelling approach that is used throughout this paper. Next, in Section 3 and 4 the reasoning methods themselves are presented. Section 3 addresses uncontrolled methods for belief generation, and Section 4 addresses controlled methods for belief generation. Section 5 illustrates how these reasoning methods can be used, by performing simulation experiments in two example case studies. Section 6 provides a number of basic properties that may hold for model-based reasoning methods within ambient agents. Section 7 addresses verification of basic properties as introduced in Section 3 against simulation traces, and interlevel relations between properties at different aggregation levels. Section 8 concludes the paper with a discussion.

2 Modelling Approach

This section introduces the formal modelling approach that is used throughout this paper. Section 2.1 briefly describes the Temporal Trace Language (TTL) for specification of dynamic properties (and its executable sublanguage LEADSTO), and Section 2.2 briefly explains how reasoning methods are formalised in this paper.

2.1 The Temporal Trace Language TTL

In order to execute and verify human-like ambience models, the expressive language TTL is used [7]. This predicate logical language supports formal specification and analysis of dynamic properties, covering both qualitative and quantitative aspects. TTL is built on atoms referring to states, time points and traces. A *state* of a process for (state) ontology Ont is an assignment of truth values to the set of ground atoms in the ontology. The set of all possible states for ontology Ont is denoted by STATES(Ont). To describe sequences of states, a fixed *time frame* T is assumed which is linearly ordered. A *trace* γ over state ontology Ont and time frame T is a mapping $\gamma : T \rightarrow$ STATES(Ont), i.e., a sequence of states γ_t $(t \in T)$ in STATES(Ont). The set of *dynamic properties* DYNPROP(Ont) is the set of temporal statements that can be formulated with respect to traces based on the state ontology Ont in the following manner. Given a trace γ over state ontology Ont, the state in γ at time point t is denoted by state(γ, t). These states can be related to state properties via the formally defined satisfaction relation ⊨, comparable to the Holds-predicate in the Situation Calculus: state(γ, t) ⊨ p denotes that state property p holds in trace γ at time t. Based on these statements, dynamic properties can be formulated in a sorted first-order predicate logic, using quantifiers over time and traces and the usual first-order logical connectives such as ¬, ∧, ∨, ⇒, ∀, ∃. A special software environment has been developed for TTL, featuring both a Property Editor for building and editing TTL properties and a Checking Tool that enables formal verification of such properties against a set of (simulated or empirical) traces.

Executable Format. To specify simulation models and to execute these models, the language LEADSTO [8], an executable sublanguage of TTL, is used. The basic building blocks of this language are causal relations of the format $\alpha \twoheadrightarrow_{e, f, g, h} \beta$, which means:

if	state property α holds for a certain time interval with duration g,
then	after some delay (between e and f) state property β will hold for a certain time interval of length h.

where α and β are state properties of the form 'conjunction of literals' (where a literal is an atom or the negation of an atom), and e, f, g, h non-negative real numbers.

2.2 Temporal Specification of Reasoning Methods

In this paper a dynamic perspective on reasoning is taken, following, e.g. [14]. In practical reasoning situations usually different lines of reasoning can be generated, each leading to a distinct set of conclusions. In logic semantics is usually expressed in terms of models that represent descriptions of conclusions about the world and in terms of entailment relations based on a specific class of this type of models. In the (sound) classical case each line (trace) of reasoning leads to a set of conclusions that are true in all of these models: each reasoning trace fits to each model. However, for non-classical reasoning methods the picture is different. For example, in default reasoning or abductive reasoning methods a variety of mutually contradictory conclusion sets may be possible. It depends on the chosen line of reasoning which one of these sets fits.

The general idea underlying the approach followed here, and inspired by [14] is that a particular reasoning trace can be formalised by a sequence of information states M_0, M_1, ... Here any M_t is a description of the (partial) information that has been derived up to time point t. From a dynamic perspective, an inference step, performed in time duration D is viewed as a transition $M_t \rightarrow M_{t+D}$ of a current information state M_t to a next information state Mt+D. Such a transition is usually described by application of a deduction rule or proof rule, which in the dynamic perspective on reasoning gets a temporal aspect. A particular reasoning line is formalised by a sequence $(M_t)_{t \in T}$ of subsequent information states labelled by elements of a flow of time T, which may be discrete, based on natural numbers, or continuous, based on real numbers.

An information state can be formalised by a set of statements, or as a three-valued (false, true, undefined) truth assignment to ground atoms, i.e., a partial model. In the latter case, which is followed here (as in [14]), a sequence of such information states or reasoning trace can be interpreted as a partial temporal model. A transition relating a next information state to a current one can be formalised by temporal formulae the partial temporal model has to satisfy. For example, a modus ponens deduction rule can be specified in temporal format as:

$$\text{derived(I)} \wedge \text{derived(implies(I, J))} \twoheadrightarrow \text{derived(J)}$$

So, inference rules are translated into temporal rules thus obtaining a temporal theory describing the reasoning behaviour. Each possible reasoning trace can be described by a linear time model of this theory (in temporal partial logic).

In this paper, this dynamic perspective on reasoning is applied in combination with facts that are labelled with temporal information, and models based on causal or temporal relationships that relate such facts. To express the information involved in an agent's internal reasoning processes, the ontology shown in Table 1 is used.

Table 1. Generic Ontology used within the Ambient Agent Model

Predicate	Description
belief(I:INFO_EL)	information I is believed
world_fact(I:INFO_EL)	I is a world fact
has_effect(A:ACTION, I:INFO_EL)	action A has effect I
Function to INFO_EL	**Description**
leads_to_after(I:INFO_EL, J:INFO_EL, D:REAL)	state property I leads to state property J after duration D
at(I:INFO_EL, T:TIME)	state property I holds at time T

As an example belief(leads_to_after(I:INFO_EL, J:INFO_EL, D:REAL)) is an expression based on this ontology which represents that the agent has the knowledge that state property I leads to state property J with a certain time delay specified by D. An example of a kind of dynamic modus ponens rule can be specified as

$$\text{belief(at(I, T))} \wedge \text{belief(leads\_to\_after(I, J, D))} \rightarrow \text{belief(at(J, T+D))}$$

This temporal rule states that if it is believed (by the agent) that I holds at T and that I leads to J after duration D, then it will be believed that J holds at T + D. This representation format will be used to formalise this and other types of model-based reasoning methods, as will be shown more extensively in Sections 3 and 4.

3   Model-Based Reasoning Methods for Belief Generation

Two types of reasoning methods to generate beliefs can be distinguished:

- *Forward reasoning methods for belief generation*
  These are reasoning methods that follow the direction of time and causality, deriving from beliefs about properties at certain time points, new beliefs about properties at later time points.
- *Backward reasoning methods for belief generation*
  These are reasoning methods that follow the opposite direction of time and causality, deriving from beliefs about properties at certain time points, new beliefs about properties at earlier time points.

In Section 3.1 the forward reasoning methods for belief generation are discussed, in Section 3.2 the backward reasoning methods.

3.1 Forward Reasoning Methods for Belief Generation

Forward reasoning methods are often used to make predictions on future states, or on making an estimation of the current state based on information acquired in the past. The first reasoning method is one that occurs in the literature in many variants, in different contexts and under different names, varying from, for example, computational (numerical) simulation based on difference or differential equations, qualitative simulation, causal reasoning, execution of executable temporal logic formulae, and forward chaining in rule-based reasoning, to generation of traces by transition systems and finite automata. The basic specification of this reasoning method can be expressed as follows.

Belief Generation based on Positive Forward Simulation

If it is believed that I holds at T and that I leads to J after duration D, then it is believed that J holds after D.
∀I,J:INFO_EL ∀D:REAL ∀T:TIME
belief(at(I, T)) ∧ belief(leads_to_after(I, J, D)) —» belief(at(J, T+D))
If it is believed that I1 holds at T and that I2 holds at T, then it is believed that I1 and I2 holds at T.
belief(at(I1,T)) ∧ belief(at(I2, T)) —» belief(at(and(I1, I2), T))

Note that, if the initial beliefs are assumed correct, belief correctness holds for leads to beliefs, and positive forward correctness of leads to relationships holds, then all beliefs generated in this way are correct. A second way of belief generation by forward simulation addresses the propagation of negations. This is expressed as follows.

Belief Generation based on Single Source Negative Forward Simulation

If it is believed that I does not hold at T and that I leads to J after duration D, then it is believed that J does not hold after D.
∀I,J:INFO_EL ∀D:REAL ∀T:TIME
belief(at(not(I), T)) ∧ belief(leads_to_after(I, J, D)) —» belief(at(not(J), T+D)))
If it is believed that I1 (resp. I2) does not hold at T, then it is believed that I1 and I2 does not hold at T.
belief((at(not(I1),T))) —» belief(at(not(and(I1, I2)), T))
belief(at(not(I2),T)) —» belief(at(not(and(I1, I2)), T))

Note that this only provides correct beliefs when the initial beliefs are assumed correct, belief correctness holds for leads to beliefs, and single source negative forward correctness holds for the leads to relationships.

Belief Generation based on Multiple Source Negative Forward Simulation

If for any J and time T, for every I that is believed to lead to J after some duration D, it is believed that I does not hold before duration D, then it is believed that J does not hold.
∀I,J:INFO_EL ∀D:REAL ∀T:TIME
∀I, D [belief(leads_to_after(I, J, D)) → belief(at(not(I), t-D)] —» belief(at(not(J), T))
If it is believed that I1 (resp. I2) does not hold at T, then it is believed that I1 and I2 does not hold at T.
belief(at(not(I1),T)) —» belief(at(not(and(I1, I2)), T))
belief(at(not(I2),T)) —» belief(at(not(and(I1, I2)), T))

This provides correct beliefs when the initial beliefs are assumed correct, belief correctness holds for leads to beliefs, and multiple source negative forward correctness holds for the leads to relationships.

3.2 Backward Reasoning Methods for Belief Generation

The basic specification of a backward reasoning method is specified as follows.

Belief Generation based on Modus Tollens Inverse Simulation

If it is believed that J does not hold at T and that I leads to J after duration D, then it is believed that I does not hold before duration D.
∀I,J:INFO_EL ∀D:REAL ∀T:TIME

belief(at(not(J), T)) ∧ belief(leads_to_after(I, J, D)) —⟫ belief(at(not(I), T-D))

If it is believed that not I1 and I2 holds at T and that I2 (resp. I1) holds at T, then it is believed that I1 (resp. I2) does not hold at T.

belief(at(not(and(I1, I2), T)) ∧ belief(at(I2, T)) —⟫ belief(at(not(I1), T))

belief(at(not(and(I1, I2), T)) ∧ belief(at(I1, T)) —⟫ belief(at(not(I2), T))

Belief Generation based on Simple Abduction

If it is believed that J holds at T and that I leads to J after duration D, then it is believed that I holds before duration D.

∀I,J:INFO_EL ∀D:REAL ∀T:TIME

belief(at(J, T)) ∧ belief(leads_to_after(I, J, D)) —⟫ belief(at(I, T-D))

If it is believed that I1 and I2 holds at T, then it is believed that I1 holds at T and that I2 holds at T.

belief(at(and(I1, I2), T)) —⟫ belief(at(I1,T)) ∧ belief(at(I2, T))

As another option, an abductive causal reasoning method can be internally represented in a simplified form as follows.

Belief Generation based on Multiple Effect Abduction

If for any I and time T, for every J for which it is believed that I leads to J after some duration D, it is believed that J holds after duration D, then it is believed that I holds at T.

∀I:INFO_EL ∀T:TIME

∀J [belief(leads_to_after(I, J, D)) → belief(at(J, T+D))] —⟫ belief(at(I, T))

If it is believed that I1 and I2 holds at T, then it is believed that I1 holds at T and that I2 holds at T.

belief(at(and(I1, I2), T)) —⟫ belief(at(I1,T)) ∧ belief(at(I2, T))

Belief Generation based on Context-Supported Abduction

If it is believed that J holds at T and that I2 holds at T and that I1 and I2 leads to J after duration D, then it is believed that I1 holds before duration D.

∀I,J:INFO_EL ∀D:REAL ∀T:TIME

belief(at(J, T)) ∧ belief(at(I2, T-D)) ∧ belief(leads_to_after(and(I1, I2), J, D)) —⟫ belief(at(I1, T-D))

If it is believed that I1 and I2 holds at T, then it is believed that I1 holds at T and that I2 holds at T.

belief(at(and(I1, I2), T)) —⟫ belief(at(I1,T)) ∧ belief(at(I2, T))

4 Controlling Belief Generation

An uncontrolled belief generation approach may easily lead to a combinatorial explosion of generated beliefs, for example, based on all conjunctions that can be formed. Therefore, controlled approaches where selection is done in some stage of the process are usually more effective. Often more specific knowledge is available based on which belief generation can leave out of consideration some (or most) of the possible beliefs that can be generated. To incorporate such selections, the following three approaches are possible: *selection afterwards overall, selection afterwards step by step, selection before*. Each of these options is discussed in more detail. Furthermore, it is discussed what selection criteria can be used to make such a selection.

4.1 Belief Generation Selection

Selection Afterwards Overall. In this approach first (candidate) beliefs are generated in an uncontrolled manner, and after that a selection process is performed based on some selection criterion. Two examples, one for a forward belief generation form and one for a backward belief generation form are as follows.

Controlled Belief Generation based on Positive Forward Simulation by Selection Afterwards Overall

If it is believed that I holds at T and that I leads to J after duration D, then it is believed that J holds after D.

∀I,J:INFO_EL ∀D:REAL ∀T:TIME

belief(at(I, T)) ∧ belief(leads_to_after(I, J, D)) —↠ belief(at(J, T+D))
If it is believed that I1 holds at T and that I2 holds at T, then it is believed that I1 and I2 holds at T.
belief(at(I1,T)) ∧ belief(at(I2, T)) —↠ belief(at(and(I1, I2), T))
If I is a belief and selection criterion s is fulfilled, then I is a selected belief.
belief(at(I, T)) ∧ s —↠ selected_belief(at(I, T))

Controlled Belief Generation based on Multiple Effect Abduction by Selection Afterwards Overall

If for any I and time T, for every J for which it is believed that I leads to J after some duration D, it is believed that J holds after duration D, then it is believed that I holds at T.
∀I:INFO_EL ∀T:TIME
∀J [belief(leads_to_after(I, J, D)) → belief(at(J, T+D))] —↠ belief(at(I, T))
If it is believed that I1 and I2 holds at T, then it is believed that I1 holds at T and that I2 holds at T.
belief(at(and(I1, I2), T)) —↠ belief(at(I1,T)) ∧ belief(at(I2, T))
If I is a belief and selection criterion s is fulfilled, then I is a selected belief.
belief(at(I, T)) ∧ s —↠ selected_belief(at(I, T))

This approach to control can only be applied when the number of beliefs that is generated in an uncontrolled manner is small. Otherwise more local approaches are better candidates to consider.

Selection Afterwards Step by Step. The step by step variant of selection afterwards performs the selection immediately after a belief has been generated. By such a local selection it is achieved that beliefs that are not selected can not be used in further belief generation processes, thus limiting these processes. The approach uses the temporal selection rule given above together with a slightly adapted form of specification to generate beliefs. Again two examples, one for a forward belief generation form and one for a backward belief generation form are as follows.

Controlled Bel. Generation based on Positive Forward Simulation by Selection Aft. Step by Step

If it is believed that I holds at T and that I leads to J after duration D, then it is believed that J holds after D.
∀I,J:INFO_EL ∀D:REAL ∀T:TIME
selected_belief(at(I, T)) ∧ belief(leads_to_after(I, J, D)) —↠ belief(at(J, T+D))
If it is believed that I1 holds at T and that I2 holds at T, then it is believed that I1 and I2 holds at T.
selected_belief(at(I1,T)) ∧ selected_belief(at(I2, T)) —↠ belief(at(and(I1, I2), T))
If I is a belief and selection criterion s is fulfilled, then I is a selected belief.
belief(at(I, T)) ∧ s —↠ selected_belief(at(I, T))

Controlled Belief Generation based on Multiple Effect Abduction by Selection Aft. Step by Step

If for any I and time T, for every J for which it is believed that I leads to J after some duration D, it is believed that J holds after duration D, then it is believed that I holds at T.
∀I:INFO_EL ∀T:TIME
∀J [belief(leads_to_after(I, J, D)) → selected_belief(at(J, T+D))] —↠ belief(at(I, T))
If it is believed that I1 and I2 holds at T, then it is believed that I1 holds at T and that I2 holds at T.
selected_belief(at(and(I1, I2), T)) —↠ belief(at(I1,T)) ∧ belief(at(I2, T))
If I is a belief and selection criterion s is fulfilled, then I is a selected belief.
belief(at(I, T)) ∧ s —↠ selected_belief(at(I, T))

This selection approach may be much more efficient than the approach based on selection afterwards overall.

Selection Before. The approach of selection afterwards step by step can be slightly modified by not selecting the belief just after its generation, but just before. This allows for a still more economic process of focus generation. Again two examples, one for a forward belief generation form and one for a backward belief generation form are as follows.

Controlled Belief Generation based on Positive Forward Simulation by Selection Before

If the belief that I holds at T was selected and it is believed that I leads to J after duration D, and selection criterion s1 holds, then the belief that J holds after D is selected.

∀I,J:INFO_EL ∀D:REAL ∀T:TIME

selected_belief(at(I, T)) ∧ belief(leads_to_after(I, J, D)) ∧ s1 —↠ selected_belief(at(J, T+D))

If the beliefs that I1 holds at T and that I2 holds at T were selected, and selection criterion s2 holds, then the conjunction of I1 and I2 at T is a selected belief.

selected_belief(at(I1,T)) ∧ selected_belief(at(I2, T)) ∧ s2 —↠ selected_belief(at(and(I1, I2), T))

Controlled Belief Generation based on Multiple Effect Abduction by Selection Before

If for any I and time T, for every J for which it is believed that I leads to J after some duration D, the belief that J holds after duration D was selected, and selection criterion s1 holds, then it the belief that I holds at T is a selected belief.

∀I:INFO_EL ∀T:TIME

∀J [belief(leads_to_after(I, J, D)) → selected_belief(at(J, T+D))] ∧ s1 —↠ selected_belief(at(I, T))

If the beliefs that I1 and I2 holds at T were selected, and selection criterion s2 holds then the belief that I1 holds at T is a selected belief.

selected_belief(at(and(I1, I2), T)) ∧ s2 —↠ selected_belief(at(I1,T))

If the beliefs that I1 and I2 holds at T were selected, and selection criterion s2 holds then the belief that I2 holds at T is a selected belief

selected_belief(at(and(I1, I2), T)) ∧ s3 —↠ selected_belief(at(I2, T))

4.2 Selection Criteria in Reasoning Methods for Belief Generation

Selection criteria needed for controlled belief generation can be specified in different manners. A simple manner is by assuming that the agent has knowledge which beliefs are relevant, expressed by a predicate in_focus. If this assumption is made, then any selection criterion s can be expressed as in_focus(I), where I is the property for which a belief is considered. The general idea is that if a belief can be generated, it is selected (only) when it is in focus. For example, for the two methods for selection afterwards, the temporal rule will be expressed as:

belief(at(I, T)) ∧ in_focus(I)   —↠ selected_belief(at(I, T))

For the method based on selection before, based on focus information the temporal rules will be expressed for the forward example by:

∀I,J:INFO_EL ∀D:REAL ∀T:TIME

selected_belief(at(I, T)) ∧ belief(leads_to_after(I, J, D)) ∧ in_focus(J)   —↠ selected_belief(at(J, T+D))

selected_belief(at(I1,T)) ∧ selected_belief(at(I2, T)) ∧ in_focus(and(I1, I2)) —↠ selected_belief(at(and(I1, I2), T))

For the backward example of the method based on selection before, the temporal rules will be expressed by:

∀I:INFO_EL ∀T:TIME

∀J [belief(leads_to_after(I, J, D)) → selected_belief(at(J, T+D))] ∧ in_focus(I)   —↠ selected_belief(at(I, T))

selected_belief(at(and(I1, I2), T)) ∧ in_focus(I1)   —↠ selected_belief(at(I1,T))

selected_belief(at(and(I1, I2), T)) ∧ in_focus(I2)   —↠ selected_belief(at(I2, T))

It is beyond the scope of this paper whether such foci may be static or dynamic and how they can be determined by an agent. For cases that such general focus information is not available, the selection criteria can be specified in different ways.

5 Simulation

This section illustrates for a number of the reasoning methods provided in the previous sections how they can be used within ambient agents that perform model-based reasoning. This is done by means of two example case studies, each involving an ambient system that uses a causal dynamic model to represent the behaviour of a human, and uses the reasoning methods to determine the state of the human in a particular situation. Section 5.1 focuses on a system that monitors the state of car drivers in order to avoid unsafe driving. Section 5.2 addresses an ergonomic system that monitors the stress level of office employees. Both case studies have been formalised and, using the LEADSTO simulation software [8], have been used to generate a number of simulation traces. In this section, for each model one example simulation trace is shown. More simulation traces can be found in the Appendix on[1].

5.1 Ambient Driver Model

The example model used as an illustration in this section is inspired by a system designed by Toyota which monitors drivers in order to avoid unsafe driving. The system can basically measure drug level in the sweat of a driver (e.g., via a sensor at the steering wheel, or at an ankle belt), and monitor steering operations and the gaze of the driver. Note that the system is still in the experimental phase. The model used in this paper describes how a high drug intake leads to a high drug level in the blood and this leads to physiological and behavioural consequences: (1) physiological: a high drug level (or a substance relating to the drug) in the sweat, (2) behavioural: abnormal steering operation and an unfocused gaze. The dynamic model is represented within the ambient agent by the following beliefs (where D is an arbitrary time delay):

```
belief(leads_to_after(drug_intake_high, drug_in_blood_high, D)
belief(leads_to_after(drug_in_blood_high, drug_in_sweat_high, D)
belief(leads_to_after(drug_in_blood_high, abnormal_steering_operation, D)
belief(leads_to_after(drug_in_blood_high, unfocused_gaze, D)
```

Figure 1 shows this dynamical model in a graphical form.

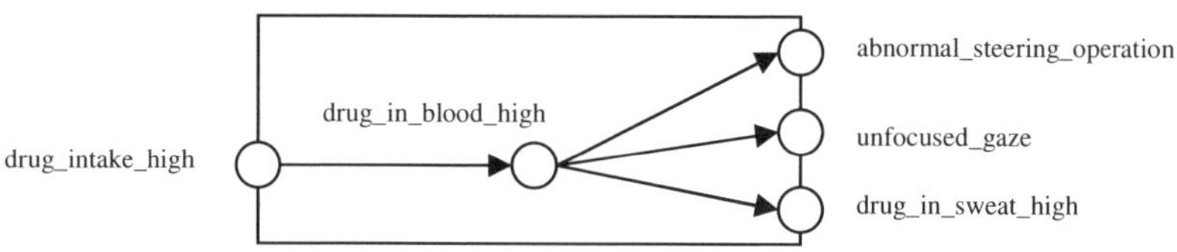

Fig. 1. Graphical representation of the dynamical model

By applying the different reasoning methods specified in Section 3 and 4, the state of the driver and the expected consequences can be derived. In the simulations below the controlled belief generation method has been used based on selection before beliefs are generated; every temporal rule requires that certain selection criteria are met and that the belief to be derived is in focus. In the following simulations, for the sake of simplicity all information is desired, therefore all derivable beliefs are in focus. The

---

[1] http://www.cs.vu.nl/~mhoogen/reasoning/appendix-rm-ami.pdf

selection criteria involve knowledge about the number of effects and sources that are required to draw conclusions. The knowledge used in this model is the following.

```
sufficient_evidence_for(and(abnormal_steering_operation, unfocused_gaze), drug_in_blood_high)
sufficient_evidence_for(drug_in_sweat_high, drug_in_blood_high)
sufficient_evidence_for(drug_in_blood_high, drug_intake_high)
in_focus(drug_intake_high); in_focus(drug_in_blood_high); in_focus(drug_in_sweat_high);
in_focus(abnormal_steering_operation); in_focus(unfocused_gaze)
```

Here, the predicate sufficient_evidence_for(P, Q) represents the belief that expression P is sufficient evidence for the system to derive Q. An example simulation trace is shown in Figure 2. In the Figure, the left side shows the atoms that occur during the simulation, whereas the right side represents a time line where a grey box indicates an atom is true at that time point, and a light box indicates false. In this trace, it is known (by observation) that the driver is steering abnormally and that the driver's gaze is unfocused. Since these two beliefs are sufficient evidence for a high drug level in the blood, using the reasoning method Belief Generation based on Multiple Effect Abduction, at(drug_in_blood_high, 1) becomes a selected belief at time point 3. Given this derived belief, the belief can be deduced that the drug level in the sweat of the driver is high, using Positive Forward Simulation. At the same time (time point 4), the reasoning method Simple Abduction determines the belief that the drug intake of the driver must have been high.

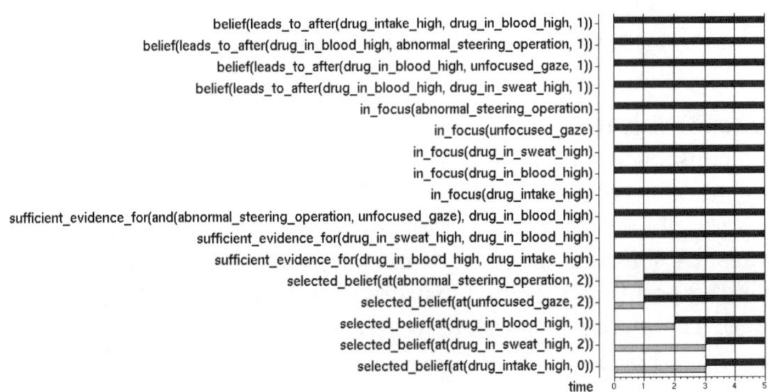

Fig. 2. Simulation Trace: abnormal steering and unfocused gaze detected

5.2 Ambient Stress Model

The example model used in this section is inspired by ergonomic systems that monitor the activities of office employees in their workspace, e.g., in order to avoid RSI (for example, WorkPace, see http://workpace.com/). Such systems may measure various types of information. In this section, three types of measurable (sensor) information are taken into account, namely *actions* (e.g., mouse clicks or key strokes), *biological aspects* (e.g., heart beat, temperature, or skin conductivity), and *activities* (e.g., incoming e-mails, telephone calls, or electronic agenda items). The model considered here describes how (the observation of) a certain activity can lead to a high level of stress and this leads to biological/physiological and behavioural consequences: (1) biological: called here 'high biological aspect' (e.g., increased heart rate) (2) behavioural: changed action (e.g., high number of keystrokes per second). The dynamical model is represented within the ambient agent by the following beliefs:

```
belief(leads_to_after(activity, observes(activity), D))
belief(leads_to_after(observes(activity), preparedness_to_act, D))
belief(leads_to_after(observes(activity), stress(high), D))
belief(leads_to_after(preparedness_to_act, stress(high), D))
belief(leads_to_after(stress(high), preparedness_to_act, D))
belief(leads_to_after(preparedness_to_act, action, D))
belief(leads_to_after(stress(high), biological_aspect, D))
```

Figure 3 shows this dynamical model in a graphical form.

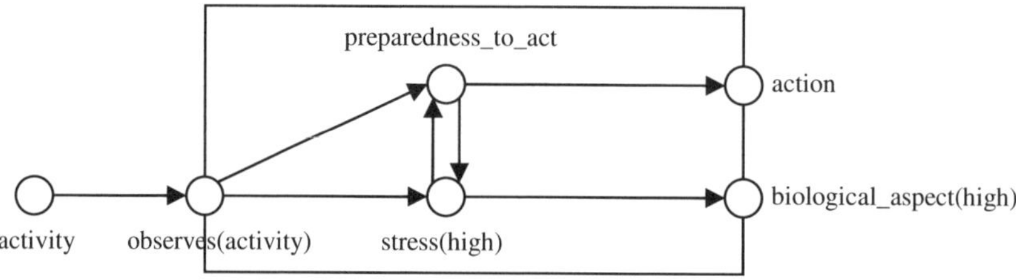

Fig. 3. Graphical representation of the dynamical model

Similar to Section 5.1, by applying the different reasoning methods specified earlier, the expected consequences for the state of the human and can be derived. A number of simulation traces have been generated, each with different settings for the selection criteria, for example sufficient_evidence_for(biological_aspect(high), stress(high)) or in_focus(activity). In other words, by selecting different combinations of these criteria, different reasoning steps will be performed. Notice that the model considered here contains a cycle (see Figure 3). Therefore it is possible to derive an infinite number of beliefs for different time points. For example, if at(preparedness_to_act, 8) is believed, then by simple Positive Forward Simulation also at(stress(high), 9) would be derived, after which at(preparedness_to_act, 10) would be derived, and so on. However, it is not conceptually realistic, nor desirable that an agent attempts to derive beliefs about time points very far in the future. Therefore, by means of the in_focus predicate, an indication of a focus time interval has been specified, for example by statements like in_focus(at(preparedness_to_act, 8)).

An example simulation trace is shown in Figure 4. This trace uses as foci all possible information between time point 0 and 10. These foci have been derived using the following rule: in_focus(I) ∧ 0 ≤ T ≤ 10 ⟶ in_focus(at(I, T)). The only initially available knowledge that is present in this trace is at(action, 5). As shown in the figure, both Positive Forward Simulation and Simple Abduction are performed several times, eventually leading to all possible derivable information between time point 0 and 10.

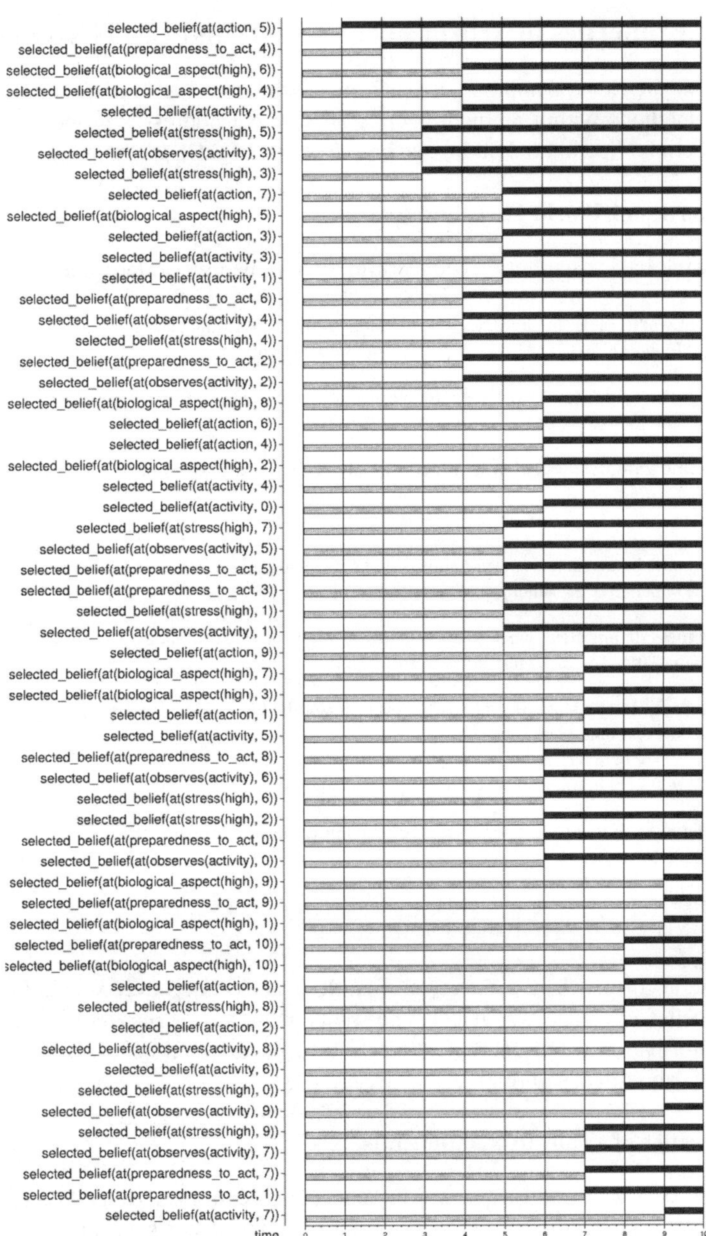

Fig. 4. Simulation Trace: Employee performs active behaviour

6 Basic Properties of World Facts, Beliefs and Leads To Relations

This section provides a number of basic properties that may hold for model-based reasoning methods within ambient agents. Section 6.1 addresses properties of world facts and beliefs; Section 6.2 addresses properties of LEADSTO relations.

6.1 Properties of World Facts and Beliefs

The following basic assumptions concerning two-valued world facts may hold:

Consistency of world facts In any state, it never happens that a world fact and its negation both hold.
not [state(γ, t) |= world_fact(I) & state(γ, t) |= world_fact(not(I))]

Completeness of world facts In any state, for any world fact it holds or its negation holds.
state(γ, t) |= world_fact(I) | state(γ, t) |= world_fact(not(I))

Consistency and completeness of world facts In any state, for any world fact it holds if and only if its negation does not hold
state(γ, t) |= world_fact(I) $\Leftrightarrow$ not state(γ, t) |= world_fact(not(I))

Belief consistency In any state, it never happens that a fact and its negation are both believed.
not [state(γ, t) |= belief(I) & state(γ, t) |= belief(not(I))]

Belief correctness In any state, when a fact is believed it holds as a world fact.
state(γ, t) |= belief(at(I, t')) $\Rightarrow$ state(γ, t') |= world_fact(I)

Belief persistence In any state, if a fact is believed, it will be believed at any later time point, unless its negation is believed at that time point.
$\forall$t, t'$\geq$t [state(γ, t) |= belief(I) & not state(γ, t') |= belief(not(I)) $\Rightarrow$ state(γ, t') |= belief(I)]
$\forall$t, t'$\geq$t [state(γ, t) |= belief(not(I)) & not state(γ, t') |= belief(I) $\Rightarrow$ state(γ, t') |= belief(not(I))]

Belief completeness For any state, any fact is believed or its negation is believed.
state(γ, t) |= belief(I) | state(γ, t) |= belief(not(I))

Belief coverage In any state, any true world fact is believed.
state(γ, t) |= world_fact(I) $\Rightarrow$ state(γ, t) |= belief(I)

In the general form, where a universal quantifier is assumed over I, belief completeness and belief coverage will usually not hold. However, it may hold for a specific class of information I. For example, sometimes it is assumed that the agent has complete beliefs about leads to relationships.

6.2 Properties of Leads to Relationships

The leads_to_after relationship expresses the conceptual core of a wide class of dynamic modelling concepts that occur in the literature in different contexts and under different names; see also [10]. Examples of such dynamical modelling concepts are, computational numerical modelling by difference or differential equations, qualitative dynamic modelling, causal relationships, temporal logic specifications, rule-based representations, Petri net representations, transition systems and finite automata. Often, either explicitly or implicitly the general assumption is made that when facts are true in the world, the facts to which they lead are also true in the world. This property is expressed as follows, also formulated by contraposition into a logically equivalent one:

Positive forward correctness If a world fact I holds in a state and it leads to another world fact J after duration D, then in the state after duration D this J will hold
state(γ, t) $\models$ world_fact(I) & state(γ, t) $\models$ world_fact(leads_to_after(I, J, D)) $\Rightarrow$ state(γ, t+D) $\models$ world_fact(J)

Negative backward correctness If a world fact J does not hold in a state and another world fact I leads to J after duration D, then in the state before duration D this I will not hold
state(γ, t) $\models$ world_fact(not(J)) & state(γ, t) $\models$ world_fact(leads_to_after(I, J, D)) $\Rightarrow$
state(γ, t-D) $\models$ world_fact(not(I))

Sometimes, also the more specific assumption is made that a world fact can be true *only* when a world fact preceding it via a leads to relation is true. This assumption can be seen as a temporal variant of a Closed World Assumption.

Negative forward correctness (single source) If a world fact I doers not hold in a state and it leads to another world fact J after duration D, then in the state after duration D this J will not hold
state(γ, t) $\models$ world_fact(not(I)) & state(γ, t) $\models$ world_fact(leads_to_after(I, J, D)) $\Rightarrow$
state(γ, t+D) $\models$ world_fact(not(J))

Positive backward correctness (single source) If a world fact J holds in a state and another world fact I leads to J after duration D, then in the state before duration D this I will hold
state(γ, t) $\models$ world_fact(J) & state(γ, t) $\models$ world_fact(leads_to_after(I, J, D)) $\Rightarrow$ state(γ, t-D) $\models$ world_fact(I)

The latter property can be formulated by contraposition into a logically equivalent property of the former one. These properties play a role in abductive reasoning methods, and automated explanation generation (in particular for why-explanations: answers on questions such as 'Why does J hold?'). The latter two properties may not be fulfilled in cases that two (or multiple) non-equivalent world facts I1 and I2 exist that each lead to a world fact J. If I1 holds, and it leads to the truth of J, then it may well be the case that I2 never was true. A more complete property to cover such cases is the following.

Negative forward correctness (multiple sources) If for a world fact J, for every world fact I which leads to J after a duration D it does not hold in the state before duration D, then in the state after duration D this J will not hold
$\forall$I, D [state(γ, t-D) $\models$ world_fact(leads_to_after(I, J, D)) $\Rightarrow$ state(γ, t-D) $\models$ world_fact(not(I))]
$\Rightarrow$ state(γ, t) $\models$ world_fact(not(J))

Positive backward correctness (multiple sources) If a world fact J holds in a state, then there exists a world fact I which leads to J after a duration D which holds in the state before duration D.
state(γ, t) $\models$ world_fact(J)
$\Rightarrow$ $\exists$I, D [state(γ, t-D) $\models$ world_fact(leads_to_after(I, J, D)) & state(γ, t-D) $\models$ world_fact(I)]

To obtain a logical foundation for a temporal variant of the Closed World Assumption in such situations in the context of executable temporal logic, in [13] the notion of temporal completion was introduced, as a temporal variant of Clark's completion in logic programming.

7 Formal Analysis of Dynamic Properties

This section shows how it can be verified that the reasoning methods introduced in Section 3 and 4 (and simulation traces generated on the basis of these methods) satisfy certain basic properties as introduced in Section 6. This is done by establishing logical (inter-level) relationships between a *global property* (GP) of reasoning methods on the one hand, and the basic reasoning steps (or *local properties*, LP's) on the other hand, in such a way that the combination of reasoning steps (logically) entails the global property. In order to establish such inter-level relationships, also certain *intermediate properties* (IP's) are constructed, which can be used as intermediate steps in the proof. Here, the focus is on one particular property from Section 6, namely the Belief Correctness property. This global property for belief generation is expressed below in GP1 and states that all beliefs should be correct. This should hold for all reasoning intervals within the trace (i.e. starting at an observation interval, and the reasoning period thereafter without new observation input). Note that all variables γ that are not explicitly declared are assumed to be universally quantified. Moreover, E is assumed to be the duration of a reasoning step.

GP1 (Belief Correctness)

For all time points t1 and t2 later than t1 whereby at t1 an observation is received, and between t1 and t2 no new observations are received, GP1(t1, t2) holds.

GP1 ≡ ∀t1, t2 ≥ t1
[state(γ, t1) |= observation_interval &
¬state(γ, t2) |= observation_interval &
∀t' < t2 & t' > t1 [state(γ, t2) |= ¬observation_interval]] ⇒ GP1(t1, t2)

The specification of the global property for an interval is expressed below.

GP1(t1, t2) (Belief Correctness from t1 to t2)

Everything that is believed to hold at T at time point t' between t1 and t2, indeed holds at that time point T.

GP1(t1, t2) ≡ ∀I, T, t' ≥ t1 & t' ≤ t2 state(γ, t') |= belief(at(I, T)) ⇒ state(γ, T) |= world_fact(I)

In order to prove that property GP1 indeed holds, a proof by means of induction is used. The basis step of this proof is specified in property LP1, whereby the beliefs during the observation interval need to be correct.

LP1(t) (Belief Correctness Induction Basis)

If time point t is part of the observation interval, then everything that at time point t is believed to hold at time point T, indeed holds at time point T.

LP1(t) ≡
state(γ, t) |= observation_interval ⇒ [∀I,T state(γ, t) |= belief(at(I, T)) ⇒ state(γ, T) |= world_fact(I)]

Furthermore, the induction step includes that if the global property holds from a time point t to the same time point, then the property should also hold between t and t + E.

IP1 (Belief Correctness Induction Step)

For all time points t, if GP1(t, t) holds, then also GP1(t, t+E) holds.

IP1 ≡ ∀t GP1(t, t) ⇒ GP1(t, t+E)

In order to prove that this induction step indeed holds, the following three properties are specified: IP2, LP2, and LP3. First of all, the *grounding* of the belief generation (IP2) which states that for all beliefs that have not been generated since the last observation interval, they should either have been derived by means of forward reasoning, or by means of abduction.

IP2 (Belief Generation Grounding)

For all time points t+E, if information element J is believed to hold at time point T and J was not believed during the last observation interval, then either this was derived by applying a forward leadsto rule, or by means of abduction.

IP2 ≡ ∀t,t0,J,T
[state(γ, t) |= belief(at(J, T)) & last_observation_interval(t, t0) & ¬state(γ, t0) |= belief(at(J, T)) ⇒ ∃I,t2, D
[state(γ, t2) |= belief(at(I, T-D)) & state(γ, t2) |= belief(leads_to_after(I, J, D)) |
 state(γ, t2) |= belief(at(I, T+D)) & state(γ, t2) |= belief(leads_to_after(J, I, D))]]

Property LP2 expresses the correctness of the model believed, that should correspond with the model present in the world.

LP2 (Model Representation Correctness)

For all time points t, if it is believed that I leads to J after duration D, then I indeed leads to J after duration D.

LP2 ≡ ∀t,I,J,D
state(γ, t) |= belief(leads_to_after(I, J, D)) ⇒ state(γ, t) |= world_fact(leads_to_after(I, J, D))

The correctness of the derivations within the world is expressed in LP3.

LP3 (Positive Forward Correctness)

For all time points t, if information element I holds and I leads to J after duration D, then at time point t+D information element J holds.

LP3 ≡ ∀t,I,J,T,D
state(γ, t) |= world_fact(I) & state(γ, t) |= world_fact(leads_to_after(I, J, D)) ⇒ state(γ, t+D) |= world_fact(J)

The final properties specified (LP4 and LP5) are used to ground property IP2. LP4 expresses that if a certain belief concerning an information element holds, and from this belief another belief concerning an information element can be derived, then this is the case at some time point t2.

LP4 (Belief Generation based on Positive Forward Simulation)

For all time points t, if information element I is believed to hold at time point T and it is believed that I leads to J after duration D, then there exists a time point t2 information element J is believed to hold at time point T+D.

LP4 ≡ ∀t1,t2,I,J,T,D
state(γ, t1) |= belief(at(I, T)) & state(γ, t1) |= belief(leads_to_after(I, J, D)) ⇒ state(γ, t2) |= belief(at(J, T+D))

Property LP5 specifies how beliefs can be generated based on abduction.

LP5 (Belief Generation based on Abduction)

For all time points t, if information element J is believed to hold at time point T and it is believed that I leads to J after duration D, then there exists a time point t2 information element I is believed to hold at time point T-D.

LP4 ≡ ∀t1,t2,I,J,T,D
state(γ, t1) |= belief(at(J, T)) & state(γ, t1) |= belief(leads_to_after(I, J, D)) ⇒ state(γ, t2) |= belief(at(I, T-D))

Figure 5 depicts the relations between the various properties by means of an AND tree. Here, if a certain property is connected to properties at a lower level, this indicates that the properties at the lower level together logically imply the higher level property. Note: LP4G and LP5G are the *grounding*[2] variant of LP4 and LP5 respectively, which is why they are depicted in grey.

Figure 5 shows that global property GP1 can be related (by logical relations, as often used in mathematical proof) to a set of local properties (LPs) of the reasoning methods put forward in Section 3 and 4. Note that it is not claimed here that GP1 holds for all reasoning methods, but that it holds for those methods that satisfy the lower level properties (LP1, LP4G, LP5G, LP2, and LP3). Such inter-level relations can be useful for *diagnosis of dysfunctioning* of a reasoning process. For example,

---

[2] The grounding variant of an executable property states that there is no other property with the same consequent. For example, the grounding variant of A ⇒ B states that there is no other property with B in its consequent, thus B ⇒ A can be derived.

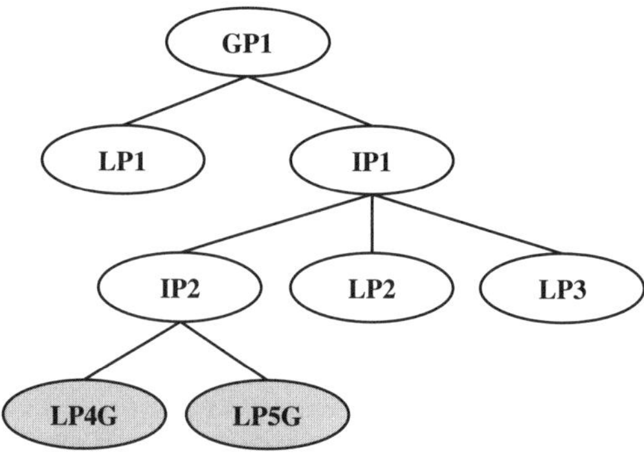

Fig. 5. Proof of GP1 depicted by means of an AND tree

suppose for a given reasoning trace (obtained either by simulation, such as in Section 5, or by other means, e.g. based on empirical material of an existing ambient system) that the dynamic property GP1 does not hold, i.e., not all beliefs are correct. Given the AND-tree structure in Figure 5, at least one of the children nodes of GP1 will not hold, which means that either LP1 or IP1 will not hold. Suppose by further checking it is found that IP1 does not hold. Then the diagnostic process can be continued by focusing on this property. It follows that either IP2, LP2, or LP3 does not hold. This process can be continued until the cause of the error is localised.

The process mentioned above is based on the assumption that it is possible to (automatically) check any property against a trace. To this end, the TTL Checker Tool [5] can be used (and has indeed been used). For the traces presented in Section 5 all properties shown in Figure 5 were checked, and turned out to hold.

8 Discussion

When ambient agents need to have knowledge about human behaviours and states over time, it is useful when they possess explicitly represented causal and dynamical models about the human's processes. Once an ambient agent has such a model, a number of logical reasoning methods can be based on such a model, and formally specified as part of the agent design, as shown in this paper. The reasoning methods included cover, for example, causal and numerical simulation, qualitative reasoning and simulation, and abductive reasoning. In several simulation experiments, example reasoning patterns were shown based on this, thus showing reusability of the ambient agent design. These simulation traces have been formally analysed and verified.

In the general abductive reasoning framework, integrity constraints can be specified (see e.g. [3, 12]). Such constraints can also be specified using the approach specified in this paper, namely by incorporating these by means of the focus mechanism specified in Section 4.2. Note that the notion of a focus is not only meant to avoid integrity constraints not being satisfied, but is also meant as a way to direct the reasoning process in an appropriate and efficient way.

In [4] temporal reasoning is combined with an Active Database (ADB) for the detection of complex events in Smart Homes. The focus of that research is the combination of ADB and temporal reasoning. There is no selection mechanism in that paper as in the current work: the focus mechanism. Another example of temporal reasoning in Ambient Intelligence [19] developed a multi-agent system based on a knowledge-goal-plan (KGP) agent for transparent communication between users and an Ambient Intelligence device. They have based their reasoning model on well-known reasoning techniques such as Abductive Logic Programming and Logic Programming with Priorities. In the current work however, the focus is at developing the underlying reasoning methods that are useful in Ambient Intelligence applications.

Although the proposed reasoning methods have been applied successfully in two case studies, the examples addressed were modelled at an abstract, conceptual level. In future work, more complex and realistic case studies will be performed. In these case studies, the possibilities to incorporate the proposed reasoning methods in real artefacts in the environment will be explored. A specific question that will be addressed is to what extent the reasoning methods are able to deal with dynamic learning of new knowledge.

References

1. Aarts, E., Collier, R.W., van Loenen, E., de Ruyter, B. (eds.): EUSAI 2003. LNCS, vol. 2875, p. 432. Springer, Heidelberg (2003)
2. Aarts, E., Harwig, R., Schuurmans, M.: Ambient Intelligence. In: Denning, P. (ed.) The Invisible Future, pp. 235–250. McGraw Hill, New York (2001)
3. Abdennadher, S., Christiansen, H.: An Experimental CLP Platform for Integrity Constraints and Abduction, In: Fourth International Conference on Flexible Query Answering Systems, FQAS 2000, Warsaw, Poland (2000)
4. Augusto, J., Nugent, C.: The use of temporal reasoning and management of complex events in smart homes. In: de Mantaras, R.L., Saitta, L. (eds.) Proceedings of European Conference on Artificial Intelligence (ECAI 2004), August 22-27, 2004, pp. 778–782. IOS Press, Amsterdam, The Netherlands (2004)
5. Bosse, T., Delfos, M.F., Jonker, C.M., Treur, J.: Analysis of Adaptive Dynamical Systems for Eating Regulation Disorders. Simulation Journal (Transactions of the Society for Modelling and Simulation) 82, 159–171 (2006)
6. Bosse, T., Gerritsen, C., Treur, J.: Integration of Biological, Psychological, and Social Aspects in Agent-Based Simulation of a Violent Psychopath. In: Shi, Y., van Albada, G.D., Dongarra, J., Sloot, P.M.A. (eds.) ICCS 2007. LNCS, vol. 4488, pp. 888–895. Springer, Heidelberg (2007)
7. Bosse, T., Jonker, C.M., Meij, L., van der Sharpanskykh, A., Treur, J.: Specification and Verification of Dynamics in Cognitive Agent Models. In: Nishida, T., et al. (eds.) Proceedings of the Sixth International Conference on Intelligent Agent Technology, IAT 2006, pp. 247–254. IEEE Computer Society Press, Los Alamitos (2006)
8. Bosse, T., Jonker, C.M., Meij, L., van der Treur, J.: A Language and Environment for Analysis of Dynamics by Simulation. International Journal of Artificial Intelligence Tools 16, 435–464 (2007)

9. Bosse, T., Sharpanskykh, A., Treur, J.: Integrating Agent Models and Dynamical Systems. In: Baldoni, M., Son, T.C., Riemsdijk, M.B., van Winikoff, M. (eds.) Declarative Agent Languages and Technologies V, Proceedings of the Fifth International Workshop on Declarative Agent Languages and Technologies, DALT 2007. LNCS (LNAI), vol. 4897, pp. 50–68. Springer Verlag, Heidelberg (2008)

10. Bosse, T., Treur, J.: Higher-Order Potentialities and their Reducers: A Philosophical Foundation Unifying Dynamic Modelling Methods. In: Veloso, M.M. (ed.) Proceedings of the Twentieth International Joint Conference on Artificial Intelligence, IJCAI 2007, pp. 262–267. AAAI Press, Menlo Park (2007)

11. Brazier, F.M.T., Jonker, C.M., Treur, J.: Compositional Design and Reuse of a Generic Agent Model. Applied Artificial Intelligence Journal 14, 491–538 (2000)

12. Endriss, U., Mancarella, P., Sadri, F., Terreni, G., Toni, F.: Abductive logic programming with ciff: Implementation and applications. In: Proceedings of the Convegno Italiano di Logica Computazionale CILC-2004, University of Parma (2004)

13. Engelfriet, J., Jonker, C.M., Treur, J.: Compositional Verification of Multi-Agent Systems in Temporal Multi-Epistemic Logic. Journal of Logic, Language and Information 11, 195–225 (2002)

14. Engelfriet, J., Treur, J.: Specification of Nonmonotonic Reasoning. Journal of Applied Non-Classical Logics 10, 7–27 (2000)

15. Green, D.J.: Realtime Compliance Management Using a Wireless Realtime Pillbottle - A Report on the Pilot Study of SIMPILL. In: Proc. of the International Conference for eHealth, Telemedicine and Health, Med-e-Tel 2005, Luxemburg (2005)

16. Gross, J.J. (ed.): Handbook of emotion regulation. Guilford Press, New York (2007)

17. Josephson, J.R., Josephson, S.G. (eds.): Abductive Inference: Computation, Philosophy, Technology. Cambridge University Press, New York (1996)

18. Riva, G., Vatalaro, F., Davide, F., Alcañiz, M. (eds.): Ambient Intelligence. IOS Press, Amsterdam (2005)

19. Stathis, K., Toni, F.: Ambient Intelligence Using KGP Agents. In: Markopoulos, P., Eggen, B., Aarts, E., Crowley, J.L. (eds.) EUSAI 2004. LNCS, vol. 3295, pp. 351–362. Springer, Heidelberg (2004)

Amigo Architecture: Service Oriented Architecture for Intelligent Future In-Home Networks

Maddy Janse[1], Peter Vink[1], and Nikolaos Georgantas[2]

[1] Philips Research, High Tech Campus 5, 5656 AE Eindhoven, The Netherlands
[2] INRIA Paris-Rocquencourt, Domaine de Voluceau, B.P. 105,
78153 Le Chesnay Cedex, France

Abstract. The Amigo architecture follows the paradigm of Service orientation, which allows developing software as services delivered and consumed on demand. The benefit of this approach lies in the looser coupling of the software components making up an application. Discovery mechanisms can be used for finding and selecting the functionality that a client is looking for. Many protocols already exist in the area of Service orientation; the Amigo project has chosen to support a number of the important protocols for discovery and communication in an interoperable way, which allows programmers to select the protocol of their choice while they can still access functionality of services using different methods. This paper gives an introductory overview of the Amigo middleware and shows how this Amigo architecture can provide easy and effective integration of services in today's home through middleware that dynamically integrates heterogeneous systems and through intelligent user services that improve the usability and attractiveness of the system.

Keywords: Service Oriented Architecture, Ambient Intelligence, networked home, interoperability, semantic modelling.

1 Introduction

The Amigo project develops middleware that dynamically integrates heterogeneous systems to achieve interoperability between services and devices. For example, home appliances (heating systems, lighting systems, washing machines, refrigerators), multimedia players and renderers (that communicate by means of UPnP) and personal devices (mobile phones, PDA's) are connected in the home network to work in an interoperable way. This interoperability across different application domains can also be extended across different homes and locations. The Amigo project is a joint effort of fifteen European companies and research organizations in mobile and home networking, software development, consumer electronics and domestic appliances.

The Amigo Open Source Software follows the paradigm of Service Orientation, which allows developing software as services that are delivered and consumed on demand. The benefit of this approach lies in the loose coupling of the software components that make up an application. Discovery mechanisms can be used for finding and selecting the functionality that a client is looking for. Many protocols already exist in the area of Service Orientation. The Amigo project supports a number of these

M. Mühlhäuser et al. (Eds.): AmI 2007 Workshops, CCIS 11, pp. 371–378, 2008.

important protocols for discovery and communication in an interoperable way. This makes it possible for programmers to select the protocol of their choice while they can still access the functionality of services that are using different methods.

2 Amigo Architecture

The Amigo service-oriented architecture consists of a Base Middleware layer, an Intelligent User Services layer, and a programming and deployment framework (Figure 1). The Base Middleware contains the functionality that is needed to facilitate a networked environment. The Intelligent User Services contain the functionality that is needed to facilitate an ambient in-house network. The programming and deployment framework contains modules that facilitate developers in creating an Amigo aware service by providing support for interoperability, security and finding and exporting context information.

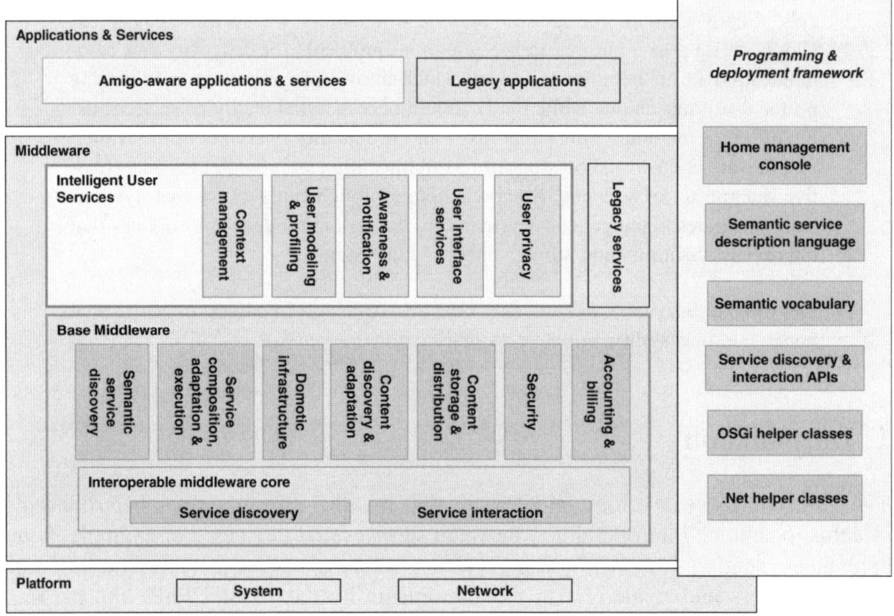

Fig. 1. Amigo architecture

The Amigo Base Middleware is a comprehensive and flexible middleware solution for the networked home that can integrate the most important existing technologies in terms of service platforms, middleware protocols, and programming paradigms. This solution is based on the semantics that is used to communicate and discover available services and devices in the network, including the ones that are based on existing communication and discovery standards, such as UPnP, WS, or SLP. Existing hardware and software and new services can be discovered and composed independently.

The Base Middleware enables interoperability and integrates heterogeneous service platforms. It provides a generalized use of semantics to represent functional, non-functional and architectural features. Semantic technologies allow for automated reasoning on represented concepts, thus providing the basis for resolution of device and service heterogeneity, service discovery and composition, context-awareness, content discovery and distribution. Advanced mechanisms for ad hoc composition of heterogeneous home resources towards complex applications are integrated. The security mechanisms for authentication, authorisation, and encryption are also provided by the Base Middleware.

Through its Programming and Deployment Framework, the Base Middleware offers modules that facilitate the development of Amigo-aware services in .NET or Java by providing support for interoperability, security and service description to service developers. Amigo supports and abstracts over several important protocols used for discovery and communication. Therefore, heterogeneous services can be integrated into the networked home independently of their underlying software and hardware technologies. A number of the important protocols for discovery and communication are supported in an interoperable way. This allows programmers to select the protocol of their choice while they can still access functionality of services by using different methods. Developers can work, for example, with an 'AmigoService class' which is provided in both C# as well as java. Target networked services come from the four application domains of the Amigo home, i.e., from the Personal Computing (PC), Mobile Computing, Consumer Electronics (CE) and Home Automation domains. The middleware protocols being bridged include: (i) service-oriented interaction protocols, such as those offered by Web Services (SOAP), UPnP (SOAP), and RMI-based infrastructures; and (ii) service discovery protocols such as SLP, UPnP and WS-Discovery. Additional middleware-related protocols being integrated embrace the control/command protocols from the Home Automation domain. This implies that the Amigo system wraps domotic protocols in such a way that they are discovered and controlled by using any of the above methods. For example, an X10 protocol that is used to control a lighting system can be wrapped and offered as a service that runs on an Amigo gateway.

The Intelligent User Services contain the functionality that is needed to facilitate an ambient in-home network. They broker between users and service providers, and provide context information, combine multiple sources of information and make pattern-based predictions. Information is tailored to user profiles and adapts to the user's situation and changes in the context.

Through their Context Management Service (CMS), the Intelligent User Services deal with the collection of data for establishing context information and transform them into appropriate formats that can be used for further processing. Context sources are, for example, basic sensor data on location, emotional states, environmental parameters, but also data on the presence of people (local and remote) that are derived from the existence of voices (speech detection and recognition front end) and acoustic scene analysis. This also includes detecting gestures of people and movements of objects. In all cases, it is necessary to recognize multiple users and multiple objects and being able to differentiate between them. CMS takes input from a range of different sources, transforms and aggregates them so that it can be used in a higher-level format by other services. Major challenges are to find the appropriate units of aggregation and the mechanism for dealing with missing data. Transformation mechanisms, context representation formalisms, and context ontologies are major components of the context management service, which together with semantic service descriptions allow inferring service parameters by reasoning from this context knowledge. Aggregated context data are also used to derive interaction histories and can be used – in combination with the User Modeling and Profiling Service (UMPS) – to offer predictions about anticipated contexts.

Through their User Modeling and Profiling Service (UMPS), the Intelligent User Services provide personalization and the corresponding personalized services by combining the necessary context information with information about the users. This is done by exploiting profile and preference information that is explicitly provided by the users and, in addition, by deriving user models on the basis of previous interaction, location, and activity histories. User interaction in Amigo is multimodal and includes speech and gestures. This service takes into account the guidelines developed in the task on Privacy and Personal Security Issues (PPS) and addresses the needed "privacy enhancing technology" to be used by other services.

Through their Awareness and Notification Service (ANS), the Intelligent User Services enable to develop applications that allow users to stay aware of any significant change in context with minimal effort. From the system viewpoint, ANS makes application layer services aware of context changes by notifying them. The benefit of using ANS is that applications do not have to care about subscribing to and monitoring of context data. These tasks are handled by ANS. In order to be notified, applications have to register monitoring rules. Once an application has set its monitoring rules, ANS constantly checks them. If one rule evaluates to true, ANS notifies the application accordingly. From the user perspective ANS provides notifications based on the user's preferences and their current context. In order to be notified appropriately, users create an individual user notification profile by using UMPS. The profile describes how and when a user wants to be notified. Before ANS sends a notification to an application, the service checks the notification profile of the user that is to be notified. Based on this profile, ANS sends a notification with an appropriate rendering of intensity. The application receiving the ANS notification implements the notification of the user according to the intensity, for example, using an "ambi-light" for an ambient notification.

Finally, through their User Interface Service (UIS), the Intelligent User Services handle the devices to present their contents and interaction modalities, and cope with explicit as well as implicit user interactions. UIS is informed by UMPS with its privacy enhancing. In the UIS context, an interaction framework was developed that allows for flexible combination and dynamic coupling of multiple devices so that services can be offered in a context-aware fashion, i.e., selection of appropriate devices depending on their "display" and multimodal presentation capabilities. This way, the devices can be adaptive and assume the role of 'smart artifacts' acting in an ambient intelligent environment.

One of the characteristics of the Amigo environment is its multiple-user aspect and the distributed applications for sharing information within and between different locations. This includes the remote presence and ambient sharing, thus linking spaces at different locations, the detection of multiple users in one and different locations. One has to observe that there are different notions of distribution: the distribution within the home, e.g., in different rooms of the same building (in this case the home), the distribution between different homes, and distribution between the home and being outside the home in a mobile context. In all situations, users are able to operate their distributed devices and get in touch with each other's distributed services. This is accomplished by the communication framework CHESS (Community CE-HTML based Experience Sharing Service), which provides the support for remote user interfaces and handles the gateways, the communities, the link to UIS, the service discovery, and integration of the services.

3   Overview of the Amigo Components

The Amigo software components can be divided into a set of core components which provide the basic functionality and a set of additional components that provide supporting or advanced functionality. Extensive tutorials are available from the Amigo website (http://www.extra.research.philips.com/amigochallenge) for the core components.

An overview of the Amigo components:

Programming and Deployment Framework
The .NET / OSGi programming framework is an essential part of the Amigo Software which will be used as a basis by nearly all application/component developers. The goal of the framework is to support developers to write their application or component software in a short timeframe by relieving them of time consuming and complex tasks, such as protocol-specific details for remote communication and discovery.

Context Management Service
The Amigo Context Management Service (CMS) is an open infrastructure for managing context information. The role of the CMS is to acquire information coming from various sources, such as physical sensors, user activities, and applications in process or internet applications and to subsequently combine or abstract these pieces of information into "context information" to be provided to context aware services.

Awareness and Notification
The Awareness and Notification Service (ANS) provides the basic functionality required to develop applications allowing people and other applications to stay aware of any significant change in context with minimal effort. ANS is able to keep track of changes in various types of context, for example activities and presence of people. ANS makes application layer services aware of context changes by notifying them. Applications register monitoring rules that specify what changes in context should be notified to them. From the user perspective, the Awareness and Notification Service provides notifications with appropriate rendering of intensity, based on the user's preferences and current context.

Security
This component provides access to the Amigo authentication and authorization service. It encapsulates the communication and cryptographic primitives that are used for device/user registration, authentication, and authorization with the centralized Amigo security service.

User Modeling and Profiling

User modeling and profiling provides the methodology to enhance the effectiveness and usability of services and interfaces in order to (a) tailor information presentation to user and context, (b) reason about user's future behavior, (c) help the user to find relevant information, (d) adapt interface features to the user and the context in which it is used, (e) indicate interface features and information presentation features for their adaptation to a multi-user environment. These goals are achieved by constructing, maintaining and exploiting user models and profiles, which are explicit representations of individual user's preferences.

Interoperable Service Discovery & Interaction Middleware Core

The role of the interoperable service discovery & interaction (SD&I) middleware is to identify the discovery and interaction middleware protocols that execute on the network and to translate the incoming/outgoing messages of one protocol into messages of another, target protocol. The system parses the incoming/outgoing message and, after having interpreted the semantics of the message, it generates a list of semantic events and uses this list to reconstruct a message for the target protocol, matching the semantics of the original message. The interoperable SD&I middleware acts in a transparent way with regard to discovery and interaction middleware protocols and with regard to services running on top of them. The supported service discovery protocols are UPnP, SLP and WS-Discovery, while the supported service interaction protocols are SOAP and RMI.

Domotic Infrastructure

The Amigo Domotic Infrastructure aims at presenting heterogeneous physical hardware devices as unified software services using standard service technologies. Nowadays, there is a great diversity of physical device technologies and protocols. Further, there are a number of service technologies that should be supported within the Amigo system. Therefore, the purpose of the Amigo Domotic Infrastructure is to enable the integration of different device technologies presenting them by means of software services, but isolating the final users (service clients) from the specific base technologies.

Content Distribution

The Content Distribution service provides available content in the Amigo home to Amigo services and applications according to the DLNA standard. This is done by gathering available content descriptions (not the actual content to avoid time-consuming and unnecessary copying of content) from UPnP Digital Media Servers (like Windows Media Connect, etc.). Moreover, it has the ability to provide content in a format which suits the renderer's capabilities in the best possible way.

Content Storage

This component offers a generic storage service to other components and applications inside an Amigo system. There is no restriction on the kind of content that can be stored, and each component or application can open and control access to a sub-store inside the Data Store. It supports also notifications on changes in a sub-store. Data is automatically backed up and restored when necessary.

Accounting and Billing
The Accounting and Billing component of the Amigo middleware offers a basic service for managing IPDR documents. Authorized applications will be able to introduce, search for and filter and share IPDR documents via the Accounting and Billing Service. This component offers validation of IPDR documents as well as service specific IPDR schema caching. Furthermore it enables advanced searches with criteria based on IPDR creation time, service type and service specific element matching.

User Interface Services
Encompasses several interface related services, such as a multimodal dialogue manager and services supporting interaction via specific modalities (e.g., speech, GUI, gesture).

Semantic Service Description, Discovery, Composition, Adaptation and Execution
This component offers a comprehensive approach to semantic service description, discovery, composition, adaptation and execution in the Amigo home, collectively called SD-SDCAE, using the Amigo-S language, thereby enabling integration of heterogeneous services into complex services based on their abstract specification.

Semantic Vocabulary-VantagePoint tool
The VantagePoint component is a Java application that can visualize, query and edit OWL ontologies that model a user-specified physical environment.

Home Management Console
The management console provides a single point of control and diagnostics for the whole connected home. It is able to connect (remotely) to the different deployment platforms on the devices for control (software update) and diagnostic purposes.

4   Advantages of the Amigo Solution

The Amigo Architecture [1, 2, 3] offers interoperability at several levels; it integrates the most important existing technologies in terms of service platforms, programming paradigms, middleware protocols. A large part of the Amigo middleware is made available as Open Source Software. Amigo offers support between heterogeneous service platforms. The Amigo Services move intelligence into the network, which enables thin client approach. The Intelligent User Services allow applications to become context aware, personalized, multi-modal and privacy aware. The use of semantics has been generalized to combine representation of functional, non-functional and architectural aspects of a home network. Examples of the common semantics are User, Space, Location, Service (Application/Device) etc. These concepts are used to create higher level information such as "Context information", "User Profiles", "User dialogues", "Notification rules" and "Privacy rules", which represent the data that is processed in the intelligent user interfaces. Reference [2] describes the Amigo vocabulary; it introduces the complete set of Amigo Concepts (some of which were shown in the list above) and their relationship. It forms the base that is needed for enhanced (context-aware) service discovery, but is also the guideline that is used whenever data is passed between Amigo Services. The Amigo Architecture, which was defined at the beginning of the project, is used as a solid base for creating Amigo Services that share the same concepts and interfaces while offering a rich variety of functionalities.

Acknowledgement

The Amigo project is funded by the European Commission as an integrated project (IP) in the Sixth Framework Programme under the contract number IST 004182. The Amigo partners are: Philips, Fagor Electrodomesticos, France Telecom, Fraunhofer IMS, Fraunhofer SIT, Ikerlan, INRIA, Italdesign-Giugiaro, SingularLogic, Europaeisches Microsoft Innovation Center, Telematica Instituut, ICCS-NTUA, Telefonica, Univ. Paderborn, VTT.

References

[1] Amigo Deliverable D2.1: Specification of the Amigo Abstract Middleware Architecture (April 2005)
[2] Amigo Deliverable D3.2: Amigo Middleware Core: Prototype Implementation & Documentation (March 2006)
[3] Amigo Deliverable D2.3: Specification of the Amigo Abstract System Architecture (May 2005)

Sharing Intelligent Services between Homes[*]

Henk Eertink[1], Remco Poortinga[1], Tom Broens[2],
Stephan Tobies[3], Andrew Tokmakoff[4], and Aart van Halteren[4]

[1] Telematica Instituut, PO Box 589, 7500 AN Enschede, The Netherlands
[2] Universiteit Twente, CTIT, PO Box 217, 7500 AE Enschede, The Netherlands
[3] European Microsoft Innovation Center, Ritterstrasse 23, 52072 Aachen, Germany
[4] Philips Research, High Tech Campus 5, 5656 AE Eindhoven, The Netherlands
{Henk.Eertink,Remco.Poortinga}@telin.nl,
T.H.F.Broens@ewi.utwente.nl, Stephan.Tobies@microsoft.com,
{Andrew.Tokmakoff,Aart.van.Halteren}@philips.com

Abstract. The user's environment is increasingly enriched with computing devices that offer services that aid users in their daily activities. Current use of these services is either public (i.e. unrestricted), or requires explicit registration. In the first case, user control and security are sacrificed whilst in the second ease of use and flexibility is limited. In this paper, we extend the perspective of user-centric computing in offering guests a simple and transparent way to access their home services from a visited intelligent environment. We provide the users with a Personal Access Device (PAD) that facilitates creation of trust between the user's own home and a visited intelligent environment. This enables seamless access to home services from the visited environment.

1 Introduction

Ubiquitous computing is about embedding computational capabilities in various kinds of objects and the surroundings in order to improve the wellbeing of users. Currently, various service access-control techniques exist that can be applied to this domain (e.g. based on imprinting devices with shared secrets that only allow access by providing compatible credentials). However, these access-control techniques typically restrict access to a well-managed collection of individuals and devices that have undergone the same imprinting techniques, making it cumbersome to provide access to guests, and even more difficult to provide secure access by guests to their home services. In this paper we describe our approach to doing this in a user-friendly manner, in which our goal is to create a dynamic and trusted association between the home environment of the guests and the visited environment, using a Personal Access Device (PAD) that acts as a trust-bridge. This association supports service discovery and service usage between the homes, allowing the guests to use their own services as if at home, using the devices available in the visited environment. In the figure below this is illustrated by having a guest with a PAD publish its services in the visited homes.

---

[*] This work was partly supported by the European Commission as part of the IST-IP AMIGO project under contract IST–004182.

M. Mühlhäuser et al. (Eds.): AmI 2007 Workshops, CCIS 11, pp. 379–384, 2008.

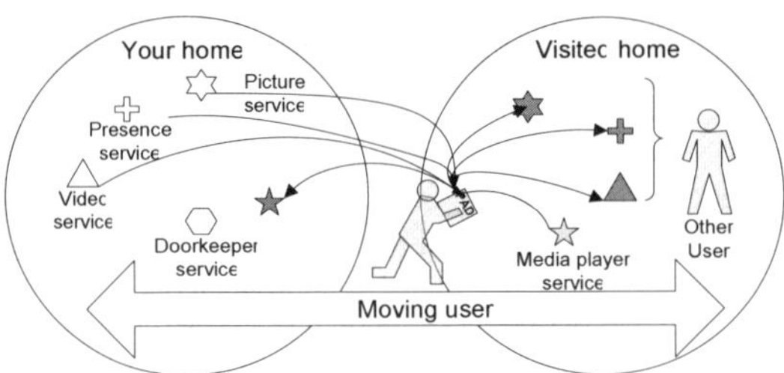

Fig. 1. Linking two homes using a PAD

Our work is part of the IST-FP6 Amigo project [1] that focuses on creating an in-home service architecture [3] to enable the intelligent home. We consider sharing services between different homes as a major aspect of intelligent homes. Our work is motivated from user-studies like the work of Röcker et al [4], which conclude that the foremost requirements for such environments, and consequently the PAD, are:

> " 1.   *The user must always remain in control of the system and never the other way around.*
> 2.   *The system must be secure, safe and protect the privacy of all users.*
> 3.   *The system must provide an added value over existing systems.*
> 4.   *The home comfort should always be maintained and not be subversive to the system.*
> 5.   *The system should provide concurrently the appropriate information to the right persons for the appropriate occasion at different locations, i. e., filter information, provide resumes, according to user preferences (note that people refer to existing services that they know)."*

If we translate that to home-to-home services, we have to balance security and trust (requirement 2), with ease of use (requirements 3 and 4), without giving automatic access to services (requirement 1), but still support visitors with appropriate information and tools in order to increase comfort (requirements 3 and 5).

2   Extended-Home Architecture

The objective of our 'extended-home architecture' is to enable secure access to guests. As already mentioned in the introduction, this should be two-way communication, meaning that home services can be accessed from the visited home and the other way around. For this we use a personal access device, called PAD, to act as a trust-bridge between the two homes. The visited home will grant the PAD limited, guest-level, access to a subset of its services needed to associate the peer houses. This means that the PAD will be able to discover these services in the visited home, and to publish them in its own home. Furthermore, the PAD is able to publish (a subset of) its home services in the visited home, allowing its owner to access his own services from within the remote domain (e.g. his presence service, or a content service). The PAD does not act as a network bridge or proxy, since that would require too many resources on the PAD. Instead, the PAD only operates as a service and trust *broker*;

the actual service usage is performed over the public Internet, directly from devices in the visited home to services in the other home.

2.1   Trust Establishment between Homes

The key functionality of the PAD is the establishment of trust between two homes. The PAD is always a member of its own home domain; it shares credentials with the home security service – a shared secret S_H – that identifies the device as a PAD towards its home. To be able to bridge trust between its own home and the visited home, temporary access of the PAD device to the services in the visited home is required. For this, the PAD has to be registered with the visited home and thus share a secret S_V with the security service of the visited home. In the following, we describe the specifics of this registration procedure and show how to use the secrets S_H and S_V to allow general access between the visited and the home domain.

We require explicit interactions to register the PAD in this visited environment. This is necessary, because in our service architecture, service-access is restricted to trusted entities (devices that share credentials with the security service). Guests therefore need to be 'approved' users, so a sign-in procedure in the visited environment is required. The basic elements of this procedure are to first gain access to the visited domain's network and then to establish the shared secret.

Obtaining access to the visited home

For trust-establishment, we need several ingredients, as illustrated in Figure 2. The first step is to obtain network access to the visited home. For wireless networks, this typically requires access to the network's configuration data like SSID and possibly encryption keys. Our scenario describes dynamic associations between homes; hence there is no a priori knowledge of the credentials needed by the PAD to join the wireless network. This creates a chicken-and-egg problem, since the PAD has to connect to the wireless network in order to initiate the (security) association between the two homes. Near-field communication (like RFID tags) is used between the PAD and a local authentication device (LAD); interaction 1 in Figure 2. The RFID tag contains a Bluetooth endpoint reference, which can be used to establish a serial connection between the LAD and the PAD. The LAD requests a temporary token for the PAD at the security service (interaction 3), and uses the serial connection towards the PAD to configure the PAD with this security token and the wireless LAN configuration information (interaction 4). Without any additional authorization, this procedure would enable any device capable of communication with the LAD's Bluetooth endpoint to obtain guest access rights to the home. Clearly, this is undesirable. One way to safeguard against such an attack is to require authorization of the Bluetooth connection on the LAD side from a registered user of the visited home (interaction 2). Alternatively, proof that the visiting device is actually physically present could be sufficient to allow limited home access. This can easily be achieved by augmenting the data on the RFID tag with some fresh random data that is updated after each swipe, which can then be used for a limited time to prove that the visiting device has been able to access the RFID tag. Regardless of the used mode of authorization, the PAD has obtained access to the visited network and is able to use the visited home's services.

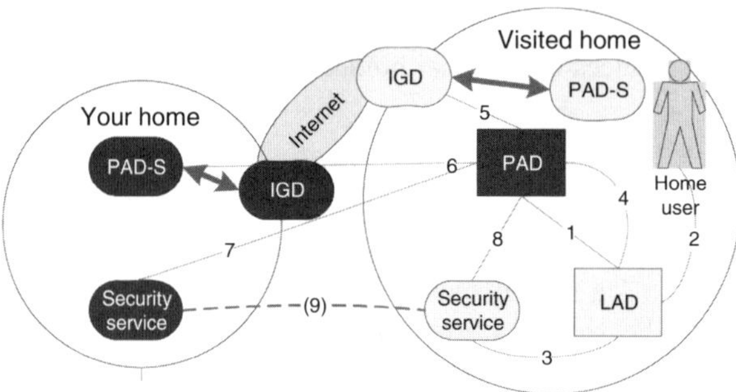

Fig. 2. Trust establishment between pervasive environments

Joining the homes

Once the PAD is registered in the visited home, it contacts the PAD-S that opens the Internet Gateway of the PAD's home for access from the visited environment (interaction 6; explained in the next section). Subsequently the PAD contacts the security service in its own home (interaction 7) to requests a temporary *join token* S_J and relays it to the security service of the visited home, together with the public address of home's security service (interaction 8). Note that the PAD can use its shared secrets S_H and S_V to encrypt and authenticate the request and transmission of S_J from its home security service to the security service of the visited home. Both the PAD and the visited security service have an active role in this process and thus explicit user approval from either domain can be built into the process to prevent unintended joining of the homes.

Once the homes are joined and can communicate securely using S_J, they cooperate by issuing tickets to the services in their respective domain that are sent to the security service of the other domain and from there are handed out to the users of the services (interaction 9). No communication through the PAD is required for this process.

2.2 Publishing and Using Home Services in the Visited Environment

Once the PAD has enabled secure communication between the security services of both domains, it will publish its home services in the visited environment. The PAD asks the PAD-S at its home, over the trusted connection, to discover services available for export, after which the PAD publishes these services in the visited network. Two practical issues have to be resolved in order for this scenario to work: (i) the firewall of any of the environments may refuse incoming traffic, and (ii) current home networks typically perform Network Address Translation (NAT)[2] at the border which also inhibits communication towards services within the home. To solve these issues, we use the UPnP Internet Gateway Device (IGD) [5] service to create well-defined and specific exposed service access points. The IGD service configures mappings between a protected service (identified with an IP-address and a port number) and a globally accessible service access point (identified with the external IP address of the home and an arbitrary port).

Our approach therefore is as follows:

1. The PAD discovers the visited IGD-service, and obtains the external IP address of the visited network (Interaction 5 in Figure 2).
2. The PAD registers this public IP address at the PAD-S @home. (6)
3. The PAD-S discovers the *exportable* services in its own home. A service can indicate whether it is exportable by setting a Boolean property with a name *exportable* to *true*. For each of these services, the PAD-S registers a mapping to a public port using the IGD service. It returns the list of services, with the public address and port assignments, to the PAD.
4. The PAD publishes these services, together with their public service access points, in the visited home. The *exportable* properties are renamed to *exported*, to avoid these services from being republished in their own home. This is all part of Interaction 6.

So, for instance, if we have an exportable content aggregation service at home, that collects all content from several devices, this service will be published in the visited environment. In the same way, the PAD can also request the PAD-S at the visited home to map *exportable* services to externally visible URIs (ignoring the already exported services which had their *exportable* property renamed to *exported*), and register these at the PAD-S in its own home. Subsequently, the home PAD-S can publish these services in the PAD's home. The PAD home's security service, joined with the other home's security service, enables home members and/or home devices to access these services.

Figure 3 shows how the joined security services cooperate to issue tickets across domain boundaries. To a service from the home of the PAD, a client at the visited location requests a ticket from the security service of the visited domain (interaction 1). After authenticating the requestor, the ticket request is forwarded to the security service in the PAD's home (2), which either denies the access or grants a ticket. This ticket is sent back to the requesting security service (3). From there it is passed to the requestor (4), which can now use the ticket to access the service (5). The ticket request sent in interaction 2 is clearly visible as coming from a remote home and thus access limitations can easily be configured in the security service that creates the tickets for its local services. The control remains with the security service of the PAD's home.

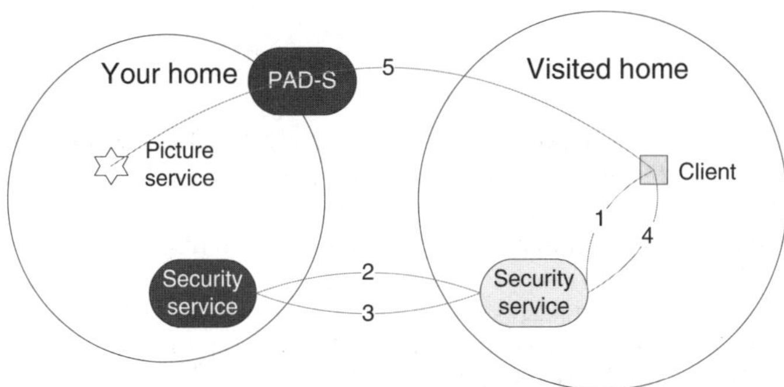

Fig. 3. Federated client authorization

3 Conclusions

In this paper we described a user-friendly approach for establishing temporary secure associations between two ubiquitous computing environments. This enables controlled and user-friendly access to home services and home content using the devices and services in your current environment. For this, we introduce a Personal Access Device (PAD) that acts as a service and trust broker between the two environments. We have shown that:

- our concept is transparent for all services, and is application independent
- it does not break role-based access-control rules defined in each of the connected environments
- it supports dynamic anonymous, yet secure, access in the visited environment; authentication is done using near-field communication without the need for explicit registration
- it provides a number of ways for user-consent: both for the guest (not to allow uncontrolled access to his home service) and for the hospitality-provider (to forbid access to strangers)
- the trust-association between the two homes is automatically removed when the guests leave the other home
- it has no significant scalability issues: there is no need for global service directories; only home-to-home brokerage is required. This only involves signaling during the service discovery phase, which is quite manageable.

Both homes need to deploy a compatible, role-based access, security service – with a (limited) set of standard roles – and a service discovery service. We are currently validating our approach using more controlled experiments, in order to get both quantitative data and end-user validation results.

The PAD concept has been realized on a belt-size computer and on smart phones and tested with several services, using the AMIGO OSGi-based middleware. Currently the exportable services in the visited home are not published in the guest's home. This means, for instance, that a phone call to the guest's home cannot automatically be redirected to the nearest audio service in the visited home. We are currently working on this extension.

References

[1] Amigo project, http://www.amigo-project.org/
[2] Egevang, K., et al.: The IP Network Address Translator (NAT). RFC 1631 (May 1994)
[3] Georgantas, N., Ben Mokhtar, S., Bromberg, Y.-D., Issarny, V., Kalaoja, J., Kantarovitch, J., Gérodolle, A., Mevissen, R.: The Amigo Service Architecture for the Open Networked Home Environment. In: Proceedings of 5th Working IEEE/IFIP Conference on Software Architecture (WICSA) (2005)
[4] Röcker, C., Janse, M.D., Portolan, N., Streitz, N.: User requirements for Intelligent Home Environments: A Scenario-Driven Approach and Empirical Cross-Cultural Study. In: SOC-EUSAI 2005, Grenoble (France) (October 2005)
[5] UPnP Forum, Internet Gateway Device (IGD) Standardized Device Control Protocol V1.0 (November 2001), http://www.upnp.org/standardizeddcps/igd.asp

Amigo Aware Services

Graham Thomson, Sébastien Bianco, Sonia Ben Mokhtar,
Nikolaos Georgantas, and Valérie Issarny

ARLES Project-Team,
INRIA Paris - Rocquencourt,
11 domaine de Voluceau
BP 105, 78153 Le Chesnay Cedex, France

Abstract. We offer a comprehensive approach to semantic service description, discovery, composition, adaptation and execution in the Amigo home, collectively called SD-SDCAE, which enables integration of heterogeneous services of the networked home environment into complex user tasks based on their abstract specification. We demonstrate SD-SDCAE with an application scenario that dynamically composes home services and devices.

1 Introduction

We have developed a comprehensive to Service Description Service Discovery, workflow-based Composition, Adaptation and Execution, which we call SD-SDCAE. The SD-SDCAE solution aims to enable user applications to exploit services deployed in the Amigo home. In the static case, we know in advance which single or multiple services we need to invoke or to compose. We also know the interfaces and the behaviour (i.e., workflow) of these services. These services may be looked up by name and invoked employing the basic service discovery and service interaction. However, in the dynamic case, we do not know in advance which services to employ nor their exact interfaces and behaviours. We thus rely on discovery of services based on the semantics of required capabilities.

2 Amigo-S Description Language

Within SD-SDCAE, services are described using the Amigo-S description language - a declarative language we have developed for the semantic specification of Amigo services. Amigo-S uses OWL-S as a basis. The Ontology Web Language (OWL) is a recommendation by W3C supporting formal description of ontologies and reasoning on them. An ontology can represent concepts of any knowledge domain and relations between them. OWL-Services (OWL-S) is an OWL-based ontology for semantically specifying Web services [1].

However, OWL-S cannot be used as-is for describing Amigo-aware services for several reasons. Firstly, the only concrete grounding with an interaction protocol that is defined in OWL-S is the mapping of OWL-S processes to WSDL

M. Mühlhäuser et al. (Eds.): AmI 2007 Workshops, CCIS 11, pp. 385–390, 2008.

operations. Indeed, OWL-S has been defined for semantically describing Web services. In the Amigo home, Web services will be used together with other technologies, and we need a semantic description language that could be used for all of them, independently of the underlying technology. Thus, OWL-S is extended by enabling several groundings to be employed for a service.

Secondly, OWL-S lacks support for describing context-ware and quality of service related information, which are key non-functional properties that we want to describe for Amigo-aware services. Therefore, included in the Amigo-S language are generic classes for describing such non-functional properties. In addition, it is desired for Amigo-S to have the possibility of specifying these properties globally for all the functionalities that an Amigo service provides, as well as individually for each capability. Thus, OWL-S is extended such that these properties could be expressed at different levels.

The semantic concepts and vocabulary used in Amigo-S service descriptions are provided by a common set of vocabulary ontologies. These vocabularies are modularly-defined to support maintainability and future evolution of concepts related to the Amigo home. The vocabularies include the Amigo Core Concepts which define the basic vocabulary that helps to tie the other vocabularies together, Devices and Platforms that provides a classification of different platforms hosted by devices and a generic classification of device types and their states, Functional Capabilities which includes several concepts representing the function of an individual capability, Quality of Service which defines a range of QoS parameters, User Context and Physical Context which attempts to model all context parameters that may potentially be related to the Amigo user and the generic parameters that are related to the elements of the physical environment respectively, and the Multimedia vocabulary that describes the different types of content that can be processed by the devices in an Amigo home. There are also several other domain-specific vocabularies defined.

By incorporating shared, semantic concepts from common vocabulary ontologies in Amigo-S service descriptions, we can promote a high level of interoperability between different Amigo services and applications. Please refer to [2] for further information on Amigo-S and the available vocabularies.

3   SD-SDCAE

Figure 1 shows the high-level architecture of SD-SDCAE. Figure 1 a) shows the main components within SD-SDCAE. These include a user's device, which hosts the application which exploits SD-SDCAE, other remote devices, which host the services that the application wishes to use, and the Amigo home server, which host the SD-SDCAE Semantic Service Repository and Execution Engine. This configuration is flexible however, and can be reconfigured to suit the need of a deployment. The repository and execution can be hosted on independent machines, for example, should a particular deployment require it. Similarly, common services and/or application could be hosted on the Amigo home server.

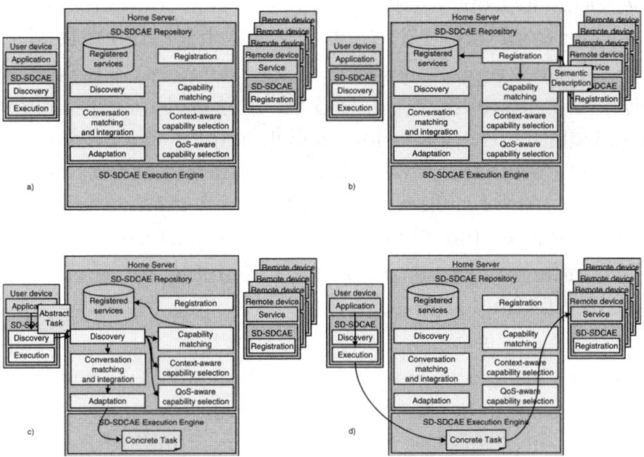

Fig. 1. The SD-SDCAE high-level architecture

Figures 1 b) to d) show the basic steps involved in registering services, dynamically composing and application using the available services, and executing the application, respectively.

Figure 1 b) shows a service registering itself with the Amigo Semantic Service Repository. The first step in this phase is that the service discovers the repository. The repository appears in the Amigo home network as a basic Amigo service, and can be discover using the standard Amigo basic service discovery mechanisms [3]. Next the service registers itself by passing its Amigo-S semantic service description to the repository.

Providing an Amigo-S semantic service description for a service provides several features and advantages to the Amigo application developer:

- It allows semantic service descriptions to be created for basic services, where the service provides a collection of atomic capabilities. This allows the service to be discovered via semantic matching at both the service and capability levels, increasing the service's availability and promoting its interoperability.
- Semantic service descriptions can provide semantic concepts for a whole service, for each capability and its inputs and outputs, and optionally its pre-conditions and effects.
- It allows semantic descriptions of conversation-based services, where the capabilities the service provides are described as a workflow of sub-capabilities. This allows the expression of data and control dependencies between the services capabilities.
- Complex workflows can be created by composing capabilities using a variety of control constructs, e.g. Sequence, Choice.
- Context parameters can be described for a service, both at the level of individual capabilities, and for the service as a whole. Then, the service can be incorporated by the context-aware discovery mechanisms [3], which enables an application to

optimise service selection based on services current context, and frees the application developer from the need to actively search for the optimal service.

- The quality of service parameters a service supports can be described both at the individual capability level, and for the service as a whole. This makes the service available to applications which employ the priority-based quality of service selection model provided by the Quality of Service Aware Service Selection Tool (QASST) [3], which allows the Amigo middleware to serve as many requests as possible while satisfying the majority of Amigo users.
- Multiple groundings can be supported, enabling interoperability between different service technologies.

Figure 1 c) shows an application being dynamically composed, based on the services currently available in the repository. Again, the first step in this phase is that the application discovers the repository using standard Amigo basic service discovery. Then the application passes an abstract task, which describes the parts of the application that rely on external services available in the environment to run in an abstract way, to the repository. The repository then attempts to select suitable services based on matching the capabilities, context-aware parameters, and QoS parameters declared for the provided services, against those requested in the abstract task. If suitable services are found, the repository than attempts to compose and if necessary, adapt the available services to fit the workflow of capabilities required by the abstract task. Finally, if a successful composition is found, the concrete task - the version of the abstract task now instantiated with real service capabilities, is deployed on the home server.

Figure 1 d) shows an application executing the dynamically composed service, the concrete task, that realises the abstract task in the previous phase. The concrete task appears as a regular Amigo service, and be discovery and executed as such. In fact, other external applications could use the newly-composed service, should it match their task description. When a capability of the task is executed, the SD-SDCAE Execution Engine automatically orchestrates the execution of each of the composite service capabilities that feature in the task capability's workflow, one or more remote devices.

Describing the service-based parts of application as a task offers the following features and advantages to the user:

- A task provides an abstract description of the required capabilities of an application. In doing so, we are not bound to any particular remote service in terms of the capabilities provided or the specific orchestration of these capabilities, increasing the availability and promoting interoperability of the potentially matching services.
- The required capabilities of a task can be identified by the semantic of the capability and of its inputs and outputs. This allows concrete details of the services provided capabilities used in a composition to be reliably and automatically adapted to the needs of the required capabilities in the absence of an exact match.

- An application may invoke capabilities of varying complexity, from lightweight atomic calls to complex, interleaved conversations (i.e. service workflows), for one or many tasks from within the same application.
- The conversation (workflow) of a required capability of a task is reconstituted by weaving together the conversations (workflows) of the provided capabilities of the available services. This offers automatic and reliable service composition, while offering fine-grained control over the placement of capabilities in the task, and guaranteeing that the data and control dependencies of each of the provided capabilities are preserved.
- The resulting (composed) service is generated as an executable ActiveBPEL bundle and automatically deployed. Orchestration of the execution of the composed service is handled automatically by the ActiveBPEL execution engine.

4   Application Scenario

In this section we demonstrate a video streaming application that exploits SD-SDCAE that integrates a media server, a media renderer, a display shared by two users, and the users personal remote controls. We show how the best choice of display is picked to play a video clip, where the best choice depends on the users' current context, the manner in which the display is currently being used, and being granted permission to use a certain display may involve interaction with the display's current user.

Figure 2 shows a graphical representation of the abstract task. We can see the workflow of capabilities is requires to run. Figure 3 gives a graphical representation of the services available in the repository, showing the workflows of their capabilities. Figure 4 demonstrates how the workflows of the services are composed to dynamically construct a workflow matching that of the task. The concrete task can then be executed as if it were basic Amigo service, and it will automatically and transparently orchestrate the execution of the composite services' capabilities.

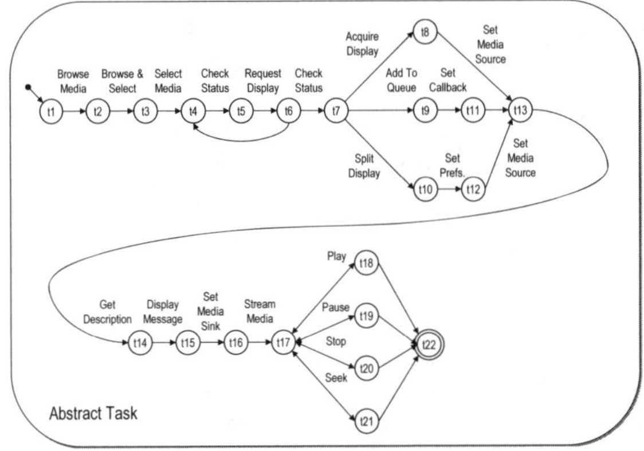

Fig. 2. The abstract task

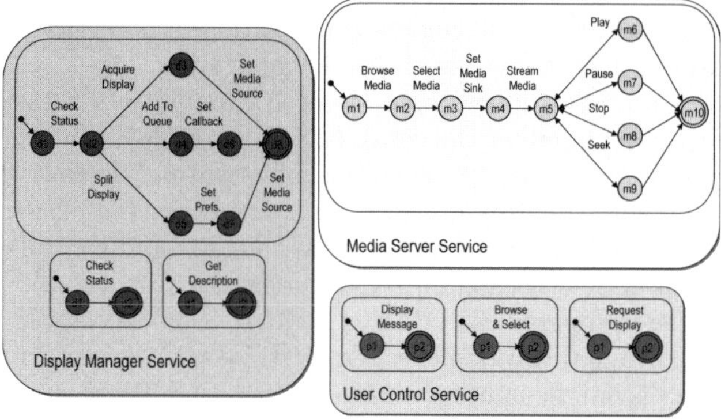

Fig. 3. The workflows of several services' capabilities

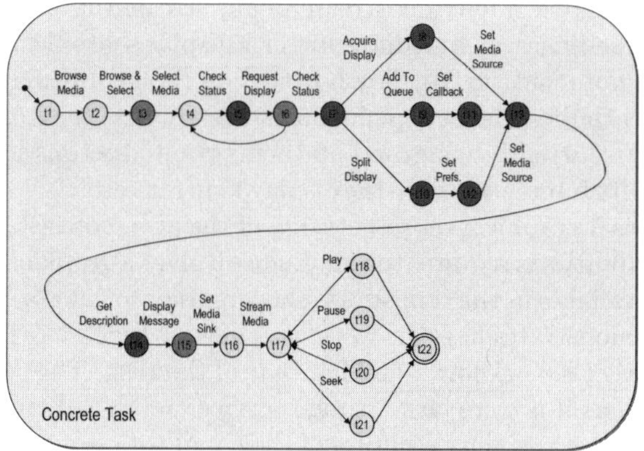

Fig. 4. The concrete task

5   Additional Information

Additional information is available online at:
http://www.hitech-projects.com/euprojects/amigo.

References

1. OWL-S, http://www.daml.org/services/owl-s/1.1/
2. Amigo Consortium. Amigo D3.2: Amigo middleware core: Prototype implementation and documentation (March 2006), available at
   http://www.hitech-projects.com/euprojects/amigo/deliverables.htm
3. Amigo Consortium. Amigo D3.4: Amigo overall middleware: First prototype implementation and documentation (May 2007), available at
   http://www.hitech-projects.com/euprojects/amigo/deliverables.htm

Ambient Communication and Context-Aware Presence Management[*]

Stanislaw Borkowski, Thibaud Flury, Anne Gerodolle, and Gilles Privat

Orange Labs/France Telecom R&D
{stan.borkowski,thibaud.flury,anne.gerodolle,
gilles.privat}@orange-ftgroup.com

Abstract. Ambient communication adapts interpersonal remote communication to the activities of users and supports interactions that come as close as possible to face to face communication. Elements of both user, physical environment and system context are taken into account to support adaptation of the communication setup and to offer implicit and intuitive interaction with the system. User presence and availability are two of the key elements of context information used by ambient communication systems. In this paper, we discuss our approach to context-aware user presence management, and describe an implementation of a presence management service. This software leverages middleware and services developed by the Amigo project to estimate user presence and availability with respect to communication applications. We also show an example of a visual communication application using interfaces distributed in the user's environment to support spatial interaction functionalities.

Keywords: Ambient Intelligence, Smart Spaces, Communication, Presence, Context-awareness, Activity detection.

1 Introduction

Ambient communication draws upon converging technology evolutions that offer both ubiquitous broadband network access and enriched interaction between the physical environment and the information world.

Departing radically from such trends as virtual reality or immersive telepresence, ambient communication propounds a vision of communication that leaves priority to user activities in their familiar environment and lets communication recede in the background, adapting unobtrusively to their time, space and attention [1].

This adaptiveness calls for a new role of *context* in communication, on a par with and inseparable from *content* proper. In this view, context is anchored in the physical environment of communicating parties, and brings remote communication as transparently close as possible to face to face communication.

Presence is such a key element of context that opens up new modes of communication. Beyond its primary use in instant messaging, it may now be seen as an enabler for new *presence-aware* modes of communication, but has still mostly been dealt with

---

[*] This work was partly funded by the IST-004182 Amigo project.

M. Mühlhäuser et al. (Eds.): AmI 2007 Workshops, CCIS 11, pp. 391–396, 2008.
© Springer-Verlag Berlin Heidelberg 2008

as resulting from explicit user interaction and directly related to network connectivity. Building upon the context management framework of the Amigo project [3] and distributed presence management protocols, we propose here to integrate seamlessly in ambient communication an enlarged notion of presence based on physical context that makes it possible for communication to move back and forth smoothly between context and content, between phatic[1] and focused communication.

2 Related Work

Presence management was first introduced in Instant Messaging (IM) applications. It is now common for all communication systems (VoIP, CSCW, etc.), but it also becomes integrated into "presence-enabled" applications, such as MS Office suite, which in principle were not designed for communication purposes [4].

In these applications presence is typically associated with a state of technical connectivity with respect to the target system or application. The presence is estimated based only on data entered explicitly by the user or on data that can be directly acquired by the application, e.g. an editor can detect user presence thanks to keyboard activity.

Some research projects [6] have tried to integrate context data (potentially obtained from implicit interaction) related to user's activity detected through sensors deployed in the environment or through re-use of information obtained by other systems. However, in these approaches, presence remains limited to a few discrete states, which is rather inadequate given the multidimensional and continuous nature of presence. Typically the notion of presence is limited to practical availability, even when context data is taken into account.

Non-objective dimensions of presence such as intentness or willingness to communicate are much more difficult to estimate. Mapping these to predefined (and cultur-ally biased) ontologies as attempted by a few standards (e.g. the notions of "moods" in XMPP /XEP and SIMPLE/RPID), is a heavy-handed and ultimately pointless approach, as no user will bother to enter these manually, and no automatic detection system could ever match to such categories.

In this article, we propose a presence management service based on a presence model that is richer than present-day IM presence systems, and more open-ended than proposed "rich presence" standards.

3 Presence Management Service

A number of application demonstrators in the Amigo project are designed to support remotely distributed parties in sharing ambience or activities.

In collocated situation, the time for starting an activity is chosen based on the observation of activity protagonists' context. Typically, one would propose a friend to

---

[1] Phatic communication is communication without content proper, or with content that should not be taken literally, as conveyed by such ritual phrases as "how do you do", handshakes, salutes, etc. Much like signalling or control packets in network protocols, it opens up or keeps active a communication "channel" between persons.

play a game or to watch a movie only when the two parties would not be engaged in other activities, i.e. they would be available for playing a game.

Sharing an ambience or mood is natural and transparent when sharing the same physical space, but in remote situations it becomes difficult and potentially intrusive. Direct audio-visual communication offers much smaller bandwidth for interaction and may intrude on people's private sphere. Communicating context information such as user presence or availability or activity, together with content proper is precious for ambience and activity sharing.

In this section, we present a Presence Management Service (PMS) designed to support ambience and activity sharing applications in conveying information about user presence.

3.1 Presence Model

Presence for ambient communication is considered as a multidimensional piece of context information characterizing to what extent the user is ready to communicate. Willingness to communicate, user attention, availability, intentness with respect to the communication, availability of communication and interaction resources, can all be considered as components of this multidimensional notion of user presence.

We restrict it here to a two-dimensional presence model that combines two parameters; user ability to communicate and user "awareness".

The ability to communicate depends on the existence of interaction resources needed for communication. It is defined over four states corresponding to the following situations:

1. The user is unable to communicate if there are no interaction resources that could support the communication.
2. The user can receive messages or notifications, but there are no resources allowing her/him to respond immediately.
3. The user can send messages or notifications, but no resources can support the interlocutor's response.
4. The user is in proximity of sufficient resources to both send and receive communications.

User awareness is defined on a linear scale from 0 to 1. It is meant to capture the user's willingness to communicate, i.e. awareness of 0 means that the user does not want to communicate, 100 corresponds to an urgent need to communicate. As a "state of mind" of the user, this willingness to communicate is of course impossible to reflect accurately on the basis of a purely automatic detection. It may however be partially inferred or modulated on the basis of such objective clues as the user being engaged in other activities than communication, or getting closer to devices that afford communication resources.

3.2 Implementation

The implementation of the PMS follows Service Oriented Architecture principles, and is based on the Amigo OSGi programming and deployment framework [5]. It uses standard XMPP protocol to exchange user status data between distributed instances of the PMS. It also leverages the Amigo Context Management System (CMS) [3] to acquire, aggregate and interpret user and system context.

In the following sections, we present principal features of our presence management service.

Per-application presence model

User presence can be potentially important for various applications. However, to cover all four communication ability levels defined above, each application might have different needs in terms of interaction resources. It is therefore natural that each application defines a presence model of its own. This allows for flexible per-application presence management.

Each application using the PMS must define its own presence model, as an XML document listing services required for each level of user's communication ability (i.e. emitting, receiving and both way dialog). An application registers to the PMS to receive user status changes by submitting its presence model.

Presence estimation

The PMS can estimate user presence status based on user and services location, service availability and user preferences. User ability to communicate is evaluated each time the user moves to a different area, e.g. to a room. On such event, the PMS performs a location-aware service discovery to obtain a list of services available in the area. This list is then compared with the list of services required by each application and ability level is set accordingly.

While the availability can be estimated automatically based on user and services location, the awareness is meant to be explicitly input by the user, being in most cases impossible to infer automatically from context data. Nevertheless, the PMS will modulate the awareness level when the user approaches or moves away from a device hosting services required by an application. This variation must be still validated by the user.

Presence visualization service

While the PMS is a web-service that can be used by other applications, it can also be considered as an application when combined with a visualization service. The composition of the PMS and a visualization service may allow the user to monitor presence status of remote buddies and to control her/his own status. We have developed a presence visualization service that we call PMS-GUI.

Awareness and communication abilities are computed by the PMS according to context information and are sent to all registered GUIs. The GUI shows presence of buddies as a patchwork of pictures. The more "aware" a buddy, the bigger his/her picture. Buddy's communication abilities are reflected by the color intensity of their pictures (see Figure 1).

The user may also control the awareness/ability information the PMS exposes to his/her buddies by opening a feed-back panel. The panel shows the current presence status of the user as computed by the PMS, the status exposed to buddies can be modified explicitly by dragging corresponding sliders.

The GUI allows the user to notify a buddy that he/she wants to communicate with him/her. To do so, the user first selects an application, by selecting it from the menu on the right, and then clicks on the buddy's picture. On the buddy's PMS-GUI, the image of the caller vibrates to indicate the call and the PMS notifies the selected application of the user's intention. Therefore, the presence management application, i.e. the composition of a PMS with a PMS-GUI service, can be used as a universal interface for triggering other communication applications.

Fig. 1. Snapshot of the GUI, while the user is controlling her awareness

4   Using the PMS in Ambience Sharing

We illustrate how the PMS can be used by applications supporting remote communication with the example of the Ambience Sharing application. The Ambience Sharing application is a context-adaptive extension of traditional person to person visual communication services such as videoconference. It offers a quasi-permanent communication channel supporting smooth switching between different communication modes, covering a continuous spectrum between non-communication and full communication. For further details on interactions supported by Ambience Sharing please refer to [2].

Ambience sharing integrates the PMS to help users initiating the communication. The application registers to the PMS a presence model specifying that it requires an audio and a video streaming service for outgoing communication and an audio and a video decoder service for reception. When the user is close to devices offering these services the PMS-GUI shows high level of presence. If the user touches a picture of a buddy, the selected person's PMS is alerted. Also the Ambience Sharing clients of the two parties are notified. This notification is a trigger to start the audio-visual communication. The PMS is thus used as a loosely coupled session initialization interface.

5 Conclusions

Ambient communication does not enforce any single particular mode of interaction or modality of communication: it opens up a new repertoire of interactions and communications modes for user to experiment with.

We present a new approach to user presence management that is based on a two dimensional presence model that represents user ability and willingness to communicate as two independent features. An implementation of a presence management service supporting this model is also presented, and the use of the PMS is illustrated with an ambient communication application called Ambience Sharing.

Expanding the ongoing drift from synchronous to asynchronous communication, the evolution towards ambient communication may be endorsed by a new generation of users unencumbered by the mindset of present-day communication: it will be up to them to invent collectively, using the tools that we have modestly attempted to propose, new forms of communication for tomorrow.

References

[1] Privat, G.: Ambient Communication: when devices disappear. In: 7th Workshop on Man-Machine Interfaces, Berlin (October 2007)
[2] Borkowski, S., Privat, G.: Spatial interaction in ambient communication. In: Enactive 2007, 4th International Conference on Enactive interfaces, Grenoble (November 2007)
[3] Ramparany, F., Poortinga, R., Stikic, M., Schmalenströer, J., Prante, T.: An open Context Information Management Infrastructure. In: Proceedings 3rd IET International Conference on Intelligent Environments, Ulm (September 2007)
[4] Vaughan-Nicols, S.: Presence Technology, more than just instant messaging, IEEE Computer (October 2003)
[5] Georgantas, N., et al.: The Amigo Service Architecture for the Open Networked Home Environment. In: WICSA 2005 (2005)
[6] Kranz, M., Holleis, P., Schmidt, A.: Ubiquitous presence systems. In: Proceedings 2006 ACM symposium on Applied computing, Dijon, France (2006)

Amigo Context Management Service
with Applications in
Ambient Communication Scenarios

Joerg Schmalenstroeer[1], Volker Leutnant[2], and Reinhold Haeb-Umbach[3]

University of Paderborn, Department of Communications Engineering, Germany
schmalen@nt.uni-paderborn.de, leutnant@nt.uni-paderborn.de,
haeb@nt.uni-paderborn.de

Abstract. The Amigo Context Management Service (CMS) provides an open infrastructure for the exchange of contextual information between context sources and context clients. Whereas context sources supply context information, retrieved from sensors or services within the networked home environment, context clients utilize those information to become context-aware.

An ambient communication scenario realizing follow-me elements is used to showcase how applications benefit from the combination of acoustics-based context sources and positioning sensors.

1 Introduction

Ambient intelligence (Ami) describes the vision of disappearing computer or other electric hardware while their functionality is still readily available to support users in their daily work [1]. One of the important building blocks of such a system is a communication infrastructure, a network, which connects heterogeneous devices. Currently, a major obstacle to realizing the vision is the lack of interoperability between devices of different manufacturers. The Amigo project has been set forth to overcome this by developing an open, standardized and interoperable middleware [2]. Further, demonstrators are being set up to showcase the benefits of a networked home to end-users.

Services can now be developed on top of the middleware. They can be perceived by users as "intelligent" if they adapt their behaviour according to the current context, where the term context summarizes all environmental or usage information which may be of relevance for the service's appropriate behaviour. The collection and provision of context information is thus of paramount importance for the overall system. This paper describes the Amigo project's structure to this, the Context Management Service (CMS). To demonstrate some of the potential of CMS, so called "ambient communication" has been realized, a hands-free communication system, where the call follows the user as he moves from one room to another, utilizing i/o devices (microphones, loudspeakers, screens) most appropriate with respect to the current user's location.

M. Mühlhäuser et al. (Eds.): AmI 2007 Workshops, CCIS 11, pp. 397–402, 2008.

2   Scenario

Maria recently moved out of her father's home for a job in another city. However, they want to keep their close relationship, despite the physical distance, by using an ambient communication system. When Maria comes home the system recognizes her and, according to her preferences, an audio connection to her father's system is established. As she walks through the home the audio connection follows her automatically. John hears Maria doing her homework and can talk to her when ever he wants. If cameras and displays are available, a video communication may also be established.

The aforementioned scenario places a number of requirements on the home network, and in the paper we will present the solutions proposed by the Amigo system. In the next section we will introduce the Amigo Context Management Service (CMS) and its concepts for distributing context information. Section 4 is about acoustic scene analysis as a means of gathering context information for services. In section 5 we discuss the realization of ambient communication and how it makes use of the Amigo CMS, before we finish with some conclusions drawn in section 6.

3   Amigo Context Management Service

The major task of the Amigo Context Management Service is the collection and distribution of context information for services and applications [3]. Fig. 1 gives a brief overview of the CMS architecture and its components.

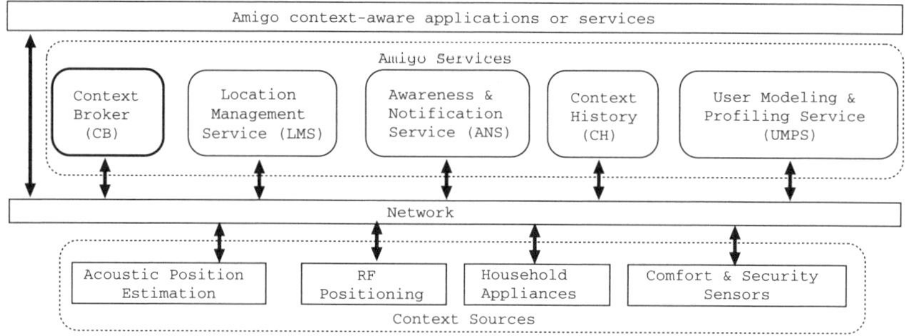

Fig. 1. Amigo CMS architecture

3.1   Amigo CMS Services

The Context Broker (CB) is the central component of the Amigo CMS services and responsible for the look up of context sources. Additionally the CMS offers the following services:

- *Awareness and Notification (ANS)*: Service for notifying applications or services about specific events.

- *Context History (CH)*: Service for recording context information and thus enabling services to exploit past context conditions.
- *User Modeling and Profiling (UMPS)*: Service for storing user preferences, based on stereotypes and configurations.
- *Location Management (LMS)*: Service providing information about user and device positions.

Each service is specialized on a certain task and provides basic data processing on context information for applications. The LMS for example, assembles a database about position information of users and devices from context sources offering location information.

3.2 Context Sources

A context source can be a sensor or a service which provides information about its current status, measurement data, database entries or usage conditions. Examples of context sources and the information they provide are:

- Sensors: temperature, air humidity, brightness, water leakage, fire detector
- Household appliances: goods available in the refrigerator
- Consumer electronics and mobile devices: usage status, login data
- Applications, Services, Databases: status
- Audio, Wlan, Bluetooth, Radio Frequency: user or device location

Each context source must implement the IContextSource interface, encapsulating physical sensors and devices, to full-fill the interoperability requirements.

There are two basic modes of data exchange between a context source and a context client (application): asynchronous and synchronous. In the asynchronous mode the application registers to context events and waits for notifications, i.e. a change of the context. Whereas in the synchronous mode the application immediately requests context information. All context information is delivered in a RDF/XML [4] description format.

The Amigo CMS reflects the dynamic nature of a networked home, where new context sources and services may be introduced in the home and others being removed. So context sources register at a central service (Context Broker) to announce their capabilities and to store a webservice reference to them. Timeout regulations guarantee that inactive context sources are removed from the list of available context sources.

3.3 Context-Aware Applications

Applications searching for context information query the CB with a RDF description of their needs for context sources and thereupon retrieve a list of references to matching sources. SPARQL [5] queries are used to request context information directly or to subscribe to events matching the SPARQL query. Applications deploying the asynchronous data exchange have to implement a notify method according to the IContextSource standard, which is called by the subscribed context source for notification.

4   Acoustic Scene Analysis

Acoustic scene analysis refers to the retrieval of all kinds of information inherent in audio signals captured by either single microphones or microphone arrays. This can be information about persons (e.g. age, gender, position, identity, mood), the environment (e.g. distortions, music) or conversations (e.g. participants, topics). In this paper we will focus on the position estimation and speaker identification tasks, since they are valuable context information in ambient communication scenarios.

4.1   Acoustic Position Estimation

Estimating the position of a speaker requires multi-channel audio signals recorded by spatially distributed microphones, either by using beamforming techniques [6] or generalized cross correlation (GCC) approaches [7].

Compared to GCC methods, beamforming has the advantage of providing an enhanced audio signal with improved Signal-to-Noise Ratio (SNR), in addition to position information. We use linearly arranged microphone arrays and Filter-Sum-Beamformer (FSB), which perform a Principal Component Analysis (PCA) and thus blindly adapt towards the loudest speaker. Each FSB delivers a Direction-of-Arrival (DoA) estimate of the speech source. As the microphone positions are known, a system of equations can be set up, whose solution delivers the speaker's location [6].

An interesting application for the acoustic positioning technique is automatic camera control in communication scenarios, where the estimate of the speaker location in combination with a face detection algorithm is utilized to steer a camera towards the speaker. Using acoustic cues in addition to visual cues allows directing the camera towards the speaker, even if the speaker is currently not in the field of view.

4.2   Speaker Diarization

A user's location is a valueable context information for the networked home environment. Among the various location estimation techniques acoustic position estimation has the advantage of being usually more precise than RF-based techniques. Further it does not require the speaker to carry a special device or wear a tag. However it demands the identification of the speaker to complement the context information. This task is referred to as speaker diarization and addresses the following question: "Who is speaking, when and where?".

Fig. 2 gives an overview of the used information sources and the chosen architecture. A Viterbi decoder is utilized to simultaneously segment and annotate the audio data, instead of performing the steps sequentially. This allows short delays and online processing of audio streams [8].

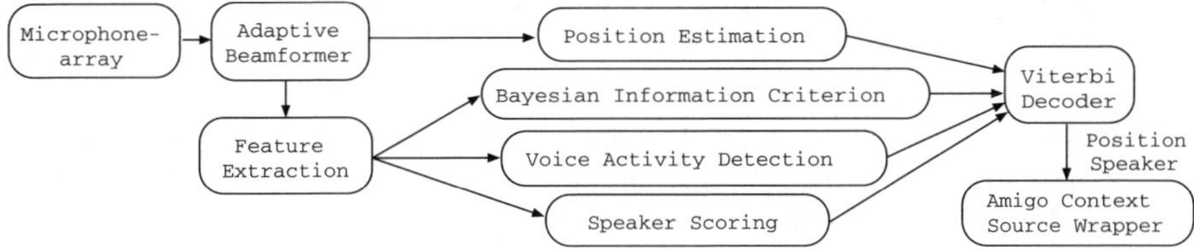

Fig. 2. Speaker diarization system architecture

5   Ambient Communication

Ambient Communication (AmCom) is the concept of virtually connecting spatially separated locations. Humans living in such environments should experience the real distance between the communication partners to a lesser extent, by developing a feeling of participating in the life of the distant partner. The communication itself moves to the background of the user's conscious attention as each partner follows his daily live.

Fig. 3 sketches the building blocks of the AmCom system developed within Amigo. It is divided in blocks responsible for audio processing and in blocks realizing the control layer, both connected via an interprocess communication (IPC). Sophisticated signal processing algorithms have been employed to realize high-quality hands-free communication, such as wideband speech coding, multi-channel echo cancellation, acoustic beamforming, noise reduction and real-time streaming. The control layer uses the Amigo middleware and services for gathering context information (e.g. location, awareness status of users) and offering services like the Seamless Audio Interface (SAInt) via Webservices to applications. The Palantir

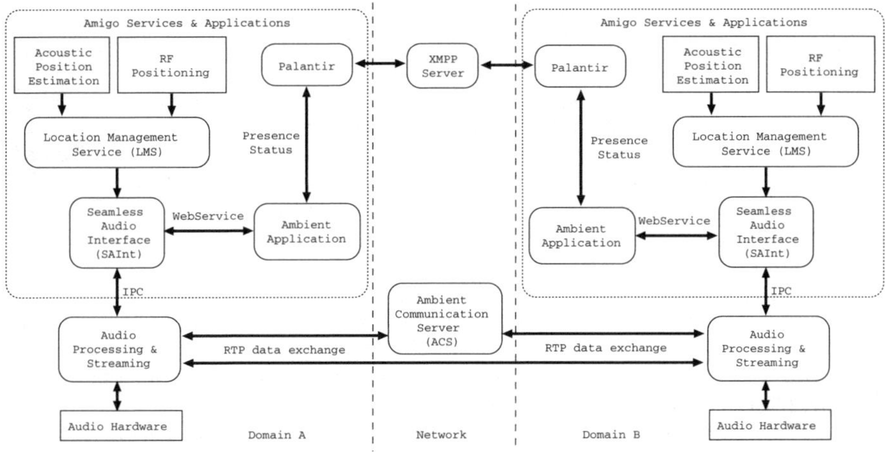

Fig. 3. System architecture for ambient communication

service exchanges context information about the users "availability and willingness to communicate" via an XMPP server and thus enables applications to control the ambient communication according to the user's current status.

One of the AmCom requirements is to be independent of terminals and to allow the user to move freely within his home. The communication follows the user ("Follow-Me") seamlessly throughout the home, configures itself according to the available hardware (audio and/or video) and does so by adhearing to privacy rules.

6   Discussion

Ambient Communication is an attractive service for the networked home environment, but it demands a certain amount of context sources and a service infrastructure providing high-level context information about the user.

The presented Amigo Context Management Service copes with these requirements by offering standard interfaces, discovery mechanisms for context sources and procedures for exchanging contextual information. Additional services like the Location Management Service (LMS) increase the range of contextual information as they encapsulate several context sources to gain improved location information. We introduced the acoustic scene analysis as a context source for the LMS and briefly discussed the technique. In contrast to common RF systems it offers position estimates without forcing the user to carry any devices. Applications, such as ambient communication, can utilize a combination of these context sources for location or proximity based services.

Acknowledgment

This work has been supported by the European union project "Amigo - Ambient intelligence for the networked home environment" [IST 4182]. For more information visit "www.amigo-project.org"

References

1. Marzano, S., Aarts, E.: The New Everyday View on Ambient Intelligence (2004)
2. Amigo Project (2007), http://www.amigo-project.org
3. Ramparany, F., Poortinga, R., Stikic, M., Schmalenstroeer, J., Prante, T.: An open Context Information Management Infrastructure - the IST-Amigo Project. In: Conference on Intelligent Environments, Ulm, Germany (2007)
4. Resource Description Format (RDF) Specifications, http://www.w3.org/RDF/
5. SPARQL Protocol and RDF Query Language, http://www.w3.org/TR/rdf-sparql-query/
6. Warsitz, E., Haeb-Umbach, R.: Acoustic Filter-and-Sum Beamforming by Adaptive Principal Component Analysis. In: ICASSP 2005, Philadelphia, USA (2005)
7. Knapp, C., Carter, G.: The generalized correlation method for estimation of time delay. IEEE Trans. ASSP 24, 320–327 (1976)
8. Schmalenstroeer, J., Haeb-Umbach, R.: Joint Speaker Segmentation, Localization and Identification for Streaming Audio. In: Interspeech 2007, Antwerp, Belgium (2007)

Amigo Approach Towards Perceived Privacy

Maddy Janse, Peter Vink, Yeo LeeChin, and Abdullah Al Mahmud

Philips Research, High Tech Campus 5, 5656 AE Eindhoven, The Netherlands

Abstract. Perceived privacy, i.e., how end-users perceive that the system affects their privacy, is one of the key aspects for the acceptance by users of ambient intelligent systems and one of the most complex to handle. Exploratory, field and conceptual design studies were conducted to generate user requirements as input and constraints for the development of mechanisms for the enforcement of privacy preferences. Based on these field studies, a model was created and a prototype was implemented in which the context, the content, and the presence of people was discovered, and shared under various privacy-sensitive conditions.

Keywords: perceived privacy, ambient intelligent system, networked home environment, extended home environment, context-aware applications.

1 Introduction

Applications in extended networked home environments are intended to facilitate the communication between users of different households and to provide them with a feeling of a shared ambiance. Connecting people in this way influences their social relationships. Home, as we know it, is a place where people can retreat from society and its social rules. Extended home applications induce intrusions in this familiar and trusted environment. Since ambient intelligent systems are by definition unobtrusive and embedded in the user's environment, users might easily forget their existence and unwillingly have their privacy violated. "Perceived privacy" or how end-users perceive that the system affects their privacy is one of the key aspects for the acceptance of ambient intelligent systems by users. It is also one of the most complex problems to handle. It is about 'how, when, and to what extent' data about people are revealed to other people within a dynamic social context. The Amigo research into perceived privacy started with user studies [1, 2]. These studies explored daily communications and their related privacy issues in the field by means of a system for presence detection and sharing that information across homes. Conceptual design studies investigated the sensitivity of masking or hiding information that is being shared between different parties in relation to the type of application. These studies provided, in addition to a set of design guidelines the following major observations on user behavior with regard to handling perceived privacy:

- People use many diverse mechanisms to preserve their social privacy,
- People share their personal information only within a small community of relatives and friends,

M. Mühlhäuser et al. (Eds.): AmI 2007 Workshops, CCIS 11, pp. 403–410, 2008.

- People need to perceive a clear benefit for information sharing,
- People control the level of detail of the information that is being shared, and they are consciously maintaining this control.

These observations resulted in a change of approach with regard to the Amigo architecture; handling privacy at the middleware service level by means of a rule-based filter that incorporated user preferences and that would use these preferences to either pass on the data or not. Such a mechanism is not sufficient for handling the user's perceived privacy because it does not offer direct user control. In particular, the type of information that is shared, the level of detail in which the information is shared, with whom that information is shared, and whether it is shared by single individuals or groups of people are crucial variables to take into account. To further investigate these implications an application implementation was developed.

2 Design Concept

The major aim is to design a privacy-aware application that is embedded in an ambient in-home network as envisioned by the Amigo project's extended home environment scenario. A content-sharing application was selected as most suitable for this purpose. In this application, context and content data are shared from various sources between different users and locations, context input is used for privacy-based decisions and context-aware feedback is given to users. A subset of the overall Amigo extended home environment scenario was selected (Table 1).

Table 1. Application Scenario

> Maria and Jerry have one child, Roberto. Jerry travels a lot for his work. They use an Amigo system to stay in touch. The system can be used from any display device that is connected to the Internet. By using the system, Maria and Jerry can be together, while they are at different locations. They can exchange information, share pictures, play games, chat, share activities, feel each other's presence and share their social context.
> Jerry is in the US on a long business trip. Maria likes to show some pictures while they are 'being together with the family' in the week-end. She has three different sets of pictures on the system. The first set of pictures is from her first marriage. She does not want anyone to see these pictures. The second set of pictures, taken at the Zoo, is recent. She wants to look at these pictures with Jerry and Roberto. The third set of pictures show the cocktails that she prepared a few days ago for their friends. She wants to look at these pictures with Jerry and not with Roberto.

This sharing application is context dependent and reacts based on the user privacy setting. Two people at different locations can share photos, location and presence. For the technical realization, existing Amigo prototypes were used and where needed extended. To maintain the home ambiance a TV was used as a display medium. Users could set their privacy preferences and navigate by means of a few buttons on a TV remote control. The user interface is built with CE-HTML (a CEA/DLNA standard).

2.1 Conceptual Model

The following design constraints were assumed:

- Context information is retrieved from the environment.
- Different control points are used to allow users to control which information they are sharing with their contacts and how that information is shared.
- The application should allow users to share information and activities with their contacts at other locations. This information includes content, for example the user's photos, context information, for example, the user's exact or approximate location, and the user's social situation.
- The application will use context information as data to be shared and as data to control the privacy settings, i.e., sharing depend on context.
- Feedback to the user regarding content and context changes should be represented in different ways, for example, by different icons and/or light colors.

The crucial components for handling perceived privacy in the Amigo extended home environment are: the services, the applications, the control, the user and the user's contacts (Figure 1). The information flow between these components results in a context dependent setting, i.e., 'how the application reacts is context dependent'.

The service component collects and provides contextual information about the environment and its users, for example, about the house and its inhabitants, such as, recognizing the persons and knowing their activities. The impact of the service component is mostly determined by the sensitivity of the data that it provides. The control component allows users to control the flow of data between components. It provides an interface for setting privacy preferences. Default values can be used when a user has not specified any privacy preferences or when the absence of data is privacy sensitive. The application component provides access to contextual information. Privacy settings will differ per application and per application usage. Contacts communicate with the user; they constitute, for example, the user's family, friends, or any other contact defined by the user. Contacts also have a context dependent factor. The user is also a component in this model, as preference settings differ per person and their context is a dependent factor. Different value combinations of these components create different settings.

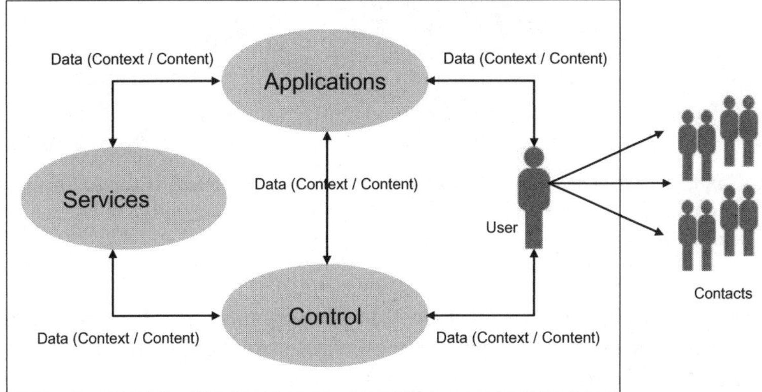

Fig. 1. Context Dependent Setting - Components context-aware sharing application

The following example illustrates the role of these components for part of the application scenario:

> if Maria [users] is in her room [services (context)] and
> is using a sharing application [applications], and
> her husband Jerry is alone [services (context)]
> at another location [contacts] and
> is also logged in to an application [applications],
> then use setting A- share photos [setting (context dependent)].

In this example, two different services and applications are running at the same time at two different locations. Setting A is a decision made at Maria's location to determine the dissemination of the information (in this case, to share photos).

2.2 Sharing Information

Information about presence, location, and content of a user is shared. Presence refers to the status of a user. This status can have different values, e.g., 'is online', 'is away', 'is busy' or 'is offline'. Location refers to where a person is located at a specified point in time. Different sources of location information can have different levels of detail, e.g., "room", "building", and "city", for the physical location. Furthermore, they can have the value "known location", and "do not share". These values can be based on agreements between users. In this way, users have control over the precision by which their location context will be disclosed to other people. The value 'known location', which is comparable to Lederer et al.'s (2003) [3] 'vague location' ordinal precision level, can be used as a custom location setting to simplify the preferences setting for the user and different levels of detail can be shared depending on the character of relationships between persons. This implies that users maintain control by configuring their preference settings with regard to 'who will see what and when'. The application will react according to these preferences setting.

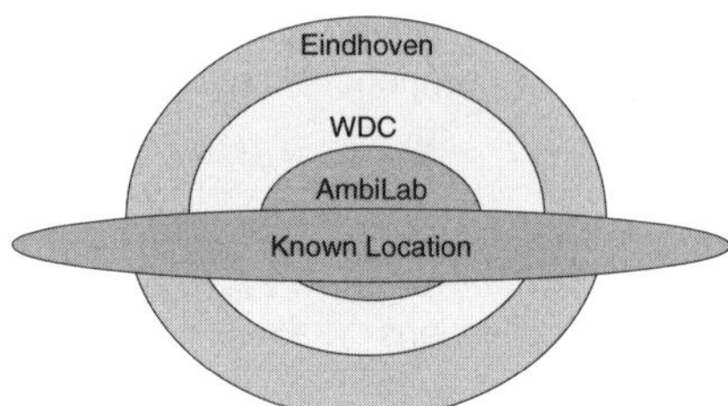

Fig. 2. Example of different levels of precision for location. AmbiLab is the room, WDC is the building, and Eindhoven is the city. Each of these levels can have a within value that is 'known location' and that may be shared or not shared.

Content refers to information of interest to persons. Content can have different values for sharing. For example for photos, these values can be: private, public, or conditionally specified like sharing with X when X is alone.

2.3 Presenting Context Information

The information that is being shared about presence, location and content is presented in relation to the context. From the many available choices for the presentation of this information, the use of icons, colored text and colored light was selected, mainly for feasibility reasons. The presence status of an individual person is presented by means of colored text on the TV display. The joined presence status and activities is presented by means of colored lights, i.e., presentation without explicit interruption and integration of prior defined agreements and social conventions. Different colors represent different contexts; for example, being logged on or not in the sharing application, or whether someone else is in the same room as the user or not. In this way, the user in location B gets information about location A. These presence settings represent a compound context; they combine different information sources: activity, availability and location of more than one person. The photo-sharing application is presented by means of photo icons.

3 Implementation

Different services and applications are installed in two different Amigo homes (Figure 3). Each home has three main components, the Amigo server, the Amigo client and the Internet. In the prototype, information is shared between the Amigo server which is running various Amigo Intelligent User Services, the Amigo client, which is running the privacy aware applications, and between the two homes, A and B.

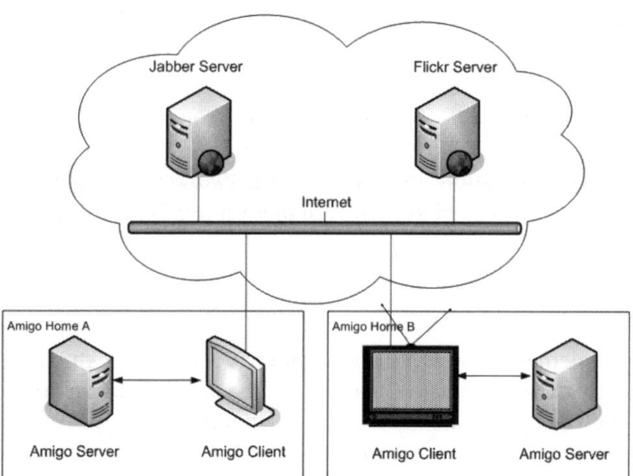

Fig. 3. Information sharing between two Amigo homes

The Amigo server consists of different services running in the home. It functions as a centralized database that stores contextual information about the home and its inhabitants and provides different types of information to the client, e.g., the location of the user. The Intelligent User Services [4, 5] from the Amigo middleware are used to retrieve contextual information and user profiles. The Context Management Service (CMS) is used to track the location of a user and store this location information on the server. The User Modeling and Profiling Service (UMPS) is used to reason on user context and feedback and to store user profiles and privacy preference settings.

The Amigo Client consists of different applications that are running in the home. These applications are, for example, a content sharing application, a lighting application (LivingColor light), and a game application. Users can set their application and location privacy preferences using the interfaces from the application. Users receive feedback from the application interface. Different user states are presented by different colors of light, e.g., online/offline/sharing photos. The Amigo client can be any display device that is connected to the Amigo server and the Internet; in this case a CE-HTML enabled television. Context information is shared between two homes through an application and the Internet.

The Internet is used to connect the homes. The Jabber server is used to store the user's contacts information. The Flickr Server [6] is used to upload and store the content; in this case, the user's photos, which have privacy-level tags. The application communicates via a Jabber server (Jabber Software Foundation, 2006 [7]). It exchanges messages on user location information, user availability and application activity between the homes. The user's availability is shown as the user's current status, e.g., is online, is away, is busy or is offline. The Jabber Server is also used for initialization of a photo sharing request and establishing the connection between the two homes.

Users are given control over which information is to be shared. Before information is passed from one component to another, it will first go through privacy decision points (PDP). PDPs consist of rule-based software that checks against the user privacy preferences that are stored in the UMPS. They control the information that is being shared between different applications across different homes. Users can modify their privacy settings from the privacy preferences interface. The PDP is enforced to make sure that the application will react according to these privacy settings and the presence and location of the user (user context). The set of photos adapts when the context of the user changes.

In sum, this implementation provides a real networked environment in which we can explore the consequences of system variables on user's perceived privacy.

4 Discussion

The prototype implementation was demonstrated as a walkthrough based on the initial usage scenario to expert users to generate feedback with regard to the initial user requirements and design guidelines. Such a running prototype system provides a much better carrier for eliciting user feedback with regard to privacy considerations than design concepts and visualizations. It has the advantages of demonstrating the consequences of changes in context and can support the exploration of different situations.

The experts that participated in the walkthrough had very different backgrounds, among others, user system interaction; security and encryption; software engineering; system architecture; and CE applications. They trusted the system. They trusted it even more than they trusted other users. One of their quotes: *"If I know the capability of the system I will trust it; I will have less trust in the people who will be using it*". It was also stated that the system *"will be trustworthy if it takes a conservative decision"*. This implies that the default value for the privacy setting should be very rigid. It is not desirable that other people know what these settings are. They also wanted a central control or setting to control the application themselves. Another issue regarding trust was expressed as: *"Can you trust the system that it is sufficiently aware of the context to adapt automatically to the right setting?"* Being sufficiently aware is the crux that needs more exploration and research work.

The relation between system autonomy and privacy is another critical factor. Being able to cheat was one of the requirements revealed by the user studies. Setting different privacy preferences and changing them during a session elicited discussions on how this might affect people's social relationships. With regard to the level of detail for the preference settings it was clear that different levels have different meanings for different people. The following verbalizations illustrate these points: *"People don't need to know that you have set some kind of privacy setting for them"*; *"If I change my privacy setting for a particular friend, people will infer something, as if I wish to hide something"*; *"If I really wanted to show my privacy settings, I should be able to override them, by having a kind of 'don't embarrass-me' button"*.

Presenting the context information by means of colored light provides opportunities for personal and intimate ambiance sharing. For this the system should be flexible. The prototype only used one light per room, but participants actually desired to have a light presentation for each individual person.

The different levels of precision that were maintained in the application for the disclosure of personal information need further exploration. It is quite clear that people require control over their personal information and that they like to vary this level of detail depending on the context at hand. These levels are different for each individual. It appears that people require about 3 levels of detail, but that these levels are at different depth for each individual. These settings might potentially cause social embarrassments and conflicts.

In sum, the application implementation made it possible to explore and experiment with privacy settings in a context-aware environment enabled by the Amigo middleware. The results highlight the need for more exploration in different settings and conditions. But it also identified that some privacy controls should be handled in a generic fashion, such as employing privacy rules and that next steps in this research need to focus on constructing more generic models.

Acknowledgement

The Amigo project is funded by the European Commission as an integrated project (IP) in the Sixth Framework Programme under the contract number IST 004182. The Amigo partners are: Philips, Fagor Electrodomesticos, France Telecom, Fraunhofer IMS, Fraunhofer SIT, Ikerlan, INRIA, Italdesign-Giugiaro, SingularLogic, Europaeisches Microsoft Innovation Center, Telematica Instituut, ICCS-NTUA, Telefonica, Univ. Paderborn, VTT.

References

[1] Amigo Deliverable D4.7. In: Janse, M., et al. (eds.) Intelligent User Services – Privacy and personal security, IST-004182 Amigo (2007)

[2] Janse, M.D., Vink, P., Soute, I., Boland, H.: Perceived Privacy in Ambient Intelligent Environments. In: Proceedings of the Context Awareness and Trust 2007 Workshop, CAT 2007, Moncton, New Brunswick, Canada, July 20, (2007) (On-line CEUR-WS proceedings ISSN 16113-0073)

[3] Lederer, S., Hong, J.I., Jiang, X., Dey, A.K., Landay, J.A., Mankoff, J.: Towards Privacy for Ubiquitous Computing, Technical Report UCB-CSD-03-1283, Computer Science Division, University of California, Berkeley (2003)

[4] Amigo Deliverable D4.7. In: Vink, P., et al. (eds.) Intelligent User Services – Context Management Service, IST-004182 Amigo (2007)

[5] Amigo Deliverable D4.7: Intelligent User Services – User Modeling and Profiling Service. Otilia Kocsis & Elena Vidjiounaite. IST-004182 Amigo (2007)

[6] http://flickr.com/

[7] Jaber software foundation, http://www.jabber.org

Ontology Based Service Modelling for Composability in Smart Home Environments

Ioanna Roussaki[1], Ioannis Papaioannou[1], Dimitrios Tsesmetzis[1], Julia Kantorovitch[2], Jarmo Kalaoja[2], and Remco Poortinga[3]

[1] School of Electrical & Computer Engineering, National Technical University of Athens, 9 Heroon Polytechneiou Str, 157-73 Zographou, Athens, Greece
{nanario,jpapai,dtsesme}@telecom.ntua.gr
[2] The Technical Research Centre of Finland (VTT), Kaitoväylä 1, 90570 Oulu, Finland
{Julia.Kantorovitch,Jarmo.Kalaoja}@vtt.fi
[3] Telematica Instituut (Telin), P.O. Box 589, 7500 AN Enschede, Netherlands
Remco.Poortinga@telin.nl

Abstract. The ontology-based semantic approaches are gradually gaining momentum in ambient intelligent environments such as smart homes, smart cars, intelligent offices, etc. In spite of the significant research work carried out in the ontology design and application field, several issues remain unresolved. The ontologies mainly focus on specific context information features. The capabilities of services from different functional domains are rarely addressed and are not aligned with context ontologies. No attempt has been made to integrate the existing ontologies, facilitating their future extension with emerging new technologies for networks, devices, software architectures and platforms. Moreover, the application developer support facilitating better understanding of semantic technologies is still in its infancy. The research work presented in this paper tackles the aforementioned issues.

Keywords: Ontology specification, service architecture, service modelling, service developer support, Intelligent Home.

1 Introduction

Ontologies are essential in ambient intelligence (AmI) environments, as they act as the means for describing the services provided by networked devices, sensors and appliances, thus facilitating their seamless automatic communication to support the users in their everyday tasks. Several research projects currently address the ontology requirements for AmI environments. Nevertheless, numerous problems remain unresolved. The designed ontologies focus mainly on very specific service aspects, e.g. modelling context [1] or QoS related service properties [2]. The capabilities of the services from different functional domains, such as personal computing, mobile, consumer electronics, and home automation (i.e. domotic) are addressed in a minor degree and are not aligned with context ontologies. No attempts have been made to integrate the existing ontologies in the domain of interest and facilitate their integration with emerging new technologies for networks, devices and software architectures and platforms. Moreover, even narrow ontologies can be very complex and are thus

M. Mühlhäuser et al. (Eds.): AmI 2007 Workshops, CCIS 11, pp. 411–420, 2008.

far from being accessible for many domain experts such as application developers. Therefore, service modelling using the semantic knowledge sources and available service semantic description languages can be time and effort consuming process. Thus, tools are required for the adoption of semantic technologies and service developer support. The research presented hereafter aims to study and address the issues above and is based on the work carried out in the Amigo project [3].

The main objective of the Amigo project is to develop an Ambient Intelligent networked system that effectively integrates heterogeneous devices and services residing in the home domain. The Amigo architecture adopts a service-oriented style. The semantic-based applications and the middleware layer interoperability mechanisms are the key elements of the Amigo architecture. The Amigo ontologies[1] enable the effective description of the heterogeneous services and resources residing in the AmI home. The ontology-based service discovery and dynamic service composition are additional challenges addressed in the project. Rich representation of service capabilities with non-functional parameters such as QoS and context enable the automatic service discovery and composition. A significant contribution of this research work is the robust ontology architecture designed, which aggregates the main core taxonomies and concepts necessary to semantically describe the services presented at home and the associated tool helping application developer in designing of intelligent semantically rich applications. The remainder of this paper is structured as follows. The architecture and modularization principles for the ontology engineering are introduced in Section 2. The Amigo core concepts, the Device, Platform, and Multimedia vocabularies are briefly exposed in Section 3. The Amigo vocabulary ontologies representing the functional and non-functional service capabilities are described in Section 4. In Section 5 the VantagePoint tool is described that has been developed to support visualised tool-aided semantic service modelling. Finally, Section 6 provides the paper conclusions and presents future research plans.

2 Architecture and Modularization Principles

The main rationale behind the overall architecture is that vocabularies should support maintainability and future evolution of concepts related to Amigo or any other home environment. The modularisation of service description vocabularies is mainly based on the specificity of the concepts defined by the vocabulary. Thus, three ontology levels are distinguished in Amigo:

- The *Core Concepts Ontologies*, the concepts defined be which are considered to be common for various fields. These ontologies are also known as "Upper-level" or "Top-level" ontologies.
- The *Core Domain Ontologies* that define concepts which are common across a specific collection of domains.
- The *Domain Ontologies* express conceptualizations that address the needs exclusively of a specific application domain. The concepts in domain ontologies are often defined as specializations of concepts in the Core Concepts and Core Domain ontologies.

---

[1] The complete Amigo ontologies (with guide for users and service developers) are publicly available at the Amigo homepage: http://amigo.gforge.inria.fr/home/index.html.

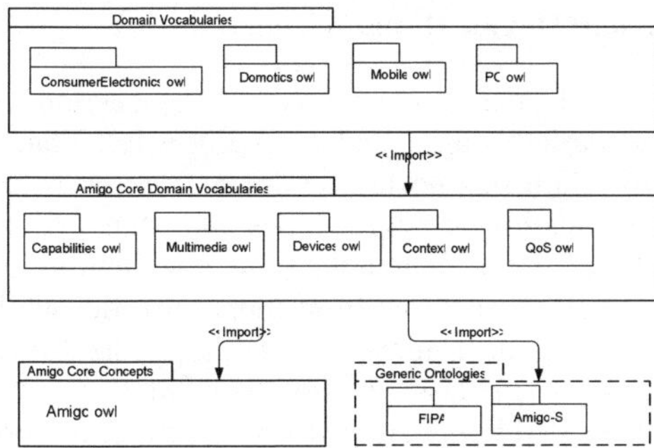

Fig. 1. Service description vocabularies' classification and dependencies

The borderline between core and domain ontologies is not clearly defined, because core ontologies tend to be generic within a domain. The service modelling vocabularies described here can be classified mainly into the last two categories. All vocabulary ontologies have been developed using OWL (http://www.w3.org/TR/owl-ref/). Its import mechanism is used to enable references on concepts from more generic ontology modules to more specialised ontologies. An ontology module can be specialised by subclassing the concepts defined in the imported file. Separate namespaces are used to prevent naming conflicts. Fig. 1 depicts the import hierarchy of the Amigo Service Description Vocabulary Ontologies.

3 Core Amigo Concepts

The Amigo core concepts define the basic vocabulary that "ties" the other vocabularies together. To keep the vocabularies modular, they avoid unnecessary references and use the core concepts when possible. The vocabularies can use the classes and property types in the Amigo core vocabulary, either directly or through sub-classing of classes and properties. The sub-classing of property types is recommended when restrictions on domain and range of relations between individuals are required. The Amigo core concepts are presented in Fig. 2.

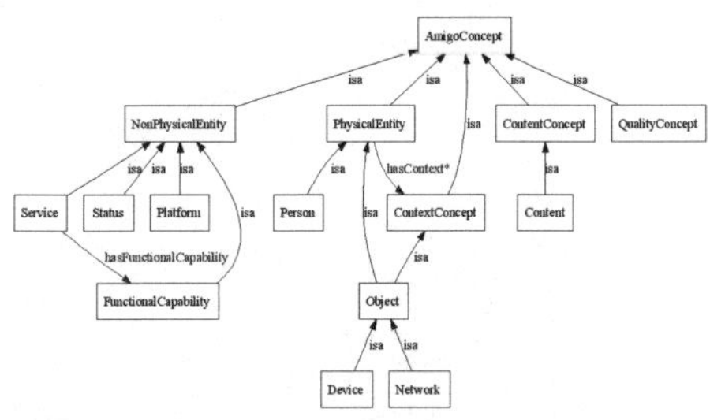

Fig. 2. Core Amigo ontology concepts

3.1 Amigo Platform and Device Domain Vocabularies

The main classifications of generic platforms and devices are described in the platform and device vocabularies (Fig. 3 and 4 respectively). Platform vocabulary provides a classification of platforms hosted by devices, whereas the device vocabulary provides a generic classification of device types and states. Although these concepts can be used to characterize the device context, the vocabularies are still very generic. The integration of descriptor structures from more specific ontology languages such as FIPA device profiles can be achieved by defining the FIPA compatible device related quality concepts as subclass of Amigo:QualityConcept (Fig. 5). However, several aspects of this are still being studied taking into consideration the QoS, Multimedia and Consumer Electronics vocabularies.

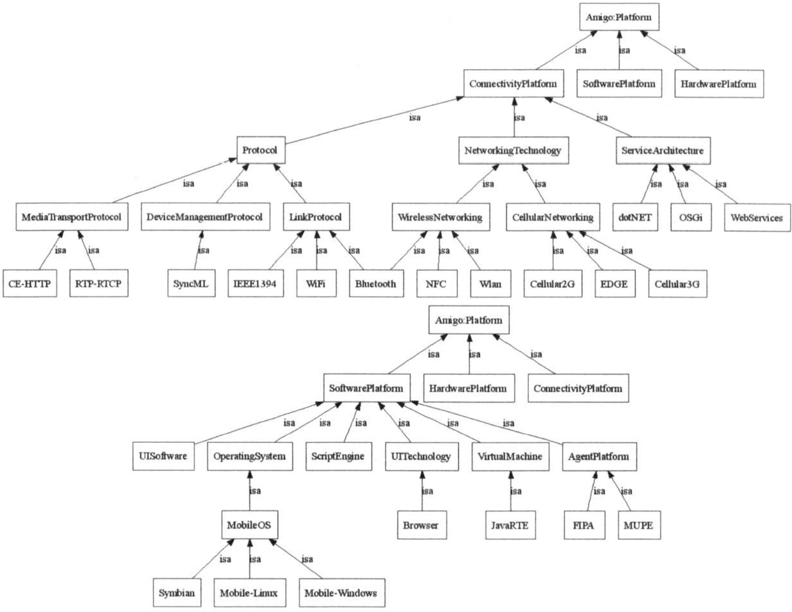

Fig. 3. The Amigo platform vocabulary ontology

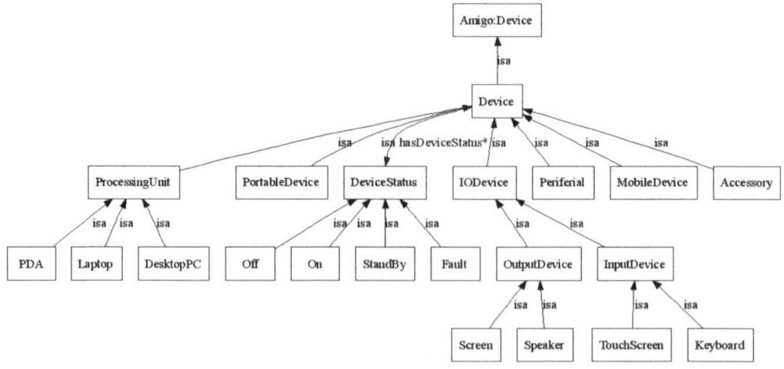

Fig. 4. The device vocabulary ontology

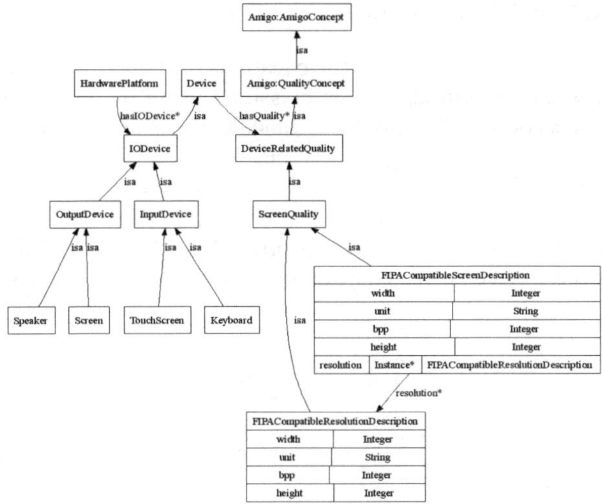

Fig. 5. An example of integration of FIPA compatible screen descriptors to the Amigo device vocabulary ontology

3.2 Multimedia Domain Vocabulary

Multimedia vocabulary describes the various content types that can be processed by the devices inside the Amigo home. The design & development of such a multimedia domain vocabulary ontology is extremely useful in terms of content adaptation and integration on the one side, and it facilitates the diverse requirements originated by the Amigo designers with regards to content and the corresponding devices that deliver it. The multimedia ontology is depicted in Fig. 6.

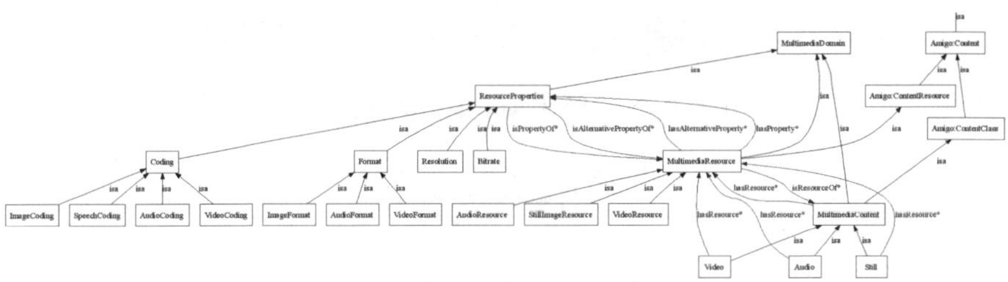

Fig. 6. The multimedia domain ontology

4   Amigo Functional and Non-functional Capabilities Vocabularies

This section briefly describes the Amigo vocabulary ontologies representing the functional service capabilities, and the ones expressing the non-functional capabilities, i.e. the Quality of Service (QoS) and the Context related capabilities.

4.1 Functional Capabilities Vocabularies

These vocabularies refine the functional capabilities of the entities in Amigo Core Concepts. Functional capabilities can be classified using the taxonomy provided by the Amigo core vocabulary. To link these functional capabilities with semantic software service description languages, this classification is extended by two new concepts: the ServiceProfileCapability and the ServiceCapability. These concepts represent the roles of functional capabilities, when offered by a software service. This distinction enables reasoning on service profile hierarchy and capabilities provided and required by the service profiles during the semantic service discovery process.

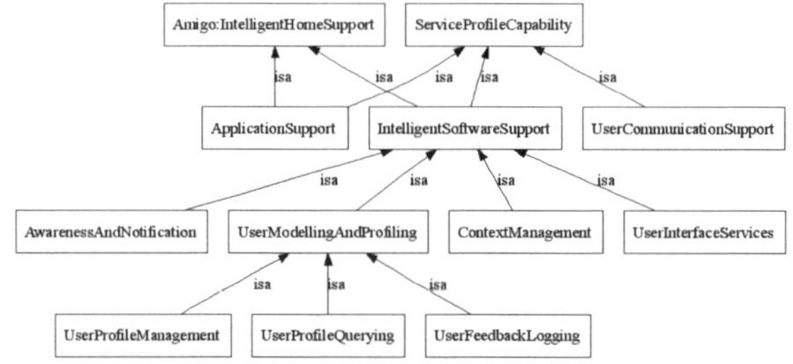

Fig. 7. Part of ProfileCapability ontology hierarchy

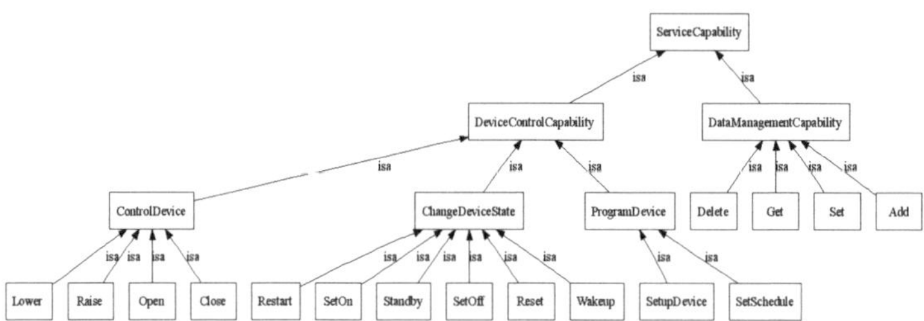

Fig. 8. Part of ServiceCapability hierarchy

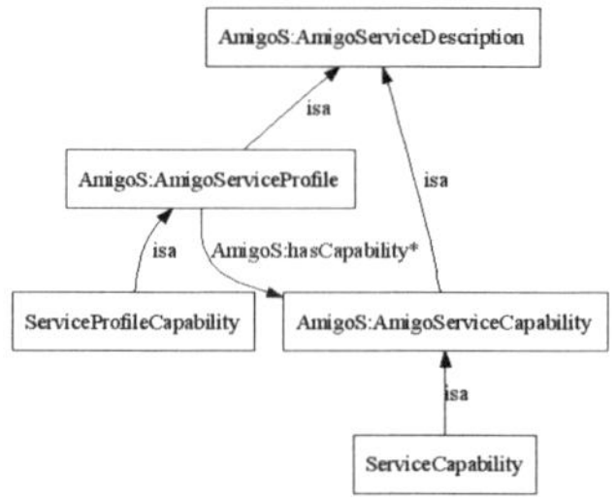

Fig. 9. Linking vocabularies with the service description language

The hierarchy under ServiceProfileCapability (Fig. 7) describes the functional capabilities that can be used to classify profiles presented by software services. This also includes the set of intelligent services provided by the upper layer of the Amigo middleware. The hierarchy under ServiceCapability (Fig. 8) represents the functional capabilities provided or required by a service and is expressed as part of its profile. Fig. 9 links these two concept hierarchies with a service description language.

4.2 Non-functional Capabilities Vocabularies

The QoS classification illustrated in Fig. 10 can be used to represent part of the service profiles, to providing additional information with regards to their QoS capabilities [4]. Furthermore, it can be used to describe the QoS preferences of users.

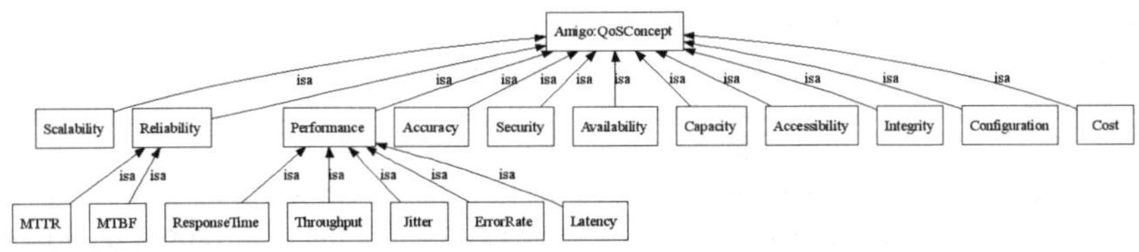

Fig. 10. Part of the QoS vocabulary ontology

The classification depicted in Fig. 11 presents the overall hierarchy of the six context domains. In Fig. 12, the Physical Context vocabulary depicted describes entities concerning time, space or environment profiles, whereas the User Context vocabulary illustrated in Fig. 13 describes the User entity and is used for creating, and altering the profile of the Amigo User.

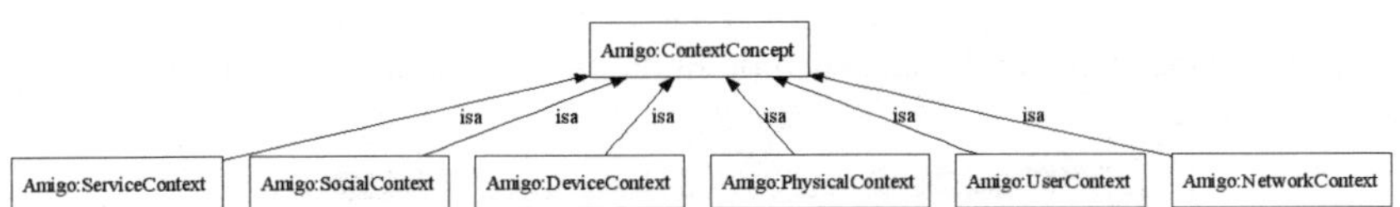

Fig. 11. Core context semantic domains

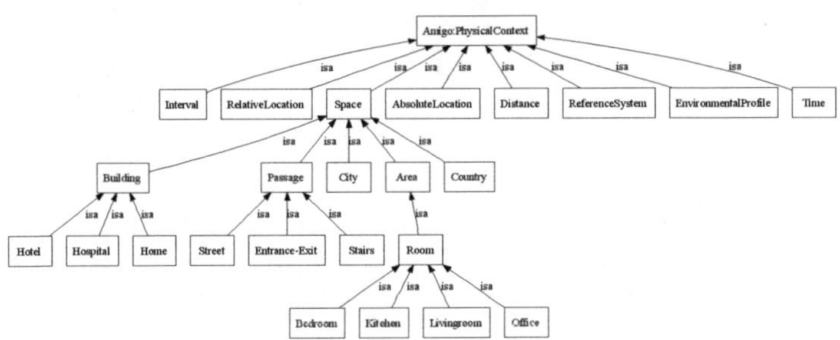

Fig. 12. Physical Context vocabulary ontology

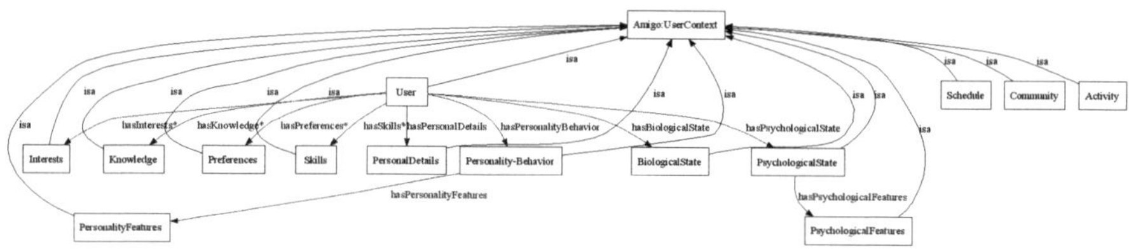

Fig. 13. Part of the User Context vocabulary

5   Interactive Ontology Visualization

As one may easily observe in Fig. 2-13, the Amigo ontologies are quit complex, thus not being very user friendly for non-experts in OWL. To make such ontologies widely usable for service modellers, they first need to be easily interpretable. Information visualization is concerned with presenting data to users, by means of interactive or animated digital images, thus improving their understanding. Therefore, visual interpretation of semantic information models of services and applications in dynamic networked home would help users (service developers, researchers) to better understand the data represented by ontologies. Several open source software and commercial tools to support ontology development and visualization are available, such as Ontoviz (http://protege.cim3.net/cgi-bin/wiki.pl?OntoViz) and Jambalaya (http:// www.thechiselgroup.org/jambalaya), which are used by ontology editors such as Protégé [5]. These visualization approaches are domain independent. However, they are graph based and are limited to showing mainly the structural relations of ontology classes and instances. These tools and are not well suited for understanding semantic relations in complex dynamic application scenarios. To address this, the VantagePoint tool [6] has been developed, which allows visualization of ontology models related to AmI services in dynamic networked home related application scenarios, also providing visual editing and interaction user interfaces for these models. It also offers means to create domain specific libraries of semantic information (e.g. device

Fig. 14. The isometric view of the Amigo house

types and services hosted by devices, context, user preferences) and to dynamically import external OWL Ontologies. The ontologies developed and discussed in Sections 3 and 4 have been used for this purpose.

VantagePoint can represent for example a real-world home or laboratory environment as in Fig.14. A developer can use the visualizations to create contextual scenarios related to AmI applications, in order to gain better understanding of the semantic models associated to the services that the application uses. The Jena (http://jena.sourceforge.net/) semantic web Java-based framework is used to manage and to query OWL ontologies. VantagePoint offers a convenient user interface to specify a query based on SPARQL (http://www.w3.org/TR/rdf-sparql-query/). More advanced developers can specify their own sophisticated queries. For the less semantics-familiar developers, VantagePoint provides some predefined sets of query templates. Therefore, information such as services of particular areas deployed by specific devices, or information related to the persons in the AmI home can be easily obtained. For example, the developer can write and test a free form query statement to find out the services available (deployed by the devices in area) in selected area:

SELECT ?x ?y
   WHERE {<#INSTANCE#> <#contains> ?x. ?x <#deploysService> ?y}
The result of the query (by selecting an area in the AmI home) is visualised in Fig. 14.

6   Conclusions

This paper deals with the ontology modelling for AmI home environments. A significant contribution of this research is the robust ontology architecture designed, which aggregates the core taxonomies and concepts necessary to semantically describe the services present at home. This facilitates the automatic service discovery, composition and communication in the AmI home. The modularization principle has been introduced, while means of integrating existing ontologies have been also demonstrated. This kind of modularization enables the integration of existing ontologies in the home domain and the introduction of new ones, in order to describe the emerging technologies of home devices, networks, services and platforms. This paper further elaborates on the VantagePoint tool implemented that offers a user-friendly visual interface enabling developers to easily model the smart home environment and relevant services and applications. The presented semantic framework has been developed and evaluated. The prototype implemented aims, among others, to validate the introduced ontologies by using them in dynamic service discovery and composition in a smart home laboratory [7]. It lies among our future plans to apply our ontologies in the automatic service configuration domain.

References

1. Sirin, F., Parsia, B., Hendler, J.: Filtering and selecting semantic web services with interactive composition techniques. IEEE Intelligent Systems 19(4), 42–49 (2004)
2. Maximilien, W.M., Singh, M.P.: A framework and ontology for dynamic web services selection. IEEE Internet Computing 8(5), 84–93 (2004)

3. Amigo Project homepage, `http://www.amigo-project.org`
4. Tsesmetzis, D., Roussaki, I., Papaioannou., I., Anagnostou, M.: QoS awareness support in Web-Service semantics. In: International Conference on Internet and Web Applications and Services, Guadeloupe, French Caribbean 128–134 (2006)
5. Protégé ontology editor and knowledge-base framework, `http://protege.stanford.edu/`
6. Niskanen, I., Kalaoja, J., Kantorovitch, J., Piirainen, T.: An Interactive Ontology Visualization Approach for the Networked Home Environment. International Journal of Computer and Information Science and Engineering 1(2), 102–107 (2007)
7. Philips Homelab homepage, `http://www.research.philips.com/technologies/misc/homelab/`

Amigo Interoperability Framework: Dynamically Integrating Heterogeneous Devices and Services

Graham Thomson[1], Daniele Sacchetti[1],
Yérom-David Bromberg[1], Jorge Parra[2],
Nikolaos Georgantas[1], and Valérie Issarny[1]

[1] ARLES Project-Team,
INRIA Paris - Rocquencourt,
11 domaine de Voluceau
BP 105, 78153 Le Chesnay Cedex,
France
[2] IKERLAN S. Coop.,
Apdo. 146,
Po. J. Ma. Arizmendiarrieta, 2,
20500 Arrasate-Mondragón,
Gipuzkoa,
España

Abstract. The Amigo Interoperability Framework provides middleware-layer mechanisms that enable integrating heterogeneous networked devices and services. It includes a service discovery and interaction interoperability architecture and a domotic architecture, which have been tested in combination in a proof-of-concept prototype.

Keywords: Interoperability, inter-working, service discovery protocol, service interaction protocol, domotic device.

1   Introduction

The Amigo Interoperability Framework provides middleware-layer mechanisms that allow for integrating heterogeneous services in the networked home independently of their underlying software and hardware technologies. Integration is achieved by bridging between the service (discovery and interaction) protocols run by the various devices.

Target networked services come from the four application domains of the Amigo home, i.e., from the Personal Computing (PC), Mobile Computing, Consumer Electronics (CE) and Home Automation domains.

The middleware protocols being bridged include:

- service-oriented interaction protocols, such as those offered by Web Services (SOAP), UPnP (SOAP), and RMI-based infrastructures.
- service discovery protocols such as SLP, UPnP and WS-Discovery.

M. Mühlhäuser et al. (Eds.): AmI 2007 Workshops, CCIS 11, pp. 421–425, 2008.

Additional middleware-related protocols being integrated embrace the control / command protocols from the Home Automation domain.

The developed domotic infrastructure aims at enabling the integration of different device technologies (e.g., BDF - Fagor Domotic Bus, EIB - European Installation Bus), exposing them by means of standard service platforms (UPnP, Web Services), and isolating at the same time the service clients from the specific low-level device technologies.

Control protocols for multimedia content distribution from the CE domain are also implicitly supported based on the bridging of service discovery and interaction protocols.

A proof-of-concept prototype of the Amigo Interoperability Framework that integrates services from different domains is depicted in Figure 1.

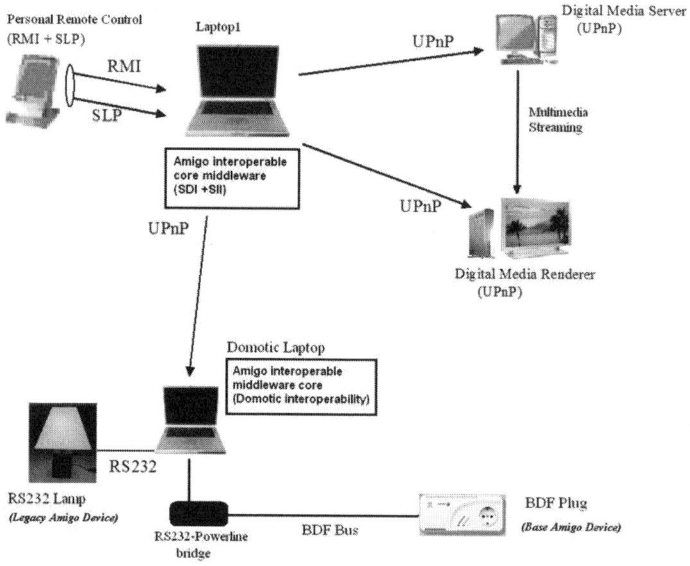

Fig. 1. The architecture of the proof-of-concept prototype of the Interoperability Framework

2   Interoperability Framework Description

As shown in Figure 2, the service discovery interoperability component [1,2] employs a monitor and an instantiator component, which, respectively, detect the service discovery protocols (SDPs) present in the environment and instantiate appropriate SDP units.

Inside a SDP unit, a parser component generates semantic events from input protocol messages, and a composer component generates output protocol messages from semantic events.

Interoperability between two SDPs is realized by combining a parser and a composer from each SDP in either direction. Semantic events represent common features among all SDPs.

For service interaction interoperability [1,2], as shown in Figure 2, the service discovery interoperability function is first employed by a client for obtaining the description and reference of a remote service.

Then, a generator component dynamically instantiates a stub from the description and reference of the service. The stub acts as an intermediary between the client and the remote service for invocation of the service. The stub contains two service interaction protocol units, which are similar in structure and functionality to SDP units.

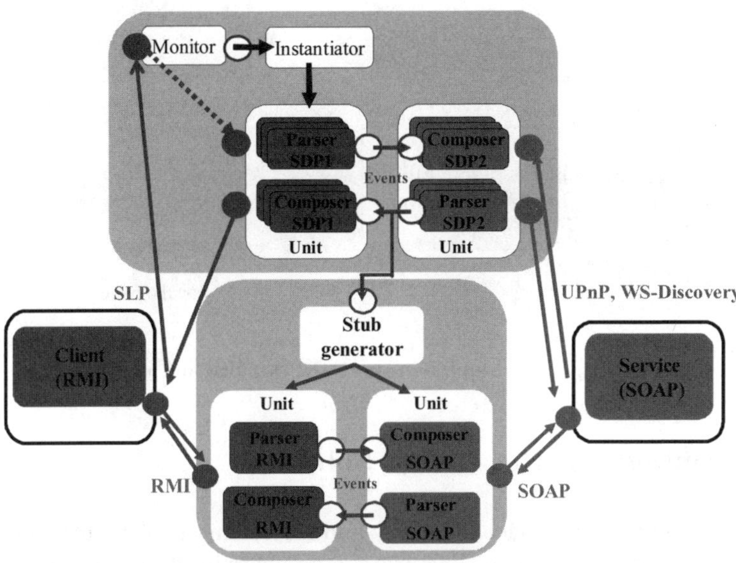

Fig. 2. The architecture of the service discovery and service interaction interoperability components

The domotic infrastructure [1], as shown in Figure 3, comprises a number of layers that decouple the low-level domotic technologies from the high-level service platforms. Low-level drivers for base technologies (BDF, EIB) extract the required information about the domotic devices.

This information is translated into an abstract intermediate service description, independent of specific domotic technologies, which is the Domotic Service Model.

High-level drivers dynamically instantiate high-level proxies (UPnP, Web Services) from the generic Domotic Service Model descriptions.

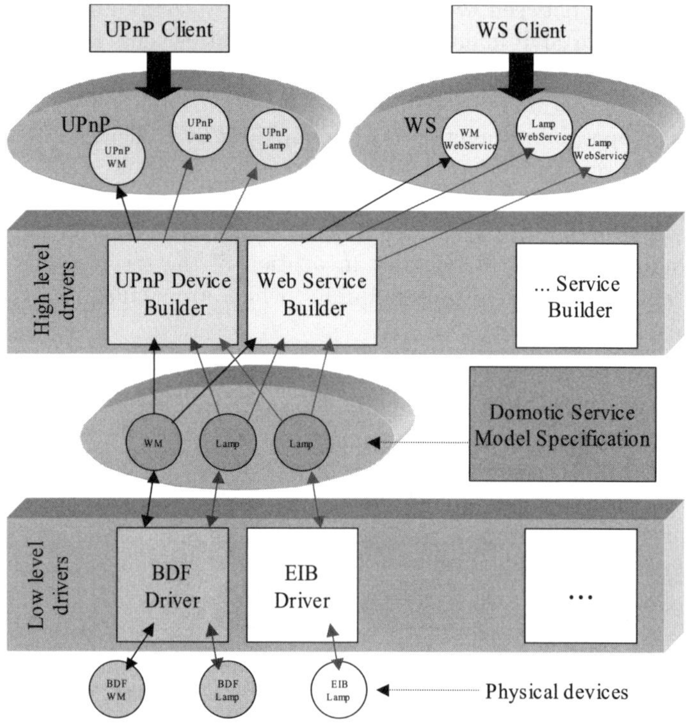

Fig. 3. The layered architecture of the domotic infrastructure

3   Advantages of the Amigo Solution

The Amigo solution to service discovery and service interaction interoperability ensures inter-working between the most common service discovery (SLP, UPnP, WS-Discovery) and service interaction (RMI, SOAP) protocols.

The Amigo approach to the domotic infrastructure exposes heterogeneous domotic devices as UPnP or Web services.

Both approaches as a whole enable integration of a large set of heterogeneous device and service technologies. A combination of both approaches has been implemented in the proof-of-concept prototype of Figure 1.

4   New to This Approach

The Amigo Interoperability Framework integrates a number of novel features. Service discovery and service interaction interoperability are supported transparently for concerned devices and services, as the inter-working mechanisms intervene between the native middleware and the underlying network protocol stack.

These mechanisms are flexible and extensible: they may be deployed on the client or service host or on an intermediate networked node; they may further be dynamically instantiated.

We have employed C as the programming language for these mechanisms for achieving independence of any platform or execution environment such as the JVM.

Further, our solution is specifically designed for open networked resource-constrained environments.

Finally, the domotic infrastructure enables easy incorporation of other low-level bus or high-level service technologies.

5   Conclusions

The Amigo Interoperability Framework enables device and service interoperability. It has already been made available as open-source software at https://gforge.inria.fr/projects/amigo/.

Projects based on the Amigo Interoperability Framework may be entered into the Amigo Challenge programming competition. Details of the Amigo Challenge are available at http://www.extra.research.philips.com/amigochallenge/.

6   Additional Information

Additional information is available online at:
http://www.hitech-projects.com/euprojects/amigo.

References

1. Amigo Consortium. Deliverable D3.3: Amigo middleware core enhanced: Prototype implementation and documentation (October 2006), Available at
   `http://www.hitech-projects.com/euprojects/amigo/deliverables.htm`
2. Bromberg, Y.-D., Issarny, V.: Indiss: Interoperable discovery system for networked services. In: Proceedings of the ACM/IFIP/USENIX 6th International Middleware Conference, Grenoble, France (November 2005)

WASP – Wirelessly Accessible Sensor Populations: A Project Overview

Peter van der Stok[1], Holger Karl[2], Fabio De Ambroggi[3],
Jean-Dominique Decotignie[4], Frank Siegemund[5], Kees Lokhorst[6],
and Michael Hellenschmidt[7]

[1] Philips Research Laboratories, Eindhoven, The Netherlands
`peter.van.der.stok@philips.com`
[2] Computer Networks Group, University of Paderborn, Germany
`holger.karl@upb.de`
[3] ST Microelectronics, Italy
`fabio.deambroggi@st.com`
[4] Swiss Center for Electronics and Microtechnologie CSEM, Neuchâtel, Switzerland
`jean-dominique.decotignie@csem.ch`
[5] European Microsoft Innovation Center, Aachen, Germany
`franksie@microsoft.com`
[6] Animal Sciences Group of Wageningen UR, The Netherlands
`kees.lokhorst@wur.nl`
[7] Fraunhofer Institute for Computer Graphics Research IGD, Darmstadt, Germany
`michael.hellenschmidt@igd.fraunhofer.de`

Abstract. This article presents an overview of the integrated project WASP that deals with the research and development of Wirelessly Accessible Sensor Populations. WASP is a European project of the Embedded Systems Strategic Objective in Framework Programme 6 of the European Union. WASP is covering the complete technology chain from sensor node hardware to the implementation of applications. The article illustrates the integrated approach of WASP by subsuming the variety of research and development issues that are addressed to reach the ambitious project goal: the provision of a complete system view for building large populations of collaborating objects.

1 A WASP Introduction

An important class of collaborating objects is represented by the myriad of wireless sensors, which will constitute the infrastructure for the ambient intelligence vision. The academic world actively investigates the technology for Wireless Sensor Networks (WSN). Industry is reluctant to use these results from academic research. A major cause is the magnitude of the mismatch between research at the application level and the node and network level. The WASP project [1] aims at narrowing this mismatch by covering the whole range from basic hardware, sensors, processor, communication, the packaging of the nodes, the organization of the nodes, to the information distribution and a selection of applications.

M. Mühlhäuser et al. (Eds.): AmI 2007 Workshops, CCIS 11, pp. 426–429, 2008.

The emphasis in the project is in the self-organization and the services that link the application to the sensor network. Research into the nodes themselves is needed because there is a strong link between the required flexibility and the hardware design. Research into the applications is necessary as the properties of the required service will influence the configuration of both sensor network and application for optimum efficiency and functionality.

Not all design decisions can be handled in isolation as they depend on the hardware costs involved in making a sensor and the market size for sensors of a given type. The general goal of the project is the provision of a complete system view for building large populations of collaborating objects. The impact on European industry and research will come from the provision of an European alternative to the WSNs originating in the USA. The WASP results will be well suited for adoption by SMEs (small and medium-sized enterprises). The consortium defines an active programme to approach the appropriate SMEs and to familiarize them with the WASP results [2]. Three business areas, selected for their societal relevance and technical differences, validate the results of the project. Figure 1 illustrates the integrated approach of the WASP project, covering the complete chain from the physical nodes to the implementation of real life prototypes. The three business areas – assisted road transport, elderly care and herd health control (Figure 1 right) – are chosen because of their societal and economic relevance for the European society (refer to [3,4]).

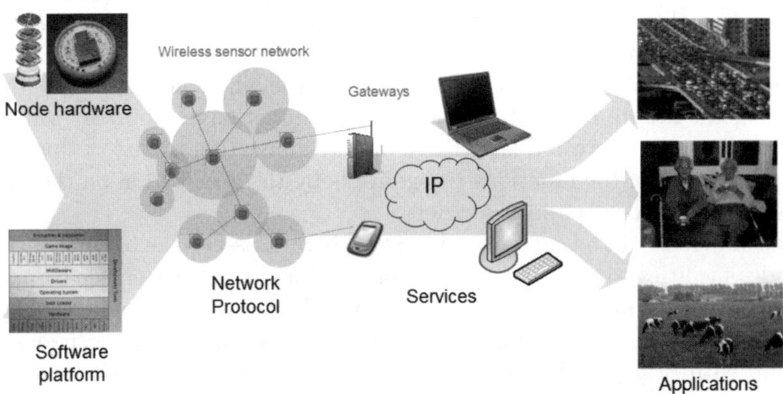

Fig. 1. Architectural View on the WASP approach

2   The WASP Research Topics

WASP seeks to optimize wireless sensor network technologies in order to facilitate and speed up the development of applications using distributed sensor ensembles. Consequently different research and development topics form the integrated approach of the WASP project. Figure 1 illustrates the discrimination into node hardware, software platforms, network protocols, services and applications. Taken together these topics constitute an integrated technology chain for implementing applications using a plurality of wireless sensors.

The **node hardware** has to be small and self-containing, but offering a variety of different sensor modes and communication techniques in order to be appropriate for the chosen application scenarios. Therefore, WASP focuses on the design of MAC portability to support the communication between nodes, the integration of sensors designed to measure physical parameters like pressure, humidity and others, and the design of the processors, which activate the hardware and support the sensor-related software. Finally, the packaging to make the sensor node a flexible, extendable sensor node, and the generation (e. g. by scavenging) and the storage of energy are considered. The emphasis is on exploiting the state of the art to make the projected flexibility possible.

The **software platform** on the nodes will provide the software infrastructure on top of the configurable hardware node and the network connections to support efficient data collection and resource consumption optimisations. The research work here focuses on local optimisations and provides hooks to higher-level optimisation strategies. The activity is essential to a viable deployment of sensor networks. It also provides the frameworks in which the network-wide optimisations can be executed. On top of that, the **networking protocols** provide abstractions to hide the individual nodes and the network topology. The applications do not address the individual nodes or handle the network topology, but they access the services, the functions of the virtual moving objects they need to invoke. The abstractions also minimise the user involvement in setting up and operating the network. The sheer size of the network excludes setting and configuring individual elements by hand, let alone the whole network configuration. Assuring the secure recognition and access of functions within the sensor network without configuration knowledge by the application is part of this activity. The granularity of the functions recognisable by the application on the different parts of the network is addressed here.

The **services** can be categorized in three main classes. The optimisation class provides facilities to optimise the network and node settings either by applying network-wide optimisation strategies or by adapting specific node parameters based on a given node grouping. The gateway class allows sensor nodes to co-operate with other kinds of computing devices and a surrounding networking infrastructure if available. Hence, gateway services provide access to the sensors by means of mobile user devices or possibly over IP-based networks from remote computers. The emphasis is on secure and privacy-conserving interactions with the sensors. The maintenance class aims at helping programmers to develop, test and deploy applications as well as to supervise the status of a wireless sensor network.

Finally, the **applications** guide the design and validate the results of WASP. They provide guidelines on the detection of specialised functions dependent on the physiological aspects of the measured physical parameters. They also guide the required abstraction to be accessible to the services. Four extra-functional aspects were selected that guide the decision making process across all activities in the project: reduced energy consumption, timeliness, efficiency and security.

3   Summary

The WASP project – a 6th Framework Programme project of the European Information Society Technologies [5] – aims at the development of an autonomous and intelligent infrastructure, which incorporates a wireless sensor network. The main focus lies on the implementation of a cost-efficient infrastructure that encourages application-driven optimisation of the network composed of generic nodes. The deployment of the developed infrastructure within a prototype will be done – based on selected applications – to validate both the sensor network design and the genericity of the offered design.

Furthermore, WASP seeks provide a consistent chain of software components to support energy-optimization, security, quality of service (QoS) guarantees, and the specification of trade-off preferences by the application. Application developers will be supported by design-rules for configurable sensor nodes, for implementing their applications and for optimizing communication strategies with respect to energy-efficiency and reliability.

Acknowledgements

This work is partially financed by the European Commission under the FP 6 IST Project "Wirelessly Accessible Sensor Populations (WASP)" under contract IST-034963. The authors would like to thank all WASP project members for their contributions and discussions during project workshops and meetings.

References

1. WASP, Wirelessly Accessible Sensor Populations, IST-2006-034963, Project Homepage, `http://www.wasp-project.org`
2. Industrial Workshop on Wirelessly Accessible Sensor Populations, Fraunhofer IGD, Darmstadt, Germany, (September 27, 2007),
   `http://www.igd.fhg.de/igd-a1/wasp/`
3. Facing The Challenge. The Lisbon strategy for growth and employment. Report from the High Level Group chaired by Wim Kok, Office for Official Publications of the European Communities (November 2004), `http://ec.europa.eu/growthandjobs/pdf/kok_report_en.pdf`, ISBN 92-894-7054-2
4. Baroso, Verheugen: Working together for growth and jobs: A new start for the Lisbon Strategy Brussels (February 2, 2005), `http://eur-lex.europa.eu/LexUriServ/site/en/com/2005/com2005_0024en01.pdf`
5. Information Society Technologies (IST), Embedded Systems,
   `http://cordis.europa.eu/ist/embedded/`

The WASP Architecture for Wireless Sensor Networks

Johan Lukkien[1], Frank Siegemund[2], Richard Verhoeven[1], Remi Bosman[1],
Laurent Gomez[3], and Michael Hellenschmidt[4]

[1] Einhoven University of Technology, Eindhoven, The Netherlands
`j.j.lukkien@tue.nl`
[2] European Microsoft Innovation Center, Aachen, Germany
`franksie@microsoft.com`
[3] SAP Research, Mougins, France
`laurent.gomez@sap.com`
[4] Fraunhofer Institute for Computer Graphics Research IGD, Darmstadt, Germany
`michael.hellenschmidt@igd.fraunhofer.de`

Abstract. This paper presents some intermediate results of the EU-IST
project WASP that aims to develop an integrated model for implementing applications using wireless sensor networks. In this paper we present
our approach to programming sensor networks. The main contribution
concerns the separation of three abstraction levels leaving more room for
standardization than with current practices. In addition, we propose to
program the network from an overall perspective rather than programming individual nodes. For doing this we present two programming models that complement one another. The proposed programming model is
event-based, corresponding closely to the nature of wireless sensors. The
paper shows our approaches by giving several examples and ends with
a description of wireless sensor networks related services and gives an
outlook on future work.

1 Introduction

The vision of wireless sensor networks is to deploy networks of ubiquitous and
intelligent sensors in order to gather information from an environment or to run
highly decentralized applications. A wide application range is foreseen where
the focus lies on long-term monitoring, and operation under harsh or difficult
environment conditions. In this way data can be gathered or monitoring solutions
can be created that are not possible with current standard approaches.

An important aspect in this field concerns programming such a network towards a specific task. While in conventional distributed programming individual
machines are by themselves powerful workstations, this is not true for wireless
sensors. Much more than in regular computer systems, the value of a sensor
network comes from the collaboration among the nodes. Also, this collaboration
and possible tradeoffs therein are of dominant importance from a performance
perspective. One might say that the application is, in fact, this collaboration.

M. Mühlhäuser et al. (Eds.): AmI 2007 Workshops, CCIS 11, pp. 430–447, 2008.

This poses several problems that form roadblocks to successful and massive deployment.

First, it is not easy to program applications because of the inconsistent behavior of individual nodes. In the majority of cases the conceptual picture of the application is blurred, because the logic of the network functionality is spread over a large set of individual node programs. In addition, the technical know-how required to program such sensors mostly restricts the application of sensor networks to teams of experts. Effort spent in programming one type of node does not necessarily carry over to a different type of node. This holds especially for sensor networks with a high degree of heterogeneity. Thirdly, wireless sensors provide only a few abstractions to programmers such as operating systems, network stacks and/or libraries, though simple versions exist. Finally, the program deployment procedure is non-trivial because of the absence of regular interfaces, the large numbers of nodes, the embedding into the environment and the limited resources available inside the nodes.

Within the European IST Project WASP (Wirelessly Accessible Sensor Populations) one of the objectives is to provide an integrated approach to programming and deploying wireless sensor networks. It should become easier, quicker and more reliable to establish useful applications in a sensor network, which is of crucial importance in order for these networks to become really ubiquitous. In our view this means that, rather than programming the individual nodes to arrive at the reasonable global behavior, we should start from this global behavior and derive node code/instructions from that.

The idea of using a programming model at the level of an entire network has a profound consequence on the program translation and deployment procedure. Regarding the translation, instructions for individual nodes should be derived from the program code. Regarding the deployment, efficient deployment to a wide range of target architectures should remain possible. For example, deployment towards sensor nodes with limited resources, without any behavior updated and only a few communications must be possible, as well as deployment towards sensors that have many resources and change functions regularly. The first corresponds to e. g. a fire monitoring sensor out in the forest, the second to a health monitoring sensor that is charged overnight. It is a challenge to use the same programming model for admitting both types of deployment without performance penalties.

Changing, adapting or renewing the functions on a sensor node is considered to be a vital ingredient of sensor operation, for a variety of reasons. A first reason for this is just the need for refreshing the program code towards a new version. This is difficult because of the number of sensors and their embedding which makes them difficult to reach and control. The second reason is the ability to respond to sensed conditions or new queries coming from the user-level applications. E.g., a fire-alert monitoring sensor network may adapt its alert level to observed humidity or temperature. A third reason for adaptive behavior is the ability to blend in in a new environment, i.e., to establish cooperation in a new environment and/or with new devices.

2   Principles and Design Guidelines

The WASP programming model will support the programming of an entire network. We aim for integrated knowledge, contained in the node instructions to be derived from the program. Consequently, node control is externalized. The following issues are strongly influencing the choices in our programming model and our architectural design.

Node knowledge
Any system comes with assumptions about its environment and wireless sensor nodes are no exception to this. In the context of the current discussion this environment concerns neighboring nodes or, more general, the services (functions) a node can use from this environment. At one extreme a node knows exactly which services or functions it will utilise and what these services look like and how connections with neighbors are set up; the knowledge it has is integrated with the code upon deployment. We call this *integrated knowledge*. At the other extreme, a node needs to learn from external sources (e. g. a service description or ontology). Hence it starts with *zero knowledge* and starts understanding how to use its neighbors based on descriptions. From a programming perspective, the integrated knowledge case corresponds to developing a program for all nodes in a network by a single party. In the zero knowledge case nodes are integrated that were developed by several parties independently. Somewhat in the middle is the use of a standard defining the functions in the nodes. Clearly, the zero-knowledge programming paradigm has high complexity (as nodes must be able to dynamically understand the services surrounding them) and high flexibility whereas it is the other way around with the integrated knowledge.

Node control
Closely related to the issue of knowledge is the question where control lies. When considering control we think about which entity is in control of decisions a node takes or more generally, the entity in control of a nodes' behavior. There are again two extreme choices. First, a node can be completely independent of its environment and decide by itself on its activities (e. g. it performs computations and initiates interactions autonomously). Alternatively, a node can be completely passive awaiting instructions from outside (e. g. from an orchestrator or other nodes). A fair tradeoff between these two extremes is a configurable node that would remain passive until an external entity configures it to start interaction. An example of this is an orchestrator binding a node service to another node. After this configuration the node has some form of internal control over the interaction. Note that having a too high degree of internal control will limit the reusability of nodes, though their ability to operate independent of the rest of the network increases. But too much internal control is affecting overall optimization. For example, if nodes have full internal control, then there is no mediating party which can prevent conflicts around resources. Therefore, in terms of complexity and flexibility, internal control is inflexible as decisions and functions are predefined. Thus, the configurable control is most flexible at the expense of extra complexity, realizing this configuration based on external instructions.

Adaptivity

The configurability touches upon a third issue, the node adaptivity. In general this refers to node behavior that changes according to state changes. Also it includes installing new behavior at nodes. The latter boils down to the ability to upload code; the former may be done by making the node program take this state into account. In sensor networks the phase of 'normal' behavior that include simple state-dependent behavior is considered to be the norm; the updating is the exception. Therefore it seems natural to separate the two: a node can be switched to configuration mode during which it receives the information to perform the functions it needs to perform. This can go as far as uploading a new binary. After that it moves to the run mode in which it executes its functions in an optimized way. Hence, while in configuration mode we may use advanced concepts like virtual machines and interpreted code, while in run mode we have optimized execution without interpretation.

Interoperability

Programming also brings the issue of node diversity and portability. It would be nice if all existing nodes could be programmed on the same footing. From experience over the last years we have learned that the network is a good place for standardization. By defining a protocol, all nodes that adhere to the protocol can cooperate independent of their internal organization. Node functions are then defined at the network and they are approached through the network in a service oriented manner.

Addressing

A last point is the notion of content-base addressing. The idea behind this is that in sensor networks destinations for information are selected based on that information itself. Although the idea is nice, the implementation is not obvious. The programming model determines to a large extent whether an efficient realization is possible. This topic is not in the focus of this paper.

3   Architecture and Design

Three abstraction levels

An important aspect of our approach is that we distinguish three abstraction levels: node, network and application, see Figure 1 and Figure 4. Each abstraction level comes with a set of concepts and primitives. The node level represents the abstraction level delivered by OS and libraries. Mostly it is dependent on the architecture of the sensor and offers instruction-set dependencies. The application level is the abstraction level of the network application. Here concepts of much higher abstraction have been proposed, e. g. Linda-type tuple spaces [2], agents [16] and databases [13,12]. The network abstraction level is in between and is characterized by layout and semantics of messages and how nodes expose themselves on the network. This abstraction level is often not fully developed. Rather we find two approaches to relate application and node abstraction. The first is by pushing the application abstraction towards the node by developing a

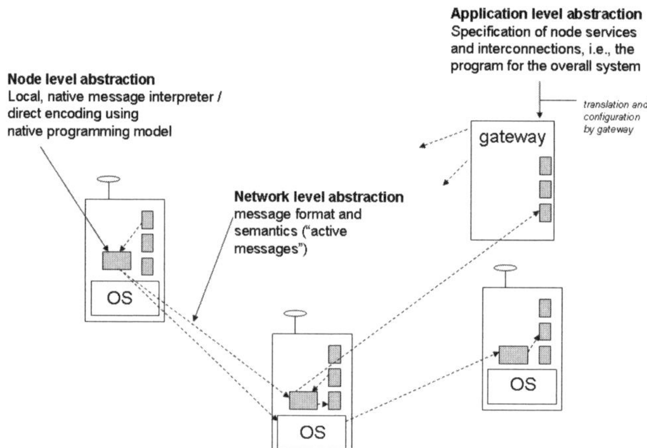

Fig. 1. A simplified picture of a sensor network describing three logical levels of abstraction. Programs running on nodes are written in a native language, particularly targeted towards the architecture, OS and ISA at hand. The network level comprises message format and semantics. We aim for messages being entirely self-contained, not needing additional context for their handling. The application level represents the specification of the wanted behavior of the network as a whole.

library that yields the same concepts in the node as there are in the application level. This just means that node programming becomes easier. The library then hides the implementation details of communication and distributed processing. The other is to have an interpretation engine on the nodes which realizes the processing needed for the application program. In both cases the used protocols and message meanings are implicit.

In our approach we regard the network abstraction level as intermediate; message layout and message semantics have the intent not to sacrifice performance or expressive power. This means that it should still remain possible to map different application programming models to this network level with no more cost than a direct implementation as is currently done. When we achieve this we have established an important step towards standardization since this network level abstraction can be independent of OS, ISA or language binding. Summarizing in short, nodes expose services on the network that represent a call interface and/or an event interface. By making a logical connection between a service event in one node and a service call in another node (called a subscription), cross-node eventing is realized. This is the only interaction possible.

Application programming model
Our application level programming model consists of two parts: first the definition of the services that must be installed on each node and second the interconnections between these. Each service consists of a collection of event generators and/or responses to events (message receipts, timers or sensor interrupts). These responses

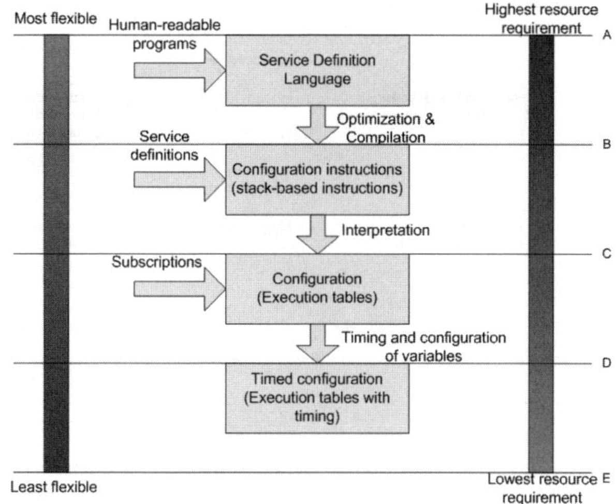

Fig. 2. An overview of the different deployment phases. There are several deployment strategies (A-E). All phases above the chosen line are done at design time and everything below the line at runtime. The various levels show the trade-off between flexibility and resource usage.

take the form of a state change and generation of new events. As such they can be realized by table-driven execution. The intent is to have an optimized implementation in the form of tables, but to hide this from the programmer through the compilation and deployment procedure.

Deployment procedure

Overall, in our approach the use of a sensor network proceeds through three phases. During the *development phase* the application program is designed as a set of cooperating services. These are compiled and installed during the *deployment phase*. The third phase is the *run-time phase*, which represent the normal operation of nodes during their lifetime, according to our network execution model. The translation process is highlighted in Figure 2 in the centre. The program is translated into a set of configuration instructions that can be executed by a stack machine. Interpreting these instructions has the effect that nodes are configured with the services in the program. Also connections between services are established. This configuration subsequently determines the run-phase of a sensor network. Communication is achieved via standardized messages, whereas the format and meaning being partially standard and partially determined by the translation process. The run-time execution therefore is meant to interpret these messages. Note, that it is not necessary to have all these steps as optimized as possible, because this depends on the required flexibility in the lifecycle and the available resources.

Typically this means trading flexibility and performance for abstraction. This is depicted in Figure 2 where each lower level (A,. . .,E) sacrifices some flexibility

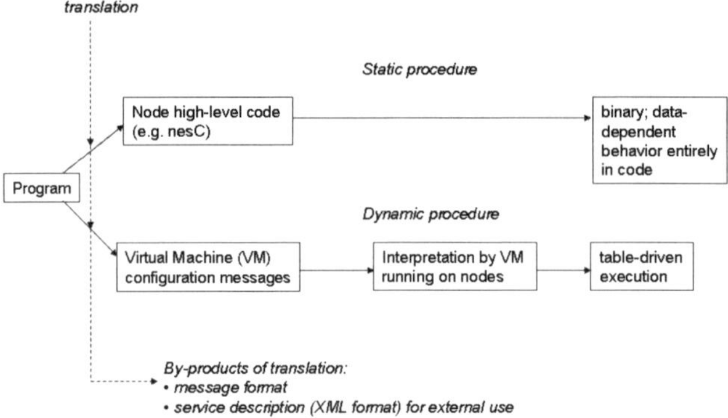

Fig. 3. During the deployment phase the code for the nodes is extracted from the application program and sent towards the nodes. This can be entirely static or through dynamic updates.

and fixes more at design time. Everything above a line is done at design time and everything below the line at runtime. At the top level (A) the high level sensor network language (see also section 4) describes how an entire sensor network should behave by defining services on sensor nodes and by subscribing nodes to those services. The interpretation of these programs directly on sensor nodes would places a serious burden on the resources of a node and assumes thus a rather unrealistic situation.

The second level (B) compiles the high level language into byte code for a virtual machine. Here, global optimizations could be performed before sending the byte code to exactly those nodes that need it. The result of the interpretation of the byte code is that the node is configured to run the loaded service and/or to subscribe to a service. Thus, tables are constructed that determine the response to events, where events consist of time triggers, sensor triggers or message receipts. Hence, the virtual machine operates only when the node is in a configuration mode (in contrast to the use of a virtual machine in e. g. Maté [11]). Consequently nodes can be in two modes: configuration mode when interpreting configuration instructions and run-mode corresponding to regular execution. Level (C) generates the result of interpreting the byte code (i.e. execution tables) directly. This can be done by generating code in a native language (e. g. nesC) and subsequently compiling this to node binary format. Alternatively, these execution tables can be generated directly at the expense of taking lots of details of the node into account. The execution tables do not specify a fixed schedule. Rather services await subscriptions and based on those dynamic subscriptions a schedule is computed that determines when to perform actions (e. g. reading a sensor value or sending a notification to subscribers).

In case the subscriptions do not change at runtime the schedule of each node can be pre-computed and the timed configuration can be stored directly on a node (level (D)). Thus, an optimized configuration can be placed into a node, again either through generation of a native program or through generating binaries directly. Furthermore optimizations could be achieved, e. g. if a service has no subscribers it does not need to be loaded or sensor polling intervals can be pre-computed such that there is a maximum overlap of notification deadlines of various subscriptions. The final level (E) corresponds to the direct programming of sensor nodes as it is represented by current practice.

The deployment phase is depicted in another way in Figure 3. A side-effect of the translation could be that a message format is determined that fills in the application-specific details. We prefer an XML-based service description that is generated for reference and processing by more powerful machines than the sensors themselves. For the follow-up discussion in this paper we follow deployment phase (B); we observe, however, that the other, more optimizing approaches, are still possible and can in fact be based on this approach.

4   Language

The following sections introduce the WASP programming model using an event-based mechanism. First, a high level language basing on event-condition action (ECA) rules is described followed by an integrated .NET-based programming model. They are defined as the top layer of our three abstraction levels (Figure 4 right). The WASP model makes it possible for an application programmer to write a distributed sensor application by using an high-level programming language. A runtime then makes sure that sensor-specific code is executed as low-level machine code on the sensors. Figure 4 (left) subsumes the main principles of our approach. The entire application code is compiled into program and configuration messages that finally define the different handler and subscription methods on the nodes.

Although the two proposed programming models use different programming concepts, the results with respect to the network behavior are similar. First, a gateway is used to transmit configuration messages into the sensor network. Afterwards, the sensor data is transmitted based on the subscriptions that are established during the configuration phase. Assumed that the protocol of the exchanged messages is standardized, nodes can cooperate independent of the development environment. The tool support of the different programming models can also be combined when the intermediate results are well defined. For example, the algorithm that determines the deployment in the programming model will produce a mapping of filters to nodes, together with a subscription pattern that connects data sources to data sinks. This mapping can be used by the ECA-rule based programming model to generate the configuration messages that the gateway needs to send in order to run the application.

4.1   ECA-Rule Based Programming Model

In this section we describe our high level programming language by examining the details of a scenario. As running example we will use the case of a farmer

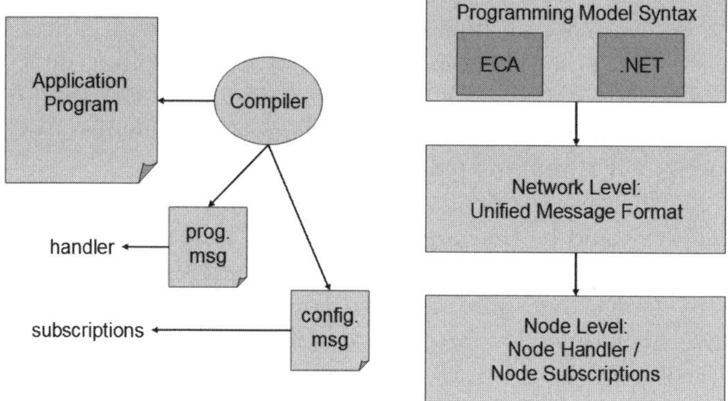

Fig. 4. Fundamental scheme of the WASP programming model (left) and the main abstraction levels of the programming architecture (right)

monitoring his herd (see Figure 5). Each of the cows will be equipped with several sensors such as temperature sensors, pH value sensors etc. One of the use cases is that the farmer wants a warning within 5 minutes whenever the pH value drops below 5 and the temperature of the cow rises above 38.

A program for sensor networks consists of a series of service definitions and service subscriptions (see Figure 4). The definitions and subscriptions are executed on nodes specified by means of a FOR clause and takes the form:

$$FOR\ [\langle Scope\rangle | \langle Selector\rangle | \langle Predicate\rangle]$$

The bracketed expression is a list comprehension augmented with a selector. The selector picks some nodes from all nodes in the scope for which the predicate holds. The scope is typically $Network$, which refers to all nodes in the sensor network. Therefore, the list comprehension which specifies the entire network is given by the expression $[Network | * | true]$ or (leaving out the predicate) $[Network | *]$.

The predicate acts as a filter, if the predicate is true for a node in the scope then the node is part of the comprehension. E.g. $[Network | * | nodeType =$ $"cowNeckNode"]$ selects all nodes in the network for which the $nodeType$ field equals $"cowNeckNode"$. The selector is used to select one or more elements from the comprehension. To indicate that only one random node from the comprehension should execute the associated statement, one would replace the star by one. As an example, we give the expression which refers to exactly one node (selected randomly) of type sink: $[Network | 1 | nodeType = "sink"]$.

Finally services have to be defined. A service definition describes a unit of functionality offered by a sensor (e. g. querying of the temperature or sending an alarm if the temperature exceeds some threshold). In our example, we need three services: Two for providing the temperature and pH values and one for sending out alerts. We call this service $TempPHAlert$ and define this service on the neck

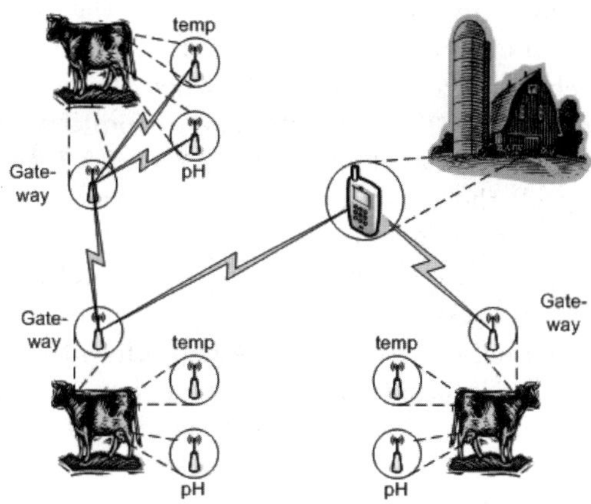

Fig. 5. Wireless sensor network for monitoring cow health. Each cow is equipped with a temperature sensor, pH sensor and a gateway. Whenever the temperature and pH values exceed their respective thresholds the smart phone or PDA of the farmer is notified.

nodes of all the cows, which will function as gateways. To prevent the node from repeatedly sending alarms, we restrict the service from re-firing until an end condition has occurred (in this case, the temperature and pH values having returned to normal). Below we show the program code for the temperature service and the alert service, the pH service is similar to the temperature service.

```
SERVICE Temperature($TempUpdate, $MaxTemp)
FOR [Network|*|Has(Temperature)]
ON EVENT $MaxTemp < Temperature
DO SendToSubscribers($TempUpdate, Temperature)

SERVICE TempPHAlert($MaxTemp, $MinPH)
FOR [Network|*|nodeType="cowNeckNode"]
DEFINE
    LastTemp := None
    LastPH := None
ON EVENT ($MaxTemp < LastTemp) && (LastPH < $MinPH) DO
    SendToSubscribers(Notify, ("TempPH Alert", self.Time))
ON EVENTEND (LastTemp < $MaxTemp) && ($MinPH < LastPH) DO
    SendToSubscribers(Notify, ("TempPH Alert", self.Time))
ACTION UpdatePH(pHvar) DO
    LastPH := phvar
ACTION UpdateTemp(tempvar) DO
    LastTemp := tempvar
```

A service consists of three parts. The service state (i.e., a set of variables), a set of generated events and a set of actions. The state variables are global for the entire service (note: only for the service, not for the node). The generated events are similar to an event condition action (ECA) system (see [1] for a nice overview). The ON EVENT clause indicates when the action specified by the DO clause is triggered. Note that the event and condition are combined here. More precisely, the trigger for evaluating the ON EVENT clause comes from a compiled schedule of all the subscriptions to this service. This is described in more detail in the description of subscriptions. An EVENTEND clause prevents the service from being executed again until its condition becomes true.

Whenever an event is sent out by calling *SendToSubscribers*, an action handler must be supplied which indicates to receiving nodes how to handle the message. Such an event handler is either a built-in event handler such as the subscription handler, the bytecode interpreter or an event handler defined by an ACTION clause. The name of a service (e. g. TempPHAlert) is its unique ID which is used in subscriptions. As a consequence, any two services on a single node must have different names. After the name of a service a parameter list supplies all subscription variables which the service accepts.

The compiler for this language will replace all names and values with constants such that only short IDs are transmitted over the network. The following listing shows an example of how the Temperature service definition could look like in byte code.

```
SERV  1          # define service Temperature
PUSHV 1          # push variable $MaxTemp
CALL  4          # Call Temperature
LESS             # $MaxTemp < Temperature
PUSHV 0          # push variable $TempUpdate
CALL  4          # push Temperature
NTFY             # SendToSubscribers($Handler, Temperature)
DEFE             # define event
POP              # Remove service from stack
```

Note that these byte code instructions are geared towards configuration not execution. Some instructions, such as *PUSHV*, *CALL*, *LESS*, and *NTFY*, do not directly manipulate the expression stack, but configure execution tables which establish the corresponding effect at a later time (when the service is run). The payload of a message which executes the above service definition would be fifteen bytes long (the BytecodeHandlerID (0) followed by fourteen bytes for the instructions and their arguments). The exact definition of the byte code and the compiler are current work in progress.

Now we need to establish some subscriptions. The alert service needs to subscribe to the temperature service and the pH service and the smart phone of the farmer (the "sink") to the alarm service. We only show the alarm subscription.

```
SUBSCRIPTION
    CowTempPHAlertGateway
FOR
    [Network|1|nodeType="sink"]
```

```
WITH
(   service: TempPHAlert,
    on: [Network|*|nodeType="cowNeckNode"],
    deadline: 5min,
    minimumSamplePeriod: 50s,
    maximumSamplePeriod: 60s,
    sendPriority: "Normal",
    executePriority: "Normal",
    $TempVar: 38,
    $PHVar: 5
)
```

In general, nodes subscribe to services offered by other nodes. Thereby subscriptions are specified for a range of nodes just like the for-clause defines services for a range of nodes. Subscriptions allow insertion of filter and priority criteria such as thresholds when to send an event and deadlines when it must arrive. These parameterized subscriptions enable nodes to only send events when needed, in order to avoid wasting energy. This is based on the assumption that testing a criteria uses less energy than sending a message and that events are generated more frequently than they are interesting. Consequently, subscriptions determine the scheduling of a node. When there are no subscriptions and the service is free of side-effects then it doesn't need to run at all. In our example the subscription by the node of type sink specifies a minimum period of 50 seconds and a maximum period of 60 seconds. If this is the only subscription the sensor will typically be read every 60 seconds (taking the maximum to minimize energy usage). Now, suppose that there was another node which subscribes to the sensor value with a sample period of 28 seconds. Because of the overlap between sampling periods $(2 * 28 \in [50, 60])$, the sensor only needs to be read every 28 seconds and alternate between notifying only the logging node and both the logging node and the farmers smart phone.

4.2   Integrated .NET-Based Programming Model

In the previous section, a domain-specific language based on Event-Condition-Action rules for writing sensor programs was introduced. Besides this approach, the WASP project is also evaluating a design alternative where developers can program distributed sensor applications using an existing high-level language such as C# (or Java.) The general programming process of the .NET-based programming model falls in category (C) in Fig. 2. In summary, the main features of the programming model are:

- Using high-level programming languages for programming distributed sensor applications without the overhead of virtual machines on sensor nodes
- Runtime environment for deploying code on distributed sensor nodes
- Lightweight virtualization layer on sensor nodes

The design of the programming model contains the following parts: (1) a .NET class library, (2) a code analysis and generation tool that translates .NET

442   J. Lukkien et al.

Intermediate Language (.NET IL) to machine code that is directly executable on sensor nodes, (3) a deployment and runtime environment and (4) a dynamic linker and lightweight virtualization layer on sensor nodes. A programmer writes an application in C# using the .NET class library provided by our framework. Here, the developer creates a data flow graph that describes how sensory data is retrieved and processed. Data sources, filters, and data sinks comprise the nodes of the graph. There is an edge between two nodes if the output of one node serves as the input of another node. The result of the compilation process of such a program is a .NET assembly. Given this assembly, the individual components of the above data flow graph must be deployed on concrete sensor nodes. This can take place either (1) as part of a one-time deployment process or (2) dynamically during runtime.

As part of the deployment process, machine code – using the standard ELF format in our prototypical implementation – is loaded onto sensor nodes. This process involves a dynamic linking process as described in [4]. In other words, the code deployed on a sensor node is no complete program – in the sense of a typical sensor deployment – but contains function calls that must be mapped onto specific calls of the operating system running on the sensor node. A consequence of this is also that multiple application fragments can be loaded onto a single sensor node. A single sensor node can thus participate in multiple applications.

Considering the farmer monitoring example described in Sect. 4.1, a programmer writes an application in .NET on a development machine using the class library that is provided as part of our framework. As the topology of the sensor nodes in this application is known at development time, the application can be decomposed and the deployment environment can statically determine which part of the application must be deployed on what sensor node. This deployment will not change during runtime. Thus, the developer can directly store identified application components on the sensor nodes. After the deployment of application components, the newly programmed sensor nodes are installed on the body of the cows. Dynamic deployment processes are also possible by means of a gateway computer that can deploy application parts during runtime in an ad-hoc fashion.

The class library allows programmers to construct a data flow graph (nodes and edges, $G = (V, E)$) of their application based on an event-based model. Nodes are either data sources, filters, or data sinks. Data sources are typically sensors that provide observations about their environment. Filters transform a set of inputs to an output; the main part of an application is programmed as filters. Filters can fire when certain conditions are met on the provided inputs, and they can contain and maintain state.

The following code illustrates a subset of a provided filter class with only one input:

```
public abstract class Filter<T,S> : DataSource<T>,ISubscriber<T>{
  protected DataSource<T> m_DataSource;
  protected S m_ResultData;

  public Filter(DataSource<T> ds) {m_DataSource = ds;}
```

```
public abstract bool ApplyFilter(T notification);
  ...
}
```

Besides support for filters, the class library provides a set of predefined sensor data sources, for example for temperature, accelerometers, and microphone sensors. Given the base Filter class and a description of data sources, a programmer can write the actual application logic.

After data sources, filters and sinks have been programmed, a developer connects nodes in the data flow graph through subscriptions. Subscriptions can be dynamic. This means that it is not necessary to connect a filter with one concrete sensor, but it is possible to connect a filter to all currently available sensors of a specific type or to a set of sensor nodes that conform to a certain condition. The deployment process, which maps a data flow graph onto a concrete network topology, operates on three main inputs: (1) a data flow graph $G = (V, E)$ as described by the application, (2) a topology $T = (N, F)$ that describes how sensors, gateways and backend systems are connected, and (3) a description of device capabilities. The topology can be a static description (for example in the form of an XML file) of how a certain set of sensors will be installed in an environment. For example, in the case of the cow monitoring scenario, this is a description about how the sensor nodes are installed on a cow. In the case of a body sensor network in the WASP healthcare scenario, it simply describes the star topology between a mobile communication hub and body-worn sensors. Besides these static topologies, a topology can also be dynamically determined during runtime. This means that a topology discovery algorithm must be executed during runtime.

Finally, the deployment algorithm operates on the data flow graph $G = (V, E)$, the topology $T = (N, F)$, and a function $g : N \rightarrow \mathfrak{P}(V)$ that maps each node in the topology to a set of sensors installed on that node. The algorithm for finding a deployment needs to solve an optimization problem. The optimization problem can be formulated in many different ways but in a basic form the algorithm looks like the following:

---

if no static topology **do**
    determine Topology $T = (N, F)$
    determine mapping $g : N \rightarrow \mathfrak{P}(V)$
fi
determine cost $c(f, n)$ of executing filter $f \in V$ on node $n \in N$
find mapping $h : V \rightarrow N$ of filters to nodes
minimize $\sum_{f \in V} c(f, h(f))$

---

5   Other WASP Aspects

This section subsumes some aspects of wireless sensor networks that are considered in the WASP project. They are responsible for mediation and information gathering from and to sensor nodes, for allowing access to overall sensor ensemble information and for ensuring access security and for secure information flow.

Gateway services in WASP (see Figure 6) are mediating between powerful backend systems and resource-constrained sensor nodes. A gateway device can either be a mobile or a stationary computer that is in wireless communication range of the sensor nodes. Gateways are responsible for integrating a range of different sensors into existing computing infrastructures. In WASP, this integration is done at the service layer by making use of a service model that we have designed in the project. Backend applications implement a Web Service-based grounding of the WASP service model, while sensor nodes use a grounding with very lightweight protocols. The main purpose of gateways is thus to map between the different groundings in our service model.

Maintenance services in WASP are responsible for monitoring status information of a sensor network. This comprises the assessment of an entire node ensemble, access to information about the nature and operability of single nodes as well as the addressing of individual nodes and their services. Calling of services on the nodes will be able by means of graphical user interfaces. Information about the node ensemble will be illustrated to the user in different ways: location-based resp. topology-based visualization will provide information about the physical coherence of the node ensemble, whereas service-based and content-based visualization provides information about service-provider and service-consumer relation or information about information sources and sinks (and thus information about the information flow in the node ensemble).

Security services in WASP aims at providing secure and trusted wireless sensor data from sensor node to business applications. Within WASP, we identified three main security requirements from the targeted business domains (e. g. automotive, healthcare, agricultural): (i) context aware access control, (ii) authentication of actors (e. g. sink, gateway, business application), (iii) and trust assessment of processed sensor data [8]. We then propose an efficient scheme for access control for wireless sensor data, which fulfils requirements related to constraints on sensor nodes (e. g. battery, CPU, RAM). In addition, we develop a secret handshake matching for mutual authentication of gateways and business applications. Besides, we define operator on subjective logic in order to assess trustworthiness of sensor data at acquisition, processing and delivery to business applications.

6   Related Work

A significant number of methods have been proposed to program sensors and networks of sensors. The TinyOS [9] operating system together with the nesC [7] programming language defines an event-driven concurrency model designed specifically for low-resource devices. Interaction between components is solely through these functional interfaces, via commands ("calls") or events ("callbacks"). No locking abstraction is provided; instead the system requires the

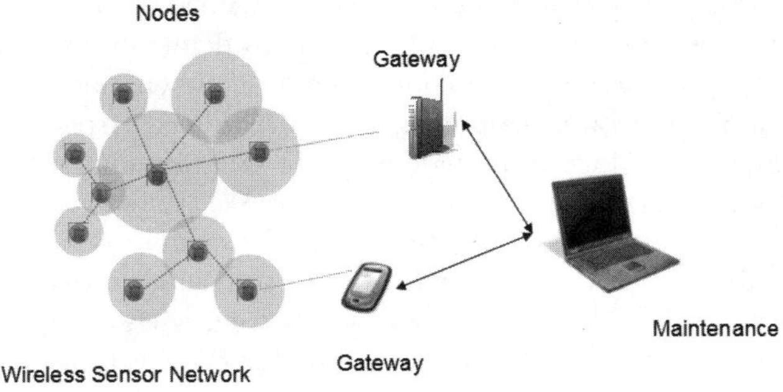

Fig. 6. Simplified illustration of the sensor node ensemble architecture describing the interconnection of the node ensemble, the gateways and the maintenance service

programmer to explicitly deal with wakeup events. No memory management, scheduler or protection is provided by TinyOS and, as such, the system can be regarded as providing merely a library of abstractions. Applications are specified by gluing component interfaces together. Hardware diversity is addressed by having sufficient abstraction to permit portability. Though TinyOS does not define specific OS services, a set of standard services (and components) have been accepted. In contrast, FreeRTOS [6] is a more traditional OS that supports multithreading, basic memory management and task synchronization primitives. It is designed to have a small footprint and has been ported to a variety of sensor nodes. Nodes are programmed in C.

A large body of work exists on how to program sensor-based systems. In the area of programming models for Wireless Sensor Networks (WSN), four main approaches can be identified: (1) programming based on event-based systems [4], (2) data-centric approaches focusing on abstractions such as databases and tuple spaces [14,13], (3) agent-based programming techniques [5,15], and (4) virtual machines (e. g. VMStar [10] and Maté [11]). Especially the latter is meant to reduce program size, to enhance protection and improve portability. Instructions of the virtual machine are application specific. The Maté virtual machine runs on top of TinyOS and provides a synchronous view on event handling. It abstracts from message routing issues. Maté does not come with a programming language; it uses scripts to control the virtual machine. Concluding, we see largely two approaches: programming individual nodes (letting the network task 'emerge') or programming at the network level while standardizing the node program to an interpreter.

7   Conclusions

This paper is presenting the results of in-depth discussions and work in the WASP project, mainly of the work package that is dealing with the development of an entire programming model by including the services of the nodes.

Furthermore overall node ensemble services like gateways, maintenance devices and security issues are considered. The goal is to define an architecture model that allows the programming and configuring of node ensembles from the perspective of an application programmer. Thus, from our perspective, the goal of virtual machine technology to provide a simple programming model on sensors based on a high-level language is very convincing. We try to extend existing work in this area along two dimensions: First, virtual machines typically target only one sensor node while the programming model presented in this paper is about programming distributed sensor applications. Second, virtual machines typically pose a considerable overhead on resource constrained sensor nodes. In contrast, our approach is to expose a high-level language environment to programmers, but we do not assume the presence of a virtual machine on the sensor nodes. In the research domain of context-aware computing, a range of context frameworks have been proposed that are used to program sensor-based applications. In the work of Dey [3] context-aware applications are constructed in terms of context widgets, interpreters and context aggregators. Consequently the WASP idea is to provide an event-based abstraction for dealing with sensory data as it is presented in the programming model in this paper.

First and foremost, in this paper we have looked at the issue of programming a wireless network from the perspective of an application programmer. From this perspective we look at the network as a single entity. We defined an event-based approach based on service-oriented concepts. We analyzed the possibilities of deploying such a program and identified several alternatives, ranging from entirely static to fully adaptive deployment. A major contribution of our work is the introduction of an intermediate abstraction level at the network level. This has as an advantage that standardization is possible without regard to sensor type, OS or programming language. In this paper we present two different programming models (based on ECA rules and .NET architectures) that are not competing with each other but offering possible WASP users two convincing entry points to work with the WASP sensor node architecture.

Future work concerns working on the currently open ends. We are in the process of defining the language syntax more formally and developing a compiler. We must define the execution tables and experiment further with the network abstraction level and message execution to aim for high efficiency. Our aim is to develop several use cases entirely from the global network perspective with no loss of efficiency.

Acknowledgements

This work is partially financed by the European Commission under the Framework 6 IST Project "Wirelessly Accessible Sensor Populations (WASP) under contract IST-034963. The authors like to thank all WASP participants for their contributions and discussions during project workshops and meetings.

References

1. Alferes, J.J., Banti, F., Brogi, A.: An Event-Condition-Action Logic Programming Language. In: Fisher, M., van der Hoek, W., Konev, B., Lisitsa, A. (eds.) JELIA 2006. LNCS (LNAI), vol. 4160, pp. 29–42. Springer, Heidelberg (2006)
2. Carriero, N., Gelernter, D.: Linda in context. Communications of the ACM 32(4), 444–458 (1989)
3. Dey, A.K.: Providing Architectural Support for Building Context-Aware Applications. Ph.D. thesis, College of Computing, Georgia Institute of Technology (December 2000)
4. Dunkels, A., Finne, N., Eriksson, J., Voigt, T.: Run-time dynamic linking for reprogramming wireless sensor networks. In: Proceedings of the Fourth ACM Conference on Embedded Networked Sensor Systems (SenSys 2006), Boulder, Colorado, USA (November 2006)
5. Fok, C.-L., Roman, G.-C., Lu, C.: Agilla: A Mobile Agent Middleware for Sensor Networks, Technical Report, Washington University in St. Louis, WUCSE-2006-16 (2006)
6. FreeRTOS Homepage, http://www.freertos.org
7. Gay, D., Levis, P., von Behren, R., Welsh, M., Brewer, E., Culler, D.: The nesC language: A holistic approach to networked embedded systems. In: Proceedings of the ACM SIGPLAN 2003 conference on Programming language design and implementation, San Diego, pp. 1–11 (2003)
8. Gomez, L., Laube, A.: Design Guidelines for the Integration of Wireless Sensor Networks with Business Applications. In: Proceedings of the 1st International Conference on MOBILe Wireless MiddleWARE, Operating Systems, and Applications (2008)
9. Hill, J., Szewczyk, R., Woo, A., Hollar, S., Culler, D., Pister, K.: System Architecture Directions for Networked Sensors. In: Proceedings of Ninth International Conference on Architectural Support for Programming Languages and Operating Systems (ASPLOS) (November 2000)
10. Koshy, J., Pandey, R.: VMSTAR: synthesizing scalable runtime environments for sensor networks. In: Proceedings 3rd international conference on embedded sensor networks (2005)
11. Levis, P., Culler, D.: A tiny virtual machine for sensor networks. In: Proceedings of the 10th international conference on Architectural support for programming languages and operating systems, pp. 85–95. ACM Press, New York (2002)
12. Madden, S.: Query Processing for Streaming Sensor Data (2002)
13. Madden, S.R., Franklin, M.J., Hellerstein, J.M., Hing, W.: TinyDB: an acquisitional query processing system for sensor networks. ACM Transactions on Database Systems 30(1) (2005)
14. Siegemund, F.: A Context-Aware Communication Platform for Smart Objects. In: Proceeding Pervasive 2005, Vienna (2005)
15. Yao, Y., Gehrke, J.: The cougar approach to in-network query processing in sensor networks. ACM Sigmod Record 31(3), 9–18 (2002)
16. Wooldridge, M.: Introduction to multi-agent systems. John Wiley & Sons, Chichester (2002)

Conjoint PERSONA – SOPRANO Workshop[*]

Elena Avatangelou[1], Rochi Febo Dommarco[2], Michael Klein[3], Sonja Müller[4],
Claus F. Nielsen[5], Ma Pilar Sala Soriano[6], Andreas Schmidt[7],
Mohammad-Reza Tazari[8], and Reiner Wichert[8]

[1] EXODUS S.A., Farantaton 6-10, 11527, Athens, Greece
[2] Vodafone Omnitel N.V., Via Lorenteggio 280/2, 20147 Milano, Italy
[3] CAS Software AG, Wilhelm-Schickard-Str. 10-12, 76131 Karlsruhe, Germany
[4] empirica Gesellschaft für Kommunikations- und Technologieforschung mbH.
Oxfordstr. 2 - 53111 Bonn, Germany
[5] Region Syddanmark, Rugaardsvej 15, 2., 5000 Odense C, Denmark
[6] ITACA – TSB, Univ. Polit. Valencia, Camino de Vera s/n - 46022 Valencia, Spain
[7] FZI Research Centre for Information Technologies, Haid-und-Neu-Str. 10-14, 76131
Karlsruhe, Germany
[8] Fraunhofer-Institut Graphische Datenverarbeitung, Fraunhoferstr. 5,
64283 Darmstadt, Germany

Abstract. Being both EU-IST integrated projects in the field of AAL, PERSONA and SOPRANO organized a conjoint workshop on the occasion of the AmI-07 conference in order for the researchers of the projects to exchange insights of the approaches to the key field challenges, the achievements so far in each of the projects, and possible synergies in the future. Here, we summarize the exchanged info and the workshop results. The paper gives a good overview of the two projects and their status by the end of October 2007.

Keywords: EU-IST integrated project, ambient intelligence, assisted living, use cases and scenarios, architectural design, technological approach.

1 Introduction

This EU Project Workshop has been a conjoint activity of the EU-IST integrated projects (FP6, IST-2006-6.2.2 Ambient Assisted Living (AAL) in the Ageing Society) PERSONA (Contract No. 045459) and SOPRANO (Contract No. 045212), both started in January 2007 with the goal to realize an Ambient Intelligence (AmI) solution for assisting elderly people throughout the life.

The project PERSONA aims at advancing the paradigm of Ambient Intelligence through the harmonisation of Ambient Assisted Living (AAL) technologies and concepts for the development of sustainable and affordable solutions for the social inclusion and independent living of senior citizens, integrated in a common semantic framework. PERSONA is developing a scalable open standard technological platform for building and hosting a broad range of AAL services, demonstrating and testing the

---

[*] The work published in this paper has been partly funded by the E.C. within the PERSONA and SOPRANO IPs under Framework Programme 6.

M. Mühlhäuser et al. (Eds.): AmI 2007 Workshops, CCIS 11, pp. 448–464, 2008.

concept in real life implementations, assessing their social impact, and establishing the initial business strategy for future deployment of the proposed technologies and services. Aiming at proposing an AAL system reference architecture, the PERSONA technical platform is exploiting and incorporating a broad range of relevant technologies, such as micro- and nano-electronics, embedded and distributed (bio)sensors / systems, communication and network technologies, energy control technologies, human-machine interfaces, and intelligent software tools for decision support.

The project SOPRANO aims to design and develop innovative, context-aware, smart services with natural and comfortable interfaces for older people with the goal to extend the time, in which they can live independently and autonomously in their homes. SOPRANO seeks to extend today's RTD methods by integrating design-for-all paradigms: from requirements, iterative prototyping and usability tests. Research is expected to strongly advance global knowledge in semantic IT, RFID location, remote diagnostics, radar and integration architectures. A new AAL architecture is to support pro-active assistance based on situational analysis fed by user input and local monitoring. Responses are to follow agreed rules and seamless access provided to external professionals. Safety and security is strongly enhanced with adherence to stringent reliability standards. Multiple modalities and dialogue adaptations to cognitive ageing help meet special accessibility and usability needs.

The workshop was organized as an exchange platform for researchers and scientists of SOPRANO and PERSONA to meet and discuss topics, such as:

- Ambient Intelligence use cases that destine the requirements for future technology research
- Ambient Intelligence technologies that will be applied with respect to the projects' application set
- Ambient Assisted Living architectures that enable the communication and cooperation of the identified devices and applications
- Field trial approaches for validation and enhancement of technology outcomes.

Furthermore, this workshop was expected to facilitate the establishment of communication and cooperation between the SOPRANO and PERSONA project members. Members of the two projects' advisory boards along with work package and task leaders and other selected project members were invited to participate. The following is a kind of report summarizing the presented material and the workshop results.

2 Summary of PERSONA Presentations

2.1 PERSONA Overview

PERSONA aims at advancing the paradigm of Ambient Intelligence through the harmonisation of Ambient Assisted Living (AAL) technologies and concepts for the development of sustainable and affordable solutions for the social inclusion and independent living of Senior Citizens, integrated in a common semantic framework.

It will develop a scalable open standard technological platform on which a broad range of AAL Services can be deployed, to demonstrate and test the concept in real life implementations, assessing their social impact and establishing an initial business strategy for future deployment of the proposed technologies and services.

To meet its objectives, the project is faced with the following challenges:

- To find solutions and develop AAL Services for social inclusion, for support in daily life activities, for early risk detection, for personal protection from health and environmental risks, for support in mobility.
- To develop a technological platform that allows the seamless and natural access to those services indicated above.
- To create psychologically pleasant and easy-to-use integrated solutions.
- To demonstrate that the solutions found are affordable and sustainable for all the actors and stakeholders involved: elderly citizens, welfare systems, service providers in the AAL market.

The PERSONA technological platform will exploit and incorporate a broad range of relevant technologies which are developed and integrated in the project: AAL system reference architecture, micro- and nano-electronics, embedded systems (e.g. as in smart textiles), Human Machine Interfaces (display technologies, natural language communication), Communication (e.g. body area network, wireless sensor networks), software, web & network technologies (e.g. tele-services), biosensors (to measure physiological data), embedded and distributed sensors (to observe activity patterns, nutrition, gait, sleep), energy generation and control technologies (energy harvesting), and intelligent software tools for decision support.

An important measure of success for the project will come from the outcome of the evaluation and validation in extensive test-beds and trials in Spain, Italy, and Denmark.

Over a time frame of 42 months, PERSONA will be developed through a Consortium, led by VODAFONE. This consortium will bring together a group of leading organisations from all over Europe, contributing to the project with all the technological, scientific, sociological and business expertise required.

2.2 PERSONA User Experience Vision

As stated in the project mission, PERSONA is devoted to empower people to feel included, secure, protected and supported, by development of Ambient Assisted Living products and services for the achievement of more autonomy and quality in their lives.

People that will benefit for these AAL services are seniors that need any kind of assistance and help to continue living in their home, with an acceptable level of autonomy and do want to preserve the freedom of making their own decisions in all relative of their life.

In consequence, to succeed in this mission we need:

- To understand users' desires, needs, motivations and contexts
- To understand business, technical, and domain requirements and constraints
- To translate this knowledge in AAL services whose form, content and behaviour is useful, usable, and desirable as well as economically viable and technically feasible.

However, there are many obstacles we should overcome in our way to successfully implement such services. In the context of ICT projects, where carrying user-driven innovation is always a challenge, we need to define specific procedures to involve end-users in all the stages of development; but it could happen that our end-users can't comprehend the future technology. On the other hand, technology-oriented researchers can be very far from reality.

In order to put all these pieces together for them to work efficiently, PERSONA project adopted the strategy of defining an Activity Line specifically devoted to take care of the PERSONA's vision regarding user experience within the development process. The objectives are:

- To involve in an active way end-users & stakeholders in the different phases of the project to gain insights to understand:

  - Why people would embrace a particular AAL service
  - What these services should be about
  - Who are involved as stakeholder in these services
  - Where in the context of people's daily life they access these services
  - How do they interact with these services

- To set up pilot sites to gather continuous feedback from users. three sites have been defined:

  - Odense municipality (Denmark)
  - Comunità Montana delle Valli del Taro e del Ceno (Italy)
  - Valencia region (Spain)

- To develop common methodology for assessment and evaluation activities

- To organize the Group of External Experts & Users, that will address the interactions of PERSONA members with users, experts and stakeholders

2.3 PERSONA Requirements Collection

As AAL services are innovative in nature, standard user requirement collection methods are not enough and need to be complemented with new user experience methodologies that enable continuous end-user insights and feedback along the project. Consequently, in every phase of the project, iterative user experience loops will be integrated taking different users and stakeholders into account.

According to the analysis made in advance on the services of high potential impact for independent living of senior citizen, four categories of AAL Services have been identified as starting point for user requirement gathering:

- Social integration: services in this category aim at alleviating loneliness & isolation by empowering social contact and sharing of vital experiences
- Daily activities: services in this category aim at improving independence at home by supporting the realization of daily activities
- Safety & protection: services in this category aim at creating safe environment by detecting risk situation occurrence and taking care of them
- Mobility: services in this category aim at supporting life outside home by providing contextualized information and guidance.

PERSONA space	Body	Home	Neighbourhood	Village
User need	Support for personal care, physiological activities, self administration	Support for Instrumental ADL mainly housekeeping	Support for shopping and remainders of appointments. Planning social activities	Very similar to Neighbourhood
Issues	• Personal Care • Personal Hygiene • Comfort in dressing • Sleep period supervision	• Cooking assistance • Support for running a house	• Shopping in the supermarket • Remainder tool • Social activities/events agenda	
AAL services	• Caregiver support • Weather info • safety services • Health services	• Cooking assistance service (recipes, shopping lists, meal storage list) • Shopping list/shopping (e-commerce) • Housekeeping service (cleaning, ironing, washing)	• E-commerce services • Leisure activities services • Agenda coordinator service	

Fig. 1. Example of AAL Service matrix for Daily Activities category

During the first iteration, each PERSONA AAL Service category was considered as a "context of use" and following aspects were defined and discussed in detail to compose a matrix related to the four spaces where the services could be provided (body, house, neighbourhood and village):

– User needs: define the main goal of senior citizens in each of the spaces and for all the categories of services.
– Issues that needs to be taken into account to cover user needs
– AAL Services: formalize how to address the issues to support the end-users in achieving their goals.

The next step was to illustrate each AAL Service by means of the definition of Scenarios ("A day in the life of…" tool). These scenarios describe how an end-user interacts with an AAL Service in a context of use. As a result, 16 promising use scenarios were produced as the first description of user requirements, combining our hypothesis based on our experiences in the field as well as real situations of elderly from the pilot sites which have been discussed and analysed in expert workshops.

The second iteration consisted of an enrichment process of the scenarios formerly defined. It started with prioritization of the current 16 scenarios according to its technical relevance and end-user interest. Eight scenarios were selected for improvement, technical requirements were included in the definition and functionalities that cover user-needs were described together with detailed interaction flows between systems, devices and end-users.

The result has been used as base to develop mock-ups to be validated by end user collectives to provide feedback of user experience to the AAL service specification. This evaluation will be done in the first six month of 2008.

2.4 PERSONA Technological Goals, Approach, and Achievements

The technological goal of the PERSONA project is to develop a scalable open standard platform for AAL based on a reference architecture for AmI systems comprising

– a self-organizing middleware,
– a framework supporting context-awareness,
– service-orientation (discovery, composition, provision, and orchestration),
– multimedia integration and content adaptation, and
– integration of embedded sensors and actuators.

As the number of research projects and industrial labs dedicated to AmI systems is constantly increasing, PERSONA decided to be a pioneer in identifying reusable results in the areas of architecture and middleware and chose an appropriate methodology for this purpose (see Fig. 2).

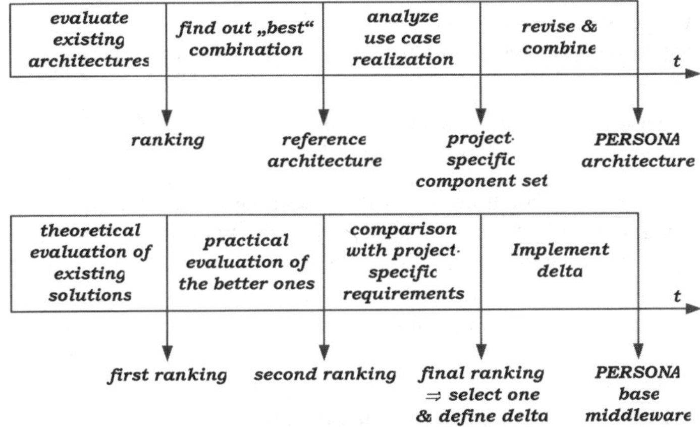

Fig. 2. Methodology for reusing solutions for architecture (above) and middleware (below) fulfilling PERSONA requirements

Starting with an abstract view on the physical architecture of AmI environments as a dynamic ensemble of networked nodes (see Fig. 3) and based on an understanding of *middleware* as the gluing software facilitating the integration of, and the collaboration among the nodes comprising an AmI system (cf. [**Error! Reference source not found.**]), we gathered over 30 R&D projects with promising solutions in these two fields. After two quick iterations for filtering out those with comparatively less significant outcomes, this list was reduced to six: Oxygen (launched by MIT in 1999, still continuing), EMBASSI (1999–2003, a German national "seminal" research project), DynAMITE (2003–06, a German national research project), RUNES (2004–07, EU-IST project), AMIGO (2004–08, EU-IST project), and ASK-IT (2004–08, EU-IST project).

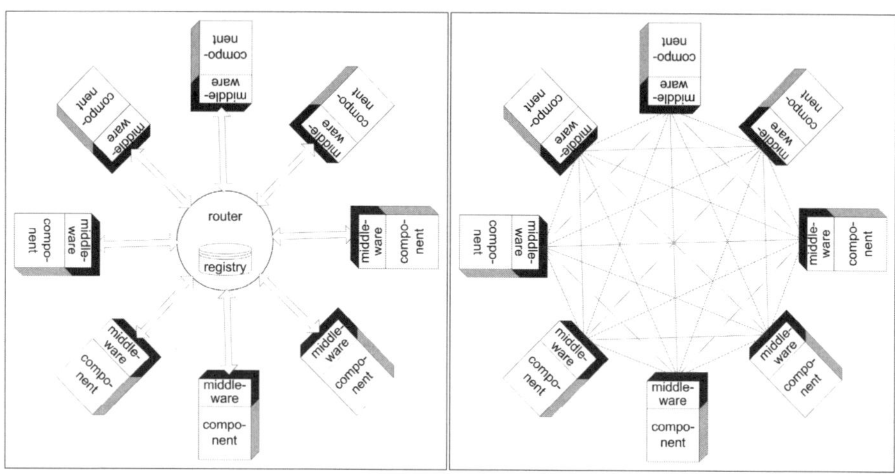

Fig. 3. An abstract view on the physical architecture in AmI environments as a dynamic ensemble of networked nodes, whether structured (left) or ad-hoc / peer-to-peer (right)

To guarantee a purposeful evaluation of the competing solutions, we defined a set of criteria for each of the two fields. In the field of architectural design, these were:

- Consideration of functional elements that facilitate the explicit, hybrid and multi-channel interaction of the users with the system, support context-awareness in all layers of the system and adaptability in the presentation layers, and hide the complexity of utilizing services from the users accessing them (cf. the concept of service brokerage in [7, 8]). Other integral functional elements could support QoS-awareness, identity management and privacy-awareness, among others.
- Regarding the domain-specific integrable components, guaranteeing a high-level of flexibility in the distribution of functionality and facilitating the integration of arbitrary numbers of sensors, actuators, control units, appliances, and applications into the system.
- Regarding the design techniques, the most important characteristic of an architecture is its modularity, because it leads to better distribution and extensibility of the system, higher maintainability / dependability, and greater possibility for reusing existing and composing new functionality.

The evaluation criteria for middleware comprised:

- Mechanisms supporting ad-hoc networking and self-organization of the components based on automatic service discovery and binding resp. service composition, on one hand, and aggregation of low-level events to deduce more high-level events, on the other hand.
- Supporting different communication paradigms, such as events, calls, streams, and transactions.
- At the technical level, stability and diagnosis, efficiency and performance, completeness versus complexity of the API, and level of dependency on platform and network layers.

Our studies showed that a combination of the data-flow-based approach of EMBASSI [2] and the service oriented approach of AMIGO [1] could lead to an optimized solution for AmI systems. Based on this conclusion, we worked out the architecture shown in Fig. 4.

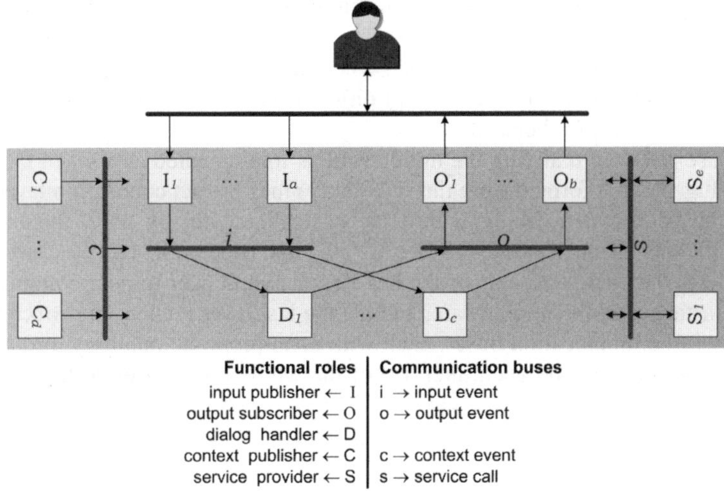

Fig. 4. The derived logical architecture for the PERSONA system

The architecture models the basic data flow in AmI systems: The explicit user input through *input publishers* and the contextual / situational events posted by *context publishers* trigger dialogs that will finally terminate with explicit system output through *output subscribers* and / or changes in the environment performed by service providers. The *dialog handlers* (formally equivalent to simultaneously playing the role of input resp. context subscriber, output publisher, and service client) are therefore responsible for the behavior of the whole system. All functionality not leading to context, input, or output events or their direct processing is abstracted as *service*, which is equivalent to the AMIGO approach; the way how this separation is considered relies however on the EMBASSI approach.

Fig. 4 defines furthermore the communication buses which reflect the loose connections needed in a dynamic environment and represent, in a modular way, the need for interface / ontology definitions, protocol specifications for communication, and strategies for "dispatching incoming messages" to an appropriate (set of) receiver(s). The horizontal arrows attached to the vertical buses symbolize the availability of services and context in the whole system, independent from any layering. For example, the input and output layers may access the s-bus for utilizing transformation services, such as ASR or TTS and the dialog handling layer accesses the s-bus, mainly for procurement of application services to the user.

The buses are realized by a middleware that must be integrated into each component, whether a (standard[2] or an application-specific) software component or a physical component, such as a sensor, an actuator, an appliance, or a device. (see also Fig. 3). Each such node may be so simple that it plays only one of the above mentioned functional roles and hence registers to only one bus or so complex with several functional roles that it must register to several buses each with different roles. Through the cooperation of different instances of the middleware, local pieces of the same bus will find each other and so will be able to cooperate with each other based on strategies specific to each bus so that the distribution of functionality in different nodes will remain hidden from the view point of the bus members.

The base software realizing the middleware is implemented as a set of OSGi bundles (see Fig. 5). It is formed from three APIs: (1) the abstract connection layer (ACL) realizes the ad-hoc networking within the ensemble with, by now, three concrete implementations using Remote-OSGi[3], UPnP, and Bluetooth, (2) the Sodapop [2] layer realizes the basic concepts of the bus structure and peer-to-peer communication between instances of the middleware, and (3) the last layer realizes the concrete PERSONA set of communication buses, each with an appropriate ontology, protocol, and strategy[4], and provides the open interface of the whole middleware to the application layer.

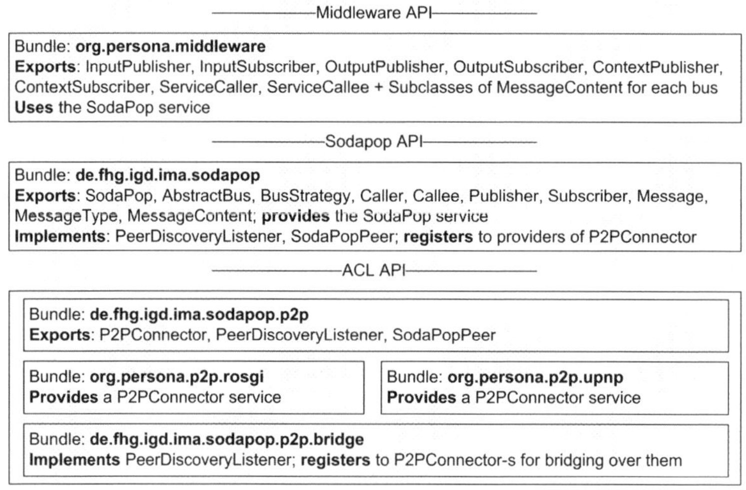

Fig. 5. The set of OSGi bundles realizing the PERSONA middlewar

---

[2] PERSONA has identified six standard components that are currently under discussion for providing their specifications: a rule-based context reasoner, a dialog manager as the default dialog handler, a service orchestrator for managing and performing composite services, a profiling component, a privacy-aware identity and security manager, and an AAL space gateway.

[3] http://r-osgi.sourceforge.net/

[4] The specification of these ontologies, protocols, and strategies is almost finalized; however, discussing them here would go far beyond the scope of this report.

3 Summary of SOPRANO Presentations

3.1 SOPRANO Overview

"Service-oriented Programmable Smart Environments for Older Europeans" (SO-PRANO) is an Integrated Project in the European Commission's 6th Framework Programme. SOPRANO's aim is to enable older Europeans to lead a more independent life in their familiar environment. As an approach, SOPRANO will develop a next generation of smart homes based on ambient intelligence. Very important is the positive mindset of the project: the resulting system will not only act in problematic (e.g. fall, burglary) or emergency cases (e.g. health problems, fire) but will focus with the same attention on improving the quality of everyday life of elderly people.

Research within SOPRANO focuses on three pillars:

– to design the next generation of systems for ambient assisted living in Europe: highly innovative context-aware, smart home environment services with natural and comfortable interfaces for older people at an affordable cost, meeting requirements of users, of family carers and Europe's over-stretched care providers so as to significantly extend the time during which elderly people can live independently in their preferred environment;
– to set up large-scale, visible demonstrations of innovative AAL systems showing their viability in European markets - markets both for care provision and smart-home comfort;
– to adapt and extend state-of-the-art Experience & Application Research (E&AR) methods, integrating design-for-all components and providing innovative tools to create a new, consistently user-centred design methodology. Design-for-all is incorporated both to combat stigma and to reap economies of scale. These and design decisions informed by cost-benefit analysis in the project will help ensure SO-PRANO solutions are cost effective.

A key feature of the methodology will be the frequent, active and strong involvement of older users throughout the entire R&D process, using scenarios, prototypes, test environments and implementations in real home settings, culminating in large-scale validation and demonstration of the innovative service-oriented smart living environments in real life settings with 600 users across four countries.

The SOPRANO environment will assist users in carrying out daily activities, monitor key vital signs and user activity - to detect situations calling for pro-active assistance- and provide strongly enhanced safety and security at home - not least by observing the most stringent of Europe's social alarm reliability standards. Through rule-based local monitoring and integration of external service provision, users will have the most effective access to social, medical and emergency services imaginable.

The technical core of the system in each house will be the SOPRANO Ambient Middleware (SAM), which receives the user commands and sensor inputs, enriches them semantically and triggers appropriate reactions via actuators in the house. SO-PRANO adopts a novel ontology-centred design approach for this component in order to get an intelligently acting, but also deterministic and economically scalable module.

First prototypes of SORPANO houses based on SAM are expected in June 2008. The evaluation of the developed concepts is also planned in this year, both in a large-scale field trial in 300 homes with restricted functionality and a fully-functional trial in dedicated smart home laboratory environments.

The SOPRANO consortium of enterprises, public bodies and (university) research institutes comprises of 25 partners from 7 European countries, namely Greece, Germany, UK, Netherlands, Spain, Slovenia and Ireland, having expertise in:

- systems integration, software architecture, voice recognition, sensing systems, semantic ICT and a range of other technology domains;
- human factors, gerontology, user needs analysis and evaluation;
- social care of older people
- telecare and assistive technologies.

The project started in January 2007 and will last 40 months.

3.2 The Need for Ambient Assisted Living

Over the last decade, considerable RTD efforts have been pursued by the European Commission, national governments and relevant industries to provide an adequate technology response to these challenges. In terms of technology uses, the so called "independent living" or "assisted living" domain today comprises a heterogeneous field of applications ranging from quite simple devices such as intelligent medication dispensers to complex systems such as networked homes and interactive services. Some are relatively mature and some are still under development.

When it comes to more complex systems in particular, the potential ICT generally holds in relation to independent living – e.g. in terms of quality of life for care recipients – are very likely to be not enough for the sustained success of ICT enabled social and medical support services.

Experiences from previous research suggest for instance that organisational, cultural and other non-technological issues come into the play if ICTs are to be successfully introduced into day-today practice. But also in relation to the technology itself, up to now all too often simplistic assumptions have been made in relation to the needs and aspiration of those who's independence is ultimately to be supported in one way or another, and of those who provide assistance to them as well. There is for instance some evidence that many older people, despite being in need of some help, are wary of giving outsiders intimate insight into and access to their homes. It seems very likely that they would accept technology based help more readily if they had more say in what information is sent out, to whom and under what circumstances. Also, the complexity and novelty of many systems and devices that have been developed during recent years seem to threaten many older people with exclusion from their uses.

At the same time, recent research suggests that a large segment of the growing number of older people in Europe can be offered ICT enabled support services which considerably improve their quality of life, provided usability of ICT systems can be equally improved. The opportunity to do so is given by recent developments in ambient intelligence and new abilities of software systems to communicate with users in something approaching natural human to human interaction. Against this background, SOPRANO aims at taking a leap forward in the way users can interact with and take charge of their living environment and in the way professional care personnel can support them when called on to do so. In that sense, the SOPRANO system is not to act as a traditional "smart home", passively receiving user commands, nor as pure "remote care", monitoring user activity to alert outside staff to a need for action. Instead, SOPRANO shall act as an informed, friendly agent, taking orders, giving advice or reminders and ready to help, and get help, when needed.

3.3 Use Case Development and Participatory Requirements Engineering

Home technologies must be designed having the needs of older people in mind if these are ultimately to be successful in supporting their independence. Therefore, an extensive program of user-related research has been implemented during the first year of the overall project.

Work started with the conduction of an extensive literature review. Here the focus was on gaining a better understanding of physical and other changes that tend to come with the process of human ageing and their potential impacts on a person's experience of life in old age. This preparatory exercise was to lay the ground for the identification of key challenges to independent living, with a view to identifying options for the provision of an adequate technological response to these.

Further to this, a repository of generic situations potentially threatening older peoples' independence or quality of life was compiled on the basis of the knowledge gained from the literature, and on the basis of feedback received from those project partners who have experiences in providing support services to older people.

The next step in requirements elicitation focused on involving potential users of the SOPRANO system in order to gather their feedback on a) key challenges to independence/quality of life and b) initial ideas on how technology could be harnessed to better cope with these challenges. To this end a qualitative methodological approach was adopted, involving both focus groups and individual interviews. The "situations inventory" compiled earlier in the project was used for triggering responses and stimulating lively discussions at the part of the participants. Overall, 14 dedicated focus groups (with more than 90 end users) were conducted with older people, informal carers and care professionals in the UK, the Netherlands, Spain and Germany. Individual interviews with older people took place in Germany, Spain and the Netherlands.

Key themes that emerged from these activities for further consideration in the SOPRANO design process included both technical and non-include aspects. Amongst others, these include the issues:

- *Social isolation/loneliness*: Perhaps one of the biggest problems mentioned at the part of the users concerns social isolation resulting in many negative outcomes such as loneliness, depression or the feeling of being cut-off. An aspect motioned in this context as well concerns the feeling of boredom which seems to be related with a feeling of being socially excluded in many cases.
- *Safety and Security*: Another challenge that was frequently mentioned concerns the desire for safety and security. Important issues that were highlighted in this context include for example falls, disorientation, control of household equipment or receiving help in the case of emergency.
- *Forgetfulness*: Forgetfulness seems to be a challenge to independence for many and concerns for example taking medication or finding objects in the house. Particular

issues that were mentioned around taking medication are multi facetted and relate to forgetting to take the correct medicine at the right time and to find the medicine in the house, but also to undesired side effects when taking different kinds of medicine. Also, some people seem to have problems in handling or managing their appointments or a normal calendar.

- *Keeping healthy and active*: Challenges were also reported in relation to keeping healthy and active in later life, e.g. when it comes to physical and mental activity and exercise, good nutrition, good routines (such as sleep patterns) and, again adherence to appropriate medications. Some people reported difficulties in adhering to specific regimes that have been determined by health professionals, including rehabilitation programmes.

- *Community participation/contribution to local communities*: During a UK focus group there was a strong emphasis on the desire to participate in local government activities and informal and semi-formal support networks. While this seems a somewhat unique view, this outcome points into the direction that community participation and contribution to local communities should not be underestimated.

- *Accessing information/keeping up to date*: Keeping up to date seems to be a crucial issue for many as well. Here, access to local news or the possibility to read newspapers were emphasised, as was the need to find tradesmen to do little jobs around the home, such decorating, cleaning, repairs, etc.

- *Getting access to shops and services*: People often seem to have difficulty getting out of the house for shopping banking pensions, etc. These kinds of services and support are usually outside the remit of local authorities so that the person in need to support has to manage getting such things done on his/her own, or is dependent on others or voluntary organisations.

- *Checking up on care provision*: Local authorities can be purchasers and/or direct providers of care at home. As care is provided in the community within the person's own home, it seems not always easy to ensure that the right amount and right quality of care is delivered.

- *Mobility inside and outside the home*: Keeping mobile outside the home was mentioned as a problem area as well. This concerns on the one hand being able to walk as long as possible and the use of public transport on the other hand. Mobility restrictions were reported especially common in winter and evenings.

The hitherto sketched work with older people, informal carers and care professionals revealed a set of key challenges to older peoples' independence and quality of life where some kind of technology-based response was seen as having great potential to provide practical help.

A set of use cases were developed to effectively capture functional requirements on the technical SOPRANO system by describing interactions between one or more users and the system itself. These scenarios not only reflect functionalities of the technical system under design but also the processes, actions and interaction of 'components' of the overall socio-technical system.

3.4 Ontology-Centered Design and Architecture

The technical core of the project is the SORPANO Ambient Middleware (SAM) [3], which will be installed in each of the houses and provides its intelligence by receiving user commands and inputs from sensors, enriching them semantically and providing appropriate reactions via actuators in the house. Planned are sensors for e.g. smoke, temperature, door status, location of the user by radar or RFID, her health status and so on. Planned actuators are speech synthesizers, digital TVs with avatars, device regulators (for switching devices on/off or modifying their behaviour), emergency calls to a central and more. Additionally the more static context of the house and the user shall be taken into considerations when performing concrete actions.

As SAM is supposed to be an integrating component in an open service infrastructure, a novel design approach was chosen for it to ensure semantic coherence: the *ontology-centred design* methodology, in which the ontology (i.e. the formal specification of a shared data model and vocabulary) is considered as a mediating artefact in the design discourse [5]. As a practical consequence, the ontology (see Fig. 6) was developed as a as the first step in order to serve as the basis for the subsequent design decisions - as opposed to other ontology-based approaches. The ontology is used as a blueprint for the internal data structures of the components, a guideline for the communication between components by helping to define interfaces and exchanged data structures as well as a communication vehicle between the technical system and the typically non-technical user.

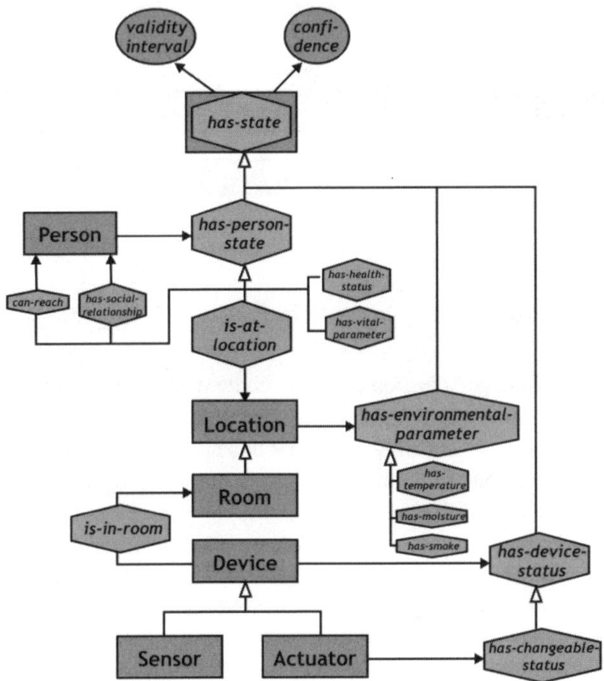

Fig. 6. Core concepts and properties of the SOPRANO context ontology (in an extended ER notation from [6])

From the architectural point of view (see Fig. 7), the ontology is used in the following ways: The contract with sensor components specifies that they provide basically state update messages (e.g. temperature is 23 degrees, fridge door is open) to the context manager (which is responsible for providing a consistent and up-to-date view on the current context, abstracting low-level sensor information into higher-level status information). This can be done via push mechanisms (the sensors sends state information to the context manager) or pull mechanisms (the context manager can query the sensor). The context manager updates the global context with this information and possibly aggregates it to other state information.

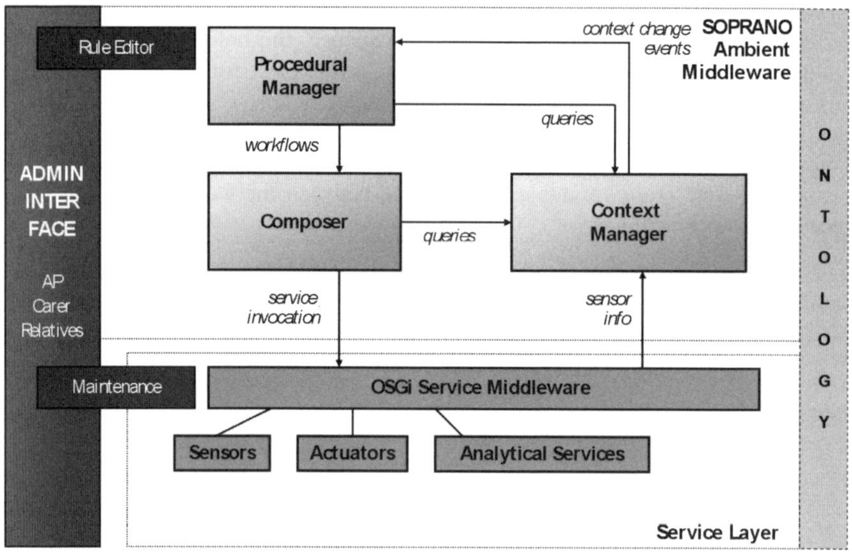

Fig. 7. Service-Oriented Architecture of SOPRANO

The Procedural Manager (responsible for context-aware system responses) registers with the Context Manager for changes to the state (e.g. AP has fallen, temperature in kitchen has fallen from medium to low, AP has not left apartment for more than 24 hours). Based on these context changes, the procedural manager can select predefined workflows whose basic building blocks are made up of goals as desirable target states (e.g. *neighbour informed*, if not possible or no reaction after 15 minutes: *relatives informed*, if not possible *service centre informed*). Based on these abstract target states, the Composer selects appropriate services described according to the state changes they can achieve.

This state-centric core of the SOPRANO ontology can be expressed in a subset of OWL Lite and thus allows for efficient implementation on top of relational databases. Subcomponents, though, might benefit from representing additional background knowledge in the ontology, e.g., for context aggregation.

4 Summary and Outlook

The workshop has brought together stakeholder representatives from the two projects and has provided an opportunity to exchange experiences made so far in relation to both requirements elicitation and system design.

Representatives from both projects agreed that successful research in the AAL field should have a strong involvement of users during the whole RTD process, and that a multi-disciplinary approach also involving experts from various disciplines is necessary. The workshop has also clearly identified that a number of research issues will need to be addressed to fully exploit the long term potential of AAL.

The two projects have used different approaches to elicit requirements but they have identified a very similar set of services useful to support independent living. This fact was acknowledged very positively by both of the projects.

One of the differences that have emerged is that PERSONA has an additional focus on mobility support whereas SOPRANO more concentrates on supporting older people in the house. However, since technical components under development will be conceived and designed as part of a socio-technical system, SOPRANO also considers mobility components, although with a less strong focus than PERSONA. This difference is also reflected in the technological solutions adopted where the SO-PRANO middleware is a centralized solution and the PERSONA middleware is a peer-to-peer architecture. Nevertheless, both SOPRANO and PERSONA middleware are based on the OSGi gateway architecture.

SOPRANO will initiate early field trials in 2008. It will be very interesting for PERSONA to further exchange experiences for the preparation of the PERSONA trials that will start in the middle of 2009.

In order to further promote experience exchange between the two projects, it was suggested to:

– organize regular meetings in order to stay up-to-date with the respective progress,
– organize an exchange of expertise to evaluate the respective platform and services,
– consider the production of a joint public study on the user needs, and
– consider the definition of a joint public reference architecture for the middleware.

References

1. Georgantas, N., Ben Mokhtar, S., Bromberg, Y., Issarny, V., Kalaoja, J., Kantarovitch, J., Géro-dolle, A., Mevissen, R.: The Amigo Service Architecture for the Open Networked Home Environment. In: IEEE WICSA 2005, pp. 295–296 (2005)
2. Hellenschmidt, M., Kirste, T.: A Generic Topology for Ambient Intelligence. In: EUSAI, Eindhoven, Niederlande, pp. 112–123 (2004)
3. Klein, M., Schmidt, A., Lauer, R.: Ontology-Centred Design of an Ambient Middleware for Assisted Living: The Case of SOPRANO. In: Hertzberg, J., Beetz, M., Englert, R. (eds.) KI 2007. LNCS (LNAI), vol. 4667, Springer, Heidelberg (2007)
4. Krakowiak, S.: Middleware Architecture with Patterns and Frameworks. INRIA Rhône-Alpes, France (May 22, 2007), `http://sardes.inrialpes.fr/~krakowia/MW-Book/`

5. Schmidt, A.: Impact of Context-Awareness on the Architecture of E-Learning Solutions. In: Pahl, C. (ed.) Architecture Solutions for E-Learning Systems, IGI Publishing (2007)
6. Schmidt, A., Kunzmann, C.: Towards a Towards a Human Resource Development Ontology for Combining Competence Management and Technology-Enhanced Workplace Learning. In: Meersman, R., Tari, Z., Herrero, P. (eds.) OTM 2006 Workshops. LNCS, vol. 4278, pp. 1078–1087. Springer, Heidelberg (2006)
7. Tazari, M.R., Plößer, K.: User-Centric Service Brokerage in a Personal Multi-Agent Environment. In: IEEE KIMAS 2003, Cambridge, MA, (USA) (October 2003)
8. Tazari, M.R., Thiergen, S.: servingo: a Service Portal on the Occasion of the FIFA World Cup 2006. In: IWWPST 2006, Münster (Germany) (September 2006)

KDubiq Workshop at the European Conference for Ambient Intelligence 2007

Michael May[1], Codrina Lauth[1], and Rasmus Pedersen[2]

[1] Fraunhofer Institute for Intelligent Analysis and Information Systems
St. Augustin, Germany
`Michael.May@iais.fraunhofer.de, Codrina.Lauth@iais.fraunhofer.de`
[2] Copenhagen Business School
Dept. for Embedded Systems, WSN Lab., Denmark
`rup.inf@cbs.dk`

1 Organizers

Michael May & Codrina Lauth
Fraunhofer Institute for Intelligent Analysis and Information Systems
St. Augustin, Germany
Michael.May@iais.fraunhofer.de
Codrina.Lauth@iais.fraunhofer.de

Rasmus Pedersen
Copenhagen Business School
Dept. for Embedded Systems, WSN Lab.
Denmark
rup.inf@cbs.dk

2 What Is KDubiq?

In order to explore how the next generation of information intensive, distributed and ubiquitous systems will look like, we need to establish a common ground for relevant research that has been carried out by several interrelated communities, e.g. ubiquitous Data Mining/Machine Learning, Semantic Web, Ubiquitous Computing and Embedded Systems.

KDubiq - Knowledge Discovery in Ubiquitous Environments - is a European funded Coordination Action[1]. The KDubiq project has started in December 2005 and will last until May 2008. The project is supporting and coordinating research and networking activities in the emerging area of Ubiquitous Knowledge Discovery. The main objective is to bridge the gap between these communities by supporting common activities and seeking new relevant research and application

---

[1] Funded by the European Commission under IST (Information Society Technology), FET Open (Future and Emerging Technologies) in the 6th Framework Programme under the number IST-6FP-021321.

M. Mühlhäuser et al. (Eds.): AmI 2007 Workshops, CCIS 11, pp. 465–467, 2008.

challenges for knowledge discovery (data mining) in the fields of ubiquitous computing. The analysis of data in various distributed and ubiquitous environments such as: sensor networks, peer-to-peer networks, embedded systems, mobile computing devices, grid computing platforms among others, demands new types of knowledge discovery algorithms that include real-time context knowledge and allow quick adaptability to non-stationary-distributions and heterogeneity of data sources.

The KDubiq members are working on setting up a long term research agenda for Ubiquitous Knowledge Discovery with special focus to industry research and transfer of research results to industry applications. KDubiq is a project very much focused towards embedded and ubiquitous applications. It is not necessarily including the whole data mining and machine learning landscape.

The final result of this project will be a joint book a Blueprint on Ubiquitous Knowledge Discovery, including all relevant topics in these areas. For this purpose, Six Working Groups (WG) are reflecting the **design space** for building Ubiquitous Knowledge Discovery Systems.

3 Workshop Objectives

The KDubiq Workshop at AmI 2007 has focused on giving a detailed overview about the relevant research and applications done within the Data Mining and Machine Learning Community, including state-of-art research results in ubiquitous and distributed Knowledge Discovery, with special focus on current applications:

- Distributed Data Mining in Ubiquitous Environments like P2P, Grids, Social Networks
- Data Stream Mining
- Intelligent monitoring with small wireless devices, WSN (e.g. lego mindstorms)
- Privacy and Security issues related to ubiquitous data mining

Ubiquitous Knowledge Discovery is an emerging and highly interdisciplinary research field. Therefore KDubiq members were looking for the open exchange and discussions for new research and applications challenges from the AmI Community, where intelligent machine learning techniques makes the difference.

The workshop started with a general **Overview about the KDubiq project and current research and application challenges in Ubiquitous Knowledge Discovery** by Michael May. Joao Gama (Univ. Porto) focused on **Issues on Learning from Data Streams**. He stressed that many mining problems in ubiquitous Knowledge Discovery take the form of a streaming problem. Rasmus Pedersen (Copenhagen Business School) gave an introduction on **TinyOS for Lego MINDSTORMS**. Compared to other devices, Mindstorms form an environment that is rich yet from the hardware perspective easy to setup. He discussed the application of Support Vector Machines in this scenario. The talk by Assaf Schuster (Technion Univ.) on **Mining in Grids Systems,PeertoPeer and Sensor**

Networks introduced a number of distributed algorithms in different kinds of distributed environments. The talk showed that some traditional learning problems are completely transformed and require fresh solutions if they are transferred to a distributed domain. Michael Wurst (Univ. Dortmund), in his talk **NEMOZ P2P Organization of Media Based on Distributed Data Mining**, gave an example of a specific distributed mining application in a web 2.0 context. Ycel Saygin Sabanci Univ. talked about **Privacy and Security in the Age of Ubiquitous Knowledge Discovery**, stressing also the role of spatial data. The workshop finished with an open discussion.

Author Index

Printing: Mercedes-Druck, Berlin
Binding: Stein+Lehmann, Berlin